THE ADVENTURE OF THE REAL

THE ADVENTURE

Jean Rouch services his Aaton in the office of the Comité du film ethnographique, Musée de l'Homme, March 1990.

OF THE REAL

Jean Rouch and the Craft of Ethnographic Cinema

PAUL HENLEY

THE UNIVERSITY OF CHICAGO PRESS   Chicago and London

PAUL HENLEY is director of the Granada Centre for Visual Anthropology, professor of visual anthropology at the University of Manchester, and a documentary filmmaker.

The University of Chicago Press, Chicago 60637
The University of Chicago Press, Ltd., London
© 2009 by The University of Chicago
All rights reserved. Published 2009
Printed in the United States of America

18 17 16 15 14 13 12 11 10 09   1 2 3 4 5

ISBN-13: 978-0-226-32714-3 (cloth)
ISBN-13: 978-0-226-32715-0 (paper)
ISBN-10: 0-226-32714-0 (cloth)
ISBN-10: 0-226-32715-9 (paper)

Library of Congress Cataloging-in-Publication Data

Henley, Paul.
      The adventure of the real : Jean Rouch and the craft of ethnographic
   cinema / Paul Henley.
          p. cm.
      Includes bibliographical references and index.
      Includes filmography of Jean Rouch.
      ISBN-13: 978-0-226-32714-3 (cloth : alk. paper)
      ISBN-10: 0-226-32714-0 (cloth : alk. paper)
      ISBN-13: 978-0-226-32715-0 (pbk. : alk. paper)
      ISBN-10: 0-226-32715-9 (pbk. : alk. paper) 1. Rouch, Jean.
   2. Cinematographers—France. 3. Ethnologists—France.
   4. Ethnographic films—Africa, West. 5. Motion pictures in ethnology—
   Africa, West. I. Title.
PN1998.3.R674H46 2009
791.4302′33092—dc22

                                                    2009028839

♾ The paper used in this publication meets the minimum requirements of
the American National Standard for Information Sciences—Permanence
of Paper for Printed Library Materials, ANSI Z39.48-1992.

To Françoise Foucault and Laurent Pellé

CONTENTS

PREFACE

Cinema is an Adventure, but the difficulty is that it is an adventure that you have to strive continually to control.   JEAN ROUCH, 1965[1]

A chronicle of the Rouchian adventure is certainly an exciting prospect, but it is one that I approach with caution. One never admires without reservation. Any tribute carries within it an element of denunciation. No eulogy deserves to be trusted unless it is combined with a certain degree of meanness.
                    CLAUDE JUTRA, 1960[2]

The Adventure of the Real

The very nature of ethnographic cinema—how it is practiced, how it is talked about, where its limits are deemed to lie—has been profoundly shaped by the work of the late Jean Rouch. When he died in a road accident near Tahoua, Niger, in February 2004, at the age of eighty-six, this genre of filmmaking was deprived of its most eminent figure, arguably its most original genius, and certainly its most prolific practitioner. In the course of a sixty-year career beginning with his first tentative ethnographic report published in a French colonial journal in 1943 and ending with his last film, poignantly entitled *Le rêve plus fort que la mort* (*The Dream More Powerful Than Death*) and released in 2002, Rouch produced over one hundred completed films and almost as many published texts. While a handful of these films have been widely distributed, reaching far beyond the confines of academic anthropology, the great majority remain little known and difficult to see, particularly in the English-speaking world.

Early on in his career, in 1947, while still a doctoral student, Rouch was appointed to a post at the Centre National de la Recherche Scientifique (CNRS), the most prestigious research institution in France. By this time, he was also already closely associated with the Musée de l'Homme.

Forming part of the grand Palais de Chaillot, situated on a hill overlooking the Eiffel Tower and the Champs de Mars, the Musée de l'Homme was, until very recently, the premier anthropological museum in France.[3] The Musée would become the seat of the Comité du film ethnographique, which was established in 1952 by various luminaries of the worlds of cinema and anthropology. Rouch was appointed its general secretary and he remained so for the rest of his life. The Comité, which at the time of writing still operates from a modest office fashioned out of a sort of storeroom at the head of the principal staircase, acted as the producer of most of his subsequent films.

Apart from a brief interlude in 1951–1953, when he was temporarily expelled for failing to complete his doctoral thesis on time, largely due to the call of competing filmmaking activities, Rouch's appointment to a position at the CNRS gave him the freedom for the rest of his life to pursue his anthropological and filmmaking interests more or less as he saw fit. When he was in Paris, he would often preside at a celebrated series of seminars. "Human Sciences and the Cinema," that took place on Saturday mornings at the Cinémathèque française, then still located just across the small plaza beside the Musée, in the other wing of the Palais de Chaillot. He also played a leading role in the creation of the practice-based doctoral programs in cinema at both the Sorbonne and Nanterre campuses of the University of Paris, and he directed the film theses of many of the students in these programs. Indeed, he was very generous with his time in encouraging young filmmakers generally, not only in France but elsewhere as well. Among many other initiatives, he was instrumental in the establishment of the Ateliers Varan, which are based in Paris and are dedicated to the organization of documentary short courses there and in the Third World.[4] But compared to most academics in what the French call the "Anglo-Saxon" world, he was not heavily encumbered by teaching obligations.[5] These circumstances enabled him to spend part of almost every year of his career on a filmmaking expedition, mostly to West Africa. But for all his travels, Rouch remained deeply attached to his particular stamping grounds in Paris.

The most immediately striking feature of Jean Rouch's oeuvre is its sheer volume. Toward the end of his life, he would often assert that he had made 130 or even 140 films. And indeed, if one compiles a list of all the films that Rouch ever worked on, such as the one that is offered in appendix 1 of this book, it is certainly the case that the total is of this order, perhaps even slightly more. But these figures should be treated with a certain degree of caution. Not all of these films could be considered ethnographic, even the in loosest sense of the term. Although Rouch may be best known as an ethnographic filmmaker, he also made a large number

FIGURE 0.1. Rouch's Paris. *Top left*, the Musée de l'Homme in the south wing of the Palais de Chaillot. At the base of the statue are the umbrellas of the restaurant featured in *Chronicle of a Summer*. *Top right*, the view from the window behind the Musée cinema. Rouch had a particular fascination with the Eiffel Tower and made it the subject of his late film, *Le Beau Navire*, based on a poem by Baudelaire of the same name. *Bottom*, the Café Bal Bullier, close to Rouch's apartment in the rue Montparnasse, where, in his later years, he was always available for breakfast-time meetings whenever he was in town. Previously, it had been the Café de la Croix Rouge, close to his earlier apartment in the rue de Grenelle. All photographs © Paul Henley.

of films that can only be classified as "ethnographic" by stretching this already very elastic term to breaking point. These other films were on an eclectic variety of subjects and were mostly relatively short. They included films about economic or social development projects, a broad variety of political or cultural events, even three promotional films for a West African car dealer. In the latter part of his career, he also made a dozen interview-based portrait films and produced a number of "ciné-poems" and "promenades inspirées" about Paris and elsewhere, though these too were all relatively short works. Much more substantial were his fiction films, mostly feature-length and numbering seventeen in total, which he began to make from the late 1950s onward. But although dealing in most cases with cultural themes, broadly defined, no more than half of these were based on specialist ethnographic knowledge.

When all these other films are subtracted from the Rouchian filmography, one is left with a corpus of around 80–85 films that could be described as broadly ethnographic. But of these, about thirty-five remain incomplete, existing only in the form of double-band copies, that is, with picture and sound stored on two independent 16mm tracks—one on film, the other on magnetic tape—that require a specialist double-headed projector to be screened.[6] While some of these incomplete works appear to have been subject to a considerable degree of editing, others consist of little more than titles given to a set of synchronized rushes. Yet even if all these incomplete works are also removed from the list of Rouch's films, one remains with a final tally of around fifty films, which still makes him the most productive of all ethnographic filmmakers, living or dead.

Rouch was also a prolific photographer, particularly in the early stages of his career. In 1954, he published Le Niger en pirogue (The Niger by Canoe), a brief account of his descent by canoe of the 2,500 miles of the Niger River with two wartime friends in 1946–1947, which was supported by a collection of sixty-four black-and-white photographs taken on this and subsequent expeditions. To the best of my knowledge, this is the only substantial collection of Rouch's photographs that has been published to date, but in 2000, the Comité du film ethnographique combined forces with the Muséum national d'Histoire naturelle to put on an exhibition of his photographs. This led the distinguished French photojournalist and filmmaker Raymond Depardon to place Rouch, as a photographer, in the same elevated category as Pierre Verger and Cartier-Bresson.[7] Following his death, Rouch's substantial collection of photographs was deposited with the Bibliothèque nationale de France where they are in the process of being cataloged. A modest selection is scattered through this book with the kind permission of Rouch's widow, Jocelyne Lamothe, the Fondation Jean Rouch, and the Comité du film ethnographique.

Rouch's publications were almost as numerous and were certainly as eclectic as his films. His most substantial ethnographic text was his doctoral thesis, defended in 1952, first published in 1960, and then republished in an extensively annotated second edition in 1989. Also based on his doctoral research was a historical memoir of some hundred pages published in a French colonial journal in 1953, as well as a short general book of a similar length published in 1954. Apart from his doctoral research, Rouch's most significant published work was an extensive statistical report on migration within West Africa, running to almost two hundred pages. This appeared in 1956 in the *Journal de la Société des Africanistes* and complemented the films that he made during this period. He also published over one hundred shorter texts, including a considerable quantity of academic articles and reports on migration as well as numerous articles about ethnographic filmmaking and cinema more generally. He also edited three catalogs of ethnographic film for UNESCO, one on French ethnographic films (1955), another on films about Africa and African cinema (1966), and a third concerning films about religion in the Pacific region (1970). Only a small selection of Rouch's publications are referred to in this book, and these are listed at the head of the reference section, but more substantial bibliographies are available elsewhere.[8]

In addition, particularly in the latter phase of his life, Rouch gave a great many interviews ranging across a broad range of subjects in both anthropology and cinema. Those referred to in this book are listed in the references section under the name of the interviewer, when this is given, and in the few cases when it is not given, under Rouch's own name. Rouch was also the subject of at least fifteen personal portrait or interview films. Those of which I am aware, plus a number of films about Rouch's West African associates talking about Rouch, are listed in appendix 3. When these films are referred to in footnotes in this book, the names of the makers are italicized.

As Christopher Thompson has pointed out, a recurrent feature of Rouch's writing and speaking about his filmmaking activities is the idea of adventure.[9] However, in French, the term *l'aventure* carries a layer of connotation that the equivalent English term generally does not. While *l'aventure* can denote, as the English term does, an amusing escapade or intrepid exploration of one kind or another, it can also be used to suggest a variety of more poetic meanings, ranging from romantic liaisons (often with a *frisson* of the illicit) to some sort of transcendent existential quest, particularly so, in the last case, when spelt with a capital A, as in Rouch's remark quoted in the epigraph to this preface. Rouch may well have inherited a taste for adventure–as–intrepid–exploration from his meteorologist father, Jules, who spent two years in the Antarctic on the survey vessel *Pourquoi Pas?* captained by Jean-Baptiste Charcot.[10] But it was through his encounter with Surrealism that he developed a more poetic sense of *l'Aventure*. This first occurred in the mid-1930s, when Rouch was still an adolescent, but its effects can be discerned in his work throughout his career, up to and including his very last completed film, *Le rêve plus fort que la mort*, released in 2002.

For the intrepid explorer of the exterior world, in the mold of Rouch *père* perhaps, the chance and risk that are implicit in any adventure are qualities that may be appreciated for their own sake, but in the last analysis they must be overcome if the expedition is to achieve its goals. For Rouch *fils*, on the other hand, as for the Surrealists, chance and risk were the very stuff of any artistic *Aventure*, since it was these conditions that he regarded as most likely to produce unexpected discoveries about what most interested him, namely, the dreams and fantasies that underlie the everyday experience of reality. Far from seeking to overcome chance and risk then, Rouch saw them as providing an opportunity to be indulged whenever possible.

However, in contrast to many of the Surrealist visual artists, Rouch's filmmaking aesthetic remained, for the most part, resolutely realist. The standard conventions of space and time were generally respected in his films, and when this was not possible, they were carefully recreated. Although he would sometimes draw an analogy between the intentions underlying his work and those of Salvador Dalí or René Magritte, there are no flaccid watch faces in his films, nor elephants with stilt-like legs, and a pipe is almost always straightforwardly a pipe. Metaphors and other symbolic associations, or ironic juxtapositions as recommended by the intellectual ancestor of Surrealism, the Comte de Lautréamont, are few and far between. Rather than depict the surreal directly, Rouch's aim was to exploit the capacity of the filmmaking apparatus to reproduce the world in a literal, indexical manner in order to document the manifestation of the surreal in the forms of the real or, as he put it much more poetically in a 1967 interview, to produce a "postcard at the service of the imaginary."[11] It is in this sense, I suggest, that his life project can be conceived as one long and constantly experimental *Aventure*, one that involved the intrepid exploration not only of the exterior world in Africa but also of the recesses of the imaginary, an evocation of the surreal, but of the surreal as made manifest in the real.

The Literature on the Work of Jean Rouch

The work of Jean Rouch has already been the subject of much commentary and exegesis, both in France and the English-speaking world, though, in general, the French literature on Rouch is very much earlier. For, in France, Rouch was probably at the height of his fame in the early 1960s. From the mid-1950s, his reputation had really begun to spread outside the narrow world of anthropology when, with the support of the producer Pierre Braunberger, a number of his films were blown up to 35mm from their original 16mm format and given a cinema release. In this form, they also began to circulate at film festivals outside France and were awarded various prestigious international prizes. One of his films, *Moi, un Noir,* an improvisational semifictionalized account of the life of a casual dockworker in Abidjan, the capital of the Ivory Coast, won France's most prestigious film prize, the Prix Louis Delluc, in 1959. The methods that Rouch used in this film greatly impressed the leading figures of what was then the avant-garde of French cinema, the New Wave. Jean-Luc Godard was particularly taken with Rouch's approach and in April 1959 wrote an adulatory piece about *Moi, un Noir* for *Cahiers du Cinéma,* the principal forum of the New Wave filmmakers. When Godard came to shoot his own first full-length feature, *À bout de souffle* in August–September of the same year, his own methods had clearly been greatly influenced by those of Rouch.

The reputation that Rouch had established for innovative filmmaking on the basis of his African films was further consolidated by the release, in 1961, of *Chronicle of a Summer,* the so-called experiment in *cinéma-vérité,* which Rouch had shot the previous year in collaboration with the sociologist Edgar Morin. This film was instrumental in putting the ambiguous but widely deployed term *cinéma-vérité* into circulation. Although highly controversial and much decried as well as praised at the time, *Chronicle* secured Rouch's place as one of the leading figures of French cinema of the day, though his reputation in the English-speaking cinema world at this point was still minimal.[12] Through the early years of the 1960s, his works became a regular subject of discussion in the pages of *Cahiers du Cinéma* and similar publications. But as the 1960s progressed and turned into the 1970s, the attention given to his work in these media gradually declined. However, his public profile was still sufficiently great in 1979 for there to be a major retrospective screening of his works at the Centre Georges Pompidou, while in 1981, the Ministry of Foreign Affairs issued an 8.5 hour selection of his films on videotape accompanied by an informative booklet.[13] A special edition of the screen studies journal *CinémAction* dedicated exclusively to his work was published the following year.

But if Rouch's profile still remained relatively high in cinema circles in France in the early 1980s, albeit somewhat declined from its apogee, this was not matched by his reputation among anthropologists. In preparing the special edition of *CinémAction*, the editor, René Prédal approached various leading French anthropologists for a contribution but all declined because they did not want to become involved in a public polemic about the academic value of Rouch's work. Given that Rouch was only the fifth person in France to be awarded a *doctorat d'état* in anthropology, this was a considerable slight. As a result of this rebuff, the only anthropologist represented in the collection was a North American academic, George de Vos, who, seemingly, was familiar with only one of Rouch's films, *Les Maîtres fous,* his celebrated short film about the *hauka* spirit possession cult in colonial Accra.[14]

However, it was just around this time that Rouch and his work were taken up and enthusiastically embraced in the English-speaking world through the burgeoning academic subdiscipline of visual anthropology. Not only was it his filmmaking per se that attracted the attention of these Anglo-Saxon admirers, but also Rouch's interest in the subjective experience of his film subjects, his skepticism about scientific objectivity (despite his own training as an engineer), and his self-reflexive, collaborative methods, all of which, much to his surprise and even amusement, led to him being identified as an early prophet of the postmodernist turn that was then sweeping through Anglo-Saxon academia.

In fact, Rouch had been a regular visitor to North American campuses since the late 1950s, while his disagreement in the early 1960s with the leading members of the Direct Cinema documentary group about the implications of the new portable synchronous-sound technology had been featured in the North American screen studies literature.[15] But it was not until the turn of the 1980s that his work became the subject of extended critical comment in the anglophone anthropological literature. A collection of articles published in 1979 under the title *Anthropology, Reality, Cinema: The Films of Jean Rouch* and edited by the screenwriter Michael Eaton, then recently graduated with a degree in social anthropology at the University of Cambridge, played a particularly important role in introducing Rouch's work to English-speaking audiences. This was followed a few years later by special editions dedicated to Rouch's work of the journals *Studies in Visual Communication,* edited by Steven Feld, and *Visual Anthropology,* edited by Jay Ruby, and published in 1985 and 1989, respectively. In 1992, Paul Stoller's monograph, *The Cinematic Griot,* provided a much-needed ethnographic context for Rouch's African films.

In the last decade or so, a number of further monographs about Jean Rouch have appeared. In France, in 1996, René Prédal edited a second special edition of *CinémAction* dedicated to Rouch's work. Although about half of this volume consists of a republication of articles from the earlier edition and is still largely written by cineastes of various kinds, it also includes contributions from two of the leading contemporary French visual anthropologists, Marc Piault and Colette Piault. Meanwhile, in the English-speaking world, there have been two major edited works in the last few years. One of these, published in 2003, is *Ciné-ethnography*, a valuable collection of articles and other materials by or about Rouch, edited by Steven Feld; the other is *Building Bridges*, edited by Joram ten Brink and published in 2007. This represents a sort of postmortem festschrift that arose out of a three-day conference and associated series of screenings of Rouch's films that ten Brink and Zemirah Moffat, of the University of Westminster, organized at the French Institute in London in October 2004.[16] More recently, in 2008, the first single-author monograph dedicated to Rouch's work as a filmmaker was published in France by the screen studies scholar Maxime Scheinfeigel. Later the same year, demonstrating the increasingly international nature of the interest in Rouch's films, a second single-author monograph was published in Rio de Janeiro by the Brazilian anthropologist and leading Amazonist specialist, Marco Antonio Gonçalves. This consists primarily of an analysis of the three principal films that Rouch produced during his period studying migration in West Africa in the 1950s—*Les Maîtres fous, Moi, un Noir*, and *Jaguar*—in the light of Rouch's ideas about the interplay between imagination and reality. Most recently of all, at least at the time of writing in 2009, a collection of articles by Rouch and interviews with him by various distinguished interlocutors has been published in Paris by the journal *Cahiers du Cinéma* under the editorship of Jean-Paul Colleyn.

The Aims of This Book

In adding to this literature, my principal aim is to make a contribution that is somewhat oblique to this substantial body of work. Although I share the general interest in Rouch as a filmmaker whose work crossed freely back and forth across the boundaries between subjective experience and objective reality, self and other, Black and White, colonizer and colonized, fact and fiction—the theme of many studies of his work— as a teacher of practical filmmaking and also as an ethnographic documentary filmmaker myself, the particular focus of my attention in this book will be on the practical processes by which Rouch actually made his films. I include here not just purely technical matters such as cinematographic or sound-recording techniques, the editorial strategies that he used to construct his narratives or his methods for delivering voice-over narration, but also the aesthetic, ethical, and even epistemological positions that he associated, with varying degrees of explicitness, with these technical procedures. Pretentiously perhaps, but conveniently, I shall refer globally to this package of techniques, strategies, and artistic-philosophical postures as Rouch's filmmaking "praxis."

Rouch was entirely self-taught as a filmmaker and was therefore never subjected to any pressure to make films according to the methods of any particular school. Also, although he may have been trained as an engineer and liked nothing better than talking about the technical problems of filmmaking, he thought of himself primarily as a poet and always emphasized the overriding importance of improvisation, of spontaneity, and more generally, of freedom from any form of constraint in filmmaking. However, notwithstanding this rhetoric, the reality is that over the years, he developed a highly systematic praxis, with its own distinctive set of technical, aesthetic, and ethical norms. The principles of this praxis are not to be found gathered together somewhere in one grand *summa* but rather have to be deduced from his many commentaries on his methods scattered unevenly over dozens of different articles and interviews, often delivered in a seemingly impromptu and partial manner. As Marc Piault has observed, rather than announce his methodology as a sort of dogma, Rouch was content to lay it out in this roundabout way and leave it up to those with sufficient determination to figure it out for themselves, in the manner of someone passing through an initiation.[17]

Perhaps the closest to a concise summary that Rouch himself produced of his filmmaking praxis is the essay "The Camera and Man." This was first prepared in 1973 for the Congress of the International Union of Anthropological and Ethnological Sciences in Chicago that gave rise to *Principles of Visual Anthropology,* edited by Paul Hockings, the volume that is widely regarded as the foundational text of the modern academic subdiscipline of visual anthropology in the Anglo-Saxon world. This essay has subsequently been published in a variety of forms.[18] Rouch produced it when he was in his mid-fifties, representing almost precisely the midpoint of his filmmaking career. Written with fluency and vigor, as if transcribed from a spontaneous spoken performance, the essay reads like a political manifesto, crackling with enthusiasm for ethnographic cinema and its future.

But, as things turned out, the publication of "The Camera and Man" coincided with what proved to be the high-water mark of Rouch's most productive period as an ethnographic filmmaker. From this point on, films of an ethnographic character begin to decline in importance in his repertoire quite rapidly. By the early 1980s, they come to an end completely. They are displaced by works such as the portrait-interviews of his friends, many of which could be described as rather whimsical, and by fictional feature films that, with two or three possible exceptions, failed to impress the majority of critics. He also made a number of short experimental films, either by himself or in conjunction with groups of young filmmakers, and these too received mixed notices. Although he shot some forty-five films in this second half of his career, almost a third of his total output, none would receive the degree of acclaim accorded to the principal works of the first half of his career. But even if Rouch had chosen to abandon his career as a filmmaker at the halfway point and had entered a monastery, his contribution to ethnographic cinema would still be far above that of most, if not all, other filmmakers.

It is the films from the more ethnographic and more acclaimed first half of Rouch's filmmaking career that will be the primary focus of this book. In addition to describing his ethnographic filmmaking praxis in a systematic way, I shall also be seeking to locate its origins in a very particular form of anthropology and to assess its relevance for present-day ethnographic filmmaking. In this sense, this book could be considered an attempt to reclaim Rouch and his work for anthropology. For when considered as a whole, the Rouchian film canon is much more ethnographic than is generally appreciated by those who rely solely on the small and rather unrepresentative selection of eighteen or so of his films that have been made available in English-language versions.[19] In fact, the great majority of his films were very conventionally ethnographic, as were the majority of his writings.

With good reason, screen studies scholars may claim Jean Rouch as a precursor to the French New Wave or the West African feature film industry. Documentarists may hail him as the inventor, with Edgar Morin, of the *cinéma-vérité* documentary. But his intellectual roots lay deeply embedded in a highly traditional form of French anthropology passed on to him by Marcel Griaule, his doctoral supervisor, and originally derived from the work of Marcel Mauss, Griaule's own supervisor. It was to expand the arena of this form of anthropology that Rouch first took up the camera, and although his success in so doing brought him into dialogue with those whose concerns were exclusively related to cinema, he himself retained the interests and intellectual loyalties of his initial training as an anthropologist. This is why it was that in the 1970s, when his fame in cinema circles was still close to its peak, he chose to make three films in homage to Marcel Mauss in which former students recollected their time at the feet of the master.

Yet although I shall be mainly concerned with the work of Jean Rouch as an ethnographic filmmaker, it is not my intention to discuss the substantive ethnographic content of his films at any length. My main objective will be to identify how his films were made rather than with what their contribution might be to the comparative ethnography of West Africa. This is because, first, my own expertise as an anthropologist concerns South America rather than West Africa, where Rouch carried out all his ethnographic work. Second, this ethnographic context has already been provided by Paul Stoller in his excellent book, *The Cinematic Griot*.[20] The only exception here concerns the key film, *Les Maîtres fous*, released in 1955. This film was the work that first brought Rouch international renown, and it continues to be the source of much controversy some fifty years later. In my view, the now-orthodox interpretation of the *hauka* spirit possession cult, which is the main subject of this film, as a powerful counter-hegemonic parody of European colonial pretensions, is seriously misplaced. Drawing on a close analysis of the film itself, as well as on the anthropological literature of the region, including Rouch's own ethnographic writings, I offer a very different reading of this film in this book.

Another way in which I would distinguish this book from many previous analyses of Rouch's work is that while it offers a fundamentally sympathetic account, what I seek to provide is a *critical* appreciation of his contribution to ethnographic filmmaking. In the anglophone anthropological literature particularly, there is a marked hagiographic tendency in the discussions of Rouch's work. Meanwhile, outside the world of anthropology, if English-speaking filmmakers have heard about Rouch's work at all, they are inclined to have a generally positive impression, though often without having actually seen any of his films. In France, by contrast, Rouch's work is subject to a broader range of critical opinion. Although he continues to be much revered in the specialist world of French visual anthropology, more broadly within modern French anthropology he is regarded by some with a relative indifference, as yesterday's man, a former "pope" of ethnographic cinema perhaps, but one who has little of relevance to say to anthropologists today. Similarly, although Rouch's contribution to cinema is still admired by many filmmakers and critics in France, there are a number who are openly critical of his work, notably certain filmmakers from francophone Africa who consider his films to be irredeemably colonialist.[21]

In this matter, I find myself very much in sympathy with Claude Jutra, the late Québecois filmmaker who followed Rouch around in 1960–1961 when Rouch was the height of his powers and whose highly amusing memoir about this experience should be read by all admirers of Rouch's work. As Jutra so rightly comments in the passage cited in the epigraph, any eulogy that is not tempered by some degree of criticism does not deserve to be trusted. As I hope will become more than evident in the course of this book, I have a great personal admiration for Jean Rouch and his work. I believe that, collectively, all ethnographic filmmakers owe him a great debt for having created, almost single-handedly, the métier of ethnographic filmmaking. But I also consider that there are certain aspects of his methods of working that are less impressive or are simply not sufficiently comprehensive for the full range of ethnographic purposes. My ultimate concern will be to distinguish the strong from the weak in the legacy that he has left behind, the true heart of his project from the cloud of legend that so often obscures it. I believe that this is necessary in order to identify those elements of Rouch's legacy that are of enduring value and that can therefore serve as an inspiration to young ethnographic filmmakers only just starting out on the "Adventure of the Real."

The Structure of the Book

I shall begin with a preliminary chapter outlining the circumstances under which, as a very young man in the late 1930s and early 1940s, Rouch was first attracted to anthropology, or ethnology as it was then known in France, and the influence upon him of the ideas of Marcel Mauss, as transmitted through his teachers, Marcel Griaule and Germaine Dieterlen. In chapter 2, I will move on to explore the connections that existed at this time between ethnology and the Surrealist movement, since it was through a prior encounter with the latter that Rouch discovered the former. Some authors have recently downplayed the significance of the links between Surrealism and anthropology in prewar Paris, but in Rouch's case, the interests and attitudes that he developed through his youthful encounter with Surrealism played an important part in molding his filmmaking method, not just during the period with which this book will be mainly concerned but right until the end of his life, several decades after Surrealism had fallen out of fashion not merely in anthropology but also in the world of the arts more broadly defined.

In chapters 3–11, I shall discuss Rouch's filmmaking activities from the mid-1940s to the mid-1970s at length. This thirty-year period can be conveniently subdivided around the crucial year of 1960 when the francophone colonies of West Africa achieved independence. Having spent most of his time in Africa prior to 1960, Rouch then moved his principal base of operations back to Paris. Though he continued to return to West Africa with remarkable regularity, he also began to make films in Paris itself, including some of his best-known works. I shall consider the films of the pre-1960 period in chapters 3–6, and these, together with the re-analysis of *Les Maîtres fous* in chapter 7, make up part 1. Then, in part 2, consisting of chapters 8–11, I will examine Rouch's work between 1960 and 1975, when he was regularly moving back and forth between Paris and West Africa, making films in both places.

Throughout parts 1 and 2, I shall be constantly referring to Rouch's filmmaking praxis as it is made manifest in particular films. In part 3, by contrast, I shall be concentrating directly on the praxis itself with the aim of identifying some general underlying principles. In chapter 12, I focus on production techniques and strategies, including the important concept of the "ciné-trance," while in chapters 13–14, I turn my attention to editing and other aspects of postproduction, a relatively neglected aspects of Rouch's praxis. In chapter 15, I shall examine exactly what Rouch meant by the concept that is so crucial to his work, "shared anthropology." The main body of the book concludes with a final chapter in which I attempt to summarize the principles of Rouch's praxis and to assess the value of the legacy that he has left for future generations of ethnographic filmmakers. This is then followed by a number of appendixes, including a very substantial listing of Rouch's films covering the whole period of his career.

ACKNOWLEDGMENTS

Many colleagues, fellow filmmakers, and friends have helped me in refining whatever may be of value in this book. Not least among these was Jean Rouch himself, whom I had the pleasure to meet on a number of different occasions. Particularly memorable were the two occasions when he came to Manchester as a guest of the Granada Centre for Visual Anthropology. On the first occasion, it was to give the 1989 Forman Lecture and on the second, in 1990, it was to participate in the Second International Festival of Ethnographic Film, which the Granada Centre hosted on behalf of the Royal Anthropological Institute (see fig. 0.2). I was also privileged to be invited the following year to be a member of the jury of the Bilan du film ethnographique, the annual film festival organized at the Musée de l'Homme by the Comité du film ethnographique. Rouch had played a leading role in creating the Bilan in 1981 and although the president of the jury was nominally the venerable octogenarian Germaine Dieterlen, in practice it was Rouch who acted as the chair and coordinator of the jury's deliberations. As at every edition of the festival from its inauguration until his death, Rouch also acted as presenter of the films and interlocutor of the filmmakers during a marathon five days of screenings, starting at ten o'clock in the morning and invariably continuing until after midnight. Most appropriately, this festival has recently been renamed the Festival international Jean Rouch.

Always considerate in his treatment of the filmmakers and subtle in his criticisms, particularly if a filmmaker were screening a first work, Rouch used this role as interlocutor as a platform from which to propagate his views about the proper conduct of ethnographic filmmaking and his seemingly inexhaustible enthusiasm for this genre of cinema. An abiding memory of many who attended the Bilan in those years will surely be the image of Rouch sitting on the left of the front row of the Musée's cinema, from first thing in the morning until late at night. When the lights went down, he would lie back in his seat and, in an almost fe-

FIGURE 0.2. Jean Rouch in a light-hearted moment in front of the pink Cadillac at the Granada Studios Tour, during the second Royal Anthropological Institute film festival, Manchester, September 1990. *To his left*, Herb di Gioia, David MacDougall, and Colin Young; *in the background, left*, the Hungarian filmmaker, Janos Tari. © Knud Fischer-Møller.

tal position, with his feet up on the stage immediately in front and a fin-ger crooked in the edge of his mouth, he would gaze up seemingly enrap-tured by the images on the large screen before him. It was with a certain nostalgic sadness that I observed, in 2006, that this front row had been removed, presumably for prosaic health and safety reasons.

Among the many others who have helped me in the preparation of this book, I would particularly like to thank Françoise Foucault and Lau-rent Pellé of the Comité du film ethnographique. Over a long period, they have been extremely generous with their time in advising me about and making available to me the films of Jean Rouch that for many years re-mained tucked away upstairs in their office at the Musée de l'Homme.[1] They were also unstintingly supportive in the final phase of the prepara-tion of this book, when I was assembling the photographic materials. I dedicate this book to them in acknowledgment not only of my own par-ticular debt, but more generally, the debt that all those interested in the work of Jean Rouch owe to them for the diligence with which they have looked after his cinematographic legacy.

I am indebted also to many others for sharing with me their knowl-edge and views about Rouch and his works in the course of many con-versations over the years. They are almost too numerous to mention, but certainly at the risk of omission, I would particularly like to thank Brice Ahounou, Glenn Bowman, Jean-Paul Colleyn, Peter Crawford, Steve Feld, Luc de Heusch, Herb di Gioia, Jim Hillier, Paul Hockings, Andrew Irving, Philippe Lourdou, David MacDougall, Alan Marcus, Steef Meyknecht, Colette Piault, Johannes Sjöberg, Paul Stoller, Lucien Taylor, Christopher Thompson, Joram ten Brink, Nadine Wanono, Richard Werbner, Colin Young, and particularly Marc Piault, the current President of the Comité du film ethnographique. I am also particularly grateful to Philippe Costantini for his many revisions to the listing of Rouch's films that appears in appendix 1, and to my Amazonist colleagues and friends, Philippe Descola and Anne-Christine Taylor, for advising me both about certain aspects of the history of French anthropology and the translation of certain key terms and concepts.

Many scholars and filmmakers will share my gratitude to the editors of Éditions Montparnasse and to their advisers, Bernard Surugue and Sophie Deswarte, for the two excellent DVD collections of Rouch's works that they have recently released. Many of the film analyses offered in these pages have been greatly facilitated by the availability of these DVDs. All those interested in Rouch's work will have been heartened by the recent announcement that in the course of 2009, the same team will be releasing another collection of DVDs, this time featuring the principal films of Rouch's work among the Dogon. Those who do not have a command of French will be particularly pleased to learn that two UK-based distribution companies, unReal and Watchmaker Films, have recently combined forces to release a whole series of Rouch's best-known films in English-language subtitled versions beginning in the course of 2009.[2]

The visual quality of this book is greatly enhanced by the many photographs, whose rights holders are acknowledged in the accompanying captions. When a caption does not carry such an acknowledgment, this is because the image is a frame-grab from one of the films discussed in the adjacent text. The quality of the book is also much enhanced by the excellent maps prepared by Peter Blore of the University of Manchester Media Centre. I am extremely grateful to Peter and all of the photographers concerned for their kind permission to use these graphic images. I am also indebted to Guillaume Fau and Georgette Ballez of the Bibliothèque nationale de France for the help that they gave me in arranging for the digital reproduction of a selection of the photographs by Jean Rouch currently held at the library, to Laurence Braunberger and Frédérique Ros of Films du Jeudi (successors to Films de la Pléiade) for providing me with various production stills associated with the Rouch films produced by their company and to my colleagues at Manchester, Andy

Lawrence, David Henderson, and Cathy Webb for their help and advice concerning the frame-grabs.

Meanwhile, the quality of the writing in this book has benefited greatly from the ministrations of Lucien Taylor, one of the readers for the University of Chicago Press, and of Alex Martin, freelance author, friend, and Oxford neighbor. I am grateful both to them and also to my editors at Chicago, T. David Brent, Laura J. Avey, and Maia M. Rigas, as well as to the design department, for their ready response to the many demands that I made of them in the final preparation of the manuscript.

But finally, and most importantly, if it had not been for the patience and support of my wife, Olivia, and of our children, Alice, William, and Richard, this text would surely never have seen the light of day.

1 : Initiation

I trace my orientation to Mauss, trying not to theorize about people in such a way as to introduce a gap between observer and observed, but to try to ask good questions, the answers to which will open up new questions.

JEAN ROUCH, 1990[1]

In the late 1930s, on the threshold of adulthood, Jean Rouch was both a would-be engineer and a would-be poet. In the event, neither engineering nor poetry would become the main thread of his life. Instead, ethnographic filmmaking would provide him with a means of combining and reconciling these youthful aspirations.

The Anthropological Encounter

Shortly before the outbreak of the Second World War, Jean Rouch was admitted to the elite bridge- and road-building *grande école*, Ponts et Chaussées. But while in his final year there, 1940–1941, with Paris by then under German occupation, he attended an introductory course in descriptive ethnography at the Musée de l'Homme. This was given by the charismatic Marcel Griaule, celebrated for his leadership of the Dakar-Djibouti Expedition of 1931–1933, and for his ethnography of the religious life of the Dogon of the Bandiagara Escarpment, a massive sandstone formation rising abruptly from the savannahs along the middle reaches of the Niger River in West Africa. These classes were accompanied by a series of "magic lantern" slide shows given by Germaine Dieterlen, colleague and enduring companion of Griaule, as well as also a leading Dogon specialist. Many years later, Rouch would claim not to have learned anything from Griaule's "austere lectures," remembering them only as a series of disaggregated ethnographic examples. But what these classes did do was confirm his developing passion for the peoples and cultures of West Africa, and establish his relationships with Griaule and Dieterlen, both of whom would be very important to him later in life.[2]

Not long afterward, Rouch would have the opportunity to go and live in West Africa himself, though under conditions that were far from his original Romantic vision of the region. Shortly before his graduation, while on holiday with a small group of his fellow engineering students on the coast of Brittany, Rouch was arrested by the German military police who thought that in strolling along the beach, they might be checking out the possibility of escaping across the Channel to England. Although they were released after only a brief detention, the experience was so unpleasant that as soon as he finished his studies Rouch took the opportunity to leave mainland France by accepting a post as a military road engineer in the Department of Public Works at Niamey, capital of the French West African colony of Niger.[3] But when he arrived in December 1941, he found that conditions in Niger were, if anything, worse than in France. Still only twenty-four, he found himself in charge of 20,000 "displaced, humiliated and brutalised" African laborers who had been press-ganged into working on what he would later call "highways of shame." In this, the most militarized and impoverished of French West African colonies, racism was rife, the governor was very pro-Vichy and the new road engineer soon came under suspicion both for his Gaullist sympathies and for his willingness to mix socially with Africans.[4]

It was in seeking to understand the world of his laborers that Rouch first began to develop his lifelong interest in their religious practices. Many of these laborers were Zerma or Sorko, both subgroups of the broader Songhay language group. The Sorko and Zerma live in what is today the western extreme of the Republic of Niger, along the middle reaches of the Niger River, though there is also a substantial population of Songhay speakers in neighboring regions of Mali, Burkina Faso and Benin. All these present-day speakers of Songhay are the descendants of the peoples who made up the precolonial Songhay empire. This was centered on Gao and Tombouctou, both of which are also on the middle Niger, but today lie within eastern Mali, somewhat to the north and west of the region in which Jean Rouch worked (see map 1). At the peak of its power in the fifteenth and sixteenth centuries, the Songhay empire stretched right across the western Sahel as far as the Atlantic coast of West Africa. But after the invasion of the region by Islamic groups emanating from Morocco in the late sixteenth century, the empire broke up into progressively smaller units. This process was exacerbated by incursions by Tuareg camel herders from the desert regions to north and by the cattle herders from the south, most commonly referred to as "Peul" in the francophone literature and "Fulan" or "Fulani" in the anglophone

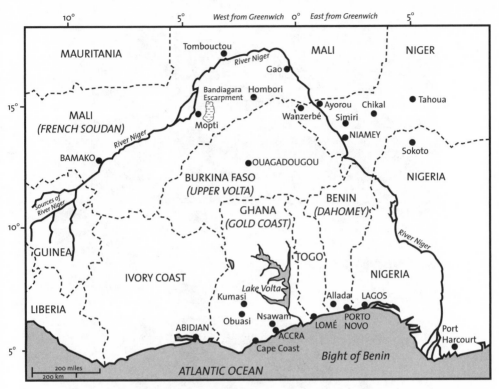

MAP 1. West Africa: principal sites of significance for Jean Rouch's work.

literature. Finally, the French colonial invasion at the end of the nine-teenth century led to the creation of international frontiers where none had existed before, and the Songhay-speaking peoples found themselves distributed across at least four different countries.[5]

In the course of his career, Rouch worked with a number of different Songhay subgroups. Of particular importance to him were the Sorko fishermen and hippopotamus hunters who live along the main chan-nel of the River Niger itself, around Ayorou and the island of Firgoun, close to the Niger-Mali border. Ayorou is famous locally for its market, which attracts the representatives of the many different ethnic groups of the region. In the early part of Rouch's career, this market town was one of his principal bases in Niger (fig. 1.1). About fifty miles further to the west, close to the border with Burkina Faso, lies the village of Wan-zerbé, celebrated for its sorcerers, the *sohantye*, whose activities were of particular interest to Rouch and about whom he made one of his best-known early films, *Les Magiciens de Wanzerbé*, released in 1949. Just to the north of Wanzerbé is Yatakala, one of the villages of the Gow sub-group, renowned for their prowess as hunters of lions, and also the sub-

FIGURE 1.1. The market at Ayorou, a meeting point for ethnic groups from all over the middle Niger region. © Fondation Jean Rouch.

a

b

c

d

FIGURE 1.2. Rouch worked with various different Songhay-speaking groups. *Top left*, a high-status Songhay woman; *top right*, a Sorko fisherman; *bottom left*, a Gow hunter; and *bottom right*, a Wanzerbé sorcerer. © Fondation Jean Rouch.

ject of one of Rouch's best-known films, *The Lion Hunters*, released in 1965 (fig. 1.2).

However, the Songhay subgroup with whom Rouch most frequently worked, certainly as a filmmaker, is the community based around Simiri, a village about fifty miles north of Niamey. This village lies in the heart of the Zerma region and in an area that suffers chronically from prolonged periods of severe drought. It was here that Rouch made another of his best-known early films, *Yenendi, les hommes qui font la pluie*, released in 1952. As its name suggests, this film concerned a *yenendi*, a rain-making ceremony. This would become a recurrent theme of the many films that he would make in the village over the next twenty years (fig. 1.3).

Until the 1960s, public ceremonial expressions of traditional, "animist" religious beliefs among the Songhay were very common, despite the fact that a significant proportion of the population had been Muslims for

FIGURE 1.3. Drummers at Simiri, performing at a spirit possession ceremony. The large drum in the centre is the *tourou*, which features in the film *Les Tambours d'avant: Tourou et Bitti* (1971). © Fondation Jean Rouch.

several centuries. However, since the 1970s, when the current fundamentalist tendency in the Muslim world first began to take hold in West Africa, public expressions of "animist" beliefs have been increasingly under pressure. Today, they have become a relative rarity, particularly in urban areas.[6] But in the 1940s and 1950s, when Rouch first started to work in the region, this historical process had hardly begun and, as Rouch himself reported it, in everyday life there was generally a very pragmatic accommodation between Islam and traditional religions: while Islam was thought to be the vehicle for contemplating issues of transcendent spirituality, it was to traditional religious practices that people would turn as a means for confronting such everyday problems as sickness, poor harvests, frustrations at work, matters of the heart and even for advice as to how to avoid military service.[7]

Both as anthropologist and filmmaker, Rouch took a particular interest in traditional practices of magic, witchcraft, and healing. But the aspect of Songhay religion that most intrigued him was spirit possession. This would become the principal subject matter of a large number of his films. He discovered that spirit possession was not only prevalent in traditional rural communities, but also in the suburbs of Niamey, and even as far afield as the cities of the Gold Coast (as Ghana was still then known) to which many Songhay migrated on a seasonal basis. Through most of 1950s, Rouch was employed by a number of colonial research agencies to study this migratory process, and out of this work arose perhaps the most celebrated of all his films, *Les Maîtres fous*, shot in 1954 and released the following year. This chronicles the annual meeting of a migrants' spirit possession cult based in Accra, capital of the Gold Coast and then probably the most economically dynamic city in West Africa.

Rouch's first encounter with Songhay spirit possession, like so much else about his life, has become the stuff of legend. Some six months after he first arrived in Niger in 1941, a number of his laborers were killed by lightning.[8] Rouch first approached a marabout, as Muslim religious specialists are known in francophone Africa, with a view to arranging a funeral for the unfortunate men. The marabout actually worked in the same Department of Public Works as Rouch, but he would have nothing to do with the victims' corpses, considering them too polluted. Rouch was then introduced to a possession cult priestess by his young Nigerien assistant, Damouré Zika. The priestess, whose name was Kalia Daoudou, was Damouré's grandmother. She suggested that before the men's bodies were taken away to be buried, a possession ceremony should be held. This began with her spraying milk from her mouth directly over the corpses and then gently rubbing it in. During the possession event that then followed, Rouch learned through the spirit medium, a frail old woman dressed in black, that it had been Dongo, the fearsome Spirit of Thunder, who had been responsible for the death of the laborers. It transpired that Dongo had told his brother, Kyirey, the Spirit of Lightning, to kill the men because they had been sleeping with local women and, more significantly for Rouch, they had been "cultivating" his lands, that is, building the roads, without seeking his permission.

In order to placate the outraged spirit, Rouch had to arrange for the sacrifice of a black bull (black being the color associated with Dongo). As he would later declare, this was not something for which his training as an engineer at Ponts et Chaussées had prepared him. But he resolved that it was also something about which he had to find out more, and shortly afterward, with Damouré's assistance, he began his first program of ethnographic research. This was structured around a series of questionnaires prepared for him in Paris by Griaule and Dieterlen and then sent out to him through a roundabout route. The first results of these investigations were published the following year in the journal of the Institut français d'Afrique noire (IFAN), a colonial research center based in Dakar, Senegal, which was in effect the capital of French West Africa at that time.[9]

Rouch's original appointment in Niamey had been for a year, but he found the colonial society there so unbearable that no sooner had he arrived than he started to pull every string that he could in order to get out of the place. But for all his efforts, it was only after the year was up that he was finally able to get transferred to Dakar. This happened to be in November 1942, the very same month that Allied troops invaded Morocco. Shortly afterwards, under the leadership of Admiral Darlan, all the French colonies of the region went over to the Allied side. These macropolitical changes had major repercussions for all French colonial personnel in North and West Africa, including Jean Rouch. Early the following year, in March 1943, he was mobilized into the local French military forces as a junior officer in the Engineers Company of the First Armoured Division. It would be another year before he actually became involved in active service and in the interim, he continued to work as a civil engineer in Senegal. In his spare time, under the auspices of Théodore Monod, the director of the IFAN, he dedicated himself to studying the anthropology and history of the region in the IFAN library. Eventually, beginning in the early summer of 1944, Rouch not only participated in the invasion of France, but later of Germany itself. The war in Europe came to an end in May 1945 and Rouch was demobilized the following August. But even before then, whilst briefly on leave over Christmas 1944, he signed up at the Sorbonne to study for a doctorate under the supervision of Marcel Griaule.[10]

The Inheritance of Marcel Mauss

At first sight, Rouch's decision to become Griaule's doctoral student seems rather strange. In contrast to most other leading anthropologists, Griaule had remained in France after the German invasion and had even accepted certain preferments from the Vichy regime. In 1942, he had been appointed to a professorial chair at the Sorbonne. Having been an aviator in his youth, he had also accepted a commission as a colonel in the Vichy air force. According to legend, he even used to give lectures in his air force uniform. This association with the Vichy regime led to his expulsion from the Musée de l'Homme after the war, though he did manage to hold on to his position at the Sorbonne. Although Rouch was generally very hostile to everything and everybody associated with the Vichy regime, he particularly appreciated Griaule's sense of humor and asked him to be his supervisor for the simple reason that he considered Griaule to be "more fun" than the other leading Africanists with whom he might have studied at that time. In later life, Rouch often referred to Griaule's smile and once compared studying ethnography with him to a game of blind-man's-buff that made him laugh so much, it almost made him ill.[11]

But while all this may have been true, there were probably also some more pragmatic reasons for this decision. Griaule was the leading French authority on the middle Niger River where Rouch wanted to work and, with Dieterlen, he had supported Rouch's own first amateur ethnographic researches during the war years. It could also have been important that Griaule was sympathetic to filmmaking, having made two films among the Dogon in the 1930s.[12] Yet although there may have been a number of good reasons for Rouch to study with Griaule, there always remained a certain ambiguity in Rouch's attitudes toward his mentor, involving a curious mixture of disdain and respect. Rouch liked to present this as an extrapolation of the traditional joking relationship between the cliff-dwelling Dogon, whom Griaule had studied, and the Songhay and the other peoples living on the fluvial savannas along the Niger River, whom he himself would study. However, as I shall describe in later chapters of this book, this seems to have been a way of masking the principal reason for Rouch's ambiguity toward his intellectual mentor, namely, the difference in their political views, not only in relation to Griaule's *vichysois* associations during the war years, but also with regard to the French colonial presence in Africa.

In notable contrast to the ambiguity in his attitudes to Griaule, Rouch always retained the highest regard for Germaine Dieterlen. In the 1960s and 1970s, they collaborated in the making of a number of major films about the Dogon, including a series of films about the Sigui, the Dogon's world renewal ritual cycle that takes place over the course of seven consecutive years. In the latter part of his career, Rouch made no less than four film portraits of Dieterlen and when they were both in Paris, they spent a great deal of time in one another's company, particularly after Rouch's first wife, Jane, died in 1987. According to some of his closest associates, when Dieterlen herself died in 1999 at the age of ninety-five, Rouch was cast into the deepest depression and never quite recaptured his celebrated joie de vivre again

The general theoretical approach to anthropology that Griaule passed on to Rouch was that of his own mentor, Marcel Mauss. Until 1940, when he suffered a mental collapse following the German invasion, Mauss was the leading anthropologist in France. The nephew of the eminent sociologist Émile Durkheim, Mauss dedicated most of his professional career to perpetuating his uncle's intellectual legacy, editing the *Année Sociologique* journal that Durkheim had founded and preparing for publication the manuscripts left behind by former students of Durkheim who had perished in the First World War. Due to these many other commitments, Mauss actually published relatively little, and always in the form of essays and articles rather than monographs. Under the modest

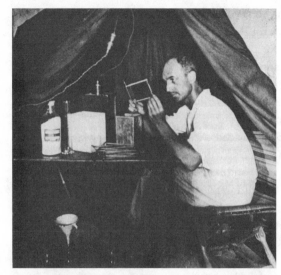

FIGURE 1.4. Jean Rouch's mentors in the field. *Top*, Marcel Griaule, 1930s, developing photographs (from the Dakar-Djibouti collection held by the Musée Quai Branly, see Clifford 1988:66). *Bottom*, Germaine Dieterlen around 1970, © Fondation Jean Rouch. Griaule and Dieterlen both told Rouch that one needs at least twenty years' experience before one can achieve a "deep knowledge" of a society's "system of thought."

title, "Essai sur le don," his most celebrated work, *The Gift*, was first published as a contribution to the *Année Sociologique* in 1923. But through his lectures and seminars, Mauss played a major role in the formation of the next generation of French anthropologists.

As Rouch himself once remarked, although Mauss was very loyal to his uncle's intellectual inheritance, there were significant differences in their respective approaches.[13] Whereas for Durkheim, ideas, beliefs, and values were little more than illusions that served to legitimate and sustain social institutions, for Mauss, these intellectual principles and their cultural variability were of primary importance. In Mauss's view, far from being mere ideological projections of social institutions, it was ideas that gave rise to social institutions in the first place. In advocating this approach, Mauss was the most influential figure in the establishment of a strongly intellectualist current in French anthropology, committed to the study of *systèmes de pensée*, literally "systems of thought." This phrase came to be used by those working in the Maussian tradition to refer to the sets of intellectual principles that they believed underlay cultural phenomena of all kinds and that could be expressed in a variety of ways. In any given society, they could be discovered not only in such abstractions as theories of cosmology and the concept of the person but also embodied in more material social practices such as subsistence activities, relationships of kinship and marriage, and even in body movements, gestures, and artifacts.[14]

From a methodological point of view, Mauss's approach involved a radical differentiation between the process of ethnographic description and the process of theoretical explanation.[15] The first stage in a research project should ideally involve the systematic accumulation of large bodies of ethnographic data. Referred to as "documents," these could be culled from a broad variety of sources, both historical and anthropological, textual as well as verbal. Indeed, everything and anything could be grist for the ethnographer's mill since, as Germaine Dieterlen once remarked, the clumsiest design scratched on a wall with a fingernail could provide an insight into ideas about the structure of the universe.[16] This process of accumulating "documents" should be as objective as possible and free from a priori explanatory concerns. Once collected, the "documents" should be subjected to a rigorous scholarly exegesis within the framework of indigenous concepts and linguistic categories. The elaboration of exogenous theoretical explanations or arguments in terms of comparative ethnography were processes that should happen later, a posteriori, rather that during the accumulation of the "documents" in the first place.

Some of the theoretical principles that Mauss identified—for example, about the forms of reciprocity in a range of human relationships or the corporeal embodiment of cultural norms—have been a source of great inspiration to subsequent generations of anthropologists. However, contemporary accounts suggest that in his lectures, Mauss often got so immersed in the ethnographic details that he never quite arrived at the elucidation of the theoretical conclusions.[17] Rouch's account of Griaule's lectures, alluded to above, suggests that they too may have suffered from the same shortcomings. More generally, in this particular anthropological school there was a decided tendency for detailed ethnographic description to be prioritized and appreciated for its own sake, while theoretical explanation and generalization were treated as matters of a second order of elaboration that should eventually—but which might not necessarily—follow.

Certainly this was true of Rouch's textual anthropology. His doctoral dissertation on the Songhay was submitted in 1952 and later published under the title *La Religion et la magie songhay*, first in 1960, and then in a substantially annotated second edition in 1989. The original dissertation was completed shortly after the publication of Dieterlen's classic work, *Essai sur la religion bambara*, and it was clearly heavily influenced by her example.[18] Not only the general approach, but even the structure and layout of Rouch's work follow those of Dieterlen's work very closely. That is, it provides a detailed but highly descriptive account of Songhay beliefs in which each element or aspect of Songhay traditional religion is described sequentially and in isolation—the general cosmology, the myths of origin associated with particular cult activities, the various roles or offices involved, the "texts" chanted, the forms of dance, the types of musical instrument, and so on. The only explanations that are offered for these practices are in terms of local legends or beliefs, often quoted verbatim. At the end of the book, in a "conclusion" of less than three pages, Rouch makes no attempt to identify any general theoretical consequences of his study. He declines to present Songhay religious ideas and practices as ideologically related to particular social or political structures. Analyses in terms of either the comparative ethnography or history of West Africa as a whole are not merely eschewed but ridiculed, albeit humorously. Instead, Rouch chooses to celebrate, in defiance of considerable evidence to the contrary to which he himself even alludes, the original and unique character of Songhay religion.[19]

As we shall see in later chapters of this book, these ideas concerning the primary importance of collecting ethnographic "documents" in as objective and rigorous a fashion as possible, derived originally from the methodology of Marcel Mauss, would later come to influence an important strand of Rouch's filmic method, notably when he worked with Germaine Dieterlen on their series of films about the Dogon Sigui ritual cycle in the 1960s and 1970s.

Fieldwork Practice

If Rouch's general intellectual formation can be traced back ultimately to Marcel Mauss, then his ideas about the actual practice of anthropology in the field were more directly influenced by the methods of Marcel Griaule. For although Mauss actively advocated the carrying out of fieldwork, his own investigations remained entirely bibliographic. Griaule, in contrast, was highly committed to fieldwork in practice as well as in principle. His ideas about how to conduct fieldwork are laid out very explicitly in his *Méthode de l'ethnographie*, a slim handbook not published until 1957, the year after his death, but drawing on his experience working with the Dogon since the 1930s.

The approach that Griaule proposes here is very different to that developed around the same time by Anglo-Saxon anthropologists, notably by Bronislaw Malinowski, which, since the 1960s, has become the orthodoxy in social and cultural anthropology generally, even in France.[20] Whereas Malinowski proposed that the fieldworker should "plunge into the life of the natives," usually alone, becoming a relatively unobtrusive "participant-observer" engaged in the day-to-day life of a community, Griaule advocated the formation of multidisciplinary teams of fieldworkers organized along quasi-military lines, who would not only maximize the collection of data within any given time period, but also at the same time triangulate the results that they were obtaining. Far from the discreet observation of life as it is lived with minimal interference, as per the Malinowskian approach, Griaule's method was highly proactive, involving intensive interrogatory interviews based on systematic questionnaires. Rather than observing the subjects interacting among themselves, Griaule preferred to work instead with a select group of elite informants, using bilingual intermediaries rather than the native language.

In an article first published in 1966, Mary Douglas provides a succinct contrast between the interview-based Griaulian approach and the more low-key participant-observation practiced around this time by British Africanist anthropologists such as herself. "Only the oblique approach will yield the results we seek," she writes. "The scrupulous setting down of informants' views merely sets up the screen which must then somehow be passed or penetrated. The kind of truths we seek to reveal are hidden from the informants themselves. Hence our attempts to develop a foxy cunning in checking statements against action." Like Brer Fox, British anthropologists tried "to lie low and to eschew direct questions. We aim to let the informants reveal, by contradiction and inconsistency, the practical social uses to which their cosmological schemes are put."[21]

The contrast between the two approaches is readily apparent from the rather droll account that Rouch himself gives of the fieldwork routines of Griaule and Dieterlen as he observed them while visiting their camp at Sanga, in the heart of the Bandiagara Escarpment, in 1950.[22] First thing in the morning, Griaule would give all members of the team their tasks for the day. While he and Dieterlen worked through questionnaires with their established informants and other researchers in the team were dispatched elsewhere, groups of traditional musicians would be summoned to perform for Rouch and his filmmaking partner and sound recordist on this particular expedition, Roger Rosfelder, also a student of Griaule. Alternatively, Rouch and Rosfelder would be sent off to film daily life in a nearby Dogon village. At noon, the whole team would meet up in the company of the Dogon informants and interpreters and would then exchange the information gathered in the morning. On the basis of these discussions—in which, Rouch emphasizes, the Dogon played an active part—Dieterlen would typically develop an inspired series of further hypotheses, which Griaule would order into a new series of questionnaires to be used in the afternoon. With perhaps just a touch of irony, Rouch compares this approach to the Socratic method of successive dialogical approximations to philosophical truth.[23]

The fieldwork approach that Rouch himself would develop, both as filmmaking and text-making anthropologist, shared certain similarities with that of his mentor. Like Griaule, Rouch returned faithfully to the same field sites in West Africa over a prolonged period. Indeed, Rouch liked to quote Griaule and Dieterlen's view that one needed at least twenty years' firsthand experience of a given society before one could begin to achieve a "deep knowledge" of its systems of thought.[24] Like Griaule, Rouch tended to rely on a key group of informants and worked largely through the medium of French, perhaps because, as he himself confessed, he was "not very good at languages."[25] In his conventional anthropological fieldwork, he often used formal questionnaires, both during his doctoral research and in the migration studies that he carried out in West Africa in the 1950s.[26] Also like Griaule, Rouch tended to focus his attention on what might be called the public cultural rhetoric of the groups whom he studied ethnographically. That is, the great majority of his films are about public ceremonial performances of one kind or another, and there is very little emphasis on private domestic life and the routines of the everyday. Partly for this reason, Rouch's films mainly concern the public world of men while the more domestic world of women remains relatively neglected.

Although Rouch rarely used interviews of any kind in his ethnographic films, one can also perhaps detect, as James Clifford has done, a certain continuity between, on the one hand, what he calls Griaule's "dialogical method," in which interrogatory questions were aimed at provoking the subjects into revealing answers and, on the other, Rouch's idea that the camera could act as a catalyst to provoke his subjects into revelatory performances.[27] Indeed, it is tempting to argue that in the same way that Griaule's proactive methods contrasted with the more passive participant-observational methods of Anglo-Saxon anthropology at the time, so too did Rouch's proactive cinematographic methods contrast with the more low-key methods of direct or observational cinema as practiced by his Anglo-Saxon filmmaking contemporaries.

These are matters that I shall explore in greater detail in subsequent chapters. As we shall see, notwithstanding these similarities between the fieldwork methods of Rouch and Griaule, in other ways their general approaches to anthropology were very different, largely on account of their very different attitudes toward the French colonial regime in Africa.

2 : The Surrealist Encounter

For me, cinema, making a film, is like Surrealist painting: the use of the most real processes of reproduction, the most photographic, but at the service of the unreal, of the bringing into being of elements of the irrational (as in Magritte, Dalí). The postcard at the service of the imaginary. JEAN ROUCH (1967)[1]

In making films, I have tried to get as close as possible to the spontaneity of the jazz players. Between my passion for the ethnology of Africa and my passion for films, there is perhaps that subtle connection, the music of jazz.
JEAN ROUCH (2001)[2]

Although it was undoubtedly a crucial influence on his future career, the extramural course at the Musée de l'Homme given by Marcel Griaule and Germaine Dieterlen in 1940–1941 was not Jean Rouch's first encounter with anthropology. In fact, he had come across Griaule's work some years previously due to his prior interest in the Surrealist movement, with which a number of leading French anthropologists of the time were associated. This mode of entry into anthropology would come to have a profound influence on Rouch's filmmaking praxis.

Complicities and Affinities

There is now a substantial literature on the intellectual climate of Paris in the late 1920s and 1930s and, more particularly, on what the anthropologist and historian Jean Jamin has called the "complicities and affinities" between Surrealism and anthropology, or rather *l'ethnologie* to use the term most commonly applied in France at that time to the study of "other cultures."[3] Although Mauss and the philosopher Lucien Lévy-Bruhl had set up the Institut d'ethnologie within the University of Paris in 1925, the practice of ethnology remained strongly centered around museums in France. As a result, French ethnology was not only particularly concerned with the collection of material objects and the interpretation of their symbolic significance, but also with the display of these objects to a nonspecialist public. This provided obvious grounds of affinity with artists of all kinds, but in the case of the Surrealists, there was also an additional complicity, namely, a common interest in the exotic Other.

One expression of this complicity lay in the fact that certain figures of the Surrealist movement attended Mauss's lectures while a number of leading anthropologists wrote for Surrealist publications. Some aspired to make original contributions to both fields of endeavor. Griaule himself tried his hand at Surrealist poetry—though not very successfully, according to Rouch.[4] Much more effective in straddling the two fields was Michel Leiris, a Surrealist author who, after studying ethnology at the Sorbonne, was appointed the "secretary-archivist" of Griaule's Dakar-Djibouti Expedition, about which he wrote a controversial semi-autobiographical travel diary, *L'Afrique fantôme*. Leiris spent most of his subsequent career working rather prosaically as an ethnologist at the Musée de l'Homme, where he occupied what Rouch described as a "miniscule" office and produced a number of conventional ethnographic monographs in the immediate postwar period. But at the same time, he continued to be a major figure on the Parisian arts and literary scene, being both a confidant and a sitter for such leading artists as Pablo Picasso, Alberto Giacometti, and Francis Bacon, as well as a coeditor with Jean-Paul Sartre of *Les Temps modernes*.[5]

One of the key meeting places between ethnology and Surrealism in the interwar period was in the pages of the ephemeral journal *Documents*. This was published over a two-year period in 1929–1930 and was edited by Leiris and Georges Bataille, the leading figure of the faction that had broken off from the Surrealist group dominated by André Breton. In effect, *Documents* was a rival to the "official" Surrealist journals, *La Révolution surréaliste*, and its successor, *Le Surréalisme au service de la révolution*. Although the mainstream Surrealist publications had also occasionally featured ethnographic items, they were much more prevalent in *Documents*. Perhaps not coincidentally, the title of the new journal was precisely the same term that Mauss used to describe the most basic unit of ethnographic description.

What is certain is that just like the lectures of both Mauss and Griaule, each number of *Documents* juxtaposed a diverse range of different bits and pieces of human cultural experience. Side by side with sober analyses of works by major artists such as Picasso, Salvador Dalí, and Paul Klee, one finds archaeological reports, eighteenth-century prints of

Siamese twins and other "freaks of nature," reproductions of the book jackets of crime novels, and photographs of all kinds—severed limbs outside an abbatoir, New York skyscrapers, carnival masks, totem poles, flies stuck on flypaper. Particularly notable are two very close close-ups of the human big toe (one male subject, aged thirty, and one female, aged twenty-four) taken by Jacques-André Boiffard, the photographer who worked with the Surrealist artist Man Ray and whose photographs of Paris had featured in André Breton's semidocumentary novel, *Nadja*. Reviews of works by Stravinsky and Rossini alternate with reviews of performances by the African American dance band, Lew Leslie's Black Birds, recordings by Duke Ellington and stills from the latest film by Sergei Eisenstein that had been banned at the Sorbonne. In the midst of this eclectic mix, there are regular ethnographic contributions from prime movers in the formation of academic anthropology in France, including such establishment figures as Paul Rivet and Georges-Henri Rivière, who together would be principally responsible for the foundation of the Musée de l'Homme in 1937. Griaule and Leiris were particularly regular contributors, as was their fellow future Dakar-Djibouti expeditionary, the musicologist André Schaeffner. Even Marcel Mauss made a brief contribution to the special issue on the work of Pablo Picasso.

Although the publication of *Documents* had by then ceased, these connections continued to exert their influence once the Dakar-Djibouti Expedition got under way. For Griaule's decision to stop off at the Bandiagara Escarpment was because this had been recommended to him by his "secretary-archivist" Leiris, who in turn had heard about the Dogon and their extraordinary masks from the North American William B. Seabrook. Self-confessed cannibal, voudou enthusiast, and bondage fetishist, as well as satellite of the Surrealist movement, Seabrook was a drinking companion of Leiris. Not long before the expedition, he had helped Leiris by commissioning a series of photographs of a naked woman in a leather bondage mask to accompany an article that Leiris wrote for *Documents* about masking.[6] It was in this way that the connections established through *Documents* were responsible for bringing about what Luc de Heusch would later describe as "the miracle that would become the founding event of French field ethnography . . . the encounter of Marcel Griaule with the most Surrealist of all the peoples of Africa."[7]

Jean Jamin, and indeed Leiris himself, have cautioned against exaggerating the extent of the mutual influence of ethnology and Surrealism in interwar Paris. While the ethnologists aspired to explain cultural Otherness within a rational scientific framework, the Surrealists sought instead a subjective immersion in the experience of the Other. Often fleeing from the values imposed on them in the course of bourgeois Catholic upbringings—which they considered discredited by the tragedy of the 1914–1918 "war to end all wars" and which they detested for the repression of sexuality associated with them—the Surrealists looked to other religions, and in particular African religions, in the hope of reconnecting with some uncorrupted elemental humanity, as much informed by sensuality and eroticism as by any notions of theology. The Surrealists despised what André Breton once called the *"regard trop souvent glacé"*—the too frequently icy outlook—of the ethnologists, and in one of the many pamphlets that the movement produced, the works of both Lévy-Bruhl and Durkheim appeared in the list of proscribed reading.[8] The relationship between ethnology and Surrealism, argues Jamin, was one of contiguity within the same critical space rather than genuine similarity, and it was marked as much by ambiguity and mistrust as by constructive dialogue. There may have been complicities and affinities, but this did not imply, he suggests, that "there were transfers of methods or concepts."[9]

Yet while this might well have been generally true, it certainly does not apply to the case of Jean Rouch. In fact, I would argue that without considering the influence of Surrealist methods and concepts, it is impossible to arrive at a proper understanding of Rouch's filmmaking praxis.

The *coup de foudre* on the rue Montparnasse

Rouch liked to relate his first encounter with ethnology as a sort of Damascene conversion, complete with blinding light, which occurred late one spring afternoon in 1934. In the rays of the setting sun reflected on the window of a bookshop at the intersection of the rues Raspail and Montparnasse, very close to where he lived with this parents, the sixteen-year-old Rouch caught sight of a display of two double-page spreads from *Minotaure*. This was the somewhat more upmarket journal that had by then replaced *Documents* but that featured much the same eclectic mix of articles on anthropology, archaeology, and the arts, with contributions by the leading Surrealist figures as well as by anthropologists and art historians. One of these spreads was from the second volume, published the previous year and featuring a series of articles about the Dakar-Djibouti Expedition, which had then only recently returned. One of the articles, by Marcel Griaule, the expedition leader, described the funeral of the great Dogon hunter Monzé, and was accompanied by a series of photographs, taken by Griaule himself, showing the masked dancers who customarily perform at such events.[10] The other double-page spread, the frontispiece from volume 5, was hot off the press and featured a color reproduction of a painting by Giorgio de Chirico, the Greek-Italian artist whose work was greatly admired by the Surrealists. Entitled *Le Duo* or *Les Mannequins de la tour rose* (*The Duo* or *The Mannequins of the Pink Tower*) and completed in 1915, this painting showed a pair of armless mannequins with mask-like faces standing on some sort of deck, with the pink tower referred to in the title in the background.

The young Rouch was intrigued by the visual similarities between the figures in the de Chirico painting and what he later recalled as "the un-forgettable photograph of the *kanaga* masks up on the roof terrace of the hunter Monzé."[11] In fact, there is no one photograph in Griaule's ar-ticle about Monzé's funeral that exactly corresponds to this description. There are certainly clear echoes between the de Chirico image and a num-ber of the photographs that accompanied Griaule's article or that ap-peared in other articles in the same edition of *Minotaure*, but the most direct correspondence is with a photograph that appears as plate 1 in Griaule's masterwork, *Masques dogons*. However, this was not actually published until some four years after Rouch's conversion experience. It would seem then that in recollecting the moment some sixty years later, Rouch conflated—quite understandably, of course—a number of different Dogon images that impressed him around the time of his late adolescence (see fig. 2.1).

But in any case, far more important for Rouch than the relatively su-perficial visual similarities that might be detected between the Dogon photographs and the de Chirico painting was what lay behind them. Sud-denly, it came to Rouch as a *"coup de foudre,"* a lightning bolt, that both sets of images provided a means of access to the marvelous that lies be-hind the everyday. In effect, both sets of masked figures represented the mysteries of the imaginary made manifest in material reality. Through this juxtaposition, the Dogon and the landscapes of the Bandiagara Es-carpment became inextricably linked in Rouch's mind with the oneiric landscapes of de Chirico, and he felt himself irresistibly drawn toward them.[12] The effects of this decisive moment would be long lasting. For it was this entirely fortuitous encounter that would lead Rouch, first, to seek out the photographer, Marcel Griaule, and to attend his lectures in the basement of the Musée de l'Homme, and then, eventually, to travel to West Africa himself.

During his student years, Rouch continued to develop his interest in Surrealism. After he was admitted to the École des Ponts et Chausées, he began to go to the *vernissages*, exhibition previews, of the leading Sur-realist artists. At one of these, he encountered Salvador Dalí and noted his green jacket and famously blue-tinted moustache. He also attended the Surrealists' poetry readings. One that he remembered particularly took place in October 1937. On this occasion, he heard Paul Éluard recite his poems in his strange reedy voice while the actor and theatre director Jean-Louis Barrault read the poems of André Breton with Breton himself sitting there, sporting his characteristic red shoelaces and listening impassively, without saying a word. But being only twenty, Rouch did not ever dare to approach these *monstres sacrés* and speak to them in person.[13]

Also central to the formation of Rouch's sensibility around this time, though perhaps less frequently commented upon, was African American jazz. This too was very much part of the same circle of exchanges in which leading figures of both anthropology and Surrealism were involved in the 1920s and 1930s. In fact, an interest in jazz was simply another refraction of the more generalized interest in *l'art nègre* that was all the rage in interwar Paris. This embraced, at one extreme, the night-club dancer Josephine Baker and African American boxers and, at the other, traditional African sculpture and voudou ritual. André Schaeffner, musicologist of the Dakar-Djibouti Expedition and renowned for his arrangement of the works of Stravinsky, was also the coauthor of one of the first books on jazz in French, published in 1926.[14] Georges-Henri Rivière, first director as well as cofounder of the Musée de l'Homme, was an accomplished jazz pianist and played at *Boeuf sur le toit*, a restaurant set up by the poet Jean Cocteau and named after a well-known Surrealist ballet. In 1931, in order to raise money for the Dakar-Djibouti Expedition, Rivière organized a boxing match between the world bantam-weight boxing champion, the African American Al Brown, and the French feather-weight champion, Roger Simondé, an encounter that Brown won easily. According to legend, Marcel Mauss himself engaged in some shadow-boxing with Al Brown before the main bout began.[15] A well-known photograph of the period shows Rivière, Al Brown, and Marcel Griaule seated together. In Griaule's hands, there is an African sculpture and he is apparently explaining something about it to the boxer.

Rouch himself was too young to attend this event but he considered his attendance in 1934 at the first concert that Louis Armstrong played in Paris to be a formative experience.[16] Once he became a student at the École des Ponts et Chaussées, he and his friends took to wearing their hair long and dressing in zoot suits, partly as a sign of their admiration for the African American musicians' dress style, and partly as a symbolic resistance to the short hair and uniforms worn by the German soldiers by then occupying the city.[17] Rouch maintained this interest in jazz for the rest of his life, finding in this music the same emphasis on spontaneity and improvisation that he appreciated in the work of the Surrealist poets. Indeed, many years later, he would claim that his ideal was to make films in the same way as Louis Armstrong played his trumpet.[18]

a

b

c

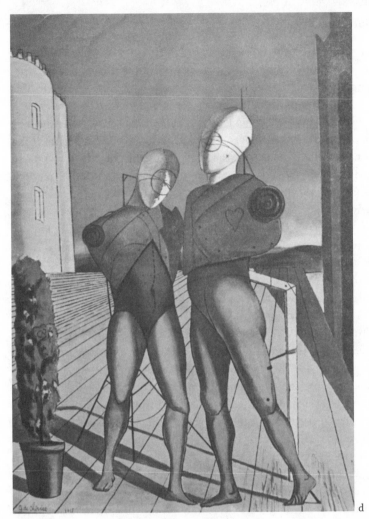

d

FIGURE 2.1. The "coup de foudre" on the rue Montparnasse. (*a*) Mourners on the terrace of Monzé's house (Griaule 1933b:32). (*b*) *Kanaga* masks at a funerary rite, with houses, granaries in the background (Griaule 1933c:50). (*c*) *Kanaga* masks on the terrace of an unnamed dead man (Griaule 1938: plate 1A). (*d*) *The Duo* or *The Mannequins of the Pink Tower*.

Rouch recalled being "struck by lightning" by the link between the images in two different editions of *Minotaure*, displayed side by side in a bookshop window: one image was a color reproduction of de Chirico's painting, *The Duo*; the other was a photograph from Marcel Griaule's report on a Dogon funeral, showing "the *kanaga* masks on the terrace of the hunter Monzé."

In fact, there is no image in Griaule's report on Monzé's funeral that exactly fits this description. It may be that Rouch was combining in his memory the three images shown *left*, which appeared in (*a*) the Monzé funeral report, (*b*) the following *Minotaure* article by Griaule on masks and (*c*) in his later work, *Masques dogons*.

The Surrealist Dream

The effect of the *coup de foudre* on rue Montparnasse remained with Rouch long after Surrealism as an artistic movement had been declared a journey that had reached its end by some of its former exponents.[19] It was an influence manifested in many different ways in his work. Most obviously, it is evident in his frequent references to the Surrealists by name, particularly to the poets, who, I would argue, had a greater influence on him than the visual artists despite the fact that he worked in a primarily visual medium himself. Among the poets, his most frequent references are to André Breton and Paul Éluard. But he was also particularly fond of alluding to Baudelaire and Rimbaud, both of whom, although writing in a somewhat earlier period, were much admired by the Surrealists and specifically claimed by Breton as precursors in his "First Surrealist Manifesto" of 1924.

Among the visual artists, Rouch liked to invoke René Magritte and Dalí, as in the epigraph above, but the visual artist to whom he probably most frequently referred was Giorgio de Chirico. Although de Chirico came to despise the Surrealists in his later years, his "metaphysical" style was much admired by Breton and his colleagues.[20] Through his passion for the work of de Chirico, Rouch also became interested in the work of Friedrich Nietzsche, whose writings had greatly influenced the painter. According to Rouch, de Chirico was directly inspired by a passage in one of Nietzsche's works, in which the statues of Turin are described as coming down from their plinths in the rays of an autumnal setting sun, to paint his celebrated series of paintings of shadowy figures in formal piazzas, "giving directly," as Rouch put it, "onto the world of dreams."[21] One of this series of paintings was *Le Duo*, the painting reproduced in *Minotaure* that played such a crucial role in first propelling Rouch toward anthropology, as described above.

These references to the Surrealist poets and artists occur both in Rouch's films and in his interviews and writings. For the most part, in the films these references are indirect, functioning more at the level of general ideas and practices. But some are quite explicit, involving direct allusions in the titles or even quotations within the films themselves. The most celebrated example of a Rouchian film title taken from a Surrealist text is surely *La Pyramide humaine* (1961), which comes from the title of a poem by Éluard that is recited at one point in the film. But Rouch later produced two less well-known films with titles that are taken from works by Surrealist precursors: *Le Couleur du temps*, a film script that Rouch wrote in 1945 and finally made into a film in 1988, shares the title of a play in verse by Guillaume Apollinaire, while *Le Beau Navire*, released in 1990, a short film about the Eiffel Tower, takes its title from a poem by Baudelaire. As for quotations within the films themselves, in *La Pyramide humaine*, in addition to the eponymous poem by Éluard, there are references to two poems by Rimbaud and one by Baudelaire. There are also a number of quotations from works by Surrealists or their precursors in *La Punition* (1963), and several passages of Baudelaire in *Les Veuves de quinze ans* (1966). Baudelaire crops up again in *Petit à Petit* (1971) when Safi Faye, playing an African prostitute in Paris, shares a passage from one of his works with a client, played by Damouré Zika, though the latter somewhat sheepishly confesses that he is not familiar with the poet's work.

In Rouch's interviews, the influence of Surrealist ideas is made manifest in his frequent references not just to adventure but to the marvelous and the mysterious and, somewhat less commonly, to the key Surrealist concepts of *hasard objectif*, "objective chance," and *les objets inquiétants*, "disturbing objects," that crop up here and there. But, above all, this influence is revealed in the constant references to dreams. These punctuate all Rouch's commentaries on his own work. Typical in this regard are his opening remarks in the major interview that he gave to Enrico Fulchignoni, published in 1981, at the time of a major retrospective of his work:

> To be able to leap from one place to another, that is my most cherished dream. To be able to go anywhere, to wander off somewhere else as one wanders about in a dream. The mobile camera, the camera that walks and flies, we all share that dream. Simply because, for me, to make a film is to write with one's eyes, one's ears, with one's body. It's to get inside, to be at the same time both invisible and present . . . We should put on the winged slippers of Arthur Rimbaud and take off to foreign lands, and from there, bring back fragments of a flying carpet that we can share with others, but that's a dream![22]

These ubiquitous references to dreams in Rouch's work are not simply a manner of speaking, nor a casual metaphor for some desirable but unattainable state of affairs. They are certainly not inspired by the Anglo-Saxon dream of self-realization or material achievement, nor by the socialist dream of a utopian society, nor even by the orthodox Freudian idea of the dream as the royal road to the unconscious amphitheatre in which fears and desires endlessly contend. Rather, these recurrent references to dreaming are inspired by the Surrealist conception of the dream, as described at length by André Breton in his various manifestos and declarations, as the medium through which the powerful creative energies within the human psyche can be unleashed and the barriers between individual subjective experience and the exterior, objective world can be broken down.

Moreover, for Rouch, as for Breton, the cinema was similar to dreaming in that it was a medium through which these effects could be achieved, be it actively, in the process of filmmaking, or more passively, in the viewing of films. Thus when he was making films, as suggested in the Fulchignoni interview cited above, Rouch aspired "to write with his whole body," to be simultaneously "both invisible and present" as if wandering in a dream. When he was viewing films, as described in the Preface to this book, he would adopt a supine, almost fetal position in the front row of the cinema and gaze up at the screen before him, seemingly in some kind of dream state then too.

Rouch's ideas about the transporting possibilities of viewing films are stated very clearly in a much-quoted passage in which he rails against the way in which an excessive concern with technique or professional equipment in ethnographic filmmaking can inhibit the potential of film to carry the viewer across cultural boundaries. Originally published in the journal *Positif* in 1955, this passage was reproduced at length in the 1975 version of his key essay, "The Camera and Man":

> [T]here are a few rare moments when the filmgoer suddenly understands an unknown language without the help of subtitles, when he participates in strange ceremonies, when he finds himself walking in towns or across terrain that he has never seen before but that he recognizes perfectly . . . A miracle such as this could only be produced by cinema . . . in the middle of the most banal film, amidst the wild collage of random events, in the meanderings of amateur cinema, a mysterious contact is established. Perhaps it is the close-up of an African smile, a Mexican winking at the camera, the gesture of a European which is so everyday that no one would dream of filming it . . . But today's filmmakers prefer not to venture along these dangerous paths, and only mediums, madmen and children dare to press the forbidden buttons.[23]

Many anthropologists would surely consider the proposition that a film-viewing experience can allow one to understand a language that one does not know or to recognize perfectly a previously unseen terrain to be little more than a mystical delusion. A more generous interpretation is that Rouch is employing a poetic metaphor here to describe the empathetic recognition of a common humanity lying beyond cultural difference of the kind that is the frequent experience of anthropologists engaged in long-term fieldwork, whether or not their relationships with their subjects are mediated by film.[24] But whatever the reservations of certain anthropologists might be, there is no doubt that Rouch's suggestion that film can reach beyond the surface of everyday cultural realities is very much in tune with the ideas of the Surrealists. Also very typical of Surrealist thinking, but also surely at odds with the *regard trop souvent glacé* of many anthropologists, is the suggestion in the last line of this passage that the insane and children enjoy some sort of privileged insight into the nature of things.

Yet if Rouch shared much in common with the Surrealists, there were also certain ways in which his views differed significantly from theirs. For one thing, he did not share the enthusiasm of at least some of his Surrealist poet-heroes for Karl Marx and Sigmund Freud. For Rouch, these men were thinkers who exploited other people's dreams rather than being dreamers themselves.[25] Overt political references are very rare in the Rouchian canon and, as he once commented, if he had any defined political posture himself, it was based on anarchism without militancy.[26] Sexuality is similarly muted in his films. Some present-day viewers have detected a certain homoerotic quality in the way in which Rouch films African male bodies and interactions, but this seems to me to be more of an index of contemporary preoccupations than evidence of any particular interest of this nature on Rouch's part. More generally, although there are some heterosexual moments in the fiction films that he made in the late 1950s and early 1960s that were relatively risqué for the time, sufficient even to attract the attention of the French censor, within his oeuvre considered as a whole, sexuality is not a dominant theme. Certainly one does not find the overt preoccupation with sexual desire and the erotic that is so central to the work of many Surrealists, particularly the visual artists.

Another feature that distinguishes Rouch's work from that of the Surrealists is that in terms of its surface visual aesthetics, it remained, for the most part, predominantly realist. As Michael Richardson, among others, has pointed out, the Surrealists were not averse to the documentation of the real.[27] As I discussed above, *Documents*, one of the principal journals of the Surrealist movement, not only had a very realist-sounding title, but its pages were filled with photographs of a highly realist character. The same was true of *Minotaure*, though perhaps to a lesser extent. But, in the hands of the Surrealists, this photographic documentation of the real, while showing the world in an indexical manner, was intended at the same time to subvert the realism of the image by suggesting the marvelous that lay behind it. For as Breton had famously put it in the "First Surrealist Manifesto," "the marvellous is always beautiful, anything marvellous is beautiful, in fact only the marvellous is beautiful." This evocation of the marvelous in the real could be achieved by simply isolating one particular moment from the flow of events, by exaggerated close-ups, or by juxtaposing the image with other images or texts. The fact that art photography was all in black and white in the heyday of Surrealism no doubt helped to suggest a symbolic burden to these realist images.

Rouch, on the other hand, not only started shooting in color as soon as he could afford it, but also had a tendency to speak about visual documentation in almost positivist terms, often expressing an overriding concern to record the features of the world as they really are, in a faithful, literal manner. Notwithstanding his evocation on occasion of Magritte and Dalí, when it came to the status of the visual image, it was more often than not the engineer and the social scientist in Rouch who dominated the Surrealist. It could be argued perhaps that his extensive recording of African spirit possession ceremonies represented a sustained project to document the irruption of the marvelous into the everyday, while he himself suggested that by distributing such films, he was fulfilling Breton's recommendation to put "disturbing objects into circulation." But only very rarely did he actually manipulate his images in a manner or to a degree that was in any way comparable to the work of Magritte or Dalí and if he ever did do so, it was only in his fiction films. Despite his profound admiration for the dreamscapes of de Chirico, even the dream sequences in his fiction films remain very straightforwardly realist. One searches in vain for anything comparable to the visual élan of *Un Chien andalou*, the classic Surrealist film on which Dalí collaborated with Luís Buñuel. In Rouch's work, the surreal lurks mostly in the wings, and even when it takes center stage, it is usually clothed in the forms of the real.

The Chance Encounter and the Creative Performance

Although the influences of Surrealism on Jean Rouch may not be very evident in the visual style of his films, they nevertheless played a very strong part in shaping his practical filmmaking methods. As Philippe Lourdou has suggested, there is, for example, a direct parallel between Rouch's methods and the Surrealists' interest in experimentation.[28] In the same way that the Surrealists set up a "Bureau of Research" and sought to advance their investigations by a series of poetical and artistic experiments, so too did Rouch conceive of his own work as a constant series of attempts to try out new ideas. This was particularly true during the period from the late 1950s to the mid-1960s, when he carried out a systematic series of film experiments to establish whether the set of methods known as *cinéma-vérité* could be applied to the making of fiction films. Secure in his tenured position at the Centre National de Recherche Scientifique (CNRS), he did not need to worry about whether these experiments were regarded as successful by film critics or other third parties. What was more important to him was to learn from these experiments and move on to the next.[29]

But perhaps the most significant way in which Surrealism influenced Rouch's practical filmmaking methods was in relation to the highly positive value that he always attributed to chance and spontaneity. One particularly important expression of this was his interest in the Surrealist notion of the *rencontre*, the chance encounter between strangers, the equivalent in human terms of the celebrated definition of beauty by the Surrealist precursor, the Comte de Lautréamont, as "the chance encounter of a sewing machine and an umbrella on a dissecting table." The Surrealists believed that such chance encounters were usually not, in fact, purely random, since the parties to the encounter, often unbeknownst to themselves, were looking for something that they suddenly recognized and therefore responded to in a very positive manner. In this way, as Michel Remy has put it, "chance encounters and coincidences signified in themselves the short-cutting of reason, the elision of all deliberate choices, and the crystallized expression of the secret laws of the subconscious." As such, they represented "the marvellous precipitate of desire—a desire that is suddenly, magically made manifest."[30]

The *rencontre* is most famously represented in the Surrealist literary canon by André Breton's chance encounter with Nadja, the eponymous heroine of his novel, with whom he falls crazily, though fleetingly, in love. A few years later, true to the research ethos of Surrealism, Breton and Paul Éluard, even conducted a survey of 140 writers, academics, and artists, in which they asked their respondents to say to what degree they considered the most significant encounters in their lives to have been merely fortuitous or, rather, required by some previous circumstance. The results were published in *Minotaure* accompanied by a drawing by Man Ray of—what else?—an umbrella and a sewing machine on a dissecting table, and the relevant quotation from Lautréamont (see fig. 2.2).[31]

The account of his *rencontre* with the juxtaposed images of Dogon masks and the dreamscape of de Chirico—a sort of *rencontre* with a *rencontre*—was but one of many stories that Rouch liked to tell about his own life in which such encounters had produced highly positive outcomes. The *rencontre* was also a theme that he pursued in his fiction films, most explicitly in two films that he shot in Paris in the 1960s, *La Punition* and *Gare du Nord*. However, it is the negative consequences that follow from the failure of one or more of the subjects to grasp the opportunity offered by a *rencontre* that acts as the *leitmotif* of both these films. In *La Punition*, a beautiful young woman, finding herself unexpectedly free to wander around Paris for a day, encounters three men, of different ages

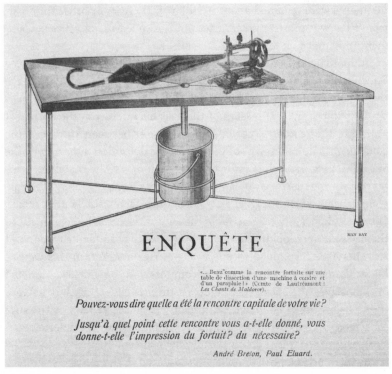

FIGURE 2.2. "As beautiful as the chance encounter on a dissecting table of a sewing machine and an umbrella." The title page of Breton and Éluard's report in *Minotaure* 3–4 (1933): 101, on their survey of personal relationships arising from chance encounters.

and backgrounds, and proposes to all three of them, one by one, that they run off with her and begin a new life together free from all constraints. But all three men refuse for a variety of banal, pragmatic reasons, leading her to conclude, sadly, that *l'amour fou*, the crazy love celebrated by André Breton, does not exist. In *Gare du Nord*, by contrast, it is the heroine, played by the same actress, who fails to grasp the opportunity to fly off anywhere in the world that is offered to her by a stranger whom she meets by chance in the street. The stranger then promptly kills himself by jumping off the railway bridge over which they are passing.[32]

The typically Surrealist moral of these stories is the importance of responding both spontaneously and positively to the opportunities thrown up by chance encounters. But, for Rouch, this was more than just a moral; it was also a practical methodology that he applied to the making of both his documentaries and his fiction films. Although he would often underline the importance of being well-prepared for any shoot through careful prior research, in the actual moment of execution, Rouch considered that the ability of both filmmaker and subjects to improvise spontaneously were of paramount importance. It was for this reason that even in the case of his fiction films, he very rarely prepared a script in anything more than rough outline. It was also for this reason that he refrained from asking his documentary subjects to rehearse or repeat any actions, while in his fictions, he tried, whenever possible, to restrict himself and the actors to a single unrehearsed take. If any action had to be repeated, he believed, the creative quality of both the performance of the subject and the performance of the filmmaker would inevitably suffer.

These are matters to which I shall be returning to in many different forms in later chapters. Suffice it to say here that one of the most cherished principles of Rouch's praxis was that if a shot were to turn out well, it required inspired, spontaneous performances on both sides of the lens that were, moreover, in harmony with one another. Over the years, he used many different analogies to describe this harmonization of performances. Sometimes he compared it to a ballet, at other times to a matador improvising his passes before the bull. But the metaphors that reveal most surely the wellspring of his cinematic praxis are those that he uses in the final section of his major interview with Enrico Fulchignoni. Here he suggests that the best parallel that he can think of for these epiphanous encounters are "those exceptional moments of a jam session between the piano of Duke Ellington and the trumpet of Louis Armstrong" and perhaps even more importantly, "the electrifying encounters between strangers described for us on occasion by André Breton."[33]

As this passage makes clear, the influence on Rouch's cinematographic practice of his adolescent encounter with Surrealism was still evident almost fifty years after the *coup de foudre* on the rue Montparnasse. It would continue to be so up to and including his final work, released in 2002. Even in its poignant title, *Le rêve plus fort que la mort*, this film showed that even at this late stage of his creative life, the strength of the Surrealist dream remained undiminished in Jean Rouch's imaginary.

PART I

THE CAMERA
AND A MAN
IN AFRICA

3 : Nothing but Cinema

Jean Rouch, it really is a great shame, always doing cinema, nothing but cinema!   MARCEL GRIAULE, quoted by Germaine Dieterlen, 1995[1]

In July 1946, before beginning his doctoral studies at the Sorbonne with Marcel Griaule, Jean Rouch returned to West Africa to spend several months traveling the length of the Niger with two wartime comrades and contemporaries from the École des Ponts et Chausées, Pierre Ponty and Jean Sauvy. Thereafter, his main base of operations would be in West Africa until the coming of independence to the francophone colonies in 1960. This period can be conveniently divided into two phases. During the first, running from 1946 to 1952, Rouch was preparing his doctoral thesis on Songhay religion. In addition to the 1946 expedition with Ponty and Sauvy, he also went on two other research missions to the Niger River and its environs, one in 1948–1949, the other in 1950–1951. This first phase will be the focus of our attention here and in the following chapter. The second phase began in 1954, after Rouch had completed his doctorate. He then became engaged in a major study of the movement of migrant workers from the edge of the Sahelian Desert to the economically dynamic cities of the British colony on the Gold Coast (later to become Ghana) and the French colony on the Ivory Coast. This second phase of what one might call Rouch's "African period", we will consider in chapters 5–7.

Through both phases of this "African period," Rouch sought to combine conventional ethnographic field research with filmmaking. His development as a filmmaker over this period was truly extraordinary. In the course of these five chapters, we shall see how, in little more than ten years and using a secondhand camera that he had picked up in the Paris Flea Market, Rouch developed his skills, without any formal training and entirely on his own initiative, such that he progressed from making modestly descriptive ethnographic films of interest primarily to specialists, to full-blown feature films that had a major impact on the New Wave of French cinema.

Although Rouch's supervisor Griaule generally supported these film-making adventures, he soon became concerned at the amount of time that they consumed, particularly as they were manifestly preventing Rouch from completing his thesis for which Griaule had high hopes. It was this, no doubt, that led to Griaule's despairing remark quoted in the epigraph and which I have used as the title of this chapter. Eventually, the delay caught up with Rouch. In 1947, he had been admitted as an *attaché de recherche* to the Centre National de Recherche Scientifique (CNRS) with the backing of Théodore Monod, his mentor during his days at the Institut Français de l'Afrique Noir (IFAN) in Senegal during the war. Although this was the lowest level of entry into the elite research cadre of French academic life, it offered the possibility of tenure. However, Paul Rivet, chair of the relevant CNRS board, and scourge of Griaule on account of the latter's connections with the wartime Vichy regime, insisted that Rouch's appointment be conditional on the completion of his thesis within three years. When Rouch failed to comply with this condition, he was dismissed from his post in early 1951.

The shock of the dismissal proved salutary. Rouch duly completed his thesis and successfully defended it in January the following year. The year after that, in 1953, he was reinstated at the CNRS at a higher level, *chargé de recherche*, and on a permanent basis. In 1960, by which time he had completed the main body of his migration research in West Africa and also published his thesis, he was promoted to *maître de recherche*. Four years later he was nominated to the highest normal category, *directeur de recherche*. With this security, Rouch was able to make films for the rest of life, unencumbered by any heavy teaching responsibilities and with relatively ready access to fieldwork funds.[2]

First Steps in Filmmaking

The first of Rouch's African expeditions, carried out in the company of Ponty and Sauvy, consisted of traveling by various forms of raft and canoe from the source of the Niger in a small swamp in Guinea, through Mali, Niger, and Nigeria, right down to the point where the river discharges into the Bight of Benin, near Port Harcourt (see map 1 above). Totaling a distance of some 2,500 miles and involving the passage of many dangerous rapids, this was a journey that had previously claimed the lives of a number of European travelers, including that of the celebrated Scottish explorer, Mungo Park, who had perished in July 1806, exactly one hundred and forty years, almost to the day, prior to the date on which Rouch

FIGURE 3.1. Rouch, aged twenty-nine, at the time of the Jeanpierjant expedition in 1946–1947. © Fondation Jean Rouch.

and his companions arrived in Africa to begin their journey in 1946. As they traveled down the river, they supported themselves by wiring newspaper articles to Agence France Presse under the collective byline Jean Pierjant.[3] They also carried out a number of minor ethnographic research projects and took a large number of photographs, which they developed using river water.

Having set out at the end of August 1946, the expeditionaries survived various perilous escapades on the upper reaches of the river, before reaching, on 25 November, the small port of Mopti, some four hundred miles to the north and east of Bamako, the capital of what was then the French Soudan, later to become Mali (see map 1 above). From here, they headed inland and paid a brief visit, of no more than a day to Griaule, Dieterlen, and their fellow research team members, Solange de Ganay and Griaule's daughter, Geneviève Calame-Griaule, at their field site at Sanga on the Bandiagara Escarpment. This was Rouch's first visit to the place that had been such an important part of his imaginary since the *coup de foudre* that had struck him on the rue Montparnasse in 1934 and that had first drawn him toward anthropology. However, Griaule was then engaged in his legendary "conversations" with the blind hunter Ogotemmêli, so they did not see much of him and they were shown around the escarpment by his daughter Geneviève instead.[4]

Rouch and his companions then returned to the Niger River and continued their journey, eventually reaching Niamey, the capital of the then-colony of Niger, in January 1947. Here they attended the wedding of Damouré Zika, Rouch's assistant during the war and, along with his new bride, Damouré joined them for a while as they traveled further downriver toward the Nigerian border. Being by then an employee of the French colonial administration, Damouré was not allowed to enter the British colony without a special permit, so on his recommendation, Rouch and his companions recruited instead a young Fulani herdsman, Lam Ibrahim Dia, then about fifteen years of age. Lam had spent part of his childhood in Nigeria as an apprentice to an elderly marabout, and he remained with Rouch and his companions for the remainder of the journey until they reached Port Harcourt at the end of March 1947.[5] It proved to be a serendipitous appointment. Damouré and Lam would become Rouch's constant companions in all his filmmaking adventures in Africa thereafter. Joined by various "third men," they would be the "stars" of most of his principal fiction films, as well as acting as his technical assistants in various capacities.

Although none of them had had any practical film training, Rouch and his companions had decided that they should take a camera with them on this expedition. Griaule offered Rouch an Edison wax-cylinder sound-recording machine and a 35mm camera weighing some twenty kilograms that he had used to make two films among the Dogon in the 1930s. But Rouch preferred to take a much lighter 16mm spring-wound Bell & Howell, a Filmo 70 equipped with some excellent Cook lenses, which he found by chance in that favorite haunt of the Surrealists, the Paris Flea Market. This camera, probably one that had been "left behind" by a departing U.S. Army news cameraman at the end of the war, was bought only on the eve of their departure after a different plan for providing themselves with film equipment had fallen through at the last moment. It was paid for by selling a gold ingot that Sauvy had picked up in Guinea in 1941, during the war, and which he had been carrying around as a sort of talisman hidden in his belt ever since. Rouch happened to know a dentist who wanted the gold—in short supply in immediate postwar Paris—in order to make up fillings for his patients. It was with the money raised from this sale that they were able to buy the Filmo 70.[6]

This was merely one of a series of fortuitous circumstances underlying Rouch's first steps as a filmmaker that he would subsequently take much pleasure in relating since they confirmed his Surrealism-inspired faith in chance and improvisation. During the flight to West Africa, at a stopover at Aguelhoc in the north of the French Soudan, the plane in which he was traveling, an old Junkers "liberated" from the Germans, crashed on takeoff, probably because the pilot was too fond of red wine. Although no one was hurt, a three-day wait then ensued. But on the same flight, there was a film crew that had just finished shooting a feature film in the very same Parisian jazz clubs that Rouch himself liked to frequent. This crew formed part of an official Musée de l'Homme expedition that was on its way to the Congo to shoot a series of 35mm films about the Pygmies. They included Edmond Séchan, who would later become one of the best-known French feature film cinematographers in the postwar years. During the delay enforced by the crash landing, Séchan showed Rouch how to load a camera magazine.[7]

In the course of the expedition itself, Rouch learned a number of further elementary filmmaking lessons. One of these was that, contrary to received wisdom, it was perfectly possible to make films without using a tripod. According to a legend that Rouch himself liked to propagate, the technique of shooting handheld was forced upon him when he lost his tripod overboard while going through some rapids early on in the trip. Paul Stoller gives a somewhat more prosaic account, suggesting that Rouch did not lose his tripod to the waters of the Niger River, but simply broke it, due to his own clumsiness.[8] Nor does this accident, whatever it may have been, appear to have occurred early on, since a photograph taken by Sauvy in late January or February 1947, toward the end of the trip, shows Rouch using a tripod to shoot the preparation of hunting arrow poison on the outskirts of a village of lion hunters to the south of Niamey. But whatever the precise timing of his abandonment of the tripod, at some point during the course of this expedition, the technique of handholding the camera became central to Rouch's filmmaking praxis and would remain so for the rest of his career (see fig. 3.2).

Yet the most important filmmaking lessons that Rouch would derive from this expedition were those that arose when he returned to Paris and set about editing the material that he had shot. One of these was that if one takes a shot of the riverbank out of one side of a traveling canoe, it will not cut together with a shot of the opposite bank taken out of the other side of the canoe. This is because in moving from one riverbank to the other, one is "crossing the line," that is, the line of movement or action represented, in this case, by the direction of the canoe's progression down the river. In a shot taken of the right bank, trees, houses, or other objects will disappear out of the frame to the right, while in a shot of the left bank, any such objects will disappear out of frame to the left. If one then juxtaposes the two shots in the edit suite, it will look as if the canoe has suddenly changed direction.

One way to avoid this problem is for the camera to pan from one bank

FIGURE 3.2. While filming the preparation of arrow poison during the 1946–1947 expedition, Rouch begins on a tripod but then adopts a hand-held technique that permits much greater intimacy. © Fondation Jean Rouch. Photographs by Jean Sauvy (2006), 104–105.

to another, thereby establishing the geography of the situation for the audience. If a pan of this kind is not available, an editor may try and get round the problem by placing one or two intermediate shots between the two riverbank shots—of passengers or goods onboard, for example. If these are shot directly looking up or down the river, that is, along the "line" of movement or in a way that gives no hint of the direction of travel, the audience will forget about the line and are therefore less likely to be confused when the second riverbank shot is cut in. But, clearly, both these possible solutions require the cameraperson to be aware of the potential problems while still on location and to shoot the necessary shots. Due to his inexperience, this was something that Rouch had failed to do.[9]

As a result of this and other inadequacies, Rouch discovered that most of the material that he had shot on the expedition was unusable. The signal exception was the footage that he had shot of hippopotamus hunting by the Sorko fishermen of Firgoun, a small island on the middle reaches of the Niger, close to the Niger-Mali border. Hippopotamus hunting on the Niger River was described by the Moroccan traveler, ibn Battûta, as early as the fourteenth century, but since the establishment of the French colony, it had been largely reserved to colonial officials and other Europeans who had been able to get the necessary permits. Rouch was able to exploit his prior connections with the local colonial authorities to get a permit on the Sorkos' behalf easily enough, but for the Sorko, it was not only the colonial authorities' permission that was necessary if the expedition was to be a success.[10] In the their view, it was also essential to arrange a possession ceremony in which they would ask the female spirit controlling the waters of the Niger, Harakoy Dikko, to concede hippopotamus prey to them. This they duly did, and Rouch was also able to film the event. This material on the Sorko of Firgoun contained the seeds of many of Rouch's later film ventures. It included not only the general sequences of hunting and spirit possession, both of which were themes that would recur main times in his work in subsequent years, but among the possession ceremony material, there were also a few brief shots of mediums possessed by the so-called *hauka* spirits. Almost ten years later, the *hauka* would be the subject of *Les Maîtres fous*, the film that truly established Rouch's international reputation as a documentarist.[11]

It was the experience of cutting this material on hippopotamus hunting that taught Rouch what was perhaps the most significant lesson of all those that he learned from his first filmmaking venture. He showed a first cut of the material, of some thirty minutes in duration, to a select audience at the Musée de l'Homme, including not only Griaule and Dieterlen, but also André Leroi-Gourhan and Claude Lévi-Strauss, who were then the director and deputy-director of the Musée, respectively. The screening was also attended by the ethnomusicologist Gilbert Rouget, with whom Rouch would later collaborate on a number of film projects. In a gesture reminiscent of the prewar associations of *l'art nègre* described in the previous chapter, Rouget invited some young French jazz musicians to come to the screening. Afterward, they asked Rouch to come and project the film at their jazz club, Le Lorientais, and to give a live commentary while they played their music and the audience danced the boogie-woogie.[12]

Confirming Rouch's faith in chance once again, it happened that the pianist at the club, one Claude Azi, was the son of the head of the news-reel company, Actualités françaises, and he arranged for Rouch to show the material to his father. The father thought most of Rouch's material was complete rubbish but he liked the hippopotamus hunting sequence and the associated possession ceremony. So he bought the rights, of-fering Rouch and his companions 60 percent of the box office takings. He then instructed his editors to cut the material down substantially in length while at the same time blowing it up from 16mm to 35mm for cin-ema release as a short to accompany a longer film. According to Rouch, this was the first European film to be treated in this way. In due course, it was distributed as part of the accompanying program to Roberto Ros-sellini's film *Stromboli*.[13]

However, in order to prepare the film for cinema audiences, in addi-tion to cutting the footage down from thirty to thirteen minutes, the newsreel editors radically reordered it and added their own material. First, they put in some stock safari movie shots of animals such as ante-lopes and leopards that were completely alien to the environment inhab-ited by the Sorko (Rouch sometimes claimed that they also included ele-phants, but this is not, in fact, the case). Then they arranged for the film to be narrated by a well-known sports commentator who brought the frenetic style that he had developed for narrating the Tour de France cy-cling marathon to his description of the hippopotamus hunt. This com-mentary track, which was punctuated with clichés about "darkest Africa" and "timeless Africa," was further "enhanced" by an excruciating library music track. Perhaps worst of all was the title that the editors gave to the new version, *Au pays des mages noirs*, which was typical of the sensa-tionalist, if not actually racist, travelogue genre of the time.[14] But from a filmmaking point of view, undoubtedly the most significant transforma-tion that the Actualités editors introduced was in relation to the narra-tive structure of the film. Believing that the possession ceremony, which had occurred in reality prior to the hunting expedition, would work bet-ter as the climax of the film, they simply moved it to the end and pre-sented it as if it were a ritual expression of thanks to the "goddess" of the river.

When he saw the result, Rouch was horrified. What had emerged from the edit suite, he would later comment, was "a monster," "a scandal." The racist innuendos were shameful, the title "absolutely abominable." It was also an ethnographic absurdity since in Africa, he claimed, people never offered thanks for food. It was a film that "should not have been made." Indeed, Rouch was so embarrassed by the film that he did not dare show it either to the Sorko or to his colleagues at the Musée de l'Homme. Many years later, in 1991, Rouch attempted to recuperate at least part of the film by recording a new commentary for the possession ceremony sequence, replacing the racist innuendo of the original with neutral ethnographic observation. But even while decrying what they had done at the time, Rouch recognized that the Actualités editors, who were turning out two such films per week, really knew their business since by placing the most dramatic material at the end of the film they had made it much more engaging, and he resolved in the future to build his own films toward a narrative climax that would occur close to the end.[15]

Filmmaking and Fieldwork

The films that Rouch made in the course of the other two principal expeditions of this first phase of his career had more clearly defined ethnographic goals than *Au pays des mages noirs* since by then he was fully engaged in his doctoral research on Songhay magic and religion. But, for the most part, these films merely expanded on the themes that had been contained in the earlier film. Moreover, he would return to these themes time and time again in the future. The general ethnographic context of the films that Rouch made during these two expeditions he would subsequently describe in a number of publications, notably in his thesis and various academic articles, but also in a series of lively popular articles that he wrote for the magazine *Franc-Tireur*. First appearing in 1951, these have recently been republished.[16]

The first of Rouch's two doctoral expeditions took place between September 1948 and March 1949 and was funded by a grant awarded as part of the celebrations marking the centenary of the abolition of slavery in France.[17] Accompanied by Damouré, Lam, and another young Nigerien, Douma Besso, who was charged with looking after the donkeys carrying supplies, Rouch rode by horseback across great swathes of Songhay territory, starting out from Ayorou on the middle Niger and reaching as far west as the Hombori Mountains in eastern French Soudan, by way of Aribinda in the northern marches of what was then still the French colony of Upper Volta (see map 1, p. 3). During this expedition, he shot the material for four films. Two of these, *Hombori* and *La Circoncision*, correspond to the French Soudan phase of the journey, in late 1948. To the best of my knowledge, these represent the only films that Rouch ever made about the Songhay-speaking populations living outside the boundaries of what is now the Republic of Niger, though, unfortunately, I have able to see neither. *La Circoncision* is reported to be a short color film of fifteen minutes that, as described by Rouch in one of the *Franc-Tireur* articles, follows some forty boys from the village of Hombori as they are taken into the bush to be circumcised. This film was apparently much ap-

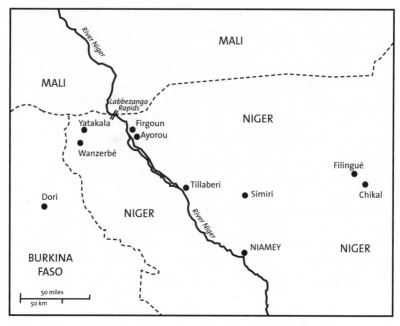

MAP 2. Western Niger: principal locations of Jean Rouch's filmmaking.

preciated by Marcel Griaule, and it won a prize at a film festival in Paris in 1950.[18] The other film shot in the French Soudan, *Hombori*, which is much longer, with a running time of sixty minutes, was thought for a long time to have been lost. But in 2007, a copy turned up at the Musée de l'Homme in a good state of conservation, though it was only a negative and there was no sound material associated with it. A preliminary viewing of this negative suggests that it offers an overall account of the expedition, featuring general views of village life and subsistence activities such as herding, ironworking, weaving, and hunting. Whether a sound track was ever prepared for this film remains uncertain.[19]

The two films that Rouch shot within Niger during the 1948–1949 expedition were more directly related to his doctoral research and are much better known. The first of these, *Les Magiciens de Wanzerbé*, was shot in December 1948 in the village of Wanzerbé, located close to the point where the borders between present-day Mali, Burkina Faso, and Niger meet (see map 2). Unusually for Rouch, it was shot in black-and-white stock, presumably because at this stage of his career, he could not always afford to use color. The principal focus of this film is on the *so-hantye* ritual specialists whom Rouch describes somewhat anachronistically as "magicians" but whom Paul Stoller and others in later texts refer to as "sorcerers."[20] An initial card assures the viewer that the film-

FIGURE 3.3 Manifestations of the power of the *sohantye* sorcerers of Wanzerbé. *Left*, a severed vulture's head, for, like vultures, the spirits of *sohantye* can fly high in the sky; *right*, the senior *sohantye* Yedyo vomits up a small chain.

maker has merely used the camera as "a pencil," directly representing what happened before him, without trickery —a device clearly intended to establish that none of the material had been staged. The main body of the film begins with a shot of a falcon in flight and then a very striking close-up of a severed vulture's head in profile that is slowly turned to look at the camera (see fig. 3.3). The voice-over, which is performed by Rouch himself, explains that the sorcerers of this village regard themselves as descendants of Si, the legendary founder of the Songhay empire (also known as Sonni Ali), who had the power, like vultures and falcons, to fly high in the sky and capture divine secrets. Preliminary scenes then show the Songhay trading with the Tuareg on market day, women collecting water, and boys playing. After about ten minutes, already a third of the way into the film, the leading sorcerers of the village are finally introduced, and one of their power objects depicting a horse and its rider, both with vulture's heads, is shown.[21]

The climax of the film is a sequence of dancing in the central plaza of the village, performed by an elderly sorcerer, Yedyo. Acting as a representative of all the Wanzerbé sorcerers, he dances to chase away the evil emanating from malignant spirits of the bush or from the *sohantye* of other villages, while his fellow sorcerers stand in a circle around him chanting praise poetry. At the climax of the dance, sensationally, Yedyo vomits up a small chain symbolizing his power, which dangles on his tongue for an instant before he swallows it again with great difficulty. This act sends the other sorcerers into a state of ecstatic frenzy, sobbing and crying violently, trembling and thrusting their arms into the air. But there is then a rather sudden change of gear and the film concludes with a sequence in which, early one morning, a group of sorcerers, along with the village headman and all the boys of the village (women and girls are excluded), go to the foot of a nearby mountain. Here they sacrifice a white calf to the mountain spirit in order to seek its help in ensuring health and fertility over the coming year.

In his thesis, Rouch comments that of all the ceremonies that he had been able to see in Africa up until that point, including all the possession ceremonies, this ceremony in Wanzerbé, on account of its gravity and its dramatic effect on the audience, was "without doubt the most beautiful and most moving." From an ethnographic point of view, Paul Stoller regards this film as one of Rouch's most important, particularly the sequence of the vomiting up of the sorcerer's chain, a seemingly miraculous act that neither he nor Rouch has been able to explain.[22] But in cinematographic terms, *Les Magiciens de Wanzerbé* suggests promise rather than polished accomplishment. Taken as a whole, the film has a certain omnibus character, typical of ethnographic expedition films at that time, exemplified particularly by the inclusion of a number of general scenes that have nothing directly to do with the main theme of the film (e.g., the Tuareg market scene and the boys' games) and many cute "postcard" shots of smiling individuals. The voice-over is also very mannered and even somewhat patronizing in tone and, moreover, is backed by an overwhelming and exoticizing sound track of drumming or chanting, presumably superimposed in the absence of any sound recorded on location. The quality of the cinematography is also rather uneven. But despite these weaknesses, there are many moments in the film, such as the remarkable shot of the severed vulture's head at the beginning, an undeniably "disturbing object" with strong Surrealist resonances, that provide clear evidence of a powerful cinematic sensibility at work.

Similar promise for the future, particularly in the quality of the cinematography, can be glimpsed in *Initiation à la danse des possédés*, the second film that Rouch made in Niger during the course of the 1948–1949 expedition. This was shot in February 1949, in Firgoun, the same island village where Rouch and his companions had shot the possession ceremony featured in *Au pays des mages noirs* during the 1946–1947 expedition. The subject is a weeklong ceremony known as a *ganandi* (literally, "to make dance"), the purpose of which is to initiate a young woman by the name of Zaba as a spirit medium.[23] Prior to the ceremony, she had been ill for some time, suffering from spells of delirium as a result of being randomly possessed by spirits. These crises had been so severe that she had lost the power of speech. The identity of the spirits troubling her had been identified in a previous ceremony, but she still needed to learn how to manage the crises induced by these spirits through performing the appropriate dance techniques. The film follows her instruction in these techniques through alternating sessions of practical train-

FIGURE 3.4 The *gasu*, a drum made from an upturned calabash and played with a cluster of sticks, which Rouch considered unique to the Songhay.

ing, periods of seclusion in a special hut, and possession dances in which initiated women also participate.

During these dances, the mediums respond to the rhythms produced by a line of drummers (one of whom in this case, unusually, is a woman) playing *gasu*, that is, drums fashioned out of half-calabashes turned upside down that are struck with a cluster of sticks. According to Rouch, this is a percussive instrument that is unique to the Songhay (see fig. 3.4).[24] These drummers, as is the Songhay custom, perform in a shelter to one side of the dance arena and are led by a man playing the *godye*. More widely distributed in West Africa than the *gasu* drums, the *godye* is a sort of violin with a sounding box fashioned out of a calabash, often clad with iguana or monitor lizard skin. It has a single string of twined horsehair that is played with a simple bow formed out of an arched stick (see fig. 3.5). The *godye* produces a disturbing but entrancing wail that the Songhay believe is much appreciated by the spirits and that therefore encourages them to approach and take possession of their mediums. As such, the *godye* is an essential feature of Songhay spirit possession and no ceremony can take place without it.[25] Fittingly, in *Initiation*, the film begins with the *godye* player's arrival by canoe from a neighboring village.

In the course of the *ganandi*, Zaba goes from being an "empty" medium who is hidden from the world—symbolized by her seclusion as well as by her closed eyes and the white scarf tied around her head while dancing in public—to one who is capable of handling possession by dancing in the manner specifically associated with a variety of different spirits. On the final day, she emerges from her seclusion hut, watched by visitors from neighboring villages who have come to witness her acceptance by the spirits. She is now without the white scarf, and her eyes are open. She is dressed in the black-and-white striped blouson worn by female initiates and completes her initiation by joining their dance. The next morning, the visitors head home, giving her gifts to "open her mouth." Having

FIGURE 3.5 *Left*, the *godye*, the instrument that the Songhay use to call the spirits, is played, *right*, with a simple bow made out of an arched stick.

been mute for a year, she is now able to speak and she thanks the *godye* player verbally, with a broad smile. He then sets off in his canoe, providing a neat "bookend" to the film.

Although still relatively primitive cinematographically, with some strangely over-exposed shots, this film showed evidence of the skills that Rouch would later develop into a fine art. As with *Les Magiciens de Wanzerbé*, it is the sound track that is the most problematic aspect. For in this case too, Rouch's commentary voice is very mannered and is accompanied by an overwhelming nonsynchronous drumming track. What makes the latter particularly awkward in this film is that these percussive effects have clearly been produced by drums based on some sort of vibrating membrane—probably the hour-glass shaped "talking drums" played under the arm that are very common in this region of Africa —rather than on the *gasu*, the upturned calabashes, that one sees in shot and that produce a very different sort of sound.

Yet whatever its shortcomings in this regard, considered as whole, *Initiation* was a remarkable achievement for an entirely self-taught filmmaker at the beginning of his career. In August 1949, a few months after he had returned from Africa, both *La Circoncision* and *Initiation* were selected for screening at an experimental film festival in Biarritz, the so-called Festival du Film Maudit.[26] Although it was without its definitive sound track—Rouch provided a live voice-over via a microphone at the screening— *Initiation* was awarded first prize in the noncommercial category by a jury presided over by the Surrealist poet, Jean Cocteau and including such influential gatekeepers to the world of French cinema as Henri Langlois, founder and president of the Cinemathèque nationale, the film critic Jacques Doniol-Valcroze, who would later found the influential screen journal, *Cahiers du Cinéma* with André Bazin, and the feature film director René Clément. In the audience were some of the future leading figures of the New Wave, including François Truffaut, Jean-Luc

Godard, and Jacques Rivette, all of whom would later be influenced by Rouch's work to some degree, though at this time, these tyros of the French cinema avant-garde were no more than teenagers and were completely unknown to the general public. It would be another two years before the launching of *Cahiers du Cinéma* on which they would cut their teeth as film critics and another decade before they would begin to make their mark as filmmakers themselves. Of more immediate significance then, at least in terms of Rouch's future career as a filmmaker, was the fact that another person at the festival was the producer Pierre Braunberger, who had supported the early work of Jean Renoir and Luis Buñuel and who would later be one of the leading producers of the films of the New Wave. Braunberger was greatly impressed by *Initiation* and, as we shall see in subsequent chapters of this book, he would become a staunch supporter of Rouch's work in the future too.[27]

4 : Encounters with Spirits

And suddenly, a sandstorm swamped all the horizons, the sky mingled with the earth, the wind tore at thatched roofs, picking up dead branches, surging into the houses as if to carry them off, and then, in the midst all this whistling, there was a terrifying crack of thunder: "That's the howling of the Dongo," said Damouré.   JEAN ROUCH, 1951[1]

No sooner had Jean Rouch returned from the successful screening of *Initiation à la danse des possédés* at the film festival in Biarritz in August 1949 than he began his "battle" to raise funds for a second doctoral fieldwork expedition. This would take place between July 1950 and June 1951 and would involve a journey from the French Soudan to the Gold Coast, passing through Niger on the way. He would be accompanied on this occasion by a fellow student of Marcel Griaule, Roger Rosfelder, a specialist on African linguistics. Six years younger than Rouch, Rosfelder was of Algerian origin and would later become a well-known writer, mostly dealing with North African themes, under the nom de plume Roger Curel (fig. 4.1). If Rouch's expedition in 1946–1947 with Pierre Ponty and Jean Sauvy had been by canoe, and his first doctoral expedition with his Nigerien associates in 1948–1949 had been mostly by horseback, Rosfelder and he had at their disposal a powerful four-wheel drive Dodge truck that Rosfelder had somehow procured in Algeria.[2]

The expedition was made possible by the fieldwork grants that Rouch received from the CNRS and IFAN, with the support of Marcel Griaule and Théodore Monod. He was also awarded a grant by the Centre national de la Cinématographie (CNC) to make three documentary films, in color, and this enabled him to commission the Sgubbi company of Paris to build a state-of-the-art portable tape recorder to record the sound track. While Rouch would continue to use the spring-wound Bell & Howell camera that he had picked up in the Paris Flea Market in 1946,

FIGURE 4.1. Roger Rosfelder at Firgoun, Niger 1951, during the shooting of the hippo-potamus hunt that features in *Bataille sur le grand fleuve*. © Fondation Jean Rouch.

Rosfelder would operate the Sgubbi. Rosfelder would also be credited as "assistant director" of the films.

Referred to as the "Acemaphone" in the film credits and as the "Zou-goubi" by Rouch's Nigerien associates, the Sgubbi replaced a sound-recording system that had to be carried around in a vehicle. According to Rouch, this was the first time that magnetic tape recordings had been made in the field in Africa. But by modern standards, it was still very heavy, weighing over thirty kilograms, so to use it in the field, it was a question of carrying it to the location, depositing it in some strategic central position and working from there, rather than walking around with it in a shoulder bag, as sound recordists would begin to do with the development of the Nagra some years later. Like the camera, the Sgubbi was spring-wound (lightweight and stable portable batteries had yet to be developed), though it could run for very much longer: while the camera only ran for at most twenty-five seconds before it had to be rewound, the Sgubbi could run for up to thirty minutes (fig. 4.2).[3]

This system was far from being synchronous: in fact, it would be another complete decade before the development of a system in which a camera and a portable tape recorder could run in perfect time with one another for any prolonged period. But the availability of this location sound contributed in a major way to the greatly increased sophistication, both in a technical and an aesthetic sense, of the three principal films that Rouch produced in the course of this second doctoral expedition—*Cimetières dans la falaise*; *Yenendi, Les hommes qui font la pluie*; and *Bataille sur le grand fleuve*. Although Rouch frequently refers to these films in his interviews and articles, they are not well known, particularly to English-speaking audiences, because, until recently, they have been very difficult to see. If they have been available at all, it has only been in the most degraded copies. However, the recent release of these films on DVD, with English subtitles in the case of *Cimetières dans la falaise* and *Bataille sur le grand fleuve*, allows one finally to appreciate their true qualities.

Filmmaking as Metaphor

The first film that Rouch and Rosfelder made together, *Cimetières dans la falaise*, came about when they visited Marcel Griaule and Germaine Dieterlen at their field station at Sanga in the Bandiagara Escarpment in August 1950.[4] At first, Griaule assigned his students the task of filming everyday life among the Dogon, which was something that Rouch found very difficult to do. All the films that he had made up until that point, and indeed, most of the films that he would make during the rest of his career, were films about performances of one kind or another, either collective ritual performances or, as in his fiction films, performances by individuals enacting their own lives or at least some fantasy construction of their lives. When asked, many years later, why this was so, he commented that to film everyday life, one had to be a very great filmmaker and that he had never hit upon a satisfactory way of doing it.[5] Whatever the precise reason for these difficulties, on this early project Rouch was pleased when Griaule suddenly changed the filmmaking commission. A Dogon man from the nearby village of Ireli had been drowned, carried off by an unexpected torrent caused by the newly arrived rains, and Griaule asked Rouch and Rosfelder to film his burial and the ritual procedures leading up to it.[6]

The film that Rouch and Rosfelder made about these ritual processes reveals the influence of Griaule and Dieterlen who appear to have written

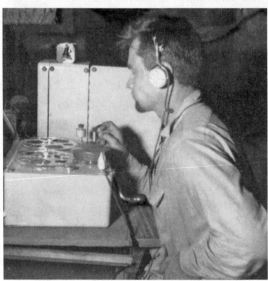

FIGURE 4.2. *Top*, Rouch and Rosfelder improvise a tracking shot. *Left*, Rosfelder records on the Sgubbi tape recorder. Although considered "portable," the Sgubbi weighed over thirty kilograms. It operated through a clockwork mechanism wound up through the handle pointing at Rosfelder's chest. © Fondation Jean Rouch.

FIGURE 4.3. Wrapped in a shroud evocative of the Dogon's checkered vegetable plots and hence metaphorically associated by Griaule and Dieterlen with germination and resurrection, the corpse is hoisted to the cemetery in the cliff face.

a narration script together.[7] This includes a number of points that make symbolic associations that are typical of their approach, as described in chapter 1 and based on the principle that, as Dieterlen put it, a design scratched on a wall can provide a clue to local conceptions of the structure of the universe.[8] There is, for example, an establishing shot early in the film, in which a woman is shown innocently carrying a square-shaped basket on her head, but which the commentary links to the Dogon's conception of the shape of the world. Later, as the corpse is about to be hoisted up the face of the cliff for burial in the cemetery above, the commentary links the checkered designs on the shroud to the similarly checkered layout of the Dogon's small agricultural plots and hence to a symbolic association of the shroud with germination and the resurrection of life (fig. 4.3).

This sensitivity to metaphor appears also to have influenced Rouch's own practice in the making of this film. It both begins and ends with some very impressive shots of cascades of water falling dramatically from the ridges along the Bandiagara Escarpment but which, before they reach the ground, are carried away on the wind as clouds of spray. In commenting later on the film, Rouch explained that he wanted these images to underline the contrast between the upward movement of the corpse as it is being hoisted up to the cliff-face cemetery that is the climax of the film and the downward movement of the cascades, as well as more generally to suggest the transience of human life. The final shot of the film pans down from the cliff face and then, in close up, moves along a stream in which a baobab flower is seen being carried out toward the savanna beyond, suggesting (albeit with dubious ethnographic accuracy) that this is the ultimate destination of the souls of the dead. Rouch later explained that he threw the baobab flower into the water himself in order to emphasize this movement.[9] As such abstract metaphorical touches are gen-

FIGURE 4.4. Rouch was apprehensive about filming the women in their grief (*left*), but Griaule reassured him that many were professional mourners anyway. *Right*, the deceased's mother shakes a broken gourd, symbolizing her loss.

erally absent from Rouch's earlier films, and even rare in his later ones, it is tempting to ascribe them, at least in part, to the influence of his mentors, Griaule and Dieterlen.

This film also represented an opportunity for Rouch to develop his technical skills. In general, the quality of his cinematography during the expedition represents a considerable advance on that of the 1948–1949 expedition. The framing is steadier, the shots are longer, and there is an effective combination of interesting shots of detail with wider shots that establish the geography of a scene. The quality of the film stock that Rouch was using appears to have been very much better. Although I have not come across any direct statement by Rouch to this effect, it is also very probable that the editing of the films from his first doctoral expedition would have helped him to shoot in a way that would make the editing of this second group both easier and more effective.

Certainly this is suggested by a story that he particularly liked to tell about the making of *Cimitières*, in which he would explain how he confronted the problem presented by the fact that while it took several minutes for the corpse of the drowned man to be hoisted up to the cliff-face cemetery, his spring-wound Bell & Howell offered only a maximum shot duration of twenty-five seconds. His solution was to make sure that every time he had to break off in order to wind up his camera, he would recommence by shooting from a slightly different angle. Once in the edit suite, he was able to use these changes of angle, supplemented by the judicious use of cuts to the deceased's mother and other women mourners looking upward—which he would have had to have made sure to capture in the moment—to cover breaks in the coverage of the hoisting up of the corpse to its final resting place. This shooting strategy was one that would only have been adopted by a filmmaker who was conscious, while still on location, of the requirements for continuity in the edit suite.[10]

A Firsthand Encounter with Dongo

This was Rouch's first film about Dogon ritual but it would not be his last. Fifteen years later, when Griaule was long dead, he would return with Dieterlen to shoot the Sigui ritual cycle and a number of funerary ceremonies over a nine-year period from 1966 to 1974.[11] But on this first occasion, after completing the shooting of *Cimetières*, Rouch and Rosfelder left Dogon country in August 1951 and headed southeast across the international frontier between the French Soudan and Upper Volta. After an exhausting trip via Ouagadougou and Fada N'Gourma, driving nonstop along roads badly affected by heavy rains, they finally crossed the Nigerien border and arrived at Niamey four days later. Here they remained for the next two months, during which time they appear to have shot one of Rouch's least known films, *Les Gens du mil*. Judging by the article that Rouch later wrote about this phase of the expedition, this film concerns both the technical and magical aspects of the Songhay's cultivation of their basic subsistence crop, a particular variety of millet well-adapted to the local conditions of very low precipitation.[12]

But in October 1950, with the arrival of the dry season, Rouch and Rosfelder joined the seasonal migrants from Niger and headed south for the Gold Coast in the four-wheel drive Dodge, accompanied by Damouré Zika, Lam Ibrahim, and two other Nigeriens. One of these additional companions was Illo Gaoudel, who, like Damouré was also a Sorko. He had previously made the trip to the Gold Coast as a migrant and would therefore serve as a guide. The other member of the group was Douma Besso, the same man who had looked after the donkeys on the 1948–1949 expedition. He would now take over the role of expedition cook from Lam since, with the Dodge, there was no longer any need to use donkeys as pack animals. The whole band remained on the Gold Coast for three months, carrying out preliminary research on migration and scouting out locations for future filmmaking ventures. But although Rouch certainly shot some rushes and Rosfelder recorded various events on the Sgubbi, this material appears never to have been made up into a freestanding film.[13]

In January 1951, they returned to Niger where Rouch and Rosfelder made two further films. Both of these, like *Cimetières*, represented but one in a series of many films that Rouch would make on the same theme. The first to be completed was *Les hommes qui font la pluie*, literally "The men who make the rain," a film also known as *Yenendi*. This was shot in late April 1951, at Simiri, a village located about fifty miles north of Niamey, in the drought-ridden savannas of the Zermaganda region (see map 2 above). As the alternate title suggests, the subject of the film was the Songhay possession ceremony known as *yenendi,* which customarily takes place annually on the fifteenth day of the seventh month of the dry season. The literal meaning of *yenendi* is "to freshen the earth" and its purpose is to persuade the spirits controlling the weather to release the rains.[14] The entire period during which Rouch was most active as a filmmaker in West Africa was a time of severe drought throughout the Sahelian region and *yenendi* were therefore particularly common. Between 1951 and 1976, Rouch returned to Simiri on many different occasions to film *yenendi,* though he also filmed them in many other locations as well. In total, Rouch made at least thirty films that feature possession ceremonies to some degree and roughly half of these concern *yenendi.*

The ceremony featured in *Les hommes qui font la pluie* took place at a ritual site just to the south of the village. Here there was a small circular thatched house dedicated to the spirits controlling the weather, in which the ritual paraphernalia of the cult were kept. Under the influence of Islam, such ritual sites had disappeared in many parts of Songhay territory, but the Zermaganda region where Simiri was located was one of those that had most staunchly resisted the marabouts and the cult continued to flourish there in its most elaborate form. Moreover, the *yenendi* shown in this film appears to have been a particularly grand enactment and was attended by Pierre Cros, a French colonial political officer in charge of the Zermaganda region. Seemingly as a result of Cros's presence, the event was also attended by more than a dozen local village leaders, some eleven *zima* priests, and a large crowd of local people. Cros was a good friend of Rouch's and is even described in the opening credits, along with Rosfelder, as an assistant director of the film.

Also featured in the opening credits are the spirits who take possession of the principal mediums during the course of the ceremony. These "starring" spirits were headed by Dongo, the Spirit of Thunder whom the Songhay believe to be principally responsible for controlling the rains and who, more generally, is considered to be the most powerful of all the many spirits in the Songhay pantheon. On this occasion, Dongo was accompanied by three of his spirit "brothers"—his elder brother Kyirey, the Spirit of Lightning; Haoussakoy, the Blacksmith Spirit who manufactures the stone projectiles that Dongo and Kyirey are said to hurl to earth; and Moussa, the Hunter Spirit, who is also the master of rain clouds. Later, they were joined by Nayanga, who is said to be as a sort of servant to this spirit "family" but who was clearly not considered sufficiently important to get a screen credit. Later still, Dongo and his brothers were joined by the Spirit of the Rainbow, the serpent Sadyara. Although he belongs to an entirely different spirit "family" from Dongo and his siblings, Sadyara is also thought to influence the weather by mounting into the sky, blocking the rain with his "back," that is, the rainbow, and then channeling the rain from the clouds down into the water wells. He is also therefore considered to be a very important spirit and is named in the opening credits.

The early part of the film consists of a series of sequences covering the arrival of the filmmakers and describing the general context of the event. The ceremony itself then begins with a number of women at the ritual site becoming possessed by the spirits. Once they have fully taken over their mediums, the spirits demand to be washed and dressed, and they are taken into the cult house for this purpose. Some hours later, at mid-day, they emerge, backward as is the habit of spirits, but spectacularly attired. They then begin to dance in front of the shelter where the musi-cians are playing the *gasu* calabash drums (fig. 4.5, *top*). These musicians are led by Wadi Godye, who is the violin player, as his second name sug-gests, but who is also the *zima* priest in overall charge of the event.

After they have danced a range of different dances—including the *kagu,* the highly animated dance named after the crested crane, a bird that, it is said, can be made to dance simply by clapping one's hands—the spirits enter into a formal dialogue with Wadi, agreeing to provide rain in exchange for various gifts and animal sacrifices. In a further effort to en-sure that Dongo releases the rain, Wadi then calls on the spirit to decant a large ceramic water jar known as a *hampi,* so that its contents flow in an east-west direction down a small, specially prepared trench representing the land and which has been filled with ritual artifacts associated with Dongo and various other ancestral spirits. Seemingly attracted by Wadi's praise songs, Dongo obligingly possesses a man by the name of Garasa, one of Wadi's fellow *zima* priests, and through Garasa's physical agency, the spirit himself, bellowing thunderously, decants the *hampi* down the trench, thereby "freshening the earth" (fig. 4.5, *bottom*).

When this happens, there is a remarkable, spontaneous outpouring of joy among the assembled crowd since the fact that Dongo himself has emptied the *hampi* is considered a sure sign that there will be good rains that year and therefore a good harvest. Finally, the next day, Wadi and the other *zima* priests return to the ritual site, where to one side of the central cult house, there is a shrine dedicated to Sadyara, the serpentine Spirit of the Rainbow, that appears to consist primarily of the stump of a dead tree. Here they sacrifice a fine-looking ram and pour a gourd full of its blood over the tree stump. All this ritual effort appears to have been effective for the film then concludes with the appearance in the sky of storks, rain clouds, and dramatic dust storms, all sure harbingers of the rain to come, until finally rain itself arrives in great torrents.

As the most powerful of the spirits that control the rain, Dongo is

FIGURE 4.5. A rain-making *yenendi*, Simiri, 1951. *Top*, the spirits arrive, led by Dongo, the Spirit of Thunder (*extreme left*), in shadow. The others are his "brothers," *from right to left*, the Spirits of Iron Making, Lightning, and Hunting, all embodied by female "horses." A musician plays a calabash drum, the *gasu*, in the shade of the shelter to the left. *Bottom*, with the assistance of Dongo, the Spirit of Thunder, the elders prepare to "freshen the earth" by decanting a *hampi*, a large water vase along a specially prepared trench. © Fondation Jean Rouch.

called upon at all *yenendi* and he is therefore a recurrent presence in the many films that Rouch made about this type of ceremony. As I described in chapter 1, Rouch's interest in spirit possession had first been sparked when he was a road engineer back in 1942 and had received a message telling him that something or somebody called "the Dongo" had been responsible for killing a number of his laborers.[15] In the course of filming *Les hommes qui font la pluie,* Rouch had an opportunity actually to

FIGURE 4.6. The Bell & Howell Filmo 70 under his arm, Jean Rouch shakes hands with Dongo, the Spirit of Thunder, embodied in a young female "horse" dressed in black, Dongo's distinctive color. © Fondation Jean Rouch.

shake hands with Dongo himself, as he was embodied during the earlier part of the day in the slight frame of a female medium (fig. 4.6). Over the years, Rouch appears to have developed a particular fascination for the Spirit of Thunder, who, in various forms, features in the belief systems of a number of West African religions, and who even made the trip across the Atlantic in the slave ships to reemerge as "Xangô" or "Shango" in the possession cults of contemporary Brazil and the Caribbean. In effect, *Les hommes qui font la pluie* was but the first of many attempts on Rouch's part to produce what he would later call a "ciné-portrait" of Dongo. This was a project that he would pursue throughout his career and, which involved showing the spirit embodied in a broad range of different mediums, of both genders and widely varying ages, in both urban and rural contexts. Almost fifty years later, right at the end of his career, when Rouch was around eighty, Dongo would make a final appearance in the very last film that Rouch shot himself, *Moi fatigué debout, moi couché*, released in 1997.[16]

Back in the early 1950s, if *Cimetières* had provided evidence of Rouch's developing camera skills, it was *Les hommes qui font la pluie* that most effectively demonstrated the advantages of using sound recorded on location. The intrusive and culturally inappropriate drumming that had been superimposed on *Les Magiciens de Wanzerbé* and *Initiation à la danse des possédés* is replaced by recordings of the very *gasu* calabash drums and the *godye* violin that one sees in shot, mixed with some elements of general ambient sound, all beautifully recorded by Rosfelder. Whilst Rouch's commentary remains extensive and is still rather mannered when compared to his later more laid-back style, there are passages when he falls completely silent and the film is sustained entirely by the music, the clapping, and the stamping, all laid over the most skilful montage of images. At certain moments, it even becomes possible to understand how it is that the mediums become entranced by this complex mosaic of rhythmic sounds to the extent of believing that their bodies have been possessed by spirits.

But perhaps the most impressive sequence of all from an editorial point of view is the one with which the film concludes. Here, a series of striking images of lowering clouds and the gathering dust storm, people hurrying home with their animals or their children, a jagged flash of lightning and trees bending before the wind, are combined with some restrained poetic remarks by Rouch on the sound track, all underlain by the sounds of howling gales and lashing rain, and a gradually intensifying singing and clapping backed by the wailing of Wadi's *godye* violin. This combination of sounds and images is so effective that one can easily sympathize with the idea that, as Rouch puts it in his voice-over, "the gods are at work," transforming the heavens and delivering the rain that was their side of the pact that they sealed with human beings in the course of the *yenendi* that has just been held.

Indeed, the editorial skill evident in this film is so much greater than in Rouch's earlier work that one cannot help wondering whether it is not just the result of his own maturation as a filmmaker, but rather an indication that someone else with greater editorial experience was involved. Certainly, around this same time, Rouch was cutting the third film that he and Rosfelder shot during the 1950–1951 expedition, *Bataille sur le grand fleuve,* with the help of Renée Lichtig, who, although still very young, was an editor of great talent. Shortly after working with Rouch, she would go on to cut for such major figures of the cinema as Jean Renoir and Eric von Stroheim. After his unfortunate experience with Actualités françaises, it would have been entirely understandable if Rouch had formed the view that a professional editor was as unnecessary to him as a professional cameraman. But the experience of working on *Bataille* with Lichtig convinced him, on the contrary, that an editor— a "second pair of eyes," as he would later put it—was essential to the success of any film project.[17] Even so, because it was not the convention in France at that time to give a screen credit to editors, Lichtig's contribution to *Bataille* is not mentioned in the film itself. The quality of the editing in *Les hommes qui font la pluie* is such that it looks as if a "second pair of eyes," perhaps even those of Lichtig, have been brought to bear on this film too. However, although Dongo and his spirit brothers get a screen credit, there is no mention of an editor.

The Origins of Shared Anthropology

The theme of *Bataille sur le grand fleuve* is yet another to which Rouch would return many times in his later oeuvre. The theme in question is hunting, in this case of hippopotami, while in his later films, it would concern the hunting of lions. Essentially, *Bataille* represents a reprise of the hippopotamus hunt of *Au pays des mages noirs,* again made possible because Rouch was able to get the necessary permit from the colonial authorities, on this occasion even persuading the head game warden to come along for the "adventure."[18] This time, however, Rouch was able to ensure that there was no inversion in the edit suite of the real temporal sequence of events and the customary appeal to the spirit controlling the waters of the Niger, Harakoy Dikko, *precedes* the hunt just as it did in reality. In addition to testifying to the same advances in the quality of cinematography and sound-recording as the other films made during the 1950–1951 expedition, *Bataille* proved that Rouch was capable of handling a story that developed over a prolonged period of time. Whereas most of his previous films had been centrally concerned with particular ritual events that had happened over the course of no more than a day or two, this film involved a tough four months in a dug-out canoe, on and off, spread out over the period February to May 1951, following the Sorko fishermen as they moved up and down the Niger River above Ayorou in search of their prey (fig. 4.7).

But these were not the only reasons why *Bataille sur le grand fleuve* represented a significant step forward for Rouch as a filmmaker. Although it is a conventional documentary in most respects, there is one sequence in *Bataille* that hints at a move toward the more fictionalized form that Rouch would develop in the next phase of his career. This is a short sequence involving Damouré Zika and Illo Gaoudel that comes toward the end of the film. It shows them walking down the river bank when suddenly they discover the tracks of the great "Bearded One," the alpha male hippopotamus that has repeatedly attacked the hunters' canoes but which, despite all their heroic efforts, has managed to elude capture. The fact that the camera is lying in wait for the protagonists on the other side of the line of the hippopotamus's tracks, coupled with the hammy reactions of Damouré and Illo as they point melodramatically to the tracks and then upstream to indicate the escape route of the "Bearded One,"

FIGURE 4.7. Hippopotamus hunting, Ayorou, 1951. The Sorko hunters use specially padded canoes to protect themselves from attacks. © Fondation Jean Rouch.

leave one in no doubt that this sequence has been enacted specifically for the benefit of the camera (fig. 4.8).[19]

But in terms of the overall development of his praxis, *Bataille* is perhaps most significant for being the first of Rouch's films that he managed to show back to the subjects successfully. This screening did not happen for some time, but when it did, the effects were dramatic. Some two and a

FIGURE 4.8. Illo and Damouré "discover" the tracks of the Bearded One.

half years after he had completed the filming of *Bataille*, Rouch returned to Ayorou accompanied by Jane George, a writer of American descent whom he had married in February 1952, as well as his regular band of Nigerien companions, including the protagonists of *Bataille*, Damouré and Illo. This visit took place during the overland trip that Rouch and Jane made between October 1953 and February 1954, starting from Paris and ending on the Gold Coast where Rouch would begin a major research project into patterns of migration from Niger and other countries on the edge of the Sahel. On their way, as Rouch and Jane passed through Niamey, they collected the Nigeriens and made a detour to Ayorou. They arrived there at the end of January 1954 and stayed about two weeks. It was during this visit that they appear to have screened *Bataille*.[20]

The arrangements for the screening were not elaborate: one evening, Rouch simply projected the film onto a white sheet in the open air. At first, the audience was interested only in the projector, but then they realized that they had to look at the sheet. By this time, Rouch had been visiting the Songhay for over a decade, but they had never really understood the nature of his work. He had given them copies of his publications but although they had stuck the photographs on their walls, they had simply ignored the texts. Even when Rouch had arranged for the schoolmaster to read out certain sections aloud, they had not properly understood. But now, in no more than a few seconds, he felt that they finally appreciated what he was trying to do.[21]

Rouch showed the film many times that night: in some versions of the story, it was three times, in others four, in some it is even claimed that there were five showings. Certain members of the audience were shocked when they saw the images of people who had since died, believing that somehow their souls had suddenly rematerialized in the form of the film. But as they began to understand the nature of the representation, they began to make more informed comments. Perhaps unconsciously revealing the influence of the Actualités françaises newsreel editors who had used the device in cutting his first hippopotamus-hunting film, Rouch had backed the commentary track of *Bataille* with a music track. But whereas they had used some banal library music, Rouch was very proud of the fact that he had used a series of local hunting melodies, known as *gawey-gawey*, recorded by Rosfelder on the Sgubbi. Indeed, a list of these sound "documents," including both the name of the melodies and of the musicians, is given in the credits at the beginning of the film.

But regardless of the fact that it was local music, the Songhay objected to its use. Sometimes Rouch reported that they considered the music inappropriate because they thought it would frighten away the hippopotami, which obviously suggests a continuing naivety about the nature of filmic representation; at other times, he presented it as a more general cultural objection that the music was at odds with the Songhay norm that hunting should be conducted in complete silence. Whatever the precise reason, he concluded that thereafter he should be more circumspect about the use of incidental music—but not, it seems, about the use of commentary, though this would surely have clashed with any Songhay norms of silence during the hunt just as much![22]

But more significant than these reactions to the music were the proposals for further films that the screening provoked. In the audience that night, there was a man by the name of Tahirou Koro, whom Rouch had met during the course of the 1950–1951 expedition and who was a celebrated lion hunter from Weyzébangou, a village close to Yatakala, some fifty miles to the west of Ayorou (see map 2, p. 44). At the end of the screening, Tahirou came up to Rouch and suggested that his film about hippopotamus hunting had been all very well but he should now come to his village and make a film about lion hunting. This would be much more exciting since he and his fellow Gow hunters were armed with no more than bows and arrows when they set out against this most dangerous of animals. This was a very attractive proposal to Rouch since he had made various failed attempts to film this form of lion hunting on his previous expeditions.[23] Although his commitment to the migration research program prevented him from taking up Tahirou's proposal immediately, it would eventually result in the making of *The Lion Hunters,* a film that Rouch shot in the course of many different expeditions between 1957 and 1965, and which we shall consider at length in chapter 10.

Even before then, the legendary first "feedback" screening at Ayorou would give rise to another film, since Damouré and Illo had very much liked seeing themselves on the screen that night and wanted to do more. Damouré suggested to Rouch that they should now make a "real film," a fictional feature "like *Zorro.*" This was a reference to the then well-known Hollywood movie character, "El Zorro," literally "the fox," the original masked crusader, who spent his time setting wrongs aright in colonial California, a role made famous by Douglas Fairbanks, Tyrone Power, and others.[24] As we shall see in the following chapter, as Rouch turned his professional attention to the study of migration to the Gold Coast, this suggestion by Damouré would indeed result in the making of a "real" fiction film, not about a man who took on the identity of a fox, but close enough. This film would be *Jaguar*, Rouch's first and prototypical "ethnofiction," and one of his greatest works.

5 : Heroes of the Modern World

They certainly came to the Gold Coast and the Ivory Coast in search of money,
but they also came in search of adventure . . . These young people are the he-
roes of the modern world. They do not bring back captives as their ancestors
did in the last century. Instead they bring back goods, marvelous stories and
tall tales. JEAN ROUCH, 1970[1]

In the period immediately following the Second World War, migration
from rural to urban areas intensified in many parts of sub-Saharan Africa. In West Africa alone, Rouch himself estimated that in the mid-
1950s, between 300,000 and 400,000 migrant workers every year made
the journey from the edge of the Sahelian Desert to Accra, Kumasi, and
other economically dynamic poles of development along the Gold Coast.
Though not in such great numbers, many others from the French colonies on the edge of the Sahel were also migrating at this time to the
coastal regions of Nigeria, Dahomey, Togo, and further to the west, the
Ivory Coast. This was a social phenomenon of major importance and
the colonial governments of the time were prepared to provide generous
funding for research into its causes and effects. Rouch was one of those
engaged to do this research, and from 1954 to 1960 he was supported by
a combination of the CNRS, IFAN, and various multinational colonial
research agencies set up to coordinate scientific programs in countries
south of the Sahara.[2]

As described in the previous chapter, in October 1953, Rouch set out
from Paris to travel overland to West Africa, accompanied by his wife
Jane whom he had married the previous year. As Jane relates in her lively
personal memoir, on the way south they visited Salvador Dalí at his atelier in Port Lligat in Catalonia before crossing the Straits of Gibraltar and
finally arriving at Niamey around the turn of the year, after many breakdowns on their way across the Sahara Desert. At Niamey, Rouch introduced Jane to his local companions, Damouré Zika, Lam Ibrahim, Illo

FIGURE 5.1. Jane Rouch in the Samreboi forest, Western Region, Gold Coast, 1954. © Fondation Jean Rouch.

Gaoudel, Douma Besso, and Tallou Mouzourane, all of whom had worked with him in one capacity or another on the films that he had made during the previous expedition with Roger Rosfelder in 1950–1951. After the brief detour to Ayorou, when they appear to have screened *Bataille sur le grand fleuve*, they then all drove south together to Lomé, capital of Togo, before entering the Gold Coast in February 1954. Here they remained until Rouch's return to France in January 1955.[3]

In November 1956, Rouch moved the principal focus of his studies of migration to Abidjan, the capital of the French colony of the Ivory Coast. Later still, he extended the range of these investigations to include Togo, Upper Volta, and Niger itself. By the time that he concluded his migration studies in 1960, all these colonies had achieved political independence, though the process of migration to the coast has continued, even if the destinations of the migrants have shifted in accordance with the political and economic vagaries of the region.[4]

In conducting his migration research, Rouch combined a number of different methods—formal questionnaires, both individual and collective, group interviews somewhat akin to what are now known as "focus groups," informal conversations with particular individuals, and, most importantly for present purposes, filmmaking. But although he was assiduous in his use of quantitative research methods, he regarded these as ultimately limited by the fact that they could not represent the subjective experience of the migrants. It was here that he saw filmmaking as playing a vitally important role.[5]

During this period, he made three major films that dealt directly with the experience of the migrants, two on the Gold Coast, *Les Maîtres fous* and *Jaguar*, the other, *Moi, un Noir*, in Abidjan, the capital of the Ivory Coast. While continuing to conduct migration research, Rouch also made another film during the period that he was based in the Ivory Coast. This was *La Pyramide humaine*, which concerned the relationships between African and European students at an elite Abidjan *lycée*. All these films were shot on 16mm film and were initially produced through the Comité du film ethnographique at the Musée de l'Homme. However, they were all subsequently blown up to 35mm for cinema release by Les Films de la Pléiade, the company of the producer Pierre Braunberger. It was these films that served to establish Rouch's reputation far beyond academic circles and launched his career as an important figure in French cinema and beyond. In this chapter, I shall refer primarily to the Gold Coast films, *Les Maîtres fous* and *Jaguar*, leaving further discussion of his Ivory Coast works until chapter 6.

Remarkably, these were not the only films that Rouch made during the period of his migration research. Among the others was *Mammy Water*, shot in 1954, though not finally released until 1966. This is an engaging if rather episodic documentary about certain aspects of the life of the Fanti fishermen who live around Cape Coast, southwest of Accra, on the Gold Coast. Considerably more substantial, but also relatively conventional was *The Lion Hunters*. This was shot over a seven-year period, beginning in 1958, in the dry savannas to the west of the middle Niger, among the Gow hunters of Yatakala. He also made *Baby Ghana*, a short film about Ghanaian independence, and two ethnographic films outside his own research area. One of the latter, *Moro Naba*, shot opportunistically in late 1957, followed the funeral of the traditional chief of the Mossi, a major ethnic group of what was then the French colony of Upper Volta. The other, *Sakpata*, was made in collaboration with the ethnomusicologist Gilbert Rouget in 1958, though it was not released until 1963. This followed the initiation of three young girls into a voudou cult in a village in the traditional kingdom of Allada, southern Dahomey. But with

FIGURE 5.2. Jean
Rouch in Saremboi
forest, Western Region,
Gold Coast, 1954, as
ever carrying his Bell
& Howell. © Fondation
Jean Rouch.

the exception of *The Lion Hunters*, which is one of Rouch's major works
and a highly estimable film that we shall return to in chapter 10, none of
these is as significant in the development of his praxis as the films that
he made based on his migration research.

Migration as Adventure

The two films that Rouch produced about migrants to the Gold Coast,
Les Maîtres fous and *Jaguar*, were made at a time of considerable political
turmoil in the British colony. This was the period when Kwame Nkrumah's Convention People's Party (CPP) was vying with a number of other
political groupings to take power following independence from Britain,
which finally came in 1957. Although Rouch generally eschewed political
topics in his films, there are some brief references to this ferment of
political activity in *Jaguar*.[6]

Les Maîtres fous is a short film documenting the activities of the *hauka*
spirit possession cult to which many Nigerien migrants on the Gold Coast
belonged (fig. 5.3). The subject of the film is the annual gathering of cult
members that took place near Nsawam, a small town about twenty-five
miles north of Accra on August 15, 1954.[7] Whereas most ethnographic
films of the day sought to record the traditional and the customary in
rural areas, *Les Maîtres fous* celebrates what Rouch refers to in the opening commentary as "the great adventure of African cities." As such, it
represented a new departure not only within Rouch's own work but also

FIGURE 5.3. A *hauka* medium in Accra, possessed by the Spirit of the Wicked Major Mugu, cracks a whip fashioned from a truck fan belt. © Fondation Jean Rouch.

within the genre of ethnographic documentary while at the same time linking up with important new developments going on in Africanist anthropology more generally.[8]

But from the moment of its first release in 1955, *Les Maîtres fous* became the subject of intense controversy. For, in the course of the film, as the adepts of the cult become possessed by the *hauka* spirits, they mimic the manners and dress of certain colonial authorities and, in this condition, they prance about in the most bizarre manner, foaming at the mouth, and burning themselves with flaming torches. At the culminating moment, they sacrifice a dog, throwing themselves forward to drink its blood. The film was immediately banned by the Gold Coast colonial authorities on the grounds that it portrayed cruelty to animals and lack of respect for the colonial regime. The film was also denounced by leading intellectuals in Paris, both European and African, including even Rouch's own supervisor, Marcel Griaule, because it showed Africans behaving in ways that they believed would pander to European racist prejudices. But over the intervening years, *Les Maîtres fous* has been progressively rehabilitated and in both the anthropological and screen studies literature, the most commonly accepted view today is that this film, far from being racist, provides a unique account of a powerful counter-hegemonic parody of European colonialism in Africa.

Although this was an interpretation encouraged, if not actually espoused, by Rouch himself, particularly in his later years, in my view, it is seriously misplaced. But I shall not pursue this matter here since, given its importance in the Rouchian canon, I propose to dedicate the whole of chapter 7 to a detailed analysis of this film. In the course of this analysis, I shall present a rather different interpretation of the *hauka* cult.

The other film that Rouch made about Nigerien migrants to the Gold Coast in this period, *Jaguar*, could hardly be more different. Although there are some establishing shots of Accra and Kumasi that are common to both films, *Les Maîtres fous* was mostly shot over a single day, whereas the main body of *Jaguar* was shot over the course of the whole year that Rouch was on the Gold Coast from February 1954 to January 1955, with the final version of the voice-over commentary not being completed until 1960.[9] While *Les Maîtres fous* is a short film of less than thirty minutes' duration, which was edited and released relatively quickly, *Jaguar* is a feature-length film of eighty-eight minutes in its final form and Rouch was not able to assemble the budget for its postproduction until the late 1960s, long after the colonial world it depicted had been brought to an end. But perhaps the greatest difference between the two films is in their general tone. Whereas *Les Maîtres fous* is a serious, realist documentary that often shocks its viewers, *Jaguar* is a light-hearted, fictionalized road movie that mostly provokes reactions of delight.

The principal protagonists of *Jaguar* are three young men, played by Damouré, Lam, and Illo, who leave the market town of Ayorou on the middle Niger and take off for what the Songhay call the "*kourmi.*" This is a reference to the luxuriant tropical forest of the Guinea Coast that contrasts so markedly with the arid semidesert in which the Songhay themselves live.[10] Here, the three protagonists have all kinds of adventures as casual laborers and market traders in Kumasi and Accra, before eventually returning, many months later, to their home villages. The following day, they gain great personal prestige by distributing all the merchandise that they have brought back with them and then, without further ado, they return to their traditional subsistence activities.

The film opens with Rouch's voice saying to an interlocutor by the name of Adamou, "We are going to tell you a story," and the three protagonists are then introduced, one by one.[11] Apart from this reference to storytelling, there is no direct clue in the film itself that it is fiction-alized. There are certain scenes that any filmmaker would immediately recognize as enactments, but an uninformed general spectator could readily be forgiven for assuming that he or she is looking at a "straight" documentary, particularly given the conventions of the time. In fact, al-though the protagonists are shown as if walking for more than a month to reach the Gold Coast, in reality they traveled throughout the journey in Rouch's Land Rover. Similarly, although they are shown working in various casual laboring jobs in Kumasi and Accra, they never received payment for doing these jobs, which in any case they only performed briefly for the purposes of the filming. Instead, Damouré was receiving a salary from his post as a minor civil servant back in Niger, while his com-panions were paid by Rouch out of the film budget.[12]

Despite the reservations of Jane, who felt that he should stick to re-portage, Rouch decided to shoot this film as a fiction because he felt that it would be impossible to show the full range of the migrants' experience within the limitations of a conventional documentary.[13] Although the making of a fiction film was an entirely new departure for Rouch, there had been a clear hint of a movement in that direction in the making of *Bataille sur le grand fleuve* in 1951, as mentioned in the previous chapter. Even in *Cimetières dans la falaise*, shot the year before that, the throwing of the baobab flower into the stream in order to reinforce the symbolic significance of the final shot already indicated an interest on Rouch's part in going beyond impassive scientific description. However, if *Jaguar* is a fiction, it is a fiction without a screenplay: for, drawing on his Surrealist background, Rouch resolved that it should be based on improvisation and chance instead. The general idea was concocted in discussion with the three principal protagonists. Rouch later reported that when they actually began filming, all that they had decided upon was that the trip would begin and end at Ayorou, and that the migrants would immedi-ately give away everything that they had brought back with them. All the other incidents in the film were then made up as they went along, with Damouré, Lam, and Illo improvising their performances in each situa-tion, following a preliminary discussion with Rouch himself.[14]

But as was so often the case with Rouch's improvisations, the ground was very well laid beforehand. Although only Illo had previously made the journey to the Gold Coast as a genuine migrant, Rouch had taken all three of the principal protagonists on a reconnaissance trip to the Gold Coast in the course of his 1950–1951 expedition with Roger Rosfelder. From a series of popular articles that Rouch wrote about that journey, as well as from Damouré's travel diary, it is clear that they visited many of the same places, or at least places that were similar, to those that they would later use as locations for *Jaguar*. On the way south, they visited the Somba, the ethnic group of northern Dahomey celebrated for wearing very little other than penis sheaths – "buttocks in the air," as Damouré describes them—who would later feature in *Jaguar*. They then continued their journey and entered the Gold Coast, via Lomé on the Togolese coast, and made fun of the border guards, just as they do in the film. Once in Accra, they met Moukaila, one of the priests who would later feature in *Les Maîtres fous*, and attended a *hauka* ceremony: Illo even became possessed. They visited a gold mine at Prestea in the Western Region of the Gold Coast and discovered Zerma migrants working as miners there; later, in *Jaguar*, Lam would play the role of a migrant gold miner, not in fact in Prestea, but in Obuasi, a similar mining complex in the western Gold Coast. True to Rouch's background as a road engineer, they inspected various bridges, as they also do in the film. Indeed, there is a certain ambiguity about Damouré's diary entries, such that one possible reading of them is that Rouch even filmed certain scenes of *Jaguar* during the course of this reconnaissance trip (fig. 5.4).[15]

Narratively, the film is structured by the chronology of the journey and held together, in the absence of any synchronous sound, by a remarkable commentary that Damouré and Lam improvised in response to a silent projection of a workprint of the film. This they did on two separate occasions, once in a sound studio in Accra in 1957, and then again in 1960. A combination of the two performances was used in the preparation of the sound track of the hundred-minute version of the film that Rouch produced for the Venice Film Festival in 1967. Despite the time lag between the two recordings, Damouré and Lam were able to switch back into their film personae without any difficulty, so notwithstanding the differences in the quality of the recordings—partly due to changes in their voices and partly due to differences in the sound-recording technology—Rouch was able to mix the two tracks, along with some asynchronous "wild tracks" recorded during the production, some music and some studio sound effects, to produce an highly effective sound track.[16]

Heroes of the Modern World

The improvisational techniques used in *Jaguar* became the model for all Rouch's subsequent fiction films, even though it was actually released after a number of these later works because Rouch had to wait many years before he could assemble the budget necessary for the postproduction of the film. Rouch referred initially to these fictional works as his "ciné-fictions" or more playfully as "science fictions," since they were

FIGURE 5.4. *Top*,
Zerma migrants as gold
miners at Prestea, which
Rouch visited on the re-
search trip to the Gold
Coast in 1951. *Bottom*,
Lam playing the role of
gold miner for *Jaguar*,
shot in 1954. © Fonda-
tion Jean Rouch.

based, at least in some cases, on ethnographic, statistical, or historical
research. Subsequently however, Rouch's way of working in a fictional
mode has come to be referred to in the literature by the somewhat ambiguous term "ethnofiction."[17]

    Jaguar is also sometimes cited as an example of "reverse anthropol-
ogy," a mirror in which the Other of the European imaginary meets its
own Other. But if this is true, it is so only in a qualified way. For the
Others whom the three adventurers meet in *Jaguar* do not actually include any Europeans. First among these others are the Somba, whose

FIGURE 5.5. "The great adventure of African cities": the Red Spots high-life dance band. © Fondation Jean Rouch.

nakedness and fetishistic religion impress the travelers greatly. However, as good Muslims, they reason that this is how Allah must have wished the Somba to be, and therefore there can be nothing wrong with these strange customs. Later, in the cities, they meet Hausa, Yoruba, Ashanti, and Ga, as well as migrants from all over West Africa, including many of their fellow Songhay. They swim in the sea for the first time, marvel at the vast size of Kumasi market, enjoy the bars with exotic names and suggestive images of stylish women, marvel at the propensity of local people to dance not just at political meetings, but even at funerals and generally enjoy "the great adventure" of an African city (fig. 5.5).

Finally, they set up a trinket stall in the Kumasi market, giving it the charming name, *Petit à petit, l'oiseau fait son bonnet*, literally, "Little by little, the bird makes its bonnet." This seems like it might be a reference to some traditional French saying, but in fact, it was a name made up by Damouré who thought of the bird's bonnet as being a metaphor for the

FIGURE 5.6. The Petit à Petit trinket stall, Kumasi market, 1954. *From left to right*, Damouré, Lam, and Douma Besso. Their names and that of Illo appear on the board above, along with the name of the stall itself, devised by Damouré. © Fondation Jean Rouch.

turban that a successful man would wear (fig. 5.6). As Rouch discovered during his migration research, many Songhay made a living from such *nyama-nyama* stalls, as they were known. It was a métier much appreciated by the francophone migrants because it required very little capital to get started, though to be successful, one had to be something of showman, as Damouré demonstrates in the film. Once he and his partners have sold off their stock, they make the long journey home, running the gauntlet of the many customs posts on the way that threaten to fleece them of everything that they have earned.[18]

Yet despite the fact that most of the film is set in a colonial city, among the hundreds, possibly thousands of people who appear in the film, not a single one is evidently European. It is true that in the scene in the Obuasi gold mine, Lam meets a miner who also comes from Niger, played by another of Rouch's associates, Douma Besso, and they discuss how the British mine owners are robbing the Africans of their gold. However, this skepticism toward wealth and power is also manifest in the disrespectful commentary over a scene in which the Kwame Nkrumah and his leading political associates are shown preparing for a photo call on the steps of the parliament building during the Legislative Assembly meet-

FIGURE 5.7. Kwame Nkrumah, leader of the Convention People's Party, and later first prime minister of the independent nation of Ghana, on the steps of the Legislative Assembly, Accra, July 1954. © Fondation Jean Rouch.

ing in July 1954 (fig. 5.7). Having commented that Nkrumah looks well-fed enough, as do all his ministers, implying that they are growing fat at other people's expense, Damouré and Lam conclude that he is not so much the "prime minister" as "the prime arse-hole." Although this may represent a certain kind of reflection on alterity, it could hardly be said to constitute "reverse anthropology."

In my view, the main achievements of *Jaguar* lie elsewhere. First, in common with *Les Maîtres fous*, *Jaguar* acknowledges that rural Africans were already tied into a much wider world, both politically and economically. Much more important, it presents the migrants not as passive victims of this process but rather as active participants: they are "heroes of the modern world," as Rouch puts it in the passage of commentary toward the end of the film that is quoted in the epigraph to this chapter. These men certainly took to the road in search of money and material goods but also in search of adventure. In doing so, Rouch adds in the same section of commentary, they were following in the footsteps of their ancestors who had taken the very same roads south in order to fight as mercenaries in the seemingly endless interethnic skirmishes connected with the slave trade that were still going on immediately prior to the European colonial pacification of the area in the late nineteenth century.

This argument was central to the major report based on his migration research that Rouch published in the *Journal de la Société des Africanistes* in 1956. Many years later, in 1988, he was taken to task by Thomas M. Painter for overemphasizing the historical continuity between the migrants' taste for adventure and the motivations of their nineteenth-century mercenary ancestors rather than focusing on the effects of the still-extant French colonial regime in Niger. In particular, Painter accuses Rouch of selective attention in not emphasizing the importance of a severe head tax imposed on everyone over six years of age in Niger that, in effect, obliged young men to migrate in order to earn the money necessary to pay it off.[19] Rouch did not take kindly to this criticism, but to a third party, their respective arguments do not seem to be entirely incompatible. While there were no doubt certain "push" factors behind the migration, including not only the taxation but also the chronically fragile state of agriculture on the edge of the Sahel, there also appear to have been strong "pull" factors, including particularly the subjects' desire to see the world. Indeed, in the conclusion to his report, Rouch lists both the need to pay colonial taxes and the historically conditioned desire for adventure as reasons for Songhay-Zerma migration.[20]

Interestingly, in her personal memoir, Jane Rouch comments that whenever she spoke to francophone migrants on the Gold Coast, taxation and the rudeness of French colonial officers were factors that they always cited as the reasons why they had migrated. The need to earn money in order to be able to pay taxes is also the principal reason for this migration that is cited by Damouré in a film interview that he gave to Berit Madsen and Anne-Mette Jørgensen in 2003. But while the priority that Rouch gives to the attractions of adventure in the film could possibly be put down to his Romantic inclinations, it might also be, as he himself suggests, that being an ethnographer in the Maussian tradition, he assigned particular significance to his subjects' own constructions of their experience in which, notwithstanding Damouré's recollections some fifty years later, the thirst for adventure may have featured at least as strongly as more material concerns.[21]

This relates to the second and perhaps even more important achievement of *Jaguar*, namely, that it succeeds in representing its principal subjects not as exotic curiosities, as in previous genres of ethnographic film and even, to some extent, in *Les Maîtres fous*, nor as mere Durkheimian social facts, as in Rouch's statistical reports on migration, but rather as human beings with idiosyncratic characters and attitudes and—particularly importantly for Rouch—their own dreams and fantasies. This interest in fantasy is exemplified in the very title of the film, which is taken from the title of a multilingual hit song that is played at various points on the sound track.[22] In the immediate context of this song,

FIGURE 5.8. Damouré shown demonstrating the "jaguar" walk in a series of jump cuts.

the term "jaguar" refers to a particular form of fashionable urban cool. As Damouré and Lam comment on the sound track, "jaguar" was the English-language equivalent of "zazouman," a style of dress and comportment associated in francophone countries with African American jazzmen.[23] In a series of jump cuts, Rouch shows Damouré giving a demonstration of this cool in *Jaguar*, at least as it applied to men: it meant to be fashionably dressed and to parade oneself about town, smoking casually, being looked at while looking about oneself (fig. 5.8).

For women, on the other hand, being "jaguar" was synonymous with being a streetwalker in another sense, that is, being a particular kind of high-class prostitute. As Rouch explains in his migration report, these women were typically very young, expected large payments and dressed in a particular way, wearing low-cut blouses, short skirts, and European shoes. Their clients were mostly Europeans and Arabs, but any self-regarding Songhay migrant would aspire to enjoy their company at least once during his time on the Gold Coast. Jane Rouch also gives a series of amusing examples of the connotations of the term "jaguar" in 1950s Accra. According to her, among men, not only jazzmen but also skillful boxers were considered "jaguar," while among women, Hollywood film stars, even though they were all white in those days, could also be "jaguar" if they were considered particularly sexy.[24]

However, the ultimate reference of "jaguar" kin 1950s Accra was not to a particular form of comportment, but rather to the classic British sports car of that name, an unimaginable luxury for most urban migrants, but one to which many aspired and one which, almost incredibly, a very few, according to Rouch, actually achieved.[25] The refrain of the song, which takes various forms, refers to a series of other such aspirations, some more improbable than others. One of these refrains is "Jaguar—fridge full, Jaguar—fridge full," which is played over the image of Damouré as he begins his cock-walk through the streets. A migrant with a refrigerator full of food would have been only a slightly less fantastic idea for a Songhay migrant than the idea of owning a Jaguar sports car. At the end of Damouré's demonstration, the refrain changes slightly to "Jaguar—freedom, Jaguar—fridge full," which provides a convenient segue into a sequence in which Damouré attends a political rally addressed by Kwame Nkrumah calling for political independence.[26] This aspiration, at least, did come to pass, though it was a dream that would later turn into a nightmare.[27]

Yet although *Jaguar* was based on fictionalization and fantasy, for all that it was "one big joke," as he would later put it, Rouch felt that the film gave a much more valuable account of the phenomenon of Gold Coast migration than his detailed statistical monograph with all its facts and figures. "When I compare the monograph to *Jaguar*," he observed in an interview given in 1967, "I realize that the most truthful testimony is that of *Jaguar* in the sense that in the monograph, the human dimension is completely lacking. This was something that really impressed me . . . We had entered into a domain that was not reality, but rather the provocation of reality, one that revealed that reality."[28] This insight was something that Rouch would pursue in a variety of ways for the rest of his career.

6 : Dreams of Black and White

Look at that! I am dreaming that one day—like all other men, like everybody, like all those who are rich—I too will have a wife, a house, a vehicle.

OUMAROU GANDA as Robinson in *Moi, un Noir* (1960), commenting on a shot of himself sleeping on the pavement

In November 1956, Rouch moved to the French colony on the Ivory Coast to begin a new phase of his migration research. Over the next four years, Abidjan, the capital, would become the principal location of his filmmaking activities. Throughout this period, he continued to shoot in Niger, and he also made minor films in Upper Volta, Togo, and back on the Gold Coast, but it was the two major films that he made in Abidjan that were his most significant works. Both were ethnofictions, involving a further development of the improvisational techniques that he had employed in *Jaguar.* The first, *Moi, un Noir,* was shot over the course of six months in 1957, though it was not released in its definitive form until 1960. The other, *La Pyramide humaine*, was shot in 1959–1960 and was not finally released until 1961. If *Les Maîtres fous* had confirmed Rouch's reputation as a documentarist, it would be these two films that would establish Rouch as a major figure of French fictional cinema and one whose methods would have a major impact on the emergent New Wave.

The shooting of *Moi, un Noir* and *La Pyramide humaine* coincided with a period of major political change in West Africa. In June 1956, the degree of local self-government in the colonies of French West Africa had been greatly extended with the intention that this would lead eventually to independence. But as a result of the political crisis in Algeria in May 1958, which led to the return to power of General Charles de Gaulle and the establishment of the Fifth Republic later that year, the process of decolonization suddenly became much more rapid. Within two years, all French colonies in West Africa, including the Ivory Coast, had achieved independence. Although there is no direct reference to these momentous macropolitical events in the films, their offscreen presence is echoed in the theme of race relations between Africans and Europeans that runs through both films, mostly only implicitly in *Moi, un Noir,* but quite directly and explicitly in *La Pyramide humaine.*

Migration as Tribulation

Rouch often traced the genesis of *Moi, un Noir* to the occasion when he screened a preliminary version of *Jaguar* to a group of Nigeriens living in Treichville, the rundown quartier of Abidjan where many of the migrants lived. Among the audience was a certain Oumarou Ganda, a young man who normally made his living as a dockworker but whom Rouch had taken on as a research assistant. "It's clear that your hero hasn't lived the life of an immigrant," he told Rouch afterward, referring to Damouré Zika. "He doesn't know what it means. Here, we really do know." Provoked by this comment, Rouch resolved to make another film along the same lines as *Jaguar*, employing the same techniques, based around the lives of Oumarou and his friends.[1]

FIGURE 6.1. *Top*, Oumarou Ganda, alias Edward G. Robinson, and his friends. *Bottom*, Petit Touré, alias Eddie Constantine, aka "Lemmy Caution, US Federal Agent."

The original working title for *Moi, un Noir* was *Le Zazouman de Treich-ville*. Given that "zazouman" is the French equivalent of the term "jag-uar," this suggests that Rouch's original intention was simply to make a reprise of the earlier film in a new location. There are, however, a number of important differences between the two films. As Oumarou so bluntly observed, the protagonists in *Jaguar* were merely playing the role of migrants, while in *Moi, un Noir,* even if during the actual period of the shoot he was no longer making a living as a dockworker, Oumarou is di-rectly acting out the reality of what had until then been his everyday life. Whereas the ethnic affiliations of all the main characters in *Jaguar* are emphasized, Oumarou is not associated in *Moi, un Noir* with any par-ticular ethnic group, either by himself or by Rouch in voice-over, although he was in fact a Zerma. Instead, he is presented simply as a member of the general urban proletariat of Niamey. Having served in the French co-lonial army in Indochina for four years from the age of sixteen, he had returned home in 1955 to find himself without a job and, according to Rouch's voice-over, rejected by his father for having lost the war. He had therefore migrated to Abidjan to find work, but even there, his circum-stances remained highly precarious.[2]

Whereas *Jaguar* presents migration as a marvelous escapade, *Moi, un Noir* is altogether more serious in tone. There is no reference here to "the great adventure of African cities," as in the opening sequence of *Les Maîtres fous*. Instead, narrating over the initial image of a group of young men in rags lying on a pavement, Rouch comments, "This is one of the diseases of the new cities of Africa—young people without jobs." While the protagonists of *Jaguar* remain confident of their own identities, even while marveling at the strange and exciting world that they encounter, Rouch observes that these young migrants to Abidjan, "caught between animism and mechanization, between Islam and alcohol, have not re-nounced their traditional beliefs but are devotees of the new idols—box-ing and cinema." Whereas the migrants to the Gold Coast in *Jaguar* ap-pear to be having a whale of a time, the life of the migrants to Abidjan as presented in *Moi, un Noir* is marked by poverty, exploitation, and conflict with the authorities. This is only partially alleviated by the companion-ship afforded by the Nigerien migrant fraternity, as well as by dancing and visits to the beach on the weekend, and by a fantasy life that allows them to imagine that they are film stars or boxing champions.

Through his migration research, Rouch became aware that conditions for Nigerien migrants in Abidjan were particularly tough. Although he never produced anything that quite matched in length or detail the ac-count published in the *Journal de la Société des Africanistes* about his work on the Gold Coast, he wrote a number of shorter reports and articles on his Ivoirian research. One of his discoveries was that the Nigerien migrants were principally exploited, not directly by Europeans as one might imagine, but by indigenous Ivoirians. Oumarou was but one of the many casual Nigeriens workers who were, in effect, under the control of Ivoirian gangmasters who hired them out to employers as they needed them.[3] However, although Oumarou and other Nigeriens are shown at work, and Oumarou complains bitterly about his working conditions on the sound track, there is no allusion to this or any other more political aspect of labor relations in the film, apart from a brief shot of a trade union march.

In fact, although there are indeed some early scenes showing the world of work, most of the film is concerned with the migrants' leisure activities and their hopes, dreams, and fantasies. A montage sequence early in the film reminds us that these are profoundly shaped by cultural influences emanating from the international metropolises: with a ballad in French in the background, sung in an African accent and celebrating the beauties of Abidjan, we are presented in quick succession with a series of shop signs alluding to various quartiers of Paris, as well as to Chicago and Hollywood, followed by a series of hand-painted cinema posters advertising cowboy movies, while on the sound track, the ballad is displaced by the sound of galloping hoofs and pistol shots. This cultural syncretism is also evident in the Caribbean influences on the music that the protagonists listen to in the bars at night and in some of the songs on the sound track. When Robinson cannot pay his bill after drinking beer into the early hours of morning, the establishment from which he is ejected is the "Bar Mexico."

These cosmopolitan influences on the migrants' fantasy life are also reflected in the film star nicknames that, as foreigners, they assume in order to hide their identities. Oumarou adopts the nickname "Edward G. Robinson" because, he explains, his friends think that he looks like the film star of that name (though apart from the fact that both the star and Oumarou are diminutive in stature, the resemblance is not immediately obvious). Oumarou's friend and the principal costar of *Moi, un Noir*, Petit Touré, who plays the role of a peddler of imported cloths and an enthusiastic ladies' man, calls himself "Eddie Constantine," after an American actor who was a leading star of French B movies in the 1950s and best known for playing the hard-living, suave-talking, womanizing detective, Lemmy Caution, US federal agent. Unlike Oumarou, whose screen role reprised his work in real life prior to making the film, Petit Touré was not actually a street peddler. In fact, he was an office clerk from Abengourou, a town close to the border with Ghana, whom Rouch had also recruited as a migration research assistant. The third member of the trio of friends, a very tall taxicab driver and former professional boxer, Alassane Maïga, is known simply as "Tarzan," while the girl whom Oumarou fervently hopes to make his wife, identified delicately in the credits as Mademoiselle Gambi, is known by the nickname "Dorothy Lamour."[4]

Africa Speaks

In the introductory commentary, Rouch explains that in order to make the film, he followed this small group of Nigerien migrants over a six-month period. The protagonists were encouraged to improvise their own lives, doing whatever they wanted to do, saying whatever they wanted to say. In the editorial construction of the film, this material is presented as if it were all taking place over the course of a single long weekend. As a result, the weekend seems extremely action-packed as material shot over several months is compressed into no more than a couple of days. But it is a device that allows Rouch to contrast the rigors of the migrants' working week (which extends until Saturday midday), with the richness and variety of their leisure activities over the weekend.

Each day of this weekend is introduced by a title card, through which Rouch contextualizes what will happen during that day. But otherwise the film is narrated by Oumarou Ganda and Petit Touré themselves, who, in the same manner as Damouré and Lam did for *Jaguar*, recorded their commentaries in response to a silent projection of a preliminary version of the edited film. Rouch later explained that this voice-over commentary played a large part in establishing the somber tone of the film. It was performed at the studios of Radio Abidjan after a three-month period during which Petit Touré had been serving a prison sentence for assaulting a police officer. This imprisonment had brought the filming to a premature end and had led to both of the principal protagonists taking a much more negative view of their lives—though strangely, as far as the tone of the commentary is concerned, it seems to have affected Robinson more than Eddie Constantine, the one who had actually been imprisoned. But while somewhat somber in tone overall, this voice-over is extremely well performed by the two protagonists, with many lively, light-hearted passages. There are even some brief moments when almost perfect postsynchronized dialogue is achieved.[5]

In terms of the development of Rouch's stylistic repertoire, this film is particularly notable for its two fully fledged dream sequences. Rouch had made a relatively modest first step in this direction in *Jaguar* in the scene in which Damouré is shown approaching Accra standing in the back of open-topped truck and he imagines that his beauty is being acknowledged by a vast crowd. There is then the sound of a mighty roaring

and cheering on the sound track when in reality the roadside is virtually empty. In *Moi, un Noir*, the dream sequences are presented in image
as well as sound and are considerably more elaborate. The first such sequence occurs when Robinson dreams that he is "Edward G. Sugar Ray
Robinson" and is challenging for the world super-featherweight title.
With his friend "Tarzan" acting as his trainer, he enters the ring with
this name emblazoned on the back of his boxer's dressing gown. Then,
in a speeded-up passage, he swiftly defeats his rival, played by another
Nigerien migrant, knocking him out for the count. But fantasy quickly
turns back to reality, or at least the diegetic reality of the film, and we
discover that Robinson is no more than an anonymous member of the
crowd watching a real boxing match.

Later, asleep in a drunken stupor outside the Bar Mexico, Robinson
dreams that he has set up house with Dorothy Lamour and that she is inviting him into her bed. First, she drops down the bodice of her dress to
reveal her shapely bosom. Then, in the last shot of the sequence—surely
very risqué for the time, and certainly unprecedented in the canon of
ethnographic film—she is shown lying down while the shot is executed
from the angle of an approaching lover, looking up to her face through
the cleavage of her breasts. But, alas, this too turns out to be an illusion for, in the diegetic reality of the film, Dorothy Lamour has spent
the night in the arms of an Italian sailor who has paid handsomely for
her services. The following morning, when Robinson goes round to her
house and finds the Italian there, they engage in a ragged fistfight in the
rain and the dirt of the street outside. In the end, Robinson is bested, and
he has to slope off back to work, his head bowed.[6]

While both these dream sequences are well executed, perhaps the
most impressive sequence in the film from a technical point of view is
one of the least fictionalized. This is the lengthy sequence (approximately
ten minutes) covering a series of events held on the Sunday afternoon
at the house of the "*goumbé*," a cultural and mutual aid association organized by the Nigerien migrants.[7] These events begin with a number of
competitive performances, including dancing to drum rhythms by teams
of men and singing solos by women. On the sound track, Robinson explains that the tasseled shirts and trousers worn by some of the men
are supposed to be cowboy costumes. Later, the performers ride their
bicycles as if they were cowboys' horses, somehow managing to stand
stationary on them with one foot on the wheel, the other on the pedal,
as if they were standing up in stirrups. In the evening, there is a dancing competition for couples, which is won by Eddie Constantine and his
partner, the beautiful Nathalie, who are then declared "King and Queen
of the *Goumbé*." The evening ends with the playing of the kind of music

FIGURE 6.2. The dream and reality. *Top,* Dorothy Lamour invites Robinson into her bed. *Bottom*, he fights with her Italian client in the harsh light of morning.

normally performed at traditional possession ceremonies, involving the whine of the single-string *godye* violin, accompanied by the clattering percussion provided by a line of *gasu* drums, that is, upturned calabashes on the ground. The cinematography in this sequence is remarkable, as it is in this film as whole. Particularly memorable is the point-of-view shot of Nathalie during the dance competition when she appears to be literally dancing with Rouch behind the camera. Indeed, it is arguable that purely from a cinematographic point of view, *Moi, un Noir* represents the pinnacle of Rouch's achievement as a cameraman.

The influence on the filmmakers of the New Wave of the cinematographic technique that Rouch deployed in this film has often been commented upon, particularly in relation to the final sequence of the film in which Robinson both relates and enacts his wartime experiences in Indochina for his friend, Petit Jules, as they walk alongside the lagoon. This sequence is made up of a series of tracking shots that Rouch executed handheld, moving alongside the protagonists in a car, all shot in wide angle in order to minimize the effect of bumps, and linked only by jump

FIGURE 6.3. Robinson and his friends play in the Atlantic breakers on the weekend, but he is troubled. How can he marry Dorothy Lamour when he is so poor?

cuts. When the producer Pierre Braunberger first saw this sequence, he suggested putting in some cutaways of newsreel from Vietnam to cover these jump cuts. Rouch thought that this would be a disaster, so Braunberger suggested that they ask the opinion of François Truffaut, whose films he also produced. But Truffaut, far from taking Braunberger's side, was so impressed that he decided that he would end *Les Quatre Cents Coups*, which he was editing at the time, in a similar way.[8]

The shooting in this film also has many other merits. Although the panning is a little rocky, as ever in Rouch's films, due to his antipathy toward the tripod even when shooting big panoramas or buildings, the sheer profusion and variety of visually interesting shots is very impressive. The intimacy and delicacy of the close-ups of the principal protagonists are often extraordinary. A scene that is particularly memorable for the quality of both cinematography and editing is when Robinson goes to the beach with his friends on the Saturday afternoon and they all frolic athletically in the deep blue waves breaking on the shore. Later in the same scene, they go to wash off the salt in the nearby freshwater river.

Rouch is clearly shooting while standing waist-deep in the water himself, which I suspect may have been some kind of first in the annals of ethnographic film, if not documentary generally. But these idyllic shots of high jinks in the water are then followed by a series of subtle close-ups of the protagonists as Robinson reflects in the voice-over on the difficulties of his life.

However, in my view, the most striking aspect of Rouch's cinematography in this film is the way in which he uses lighting. In general, there are not many examples of the creative use of lighting in Rouch's films, either before or after this point in career. But in this film, he seems to have gone to particular trouble to use light in an imaginative way. Both the main characters are first introduced in lit night-time shots; Robinson, who first appears beneath the Treichville train station sign, is a little out of focus, but the shot introducing Eddie Constantine, lit from below, is magnificent (see fig. 6.1 above). There are many other interesting examples of lighting in the bar scenes and many highly atmospheric night-time establishing shots.

But perhaps the most impressive sequence of all from a lighting point of view is the scene in which Robinson and Tarzan do their sparring on Friday evening. There is very little light falling on the subjects, but it is just enough to highlight their faces and limbs as they move about energetically in the darkness. This minimal lighting, accompanied by their pants and grunts, communicates a powerful sense of the intense physicality of their movements. In a review of the film, Jean-Luc Godard expressed his great admiration for this particular scene, comparing Rouch's aesthetic vision to that of Richard Avedon, the celebrated photographer of high fashion.[9]

The sound track of this film is also skillfully constructed. The credits suggest that rather than use his trusty Nigerien friends as sound recordists (though Lam gets the unusual credit of "marabout-consultant"), on this occasion Rouch worked with a professional sound recordist, André Lubin. But it is the sophistication of the postproduction sound that is most remarkable when compared to Rouch's earlier films. The final sound track is made up of a complex mix of the improvised voice-overs by the protagonists, Rouch's own commentary voice, a profusion of "wild track" field sound recordings, and a variety of special effects, not to mention a highly diverse catalog of songs, which not only enrich the sound track but also have the advantage of covering breaks or unevenness in the other sound effects. In developing this dense tapestry of sound, Rouch appears to have been greatly assisted and inspired by the editor, Marie-Josèphe Yoyotte.[10]

When *Moi, un Noir* was released, it received a rapturous critical welcome. Jean-Luc Godard wrote no less than three notices about the film for *Cahiers du Cinéma*, including a particularly eulogistic full-length review that appeared in April 1959 under the title "Africa Speaks to You about the Ends and the Means." Godard was particularly struck by the effects that Rouch had managed to achieve simply by relying on improvisation by nonprofessional actors. Whereas others, such as the Italian Neorealists, Pirandello, and Stanislavsky had sought to achieve such effects by careful calculation, Rouch had achieved them by trusting to chance. Playing on the fact that in French the name of Joan of Arc is written as Jeanne, the female form of Jean, Godard declared that like the national heroine, Rouch would come to the rescue, not of France perhaps, but certainly of French cinema, by opening the door on a completely new way of making films.[11]

But what also impressed Godard, in common with the majority of other critics, was not only the technical and stylistic effects that Rouch had managed to achieve by his informal, improvisational methods but also the fact that this was the first time—given that *Jaguar* remained unfinished and had only been shown in public in the Cinemathèque—that a feature film had provided general French audiences with the opportunity to hear Africans describing their life experiences in their own voices. The combination of these two qualities led to *Moi, un Noir* being awarded the most prestigious film prize in France, the Prix Louis Delluc, for 1959. Rouch, however, was not there to collect the prize in person, for by then he had already returned to the drought-ridden savannas of the middle Niger River to continue working on the film that would eventually become *The Lion Hunters*.

A Difficult Story

The final film that Rouch made in his "African" period, *La Pyramide humaine*, was shot at the very height of the process of decolonization on the Ivory Coast in 1959–60. It was in this climate that Rouch set about making a film about what he calls, in the opening commentary, "a difficult story of friendship between Whites and Blacks."

In terms of content, *La Pyramide humaine* is very different from the previous films that Rouch made during his migration research. First, although one or two of the characters had migrated to Abidjan at some point in the past, the film has nothing to do with rural-urban migration as such. Secondly, if European protagonists had been completely absent from *Jaguar*, and in *Moi, un Noir*, had been represented only by the Italian sailor and a few passing extras, in *La Pyramide humaine* the relationship between Africans and Europeans is central to the action of the film. Third, whereas Rouch's earlier films had charted the experiences of the relatively poor or socially marginal, the protagonists of this film are pupils at an elite Abidjan *lycée*. As such, Rouch saw it as an opportunity to counter the accusation that he only ever filmed the lumpen proletariat.[12]

But perhaps the most important distinguishing characteristic of *La Pyramide humaine* concerns the relationship between enactment and reality. In the case of his earlier ethnofictions, even though they were extensively fictionalized, they had nevertheless reflected an underlying ethnographic reality. Robinson was acting out his own life prior to meeting Rouch, and while Damouré and Lam may never have been on a migratory journey to the Gold Coast before the making of *Jaguar*, many people like them did make such journeys, and they themselves would have been very likely to have done so at some point, even without Rouch's intervention.

In contrast, in *La Pyramide humaine* the action was entirely fictional. Prior to the making of the film, though the two groups of pupils were mostly in the same school year, sat side by side in the same classroom, and even shared common professional ambitions, they had very little to do with one another. Therefore, in order to explore the possibilities of interracial friendship, Rouch was obliged to provoke some sort of contact between the Africans and the Europeans. In this way, "instead of reflecting reality," as Rouch puts it in a crucial early commentary line, *La Pyramide humaine* "created another reality." Yet although the film was a fiction in this sense, Rouch claimed that it was a fiction that changed the protagonists' attitudes toward race in the real world. Later in his career, he would come to employ the term "psychodrama" to refer this process whereby the protagonists are provoked by the requirements of making a film into improvising a reality that otherwise would not exist but that then acts back on and affects their everyday reality.[13]

La Pyramide humaine was also different from Rouch's earlier works of ethnofiction in the sense that it was first of his films that he did not shoot entirely himself. In an interesting memoir written shortly after the shoot was completed, Rouch explains that the sixteen hours of rushes were shot in three different stages. Each of these corresponded to a different school vacation so that nobody could accuse him of interrupting the pupils' studies. Even so, for reasons that remained obscure, the Ivory Coast government forbade him to shoot in the *lycée* itself, so he had to recreate the classroom scenes in another, half-constructed building. Perhaps due to this implicit official disapproval or simply because the shoot occurred

FIGURE 6.4. The classroom set up in a half-constructed building when permission to film in the Cocody *lycée* itself was refused. Later the props were transferred to Paris for the final phase of the shoot. At first, the pupils remained in separate racial groups, as in real life, but as the film progressed, they began to share desks. © Films du Jeudi.

during the vacation, the schoolteacher never appears: a voice is heard instructing the students, but this is Rouch's own voice.

The first shoot took place in Abidjan in July 1959, during the summer vacation. This material was shot by Rouch himself, and although he was not using his faithful Bell & Howell Filmo 70 but rather a battery-driven camera that permitted longer takes, he still did not have synchronous sound.[14] The ten hours of rushes that he produced during this stage account for almost all the exterior scenes in the film and some of the interiors. The sound of these scenes was achieved through the same technical procedures that Rouch had employed in the making of *Moi, un Noir*, that is, a mixture of wild tracks, voice-overs, a little postsynchronization, and a considerable amount of music to cover the glitches.

But at some point after this first shoot, it was decided that in order to complete the film, synchronous sound was necessary for certain scenes. Probably because the situations created for the film were entirely fictional, the European *lycéens* particularly were not able to improvise voice-overs retrospectively in a sound studio with the conviction that the protagonists of Rouch's earlier ethnofictions had shown. The voice-overs that one hears in the *La Pyramide humaine* were actually scripted by

FIGURE 6.5. Nadine gets a ride from Alain. "During the vacation . . . he slept, really slept with a girl, a sensational Swedish girl, he claimed, rather pleased with himself." Although the protagonists performed the voice-overs, Rouch wrote the lines, inspired by the example of *We Are the Lambeth Boys*.

Rouch himself, even though they were then voiced by the protagonists. In drafting these voice-overs, he was inspired by examples from Karel Reisz's then recently released film about South London schoolchildren, *We Are the Lambeth Boys*, which he had seen as a member of the jury for the ethnographic section of the Festival dei Popoli in Florence in December 1959.[15]

There was also the problem that some of the scenes shot by Rouch suffered from certain technical inadequacies. In a recent interview, one of the principal protagonists, Nadine Ballot, reports that the producer Pierre Braunberger insisted that if the film was to have a commercial distribution, it was necessary to supplement Rouch's footage with material shot by a professional crew.[16] Another consideration was that Rouch wanted to include some reflexive scenes with himself on screen, which obviously required someone else to be behind the camera.

In order to record this additional material, Rouch returned to Abidjan during the Christmas vacation with a professional crew, albeit a very small one by the standards of the time. But even this second shoot failed to produce all the material necessary to produce a coherent film, so a third shoot was arranged for the Easter vacation, this time in Paris. By this time, five of the original cast had moved to Paris anyway to continue their studies, but a further five were brought over from the Ivory Coast. In Paris, a number of additional voice-overs by the protagonists were recorded, but also a number of further key scenes. These even included some of the scenes in the classroom, for which the props had been brought from Abidjan and set up in a film studio in Paris. This surely explains the rather curious variation in the lighting of the classroom scenes through the course of the film. Indeed, achieving continuity through all this different material proved extremely challenging and required six months in the edit suite to sort out.

The Generation of a Surreality

Although he was directing a professional crew for part of the shoot rather than working by himself, Rouch claims in the introductory voice-over that the techniques that he employed for generating the action of the film were the same as in the earlier ethnofictions. That is, once he had contrived the original situation whereby the two groups of pupils had some form of contact with one another, it was then left to them as actors to devise their actions and their dialogues as they saw fit, "spontaneous improvisation being the only rule of the game." But although this may have been true in a general sense, it is clear from both his own memoir and that of Nadine Ballot that at all stages, Rouch played a strong hand in setting up the situations in which the pupils would perform their improvisations, as well as in determining the general overall storyline of the film.

Early on in the film, he is shown setting up the initial situation, first with the European pupils, then with the Africans. The scene with the Europeans is shot outside, close to the banks of the lagoon. Although this was one of the scenes shot during the second shoot over the Christmas vacation, everyone pretends that they are learning about the project for the first time. Rouch explains that his eventual aim is to explore whether it is possible for there to be friendships between Blacks and Whites that are genuine and completely free of tension. For the purposes of the film, not only does he want each group to have contact with the other, which they do not normally have, but he wants certain members of each group, whatever their personal sentiments, to play the role of racists, in the same way that "if you are making a film about robbers, somebody has to play the role of the robbers." This is immediately followed in the film by a scene in which Rouch offers similar explanations to the African students. This is shot indoors, with a guitar and the sleeves of various classical music LPs arranged just a little too artfully around the walls, suggesting that this scene may have been shot in the studio in Paris as late as the Easter vacation. The acting in both scenes is very wooden—for understandable reasons, given that most of the students had been actively involved in the shoot for some months—but they do fulfill their dramaturgical purpose: after a show of being initially perplexed and worried by the fact that there is no script, both groups agree to participate in the project.

The initial plot point of the film revolves around the character played by Nadine, who wants to get to know more about the lives of her African schoolmates. In reality, Nadine was the daughter of a French banker and had grown up in Africa, but in order to explain her newfound curiosity about the Africans, she is presented in the film as a *débarquée*, that is, as having only recently got off the boat from France.[17] As her parents are living in the interior of the country, she feels free to do more or less as she pleases, without undue concern for the mores of the Abidjan European community. Despite the opposition of some of the pupils, African as well as European, she first develops a friendship with the character played by Denise Koulibali, and other friendships between the two groups then ensue. The most eloquent member of the African group, Denise was a couple of years older than most of the others members of the cast and in reality was not actually in the same class. But she was a key figure in the project, being politically well-connected as her father was an important figure in the ruling party in the Ivory Coast, the Rassemblement Démocratique Africain (RDA). Some years after the film, she herself became a government minister.[18]

An important moment in the breaking down of barriers between the two racial groups occurs when the African pupils entertain the Europeans at a dance at the Royale *goumbé*, the migrants' fraternity house that had been featured in *Moi, un Noir.* The Europeans then reciprocate with a party at Nadine's very grand house, which, in extradiegetic reality, actually belonged to the local director of the IFAN. A central figure in the *goumbé* scene is Nathalie, who in *Moi, un Noir* had been Eddie Constantine's dance partner. In this film, she shows the European pupils how to dance in an African manner. Although Nathalie was not actually one of the *lycéens*, she became a regular member of the cast thereafter. Rouch was clearly much taken by Nathalie's beauty, commenting in his memoir that whenever she appeared in the film, she lit up the screen.[19]

These contacts give rise to some interracial love affairs, which to a modern sensibility seem rather touchingly innocent. In the most risqué sequence on this topic, Nadine and Raymond, the son of a poor fisherman, walk hand in hand through the night after the party at her house, and then sit together beneath a tree. While Raymond sings a Spanish ballad, Nadine puts her head in his lap and a dream sequence unfolds. They are shown arriving by canoe at a chapel of the Harris cult, a local syncretic religion combining African and Christian elements.[20] On the sound track, Nadine recites a poem by Rimbaud. They kiss on the lips, enter the chapel, and their union is apparently blessed by the statues in the chapel. Then with a smile and a look of erotic complicity toward Raymond, Nadine brings her abundant beautiful red hair down over her face. Slightly caught up by the breeze, the mound of her hair momentarily becomes a disturbingly surreal object of desire. But then there is a cut and Nadine is shown still lying innocently in Raymond's lap, listening to his song as if it were merely a lullaby (fig. 6.6).

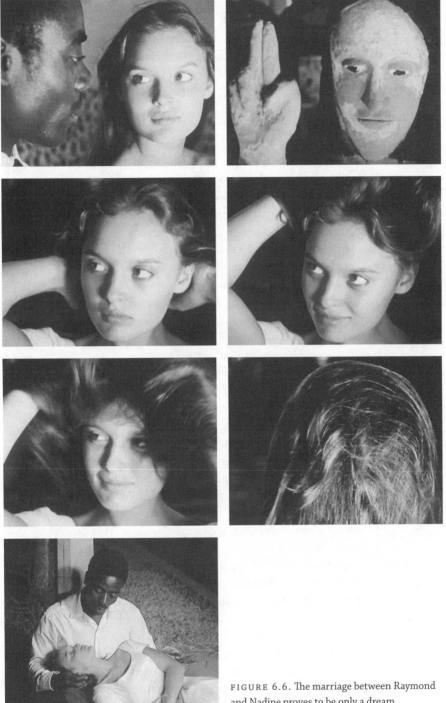

FIGURE 6.6. The marriage between Raymond and Nadine proves to be only a dream.

Although scenes such as this might seem relatively innocuous now, at the time of the film's release, they were regarded as nothing short of scandalous, if not in France itself, then certainly to the European population of the Ivory Coast where the film was initially banned because, according to Nadine Ballot, it showed African boys approaching European girls. However, although Nadine lent herself to the part of the "flirt" with considerable conviction, she did not take the possibility of such interracial love affairs very seriously. "It was, if anything, very funny," she comments in the recent interview. "It became a kind of a game. I did not believe in it all, but maybe some of the boys believed in the possibilities suggested in the film."[21]

The title of the film, *La Pyramide humaine*, is taken from a poem by the Surrealist poet Paul Éluard, which is read out in class at one point by Jean-Claude, one of the European pupils.[22] In this poem, Éluard reflects on whether his dreams of love can result in a genuine love in real life. This has an obvious immediate relevance to the love affairs going on in the film, but it also appears to be a metaphorical reference to Rouch's hopes for friendship between Africans and Europeans outside the film. As one commentator on the film has pointed out, this contrasts radically with the call by Frantz Fanon, at around this same period, for a total rupture in relations between Africans and Europeans.[23]

However, whatever the objective possibilities for interracial friendships outside the film, the friendship between the two racial groups within the film results in some arguments. At first, these relate mostly to the love affairs, and particularly to Nadine's habit of flirting with several different boys at once, both African and European, raising their hopes but, in the end, disappointing all of them. In fact, this theme becomes so prominent that it threatens to transform the film from being an imaginative exploration of race relations into little more than a high school romance with the usual complement of tiffs, frustrated sexual energies, and adolescent ramblings about relationships. Yet there is another thread to the discussions between the two groups that concerns social and political matters and this eventually leads to a heated debate about apartheid in South Africa and, more generally, about the European colonial practice of divide and rule in Africa—one of the relatively few moments when political matters are addressed head-on in the Rouchian canon (fig. 6.7).

This argument demonstrates that although they might have crossed racial boundaries in their own personal relationships in the course of making this film, they remain enmeshed in political conditions and ideologies that keep Europeans and Africans firmly apart. But before this political debate becomes too acrimonious and before, one suspects, the

FIGURE 6.7. The diegetic interracial friendships are threatened by extradiegetic political realities. Alain, *center*, later joined the Foreign Legion and was killed during the Algerian war of independence. Denise, *left*, later became a minister in the post-independence government of the Ivory Coast.

extradiegetic reality of interracial tension intrudes too strongly on the burgeoning diegetic friendships, the scene breaks off and all the protagonists are shown, together with Rouch, laughing at a screening of rushes of themselves engaged in this argument. In the commentary track, Rouch deflects the film away from these "interminable" political discussions and returns to the question of the epistemological status of the film. As the camera pans over the protagonists looking at the film, he remarks that they are discovering a previously unknown image of themselves, adding, in a telling phrase, that the fictional world of the film "has become a surreality."

The film then culminates in a scene of the whole group going for a picnic on board an old cargo ship that has run aground on the beach. In the course of this scene, Alain, one of the European boys, sees another European boy, Jean-Claude, canoodling with Nadine, and in a fit of pique, dives off the ship and apparently drowns. As a plot point, this does not make a great deal of sense. Although Alain and Jean-Claude had been shown fighting at the party at Nadine's house earlier in the film, the reasons for this remain unclear: it is vaguely intimated that it has something to do with Nadine, but in fact, as originally shot, the fight arose because, in a scene that was eliminated from the final version, Jean-Claude had previously been teasing Alain about the fact that he had failed his baccalauréat.[24] In any case, in subsequent scenes in the film, Alain is shown engaging in a rivalry not with Jean-Claude for Nadine's affections but with one of the African boys, Elola, for the affections of the beautiful African girl, Nathalie. It makes even less sense therefore that this tragic outcome of a supposed love triangle exclusively between Europeans should then result in a rupture in the film between the two racial groups as a whole.

In his memoir, Rouch admits that there is something unsatisfactory about this but metaphorically shrugs it off, commenting that this is the risk one runs in improvising films in this way.[25] Perhaps, given the prejudices of the time, it would have been just too explosive to have added a racial component to the tragic love triangle, or perhaps it was indeed simply that he found himself lumbered with rushes that did not really hang together and had to make the best of it. But whatever the case, he clearly did not want to leave the film on this pessimistic note, so in the final scene, there is a reconciliation between the two groups as they meet at the airport to see off Nadine, who has decided to return to France. Then, in an epilogue, the film shows a number of the protagonists, including the "drowned" Alain, happily walking down a street in Paris, and one is reminded that the film was but a fiction. Even so, Rouch suggests, it was a fiction that has had effects in the real world in the sense that it has helped all the participants to overcome their racial prejudices.[26]

La Pyramide humaine confirmed Rouch's developing status as a major figure of French cinema. In 1965, four years after its release, when thirty-one leading critics were asked by Cahiers du Cinéma to name the best ten French films since the end of the Second World War, seven of them included La Pyramide humaine in their lists while three more included Moi, un Noir. Jean-Luc Godard was a particular admirer, rating La Pyramide humaine second only to the Max Ophuls film, Le Plaisir, as the greatest French film of this period.[27] From an ethnographic point of view, La Pyramide humaine is perhaps the least interesting of the films that Rouch made during the period of his migration research since we discover very little about the broader social, political, or cultural contexts in which race relations are played out. But in terms of the development of Rouch's praxis, this film is of crucial importance since it prefigures a number of elements that would be central to his work in the future. As we shall see in chapters 8 and 9, the psychodrama methodology and the associated play between the fiction and reality, the incorporation into the film itself of both the initial setting up and the viewing of rushes by the protagonists, and even several of the leading characters of La Pyramide humaine, would all reappear, under various different guises, in the films that Rouch would make in the next phase of his career. But this phase would only begin after Jean Rouch had undertaken his own migration, back to Paris, just as the French colonial empire in West Africa was coming to an end.

7 : Images of Power

In Jean Rouch's immense body of work, there are a number of films that stand out particularly, but even among these, *Les Maîtres fous* is one of the most salient. Mostly filmed over the course of a single day—Sunday, August 15, 1954—this was the film that first clearly established Rouch's international renown. He shot the film with his trusty spring-wound Bell & Howell Filmo 70 purchased at the Paris Flea Market, while the sound was recorded asynchronously by his longtime Nigerien associates, Damouré Zika and Lam Ibrahim Dia on a "portable" tape recorder weighing in excess of thirty kilograms. It was edited by Suzanne Baron, a rising star of the cutting room who had already worked with Jacques Tati on *Les Vacances de M. Hulot* (1951) and who would later become Louis Malle's editor of choice.

Les Maîtres fous concerns the *hauka* spirit possession cult in and around Accra, capital of what is now the independent state of Ghana but was then still the British colony of the Gold Coast. The mediums were mostly young Songhay men who had migrated from the middle reaches of the Niger River, some 650 miles to the north in the French colony of Niger (and now an independent republic of the same name). Referred to as "Zabrama" in the film, they represented merely the most recent wave of a pattern of seasonal migration from the drought-afflicted southern margin of the Sahelian Desert to the economically dynamic cities on the coastal plains of West Africa that had been going on since at least the middle of the nineteenth century.

This chapter represents a modified version of an essay that was awarded the 2004 Curl Essay Prize of the Royal Anthropological Institute and that later appeared in a somewhat abbreviated form under the title "Spirit Possession, Power and the Absent Presence of Islam: Re-viewing *Les Maîtres fous*" in the *Journal of the Royal Anthropological Institute* (Henley 2006a). It is republished here in this form with the kind permission of Blackwell Publishing Ltd. but the original can be accessed via http://www.blackwell-synergy .com/loi/JRAI.

FIGURE 7.1. Globalization *avant la lettre*. *Top*, the Little Sisters of Christ proclaim their faith in the streets of Accra. *Bottom*, West Indian calypso plays day and night in bars with names such as "Weekend in California" and "Weekend in Havana."

Although *Les Maîtres fous* is a relatively brief film, with a running time of less than thirty minutes, it has been the subject of innumerable commentaries. Marc Piault echoes a commonly held view when he observes that *Les Maîtres fous* is a "truly foundational film, without doubt one of the cult films of both cinema and anthropology."[1] In terms of general film craft, it marked an important new phase in Rouch's development as a filmmaker, going beyond the simpler narratives of his earlier films. Whereas most ethnographic films of the day aimed to capture the last expressions of traditional rural cultural traditions under the threat of disappearance, *Les Maîtres fous* celebrates what Rouch refers to in the opening commentary as "the great adventure of African cities" and unashamedly describes a world already affected by cultural and economic globalization long before this term had entered common currency (see fig. 7.1).

But what really accounts for the interest that this film has attracted over the years is its controversial subject matter. Some fifty years after it was made, the argument about the precise meaning of the ritual event at the heart of the film continues unabated. Indeed, the film is so well known that it is barely necessary to summarize its content, though I shall do so briefly:

> Following a preliminary sequence showing the highly varied range of casual laboring jobs performed by Songhay-Zerma migrants in Accra, the film follows a group of them as they travel by rural taxi to the small town of Nsawam, about twenty-five miles north of Accra and then to the small-holding of one Mountyeba, a cacao farmer from Niger and priest of the *hauka* cult. Here, after a new member has been initiated and other more established members have offered small animal sacrifices in recompense for certain moral infringements, the *hauka* spirits are summoned and the mediums go into trance. While in this state, they assume a series of iden-tities associated with the colonial world, mostly political or military: Gov-ernor, General, Major, Corporal of the Guard, and so on, putting on pith helmets and red sashes, blowing a whistle and parading up and down with wooden models of guns. Not all these identities are high-ranking or military: one medium becomes Train Driver while another becomes Truck Driver. Nor are they all male: one man adopts the identity of Doc-tor's Wife while the only female medium adopts the identity of a certain Madame Salma, the wife of an early twentieth-century French colonial official. In these various forms, the mediums dance about, foam at the mouth, and run flaming straw torches over their torsos (fig. 7.2). At the culminating moment, they sacrifice a dog and throw themselves forward with an animalistic frenzy to drink its blood. They then put it on to boil and plunge their hands into the pot to extract pieces of meat, seemingly impervious to the pain. But next day, the film shows that they have all re-turned to normal life as smiling workers in the city.

The now-orthodox interpretation of this spirit possession ceremony and one that is almost universal in the English-language literature, is that it represents a carnivalesque parody of colonial authority figures and as such constitutes a form of counter-hegemonic cultural resistance to European colonialism. In this chapter, I shall be arguing that while such an interpretation is immediately attractive, and obviously conge-nial to postcolonial sensitivities, it is misplaced, involving a confusion of ends and means, and consequently obscuring what the ritual activity represented in *Les Maîtres fous* is really about.

The Genesis of a Counter-hegemonic Text

The first public screening of the *Les Maîtres fous*, when it was still in the form of a work print, took place sometime in early 1955, in the cinema

FIGURE 7.2. Mediums possessed by *hauka*. *Top*, Lieutenant Malia, "from the Red Sea" enters a trance. *Below*, by passing a flaming torch over his body, Corporal of the Guard proves that he is no longer an ordinary human being, but a *hauka*.

of the Musée de l'Homme, before an audience mostly composed of anthropologists and African intellectuals. It was a complete disaster. Most of those present condemned the film for encouraging racist prejudices, and urged Rouch to destroy it. The critics included even Rouch's mentor Marcel Griaule, though Rouch would later claim that it was the mimicking of the colonial authorities that most worried him. Only the Belgian anthropologist and filmmaker Luc de Heusch spoke up for the film, declaring that it was bound to become a classic of ethnographic cinema and on no account should it be destroyed.[2]

Defying the criticisms Rouch completed the film and put it into circulation. In Paris, it continued to cause offence: a commonly told story concerns the late Senegalese director Blaise Senghor who reported that when he emerged from a public screening in Paris, he sensed that other members of the audience were looking at him and thinking, "Here's another one who is going to eat a dog!"[3] Back on the Gold Coast, it was banned on the grounds not only that it showed cruelty to animals but also disrespect to the governor, the Queen's representative, and hence to the Queen herself. Many other audiences, both then and now, have found the images disturbing: Paul Stoller reports that every time that he shows the film to his students, one of them invariably vomits.[4]

But although the film still has its critics, de Heusch's prophecy has come to pass and *Les Maîtres fous* is indeed now regarded as a classic of ethnographic film, with an impact extending far beyond the realm of academic anthropology. Not only did it begin to garner various international film prizes, but also, shortly after it was released, it inspired Jean Genet in the writing of his play *Les Nègres*, in which oppressed Blacks don masks and mimic their White masters. A few years later, Peter Brook screened it to his actors when rehearsing his famous 1964 production of *Marat/Sade* in order to demonstrate to them the effect of overwhelming madness on the human body. Nor was it only in the former colonial metropoli that the film came to be acclaimed. For, according to Rouch himself, those same African colleagues who had once denounced the film as racist later came to appreciate it as the best available filmic depiction of colonialism from below. As such, he claimed, it has come to be considered an anticolonial film that is routinely screened for educational purposes in the independent Republic of Niger.[5]

Over the years, Rouch seems to have worked hard to secure this rehabilitation. Although he may have defied his friends and colleagues at the Musée in releasing the film, he would surely have been deeply troubled by their reaction. That any film of his should encourage racist attitudes toward the African subjects would have conflicted profoundly with his most fundamental principles. In order to disarm these criticisms while not compromising on the documentation of the cult, he appears to have adopted the strategy of suggesting that if there was anything shocking or ugly in the film, this should not be attributed to the African subjects but rather to the colonial society in which they lived.

A number of editorial devices deployed within the film itself encourage this interpretation. First of all, there is the main title, which plays on a series of linguistic ambiguities. For, in French, the word *maître* means both "master" as in "master and servant" and the "master" of a cult, that is, an accomplished spirit medium. The identity of the *maîtres* alluded to in the title of the film is thus ambiguous: it could refer to either the colonial masters or the mediums, or indeed to both. The adjective *fou*, meanwhile, means "mad," which on one level is an ethnographic allusion to the fact that *hauka*, the most common local term for the cult, has precisely this connotation. But on another level, it suggests that it is the political masters, the colonial authority figures represented by the mediums in trance, who are the truly insane ones.[6]

Another such device is the lengthy series of intertitles at the beginning of the film. These warn the spectators of the "violence and cruelty" they are about to see, but assure them that the objectives of the film are merely sociological, aiming to provide an uncompromised view of one of the "new religions" developed by young African migrants as a reaction to their "bruising" encounter with "the mechanical civilization" of the cities. The spectators are also assured that there is nothing subversive about the cult since the film was made at the request of the cult's priests, and it is open to all those "who really wish to play the game." If this "game" seems rather unpleasant, the spectators are reminded that it is "nothing other than the reflection of our civilization" as seen by "certain Africans."

This reference to a "game" seems to have had the unfortunate effect of suggesting to some commentators that the *hauka* cult is merely a ludic performance of some kind. In fact, this reference is an allusion to the Songhay's own term for spirit-possession rituals, *holey hori*, which can be translated, very literally, as "game of the spirits." But what this refers to is not so much the ludic quality of these rituals but rather their theatricality: Marc Piault has suggested that there is an analogy here with the way in which, in the Christian tradition, one can refer to Passion "plays." As in the case of the latter, the theatricality of these events does not mean that their purposes cannot be both entirely authentic and deeply serious.[7]

The presentation of the *hauka* cult as a reaction to the oppressive nature of "mechanical civilization" is taken up again in the commentary of the film. Over the opening sequence showing the migrants at work at their many different jobs around Accra, the commentary deploys the cacophony of urban living as a metaphor for all the stresses and strains of city life, concluding with the suggestion—running over a dramatic nighttime shot of a medium frothing at the mouth—that the migrants "from silent savannas" are "forced" to turn to the cult as refuge from all this "noise." Rouch returns to these themes in the concluding passage of commentary at the end of the film. Here, over a series of shots of smiling laborers who only yesterday had been gorging themselves on dog meat, he comments:

> When looking at these happy faces . . . one really wonders whether these men of Africa have found a panacea against mental disorders. One wonders whether they have found a way to absorb our inimical society.

Here too then, he is suggesting that if there is anything distressing about the behavior represented in the film, this should be understood as merely the Africans' response to the madness of "inimical" European colonial society (fig. 7.3).[8]

It is significant that these various editorial devices deflecting a

FIGURE 7.3. Possession as a form of defense. *Top*, the adepts take refuge from the noise of the city by calling on the "new gods." According to Muller (1971: 1472), the frothing at the mouth is the product of a systematically developed technique involving "special tongue movements." *Bottom*, next day, the adepts return to their everyday menial jobs. "When looking at these happy faces . . . one wonders whether they have found a way to absorb our inimical society."

possibly negative reaction—the titles, the commentary—are normally added toward the end of the postproduction of a film. Given that it was only a work print with an improvised commentary that was screened at the disastrous première in the Musée, it is tempting to speculate that these editorial devices in the definitive version of *Les Maîtres fous* were added subsequently, as a direct response to the harsh criticisms that the film had attracted at that first screening. But whatever the exact chronology of their addition to the film, the general line of the interpretation that they promote is the same as the one that Rouch encouraged in his many external commentaries on the film in later years.

Moreover, as time went on, these commentaries became progressively more radical. Rather than present the cult as simply a response to the various personal problems that rural migrants encountered on moving to the city, as is implied in the internal commentary of the film itself, Rouch later came to see it as a form of "group therapy" developed as "a reaction against the colonial power of the British and French authorities."[9] By 1977, he was distancing himself from the implication in his concluding comment that the cult could be interpreted as a means of psychological accommodation to colonial society, preferring instead to call it "implicitly revolutionary." However, in the same interview, he acknowledges that the *hauka* mediums "insist" that they were not engaged in mockery nor motivated by any notion of revenge, adding that he considers this to be true, "at least on the conscious level."[10] Yet by 1990, we find him describing the *hauka* performances as "unmercifully mimicking" colonial military displays.[11]

In the hands of some secondary commentators, this interpretative tendency has been taken one step further. Although Rouch's more mature understanding of the *hauka* cult may have been to see it as a reaction against colonial power rather than just against "mechanical civilization" in some more general sense, he still continued to think of it as being essentially therapeutic. In the writings of others, however, this has subtly metamorphosed into an interpretation in which the cult is presented as primarily a form of parodic resistance to the cultural hegemony of European colonialism while the therapeutic element is downplayed in importance or ignored completely.

In reassessing this film, I shall begin by identifying the grounds for doubt about the conventional view of the *hauka* ceremony in *Les Maîtres fous* as a counter-hegemonic performance that arise simply from viewing the film itself. I will then develop an alternative interpretation on the basis of an examination of the ethnographic literature on possession cults among the Songhay and a number of other peoples of West and North Africa. In doing so, I shall be relying heavily on the work of an ethnographic author of unrivalled authority on the subject of Songhay possession. This author is none other than Jean Rouch himself. In effect then, I shall be using the work of Rouch the Author to finesse and expand the reading of the *hauka* cult offered by Rouch the Filmmaker.

Some Loose Threads

My own doubts about the interpretation of the *hauka* cult as a counter-hegemonic parody of European political power were first aroused by a number of details in the film itself. There is, first of all, the extended sequence in the compound before the principal ceremony begins. After a new member has been initiated, a number of more established members make confessions to Mountyeba the priest. One confesses that he has had sexual intercourse with his friend's girlfriend and consequently has been impotent for two months while a second, clearly in a state of psychological turmoil, declares that he is unclean. A third then questions the very existence of the *hauka* spirits. The priest imposes various fines, involving the sacrifice of a ram and a number of chickens, and their blood

FIGURE 7.4. Public confessions. *Top*, "I never wash, I am unclean." *Bottom*, Mounteyba the *zima* priest imposes an animal sacrifice as a punishment.

is then spattered over the makeshift concrete altar and the painted termite mound that serves as the "palace" of the *hauka* spirit Governor (fig. 7.4). Right at the end of the film, we discover that the impotent man, who had been possessed during the ritual by the spirit known as Wicked Major Mugu, has been cured of his impotence and that his current girlfriend is "very happy" as a result. We do not learn what effect the event has had for the other "penitents," but this one case shows that there is something else going on here that has nothing directly to do with politically motivated parody.

Another reason for doubt, at least about the *sufficiency* of the interpretation of the event as a parody of European political power, lies in the particular identities of the *hauka* spirits. For not all of the mediums assume identities that would necessarily have been associated with politically powerful Europeans. Not only are some of the characters African, such as the more lowly soldiers and, it transpires, Madame Salma,[12] but in among all the political and military figures, there are also the civilian figures of the Truck Driver and the Train Driver who would probably also have been African, at least in the British colonies.[13] It is true that all these characters would have been implicated in some way in the culture of the Europeans' "mechanical civilization," but are we to assume that on these grounds, they are also being parodied in a counter-hegemonic manner? This seems rather unlikely for a variety of reasons, not least because, as we discover in the latter part of the film, a number of the mediums in everyday life are themselves low-ranking soldiers, truck drivers, and the like. So if these characters were being parodied, the mediums would, in effect, have been parodying themselves.

But perhaps the most intriguing loose end concerns the fact that a number of the most senior military figures, in addition to their military rank, are given the name "Malia." This, Rouch explains, means that they are "from the Red Sea." But why would these *hauka* spirits be identified with that thin sliver of water, lying over 2,500 miles away as the crow flies, which separates the Horn of Africa from Saudi Arabia? The mediums would surely have known about London and Paris, so if the *hauka* are parodic embodiments of colonial political authorities, why did the mediums not conceive of them as coming from these imperial capitals?

These are not the only details that provoke questions. One that has generated more comment than perhaps any other single moment of this film occurs about halfway through the principal ceremony, when a number of the mediums approach a small wooden statue of the *hauka* Governor that stands to one side of the compound where they have been dancing. The statue is bespectacled and mustachioed, a sword lies across its shoulder, and the model of a small horse stands at its foot, along with a scattering of small bottles (fig. 7.5). One of the mediums then cracks an egg over the head of statue. At this point in the commentary, Rouch asks, "Why an egg?" immediately answering, "To imitate the plume worn by British governors on their helmet." There is then a cut to a series of shots from above of the present British governor arriving at a military parade, wearing a plumed helmet of ostrich feathers (fig. 7.6). This in turn is followed by a couple of general views of the event, with Rouch commenting:

> Amid the crowd there are *hauka* dancers looking for their model. And if the order is different here from there, the protocol remains the same.

At this point, the film cuts back to the *hauka* Governor consulting in Grand Guignol manner with his "general staff" as they prepare to inspect his "palace," that is, the painted termite mound.

This cutaway to the colonial governor's parade lasts less than a minute and stands out in sharp contrast to the editorial aesthetic of the rest of this part of the film. Indeed, cutaways to a different time and place for the specific purpose of commenting on an adjacent shot are highly un-

FIGURE 7.5. *Top*, the statue of the *hauka* Governor, with model horse and perfume bottles at the base; *bottom*, the *hauka* Governor embodied in a human medium, with his attendants, one of whom, though male, is wearing a flowery woman's dress. © Fondation Jean Rouch.

FIGURE 7.6. Why an egg? *Top*, an adept cracks an egg on head of the statue; *bottom*, wearing his plumed helmet, the British governor, Sir Charles Arden-Clarke, arrives at the Trooping of the Colour.

usual in Rouch's documentary work taken as whole.[14] Commentators on the film have debated what kind of cut this is, with some arguing that it is an example of Vertovian montage while others have claimed that it must surely be Eisensteinian. Yet whatever kind of cut it may be, it has been widely interpreted, by critics from all points across the political spectrum, as evidence that the *hauka* performance represents a parodic subversion of imperial power.[15]

But this interpretation relies on the assumption that in cracking the egg over the statue, the *hauka* mediums sought to debase the colonial governor symbolically in some way. Yet there is nothing in the film itself that indicates that this is the case. Rouch himself merely comments that the broken egg was considered by the mediums to be imitative of the governor's plumes. Neither this comment, nor his subsequent suggestion over the shot of the crowd at the parade that the *hauka* dancers were there looking for their model, nor even his final observation that protocol was the same in both places, necessarily entails that the *hauka* were intending to parody the colonial governor.

Here it would clearly be a great advantage to have the *hauka* medi-

ums' own explanations as to their intentions. But in their absence, careful attention to the filmic text suggests that the cracking of an egg over
the statue, far from being symbolically debasing, was intended to have
positive connotations. For, earlier in the film, we see Mountyeba the
priest carefully breaking eggs over the *hauka* Governor's termite mound
"palace." Rouch does not explain the motivation for this either, but it
comes at the end of a sequence in which the priest is shown sprinkling
gin around the compound, including on the "palace," to purify the space
in preparation for the ritual. This suggests that the breaking of eggs on
the "palace" and later on the Governor's statue would have had some
similarly beneficial symbolic purpose.

A somewhat different question is posed by the sacrificial dog. "Why
a dog?" asks Rouch rhetorically when the unfortunate animal is first
brought into the compound. The answer is intriguing:

> Because it is a strict taboo and if they eat a dog, the *hauka* will show that
> they are stronger than the other men, whether Black or White.

So if the rite is supposed to be a challenge, Rouch seems to be suggesting, it is a challenge directed not only at Europeans but at other Africans
as well. Moreover, the Africans are mentioned first, suggesting that they
are in fact the primary audience for this demonstration of power (fig.
7.7). But which class or group of Africans could this be?

While it is possible that all these apparently dissonant details could be
reconciled with a coherent interpretation of the cult as a form of counter-
hegemonic resistance to colonial power, they suggest that there is more
going on here than any straightforward explanation in terms of anticolonial politics can account for. As such, they invite one to look beyond the
film to any literature that might throw further light on the matter.

The *Hauka* in Songhay History

But as soon as one turns to the literature, the parody-of-colonial-power
interpretation begins to look increasingly unsafe. To begin with, it is
difficult to reconcile this interpretation with the fact that the *hauka* cult
long outlived both the French and British colonial presence in West Africa. Although Nigerien migrants were expelled from Ghana some ten
years after the coming of independence in 1957, Paul Stoller reports that
in the 1980s the *hauka* cult was still flourishing back in Niger, which itself
had become independent in 1960. Here the cult has drawn followers from
all strata of Nigerien society, including even the military dictator General
Seyni Kountché who ruled the country from 1974 to 1987. Stoller himself
witnessed a ritual in which an agronomist who had studied at "several

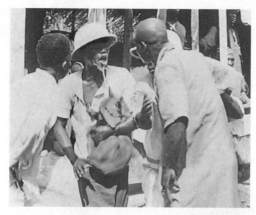

FIGURE 7.7. Why a dog? *Top*, at a "round table conference," the Wicked Major and the Governor debate whether the dog should be eaten raw or cooked; *bottom*, with no sign of fear, adepts plunge their hands into the boiling pot of dog meat, another sign that they have become *hauka*.

European and American universities" consulted some *hauka* mediums in order to find out why his career had not prospered.[16]

As a one-time leading proponent of the *hauka*-as-colonial-parody thesis, Stoller seeks to explain the postindependence survival of the cult on the grounds that although the old imperial colonies may have disappeared, Europeans continue to have a powerful presence, even if they now act as technicians, development consultants, and university lecturers.[17] But while this may well be true, it is still difficult to understand why a parody of European power, be it in the form of some long-gone imperial governor, or even in the form of a modern-day European paramedic, could be considered by an elite, university-educated Nigerien to provide a possible solution to his career problems.

The postcolonial *hauka* cults in Niger have also been studied by Jean-Pierre Olivier de Sardan, who, in sharp contrast to Stoller, firmly rejects the interpretation of the cults as a form of anticolonial counter-hegemonic resistance. He reports that in the course of conducting "hundreds" of interviews on the *hauka* with Songhay-Zerma informants, not once was such a political interpretation suggested to him, not even by those who were most critical in other regards of the colonial regime. While Olivier de Sardan acknowledges that the *hauka* spirit world is peopled to some extent by colonial figures, he points out that the notion that there is an intentional critique implicit in the enactment of these identities runs directly counter to the local understanding that it is the spirit that chooses the medium rather than vice-versa. Thus the idea that somebody would purposefully adopt a particular identity in the interests of political satire simply would not make sense in indigenous terms. Instead, Olivier de Sardan argues that the *hauka* cult should not be interpreted as a political phenomenon at all, but rather as a religious phenomenon. In proposing this argument, he claims to be returning to the point of view of the first anthropologist to study the *hauka* cult in any depth, namely, Jean Rouch himself.[18]

The credibility of the *hauka*-as-political-parody interpretation begins to unravel still further when one looks at the comparative literature. This literature shows that cults involving possession by spirits identified with Europeans are found throughout West and North Africa and even in East and Southern Africa. One of the most widespread is the *zar* cult, which has been the subject of ethnographic descriptions in both rural and urban contexts in North Africa. But although the *zar* cult typically involves possession by spirits identified with Europeans, this is not exclusively the case. Writing of the *zar* cult in the Sudan, Ioan Lewis reports that spirits associated with eminent colonial figures such as General Gordon and Lord Cromer play a leading role in the cult, but that they cohabit in the *zar* pantheon with a variety of Islamic holy men, as well as with certain modern political figures such as Gamal Abdul Nasser, the former Egyptian president, and even Sheik Yamani, the Saudi Arabian government minister who became internationally famous in the 1970s at the time of the dramatic increase in oil prices.[19]

The similarities between the *hauka* cult of West Africa and the *zar* cult practiced in a rural village in northern Sudan as described by Janice Boddy are particularly striking. Boddy's textual description of a *zar* ceremony that took place in this village in July 1976 is highly reminiscent of the ceremony portrayed cinematographically in *Les Maîtres fous* some twenty years earlier. Over the course of three days, the *zar* mediums are possessed by a succession of spirits identified with outsiders. These include spirits modelled on colonial military officers and other Europeans such as the Doctor, the Lawyer and a violent sword-wielding Roman Catholic Priest. As in *Les Maîtres fous*, there are also figures associated with modern transport, including the Aeroplane Captain and the Railway Engineer, who may or may not be modeled on Europeans. But there are also those who are clearly not modeled on Europeans, including Luliya, the Ethiopian Prostitute; the Azande Cannibal, and the Automobile Gypsy, who is one of a number of spirits identified collectively as Arab Nomads. However, there is also one very noticeable difference with the *hauka* cult as portrayed in *Les Maîtres fous*, namely, that the *zar* mediums in Boddy's account are exclusively female.[20]

A very significant feature of the *zar* cult and its various analogues is that they are frequently practiced by peoples professing Islam. In the past, the conventional view was that these possession cults represented the residue of local animist religions that had been overlain by Islam as it spread through Africa. However, more recently, Lewis has argued that while these possession cults may indeed have first developed in certain local areas, they have become so completely entwined with Islam that they have been diffused through Africa along Islamic networks.[21] The pilgrimage trail to Makkah seems to have been particularly important in this regard. According to Boddy, there is evidence that as far back as the early nineteenth century, West African pilgrims on their way to Makkah would meet with Sudanese pilgrims and that they would attend one another's possession ceremonies, resulting in the cross-fertilization of ideas and practices. She reports that in the region of northern Sudan where she herself worked, the local *zar* cult has been greatly influenced by the *bori* cult practiced by among the hausaphone peoples of eastern and central Niger.[22] These peoples are not only the immediate eastern neighbors of the Songhay-Zerma but they have also had some involvement in the *hauka* cult itself. Indeed, in the view of some specialists, the *hauka* cult is in fact nothing more than a variant of the *bori* cult.[23]

This outsiders' historical account of the origins of the *hauka* cult concurs well with the Songhays' own account. The exact details of this account vary somewhat from one source to another, but it is generally agreed that the *hauka* first came into the middle Niger region in the late 1920s when they followed a Hausa man, a veteran of the First World War, as he was returning from a pilgrimage to Makkah. Some versions tie the *hauka* to both strands of Songhay religion simultaneously, suggesting that the most powerful of the indigenous Songhay spirits, namely, Dongo, the Spirit of Thunder, was at one time Yabilan, a Black slave who, having been freed by the Prophet Mohammed, became his first muezzin. While still in Makkah, Dongo is said to have had various adulterous unions with concubine slaves and the children born of these unions later gave birth to the *hauka*, who are therefore Dongo's grandchildren. The slave grandmothers are said to have been white, which would account for the European appearance of some of the *hauka*.[24]

Whatever the precise details of their genesis, it is generally agreed among adepts of the cult that after lingering in the bush for a while, the *hauka* started possessing people in western Niger, notably in the village of Chikal, close to the town of Filingué and about a hundred miles to the northeast of the capital, Niamey (see map 2, p. 44). Although the *hauka* are said to have announced themselves at their very first appearance as associates of Dongo, they were initially vigorously rejected both by the priests of the more traditional spirit possession cults as well as by devout Muslims. Their appearance particularly troubled the French colonial authorities. Olivier de Sardan cites an official report to the effect that while in a trance, the leading *hauka* medium, a woman by the name of Zibo, "preached insubordination," encouraging people not to pay taxes and to refuse to work in the colonial forced labor gangs.[25]

On account of what they considered to be the parodying of their military institutions, the local colonial authorities concluded that the cult was potentially subversive. In 1926, the commandant of the local military garrison, one Major Horace Croccichia, attempted to put an end to the cult by locking up Zibo and her followers. But they manage to escape, taking refuge on the Gold Coast. There they continued to practice the cult, even incorporating their oppressor into the *hauka* pantheon as the evil Kommandan or Major Mugu. Also known as Korsasi, on account of Croccichia's Corsican origin, this *hauka* features in *Les Maîtres fous* as the Wicked Major, whose "horse," that is, medium, is the man whose impotence is cured over the course of the ceremony.[26]

In the view of Nicole Échard, who carried out fieldwork in the region of western Niger where the cult first broke out, albeit many years later, this first appearance of the *hauka* cult was associated with a very real political revolt against the French colonial authorities. However, while acknowledging that Échard has unrivalled authority concerning this first outbreak due to her local fieldwork experience, Olivier de Sardan insists that, even if this was not merely an illusion propagated by the French colonial authorities in their reports, as he suspects, it was the exception that proved the rule since thereafter there is virtually no reference to the cult in Nigerien colonial documents, and certainly not as the vehicle for political resistance.[27]

Some years later, around 1935, the *hauka* adepts were involved in further trouble in the Gold Coast, though this appears to have been a dispute with the adepts of rival cults rather than with the British colonial authorities as such. Certainly, after briefly banning *hauka* ceremonies on account of the social unrest that it was causing, the British allowed the cult to operate in certain designated places. Over time, the *hauka* came to be progressively accepted by the adepts of other cults and became integrated into their possession ceremonies, particularly those associated with Dongo. Eventually, they came to be considered his sentinels, providing protection to those whom he possesses and escorting people who wish to have an audience with him into the center of the dancing arena.[28]

Once the cult moved to the Gold Coast—which Rouch describes as the "Mecca" of the *hauka*—the number of different spirit identities reported in Rouch's publications becomes much greater, though this proliferation may also be no more than an index of Rouch's developing knowledge. In his first publication on the *hauka*, dating from 1943, Rouch provides a tentative list of only fifteen names, mostly denoting military ranks, and half of them identified as being from Malia, that is, the Red Sea.[29] But this was still the height of the war in Europe and Rouch would have had no access to the British colony. In his book, first published in 1960, after his studies of migration on the Gold Coast, he says that there were more than fifty established *hauka* characters, though he lists only about thirty-five in the book itself. This is clearly considerably more than the very limited selection of twelve *hauka* that actually appear in *Les Maîtres fous*. A comparison of the main *hauka* characters listed in these three sources is given in the table. Later, Rouch revised the *hauka* population upward again, stating in a 1977 interview that were "maybe one hundred" at the peak of the movement.[30]

From table 1, it is apparent that many of the *hauka* that Rouch mentions in his book are similar to those who appear in the film, that is, high-status political or military characters. They include Askandiya the Judge, Minis de Ger (from the French title, *ministre de guerre*) and even Prazidan di la Republik (from *président de la république*) who first possessed a public works laborer in Niamey in 1948. There is also King Zouri, whose name, Rouch suggests, is derived from "king of the judges," but as it is rather strange to associate judges with kingship, I suspect that this could be a derivation from "King George" since George VI was on the throne of the United Kingdom at the time. Not long afterward, in the mid- to late 1950s, when many Nigeriens were recruited to fight in the French colonial wars in Indochina and Algeria, and were based at a military transit camp at Fréjus on the Mediterranean coast of France, a new *hauka*, General Marseille, began to possess them.

However, not all these high status *hauka* are identified with Europeans. As in the case of the *zar* cults described above, the pantheon is also peopled by high-status Islamic figures. Thus there is also Dogo Malia, the Very Tall Gentleman from the Red Sea, and Istanbula, the Great Muslim from Istanbul, the greatest *hauka* of them all and considered to be their overall leader. Then there are the more lowly technical

TABLE 1. Hauka Listed in Various Works of Jean Rouch

Hauka in Rouch (1943): 15 spirit identities	Hauka in *Les Maîtres fous* (1955): 12 spirit identities	Hauka in Rouch (1960a): 50+ spirit identities
Istanboula		Istanbula: chief of all the hauka
		Dogo Malia: a great Muslim
King Zouzi Malia, King Judge/George (?)		King Zuzi
		Prazidan di la Republik: Président de la République
Goumna	Governor	Gomno
		Minis, Minis de ger: Ministre de Guerre
		Askandya: a judge
	Secretary General	Sekter
Zeneder Malia		
Zeneral Malia: General Malia	General	Zeneral Malia, Colonel
Commandant Mougou	Major Mougou: the 'Wicked' Major	Kommandan Mugu, Korsasi
Captan Malia	Captain Malia	Capitaine
Lieutenant Malia	Lieutenant Malia	Lieutenant
Lassidan Malia: Adjutant Malia		Adjutant chef, Adjutant
Serzan Malia: Sergeant Malia		Sergent-chef
Capral Gardi: Corporal of the Guard	Corporal of the Guard: General's adjutant	Kapral Gardi
		Kafrankot: corporal of the coast
		Bambara Mossi: private soldier
	Private Tiemoko: General's orderly	Tyemoko: child of Kapral Gardi
Doctor Malia	Mme Lokotoro: Doctor's wife	Lokotoro
	Train Driver	Hanga Beri: "big ears" who drives trains

(continued)

TABLE 1. *(continued)*

Hauka in Rouch (1943): 15 spirit identities	Hauka in *Les Maîtres fous* (1955): 12 spirit identities	Hauka in Rouch (1960a): 50+ spirit identities
Maymota Malia: the chauffeur	Truck Driver	Maymota Malia
		Maykuano: mechanic
		Maylanba: surveyor
		Basiru: telephone linesman
		Babule: blacksmith, "spirit" in Hausa
Mayaki		Mayaki: "warrior" in Hausa
		Wasiri: executioner, Kafuyi: marabout killer
		Maykarga: he who spends all day sitting down
Fatimata: wife of Zenender	Madame Salma: colonial wife	Fatimata Malia: wife of Zeneral Malia
		Maryama, Musukura: female spirits
		Ramatala, Andro: child spirits

characters including Maykuano the Mechanic, Maylanba the Surveyor, Babule the Blacksmith, even Basiru the Telephone Linesman. There are also a number of female characters, including Fatimata of the Red Sea and Maryama, whose names presumably derive from those of the wife of the Prophet Mohammed and the mother of Jesus, respectively. There are even at least two children, Ramatala and Andro. Finally, there are some characters that do not quite fit into any social category and seem to exemplify purely transgressive behavior, including Maykarga the One Who Always Remains Seated, Kafuyi the Killer of Marabouts, and Wasiru the Executioner.[31]

Rouch maintains that with the end of the colonial era, the elaboration of *hauka* characters came to an abrupt halt since they were essentially identified with colonial personae. He claims that their place as challenging "newcomers" from the spirit world was taken over by the so-called *sasale*, whose sexually explicit dancing and singing were as shocking to the traditionalists as the *hauka* once had been.[32] However, this report of the demise of the *hauka* is somewhat at odds with other sources. As noted above, Stoller describes the cult in operation in Niger in the 1980s, while Olivier de Sardan reports that in the 1990s new *hauka* characters were still being elaborated, the most recent being "Chinese" characters inspired by the then fashionable kung-fu movies.[33] Certainly, as apparently powerful, exotic, and aggressive characters, these martial arts heroes would conform well with the general pattern of *hauka* spirits.[34]

Whatever the historical facts on this last issue, it is clear that even in the heyday of colonialism the roster of *hauka* spirits was only to a limited extent made up of European authority figures. In this sense, the selection of *hauka* in *Les Maîtres fous* seems at first sight to be somewhat unrepresentative, since not only are there very few of them, but it includes none of the Islamic figures who were regarded by the Songhay as the most powerful of all *hauka*. But reflecting on the matter more carefully, one realizes that the Islamic figures are present after all, but they have become hybridized in the mediums' performance with the model of distant power provided by more local European authorities. This hybridization is revealed in the recurrent addition "of Malia," meaning "from the Red Sea" to many of the names. For it is, of course, on the shore of the Red Sea that the Muslim holy city of Makkah lies. This then, we can finally conclude, is the ultimate provenance of the *hauka* Governor—certainly not Tunbridge Wells or wherever else the plumed British colonial officer saluting the troops in Accra might have come from!

The *Hauka* in Songhay Religion

The idea that the *hauka* mediums whom one sees in *Les Maîtres fous* dancing wildly, foaming at the mouth and eating dog meat could be Muslims seems rather unlikely, to put it mildly. However, as reported by Rouch the Author, Stoller, and others, although they may not be as thorough in their observance as some of their neighbors, the Songhay have been influenced by Islam for almost a thousand years, at least in the larger settlements.[35] But although Allah may stand at the apex of the Songhay empyrean, he is considered an inaccessible entity who communicates with human beings only through secondary divinities. Beneath Allah, there are various classes of supernatural being found in popular versions of Islam, such as angels, djinns, and the demons associated with Satan. There is also a human ancestor cult. The aid of these other supernatural beings may be sought through the making of sacrifices and other propitiatory ritual acts, but it seems to be to the spirits reached through possession ceremonies that the Songhay most frequently turn when they seek solutions to everyday problems. In his book, Rouch claims that while there could sometimes be tensions between the practice of Islam and participation in possession ceremonies, these two aspects of religious belief were usually reconciled in a highly pragmatic way in day-to-day life.[36]

As Jean-Claude Muller pointed out in a much-cited review of *Les Maîtres fous*, the work of Rouch the Author demonstrates— somewhat in contradiction to the reference to the emergence of "new religions" by Rouch the Filmmaker—that there is a high degree of continuity between the *hauka* cult and other more traditional Songhay possession cults.[37] For a start, *holey*, the term used to refer generically to the spirits invoked in these cults, is the plural form of *holo*, which means "mad" in the Songhay language and refers to the state of a medium in a trance. Thus it is not only the mediums of the *hauka*, but all *holey* mediums who could be legitimately described by the title of *Les Maîtres fous*. But more important, Rouch the Author shows that the *hauka* are but the most recent of some six different *holey* spirit "families" that have emerged at various different points in Songhay history. A particularly striking feature of this pantheon is that like the *hauka*, and indeed like the spirits invoked in the Sudanese *zar* cult described above, most of the other five major *holey* families are also strongly associated with some element of alterity. That is, they are metaphorically associated either with other ethnic groups of the region or with anthropomorphized forces of nature, or with some combination of the two.

In summary, the main characteristics of the five other *holey* families as described by Rouch the author, supplemented here by the accounts from other sources, are as follows:[38]

(1) *tôrou*—the most ancient and prestigious family, headed by Dongo, the irascible Spirit of Thunder, who together with his mother, Harakoy Dikko, and his siblings, controls the wind, the rain, and the levels of the Niger River. The various members of Dongo's sibling group are further associated with particular ethnic Others who over the centuries have had relationships of both hostility and exchange with the Songhay-Zerma, that is, the Fulani, Tuareg, Gourmantché, Hausa, Bella, and Bariba.

(2) *hargey*—Said to have been born from the union of Harakoy Dikko and a cemetery djinn, they are "cold like corpses" and threaten pregnant women with death in labor. They are identified with Fulani and Bella.

(3) *gandyi koare*—literally, "white spirits of the bush." These spirites are associated with the Tuareg marabouts who arrived in the late sixteenth century from what is now Morocco.

(4) *gandyi bi*—literally, "black spirits of the bush." Identified with the original inhabitants of the *gourma*, that is, the right bank of the

middle reaches of the Niger. Considered very primitive, washing themselves with earth and eating excrement. Among contemporary peoples, associated with the Kurumba and Gourmantché, western neighbors of the Songhay.

(5) *hausa gandyi*—spirits identified with the left bank of the middle Niger, known as the *haoussa*. Associated with all the peoples living there, not just the ethnic group most commonly referred to by this name. Said to drive people insane before drinking their blood. Male spirits may appear dressed as females and vice versa, and both have filthy bodies.

An important point is that each of these *holey* families is believed to specialize in resolving particular problems. Thus the *tôrou*, who control the natural elements, are the ones to consult about bringing an end to drought. This consultation takes the form of a ceremony known as a *yenendi*, meaning literally "to freshen the earth" and the subject of a large number of Rouch's films.[39] On the other hand, the *gandyi bi*, the black spirits associated with the earth, are called upon for problems associated with agricultural matters. These are the spirits invoked in the celebrated short film *Les Tambours d'avant: Touru et Bitti* (1971) in which a village community seeks a remedy to the plague of locusts eating its crops.[40] However, in all cases, the consultations take much the same form, namely, the priests of the cult ask the spirits embodied in the mediums what course of action they would recommend for resolving a given problem. The remedies that the spirits propose often involve making some sort of animal sacrifice to themselves.

The Songhay refer to spirit mediums as *bari*, literally "horses," because they are said to be "mounted" by the spirits, and I suspect that this is why there is a small model of a horse at the foot of the *hauka* Governor's statue in *Les Maîtres fous*.[41] In order to become possessed, it is usually necessary to dance. The general order of dancing is the same for all *holey* cults and begins with the *windi*, a circular counterclockwise dance, led by a priest. This is the dance we see at the beginning of the ceremony in *Les Maîtres fous*. Then comes the *fimbi*, when the dancers begin to shiver all over, starting from the left foot. In *Les Maîtres fous*, we see the Corporal go through this process. Finally comes the *gani*, the full and most animated stage of the dance, when all the mediums are fully possessed.

Not only does each family of *holey* spirits have distinctive powers, but they are also said to have distinctive manners of dress, speech, bodily movement and gesticulation, and even a distinctive smell. In certain of Rouch's films, one sees mediums drinking from bottles of perfume, which may explain the small bottles at the foot of the Governor's statue in *Les Maîtres fous* (see fig. 7.5 above). All *holey* spirits are attracted by the plaintive sound of the *godye*, the one-stringed violin, but each spirit is deemed to favor a distinctive melody. In addition, certain spirits are thought to be attracted by particular sorts of percussive instrument. Although we hear the *godye* in *Les Maîtres fous* well enough, we see the musician only fleetingly, which is perhaps one of the most significant omissions of the film from a purely ethnographic point of view.[42]

When the priests sense the arrival of a particular spirit, the musicians play his or her melody only. Dancing becomes a convulsion rather than a dance. Suddenly there will be a paroxysm and the dancer will roll on the ground shouting: this is the moment when the spirit takes up residence inside the dancer. The dancer's behavior will then conform to the conventional behavioral attributes of the spirit in question. In a traditional *holey* ceremony, if it is Dongo, the Spirit of Thunder, who has arrived, the medium will look up into the sky and groan; if it is his brother Kyirey, the Spirit of Lightning and supposedly one-eyed, the dancer will close one eye.[43] In just the same way, each of the characters in *Les Maîtres fous* is identifiable by certain conventional behaviors or forms of dress: thus Captain Malia walks about with the distinctive marching gait of the British Army, Train Driver plies his way back and forth between the Governor's termite mound "palace" and the cement altar, the Corporal of the Guard carries a wooden gun, the Doctor wears a white coat, and so on.

This description of the broader practice of possession among the Songhay, even though only summary, is hopefully sufficient to confirm Muller's general argument that the *hauka* cult is only "new" in a relative sense. As a category of *holey*, the *hauka* are not that remarkable. All the *holey* spirits are "mad": the *hauka* may be particularly violent and aggressive, but none of the traditional *holey* spirits is exactly genial or beneficent. Indeed, the most aggressive and violent *holey* of all is Dongo himself, since he is both mean with the provision of rain and merciless in his killing of humans with bolts of lightning delivered by his sibling Kiriey. *Hauka* dances may look particularly "savage" and bizarre, particularly to European eyes, but they are different in degree rather than in kind from other *holey* possession dances, as shown in Rouch's many films on these more traditional forms.

It is true that there are two characteristics of the *hauka* that initially appear to mark it out as different from other *holey* cults, but on further reflection, even these are not so significant as they might appear at first sight. The first is the fact that in the *hauka* cult, the "horses" are usually men, whereas in traditional *holey* cults, they are often women. But this, Rouch explains, is because the great majority of those who migrated to coastal regions where the *hauka* cult reached its greatest development

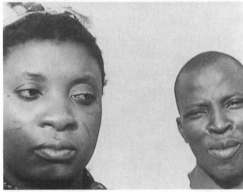

FIGURE 7.8. The day after. *Top*, in everyday life, Madame Lokotoro, the Doctor's Wife, works for an Asian shopkeeper. Images on the storefront attest to the coronation of Queen Elizabeth II the previous year. *Bottom*, the Wicked Major has been cured of his impotence and his girlfriend is said to be "very happy."

were men. When *hauka* spirits appear in rural areas, their "horses" are just as likely to be women. Even among migrant communities, women could become mediums, as represented in *Les Maîtres fous* by the "Queen" of the Accra prostitutes who is possessed by Madame Salma.

Interestingly, as in the case of the *zar* cults described by Boddy, there is no necessary correspondence between the gender of the medium and the gender of the possessing spirit and it is quite possible for women to be "horses" for male spirits. The reverse is also true, as in the case of the Doctor's Wife *hauka* in *Les Maîtres fous* who is embodied by a male medium, though Rouch describes him as a "rather effeminate boy who uses a lot of hair Vaseline," which I suspect may be 1950s code for "homosexual" (fig. 7.8). There is also at least one other male medium dressed in a very flowery woman's dress in *Les Maîtres fous*, though the identity of neither the possessing spirit nor the "horse" is commented upon by Rouch (see fig. 7.5, above).

The other characteristic of the *hauka* that seems, at first sight, to distinguish this spirit "family" from others in the Songhay pantheon is the association with a particular form of technology, namely, the apparatuses of "mechanical civilization" as exemplified by Truck Driver and Train Driver in *Les Maîtres fous* and by the longer list of technicians provided by Rouch the Author in his book. But I would suggest the control of these technological powers by the *hauka* is directly analogous to the control of natural powers by the more traditional *holey* families, most notably by the *tôrou*, who are deemed to control not just thunder, lightning, and rain, but also the powerful seasonal winds, the Harmattan and the Mousson, and the levels of the Niger River. Thus even this attribute can be considered as a variation on a theme, rather than an absolute difference.

But the element of continuity that is surely the most significant of all is the association of traditional *holey* spirits with the various ethnic Others with whom the Songhay have come into contact at certain moments in their history. In this context, the association of the *hauka* with colonial Europeans merely represents a continuation of a long-established pattern. Moreover, there is also a clear continuity in the association of these others with transgressive behavior. Only the *genji koare*, the white spirits associated with Islam, appear to be relatively benign. Other *holey* are variously said to be cold as corpses, to eat excrement, to wash themselves with dirt, to drink blood, or to be transvestites. Indeed compared to the conventional attributes of some traditional *holey*, the *hauka* predilection for dog meat, their foaming at the mouth, and their disposition to burn themselves with flaming torches could almost be considered rather tame! Certainly these attributes are well within the parameters of transgressive behavior conventionally associated with spirits in traditional Songhay religion.

The *Hauka* and the Construction of Otherness

The many continuities between the *hauka* cult and the more traditional *holey* cults suggest that if one were to offer an interpretation of the former, it should be consistent with any interpretation that one might offer for the latter. However, to suggest that parody is the motivation for all forms of *holey* possession is singularly unconvincing. It is true that there is a certain burlesque theatricality about the ceremony in *Les Maîtres fous* that a nonspecialist spectator might reasonably conclude constitutes some sort of oblique satire of colonial pretensions. But that even this degree of secondary parody is involved is firmly rejected by Olivier de Sardan. While recognizing that theatricality is common to all *holey* ceremonies, he argues that the suggestion that the mediums are intentionally parodying the colonial figures on which the *hauka* are modelled is as absurd as the suggestion that the mediums who perform Dongo as an irascible tyrant in a rain-making *yenendi* are seeking to parody the forces of nature.[44]

In helping us to understand the *holey* phenomenon more generally, Olivier de Sardan makes a telling point when he observes that the behavior typically associated with the spirits of traditional *holey* families is considerably at variance with the empirical reality of the customary behavior of the "real" ethnic Others on whom they are supposedly modeled.[45] It does indeed seem very unlikely that the Songhay-Zerma would believe, for example, that the "real" Hausa, with whom they are in regular contact and to whom they are culturally closely related, are customarily blood-drinking transvestites in the way that the *hausa gandyi* are supposed to be. Rather it would seem that this conception of the *hausa gandyi* represents an elaboration of some ideal-typical notion of alterity that bears, at most, only a partial and hyperbolic relationship to the Songhay's actual day-to-day empirical knowledge of the Hausa. Moreover, this conception of the *hausa gandyi*, in common with the conception of many of the other *holey* spirit families, is something of a composite since it refers not only to the Hausa themselves but also to all the other groups living on the *haoussa*, that is, the left bank of the Niger.

I would suggest then that a similar process of hybridic conceptual elaboration has taken place in relation to Songhay ideas about the *hauka*. In this view, the local colonial Europeans with their obvious political power and equally obvious technological power, hybridized in a composite fashion with imaginary Islamic elites originating from Makkah, offer a variety of models of what powerful other-worldly beings might be like and how they might behave. The *hauka* performances based on these models are thus not intended to be a literal representation of the "real" Europeans. To borrow Claude Lévi-Strauss's celebrated phrase with regard to Australian totems and stand it on its head, these powerful Europeans are "good to think with," not about the nature of human beings but about the nature of spirit beings. The European colonial world evoked in this modeling of the *hauka* spirit world may appear absurd, authoritarian, and violently aggressive. However, to suggest that the projection of this negative image of the colonial world is the *purpose* of the modeling is to confuse the means with the end, since the beings whom the dancers are seeking to embody are not human Others, but spirit Others.

However, as Stoller very properly insists, what is involved here is much more than a purely intellectual appropriation of the attributes of alterity. Drawing on Michael Taussig's ideas about mimesis, Stoller argues—to my mind very convincingly—that in embodying the highly conventionalized behaviors associated with the spirits in their dancing, the mediums in a *hauka* ceremony are seeking, through a process of mimetic appropriation, to gain control of the powers associated with those spirits. Their success in doing so, as the Songhay themselves see it, is demonstrated by the fact that once they are possessed by *hauka*, the mediums are capable of running flaming torches over their bodies and plunging their hands into a boiling pot of dog stew. This is a sign that they have become powerful spirit beings, not just in mind or soul, but also in body.[46]

But it is important not to conflate mimesis and parody in this specific context. Although mimesis may often be associated with parody and satire, it can also arise as a result of exaggerated respect: for, as the popular saying has it, imitation can be the sincerest form of flattery. I would not go so far as to suggest that the *hauka* mediums sought to flatter the colonial masters with their performances, but, as I noted at the beginning of this chapter, they themselves were at pains to make clear to Rouch that they certainly did not intend to mock them.[47]

Reinterpreting *Les Maîtres fous*

But if the purpose of the *hauka* cult is not parodic, how then is it to be explained? A comprehensive answer to this question would be best left to West Africanist specialists rather than attempted by an out-of-area interloper such as myself. However, I shall conclude this chapter by suggesting some lines of further enquiry.

If we consider the *hauka* cult as but the most recent of the *holey* possession cults, its purpose seems almost too obvious. For, as we saw above, the most salient characteristic of these cults, as with similar cults all over North Africa and beyond, is that they involve consultation with the spirit powers embodied in the possessed dancers in order to diagnose the causes of a range of everyday, temporal problems and then to propose a remedy for them, usually involving some form of animal sacrifice. Even Stoller, for all his advocacy of the interpretation of the *hauka* as a form of counter-hegemonic colonial discourse in his early work, has latterly emphasized this more instrumental aspect of the cult, and he has written very eloquently about this.[48] It is clear though that not all *hauka* possession rituals have an immediate instrumental purpose: some seem to be enacted merely to maintain the relationship with the spirits.[49] Nor are all *hauka* possession ceremonies concerned with serious matters. Rouch reports that some *hauka* events are little more than a form of entertainment, considered by the participants to be somewhat superior to going to the cinema.[50]

But if the purpose of maintaining a relationship with the *hauka* is to seek their aid in resolving the problems of everyday life, what kind of problems can they solve? To answer this question, we should begin by recalling that each *holey* family of spirits is considered to have a distinctive problem-solving capability. If the *hauka* have a specialization, it would appear to be in matters relating to witchcraft. Both Rouch and Stoller report that the *hauka* are thought to be particularly valuable in the detection of witches, while Olivier de Sardan explains that although Islam recognizes the existence of witchcraft, it has no way of combating its effects. As witchcraft is perceived to be particularly widespread among the Songhay-Zerma, the marabouts will reluctantly admit that the *hauka*, of whom they generally disapprove, do have a value as witch hunters.[51] While this may be a primary specialization, the *hauka* are also deemed to have other skills too. Rouch reports, for example, that they also have a reputation for giving good advice on how to avoid military service![52]

However, at first sight, there appears to be no reference whatsoever to the *hauka* witchcraft specialization in *Les Maîtres fous*. Nor does there appear to be any process of consultation with the *hauka* spirits, about witchcraft or any other matter, let alone any sacrificial offering to them. It could be that Rouch simply failed to shoot this aspect of the ceremony or, alternatively, that the ceremony shown in *Les Maîtres fous* has no particular instrumental purpose and should be construed simply as a performance aimed merely at maintaining relationships with the *hauka*. Some support for this latter interpretation can be found in the fact the ceremony in *Les Maîtres fous* is specifically identified as a special annual celebration rather than a humdrum consultation about everyday problems. We might speculate that the latter would have been dealt with during the weekly Sunday meetings back in the salt market in Accra, to which Rouch alludes right at the beginning of the film.

However, on closer consideration, it is evident that there is a process of consultation in the film and one in which there might be some allusion to witchcraft. But this takes the form not of a consultation with the spirits themselves, but rather of the extended consultation between a number of "penitents" and Mountyeba, the *zima* priest, that occurs immediately before the main possession event. Among the problems brought to Mountyeba, there is the case involving sexual impotence, a condition that is certainly sometimes thought to be caused by witchcraft in an African context.[53]

What is intriguing about this consultation is that although the *hauka* have not yet been formally called by the musicians, the way that Rouch paraphrases the penitents' speech suggests that they are not addressing Mountyeba but rather the *hauka* themselves—for example, they ask the *hauka* to strike them dead if they should transgress again. Moreover, the sacrifice of animals that Mountyeba asks for is something that the *hauka* would typically have required as a condition for their help in the alleviation of a problem. Since the *hauka* have not yet arrived, Mountyeba appears then to be acting in some sense as their representative. Some possible evidence for this is to be found in the very next scene, in which we see him pouring purificatory libations of gin and cracking eggs around the compound. For if one listens carefully, he appears to be chanting in the glossolalic combination of French and Songhay that is the distinctive language of the *hauka*.

This brings us back to the significance of the eggs. I proposed early on in this chapter that the filmic text itself suggests, contrary to the interpretations of many commentators, that the cracking of an egg on the statue of the Governor may have had positive connotations. Support for this idea can be found in Marc Piault's report that for many Sahelian groups, including the Songhay-Zerma, the egg is strongly associated with fertility and, as such, is considered a high-status gift that is offered only to the most prestigious visitors.[54] We might conclude then that the smashing of an egg on the statue, whatever the imitative rationale suggested by Rouch himself with respect to the ostrich plumes on the helmet of the colonial governor, might also be interpreted as an offering made upon the arrival of a high-status visitor, namely, the *hauka* spirit Governor.

Nor is this the only possible association of the *hauka* with fertility. Adeline Masquelier reports that among the hausaphone Mawri of Niger, whose *bori* possession cult, as we have seen, bears many similarities to the *hauka* cult and may even be the origin of it, the termite mound with its multitudinous inhabitants is regarded as a powerful symbol of fertility.[55] Would this then explain why the *hauka* Governor's "palace" in *Les Maîtres fous* should consist of a termite mound? Although the *hauka* may embody the power of "mechanical civilization," these associations suggest that they may have been considered to have some influence on natural reproductive power as well. Certainly this would make sense of the fact that as a result of his participation in the ceremony, the "penitent" who was possessed by the Wicked Major Mugu was cured of his impotence.

Finally, there is the enigma of the dog that is butchered and eaten in such a "savage" manner. In the film itself, as noted at the beginning of this chapter, Rouch explains that in eating a dog, which is highly taboo, the *hauka* aimed to show that they are stronger than other men, "whether Black or White." In an interview many years later, he added that the *hauka* ate dog "because the British would not eat dogs, just as before they had eaten wild pig, which Muslims refuse to eat."[56] Now if the *hauka* performance were conceived merely as some sort of counter-hegemonic performance, then this interpretation would perhaps suffice. But as a corollary of the various arguments that I have offered above, I would suggest that there is probably considerably more to the killing and eating of the dog in *Les Maîtres fous* than the defiance of European culinary habits.

Here I would return to the point that I made at some length concerning the many continuities between the *hauka* cult and other *holey* spirit possession cults. The first question one might ask then is whether the dog represents a sacrificial offering of the kind that is often made to the spirits during the possession ceremonies associated with other *holey* families, usually in the hope of the concession of some eventual favor, such as the release of the rains, or the withdrawal of a horde of locusts. Admittedly, Rouch makes no suggestion in the film that the dog is considered a sacrificial offering and we certainly do not see any sequence of the priests bargaining with the spirits in which it is suggested that some such sacrifice should be made. But given the presence of animal sacrifice in other *holey* possession ceremonies, one still cannot help wondering whether the slaughter of the dog may not have had some sacrificial rationale of this kind.

But even if the slaughter of the dog had no such instrumental sacrificial purpose and was merely some form of symbolic gesture, I would argue that given the continuities between the *hauka* and other *holey* cults, one should still seek to interpret its significance in terms that one could equally apply to these other cults. That is, rather than interpret the killing and grotesque consumption of the dog as a gesture of defiance aimed at an entirely absent European audience, it would be more appropriate to see it as an aspect of a more general attempt, aimed at the immediately present audience of Africans, to give a material form to otherworldly spirit beings who, by very definition, will behave in abnormal, transgressive ways. On these grounds, I suggest that instead of seeking to explain the *hauka* taste for dog meat as some sort of reaction *against* the perceived attributes of Europeans, it would be more consistent to interpret it as a hyperbolic augmentation of the attributes that the Songhay conventionally associate with Europeans in just the same way that the supposed predilection of the *hausa gandyi* for drinking blood and cross-dressing represents a hyperbolic augmentation of certain behaviors that are conventionally associated with the Hausa, or the tendency of the *gandyi bi* to wash themselves with earth and eat excrement represents a hyperbolic augmentation of certain behaviors conventionally associated with the Kurumba and Gourmantché. In all these cases, the intention is not to parody or belittle the ethnic Other but rather to draw on attributes associated with them and with the addition of certain transgressive behaviors, to build up a model of how a nonhuman spirit is likely to manifest itself when it takes a human form.

In this context, it is very pertinent that the Songhay-Zerma believe that the peoples who live to the south of them, in the region through which they pass when migrating to the Gold Coast, practice what they consider to be the despicable habit of eating dog.[57] I propose that it is this attribute of alterity that the mediums have used to elaborate their ideas about the preferred diet of the *hauka* spirits, mixing this together with the other attributes modeled on European and Islamic authority figures to produce a typically hybrid and composite conception of this particular class of *holey* spirit. By gorging themselves on dog meat, the Songhay mediums are showing themselves to have become completely Other, that is, to have become nonhuman spirit beings who can behave in outrageously transgressive ways and who can burn and scald themselves apparently without pain. While these spirit beings may partake of the names of both European and Islamic authority figures as well as some of their physical attributes, and while they may follow the dietary habits of the barbarous peoples living to the south, they are also more exotic than any of these Others, and by their transgressive behavior show themselves to be more powerful than any of these Others, be they Black or White. In exceeding all these models in combination, they have become something more powerful than any of them—they have become *hauka*.

The *Hauka* Cult as a Form of Political Expression

If this analysis is correct, then we may conclude that to interpret the *hauka* ritual portrayed in *Les Maîtres fous* merely as some parodic counterhegemonic theatrical burlesque is to fundamentally misunderstand its purposes and motivations. However, this is not to say that the *hauka* phenomenon cannot be interpreted, at the same time, as the expression of a particular political interest. Rouch once recounted how he saw a hundred or so possessed *hauka* mediums parading loudly through Kumasi, though, to his regret, he was not able to film this event because it was at night.[58] This suggests that whatever the instrumental religious purposes of the *hauka* cult, it also acted in the context of the colonial city as a vehicle for the expression of the cultural identity and solidarity of the migrants. Far from acting as a refuge from the cacophony of the multiethnic "Babylon" of the city, as Rouch suggests in opening sequence of *Les Maîtres fous*, the *hauka* cult seems to have been an energetic assertion of a particular identity that competed for the allegiance, or at least the attention, of the proletariat of colonial Accra, along with all the other groups shown in the opening sequences of the film, such as the Little Sisters of Christ proclaiming their faith, Hausa prostitutes demanding higher wages, the various brass bands, and Yoruba playing their talking drums.

This perspective on the cult opens up the possibility of recuperating something of the *hauka*-as-counter-hegemonic-performance thesis. For what the *hauka* performance appears to represent is a collective assertion of the migrants' desire, through mimetic bodily appropriation, to control the forces that govern their lives as represented in the possession ceremonies by the political and military figures, and the skilled controllers of modern technology, such as truck drivers and telephone engineers. Even in this regard, one can trace a continuity with more traditional *holey* cults. For just as in the traditional *yenendi* rain-making ceremonies in rural areas, Songhay mediums literally embody Dongo, the Spirit of Thunder, and other forces of nature, so that the priests can parley with them and try to make a deal, offering sacrificial animals and moral behavior in exchange for rain, so in *Les Maîtres fous*, we see a similar bargaining process underway, with the urban migrants offering to the *hauka* spirits, through the intermediary offices of Mountyeba, sacrificial animals and moral behavior in exchange for the spirits' help in overcoming problems of sexual impotence and psychological derangement.

Far from being an intentional parody of power, then, the *hauka* performance thus represents an aspiration on the part of men and women whose marginal circumstances make them supremely vulnerable to the vagaries of political power to gain control of that power, albeit indirectly, through religious means. In this sense, one might agree with Rouch that the *hauka* cult was indeed "implicitly revolutionary," though the harsh truth is—as Karl Marx famously remarked—that in extrapolating political power to the supernatural world, the cult probably made explicit revolution *less* rather than more likely.

"Thick Inscription" and the Place of Film in Anthropology

In juxtaposing the work of Rouch the Author and other text makers with the work of Rouch the Filmmaker in this analysis of *Les Maîtres fous*, it has certainly not been my intention to demonstrate the superiority of the former over the latter. On the contrary, it was precisely the richness of the ethnographic account in the film that stimulated this recourse to the texts in the first place. My hope is that this reinterpretation can now feed back into subsequent viewings of the film, thereby enriching the understandings that it can deliver and sending later viewers back to the texts with further ideas to pursue. What I am certainly not proposing is that if the film could somehow be made again that Rouch ought to burden it with all the ethnographic detail laid out in this chapter. By smothering it with information, this would destroy the film's capacity to communicate, even after fifty years, a vicarious but powerful experience of the ceremonial event at its heart.

It is undoubtedly the case that the dramatic nature of the subject matter is one of the main reasons why *Les Maîtres fous* continues to engage audiences so many years after it was made. But it is important to recognize that this engagement is also achieved by the sheer film craft of Rouch and his editor Suzanne Baron. Such engagement would not have been achieved if the film had been merely an unshaped ethnographic document, simply laying out visual "data" for some indeterminate analytical purpose. This molding of rushes into a filmic narrative involves, in effect, a form of rhetoric aimed at convincing the audience of a particular interpretation of the events happening within the film. But the nature of the medium of film is such that this meaning can never be definitive nor remain uncontested for long. For film has an attribute that one might describe, with apologies to Clifford Geertz, as "thick inscription," that is, the potential to record the world in a degree of complexity that can easily escape the control of the explanatory devices of the filmmaker, restricted, as these inevitably are, by the limitations of the ideologies and understandings of the time at which the film was made. A good ethnographic film, then, is one that through its analysis encourages engagement and provokes reflection but that, at the same time, through its richness of detail permits the establishment of connections of which possibly even the filmmaker him- or herself may not have been aware. As I have sought to show in this chapter, *Les Maîtres fous* is surely a magnificent example of such a film.

PART II

BETWEEN PARIS AND THE LAND OF NOWHERE

Introduction: New Technologies, New Methods

In December 1959, having spent most of the previous twenty years in Africa, and with his work on Sahelian migration winding down, Rouch was attracted to an idea put to him by Edgar Morin at the Festival dei Popoli film festival in Florence. Morin was not a practicing filmmaker himself but rather a sociologist with a specialist interest in the cinema and the ways in which it had transformed the human imaginary. He had been greatly impressed by the manner in which Rouch had used a lightweight camera and portable tape recorder in his African films to achieve a high degree of engagement with his subjects. At Florence, where they were both serving as members of the festival jury for the ethnographic section, he proposed to Rouch that they should collaborate in making a film about their own "tribe," the Parisians. The result was *Chronicle of a Summer*, the celebrated "experiment in *cinéma-vérité*," in which they not only presented an ethnographic portrait of a group of young Parisians at a crucial turning point in French history but also reflected upon the nature of the truth that can be achieved through a documentary film.

This return to work in Paris marked the beginning of a new phase in Rouch's career and as such, represents an appropriate starting point for this part of the book in which we shall be following Rouch's filmmaking adventures in the period framed by the shooting of *Chronicle of a Summer* in 1960 and the publication of "The Camera and Man" essay some fifteen years later. In reality, though, this change of location appears to have involved more of a change of emphasis than a change in kind. Over the coming years, Rouch would continue to return to West Africa with remarkable frequency, for, as his wife Jane once said of him, he would catch an airplane as readily as most other people would take a taxi.[1] These returns to West Africa would be mostly to continue his work among the Songhay in Niger, though he also shot a considerable number of films elsewhere—on the Ivory Coast, in Dahomey and Senegal, but above all in Mali, among the Dogon. These projects in themselves would have been enough to have consumed the energy of most filmmakers but, remarkably, over the same period Rouch also made a series of fiction films set in Paris.

Rouch's reputation probably reached its peak in France around this time, both in the worlds of cinema and anthropology. As early as 1955, the eminent Italian Neorealist director Roberto Rossellini had been impressed by a preliminary version of *Jaguar*, before it had any voice-over. Indeed, according to some sources, it was Rossellini who suggested to Rouch that he should ask the principal protagonists, Damouré and Lam, to perform this voice-over.[2] Two years later, Rouch and Rossellini organized a workshop in Paris together, which was attended by many of the young film critics who would later become leading figures of the New Wave.[3] As a result of the prestigious prizes awarded to *Les Maîtres fous* and *Moi, un Noir*, the cinema distribution of *Les Fils de l'eau* (a 35mm compilation of some of his earlier films), and the screening of *Jaguar* at the Cinémathèque française, Rouch's fame as a filmmaker had already spread far outside the narrow world of anthropology by the time he returned to work in Paris. But also within anthropology, Rouch's fame was riding high at this time as a result of the publication of his doctoral thesis on Songhay magic and religion by the academically prestigious publishing house PUF, the Presses Universitaires de France, in 1960.

In his amusing memoir about "catching up on Rouch" published in *Cahiers du Cinéma* in 1960–1961, the Québécois filmmaker Claude Jutra provides a portrait of a dynamic filmmaker at the height of his powers, his fingers in all sorts of pies, as in this vignette about Jutra finding Rouch in the miniscule editing suite of the Musée de l'Homme, then accessed via a gallery of glass cases containing diverse human remains, including a Jivaroan shrunken head and a Chulpa mummy:

> I found fifteen demoralized people there. Jean had given them all an appointment, all at the same time, and this time had long gone. He suddenly appears. The crowd murmurs. Jean jumps back and forth, cooking up some crazy explanation with just a sufficient glimmer of truth about it that it satisfies everybody: "I was with the Minister of Foreign Affairs, who is certainly very foreign to my affairs. We were chatting about the territories of the After-World." Everyone assails him at once. He appears to resolve every problem presented to him without opening his mouth. Even his evasions appear to offer a solution. One only needs to consult him to be reassured. People leave and get on with it, but simply by showing up, he makes this possible.

- A young man wants some tubing for an expedition to the Sahara.
- A woman invites him to an international film festival, and Jean enthusi-

astically accepts. Later, he will work out how he will manage to find himself in three countries at the same time on that date.

- A distinguished musicologist begs him for the very precious tape of Hausa singers which he recorded three years before in Tera [a village northwest of Niamey]
- Jacqueline puts her head through the door. There's a phone call for Jean in the next office. "I'm coming," he says, and does no such thing.
- With Paulin Vieyra, a Black filmmaker, he sets up a magnificent film co-production network for African countries in five minutes. All his pals are catapulted from the office into the principal posts. The budgets are established in an instant.
- [Sergio] Ricci arrives, shouting, "What's this I hear? You're sending me to Ouagadougou?" "Yes, I just got you a contract for three years. You leave on Saturday. Here's your ticket." "What? Saturday? Jean, don't even think about it! It's not possible." "Of course it is. They're expecting you in Niamey for a projection of a double-band version of *Hampi* at the RDA party congress . . ." Ricci feels like crying

In the middle of this circus, Annie [Tresgot] gives the impression that she sees nothing and hears nothing, going backward and forward on the editing table checking an awkward splice. [Jean] Ravel is transferring the sound track. Tom-tom drums reverberate around us. A distant cry rings out. It is coming from the telephone hanging on the end of its cable, and it is the distraught voice of Braunberger's secretary, who has been waiting for a quarter of an hour. "Give me a moment, I've got take a piss," says Jean. He disappears. General outcry. He will not be seen again for several days.[4]

DEVELOPMENTS IN DOCUMENTARY TECHNOLOGY

Over the period that we shall be considering in this part, Rouch's filmmaking praxis evolved in a number of significant ways. In large measure, this was due to major developments in the technology of documentary filmmaking, which Rouch himself played a leading role in bringing about. Being an engineer by training, Rouch retained a lively interest in filmmaking technology throughout his life and was on close personal terms with many of the most innovative camera and sound engineers of his day. However, this enthusiasm was strictly confined to film, and particularly 16mm film. When video technology began to appear in the 1970s, Rouch initially welcomed the possibility that it offered of democratizing the filmmaking process.[5] But later, he radically rejected it, arguing that its very ease of use, cheapness, and automatic sound-image synchronicity encouraged poor filmmaking. He also had certain well-founded reservations about the longevity of video.

But two decades earlier, Rouch had been in the vanguard of those who were looking for a way of developing sound-synchronous and portable combinations of camera and tape recorder. As early as 1950, Rouch and Roger Rosfelder had made the first magnetic tape recordings to be recorded in the field in Africa using a prototype portable machine developed by the Sgubbi Company of Paris. But these recordings had been made in conjunction with the springwound Bell & Howell camera that Rouch had bought in the Paris Flea Market some years earlier and the rushes were far from being synchronous. Moreover, although the tape recorder was considered "portable," it weighed over 30 kilograms. So rather than carrying it around alongside the camera, it was more often a question of transporting it to the location, positioning it strategically in one particular place, and then leaving it there.

As the 1950s progressed, various experiments aimed at achieving image-sound synchronicity with portable equipment were taking place not only in France but also in North America, where two groups were particularly active. In the United States, there was the so-called Direct Cinema group based in New York, which included Bob Drew, Ricky Leacock, and D. A. Pennebaker, while in Canada, there were a group of filmmakers working for the National Film Board. Rouch was in contact with both groups, and also with John Marshall, the North American ethnographic filmmaker based at Harvard University, who around the same time was experimenting with a synchronous system in making films about the San Bushmen in southern Africa.[6]

On both sides of the Atlantic, all these filmmakers were striving to overcome the same set of technical problems. The essential requirement for mobile synchronous sound was the development of cameras and tape recorders that were light enough to be carried around but which could also be guaranteed to run consistently and at exactly the same speed. This presupposed not merely the development of lightweight electric motors but also dry batteries that were powerful enough to run these motors for more than a few minutes while also being light and chemically stable. Meanwhile, power fluctuations and tape tautness, among many other factors, could also cause the speed of either the camera or the tape recorder to vary slightly during recording.

By 1960, most of these problems were close to being solved. Not only had lighter motors and portable batteries been developed, but a means of ensuring precise synchronization between camera and tape recording had also been devised. Initially, this was achieved by transmitting an electronic signal or "pilot tone" from camera to tape recorder through a cable known affectionately as an "umbilical." But this had the disadvantage that the sound recordist was obliged to remain close to the camera person, since he or she could not be any further away than the length of the umbilical. Subsequently, another system was devised whereby camera and tape recorder would each be equipped with a quartz crystal and the very precise oscillations of these would then be used to regulate their respective motors in such a way that synchronicity could be achieved on playback. This meant that it was possible to do away with the umbilical, and cameraperson and sound recordist were free to operate with much greater independence.

Initially, however, sound-image synchronization was achievable only over the duration of relatively brief takes and a great deal of sound editing still had to take place in the edit suite to achieve true "lip-sync," that is, the synchronization of voice sounds with the movement of a subject's lips, or the synchronization of any rapid movements, as in instrumental music or dance, for example. By 1965, Rouch himself reported that it was still only possible to maintain synchronicity for three minutes.[7] In fact, it would not be until toward the end of the 1960s that full synchronicity could be achieved over the entire eleven-minute duration of the standard 400-ft 16mm magazine.

A NEW WAY OF MAKING FILMS

As Rouch quickly appreciated, this new technology also required a new way of making films. Previously, in shooting with his Bell & Howell, he had been restricted to takes of a maximum duration of twenty-five seconds since this was the time that it took for the spring to unwind completely. But while rewinding between takes, he could consider his next shot and, in effect, edit in the camera by changing angle, framing, or position in relation to the subject. The longer takes that became possible with the new technology greatly increased the fidelity with which camera operators could represent the world, but if these takes were not to become tedious, adjustments in angle, framing, and position now had to be made in the course of the shot itself. In effect, it became necessary, as Rouch would later put it, "to edit through the viewfinder."

Both Rouch and the North American Direct Cinema filmmakers favored handheld techniques so that they could move around freely, but while the Direct Cinema practitioners made a particular virtue of using the zoom lens to effect changes of framing or position, Rouch much preferred the tracking shot, that is, moving himself and the camera bodily in and out in relation to the subject. By this means, he aimed to achieve a much greater intimacy with the subjects, though all this moving around also required him to coordinate closely with his sound recordists so that they could stay out of shot while still getting their microphones close enough to the subject to record good quality sound.

This way of shooting required a great deal of skill and, in 1960, in order to help him develop this new mobile camera technique, Rouch persuaded Michel Brault, a French-Canadian cameraman who had pioneered the strategy of "walking with the camera," to leave his position at the National Film Board of Canada and come to Paris and work with him. As we shall see, Brault shot a large part of *Chronicle of a Summer* and, later that same year, *La Punition*. Over the ensuing years, inspired by Brault's example, Rouch would develop a shooting praxis based on the so-called "*plan-séquence*," the sequence-shot, that is, a prolonged, unbroken shot in which one moves around with the camera, responding to the action within the frame so as to make editing unnecessary.

For Rouch, the sequence-shot, for all its inherent difficulties, became the ideal way to shoot, "a dream almost out of reach." As the 1960s unfolded and both Rouch's skills and the technology developed, sequence-shots became both more prevalent in his films and more prolonged, though it was not actually until 1971 that he finally achieved the *nec plus ultra* of the eleven-minute shot lasting the entire duration of a 400-ft. magazine.

The development of this way of working on the back of the new technology also influenced the substantive content of Rouch's films over this period. For the development of the fully synchronized sequence-shot enabled him to use film to record not only more extended stretches of music and dance, or ritual performance, but also what Marcel Mauss had called *techniques de corps*, that is, everyday bodily movements that although apparently purely biological or functional are, in fact, culturally specific, literally embodying particular cultural ideas and values. Initially, Rouch made these films in collaboration with the eminent ethnomusicologist Gilbert Rouget, and their focus was very specifically on music and dance.[8] But later, working mostly on his own, Rouch also employed the sequence-shot technique to record the percussive rhythms that the Songhay, in common with many other groups in Africa, use to structure highly demanding forms of physical labor and thereby make them tolerable.

But by far the most significant consequence of the development of fully synchronous sound, not just for Rouch but for all documentarists, was that it now became possible for the general storyline of a documentary to be carried by dialogue, either between the filmmaker and subjects, in the form of interviews, or in the form of dialogues between the subjects themselves, as in a fictional feature film. As we shall see, Rouch and Morin used both these forms of dialogue to carry the storyline of *Chronicle of Summer*. Rouch also used synchronized dialogues improvised by the protagonists to carry the storylines of the various ethnofictions that he made through the 1960s and 1970s. But notwithstanding his own use of dialogues, Rouch retained a general antipathy to what he called "chatting" in documentary films, considering it an "archaic habit" that derived from radio.[9]

The problematic status of dialogue became even more acute for Rouch when the language of the film that he was making was not French, since he also retained an aversion to subtitles, on the grounds that they "mutilate" the image, distract the viewer and are often not on the screen long enough for the full complexity of what is being said to be translated. He therefore preferred to continue with the poetic narrational voice-over format that he had developed in the presynchronous sound era. However, while this worked reasonably well when the original dialogue was itself in a poetic form—as in ritual chanting, for example—it was a cumbersome and stylistically awkward device when it consisted merely of everyday conversation, particularly if there were two or more voices involved. This was a problem that one can see Rouch struggling with through this period of his career and one that, arguably, he never satisfactorily resolved.

CINEMA AND ETHNOGRAPHIC RESEARCH

In conjunction with these technological developments and the filmmaking strategies that they enabled, one can detect a developing bifurcation in Rouch's oeuvre over the course of the 1960s and 1970s. With one significant exception, all the major films that he had made previously— be it in the 1950s during the period of his studies of migration, or before that, in the 1940s, while carrying out his doctoral fieldwork—had been associated with extensive prior ethnographic research. Although he may have deployed cinema-inspired techniques and conventions in making these films—as in the beginning-middle-end structure of *Les Maîtres fous*, or the improvisational acting in *Jaguar* and *Moi, un Noir*— they remained profoundly informed by his ethnographic knowledge of the subject matter.

The significant exception in this earlier period was *La Pyramide humaine*. Not entirely convincingly, Rouch claimed that a proposed six-month preparatory study of race relations in the Cocody *lycée* was abandoned when it was discovered that there were no race relations to be studied since the students had no contact with one another. Instead, the film itself became the research, though it turned out that the principal object of this research was not so much the social, cultural, economic, or political contexts of race relations, such as one might explore in an ethnographic study, but instead the nature of filmic reality, or more precisely, the relationship between the dreams, fantasies, and performances provoked by the process of filming and the reality of everyday experience.

As the 1960s wore on, the ethnographic and the cinematic became increasingly separate in Rouch's work. Cinematic language and ethnographic insight are still used in the service of one another in some of the earlier films of this decade, as in *The Lion Hunters* or *La Goumbé des jeunes noceurs* (*The Goumbé of the Young Revelers*), which concerns a cultural association set up by migrants from Burkina Faso in Abidjan. They are also mutually entangled in *Chronicle of a Summer*, though in a different sort of way, since the insight is based largely on the filmmakers' personal experience rather than on prior ethnographic research as such. But thereafter the cinematic and the ethnographic become increasingly separate, with the fictions becoming progressively detached from any prior research, while the ethnographic documentaries become increasingly descriptive films of record, involving minimal manipulation of the profilmic reality, be it on location or back in the edit suite.

These developments in Rouch's praxis, like Ariadne's thread in the Minotaur's labyrinth, will serve as a guide through the extraordinarily varied and abundant corpus of work that Rouch produced during the 1960s and 1970s. We will consider this work in the course of four chapters. In the first, chapter 8, we shall focus exclusively on *Chronicle of a Summer*, in acknowledgment of its importance not only in the development of Rouch's own praxis but in documentary praxis generally. In chapter 9, we shall explore how Rouch sought to apply the practical lessons that he learnt from this "experiment in *cinéma-vérité*" in making a series of three fiction films, all set in Paris, and all representing variations on the quintessentially New Wave theme of love and its relationship to personal freedom.

In the other two chapters, we will consider the films that Rouch was simultaneously making in West Africa. In chapter 10, I shall discuss his work among the Songhay, including one of his major films, *The Lion Hunters*, set in "the land of nowhere" on the frontier between Niger, Burkina Faso, and Mali. I shall also discuss *Petit à Petit*, a film that brings the two principal loci of Rouch's work together since it consists essentially of a reprise of *Jaguar*, though it features Paris rather than the cities of the Gold Coast as the destination of his regular heroes, Damouré and Lam. Finally, in chapter 11 I will examine the series of films that Rouch made in collaboration with Germaine Dieterlen about the Sigui, the world-renewal ritual cycle of the Dogon of the Bandiagara Escarpment in eastern Mali. Here I shall propose that Rouch thought of cinema as the Dogon think of the Sigui, namely, as a means of transcending the limitations of the normal human life span.

8 : Chronicle of a Violent Game

There remains the most difficult, the most moving, the most secret [aspect of social life]: wherever human feelings are at stake, wherever the individual is directly involved, wherever there are interpersonal relationships of authority, subordination, comradeship, love, hate—in other words, everything connected with the emotional fabric of human existence. There lies the great terra incognita of the sociological or ethnological cinema, of cinéma-vérité. There lies its promised land.   EDGAR MORIN, 1962[1]

While anthropologists may debate whether *Les Maîtres fous, Jaguar, The Lion Hunters*, or possibly the Dogon ritual films represent Jean Rouch's most important ethnographic work, and screen studies specialists argue the case between *Moi, un Noir* and *La Pyramide humaine* as the most influential on the development of the French New Wave, as far as documentarists generally are concerned, it would surely be *Chronicle of a Summer*, shot in 1960 and released in 1961, that would be considered the most significant of his films. Indeed, the leading media studies author, Brian Winston, goes so far as to suggest that in the English-speaking world, "*Chronique d'un été* has been, more or less, the Rouch oeuvre in its entirety; and it is pretty meaningless to question the impact of the man (at least on the mainstream of anglophone documentary production over the last half century) in terms that stray much beyond *Chronique d'un été*."[2]

Somewhat paradoxically, however, in terms of its underlying praxis, *Chronicle of a Summer* is in some ways atypical of Rouch's work as a whole. In large part, this is due to the influence of the codirector, Edgar Morin. A sociologist rather than a practicing filmmaker, Morin is a much more interesting figure than is generally acknowledged in anglophone milieux and certainly in the visual anthropology literature, in which there is a tendency to present him as no more than an over-intellectual stooge who is regularly upstaged by Rouch in the course of the film. Born in Paris in 1921, the son of Greek Sephardic Jewish immigrants, he had changed his name from Nahum to "Morin" during the Second World War when, as a member of the Resistance, he had to conceal the fact that he was a Jew. After the war, Morin was appointed to a research position in the CNRS and was already a rising figure of Parisian intellectual life by the time he came to make *Chronicle*. Prior to making the film, he was probably best known in intellectual circles for two well-received books on the effect of cinema on the human imaginary, *Le Cinéma ou l'homme imaginaire* (1956) and *Les Stars* (1957). He was also known as the editor of the leading Marxist journal *Arguments* and as the author of *Autocritique*, a personal memoir about his engagement with and subsequent expulsion from the French Communist Party. In subsequent years, Morin would come to be recognized in France as a major multidisciplinary thinker, with publications ranging across a wide range of topics including the nature of nature, consciousness, and complexity. In the many profiles of his career that are available on the Web, his participation in the making of *Chronicle* is generally only mentioned in passing and often not at all, which is symptomatic of the fact that although this film may be widely regarded by documentarists as a milestone of documentary filmmaking, it represents a relatively small part of Morin's personal curriculum vitae.[3]

Over the course of his career, Rouch shared the direction of a number of other films—notably the Sigui films, which he codirected with Germaine Dieterlen, or the research films that he directed with the ethnomusicologist Gilbert Rouget—but in these other cases, the codirectors mostly left the actual filmmaking up to him. However, this was not the case with *Chronicle*, and Rouch clearly found the sharing of directorial coauthorship particularly demanding. Although Morin and Rouch started out in general agreement about the objectives of the film and the methods that they would use, in the process of actually implementing their ideas, a number of major differences of opinion arose between them. Codirection, Rouch discovered, was not a matter of teamwork based on mutual collaboration but, as he put it, "more a violent game where disagreement is the only rule, and the solution lies in the resolution of this disagreement."[4]

The ups and downs of the cat's cradle of relationships involved in the making of *Chronicle*, as well as the many different transformations that the film went through from initial conception to final version, have been wittily recollected by Morin in a memoir written shortly after the release of the film. This "chronicle of a film," as he dubs it, provides unique insight into the process of making a "documentary" (even though he actually denies *Chronicle* that particular label) and, as such, it deserves to be read by any student of documentary filmmaking. In this chapter, I shall be relying particularly on Morin's account, supplemented by commentaries by Rouch and a number of third parties, to discuss the practical processes whereby *Chronicle* came into being. First, though, we should begin with a brief description of the film as it was finally released:

> The film follows a group of young people living in Paris in the summer of 1960, exploring their views about work, love, and happiness but also about the colonial wars then going on in Africa. Over the opening shots of the early morning rush hour in Paris, Rouch's offscreen voice identifies the film as an "experiment in *cinéma-vérité*," to which ordinary men and women have undertaken to give a few moments of their lives. In the first half of the film, the investigation proceeds by means of a variety of verbal devices, including survey-style questions in the street, mealtime discussions and intensive one-on-one interviews conducted by Morin. One of the subjects, Marceline, having been invited to walk through various locations in Paris and give free rein to her thoughts, is moved to talk about her experiences during the war when she and her father were deported to a German concentration camp. These various oral testimonies are interspersed with a few relatively brief sequences of the subjects going about their daily lives at work or home.

> About two-thirds of the way through the film, the subjects leave Paris for their summer holidays, and there is a shift in emphasis from static discussions physically anchored in one place to sequences in which the subjects are moving about, though there continues to be a heavy emphasis on dialogue. The general tone of the film also becomes more light-hearted. Several subjects are shown at the beach in the south of France, while others are shown at a picnic in Fontainebleau Forest, close to Paris, teaching their children to climb a small outcrop of rocks.

> Eventually, the subjects all return from their holidays and are shown a preliminary assembly of the rushes. The reception is much less positive than Rouch and Morin had been expecting. Some subjects think that the film completely misrepresents their lives, while others think that it is too intrusive, encouraging an immodest degree of self-revelation. Rouch and Morin are left walking up and down amid the ethnographic display cases in the Musée de l'Homme ruminating on the nature of the truth that they have brought to light.

In addition to his disagreements with Morin, Rouch also found himself constrained by the concerns of the producer, Anatole Dauman, the head of Argos Films, who seems to have acted as some sort of arbiter between the two directors but who, like all producers, also had his own agenda, namely, to complete the film "on time and in budget."[5] The form of the film was also greatly influenced by the succession of distinguished cameramen who worked on it, as well as by the important technological innovations that they and Rouch were introducing even as the film was being made. Later, in the edit suite, in the hands of several different teams of editors (about whose appointment Rouch was constantly arguing with Dauman), the rushes resulting from the pooling of these various interests and skills at the production stage underwent a further major transformation. For reasons that I shall describe below, in some senses this transformation in postproduction appears to have undermined, if not actually betrayed, the original ambitions of the directors and the cameramen. Yet despite all these different inputs and the fact that the project started out with only the vaguest of script ideas, rather like a medieval cathedral that possesses architectural harmony despite having been built by many different masons over several centuries, the film that eventually emerged from this complex set of relationships possesses a remarkable overall coherence.

"Comment vis-tu?"

Although attributions of the authorship of *Chronicle* invariably put Rouch's name first, in Morin's account it was he who first had the idea to the make the film. According to his account, in December 1959, while attending the first Festival dei Popoli in Florence as a member of the jury for the ethnographic section, he was much impressed by John Marshall's early film about the San "bushmen" of southern Africa, *The Hunters*, first released some three years previously, since it had succeeded in communicating the essential humanity of the San despite their exotic appearance and unfamiliar way of life. At the same festival, he also saw a number of films shot in urban locations, including the documentary made in South London by Karel Reisz, *We Are the Lambeth Boys*, released in 1958, which had managed to get beyond what Morin called the "Sunday best" reality of current affairs documentaries and to show what these teenagers were really like when they were simply hanging out at their youth club.

Both these films had employed, at least in part, a handheld camera to achieve their effects. Morin formed the idea of applying this technique to a film about Paris and thought that the best person to do this was Rouch since he had already developed this technique into a fine art in his African films. He had become, as Morin put it, a "filmmaker-diver who plunges into real-life situations," infiltrating communities "as a *person* and not as the director of a film crew."[6] Since Rouch was a member of the same jury at Florence, Morin proposed to him then and there that they should collaborate on a film about their own "tribe," the Parisians. As his migration work in Africa was coming to an end and he was looking for a new challenge, Rouch readily agreed. With Rouch on board, Morin later had no difficulty in selling the idea to Anatole Dauman.[7]

On his return to France, Morin published an article in January 1960 in the journal *France Observateur* entitled "For a New *Cinéma-Vérité*," linking the project with the concept of *kino-pravda* or "cinema-truth" first developed by Dziga Vertov, the Polish-Russian Constructivist filmmaker. Best known for his experimental 1929 "city film," *Man with a Movie Camera*, Vertov had later fallen foul of the Stalinist diktat in favor of Socialist Realism, and by the time that he died in 1954, he had become a marginalized and largely forgotten figure in the Soviet Union. In France, however, his ideas had been kept alive by the Marxist cinema historian Georges Sadoul, though his films remained very difficult to see and would not become readily available until the mid-1960s, sometime after *Chronicle* had been made. Indeed, Morin later confessed that at the time that he wrote the article for *France Observateur*, he was more familiar with Vertov's ideas than with his films. As for Rouch, although it seems that he may have previously had some awareness of Vertov's work, it was only after working on *Chronicle* that he began to associate his own way of working with that of Vertov. In various different guises, it was an association that he would continue to make for the rest of his life.[8]

The term *cinéma-vérité* has a checkered history in the literature on documentary filmmaking. For a period, particularly in North America in the 1960s and 1970s, it was understood to denote a documentary practice that aspired to reveal an entirely objective truth about the world and, as such, was associated with the work of the Direct Cinema filmmakers, referred to in the Introduction to this part of the book. However, this understanding is considerably at odds with the original meaning of *kino-pravda* as conceived by Vertov. He coined this term not to refer to some objective truth that could be delivered by cinematic means but rather to the distinctive way of viewing the world that had been made possible by the invention of the "ciné-eye," that is, the cinematographic apparatus. It was clearly in this latter sense that Rouch also understood the term. "For me . . . ," he once commented, "'cinema-truth' has a specific meaning in the same way that 'ciné-eye' does, designating not pure truth, but the truth particular to recorded images and sounds: 'ciné-truth.'"[9]

But while at a very general theoretical level Rouch and Vertov may have shared this view about the nature of cinematographic reality, at the level of actual practice, there seems to be very little in common between their respective filmmaking approaches. The visual aesthetic of Rouch's films, throughout his career, remained generally realist and, once the technology allowed, was based on the long take and a "normal," progressive chronology. Vertov's approach, on the other hand, as particularly exemplified by *Man with a Movie Camera*, was based on the flamboyant use of montage and a complete disregard for any conception of realism or a "normal" chronology. But perhaps even more significant are the differences between Rouch and Vertov with respect to their ideas about the precise nature of the truth made possible by the "ciné-eye." For Vertov, the term *kino-pravda* referred primarily to the process of perceiving the world: the ciné-eye could go anywhere and see anywhere. It could fly in the air with airplanes, watch from beneath as a train thundered overhead, pry into a lady's boudoir. In the edit suite, these images captured by the ciné-eye could then be transformed in all manner of ways: they could be juxtaposed in provocative ways, superimposed, speeded up or slowed down, even run backward. In this way, humanity's vision of the world could be transformed. For Rouch, on the other hand, it was not so much the perception of the world but rather the world itself that was transformed by the cinematographic process as the presence of the camera provoked the subjects into revelatory performances that were different from their normal forms of behavior.

This is a topic that I shall return to again in part 3 when I consider Rouch's shooting praxis in greater detail. Suffice it to say here that this fundamental difference between Vertov and himself about the nature of the truth made possible by the ciné-eye is something that, in my view, Rouch never fully acknowledged. Morin, on the other hand, even back in 1960, recognized in his article in *France Observateur* that there was a significant difference in the nature of the relationship that the two filmmakers sought to develop with their subjects. Whereas Rouch was the "filmmaker-diver" who "plunged" into the social world that he was filming, Vertov's strategy often consisted of filming subjects by means of a hidden camera, catching them unawares in a voyeuristic way and sometimes against their will. This aspect of the Vertovian technique, Morin suggested, was not acceptable, and in the article, as flagged even in the title, he emphasized the need to develop a *new* form of *cinéma-vérité*, one that went beyond Vertov's voyeurism and was built instead on a strategy akin to the classic anthropological fieldwork technique of participant-observation. Indeed, Morin suggested, the "true father" of this new *cinéma-vérité* was "doubtless much more Robert Flaherty than Dziga Vertov."[10]

Curiously, neither Morin in his memoir, nor Rouch—at least as far as I am aware, since he made many pronouncements on the film over the years—drew attention to the feature that, in retrospect, seems to be the most obvious formal similarity between *Man with a Movie Camera* and *Chronicle of a Summer*, namely, the quite unabashed reflexivity. Even if Vertov had sought to hide the fact that he was making a film from his subjects, he constantly reminds his audience about the process, showing not only the eponymous cameraman in shot, but also the editor, and

FIGURE 8.1. Reflexivity *à la française*. *Top*, Rouch and Morin brief Marceline with the aid of a number of bottles of wine; *bottom*, Nadine and Marceline conduct interviews in the street: "Are you happy or unhappy?" "That depends . . . have you read Descartes?"

even an audience watching the film within the film. Rouch and Morin take this reflexivity one step further, for not only do they share the process of construction of the film with the audience, but they also share the process of construction with the subjects. For Rouch, this was nothing new, representing merely a further extension of his commitment to the "shared anthropology" that he had been practicing in Africa since 1954, when he first began showing his works to his subjects. But as one might expect, given his left-wing political inclinations, Morin was also entirely sympathetic with this strategy (fig. 8.1).[11]

In addition to their common commitment to a reflexive mode of enquiry based on principles of participant observation, Morin and Rouch also shared an interest in "psychodrama" or, as Morin sometimes refers to it, "sociodrama," but which amounted to the same thing, namely, the strategy of encouraging subjects to play out their lives before the camera in order to release otherwise hidden aspects of their imaginations. As we saw in chapter 6, this was a technique that Rouch had already used quite self-consciously in *La Pyramide humaine*. Morin was also interested in the potential of this technique, though he appears to have come to it from a slightly different angle. Whereas Rouch thought of the subjects' camera-induced performances as drawing on the unconscious conceived, in the Surrealist manner, in a positive sense, as a source of creativity, Morin approached it from a more conventional psychoanalytical perspective, believing that these performances would have an effect similar to that of a psychoanalytical consultation, bringing to the surface ideas and feelings, and not necessarily positive ones, that had been banished to the unconscious by repressive psychological mechanisms. But these were differences of emphasis rather than of kind, since historically both Surrealism and psychoanalysis were drawing on a common inheritance in Freudian ideas. Moreover, both Morin and Rouch were agreed that the process of bringing out what would otherwise remain hidden in the deep recesses of a film subject's mind was, on balance, beneficial for the subject in that it would help to break down the barriers that normally obstruct social relationships.[12]

Morin and Rouch also agreed that the film should be entirely dependent on these performances provoked by the camera and that there could therefore be no script. Instead, as Morin explained in the synopsis that he wrote to obtain filming authorization from the Centre National de la Cinématographie, their aim was to gather together a number of subjects, present them with the simple question, "Comment vis-tu?," "How do you live?," and take it from there, letting the subjects' responses determine the direction that the film would then follow.[13] In an allusion to the famous play by Pirandello, he and Rouch would be "two authors in search of six characters." There would be no artificial narrative, and the film would conclude not with a title indicating "The End" but with a "To Be Continued," in recognition of the fact that the subjects' lives would go on after the filmmaking had ended.

In effect, Morin proposed, the film would not be a documentary at all, but a program of research based on "an experiment lived by its authors and its actors," clearly echoing here the intertitle close to the beginning of Man with a Movie Camera that declares that it is "an experiment in visual communication." In the course of this experiment, Morin explained, there would be no "moat" between filmmakers and subjects, since the former would participate directly in the lives of the latter. Even at this proposal stage, Morin envisaged that there would be a screening of a preliminary assembly to the subjects, as in La Pyramide humaine, the purpose of which was to attempt "the ultimate psychodrama." That is, after the screening, the subjects would be asked what they thought that they had learned about themselves or their fellow subjects, or about their relationship to the filmmakers and the filmmaking process.[14]

In short, when the "experiment" began, Morin and Rouch were largely agreed both about the objectives of the project and the methods to be employed. But as they set about actually making the film, a number of crucial differences between them soon began to emerge.

From Alienation at Work to Waterskiing

These differences between Rouch and Morin derived to some extent from their respective political postures. Throughout his career, Rouch made every effort to avoid political statements. In postindependence Africa, he argued, it would be "imperialistic" for any European to seek to impose his political values, while in France, he was never publicly associated with any particular political project. Indeed, he was deeply suspicious of those who hoped to change the world through political activism. If he had any sort of political credo, it appears to have been anarchism without militancy.[15] In contrast, Morin was a Marxist of decidedly militant inclinations. He had joined the French Communist Party at the height of the Second World War and had remained a member, albeit a somewhat dissident one, until he was expelled for his criticism of the Soviet suppression of the Hungarian uprising in 1956. At the time of filming *Chronicle*, he continued to be closely associated with various left-wing political groups, many of which openly supported the Algerians in their war of liberation against the French colony that was still in full flow at the time that *Chronicle* was being made.

Since Rouch had only recently returned from Africa, he initially allowed Morin to select the subjects and without him being fully aware of it, Morin drew almost exclusively on his own left-wing friends and associates.[16] Although the first commentary point refers merely to unspecified "men and women" lending themselves to an "experiment in *cinéma-vérité*," suggesting that they may have been randomly selected in some way, the reality was that many of them came from this very particular segment of the Parisian population. At first, Morin's principal strategy for getting answers to the question, "How do you live?" was to arrange a number of meals at his own apartment or those of his left-wing friends that brought together a few of his old comrades, some workers from the Renault factory at Billancourt and a number of left-wing students. In a series of these mealtime scenes, surrounded by evidence of good food and drink, as well as by clouds of smoke from untipped cigarettes, the subjects, accompanied by both Rouch and Morin in shot, set about discussing such heavy-duty matters as alienation in the workplace, the problems of transport workers' housing, and the Algerian war.

Although Rouch quipped that this idea for collective meals arose from Morin's "demonic greediness," Morin himself believed that the commensal bonhomie would encourage the free flow of conversation and help the subjects overcome any inhibitions that they might have about being filmed. The film crew was also encouraged to participate and in the mealtime scene dedicated to the discussion of the war in Algeria, they take a particularly active part, with the sound recordist Guy Rophé arguing that France should stand up for her rights against the Algerian independence movement while the veteran cameraman Albert Viguier, who had been director of photography on such classic works of French cinema as Marcel Carné's *Le jour se lève* (1939) and Georges Rouquier's *Lourdes et ses miracles* (1954), accuses the students of not being sufficiently engaged in the debate about the war.

Morin later explained that by including a discussion of the Algerian war at this particularly sensitive time, they were running the risk of falling foul of politically motivated censorship, and in order to forestall this, they had to exercise some censorship of their own in the edit suite. Although the mealtime debate is lively and many of the students condemn the war unreservedly, the possibility of Algerian independence is never actually mentioned. They also cut out a passage in which, in response to a direct question from Rouch, two students of military service age said they would not go to fight in Algeria if they were called up. One of these students was Régis Debray, who the following year joined the Communist Party. He would later become a confidant of Fidel Castro and a leading figure of French left-wing politics, though at the time of filming, he was still what Morin calls "an individualist in the Camus mould."[17]

The other student in this exchange was Jean-Pierre Sergent. He appears in the scene immediately prior to this mealtime discussion of the Algerian conflict, in which he and Marceline talk about the connection between the difficulties in their personal relationship, Jean-Pierre's sense of despair and their general feeling of political impotence.[18] In fact, this scene is made up of material shot on two different occasions, several months apart, though they are linked through the sound track in such a way as to suggest that both sets of rushes were shot on the same occasion. The set of rushes showing Jean-Pierre and Marceline talking about their relationship, mostly framed in a series of relatively tight close-ups, was one of the first to be shot, while the second set, shot considerably later, show Jean-Pierre on his own, studying hard for his imminent philosophy exam.

In reality, although shot at different times, both sets of rushes were originally informed by political issues directly connected to the Algerian war, though in neither case are these alluded to directly. For the reason why Jean-Pierre was shown studying so intensively—which comes first in the scene in question, though it was actually the material shot later—

was that if he had failed his philosophy exam, he would have been eligible to be called up for military service in Algeria. As for the interview material with Marceline, one of the reasons that Jean-Pierre was so depressed at this time, as he would explain much later in a 1991 interview, was that prior to becoming involved in the filming of *Chronicle*, he had been active in the *réseau Jeanson*, a clandestine network based in France that was committed to aiding the Algerian struggle for independence. Earlier that year, the French police had broken up the network and although Jean-Pierre had not been arrested, he was still feeling anxious about the possible consequences.

However, all the references to politics made by Jean-Pierre and Marceline in the edited version of this scene remain steadfastly in the domain of the general. Indeed, just as it seems that one or other of them might be about to move to the particular, there is often a blatant cutaway to Morin looking on, suggesting that a passage from the sound track has been excised at this point. In the absence of this specific political context, one is left with the vague sense that their interpersonal problems are due to some kind of existential crisis that impacts on their relationship, possibly due to the fact that Marceline is considerably older than Jean-Pierre. If this existential crisis has any link to politics, the way this scene is edited suggests that rather than having anything to do with contemporary affairs, it may be a throwback to the war years since in the last shot in the scene, the camera pans down to reveal some numbers tattooed on Marceline's forearm. Although these are not explained, they would probably be recognized by most viewers, certainly in the early 1960s, as evidence that Marceline had been a prisoner in a Nazi concentration camp.

In the early part of the shoot, these mealtime scenes alternated with intensive interrogatory interviews conducted by Morin. The most dramatic of these, conserved in the final version, was with another of Morin's friends, Marilou Parolini, who was then working as a secretary at the *Cahiers du Cinéma* office. In response to Morin's probing questions, Marilou struggles to find the words to explain her existential dilemmas, on the verge of tears and her face a constant ripple of anguish. At one point, she even talks about killing herself, though concludes that she does not even have the right to do this. This scene was shot by Rouch himself from a camera on a tripod, mostly in very tight close-up on Marilou's tortured visage. In both respects, this was diametrically opposed to his normal camera praxis. But when asked about this many years later, he did not have any very elaborate explanation for this other than that Marilou was talking very nervously and that he had shot the big close-ups "to try to get inside" (fig. 8.2).[19]

As the shooting proceeded, Rouch began to tire of this way of work-

FIGURE 8.2. While Morin interrogates, Rouch tries "to get inside" Marilou with a close-up: "I feel trapped . . . I want to free myself from alibis . . . I don't even have the right to kill myself. That would be false, completely false."

ing. He did not want to deal only in serious topics. Filming endless discussions of social problems had no interest for him—he wanted joy and gaiety. He also wanted the film to have two or three leading protagonists with whom the audience could identify. He even suggested that Morin could be one of these protagonists, the hero in search of the Holy Grail of Truth, but Morin flatly rejected this idea. On the other hand, Rouch did manage to introduce his own friends into the "cast," including Nadine Ballot, the European who had played a leading role as the *débarquée* in *La Pyramide humaine* (and who would later star in his Paris-based New Wave films) as well as Landry and Raymond, two of the Black Ivoirian *lycéens* who had also appeared in that film. Although the mealtime discussions continued, they no longer took place in Marceline's house, but outside at *Le Totem*, the restaurant on the terrace of the Musée de l'Homme. Under Rouch's influence, the main themes of the conversation also moved from alienation at the workplace and the political intricacies of the Algerian war to the more conventionally anthropological issues of Black-White sexual relationships, racism and anti-Semitism, and to the issues raised by the independence struggle going on in the Congo, which although also a delicate political subject, was much less so than the Algerian war since it was Belgian rather than French colonialism that was under attack there (fig. 8.3).

But what concerned Rouch more than anything else at this time was the development of a new technique of handheld shooting. This represented a major point of difference between the two codirectors. For Rouch was far more interested in conducting technical experiments than in any political significance that the film might have, while Morin had no interest whatsoever in technical matters.[20] But if Morin was indifferent to the technical experiments, the cameramen whom Dauman had hired for the film were positively hostile to them and they refused to shoot

FIGURE 8.3. Outside at Le Totem restaurant: Landry explains his views about the interracial conflicts in Africa (*see also fig. 0.1 above*).

handheld because they feared that the loss of technical quality would be too great. The principal cameraman, the distinguished Albert Viguier, withdrew from the shoot and insisted that his name should not be included in the final credits since he feared that this would seriously damage his reputation. For a short period, Rouch was able to employ Raoul Coutard, who had shot the handheld sequences of Jean-Luc Godard's *À bout de souffle* (which in themselves had been inspired by Rouch's own handheld shooting in *Moi, un Noir*) with the 35mm Éclair Cameflex CM3 designed by innovative camera engineer André Coutant (fig. 8.4). But when Coutard had to return to other commitments, Rouch was able to persuade Dauman, despite the latter's serious reservations about the technical experimentation, to bring over Michel Brault, who together with his colleagues at the National Film Board of Canada had been developing the technique of the handheld "walking camera."

The strategy of the "walking camera" radically transformed the shooting praxis of the film. Initially, it involved the use of a small 16mm Arriflex camera in conjunction with a newly developed wide-angle lens, which, in contrast to previous models, did not distort the image. This lens allowed the operator to minimize camera shake while at the same time maximizing the depth of field. However, the motor of the Arriflex was too noisy to use in conjunction with simultaneous sound recording, so the scenes in which it was used had to be shot mute and the sound added afterward. This was the case, for example, with the scene of Jean-Pierre Sergent studying for his philosophy exams described above. But even while the shooting of *Chronicle* was going on, Rouch and Brault were simultaneously working with André Coutant to develop an even more compact but also quieter camera based on a prototype developed for military purposes. This was the KMT Coutant-Mathot Éclair, which weighed only 1.5 kilograms but still could carry a 400-ft magazine with a ten-

FIGURE 8.4. Jean-Luc Godard's cameraman, Raoul Coutard, and his 35mm Éclair Came-flex CM3 camera, with Rouch in the Renault factory at Billancourt. Reproduced in the journal *Studies in Visual Communication* 11, no. 1 (Winter 1985): 12.

minute running time. Instead of looking through the viewfinder, the operator held the camera at chest level, relying on the wide-angle lens to achieve an acceptable degree of accuracy in the framing. The new camera remained rather bulky on account of the "blimp," a soundproofing housing that was necessary to suppress the noise of the motor so that it would not be picked up on the microphones, but it greatly improved mobility. "We could film in the middle of the street, and no one knew we were shooting except the technicians and the actors," Rouch enthused. Although the extent of the operation might seem absurdly large to us now, living as we do in an era of sound-synchronous documentaries shot by a single person on a mobile phone, in 1960, this innovation represented a major technical advance (fig. 8.5).[21]

However, at this stage, the sound track was still being recorded on an independent tape recorder that had no direct connection with the camera and was not entirely synchronous. Although the Nagra tape recorder used on *Chronicle* was genuinely portable and was a great improvement on the Sgubbi that Rouch had used earlier in his career, full synchronicity of speech could only be achieved by much careful cutting and splicing in the edit suite.[22] In order to avoid getting the sound recordist in shot while using the wide-angle lens that was an integral aspect of Brault's method of "walking with the camera," the subjects themselves often carried the tape recorder hidden in a bag slung over their shoulder—which explains

FIGURE 8.5. The "walking camera" in action. *Top*, watched by Rouch, Brault shoots mute with the Arriflex (from *Studies in Visual Communication* 11, no. 1 [Winter 1985]: 54). *Bottom*, he shoots with the KMT Coutant in its blimp. The camera assistant (*right*) carries the battery, while the tape recorder is hidden in a shoulder bag, the strap just visible on the left shoulder of Régis Debray, the subject to Brault's right. Debray was also miked up with a lavalier microphone, visible just below his right shirt collar, a shining sphere dragging down his V-neck sweater. Meanwhile, Rouch, obscured by Brault, and Morin (*far right*) direct from behind. © Argos Films.

why so many of the subjects in the film appear to favor this particular fashion accessory! Brault had also brought over with him some small Electro-voice lavalier microphones recently developed in North America that could be discreetly hung around the subject's neck or clipped on to a lapel, where they would not be readily visible to the camera (though they were still very large by present-day standards). From these hidden positions, the lavaliers could be linked to the tape recorder in the shoulder bag by a cable running under the subject's clothes.

Another innovative sound-recording technique was used in the penultimate sequence of the film, in which Rouch and Morin walk up and down amid the display cases of the Musée de l'Homme, reflecting on the significance of their "experiment." In a well-known production photograph, Rouch and Morin are shown deep in conversation with, on the left, Brault with his heavily blimped camera, seated on a makeshift dolly, apparently being pulled backward by an assistant, while in the background one can see the sound-recording team. If one looks carefully, there is a cable emerging from the bottom of Morin's trouser leg. This runs toward the sound-recording team behind, suggesting that he was miked up, and possibly Rouch as well, with a lavalier physically attached to the tape recorder by a cable. However, this photograph was taken during first take of this sequence rather than during the take that was actually used in the film. This second take was shot a few weeks later and not only are Morin's clothes noticeably different, but there is no evidence of any cables emerging from trouser legs, nor of the ubiquitous shoulder bag. Instead, there is a large microphone very obviously strapped across Rouch's midriff, angled toward Morin. This, Morin reports, was a wireless radio microphone. Presumably, it was attached to a transmitter hidden under Rouch's clothing, from whence it would have sent a signal to the out-of-shot sound recordist (fig. 8.6).[23] I suspect that this represents the first time that a radio microphone was used in an ethnographic documentary, if not in documentary filmmaking generally.

Following the transformation of the shooting praxis of the film by Brault's "walking camera" method, static interviews and sit-down meals were largely abandoned and mobility became the order of the day. One of the first triumphs of the new method was the scene of Marceline walking through Place de la Concorde recollecting the experience of being deported with her father to a German concentration camp during the Second World War. For this shot, the tape recorder was hidden underneath her raincoat and she talks down into her chest, presumably to maximize the quality of the sound picked up by the lavalier around her neck. In the immediately following scene, set in the empty Les Halles marketplace and in which she continues her *sotto voce* recollections, she is carrying a large bag

FIGURE 8.6. Technical innovations in sound recording. In the first take of the discussion scene in the Musée de l'Homme (*top*, shown on the cover of *Studies in Visual Communication* 11, no. 1 [Winter 1985]), Morin's right trouser leg is visibly hoisted up by a cable running down from a microphone, probably hidden on his jacket lapel, to the sound-recording team behind. *Middle*, a close-up view reveals that there is also apparently some cabling around Rouch's right leg and on the floor behind him. *Bottom*, by the time of the second take, shot some weeks later, which is the one used in the film, they were using a radio microphone, clearly sticking out from Rouch's midriff.

in her left hand, suggesting that for some reason it was decided to transfer the location of tape recorder. In actual fact, in neither of these shots was Brault actually walking as he filmed. Instead, with Rouch at his side, he was standing up inside Rouch's Citroën 2CV and shooting through the sunroof. The engine was turned off so that its sound would not be picked

FIGURE 8.7. Marceline recollecting her deportation to Birkenau. *Top*, at the Place de la Concorde, the shape of the tape recorder, on her left shoulder, is just visible beneath her raincoat. *Bottom*, in Les Halles marketplace, it appears to have been transferred to a bag in her left hand.

up by the microphone and the car was simply pushed along in neutral in front of Marceline by other members of the crew, including Morin, as if it were a dolly on a film set. As Marceline was carrying the tape recorder, none of the crew could actually hear what she was saying. But when they played the recording back, and heard her heartfelt story about her experiences in Birkenau, they were all reduced to tears (fig. 8.7).[24]

Shortly after the shooting of this sequence, in order to introduce some more gaiety into the subject matter, Rouch went with Brault and a number of the subjects to Saint-Tropez, a glamorous holiday destination on the Mediterranean coast of France. On the way, they shot sequences in an airplane, on a train, and in a crowd, each of which, Rouch claimed, were some sort of "first" in documentary history. None of these "firsts" actually made it into the final version, but a dramatic shot of water-skiing certainly did. All of these things are now commonplaces of documentary practice, but audiences at that time had never before seen this sort of movement in documentaries. Suddenly it seemed that the mobile camera could boldly go anywhere and film anything, and by ingenious placing of microphone and tape recorders, coupled with hard labor in the edit suite, it could deliver fully synchronous rushes (fig. 8.8).[25]

FIGURE 8.8. Catherine goes waterskiing: a first in documentary cinema? On the right, Landry, "the Black explorer of the South of France," watches a bullfight with Nadine Ballot.

Initially, Morin did not want to go to Saint-Tropez, and though Rouch finally persuaded him, further disagreements soon arose. Rouch wanted to film a Surrealist dream sequence in which Marilou, wandering alone in a cemetery at night, meets a Black man wearing a mask. She runs off and the man pursues her, but then unmasks himself only to reveal that he is Landry. The mask that Rouch wanted Landry to wear would have represented Eddie Constantine, the North American actor who featured in many French B movies in the 1950s as Lemmy Caution, US federal agent. This character was also the alter ego of Petit Touré, the costar, with Oumarou Ganda, of *Moi, un Noir*.[26] Morin was strongly against this idea as he felt that this self-evident fictionalization would undermine the credibility of the documentary footage that they had already filmed. On the other hand, he was ready to go along with another of Rouch's ideas, namely to present the Saint-Tropez material as if Landry were a Black "explorer" discovering the South of France, an idea that both links back to the central theme of *Jaguar* and anticipates that of *Petit à Petit*. Landry is shown emerging out of the sea and then attending a bullfight with Nadine (actually in Saint-Jean-de-Luz, near Biarritz, rather than in

FIGURE 8.9. Sophie, the "cover-girl," demonstrates how to walk with a *soutien gorge balcon* and how to pose for photographers on a pitching yacht. To Morin's chagrin, both she and the "snappers" were extras recruited by Argos Films.

Saint-Tropez). Later, he meets Sophie Destrade, a Brigitte Bardot look-alike, hired by Dauman specifically for the purpose. She and Landry walk alongside the harbor before she is shown on a yacht posing in front of a crowd of photographers. To the chagrin of Morin, who was uncomfortable about all this staging, even the photographers were extras recruited by Dauman (fig. 8.9).

After filming a few other scenes, some of which did not make it into the definitive version of the film, the filmmakers returned to Paris.[27] Here they continued to film for a few more weeks, despite pressure from Dauman to finish. In an attempt to tie things up, Rouch and Morin filmed the first take of themselves walking up and down amid the display cases of the Musée de l'Homme, drawing various conclusions. Finally, as foreseen in Morin's proposal, a selection of the rushes was then screened to the subjects in the cinema of the Studio Publicis, and their reactions to this material were also filmed.

These reactions turn out to be highly diverse. Some subjects say that they found the film to be false because their fellow subjects were clearly acting up for the camera, while others say that it was almost too true to life in the sense that some of the subjects had bared their innermost selves to the camera to an extent that they found indecent. Marceline claims that her moving soliloquy about her deportation to Birkenau, which had reduced the filmmakers to tears when they finally married up sound and image, had merely been playacting. One of the protagonists claims that having seen the film, there are certain people in the room whom she hopes never to meet again, but this is immediately contradicted by others who claim, on the contrary, that having seen those same characters, they are looking forward to getting to know them better. In the midst of this exchange of views, Morin seems shocked, almost angered, by the nature of this reaction. It is left to Régis Debray to tie things up by making some comments of a more intellectual character about the aesthetic merits of the film.

The Endgame: Transforming Real Time into Cinema Time

The shoot at the Publicis cinema brought to an end some six months of filming that, in total, had generated around twenty-five hours of rushes, which in the early 1960s was a vast amount for a documentary. But having worked very hard to achieve a high degree of authenticity in terms of the content, and of fidelity to the real in terms of technique, once in the edit suite, Rouch and Morin were required by the producer, Anatole Dauman, to reduce this large corpus of material to a maximum running time of no more than ninety minutes. This represented a cutting ratio of about 16:1, which is not high by present-day standards, when documentaries shot on digital video are commonly cut at a ratio of 50:1 or more, nor even by the standards of the Direct Cinema filmmakers working in North America somewhat later in the 1960s, some of whom were cutting at ratios of up to 200:1. But it was very much higher than the ratio that Rouch himself had used on his earlier documentaries.

As Morin points out in the section of his memoir dealing with the editing phase, in fact this process of reduction involved two different problems.[28] One was the matter of transforming real time into cinema time, the other was refining the meaning of the film. With regard to the latter, Morin was keen to retain hold of his original idea of basing the film on an exploration of the subjects' responses to the question "How do you live?" He therefore wanted to structure the entire film on a sequence of themes such as work, the difficulties of living, interpersonal relationships and the summer vacation. Although he shared with Rouch a concern to show how these aspects of contemporary life were experienced subjectively by the protagonists, he did not want the film to be reduced to a series of individual stories. Instead, Morin felt "there should be a dimension, not so much of the crowd, but of the global problem of life in Paris, of civilization, and so forth." He wanted the film to end with a message in the form of a montage of the subjects expressing some form of resistance, culminating in a shot of Angelo, a disaffected Renault car factory worker, striking a tree as he does his kick-boxing training in his small garden.

Rouch, on the other hand, wanted the film to be structured entirely on chronological and biographical principles. For him, the main interest of the material was not in the responses that the subjects offered to the question of how they lived, since these were almost invariably the same, namely, that they were bored with their jobs. Much more interesting, in his view, was the development of the subjects over the course of the summer. He had been hoping that events in Algeria or the Congo would reach some sort of critical climax, producing interesting effects on the subjects. But even in the absence of this, he felt that all the subjects should be introduced at the beginning of the film and that the gradual elicitation of their characters and views thereafter should provide the narrative thread of the film. For this reason, he wanted to abandon Morin's original working title, "How Do You Live?" and replace it with "Chronicle of a Summer."

There were also arguments between Rouch and Dauman, the producer. According to Morin, sometimes Dauman considered Rouch no more than "a clumsy *bricoleur*" while at other times, he thought him "an inspired improviser." Dauman wavered similarly in his opinion of Morin, sometimes considering him an effective, if neophyte, editor, while at other times "an abstract theoretician" who was "massacring the film." Dauman wanted to impose "an editor-in-chief" whose responsibility it would be to rethink the material completely so as to ensure that it would have "an incontestable technical and artistic quality." But Rouch successfully resisted this and suggested that instead he and Morin should work alternately with the editors for a period of several weeks, thereby bringing the material down to the required length by what he called—invoking the memory of his engineering teacher, Albert Caquot—a series of "successive approximations." This involved a sort of dialectic between their respective views: as each took over, he restored some of the material that had been eliminated by the other, but respected some of his excisions, while also alternately excising or respecting the other's additions.

This method eventually produced the desired result, but Rouch experienced great anguish in the edit suite, comparing it to the amputation of a limb.[29] For him, the original material derived much of its authenticity—and hence its value—from all the hesitations and awkwardnesses that are a normal part of human interaction and that, with the newly developed synchronous-sound equipment, they had so triumphantly managed to capture in the rushes. He believed that these seemingly redundant moments in fact lent value to the most essential, important moments in the material, since once they were removed and the important moments were presented without this *bavardage* as he termed it (literally, "chattering"), they somehow seemed less significant.[30] Yet as the rushes were ruthlessly pared down in the edit suite to the ninety-minute running time that Dauman insisted upon, it was precisely these aspects of the material that were among the first to go.

Rouch also resented the sheer reduction of material in and of itself: in the production phase, they had spent a great deal of time filming a day-in-the-life of Angelo, the Renault worker, with what Rouch considered wonderful results, only for this to be reduced to no more than three minutes in the final film. For Rouch, this day could have been the subject of a complete film in itself. He admitted to being deeply perplexed by what he would later call "the devil of editing": he simply could not bring himself to accept the idea that editing should consist of isolating little moments of reality from the surrounding rushes and sticking them together with other such moments to produce some meaningful representation of the world.[31]

In the end, the final version of the film represented a compromise between the respective positions of all the main parties. Rouch's title was chosen ("How Do You Live?" was considered "too television" by Dauman anyway) as was his preference for a chronologically based narrative. But the real chronology of the summer was radically manipulated so as conform, on the one hand, to Morin's concern to identify themes that went beyond individual stories and, on the other, to Dauman's concern to have a clear beginning-middle-end structure. Initially, this tripartite structure was to have been represented by the sequence proposed by Morin: "before the vacation," "the vacation," and "after the vacation." But the "after the vacation" part was later deemed too weak to end the film and it was eliminated, with the best parts being moved into the "before the vacation" part. Although it is scarcely credible, among these relocated scenes was the famous Marceline-Nadine "vox pop" sequence with which the film now begins and in which they go round asking random people in the street the same question, "Are you happy?"[32] All parties agreed that by moving this sequence to the beginning, the agenda of the "experiment in *cinéma-vérité*" would be immediately established and it would serve as an effective introduction to the series of mealtime discussions that make up a large proportion of the remainder of the prevacation part of the film. Also contrary to what one might imagine, given Rouch's supposed preoccupation with gaiety, the framing of the "vox pop" question was actually Morin's idea, though one suspects that he would have been satisfied with the answers, which were mostly in the negative. The only correspondents to declare their happiness at any length were not people randomly encountered in the street but a young couple who were actually friends of Rouch. These were the Cuénets, whom Marceline and Nadine visit in their apartment overlooking the Eiffel Tower and where they listen to the melodious sounds of a remarkable mechanical music box.

Other scenes that were moved from the post- to the prevacation part included the similarly celebrated scene of Angelo discussing racism in France with Landry, the Ivoirian student, on a staircase, in what was actually Morin's house. This comes at the end of the sequence purporting to be a day-in-the-life of Angelo. The beginning of this "day," which shows Angelo getting up and going to work, and the end, which shows him returning home up some steep steps (tape recorder in shoulder bag) were both shot after the vacation. But in the film, they frame a sequence of workers in the Renault factory that was actually shot just prior to the vacation. Both the shooting style and the visual resolution of the image in this middle part of the day-in-the-life —from which Angelo is actually absent because the filmmakers did not want to get him into trouble with the factory management by drawing too much attention to him— reflect the fact while the going and coming from work was shot by Brault in 16mm, the scene in the Renault factory was shot by Coutard in 35mm on a completely different occasion.[33]

Meanwhile, in the definitive version of the film, the original "after the vacation" part was replaced by a completely new part consisting primarily of the scene in the Studio Publicis cinema in which the subjects respond to a preliminary assembly of the film. In a first print of the film, shown at Cannes, the Musée de l'Homme and elsewhere, this was not included, despite the provision for it in Morin's original proposal, since it had been found impossible to edit. But after the screenings of the first print, when it was generally agreed that a stronger ending was required, Rouch returned to the edit suite with the material and managed to make it work. Morin and he then reshot their discussion pacing up and down among the display cases in the Musée. Before doing so, they looked at the Publicis cinema scene again so that they could appear to be responding directly to the issues raised by the subjects.

The principle issue that they consider as they walk up and down in the Musée is the claim made by some of the subjects that, throughout the production, the camera had encouraged playacting rather than showing real life. Having had some time to consider it, Rouch and Morin are at least able to put a somewhat more positive construction on this claim than Morin had been able to manage in the actual moment of filming in the Publicis cinema, when he had appeared to become angry. For what Rouch and Morin conclude is that although the subjects might question or disclaim the authenticity of the behavior provoked by the camera, perhaps these "acted" performances in fact revealed the most genuine part of themselves. Marceline might claim that she was merely playacting when speaking about her experiences of being deported with her father to Birkenau, but as witnesses to the event, they could testify that it was certainly no mere game that she was playing. And yet, there is an element of bravado about this discussion, masking what seems to be an uncertainty on the part of Rouch and Morin about what their final conclusions should be. They had hoped to make a film about love, which would encourage the audience to like those whom they had filmed, but they had discovered that even when made with sympathy, a documentary film cannot guarantee such a positive reaction.

The discussion in the Musée finally concludes on this uncertain note with a cut to Rouch and Morin saying farewell on the rain-soaked pavement of the Champs Elysées, a shot that had actually been filmed some weeks earlier, immediately after the Publicis cinema scene. As Brault follows Morin's departing back in the classical valedictory manner and the credits come up, the sound track takes us back to the Cuénets' mechanical music box and the voices of Nadine and Marceline asking, "Are you happy?" from the beginning of the film, another classical editorial device aimed at achieving a sense of narrative closure. This is finally brought about —contrary to Morin's original proposal that the film should conclude with a "To Be Continued"—with a discreet but quite unambiguous "Fin" (fig. 8.10).

From *Cinéma-vérité* to *Cinéma direct*

What then are we to make of this "experiment in *cinéma-vérité*" almost half a century after it was made? Among historians of documentary cinema, it is widely hailed as a ground-breaking work that played a pioneering role in defining a particular genre of documentary based on a mobile, handheld camera and synchronous sound. For almost the first time, a documentary film had shown ordinary people, from all walks of life, speaking spontaneously, in synch and in their own voices, about their everyday experiences. "The first time I heard a worker speak in a film," commented Jean-Luc Godard in 1962, "was in *Chronicle of a Summer*."[34]

Meanwhile, in the visual anthropology literature, even if Rouch and Morin themselves did not think about the film in quite this way at the time, *Chronicle* is widely and justifiably celebrated for its self-reflexive method that anticipates by the best part of twenty years the adoption of

FIGURE 8.10. Narrative closure. *Top*, contrary to Morin's original proposal, the film has a formal ending while sound effects remind the viewer of the beginning of the film. *Bottom*, the credits evoke the Surrealist notion of the *rencontre* with unknown strangers.

similar approaches in the production of textual anthropology. Not only do Rouch and Morin show themselves on the screen, thereby revealing the constructed nature of the representation, but they also engage the subjects actively in the process of making of the film, thereby making them its protagonists in the broadest sense of the word.[35] One might also point to the film's purely ethnographic value, which increases with the passing of the years as the world it represents approaches the horizon when it will pass out of the living memory.

But for all its many merits, *Chronicle* is a film that is positively awash with contradictions and ambiguities, many of which continue to trouble documentarists inspired by its example to this day. There is, first of all, the striking contrast between the principles governing the process of production and those applied in the postproduction phase. During the former, great efforts were made by both Rouch and Morin, albeit in their different ways, to achieve a direct representation of the real that overcame the obstacles that had previously inhibited documentarists. While Rouch sought to overcome the technical obstacles, Morin sought to overcome the more methodological impediments that resulted in most documentaries of the day presenting reality in its "Sunday best." Whatever their differences, they shared a commitment to the idea of making the film on the basis of spontaneity, without a formal script, following their own or their subjects' inspirations. But in the edit suite, under pressure from Dauman, all this was cast aside, and, as I have described, the material was radically manipulated to make it conform to highly conventional editorial procedures and to a pseudo-chronological overall structure.

In the view of some French authors commentating on the film at the time of its release, including the distinguished sociologist Lucien Goldman, the differences between Rouch and Morin were never successfully reconciled and as a result, the film must be considered a failure since both of their agendas were compromised. From an ethnographic or filmic point of view, such as these critics suggest Rouch might have adopted, the development of character is insufficient to gain an in-depth understanding of the subjects beyond their stereotypical social roles, while from a sociological perspective, as it is alleged Morin would have assumed, the analysis of Parisian society at that particular conjuncture in French history remains superficial and insufficiently contextualized.[36] While Rouch declined to respond directly to the critics, claiming (somewhat dubiously) that he always allowed his films to speak for themselves, Morin defended the film against the criticism that it lacked sociological profundity by pointing out that neither Rouch nor he had ever claimed that the film was formally "sociological." Moreover, if the film did have some sociological import, it was certainly not the sort of superficial sociological understanding that arises from conducting an opinion poll. Rather, Morin reiterated, their concern was simply to determine how such general problems as alienation at work and the difficulties of interpersonal relationships impacted on certain individuals. Nor did it matter in his view that these individuals were not statistically representative of all Parisians at the time the film was made. Just as Marx had looked to political crises, Weber to ideal-types, and Freud to pathological cases to reflect on the nature of normality, so too, Morin argued, one could look to the subjects of *Chronicle*, however atypical, to provide insights into the nature of broader social processes at the time.[37]

Chronicle continues to confound and intrigue film critics to this day. In a recent article, the French studies scholar Sam DiIorio describes the film as "both a window and a brick wall." On the one hand, he proposes, the film went further than any previous work of cinema in seeking to put into practice a particular set of ideas about realism that were widespread in French film criticism in the postwar period but which were associated particularly with the *Cahiers du Cinéma* essayist André Bazin. This set of ideas was itself inspired by the proposition central to phenomenology, the philosophical movement at the heart of French intellectual life at the time, whereby the essential truths governing existence can only be grasped through the direct experience of things in themselves. What films should be aspiring to do, therefore, in the view of these critics, was to give audiences direct access to experience, even if necessarily in a vicarious manner, so that they could achieve an understanding of the essential underlying truths implicit in that experience. In that *Chronicle*, through a combination of technological innovation and participatory research methods, moved cinema closer to a direct representation of everyday experience in the world of ordinary people, DiIorio suggests that it also moved closer to the Bazinian ideal of "Total Cinema."

But if *Chronicle* offered a window onto the world in this sense, as recommended by Bazin, DiIorio argues that it also presaged the end of the line for Bazin's particular take on phenomenological realism. For having got closer to Total Cinema than any previous exponents of the seventh art, Rouch and Morin discovered that what this threw up was not just one particular truth but many, about the significance of which even the protagonists themselves could not agree, as was so clearly demonstrated by their reactions to the screening of the film in the Publicis cinema. Moreover, in editing the film, for a mixture of political and presentational reasons, the filmmakers had been obliged to transform and, in some senses, even traduce the direct experience captured in the rushes. On these grounds, DiIorio argues that although *Chronicle* "harks back to Bazin" in its aspiration to show the world as it really exists in an unmediated, experiential fashion, "its inability to confirm a consensual real underscores the necessary artificiality of filmic realism and. . . . indirectly announces the turn away from the ideal of cinema as transparence which takes place in French film and French film criticism over the course of the 1960s." By 1968, DiIorio adds, "the enthusiasm for representational illusion had given way to the awareness of the cinematic image as a construct that can support, mirror or resist dominant ideologies."[38]

It should be said that Morin makes no mention of Bazin in his personal memoir about the making of *Chronicle*, while if Rouch was directly inspired by any specific body of theory to use film to show the world as it really is then this would probably have been Marcel Mauss's rather positivist methodological injunction to collect "documents" in as objective a manner as possible.[39] But if we accept that these phenomenological ideas would have been part of the general intellectual *zeitgeist* of Paris in the 1950s and as such are likely to have influenced Morin and possibly also Rouch, at least indirectly, then DiIorio's analysis allows one to make sense of what, in retrospect, seems an almost painfully naïve belief on the part of the filmmakers that their direct, participatory methods could somehow provide access to an undefined great Truth with a capital T.

DiIorio's analysis also helps one to make sense of the filmmakers' frustrated and uncertain soul-searching, particularly in Morin's case, about what to make of the fact that the film had failed to deliver this ultimate Truth. Although Morin energetically defended the film from its critics at the time of its release, he also somewhat dolefully recognized that his original aim—to explore the question of how individuals worked out their lives at a particular social and historical conjuncture—had been sidelined. Instead, the principal question of the film had ended up being about the nature of the truth revealed by the performances that all individuals put on as social actors, whether or not a camera is present. In this sense, one might draw a parallel, though not one made by Morin himself, with the way in which *La Pyramide humaine* also drew away from the social and the historical to focus instead on questions of truth, fantasy, and performance.

Morin had begun by assuming that cinema would reveal truths about the subjective experience of the subjects of the film that lay beyond the spectacle of everyday life. But he discovered that although the camera did indeed provoke the subjects into revealing aspects of their experience that were not ordinarily visible—as in Marceline's recollection of her traumatic wartime experiences or Marilou's confession of her existential dilemmas—there was no guarantee that these testimonies were any more true than those that they might have given under normal circumstances. Although Morin felt that this question about the nature of truth was a valuable one to have posed, he felt disappointed that the film had not delivered something closer to what he had been aiming for when they started out. By 1963, he had begun to be openly critical of the film and its deviation from his conception of its original goal, observing that "*Comment vis-tu*, misnamed *Chronique d'un été*, was, under the name *ciné-vérité*, an unsuccessful draft of a ciné-dialogue, of a ciné-communication, that revealed to me the difficulties and superficialities, the traps and the diversions of such an undertaking." Twenty years later, in the early 1980s, his views seem to have mellowed somewhat, but he was still confessing to an interviewer that although Rouch and Dauman had ended up reasonably content with the film, he remained "in a state of perplexity" about it.[40]

But of all the ambiguities about *Chronicle* that remained unresolved, perhaps the one with the most significant consequences, at least for the praxis of documentary cinema, concerned the denotatum of the term *cinéma-vérité*, which this film played a large part in putting into general circulation. Here too, although there was some common ground between Rouch and Morin, there were also some very significant differences. Where they agreed was that *cinéma-vérité* consisted of the truths brought to light through the interactions between filmmakers and subjects that take place in the course of making a film. As a result of these interactions, the subjects are inspired or provoked to express thoughts and feelings that they normally keep hidden and may be only partially aware of themselves. However, as I noted above, this interpretation of the meaning of the term *cinéma-vérité* was considerably at variance both with Vertov's original concept as well as with the most conventional understanding of the term among North American authors and filmmakers. In this sense, Rouch and Morin were indeed practicing a "new *cinéma-vérité*" as proclaimed not only in the title of Morin's original article but also on the posters for the film when it was first shown at Cannes.

Where Morin differed from Rouch was in the connection between "walking with the camera" in the Brault manner and the achievement of *cinéma-vérité*. Morin recognized that this way of working could indeed result in the revelatory epiphanies that they both regarded as the hallmark of *cinéma-vérité*, as in the case of Marceline's walk through Place de la Concorde and Les Halles. But as far as Morin was concerned, they could equally well arise through the interrogational interviews of the kind that he conducted with Marilou or through the mealtime conversations that he orchestrated with his left-wing comrades, both of which were shot and recorded in a conventional manner with the camera on a tripod in a single, static position. For Rouch, on the other hand, *cinéma-vérité* and "walking with the camera" were directly and necessarily connected. Although this technology had not been available in Vertov's day, he credited him with having "magisterially prophesied" the development of a fully mobile ciné-eye operating in tandem with a fully operational "radio-eye," that is, a microphone recording sound.[41]

Two years after the release of *Chronicle*, the documentarist Mario Ruspoli proposed that the term "*cinéma direct*" should henceforth be used instead of *cinéma-vérité* so as to avoid the widespread mistaken association of the latter with a claim to some absolute ontological truth.[42] Subsequently, some French authors have used the two terms to distinguish between the technique of "walking with the camera," which they refer to as *cinéma direct*, and the distinctive form of knowledge of the world produced by cinema, which they continue to refer to as *cinéma-vérité*. These authors include Edgar Morin, who uses this distinction to refer to *Chronicle* as a "hodgepodge" of *cinéma direct* and *cinéma-vérité*.[43] In contrast, for Rouch, in common with many other authors both in France and the English-speaking world, the new term *cinéma direct* merely referred to the technical-strategic process whereby the "theory of *cinéma-vérité*" was to be realized, and as such, there was a necessary connection between them that, for all practical intents and purposes, made them synonymous. This failure to distinguish between a technique and an epistemology has continued to bedevil a great deal of thinking and writing about this approach to documentary filmmaking ever since.

9 : New Wave Experiments

Rouch is the force behind all French cinema of the past ten years, although few people realize it . . . In a way, Rouch is more important than Godard in the evolution of the French cinema.   JACQUES RIVETTE, 1968[1]

Building on the earlier acclaim of *Moi, un Noir* and *La Pyramide humaine,* the release of *Chronicle of a Summer* in 1961 confirmed Jean Rouch as a leading figure of French cinema. Throughout the 1960s, reviews of the work of Jean Rouch, interviews with Jean Rouch, or articles by Jean Rouch would frequently appear in the pages of *Cahiers du Cinéma,* the principal mouthpiece of the New Wave.[2] Of the leading New Wave filmmakers, Jean-Luc Godard was particularly influenced by Rouch, adopting his filmmaking techniques in his own films, most notably in *À bout de souffle,* in which the handheld camera and the jump cuts are all very reminiscent of Rouch's way of working. Indeed the stylistic similarity was so great that it led one eminent *Cahiers* film critic, Luc Moullet, to describe the film as "a sort of *Moi, un Blanc*" and to suggest that Godard wanted to become "the Rouch of France."[3]

Another New Wave figure to be deeply influenced by Rouch was Jacques Rivette, whose comment about the importance of Rouch's influence is quoted in the epigraph to this chapter. Not only did Rivette share Rouch's interest in improvisation and his antipathy to formal scripts, but, as Christopher Thompson has described, there are a number of telling allusions to Rouch, only slightly disguised, in his monumental twelve-hour masterwork, *Out One. Noli me tangere* (1971). One of the characters in this film is an ethnologist played by Michel Delahaye, a *Cahiers du Cinéma* contributor who had written about Rouch's work, and who had also had a part in Rouch's own film, *Petit à Petit,* then only recently released (1970). In one of the key scenes in Rivette's film, shot on the roof of the Musée de l'Homme, Delahaye's character expresses his desire to break free from conventional ethnography, praising the initiative of a colleague who had moved from working with fishermen on the Niger River to studying Breton fishermen back in France with the help of a Nigerien. As Thompson observes, the reference to Rouch is "unmistakable." [4]

However, not all the New Wave directors were quite as enthusiastic about Rouch's work as Godard and Rivette. Notwithstanding the much commented-upon influence of the final sequence of *Moi, un Noir* on *Les Quatre Cent Coups*, François Truffaut, far from acknowledging any debt to Rouch, mentions him only in passing in his autobiographical collection of essays, *The Films in My Life*, and then only to suggest that he was greatly influenced by Roberto Rossellini.[5] Indeed, Rouch appears to have been more of a fellow traveler than a card-carrying member of the New Wave. He was a decade or so older than its leading figures, and the life experience that he brought to his filmmaking was very different. As the New Wave directors had all reached adulthood after the Second World War, they had not witnessed Surrealism at its apogee, they had none of Rouch's military experience, nor could they have any personal understanding of his twenty years of work as an anthropologist in Africa. By contrast, to use the graphic phrase of Maxime Scheinfeigel, the New Wave was as anchored in Paris as a boat tied up on the Seine.[6] Although some of the New Wave directors adopted some of the same technical procedures as Rouch, such as the use of the handheld camera and the portable Nagra tape recorder, they never handled this equipment themselves. They also normally worked in 35mm rather than in Rouch's preferred 16mm medium. But notwithstanding these differences, for a while during the first half of the 1960s, Rouch traveled along the same road as the directors of the New Wave, addressing many of the same cinematographic issues.

During this period, in addition to *Chronicle of a Summer*, Rouch made three other films in Paris: *La Punition*, first screened publicly in 1963, *Gare du Nord*, released in 1965, and *Les Veuves de quinze ans*, released in 1966. These three films represented a series of attempts to apply the methods of *cinéma-vérité* to fictional filmmaking and, as such, were a continuation of "the experiment in *cinéma-vérité*" that Rouch had announced in the opening voice-over in *Chronicle of a Summer*. More generally, this interest in experimentation can be linked, on the one hand, to Rouch's enthusiasm for the ideas of the Surrealists, who also thought of their works as a constant series of experiments, and, on the other, to the work of Dziga Vertov, whose masterwork, *Man with a Movie Camera*, was also presented as an experiment in the opening titles, and whose injunction not just to make films but to make "films that produce films" was a remark that Rouch was particularly fond of quoting.[7]

Rouch often claimed that he was more interested in the results of these experiments than in whether his films were considered successful by cinema critics. In the case of these three films, this was just as well, since they received very mixed notices. As René Prédal, editor of the two special editions of *CinémAction* dedicated to Rouch's work, comments, as tactfully as he can, "these films . . . represent the most harshly debated part of [Rouch's] work, and the one to which the adjective 'embarrassing' is most readily attached." However, Prédal himself considers this as being as much to do with the French public's greater appetite for films about Africans ruled by the Spirit of Thunder than for films about themselves and their submission to the spirit of money.[8]

But though the materialism of the French bourgeoisie is indeed a theme that crops up in all three films, money as such is not the primary focus. Rather, all three films explore, as did *Chronicle*, the themes of love, personal freedom, and the difficulty of reconciling one with the other. Interwoven with these characteristic concerns of the New Wave, there are a number of other threads that derive directly from Rouch's youthful encounter with the work of the Surrealists. The Surrealist aspiration to conjoin dreams with reality is a constant theme of all three films, even if accompanied by a certain resigned acknowledgement of the ultimately chimerical nature of the enterprise. Also important is the Surrealist idea of the potentially transformative and liberating *rencontre*, that is, the chance encounter of two people previously unknown to one another. This idea provides a crucial key to reading Rouch's films of this period, particularly the first two, *La Punition* and *Gare du Nord*.[9]

By this time, Rouch was in his middle forties, but in all three films, for reasons that are obviously intriguing, but which he himself—to the best of my knowledge—never directly commented upon, these themes are explored through the experiences of young women who, if not actually adolescents, are certainly no older than their early twenties. In *La Punition* and *Gare du Nord*, the female lead is played by Nadine Ballot, who had previously played a starring role in *La Pyramide humaine* as the *debarquée* whose ingenuous flirting unleashes the dramatic narrative of the film. She had also appeared as a relatively minor character in *Chronicle*. In *Les Veuves de quinze ans*, the third of these films, she also appears, but here too only in a secondary role.

A woman of great beauty, Nadine clearly held a particular fascination for Rouch. Although she never trained as an actress nor ever claimed to be one, Nadine's remarkable improvised performances, together with her model-like pose, her *haute couture* clothes, her engagingly troubled facial expressions, and her ambiguous persona, combining a disconcerting mixture of credulous virgin and adventurous woman of the world, give the films in which she appears a very particular character. In fact, her presence in Rouch's films over this period is so pervasive that Prédal has suggested that one can discern in them a "Nadine series" that is akin to the "Lam-Damouré series" that is a feature of his African work. This is perhaps overstating the case, but the general point is well taken.[10]

The Disappointing Adventure

The first of the three films, *La Punition,* was shot in October 1960, when Rouch was still actively involved in the cutting of *Chronicle.* As we saw in the previous chapter, although he had greatly enjoyed the shooting of *Chronicle,* Rouch found the editing phase a time of great anguish, just as he had found the editing phases of *Moi, un Noir* and *La Pyramide humaine* before that. The main reason for this anguish was the seemingly unavoidable obligation to eliminate the great majority of the material filmed, including particularly the many awkwardnesses and hesitations that Rouch felt imparted a sense of authenticity to the material as a whole and thereby underpinned the significance of the most important moments of the film. Conceived as a direct reaction to this experience of editing *Chronicle,* Rouch aimed with this new film to conserve the full complexity of a series of events shot over the course of a single day.[11]

The film was mostly shot by Michel Brault, in black and white, using the "walking camera" techniques that Rouch and he had developed together in the shooting of *Chronicle.* Later, since Brault had by then already returned to Canada, Rouch shot some additional material, mostly cutaways, to allow the material to be cut together in the edit suite. In order to achieve lip synch even while shooting in this mobile way, again as in the shooting of *Chronicle,* the lead character, played by Nadine Ballot, carried a Nagra hidden in a handbag. This was linked to a lavalier microphone hidden in her clothing at chest level and which was attached to the Nagra by a cable, visible in some shots, that passed up under her skirt. The other characters in the film were also wired up with lavaliers, and as they approached Nadine, Brault would cut and change angle, while the character concerned was plugged into the Nagra as well. Some of the wider shots are not in synch, and these are covered instead by snatches of the music of J. S. Bach played on what sounds like an electronic keyboard.

As in his African ethnofictions, *La Punition* had no formal script. Instead, Rouch devised a framework story that he laid out on a single typed sheet. The actors, none of whom was a professional, then improvised their dialogues in the various situations identified in the framework story, though they were assisted by further prompts from Rouch whenever there was a break in shooting. Contrary to his original intention, for logistical reasons to do with the availability of one of the principal protagonists, Rouch was obliged to shoot the film over two days rather than one. But in the film diegesis, the action is still presented as taking place over the course of a single day.

The narrative of the film is built around the character played by Nadine. She is a *lycéenne* who, arriving late for her philosophy class one morning, is disrespectful to the teacher and is therefore suspended from the school for the remainder of the day. As she does not dare to go home to her wealthy bourgeois parents until the evening, she is unexpectedly confronted with a day of complete freedom to wander through Paris. This idea was based on Rouch's own experience of having been dismissed from class in this way. This also fitted well with Nadine's situation since she happened to be studying philosophy at the time at a *lycée* in central Paris.

During this day of freedom, Nadine has a number of supposedly chance *rencontres* in the Bretonian manner. Rouch decided that there should be three principal encounters for a reason that he later admitted was perhaps "a bit ridiculous," namely, that a philosophy thesis should normally have three parts. The first encounter, in the morning, in the Jardin de Luxembourg close to the *lycée,* is with Jean-Claude, whom the cameraman, Michel Brault, had recruited for the project. A student of geography, he is only a few years older than Nadine herself though he clearly thinks the difference is significant because he speaks to her in a rather supercilious way. After some preliminary jousting about what they each want from life, Jean-Claude reveals that what he most seeks at that particular moment is an adventure of a physical kind with her. Moreover, he suggests that she has come to the park for a similar purpose and that her story about being expelled from the *lycée* is merely a cover. She is initially offended by this suggestion but they are soon reconciled and frolic in the park to the sound of electronic Bach. However, the conversation then becomes serious again, and Nadine suggests that they abandon everything and run off together. In response, Jean-Claude comes over all pragmatic: to talk of such an adventure is all very well, but what would they do for money? Nevertheless, he agrees to meet her again the following day and to go with her if she can provide him with a convincing reason. Nadine is clearly not impressed.

The second encounter, in the early afternoon, in the Jardin des Plantes, is with Modeste Landry, an Ivoirian friend. This is the same Landry who had previously appeared in *La Pyramide humaine* and in *Chronicle* and who would also later appear in Rouch's 1963 film, *Rose et Landry*. At the

FIGURE 9.1. In the Jardin de Luxembourg, *top*, Jean-Claude proposes an *aventure* to Nadine. Later, *bottom*, she goes for a ride with Jean-Marc: is ethnology a form of escape? From *Cahiers du Cinema* 24, no. 144 (1963): 3, 11.

time that *La Punition* was being made, he was studying at a *lycée* in the south of France. As the two friends walk through the museum within the park, Nadine is reminded of the possibility of escape by the sight of exotic stuffed animals in glass cases. She tells Landry that she is seeking a completely new experience, though she confesses sadly that she had discovered that morning, through Jean-Claude's reluctance to run off with her, that the notion of *l'amour fou* (a clear reference here to the work of André Breton) "does not exist." But Landry suggests that she is too *bourgeoise* for such fantasies and contrasts her ambition with his own: for him, it would be an adventure simply to be awarded a place at a Parisian *lycée*.

Within the diegesis of the film, the third *rencontre* takes place late on the same afternoon, while Nadine is browsing through some secondhand volumes of Chateaubriand at an open-air bookstall along the banks of the Seine. She is approached by Jean-Marc, a forty-something engineer, played by one of Rouch's friends. He initiates a conversation by asking her, patronizingly, why a young girl like her should be interested in the works

FIGURE 9.2. In Jean-Marc's apartment. Nadine lets down her hair and suggests that they should run off together, anywhere . . . but Jean-Marc thinks that her idea is no more than a girlish fantasy and firmly rejects it. (*Compare with fig. 6.6 above.*) © Films du Jeudi.

of Chateaubriand. As Jean-Claude had done earlier in the day, he implies that she must be looking to pick someone up or she would not be talking to him. She reminds him that it was he who started the conversation but nevertheless agrees to go for a drive in his Citroën DS and later, to go back to his apartment. As in the Jean-Claude encounter, there is much discussion of life projects, interspersed with speculation, heavily laden with innuendo, about what they might do in their brief period of time together. Nadine declares that she wishes to become an ethnologist, but Jean-Marc disapproves of the plan, considering it a form of evasion from reality. Once they are back in Jean-Marc's apartment, with a gesture similar to the one that featured in the dream of her "marriage" in *La Pyramide humaine*, Nadine lets down her hair and proposes, as she had done earlier in the day to Jean-Claude, that they abandon everything and run off together. But Jean-Marc considers the idea preposterous, a mere young girl's fantasy, and offers to take her home there and then (see fig. 9.2).

Finally, after leaving Jean-Marc but before going home, Nadine goes window-shopping after dark along the Champs Elysées. Here she is approached by a number of people who want to engage her in conversation. The first seems to be a genuine passer-by, but the others are evidently actors and include Elola, another Ivoirian *lycéen* who had played a leading role in *La Pyramide humaine*. In what would surely have been rather a risqué detail at the time, the last passer-by to proposition her appears to be a woman, and after this, Nadine beats a hasty retreat to her elegant home nearby.

The film as a whole is framed by three curious shots, one at the beginning and two at the end. These appear to represent the narrator of the film, that is, Rouch himself, though it is not actually Rouch who is playing the role in shot. At the beginning, we see only the narrator's feet as he picks his way through the puddles on a damp formal pathway of the Jardin de Luxembourg, before cutting abruptly and rather counterintuitively to an upper torso shot of Nadine, late for class, walking briskly in the opposite direction across a bridge over the Seine. This mysterious figure, clad in black, then appears again in the last two shots of the film, at night, after Nadine has gone home, first beneath a street lamp, and then in silhouette, with an aureole of light around his head.

This figure narrates the film through a series of six extracts from poems and other literary works, elegantly voiced by Rouch. These punctuate the film at the beginning and the end, and prior to the three encounters. The sources are not directly identified, but they touch on the recurrent metathemes of Rouch's work—adventure, mystery, the world of legend. Rouch later said that he thought of them as being more in the nature of a musical accompaniment than literary quotations as such, and that he had chosen these particular quotations because they had been important to him when he himself was studying philosophy. At the time of editing, he felt that they gave the film a certain cohesion, but on mature reflection, he concluded that they had been an error and that the film would have been better without them. Yet notwithstanding Rouch's own reservations, in my view they work very effectively to set up the tone of the immediately following sequences.

Over the opening shot of the narrator's feet, Rouch speaks some lines referring to the bittersweet experience of walking in the Jardin de Luxembourg in October. These were probably written by Baudelaire, one of Rouch's poet-heroes, who was well known for his love of the Jardin and to whom a statue is erected on its grounds. Then, shortly afterward, as Nadine walks through the Jardin after being expelled from the school, and just prior to meeting Jean-Claude by the lakeside, Rouch recites some more lines. These sound as if they might have been written by André Breton, but in fact they are extracted from *Le Grand Meaulnes*, the classic coming-of-age novel by Alain Fournier, written just before the First World War:

For the first time, here I am on the path of adventure . . . I am looking for something even more mysterious . . . Something to be found in the depths of the morning, when one has long forgotten that the clock stands somewhere between eleven and midday.

Prior to the second encounter, with Landry, as Nadine approaches the entrance of the Jardin des Plantes and is walking alongside the tall wall of the perimeter, Rouch quotes from Rimbaud's well-known poem, *Enfance*, in which the poet refers to a park surrounded by high palisades, within which "*des bêtes d'une elegance fabuleuse circulaient*"—fabulously elegant creatures are circulating. This comes immediately before a shot of a seal emerging from its pool in the zoo within the Jardin, and later, a series of long tracking shots of row upon row of exotic stuffed animals in the museum.

Later still, as Nadine first encounters Jean-Marc at the bookstall, Rouch quotes from a passage in the first chapter of *Justine*, the scandalous late eighteenth-century novel of the Marquis de Sade:

The thing that men least celebrate, that they least value, that they scorn above all in your sex, is chastity. These days, Justine, one only values things that yield some material benefit or provide delight; and what profit or what pleasure could we gain from womanly virtue?

This is surely a most ambiguous prompt for Rouch to lay over a shot of his middle-aged friend Jean-Marc chatting up Nadine, particularly when one bears in mind that in the original context, these are comments that an old libertine makes to the fourteen-year-old heroine just prior to attempting to assault her sexually.

The final poetic quotation is recited over the concluding two shots of the narrator standing in a pool of light from a street lamp: "At least waiting is an occupation. To be waiting for nothing is what is really terrible." This, finally, represents a direct reference to the work of André Breton, being a rough quotation from chapter 3 of *L'Amour fou*.[12] It strikes a note of resignation at the end of a film in which there has been a progressive decline from the initial sense of the potentially exciting adventure that might follow from a chance encounter to the final realization that, in reality, the opportunities for escape and for evading the banalities of everyday life are few and far between.

This decline is also reflected in the various titles that were given to the film. The original working title of the film was simply *Liberté*, reflecting both the liberty that the main character enjoys for a day and the freedom from conventional filmmaking constraints with which the film was made.[13] But this was later changed to *La Punition*, presumably referring to the punishment meted out to Nadine for her disrespect to the teacher, while the subtitle of the film, *Les mauvaises rencontres*—the bad encounters—is similarly pessimistic. Far from being seen as a potentially liberating experience, as originally envisaged by Breton, in this Rouchian account the *rencontre* has become something disappointing, something bad.

At the time of its first release in 1963, *La Punition* came in for a great deal of criticism from all sides, from the most intellectual critics of the *Cahiers du Cinéma* to members of the general public, who saw the film when it was broadcast on television. The criticism of the principal character, Nadine, was particularly severe. One surprisingly stern critic was Rouch's friend, Roberto Rossellini, who accused him of laziness for relying too much on the spontaneity of the actors and for not having given enough of his own shape to the material.[14]

In part, this highly negative reaction seems to have been because the audience did not know how to read the film. It was presented by Rouch as a work in which the methods of *cinéma-vérité* had been applied, but once again, this term seems to have caused great misunderstanding. For even some of the most sophisticated commentators, including Rossellini, appear to have been under the impression that in using the term *cinéma-vérité*, Rouch was referring to some literal objective truth rather than to a truth that was particular to the cinema. As a result, many members of the audience were confused about the status of the images that they were watching. *La Punition* was clearly not a documentary since the characters were very self-consciously acting for the camera in situations that had been entirely set up by the director. Given these circumstances, the critics claimed, it could not be said to represent the truth. Because of its beguiling documentary feel, some even accused the film of being a case of "*cinéma-mensonge*," cinema-falsehood, rather than *cinéma-vérité*. On the other hand, if *La Punition* was to be considered as a work of fiction, the dialogues were considered by many critics to be excessively banal.[15]

Rouch himself was unrepentant. For him, whether the film was considered a success or failure by the critics was a mere detail. He thought of the film as primarily an experiment to determine whether one could create a fiction out of reality using the filmmaking methods of *cinéma-vérité*. To his own satisfaction, *La Punition* had demonstrated that this was indeed possible, even if he was still trying to determine what the rules of this particular game should be. Moreover, he had heard that André Breton himself had seen the film when it was broadcast on television and had found in it a certain echo of his novel *Nadja*. This reaction pleased Rouch immensely. He even suggested that one of the reasons for the negative critical reaction to the film was the fact that while Breton's idea of the *rencontre* was very significant for his own generation, it had little resonance for a younger audience.

The adverse reaction to *La Punition* has continued down the years. In 1982, even Pierre Braunberger, the producer, declared that the film had been a disaster: "Let's be honest," he commented, "it's bad." Among contemporary critics, Christopher Thompson, normally a great admirer of Rouch's work, remarks that although *La Punition* is one of the most revealing of Rouch's interest in Surrealism, it is "not the best" of his films.[16] But in my view, considered as a film of its time, *La Punition* has many merits. In the first place, the shooting by Brault is as good as anything one finds in *Chronicle*. It is true that there is a certain banality about the dialogues and some of Nadine's propositions are painfully adolescent, but as the critic Luc Moullet pointed out at the time, in this sense, they are faithful to most people's real-life experience.[17] Indeed, I would argue that these dialogues have better withstood the test of time than the dialogues one finds in other films of the period—in comparison to the highly mannered exchanges of *À bout de souffle*, for example.

In order to appreciate *La Punition*, it is necessary to abandon any attempt to classify it as *either* a documentary *or* a fiction and assess it instead on the terms by which Rouch himself conceived it, that is, as a hybrid of the two. There are, for example, some interesting continuities between *La Punition* and some of the scenes in *Chronicle*—Marceline's famous walk through the Place de la Concorde reflecting on her concentration camp experience provides an obvious parallel—in which the characters are inspired by the presence of the camera to put on a performance that might be considered "false" for this reason but that, at the same time, brings to the surface certain attitudes and fantasies of the characters that would otherwise remain hidden. But if *La Punition* is similar in certain regards to *Chronicle*, which most commentators would have little hesitation in classifying as a "documentary," there are also parallels with the fictional "psychodrama" of *La Pyramide humaine*, in which the characters are invited to create an imaginary world, albeit one that is constructed out of their own real experiences.

Considered in these terms, *La Punition* can be valued not only as a cinematic work but also as an ethnographic document in that, for all its artifice, it brings to the surface certain views about social life, and in particular views about gender, in the Paris of the early 1960s. Luc Moullet is surely right to insist that if the camera had not been present, Nadine would have behaved in a completely different way. It is doubtful, for example, that she would have allowed the conversations with two unknown male strangers to have developed to the degree that they do in the film. But once one allows for this initial conceit, these improvised conversations give expression to certain attitudes that now seem very characteristic of their era. For example, there is something cloyingly patronising about the attitudes of the two men toward the young woman that seem to be very much of their time, as do their very bourgeois aspirations for a fulfilling professional career. Similarly, although there is a brief reference to the workers at Renault (no doubt a throwback to her experience of making *Chronicle*), Nadine's youthful rebellion is primarily expressed in naïve, postwar existentialist terms, unmarked by any form of Marxist rhetoric, as it would almost certainly have been if these conversations had been taking place at the same *rive gauche* locations sometime later in the 1960s.

If the encounter between Nadine and Jean-Marc had been filmed for a fiction film today, in all probability it would have ended with them taking their clothes off. But it being the early 1960s, their feints and bluffs around what they might do together in the small window of time that they have available remain entirely rhetorical. Of course, this is also a function of the circumstances of filming—one wonders what Rouch would have done if Nadine had started to take off more than her obviously very expensive headscarf—but within the limitations of this situation, we learn a good deal about their respective attitudes to life and, as much by implication as direct expression, about their ideas about appropriate relations between genders.

The Bridge of Death

Although it was not shot until 1964, some three years later, the second film of Rouch's New Wave period, *Gare du Nord*, represents a further refinement of the experiment underlying the making of *La Punition*. But whereas the earlier film was entirely Rouch's own initiative, *Gare du Nord* formed part of an omnibus film of the kind that was popular in France at the time, to which several directors contributed short "sketches." The subject of this collective film was the city of Paris, and Rouch was one of six directors involved. All the others were leading New Wave figures, including such well-known directors as Éric Rohmer, Jean-Luc Godard, and Claude Chabrol.[18]

The general title of the film was *Paris vu par . . .* and each director was responsible for a film about one particular quartier that, in Rouch's case, was the quartier round the Gare du Nord railway station. Then as now, this is a rather scruffy and rundown part of Paris, and it seems, at first sight, a rather curious choice on Rouch's part. The principal reason for this choice lies a couple of blocks to the east of the station. Here, on the rue La Fayette, there is a bridge crossing over the railway tracks leading

FIGURE 9.3. The railway bridge on the rue La Fayette, close to the Gare du Nord: "one of the most dramatic landscapes in Paris." © Paul Henley.

to the nearby Gare de l'Est. To the casual passer-by, there does not seem to be anything particularly remarkable about this bridge. But for Rouch, it represented "one of the most dramatic landscapes" in Paris (fig. 9.3).[19]

This unassuming bridge held a particular personal significance for Rouch on account of a childhood memory of crossing the bridge with his father, Jules, who on looking down at the railway tracks passing below, described them as "the tracks of death." This was a reference to the fact that many people committed suicide by jumping off the bridge just as a train was coming.[20] But there may well have been another reason why the bridge was of particular interest to Rouch. When it was built in the 1920s, it had involved what was then considered a particularly innovative use of concrete. One of three designers of the bridge was none other than Albert Caquot, Rouch's mentor at the École des Ponts et Chaussées, whose ideas about design by successive approximations he adopted as one of the guiding principles of his filmmaking praxis.[21]

As in *La Punition*, the lead character of *Gare du Nord* is played by Nadine Ballot who, just like her character in the earlier film, feels trapped in her present situation and is desperate to escape. In this film too, the idea of the Bretonian *rencontre* plays a crucial dramatic role. But whereas in *La Punition*, the two male strangers whom Nadine's character encounters had refused to accept her invitation to abandon everything and take off with her, in *Gare du Nord*, the roles are reversed. In this film, it is the character played by Nadine who refuses to accept the prospect of liberty offered by a stranger.

The film was shot in Nadine's own apartment, not actually by Rouch himself but by a professional crew acting under his direction. The cameraman was Étienne Becker, son of the fiction director, Jacques Becker, well known in France for such classics as *Casque d'or* and *Touchez-pas au grisbi*. The son would later work with Jacques Rivette, Louis Malle, and many other leading directors.[22] The total running time of the film is a mere seventeen minutes. Apart from the opening title and two relatively brief panoramic establishing shots that act as bookends, the film consists entirely of two lengthy *plans-séquences* or sequence-shots, that is, prolonged shots, unbroken by any cuts, that constitute a complete sequence or scene in themselves.

In the first sequence-shot, we are presented with Nadine's character, Odile, a young woman who longs to escape from her life in the cramped apartment with her husband, Jean-Pierre, played by the producer of the film and then up-and-coming director, Barbet Schroeder.[23] It begins with the couple having breakfast while in the background there is an incessant sound of pneumatic drilling. Whether this sound—which is present even over the opening title—was recorded in synch or mixed in later is unclear, but in either case, it is highly effective in increasing the sense of claustrophobia within the apartment. Odile hates living in the Gare du Nord quartier, and wishes she could move to the wealthy suburb of Auteuil to get away from the noise. She dreams of exotic adventures and mimics the voices of the stewardesses at Orly Airport calling the passengers to board a flight to Tehran. She says to Jean-Pierre that she would be prepared to go anywhere, just to get away. But in response to her dreams, all that her husband can offer is the distant prospect of a better house, a car, and exotic holidays but only once he has worked his way up to the head of his office. As they get dressed, they begin to quarrel, and she ends up slapping him, stalking out of the apartment and into the open-sided elevator within the stairwell. The camera, which has been running without a cut all the while, follows her into the elevator and descends with her, the light from the intervening floors briefly illuminating her face, while Jean-Pierre's voice, increasingly plaintive and distant, calls her back from above. Finally, at the bottom of the elevator shaft, the image turns pitch-black and although the screeching sound of the elevator mechanism continues seamlessly, Rouch takes advantage of this blackness to make an invisible cut, bringing to an end the first sequence-shot.

In terms of the content, the second sequence-shot represents a mirror image of the first. It begins with Odile coming out of the elevator, press-

FIGURE 9.4. *Gare du Nord*, first sequence shot: Odile and Jean-Pierre argue in their apartment and she flees down the elevator shaft.

ing the button to open the front door and then walking down the street. She crosses the road in order to take the rue La Fayette bridge over the railway tracks, when suddenly there is a great squealing of brakes and a wealthy-looking man jumps out of a car and rushes over to her. The Stranger, played by the professional actor Gilles Quéant, abandons his car in the middle of the road and walks along beside her as she continues over the bridge. Their conversation becomes an uncanny inversion of Odile's immediately prior conversation with Jean-Pierre. The stranger reveals that he has a house with a garden in Auteuil, but it is too quiet there and he wants to escape. He proposes to Odile that they should go to the airport and get on the first plane, regardless of destination. "Are you familiar with the caressing voices of the stewardesses?" he asks her (fig. 9.5). But unless she agrees to go with him immediately, he vows that he will kill himself. When actually faced with the reality of the escape that she had previously dreamed about so earnestly, Odile is unable to grasp the opportunity and refuses the Stranger's offer. Thereupon the Stranger dramatically vaults to his death over the railing of the bridge.

FIGURE 9.5. *Gare du Nord*, second sequence shot: Odile meets the Stranger, who asks, "Are you familiar with the caressing voices of the stewardesses at Orly?"

Maxine Scheinfeigel has proposed the interesting interpretation that the second half of *Gare du Nord* should be considered an oneiric inversion of the first, with Odile's descent into the darkness of the elevator shaft representing her passage into a dream state. From this perspective, she suggests, the Stranger is not actually a stranger at all, but merely a dream state inversion of the husband, Jean-Pierre, and one who offers her the opposite in terms of life possibilities. When Odile cannot accept his proposition to run off and the Stranger kills himself, this represents an ideal form of wish-fulfillment since she has managed to get rid of her husband without having to take any responsibility for the crime. While this is clearly a speculative interpretation, it implies a conjoining of dreaming and reality that one suspects that the Surrealist in Rouch would have much appreciated.[24]

Considered purely as a technical experiment, *Gare du Nord* was intended to tackle Rouch's long-running concern with what he referred to as "the problems of that devil, editing." Previously, in shooting *La Punition*, his aim had been to avoid the anguish that he had suffered in the cutting of *Chronicle*, when the great majority of the rushes had been consigned to oblivion for reasons that he considered insufficiently thought through.[25] He had begun shooting *La Punition* with no clear idea as to how long it would be, but in the edit suite, he soon discovered that even when shooting was restricted to two days, as it had been in that case, a great deal of material still had to be jettisoned. For, although they had produced over seven hours of rushes, the film had ended up being only an hour long. It had also taken him three years to get round to cutting it. He continued to be particularly interested in the effects of the *rencontre*, but he had been obliged to acknowledge the surely rather obvious point that "not all encounters are interesting, in fact, very few of them are."[26]

In preparing *Gare du Nord*, therefore, he gave much greater attention to developing a script, which, according to Nadine Ballot, he did in collaboration with her.[27] In this way, he hoped, the redundancy in the performances would be eliminated. There would still be improvisation, but it would not be in relation to the dialogue but rather in relation to the actors' movements and the reactions of the director and technicians to these movements. However, even this improvisation was not to be entirely spontaneous, since the camera movements were worked out meticulously beforehand. Also, notwithstanding Rouch's later rhetoric about the shooting of *Gare du Nord* "in real time," echoed in most of the subsequent commentaries on the film, in actual practice the production process involved a certain amount of reiteration since the first of the two sequence-shots went through seven takes before it was considered acceptable, while the second required three takes.[28]

Gare du Nord is generally much appreciated by authors who approach it from a screen studies perspective. One of the leading scholarly authorities on the New Wave, Michel Marie, has recently declared it to be "the undeniable masterwork" of the 1960s, not just in terms of the Rouchian canon but seemingly with respect to French cinema generally.[29] But while one might readily recognize that in presenting real time and diegetic cinematic time as coterminous, *Gare du Nord* represents an interesting formal experiment in fictional filmmaking, it did not really resolve the dilemmas that the "devil" of editing posed for the *cinéma-vérité* approach. In effect, given that the shooting of the two sequence-shots that make up the main body of the film involved a considerable number of retakes, the process of editing was not so much eliminated in *Gare du Nord* as transferred from the edit suite to the location. As we shall see when we turn to the ethnographic films that Rouch was making around this same period, this was also the direction in which the methodology that he employed in his African filmwork was also evolving.

Baudelaire to the Rescue

The last film that Rouch made during his "New Wave period" was *Les Veuves de quinze ans*, which was shot in 1964 and released in 1966. It formed part of a coproduction that Pierre Braunberger had arranged with partners from Canada, Italy, and Japan, whereby a filmmaker from each country would contribute a film about adolescence.[30] Rouch's contribution purports to be, as stated in the opening title card, "an essay about the adolescents of Paris in the summer of 1964," though, in fact, it deals only with adolescents from a very rich, elite stratum of Parisian society. The film suggests that these wealthy young Parisians are lost in a swirl of materialism, rock-and-roll, and drunken parties, matched only by the similarly dissolute attitudes of their parents who are too busy with their own love affairs or with their businesses to pay any attention to their children. Although these young people might enjoy sexual freedom at an early age, the film claims that only a minority of them are ever able to find true love. The ironic title of the film—literally translatable as "the fifteen-year-old widows"—appears to suggest that even before they have reached their midteens, these young people have seen it all and done it all, and are emotionally extinguished.[31]

The narrative of the film is structured around the friendship between two girls, the elegant Véronique and the more homely Marie-France. While Véronique lends herself to the world of youthful excess, Marie-France manages to resist it with the aid of regular consultations of the works of Baudelaire. Nadine Ballot also appears in the film, as a coquettish friend of the two principal characters, but only briefly, in little more than a walk-on part in which she advises them about boys (fig. 9.6). The principal characters were based on the real lives of the two leading actresses, but for the purposes of the film, they each played the life of the other. Rouch opted for this strategy following the experience of screening *Chronicle* back to the subjects, when some of them had been disturbed by the performances that they had put on for the camera.[32]

The film takes the form of an edifying morality tale. Although Véronique seems to be having all the fun, she comes to realize that the dizzy social world in which she lives is ultimately empty and meaningless.[33] By contrast, Marie-France, who behaves more soberly throughout the film (though not entirely so) is finally rewarded by receiving friendly overtures from Marc, a nice boy who comes across as some sort of alter ego of Rouch himself. Although Marc has also been sucked into the shallow world of parties to some extent and is destined to take over his father's business, he actually cares most of all about painting, the Flemish mas-

FIGURE 9.6. "When you kiss a boy, it's wonderful." Nadine gives some advice to the shy Marie-France (*left*) and the more adventurous Véronique (*right*).

ters in particular, but also the moderns and Dalí "before he went to America" (fig. 9.7). In the final scene, in a grand park, Marie-France walks off in wide-shot with a worldly-wise avuncular figure, played by Gilles Quéant, the actor who had played the Stranger in *Gare du Nord*. He explains that although the chances of achieving happiness are but one in a thousand, one might just find it if one is sufficiently courageous.

Compared to the earlier two films in Rouch's New Wave period, *Les Veuves de quinze ans* is a much less interesting cinematic experiment. In the same passage quoted in the epigraph, Jacques Rivette describes it as a "failure" though one from which other French filmmakers might learn.[34] As for Rouch himself, in an interview given in 1967, the year after *Les Veuves* had its general release, he confessed that of all the films that he had made up until that point, this was the one that he had least enjoyed making, comparing the production process to "forced labour, military service." This was because, in contrast to all his earlier films, which had been shot in 16mm and were only later blown up into 35mm for cinema release, this film was shot in 35mm, involving the full panoply of blimps, tracks for tracking shots and other heavy equipment, as well as a full professional crew. All of this meant that the production took a month to complete and the young leading actresses often froze up on set when confronted by the laborious production procedures.[35]

But although it is certainly true that some of the acting leaves much to be desired, this is not the only flaw in *Les Veuves de quinze ans*. The structure of the film consists of a series of short scenes that follow one another pell-mell without any sustained internal development, though the censorship that was imposed on certain scenes in which the young girls used bad language and criticized their families would certainly not have helped in this respect. Also, but again possibly due to the effects of censorship, the general argument of the film is rather trite in the way that is so commonly the case when the middle-aged pontificate about the sexual activities of the young.

FIGURE 9.7. Véronique is disillusioned with love, but Marie-France receives friendly overtures from Marc, perhaps some sort of alter ego of Rouch himself?

But the weakest aspect of the film by far is the dialogue. As in the case of *Gare du Nord*, in order to get round what he refers to as "the dilemma" posed by the fact that in order to edit improvised dialogues "you have to distort," Rouch wrote a dialogue script in collaboration with the actors.[36] But this has none of the fluidity of the script for the earlier film. Lumbering, and laden at every turn of phrase with self-conscious significance, this dialogue bears little relation to normal speech. The nadir is represented by the two different moments when Marie-France, aiming to deliver a cutting reprimand to another female character for what she considers her sexual misbehavior (her own mother on one occasion, Véronique on another), pulls out a weighty tome that she just happens to have about her person and, with furrowed brow, unburdens herself of a passage of bitingly misogynistic verse by Baudelaire.

Although Rouch had disliked making this film, it actually did very well at the box office. Surely not coincidentally, the producer Pierre Braunberger thought very highly of it.[37] But for all its commercial success, it turned out to be the last of Rouch's New Wave films. As we shall see in the following chapter, although he would continue to work in Paris in the second half of the 1960s, his next project would be a film with a very different ethos and a very different subject matter, namely, an ethnofiction involving his trusty Nigerien associates, Damouré Zika and Lam Ibrahim Dia, in which they explore the city of their former colonial masters.

10 : Between Paris and the Land of Nowhere

Rouch, the ethnologist! Rouch, the explorer! Rouch, the traveller! Mere ap-
pearances. Rouch has two very circumscribed habitats: Paris and Niger . . .
he has no desire to cross these boundaries that he has so carefully traced. . . .
Rouch is sedentary, a stay-at-home.   CLAUDE JUTRA (1961)[1]

In contrast to other leading figures of ethnographic cinema, such as Robert Gardner or, latterly, David and Judith MacDougall, who have made
films in several different continents, Rouch returned religiously to the
same relatively circumscribed part of West Africa throughout his life.
Even while he was being lionized as a leading figure in the world of cinema in Paris in the 1960s, Rouch continued to return to the region with
great regularity. In the extract from his memoir of "chasing after Rouch,"
quoted in the epigraph, Claude Jutra is only slightly exaggerating. For
although Rouch did work in a number of other West African countries,
notably in Mali among the Dogon, as we shall discuss at length in the
following chapter, the great majority of the films that he made in this
period were shot in Niger, almost exclusively among the Songhay. In explaining this fidelity, Rouch would often cite Griaule and Dieterlen's view
that it requires twenty or thirty years to arrive at a "deep knowledge" of
a given society.[2]

Rouch the Ethnologist!

Through the 1960s and into the early 1970s, Rouch would shoot at least
two films in West Africa every year, usually more. In the case of six of
those years, he shot five films; in 1973, he shot seven. But his most productive year appears to have been 1967, when he shot a remarkable eleven
films. As one might anticipate, not all of these films were masterpieces.
Indeed, some were technically poor. Many were no more than descriptive documentation films of possession ceremonies of between ten and

thirty minutes' duration. A substantial proportion remained unfinished and exist only as double-band prints to this day.[3] But in among the many run-of-the-mill films, there were also works of true quality.

A number of new themes and genres appeared in Rouch's West African repertoire over this period. One of these concerned social and economic development. In 1962–1963, for example, he made a number of films about agronomic and fisheries research. He also shot an unfinished film about town planning. In 1965, he made a ten-minute film about an adult literacy campaign in Mali. But Rouch himself did not have a very high opinion of this work. As he explained in an interview given in 1967, he found the making of these films "deadly boring," since they were about "supposedly serious subjects that I never managed to understand."[4] Some years later, in the 1970s, he even ventured into the world of corporate filmmaking, making three promotional films about cars for SCOA, a French trading conglomerate operating in West Africa. One of these was about the Volkswagen Beetle and the other two about the Peugeot 504. But he appears not to have taken this work too seriously either since all three have rather jocose titles.[5]

A more ethnographic theme that emerges in Rouch's work during this time concerns music, dance, and corporeal movement more generally. Given Rouch's formation as an anthropologist in the Maussian tradition, it is tempting to trace this interest to the influence of Mauss's ideas about *techniques de corps,* that is, body movements that although seemingly merely biological or functional, are in fact imbued with and molded by culturally specific ideas. This interest in corporeal movement had long been implicit in Rouch's earlier films on possession events and is also evident in his attention to the movement of boxers and dancers in *Moi, un Noir.* But through the 1960s, taking advantage of the possibilities offered by the new synchronous-sound technology to build up a film based on a series of sequence-shots, Rouch made a number of further films on this theme.

These films often involved collaboration with the leading French ethnomusicologist, Gilbert Rouget, whose own work has focused particularly on the relationship between music and trance, and whose field research was largely carried out in the traditional indigenous kingdoms of southern Benin.[6] The first of their joint works was shot in 1958 in Allada (see map 1, p. 3), before fully synchronous-sound equipment had been developed. This film concerned the initiation of novices into the cult of the voudou divinity Sakpata, a ritual process involving long periods of seclusion during which the novices are taught the chants and dances associated with this divinity. At this time, Rouch was still using a spring-wound camera that would only permit a maximum take of twenty-five seconds. However, the audio tape recorder could play for much longer, so in order to preserve the temporal integrity of the music and dancing, he and Rouget cut the film on the basis of the sound, with black leader inserted between shots to cover for the images missing when the camera was being rewound.[7]

Another of their joint works was a highly pedagogical, twenty-six-minute film shot in 1964 among the Dogon of the Bandiagara Escarpment in eastern Mali. This was *Batteries dogon: Éléments pour une étude de rythmes* (*Dogon Drums: Elements for a Study of Rhythms*). Germaine Dieterlen is credited as a codirector, along with Rouch and Rouget. This film examined a series of different rhythms played by the Dogon on percussive instruments made of wood, skin, and even stone. Described by Rouch as an exercise in *"ciné-musicologie,"* it devoted particular attention to the subtle interaction between the right and the left hands in Dogon drumming. As well as being a film of ethnographic documentation, it was also a technical experiment aimed at testing out a newly developed lightweight system for achieving synchronous sound to the degree of accuracy of one one-hundredth of a second. It was accompanied by a text published by Rouget the following year in the academic journal *L'Homme*. Indeed, without this text, most of the film is more or less incomprehensible.[8]

Somewhat later, in 1971, Rouch again collaborated with Rouget, this time exploring the relationship between dancing and percussion in African music in *Porto-Novo—La Danse des reines* (*Porto-Novo—Dance of the Queens*), a film about a possession ceremony in the capital of Benin. With the aid of slow-motion cinematography, Rouch and Rouget sought to show that once a performance really gets going, contrary to what one might expect, it is the drummers who follow the steps of the dancers rather than vice-versa.[9]

But Rouch was not only interested in the rhythms associated with formal religious or musical performances. In a number of his films, one finds sequence-shots demonstrating how Africans can use rhythm in an entirely secular context to structure heavy physical work and thereby to make it tolerable. There is a precursor to this in a brief shot in the first part of *Les Maîtres fous* (1955), in which one sees a line of men cutting grass with machetes while in the background another man beats out a rhythm with a large maraca, though this is not actually audible on the sound track of the film. With the synchronous-sound technology that became available by the 1960s, Rouch was able to show these work rhythms much more effectively. In *Un lion nommé "L'Américain"*, shot in 1968, there are two sequence-shots, one showing a man inflating a Land Rover tire with a hand pump while another beats out a rhythm on the wheel rim with two metal tools, the other showing a woman with a baby on her back rhythmically pounding millet in a large wooden mortar. Three years later, for *Architectes ayorou,* a film that is otherwise about the combination of traditional and modern house-building techniques in the small market town of Ayorou, Rouch shot a rather more elaborate version of this second sequence-shot, in which he circles around a whole group of women who are both singing and rhythmically pounding their millet at the same time. In 1973, he brought a number of such sequences together to make up a short composite film entitled *Rythme de travail (Rhythm of Work).*

But if there were some new elements in Rouch's film repertoire from 1960 onward, he also continued to make films on themes that had been central to his work in the 1940s and 1950s, including migration, spirit possession, and other forms of religious ritual. Of these, migration is the least well represented in his post-1960 work, coming down to a single film shot in Abidjan, *La Goumbé des jeunes noceurs (The Goumbé of the Young Revelers)* which was released in 1965. As I noted in chapter 6, when referring to a similar institution that features centrally in *Moi, un Noir,* the term *goumbé,* originally the name of a particular type of drum, is also used in Abidjan to refer to the economic and cultural self-help fraternities run by migrants to the city. The *goumbé* that is featured in *Moi, un Noir* was run by Nigerien migrants, while in this film, it is a *goumbé* run by migrants from Upper Volta (as Burkina Faso was then still known). This film is a conventional documentary, which, although certainly estimable, does not have the profundity of the ethnofiction *Moi, un Noir.* It shows the migrants at work, then at a meeting, and culminates in some display dancing in the evening during which, as Rouch would later show in detail in his work with Rouget, the drummers follow the dancers.

It was in shooting these dances that Rouch first experimented in his ethnographic work with sequence-shots, taking advantage of the fact that the most recent technological developments allowed him to shoot for up to three minutes while still retaining synchronicity. But after this experience, he resolved to give up making films about migrants to the coastal cities of West Africa and to concentrate instead on using this new technology to record the fast disappearing traditional cultural performances back in the regions around the middle reaches of the Niger.[10]

One of the principal ways in which Rouch used this new technology was to chronicle the elaborate Dogon ritual cycle, the Sigui, over an eight-year period, from 1966 to 1974, a project that we shall turn to in the next chapter. But even while he was engaged in this filmmaking among the Dogon, Rouch continued to pursue his longstanding interest in spirit possession among the Songhay-Zerma. All told, in the course of the

1960s and 1970s, he appears to have made perhaps as many as thirty films directly or indirectly dealing with this subject.[11] With one exception (*Porto-Novo*, referred to above), all these films were shot in Niger among the Songhay. A substantial number were shot in and around Niamey since Rouch wanted to reinforce the point that he had established as far back as *Les Maîtres fous* that possession cults were not restricted to rural contexts, but were also being actively maintained and even developed in supposedly 'modern' urban contexts as well. But at the same time as making these films in urban locations, Rouch continued to return to his former field sites in the interior, shooting perhaps as many as a dozen films in Simiri, the same village about fifty miles north of Niamey in which he had shot his first film about rainmaking, *Yenendi, les hommes qui font la pluie,* back in 1951 (see map 2, p. 44).

Many of these films about spirit possession ceremonies were works of documentation, primarily intended to assist the academic study of these phenomena. As such, they often do little more than follow the progress of the ceremonies in a series of minimally edited sequence-shots, with very little and sometimes absolutely no explanatory exegesis. A number of these films have neither credits nor even a title card. In fact, of the thirty or so films on spirit possession that Rouch made during this period of his career, at least half remain technically unfinished in the sense that they exist only as double-band prints that are very difficult to see. Even among those that were completed as married prints (that is, with sound and image combined together on the same roll of film), very few have been widely distributed.

Among these more widely distributed films is *Yenendi de Ganghel*, which was shot in 1968, but not released until 1975. The location, Ganghel, is a small Sorko fishing village some twenty miles from Niamey. In common with many of Rouch's spirit possession films of this period, *Yenendi de Ganghel* concerns a rainmaking ceremony. It formed part of a more general project that Rouch began to develop around this time to produce a "ciné-portrait" of Dongo, the Spirit of Thunder, thought by the Songhay to control the rains. Rouch aimed to achieve this by shooting as many different manifestations of Dongo as possible, showing him embodied in a range of mediums, of both genders and of many different ages. This particular *yenendi* was of special interest to Rouch because, as described in chapter 1, it was precisely here, close to Ganghel, that, in 1942, when he was working as a road engineer, he had first been introduced to spirit possession after a number of his laborers were struck by lightning and their deaths were attributed by their fellow workers to Dongo.[12] *Yenendi de Ganghel* is remarkable for a number of reasons including the fact that in the course of the ceremony, when he has become possessed by Dongo, the principal medium comes right up to the camera and acknowledges Rouch behind it. The villagers beseech Dongo for rain, but he is unrelenting and a further seven years of drought ensue.[13]

Another of Rouch's films about spirit possession from this period that is among his better-known works is *Les Tambours d'avant: Tourou et Bitti* (1972). This was shot in Simiri and concerns a possession ceremony aimed at attracting the *gandyi bi,* the Black Spirits of the Bush, in order to seek their help in combating a plague of locusts that have been attacking the villagers' crops. This film consists almost entirely of a single sequence-shot and it was the experience of making it that led Rouch to develop his notion of the "ciné-trance." For this reason, we shall return to consider this film at greater length in chapter 12.

Into the Land of Nowhere

Hunting was another theme from his earlier work that Rouch continued to explore through his filmmaking in the 1960s. But whereas his earlier films had concerned the hunting of hippopotami in the waters of the Niger River, the films of the 1960s were about the hunting of lions in the semidesert that stretches across the frontiers between Niger, Mali, and Burkina Faso. The most significant of these films, *The Lion Hunters* concerns a traditional form of hunting lions with bow and arrow, as practiced by the Gow, a Songhay subgroup. The Gow live in and around Yatakala, some fifty miles to the west of the Niger River and just north of Wanzerbé, at the edge of the vast trackless savanna that is referred to in the film, after a local usage, as the "land of nowhere" (see map 2, p. 44).

This is another film whose origins lay in the fateful screening in Ayorou, one evening in early 1954, of *Bataille sur le grand fleuve*, Rouch's early film about hippopotami hunting.[14] It so happened that Tahirou Koro, a Gow lion hunter from Weyzébangou, a village close to Yatakala, was in the audience. After the screening, Tahirou came up to Rouch and suggested that he should come to his region and make a film about lion hunting with him and his fellow hunters. It took Rouch some five years to take up the suggestion, but eventually he did so, and *The Lion Hunters* is the result, once again proving that through "shared anthropology," one film can lead to another.

The Lion Hunters has a running time of seventy-seven minutes and is not only one of the longest of Rouch's "straight" ethnographic documentaries but also a strong candidate to be considered the most accomplished of his films in this genre. It was certainly a film to which Rouch himself attached great importance, investing a vast amount of time and energy in it over the course of seven different expeditions between 1958 and 1965. On the first of these expeditions, his commitment was so great that he overexposed himself to the sun, suffered a serious bout of heat-stroke and had to spend a month in the Niamey hospital recuperating.[15] The following year, as Jean-Luc Godard reported with great admiration, instead of remaining in Paris to receive the prestigious Prix Louis Delluc for *Moi, un Noir,* Rouch preferred to take off for the Nigerien savannas to continue work on this film.[16] Thereafter, he kept returning to the location year after year, each time bringing back a provisionally edited version of the material that he had shot the previous year. Before going out to film again, he would show this to the hunters and receive their feedback and suggestions for further filming, thereby establishing a profound *complicité* with his subjects.[17]

At the time of its eventual release in 1965, *The Lion Hunters* was acclaimed by some of the leading critics of the day. For Georges Sadoul, the doyen of French cinema historians, it proved that Rouch was among the greatest of French filmmakers.[18] It was also awarded the *grand prix* at the Venice Film Festival, which, as it happens, is called the Golden Lion, after the famous winged lion emblem of the city. (This was an irony that greatly amused Rouch, and he later added the sound of a lion growling over the card announcing the award of the prize at the beginning of the film). But although *The Lion Hunters* continues to be much appreciated by some of Rouch's greatest admirers in France, there has been a tendency for it to be overlooked in recent English-language overviews of Rouch's work, even in those written by anthropologists whom one might have expected to appreciate its ethnographic qualities. For this reason, I propose to deal with it here at some length.

Although the film was actually shot over the course of seven different expeditions, it is presented as if it were made in the course of merely two. This probably accounts for the somewhat startling discontinuities in the expedition vehicles that appear in shot at various points early in the film. The film as a whole is framed by two nighttime sequences, both clearly shot at the same time, in which traditional *gawey-gawey* hunting ballads are chanted to an audience of wide-eyed listening children, accompanied by the plangent tones of the single-stringed *godye* violin. This framing device has the effect of suggesting that the film itself is a hunting story, which, in some senses, it is.

The Lion Hunters is a very densely ethnographic film, particularly in the first part, which deals with the general social context of the hunt and the technical preparations for it. This ethnographic context is delivered entirely through a voice-over spoken by Rouch and recorded at postproduction. Although it was during precisely this period that Rouch

FIGURE 10.1. "While the people of ancient times may have disappeared from the land of nowhere, the wild animals have remained."

and his colleagues were experimenting with synch-sound systems back in Paris, for this film in "the land of nowhere," he was still obliged to use a largely nonsynchronous system. However, in making this film, Rouch finally abandoned the Bell & Howell Filmo 70 that he had bought in the Flea Market in 1946 in favor of a more sophisticated 16mm Beaulieu. This provided him with a zoom facility but it was still a spring-wound camera, and the maximum length of the shots that it permitted remained no more than thirty-five seconds.[19]

After the opening *gawey-gawey* ballad, the main body of *The Lion Hunters* begins with a lengthy sequence following the journey of the filmmakers to the location on the unmarked frontier between Niger, Mali, and Burkina Faso. Rouch explained later that he wanted the film to be like an African quest for the Holy Grail or the *Chanson de Roland*, and in the commentary he stresses the remoteness and romantic mystery of this "land of nowhere."[20] Amid the lone and level sands, boundless and bare, it is revealed that a long disappeared and unknown people have left petroglyphs etched upon the broken boulders. Nothing beside remains. Even the names of the mountain have been forgotten and those that Rouch invents for them—the Mountains of the Moon, the Mountains of Crystal—establish that we are now truly in another world, where only wild animals remain. This sets the scene for the epic struggle between man and beast that will unfold in the course of the film (fig. 10.1).

But, in fact, for all its poetic resonance, this emphasis on isolation is something of a conceit in the literary sense. As the crow flies, the location was not much more than about fifty miles west of Ayorou, the market town on the banks of the Niger River where Rouch spent much of his time while in the field. It is certainly true that fifty miles can seem like a very long way when there are no roads and the terrain is criss-crossed by constantly shifting sand dunes, but as the film itself reveals, the inhabitants of this land that is supposedly "further than far," remain well connected with the outside world. Thus the poison with which they paint their arrows is distilled from a plant that they travel some three hundred miles to the south to collect, while the metal traps that they use are made even further south, by ironmongers in Ghana, based on a design brought to West Africa by the Portuguese.[21] The hunters' very names indicate that they are Muslims, at least nominally. Even the name given to the lion, the "American," suggests contact with the outside world.[22] Perhaps most amusingly, on the advice of the Spirit of the Whirlwind, whom the hunters consult through a possession ceremony at one point in the film, they attempt to attract the lion toward the trap by burying alongside it a bottle of perfume with the crass but undoubtedly cosmopolitan name, *Soir de Paris.*

Although the original inhabitants may have disappeared, the "land of nowhere" remains occupied by small groups of Fulani and Bella cattle herders. Rouch explains that they have a well-established symbiotic relationship with the lions that live nearby in the bush. They refer to them as individuals and even give them names; they know whether particular lions have mates and how many offspring they have. The lions attack their herds, but they usually carry off only the sick animals that need to be culled anyway. But from time to time, a particular lion breaks the implicit "pact" with the herders and begins to kill their animals, not to eat, but for amusement, leaving the carcass behind to rot. This is what the herders fear above all else, for soon such lions may start to attack healthy cattle. It is at this point that the herders call in the Gow, who live in Yatakala and other small villages on the edge of their grazing area. Most of the time, the Gow are sedentary cultivators of millet, but they also have an established reputation as fearless hunters of lions.[23]

The film then introduces us to the hunters, naming them as individuals and showing them in close-ups. This personalization of the subjects is consistent with a practice that Rouch first adopted many years before when shooting *Bataille sur le grand fleuve* in 1950. In *The Lion Hunters,* Tahirou Koro, the leader, and his seven fellow hunters are all given screen credits by name at the beginning of the film, along with Rouch's Nigerien "assistants," Damouré, Lam, and Tallou, and his Nigerien sound recordists, Idrissa Maïga and Moussa Hamidou. This open acknowledgment of their various contributions through the screen credits represents another expression, I would argue, of Rouch's commitment to a "shared anthropology."

Having introduced us to the hunters, the film then shows them getting ready for the hunt. Central to this is the preparation of the poison with which they paint their arrowheads. Rouch explains in the voice-

FIGURE 10.2. Tahirou Koro prepares the arrow poison. He crosses his hands so that the lion will find its limbs similarly obstructed in a trap. (*Compare with fig. 3.2 above.*)

over that the poison is distilled from the seeds of the *naagji*, a tree that only grows far to the south. Then, suddenly, with scant respect for diegetic chronology, the location of the film is abruptly transferred for a short sequence to these distant savannas where the *naagji* grows and we see the hunters collecting cuttings. With equal rapidity, we are then returned back to the diegetic present and we see Tahiru Koro, now dressed in a goat-skin loincloth and with shaven head, going through the ritually elaborate procedures involved in preparing the poison (fig. 10.2) But after all these extended preparations are complete, a diviner throws some cowrie shells and discerns that prospects for the hunt are poor, since one of the hunters is in league with the lion.

Despite this bad augury, the hunters start out the following morning, and their various techniques are described, including the placing of traps, which involves another swift extradiegetic diversion to a workshop in Ghana—with the charming name, "Suffer to Gain"—to see them being made. But all their efforts turn out to be in vain as another diviner confirms the earlier diagnosis. It seems that the traitor in their midst was born on the same day as the lion and if the lion is killed, he will die too. The hunt is abandoned at what is, in effect, the midpoint of the film.

In a curiously anachronistic device—reminiscent of the American consul's notarized statement in Cooper and Schoedsack's 1925 classic, *Grass*—the second half of the film begins "some years later" with an African holding up a telegram to the camera. Again belying the "land of nowhere" trope this has been sent from Ayorou by Tahirou, the hunters' leader, to Rouch in Abidjan, capital of the Ivory Coast. The telegram reports that a lion has been caught in a trap and that the hunters are waiting for him. Rouch returns to Yatakala with his Nigerien companions and discovers a new grave in the cemetery, belonging to the hunter who had been in league with the lion.

This traitor is certainly not one of the hunters introduced at the beginning of the film, nor is his grave in the cemetery shown. This leads me to suspect that although the Songhay may well hold the belief that a man can enter into an alliance with a lion to frustrate his fellow hunters, in this case the anonymous traitor may be no more than a fictional device that Rouch introduced in order to help with the narrative development of the film. But whatever the extradiegetic status of the hunter might have been, as far as the film is concerned, hunting can begin again with at least some hope of success since the lion's ally is now dead.

But still the hunters have difficulty in capturing the "American." They trap various other felines, then a hyena and, finally, a lion, but it is only a cub, possibly a "son" of the "American." Still they continue, and capture both of the lionesses whose tracks indicate that they are the consorts of the "American." As these various animals are caught in the traps, Rouch is unsparing in showing their suffering, zooming in on their desperate attempts to escape or to bite off the poisoned arrows that the hunters shoot into their bodies to kill them off. The hunters themselves are also afraid. For if an animal dies in anger, its soul may return to harm them. The hunter who actually shoots the final arrow runs the risk of losing a son before the year is out (fig. 10.3). So Tahirou leads the chanting to calm them during their final agonies and to seek their pardon. He sings praise songs to the hunters, to the lion, and to the poison. Once the animals are dead, he taps them on the nostril with his bow three times or puts magic powders in their orifices so that their souls may be swiftly released.

While this ritual process is going on with the second lioness, against the explicit advice of the hunters, one of the Fulani herders gets too close, and the lioness, even though still trapped, strikes him down. Although Damouré kept recording the sound, Rouch stopped filming at this point and the screen goes into a series of freeze frames. Fortunately, the other herders manage to kill the lioness with their spears before she kills her victim, but as the film image returns, it is clear that the episode has embittered the relationship between the hunters and the herders, and the hunt is again abandoned, even though the "American" is still at large.

Many years later, Rouch acknowledged that this accident probably came about as a result of his presence with a camera. Normally, the Fulani were not allowed to accompany to the hunters, but seeing that the Gow were permitting Rouch, also an outsider, to accompany them, and believing Rouch's camera to be a magic weapon with which he would be able to kill the lion, the herdsman's curiosity overcame him and he defied the Gow's warnings to stay away. But the Gow themselves, far from considering Rouch's camera an asset, believed, on the contrary, that the

FIGURE 10.3. A lion cub is caught in a trap and the youngest hunter has been chosen to kill him. But he who kills a lion runs the risk of losing a child within the year.

lions would be able to smell its odor, just as the lions were believed to be able to smell the odor of guns, and would be motivated to attack. Therefore, before allowing Rouch to set out with them, they would insist that he rub herbs over his camera in order to hide its smell.[24]

In the final part of the film, the hunters return to Yatakala where they are received as heroes, praise songs are performed in their honor, and they reenact the scenes of the hunt for the edification of the young boys.

The carcass of one of the lionesses is butchered and distributed around the community, while the skin and other body parts are preserved for sale in the markets far to the south, on the Atlantic Coast. In an interview given in 1977, Rouch claimed that the heart of the lioness, which had been directly pierced by an arrow and was therefore considered a very powerful charm, was later sold to an Ivory Coast politician for US $2,000.[25]

In the very last sequence, the film achieves a sense of narrative closure by returning to the scene with which it began, with a *gawey-gawey* singer retelling the story of the hunt and chanting the praises of the hunters who are once again picked out, one by one, by the camera. But by now the listening children have fallen asleep and over their prone bodies, Rouch brings the film to an end with the comment: "By the time that you have grown up, nobody will hunt lions with bow and arrow any longer. And so, the *gawey-gawey* hunting story is over."

An Epilogue to the Hunters' Story

By ending the film in this way, Rouch no doubt meant to imply a double meaning: not only was this particular *gawey-gawey* story finished, but so too was the custom of hunting lions with bow and arrow. But, in fact, neither proposition was quite true, for the story turned out to have an epilogue. In 1968, three years after completing the original film, Rouch returned to Yatakala to show the film to the hunters and receive their feedback. Once again, the screening of one film led to the making of another since, having been reminded that the "American" had managed to elude them, the hunters decided to set out immediately to see if they could finally capture and kill him, thereby "cleansing the shame" of their previous failures.

This second film, *Un lion nommé "L'Américain"* (*A Lion Called "The American"*), finally released in 1972 and only twenty minutes long, is but a pale shadow of the first. Ethnographically, there is nothing that is not covered in much greater detail in *The Lion Hunters*, and once again, although the hunters do trap and kill another lioness, they fail to catch the wily eponymous hero. A significant part of the film is taken up with the two sequence-shots of work rhythms described above, the first involving the inflation of a tire with a hand pump, the second of a woman pounding millet in a mortar, both of which appear to have been set up and neither of which is of any direct relevance to the main theme of the film. But notwithstanding these limitations, this is a very interesting film to consider in terms of the development of Rouch's filmmaking praxis at this time.

Whereas *The Lion Hunters* was shot on a spring-wound camera, mostly with nonsynchronous sound, *Un lion nommé "L'Américain"* was shot with fully synchronous sound, camera batteries that could sustain much longer takes, and a much improved color film stock. But, curiously, although Rouch had been using synchronous sound for some years in his ethnofictions by this point, it seems as though he had not worked out how to use the new technology in an ethnographic context such as this, in which the subjects are speaking a language that will certainly not be understood by the majority of audiences. In total contrast to *The Lion Hunters,* which was structured by wall-to-wall commentary, in this film Rouch speaks not a word. Nor does he employ subtitles and, apart from a brief moment when Tallou, one of Rouch's assistants appears in shot and speaks in broken French to explain that a herder has driven off a lion preying on his goats, the dialogue is entirely in a language that is presumably some dialect of Songhay.

This dialogue runs throughout the film. Initially, the hunters are shown discussing the significance of the tracks they detect on the sand. Damouré Zika then appears in shot and appears to orchestrate activities in some way, but the reason for this is unclear for anyone who cannot understand the language. Later, once the lioness has been discovered caught in a trap, there are many lively exchanges between the hunters and Tallou is shown squirming on the ground, shouting in a hoarse, peculiar way. Rouch later explained that at this point, overcome by fear, he had become possessed by the spirit of the "American" and that his shouts were the roars of the lion.[26] But for the great majority of viewers this will surely remain obscure unless, presumably, one understands what the others are saying.

The leader of the hunt, Tahirou, then chants at length, and the lioness finally calms down and eventually dies. Afterward, once the hunters have returned with the carcass and divided it up among the villagers, we see Damouré interviewing a man who is presumably another of the hunters, though what he says will again remain totally opaque to anyone not fluent in Songhay. There is then some further chanting by a man wearing some remarkable goggles, such as might be worn by a motorcyclist or possibly an arc-welder, before the film ends with a series of fine sequence shots of women clapping their hands and singing, led by Tahirou. In the final sequence-shot, Rouch walks backward away from the group and then, in a movement that is eerily reminiscent of the cut to the dead walrus' mates bobbing out to sea in the Flaherty classic *Nanook,* a film that much influenced Rouch, there is a pan off to the bush, to signify, I suspect, that the "American" is still out there somewhere. However, one can surmise this only if one has read about the film beforehand because unless one speaks Songhay, one would not know from the film itself that the hunters have failed to capture their prey.

In his 1975 essay, "The Camera and Man," Rouch addressed the dilemmas that the translation of the dialogues in this film presented. He explained that as a general rule, he was reluctant to use subtitles because in addition to "mutilating" the image, they cannot provide any more than a rough summary of what is being said. He felt that this was particularly a problem in relation to Tahirou's chanting in this film, which, it turns out, consists of praise-songs to the poison on the arrows. Having tried unsuccessfully to summarize what Tahirou was saying in voice-over, he concluded that it was best to leave the film without either voice-over or subtitles, suggesting that it could only be an "open door" to the stock of knowledge that, after all, it had taken the hunters themselves decades to acquire. Those who wished to learn more, he proposed, should refer to the "short pamphlet . . . which should henceforth accompany every ethnographic film."[27]

Here we are touching upon what is surely one of the most significant limitations of Rouch's ethnographic filmmaking praxis. For, in making this film, Rouch appears to have arrived at some sort of impasse: reluctant to overlay the synchronous voices of his African subjects with his own voice, but at the same time also reluctant to use subtitles, he produced a work that is in large measure incomprehensible. Nor does his suggestion about the writing of an accompanying pamphlet represent a solution since neither for this nor any other of his subsequent films did Rouch ever produce such a thing. This is an issue that we shall have reason to return to at greater length in chapter 14.[28]

The Persian Letters

The filming of *Un lion nommé "L'Américain"* came to an abrupt end when Rouch heard on the radio about *les événements*, the political unrest of May 1968. Outraged at the thought of the French police entering the Sorbonne, Rouch rushed back to Paris. Three weeks after he left, the "American" was finally and, in Rouch's view, shamefully, killed with a rifle.[29] Meanwhile, although Rouch did shoot some material on *les événements*, this was never made into a film. Instead, he worked on a feature-length ethnofiction that would bring together West Africa and Paris, the two poles of his filmmaking activity over the previous decade.

This film, *Petit à Petit*, represents a reprise of his earlier migration film, *Jaguar*, and again features the intrepid adventurers, Damouré Zika and Lam Ibrahim, but this time their destination is Paris rather than the cities of the Gold Coast. In making this film, Rouch had in mind the early eighteenth-century work, *Lettres persanes*, written by the celebrated essayist Baron de Montesquieu but purporting to be the translation of a series of letters written between 1712 and 1720 by two Persian noblemen visiting Paris. These letters had supposedly been exchanged either with a fellow Persian nobleman living in Venice or with the correspondents' wives and eunuchs in the seraglio back in Persia. Yet although there may be certain superficial parallels with Montesquieu's text, *Petit à Petit* is an altogether less serious work, being, if anything, even more of a "big joke" than *Jaguar*. However, given that the focus of the African expeditionaries' attention is a European society, this film certainly has a stronger claim than *Jaguar* to be considered an example of "reverse anthropology," though it was not based on systematic prior ethnographic research.

The title of the film derives from the name of the business that Damouré and Lam had set up in Accra in *Jaguar*. In the opening shots, Damouré is introduced galloping energetically on his horse, Tarzan, while Lam is herding cattle, just as they were shown in the opening shots of the earlier film. But by now, Petit à Petit is no longer a modest trinket stall, but has grown into a flourishing import-export business dealing in fish, cattle and agricultural produce from an office at Ayorou on the banks of the Niger River. The plot point that initiates the film narrative is the discovery that a rival firm in Niamey is building a "skyscraper" as much as four stories high. In order to outdo this rival, the members of Petit à Petit decide to dispatch Damouré to Paris to find some architects who will design a building that is at least twice that height.

Once in Paris, as well as commissioning some architects, Damouré sets about studying what life is like for people who live in multistory buildings.[30] He walks about Paris and the surrounding countryside, notebook in hand, making ethnographic observations: the air is bad, the trees are imprisoned by fences and the river Seine by an embankment, but the cows are as big as hippopotami; men have long hair, women have short hair, and although the girls are generally pretty from the waist up, they wear mini-skirts and show off their legs in brightly colored stockings in a way that is shocking to a West African Muslim.

In a much-reproduced scene that takes place on the Place Trocadéro, next to the Musée de l'Homme and overlooking the Eiffel Tower, Damouré conducts an investigation in the manner of a nineteenth-century biological anthropologist: he measures a sailor's shoulders and middle-aged man's head with calipers, estimates one girl's chest measurement and checks several sets of teeth without giving any explanation for what he is doing other than that he is a student carrying out research (fig. 10.4).[31]

FIGURE 10.4. Damouré does anthropometric research beside the Musée de l'Homme.

He sends all this information back on a series of picture postcards to his partners in Ayorou. But when he reports that the French kill chickens by electrocuting them rather than by slitting their necks in the Muslim fashion and also cook with pork fat, his colleagues fear for his mental and physical health, and Lam is sent to rescue him.

Lam arrives in Paris about 30 minutes in, around a third of the way through the film. But far from rescuing Damouré, their adventures become even more extravagant. Lam's first reluctant experience of the Métro subway system suddenly turns into a cable car ride up to the snows of the Swiss Alps. After a snowball fight, the two friends go through an arch and suddenly arrive at Camogli, an ancient Mediterranean port near Genoa (and not coincidentally, also close to the vacation apartment of Rouch and his wife, Jane). Damouré explains that it was from here that Columbus set sail to discover America, where they have even taller buildings. With a Nigerien song in the background, a series of shots then take the viewer through a tunnel and into some downtown location in California, followed by a number of shots of vast skyscrapers, also apparently in the United States. Damouré and Lam are not actually in shot

FIGURE 10.5. Lam and Damouré in their Bugatti meet Safi, in her "jaguar" car: "I'll do you a special deal!"

in this North American sequence, but one is clearly supposed to believe that they have extended their researches into multistory buildings across the Atlantic. But a couple of screen minutes later, they are seen arriving back in Paris. A verse from the "Jaguar" song then evokes Damouré's cool walk through the market at Accra, but this time they will ride through town, not in a Jaguar, but in a classic Bugatti with a retractable canvas roof, as this reminds them more of the Land Rover that they have left at home.

Shortly afterward, they meet Safi, a beautiful Senegalese "jaguar" prostitute, also driving a sports car.[32] She quickly announces her rates but offers them a bargain: "10,000 francs for a little 'bump,' 20,000 for a big 'bump.' But I'll do you a special deal: 15,000 for the pair of you" (fig. 10.5). Later, they also pick up a White French girl, Ariane, a typist whom they find moonlighting as a dancer in a cage in a nightclub. After another spin in the Bugatti, they all go floating down the Seine on a *bateau-mouche* tourist boat, accompanied by a French Canadian tramp whom Lam has befriended and who is played by the assistant director of the film, Philippe Luzuy. Inspired by the slogans of May '68 daubed on the walls along the embankment of the Seine, Safi and Ariane then engage in a discussion that now seems rather quaint but which was a subject of much debate at the time of the New Wave, namely, whether a woman can really love more than one man at a time. Overhearing their conversation, Damouré comments that he has no interest in such questions since he has always seen marriage as a matter of social obligation rather than of love anyway.

The architects have by now completed their eight-story design, with one floor for each of Damouré's six wives, plus two extra for future wives. At this point, an hour into the film, the motley crew returns to Ayorou, the builders get to work and Damouré marries both Ariane and Safi, the former in a Christian church, the latter in a traditional African ceremony. But problems soon emerge. Philippe the Tramp finds cattle herding not to his liking since it means getting up too early in the morning, and there is no wine to drink. Safi tries to set up a dressmaking business, but the local women do not like her designs and one threatens to call the police when she offers her a see-through *boubou* dress. Ariane is unhappy because the local typists resent the fact that she is paid more though she is no more competent, and she is impatient waiting her turn with the other seven wives for Damouré's attention. Philippe leaves for Québec, and Safi and Ariane set off to hitchhike to Dakar in Senegal.

The three original founders of Petit à Petit are left wondering what value all their wealth has since it clearly leads to such unhappiness. They conclude that they should hand over their company to their managers, retreat to a thatched hut on the banks of the Niger River and, just as they had done at the end of *Jaguar*, return to the lives they had led before they had even become Gold Coast migrants, let alone international import-export wheeler-dealers. So Illo returns to fishing without an outboard motor, Lam returns to herding cattle on foot, and Damouré, the "*galant*," the ladies' man, gallops off on Tarzan to visit the girls in a nearby village.

Petit à Petit was a long time in editing and was not finally released until 1971. But whereas *Jaguar* and Rouch's other earlier ethnofictions were the subject of much enthusiastic review in the pages of *Cahiers du Cinéma*, according to the catalog prepared by René Prédal, the journal remains conspicuously silent on *Petit à Petit,* apart from one interview conducted with Rouch when the film was still in production.[33] This is probably connected to the fact that although the running times are approximately the same, where *Jaguar* is sharp and witty, *Petit à Petit* seems disjointed and slack, particularly in the final third of the film when the action moves back to Ayorou. Although there are certainly some highly amusing moments in the first third of the film, particularly when Damouré is first in

FIGURE 10.6. A Surrealist moment: shooting the wedding party in the Niger River. © Films du Jeudi.

Paris on his own, more generally the humor, at least to this viewer, seems distinctly leaden.

Rouch's Surrealist inclinations reemerge in various scenes, especially in the last third of the film. At one point, the party following the weddings is shown taking place actually in the Niger River, with the guests dancing with the water halfway up their calves (fig. 10.6). In another, Ariane is seen typing away at dusk in a cage on a bluff overlooking the river. Interestingly, the original inspiration for this *mise-en-scène* came from an idea that occurred to Damouré after seeing a woman dancing in a cage in a Parisian nightclub, just as Ariane is shown doing earlier in the film. He suggested to Rouch that it would be an amusing idea to set up a similar cage back home in Niger, place a typist with a miniskirt in it, as if she were in a zoo, with a sign in cod Latin, *dactylographia parisiana,* and then charge the local Tuareg hicks twenty "balles," that is, francs, to come in and watch her type.[34] But while these surreal scenes are certainly striking, their significance for the story remains completely obscure and they therefore come over as merely ridiculous.

Rouch originally intended *Petit à Petit* to be very much longer than the ninety-two-minute version in which it is most commonly shown and which is the version blown up to 35mm for cinema distribution. An earlier 16mm version of the film also exists, consisting of three parts, each approximately seventy-five minutes long.[35] But under pressure from the producer, Pierre Braunberger, Rouch was obliged to eliminate a large number of scenes and to collapse the three parts into one for the definitive 35mm version of the film. On the basis of the descriptions given by Rouch in a 1967 interview, it seems that some of the scenes eliminated from the definitive 35mm version would have been more interesting than some of those retained: for example, one of the omitted scenes showed Damouré and Lam visiting the cemetery at Genoa where they comment on the European fear of death, and on the ironic contrast between the rich tombs inhabited by the dead and the poverty of those living in the back streets of the city. But other eliminated scenes—such as Safi eating the hand of a dead U.S. Peace Corps volunteer to support her remark that her ancestors were cannibals—probably deserve the oblivion that was visited upon them.[36]

Petit à Petit contains a great deal of fun, but considered as a whole it is difficult to disagree with Safi Faye—who would later become a distinguished feature film director in her own right—that the film is really "a bit foolish." Even those who generally admire Rouch's work acknowledge that it is a "difficult" film that requires several viewings in order to appreciate its distinctive handling of cinematic time. Much to Braunberger's chagrin, even when reduced to ninety-two minutes, it bombed at the box office in France. In Africa, on the other hand, at least according to Rouch, although the intellectuals did not like the ending since it appeared to suggest that the principal characters were choosing to go backward rather than furthering economic development, the film proved to be a great success in the popular cinemas.[37]

It is an intriguing question why there should be such a marked contrast between Petit à Petit and Jaguar. After all, the underlying concepts were similar and the principal protagonists and the filmmaker were the same. The two films were also edited relatively close together in time, even if the principal editors were varied, Josée Matarasso being the principal editor of Jaguar and the 16mm version of Petit à Petit, while Dominique Villain was the editor of the 35mm version.[38] There are a number of possible explanations, but I suspect that one of the most important is that the improvisational methods that had worked so well in the making of Jaguar were subjected to a much greater challenge under the very different conditions involved in the making of Petit à Petit. During the shooting of Jaguar, Damouré and Lam were required to improvise the action only over the duration of the twenty-five-second takes that were all that were possible with the spring-wound Bell & Howell camera that Rouch was using at that time. The sound track was then supplied later, in response to a silent screening of the assembled film, as described in chapter 5. All this was difficult enough to do and required great talent. But it would surely have been an even more demanding task to improvise *simultaneously* both the action and an interactive dialogue over the duration of the much longer takes that were possible with the battery-driven, synchronous-sound system based on the Éclair NPR that Rouch used on *Petit à Petit*.

It is little wonder then that the results were uneven. Throughout the film, Damouré demonstrates a remarkable theatrical talent, though interestingly, Rouch reports that without the presence of Lam as his straight man, even he found it very difficult to improvise. At one point, the production had to be abandoned until Lam could be brought to Paris.[39] But although some of the actors certainly have their moments, particularly Safi Faye and Moustapha Alassane, who plays one of the managers of the Petit à Petit business, the improvisations are too often rather ponderous and hammy.

But it would be unfair to attribute the weaknesses of *Petit à Petit* solely to the dramaturgical difficulties confronted by the actors. In reflecting on *Petit à Petit* from his point of view as the producer, Pierre Braunberger suggested another reason. While he recognized that Rouch was a filmmaker of genius, it was a genius that, as Braunberger put it, he did not always control. Although *Petit à Petit* was based on one of Rouch's best ideas for a film, it was not only poorly shot, Braunberger claimed, but even more poorly managed. But Braunberger also recognized that this was merely the flip side of an approach to filmmaking that accounted for the great sense of joy to be found in Rouch's films. He noted philosophically that as a civil servant who was paid at the end of every month, Rouch could do whatever he liked since he did not depend on filmmaking for a living. "For all his faults, for all his mistakes," Braunberger concluded admiringly, "he is a great figure of the cinema."[40]

11 : A Struggle Waged Against Corruption

. . . among these people, hidden behind all these forms and all these rhythms, there lies their desire to endure, a desire that came to them, according to their legends, when they became aware of the physical decomposition of death. . the art of the Dogon is a struggle waged against corruption.

MARCEL GRIAULE, 1938[1]

Filmmakers never die, for every time their work is screened, they come to life again. HENRI LANGLOIS

The Dogon of the Bandiagara Escarpment in eastern Mali held a particularly privileged place in Jean Rouch's personal imaginary. As described in chapter 2, it was a photograph of masked Dogon funerary dancers, glimpsed in a display in the window of a Parisian bookshop one spring afternoon in 1934, that led the young Rouch first to the photographer, Marcel Griaule, and his partner, Germaine Dieterlen, then to their introductory course of ethnology in the basement of the Musée de l'Homme, and from there to West Africa. Although the doctoral work that he subsequently carried out under Griaule's supervision in the immediate postwar years concerned the Songhay rather than the Dogon, Rouch made at least two expeditions to the Bandiagara Escarpment during this period. The first of these was in 1946 during his descent of the Niger with his wartime friends Pierre Ponty and Jean Sauvy when they made a very brief visit to Griaule and his colleagues at their research station at Sanga (see map 3). The second visit was in 1950, when Rouch visited Griaule and

This chapter represents a substantial reworking of an article that I contributed to *Building Bridges: The Cinema of Jean Rouch*, edited by Joram ten Brink (Henley 2007). I am very grateful to Nadine Wanono and Philippe Lourdou for their comments on a draft of that earlier version. Any inadequacies and inaccuracies that remain are, of course, entirely my responsibility.

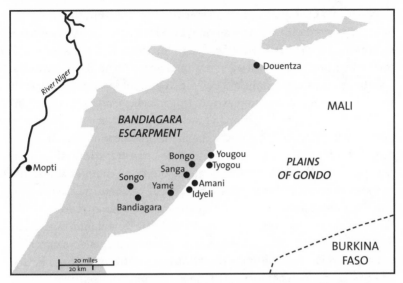

MAP 3. Bandiagara Escarpment, Mali: principal locations of Jean Rouch's filmmaking.

Dieterlen in the company of another of Griaule's supervisees, Roger Ros-felder. It was during this visit that Rouch and Rosfelder shot *Cimetières dans la falaise*, the first of many films that Rouch would come to shoot about Dogon funerary rites.[2]

But neither of these visits, nor a subsequent visit in 1964 described in the previous chapter, during which Rouch and the ethnomusicologist Gilbert Rouget tested out a new method for synchronous-sound filming in making a film about Dogon percussion, came even close to matching the vast investment of time and energy that Rouch dedicated to the film-ing of the Dogon's major ritual cycle, the Sigui, in the years between 1966 and 1974. Over this period, in the unfailing company of Germaine Dieter-len, who acted as codirector of all the films, and on occasion, by Rouget, also credited as codirector of the first of the films, Rouch returned al-most every year for at least two months to the Bandiagara Escarpment in order to follow the unfolding of the Sigui over its remarkable seven-year duration. Only in 1973 were they unable to do so, due to the effects of a particularly severe drought.

The Dogon are surely one of the most well-known of West African peoples, primarily on account of their elaborate cosmological beliefs and ritual practices, as described in the encyclopedic series of monographs published by Griaule, Dieterlen, and their various colleagues between the 1930s and the 1980s.[3] Due in part to Griaule's concern to popularize this work, a knowledge of Dogon beliefs has spread far outside the world of professional anthropology. However, within the academy, this literature has been treated with a certain amount of skepticism, not only in France, where Griaule had many enemies due to his wartime associations with the Vichy government, but also by a number of Anglo-Saxon scholars. The charge most commonly laid against Griaule, at least by the latter, is that he exaggerated the complexity of Dogon beliefs, not through any intentional process of fabrication but rather as a result of a concatenation of circumstances connected with the fieldwork encounter itself. These included, his critics suggest, a well-intentioned but overzealous concern to prove that African belief systems can be as complex and subtle as those of ancient Greece, a particular mode of enquiry based on systematic and intensive interviews conducted through interpreters, and the colonial context of this enquiry in which the Dogon informants' understandably pragmatic concern to satisfy powerful outsiders may have reinforced their own culturally conditioned concern to avoid public disagreement at any cost. These criticisms have in turn been subjected to a determined counter-critique by those directly or indirectly connected with the Griaulian project.[4]

However, in this chapter, as in this book generally, my concern is not with the ethnographic substance of Rouch's work among the Dogon so much as with the particular praxis that he deployed in making his films about the Sigui. Although this will inevitably involve some reference to Dogon ethnography in order to understand the context of Rouch's methods, I make no claim to any authority on such matters, nor do I have any defined position in the often bitter controversy that swirls around the anthropological accounts of this remarkable people.

The Context of the Sigui

At the time that Rouch and Dieterlen came to film the Sigui, the Dogon numbered about 250,000 people.[5] While then, as now, many Dogon lived on the plains to the east of the Bandiagara Escarpment, the groups with whom Rouch and Dieterlen mostly worked inhabited villages at the foot of the escarpment or on top of the plateau nearby. These Dogon practiced very limited animal husbandry and even some hunting, but they were primarily cultivators of millet. Employing a system of irrigation introduced by none other than Marcel Griaule himself, they had also developed the cultivation of onions. Both archaeological evidence and their own oral traditions suggest that the Dogon are relatively recent arrivals in the middle Niger region, having migrated there from the Mandingo Mountains, about 750 miles to the southwest, possibly in order to take refuge from the destabilizing effects of the arrival of Islam in the region some five hundred years ago. Over the years, according to Rouch, they have developed a conventional "joking relationship" with the other ethnic groups living down on the plains and along the banks of the middle Niger, involving a curious blend of teasing deprecation and respect.[6]

Among these plains-dwelling peoples are the Songhay, the group with whom Rouch carried out most of his ethnographic research. But although the Dogon and the Songhay are geographical neighbors, they are culturally very different. Their languages may have some elements in common, and in the view of some scholars, may even belong to the same language family, but they are mutually unintelligible. As Rouch himself reports, the system of patronymic clans, age grades, and related initiation ceremonies, and most significantly for the present chapter, the various cults associated with ancestral masks that are so important in traditional Dogon religion, are completely absent among the Songhay. Conversely, the Dogon do not have anything akin to the spirit possession ceremonies that are so prevalent among the Songhay and that feature in so many of Rouch's films.[7]

However, one feature that is common to both these groups is that a large proportion of their respective populations are practicing Muslims. Even at the time of the Dakar-Djibouti expedition in 1931, the celebration of the Sigui was already inhibited to some degree by the local presence of Islam.[8] But among both the Dogon and the Songhay, public ceremonial expressions of traditional "animist" religious beliefs and practices have been increasingly under pressure since the mid-1970s when the current fundamentalist tendency in the Muslim world first began to take hold in West Africa. As we shall see, although the presence of Islam was less marked when Rouch and Dieterlen were filming in the late 1960s and early 1970s, it was nonetheless still sufficiently strong to affect the performance of the Sigui at certain critical moments in the ritual cycle.

The Sigui ritual cycle is remarkable not only for the fact that it takes place over a period of seven successive years, but also because it is only enacted at interludes of sixty years. In the Dogon view, this is the conventional duration of a human generation. At the end of this period, they reckon that there will still be sufficient survivors from the previous celebration of the Sigui to instruct those born in the interim about its significance and about how it should be conducted. Germaine Dieterlen suggests that the Sigui thus acts as a sort of collective rite of passage, in which the elders of the generation aged sixty years or more initiate the members of the succeeding generation into the most sacred knowledge of the Dogon.[9]

Another distinctive feature of the Sigui is that, for the most part, only male members of the society are involved in the ritual performance per se. These male participants are considered to include even male fetuses still in their mother's wombs.[10] Women, regardless of age, are almost entirely excluded from the performance, the only exception being the so-called *yasigine*, literally "women of the Sigui," who represent one of the first beings in the Dogon cosmogony and who participate in the dancing at certain crucial moments. But while women may be excluded physically, they are symbolically represented throughout the performance of the Sigui in the ritual attire worn by the male dancers. Not only do the male dancers dress up in the clothes and jewelry of their female relatives at certain points, but also, at various stages of the cycle, they wear jerkins fashioned from strings of cowrie shells, which, according to Dieterlen, symbolize female genitalia.[11] There are also certain stages of the cycle when men sing what are conventionally regarded as women's songs and dance women's dances.

Yet another unusual feature of the Sigui is that it is peripatetic, moving from one group of villages to another with each passing year. The Dogon themselves conceive of this movement as being in an east-west direction, "on the wings of the wind." However, in strictly geographical terms, the Sigui moves in a northeast to southwest direction, along the line of the Bandiagara Escarpment. As it does so, it also moves up and down the escarpment, alternating between villages on the edge of the plain at the foot of the escarpment and those on the plateau on top of the escarpment (see map 3, p. 219). By convention, the Sigui always begins in the village of Yougou because it is associated with the death of the first Dogon ancestor to die, crushed by a massive sandstone pillar, which is said to be the one still standing not far from the village (fig. 11.1).[12] After a three-day performance at Yougou, the Sigui then goes to neighboring Dogon villages for further performances . In the second year, it is carried to a similar agglomeration of Dogon villages around Tyogou and Sanga, and further performances are enacted. And so it continues until, in the seventh year, at the extreme southwest of its trajectory, it reaches a shelter set within the cliff face close to the village of Songo. The walls of this shelter are covered with paintings of great religious significance to the Dogon and it is here that, traditionally, the circumcision of local boys would take place. From Songo, the drinking gourds are then carried back to Yougou, the village where the Sigui began, and are filled with millet beer. The ritual cycle is then considered to be complete and will not begin again for another sixty years.

In earlier times, the Sigui used to continue even further to the southwest, but already by the 1930s, when Griaule gathered the first reports on the event, this area had already been extensively Islamized and the

FIGURE 11.1. Male dancers gather at Yougou for the first year of the Sigui, observed (*above, left*), by the women. © Fondation Jean Rouch.

Sigui was no longer welcome there.[13] By the time that Rouch and Dieterlen came to film the final stages of the Sigui in the 1970s, even the villages as far to the northwest as the region around Yamé, where they filmed in the sixth year, had been strongly Islamized, making the celebration of the Sigui more complicated.

The Genesis of the Sigui Film Project

Griaule himself was never an eyewitness to the Sigui, but in the course of various different expeditions in the 1930s, he collected detailed oral accounts from those who had attended the last enactment in the first decade of the twentieth century. He would surely have hoped to live to see the next enactment himself, since he would only have been in his late sixties when it was next due to begin in 1967. But shortly before his death in 1956, when he had already had two heart attacks and knew that his days were numbered, Griaule asked Rouch to film it.[14] Later, as the time for the Sigui drew near, Dieterlen also urged him to do so. So it was that in 1966, accompanied by Ambara Dolo, one of Griaule's principal informants, Rouch and Dieterlen went to visit the Hogon, the paramount Dogon religious authority, in order to seek his permission to film the Sigui.

The Hogon duly gave his permission, but initially Rouch was wary of being drawn too far into the uncomfortable mixture of professional controversy and interpersonal tension that marked relationships between the leading French specialists on the Dogon at that time. He was also actively involved in many other projects both in Paris and among the Songhay. So he proposed to Dieterlen that he would act merely as her cameraman and only for the first year or two, before finding someone else to work with her. But, as things turned out, he became progressively drawn into the project, eventually shooting the entire cycle and sharing the directorial role with Dieterlen.[15]

Despite the obstacles put in their way by the recently independent Malian government, which was unhappy about this recording of "tribalism," as well as by Muslim Dogon who disapproved of traditional religious practices, and even by the threat of great encampments of tourists attracted in large numbers to the event, Rouch and Dieterlen went back to the Bandiagara Escarpment year after year, not only to shoot but also to screen the material shot the previous year and listen to the feedback from the Dogon. This was not without its problems: when individuals who had died in the interim appeared in shot, some members of the audience would begin to cry. There were also certain sequences that the men were concerned that the women should not see. Rouch overcame these problems by the simple expedient of putting his hand over the projector lens.

After six years, they brought one of their principal informants, Amadigné Dolo, back to Paris and worked with him in the edit suite. But then they suffered something of a set-back in the seventh and final year: the

Malian government forbade them to film since the country was in the grip of an intense drought and it was deemed inappropriate to record the celebration of festivities in which large quantities of millet beer would inevitably be consumed. Rouch and Dieterlen therefore had to content themselves with returning the following year, 1974, and filming a highly reduced reconstruction of the event.

Rouch allowed himself to become more involved in this project despite his initial reservations because, like Griaule before him, he became fascinated by the prospect of unraveling the "mystery" of the Sigui. When Dieterlen and he began, having only the oral accounts collected by Griaule to go on, they were not even sure how long the cycle lasted—it could have been anything between four and eight years. But as the project proceeded, they gradually identified a pattern that was rather different from the one that Griaule had originally discerned. In doing so, they were greatly aided by the fact that they were able to witness the complete sequence of ritual events, something that no Dogon would normally get to do. For the Dogon themselves are normally forbidden to see more than three stages of the Sigui, that is, the celebration in their own villages, in the villages from which their villages receive the Sigui and in the villages to which their own villages pass it on.

At first, the Dogon were disturbed by the fact that Rouch and Dieterlen would see more than three stages, and they insisted that they consult the Pale Fox, a powerful trickster spirit of great importance in Dogon cosmology and associated with a local nocturnal species of fox. The consultation took the form of a conventional Dogon oracular procedure. This involved drawing out a grid-like pattern in the sand at some distance from a village. With a few peanuts alongside as bait, this pattern was then left out overnight in the hope that it would be walked over by the Pale Fox. By the exact position of the animal's tracks across the pattern the following morning, the elders would be able to tell whether the Pale Fox approved of the project. In the morning, the anxious filmmakers returned to the scene to receive the verdict. Although certain difficulties were foreseen (correctly, as it turned out), the decision turned out to be favorable and Rouch and Dieterlen were given permission to continue with the filming for the full seven years.[16]

The overview that this witnessing of the complete sequence afforded, in combination with the information that they gathered both from the public feedback screenings among the Dogon, and from Ambara and Amadigné, their specialist informants, gave Rouch and Deiterlen a privileged insight into the significance of the Sigui. They were also greatly assisted by the fact that they were able to view the rushes repeatedly in the edit suite, progressively refining their understandings of the full ritual cycle as they went along. In effect, whereas even a Dogon elder would generally only have witnessed the enactment of the Sigui at most twice, and then only for part of the cycle, Rouch and Dieterlen were not only able to see the whole cycle but, due to the filmic record, to see it many times over. This placed them in a uniquely advantageous position to offer a comprehensive anthropological interpretation of the event.

As a result of these repeated viewings, Rouch and Dieterlen realized that although many features of the celebration were the same from one year to the next, there were also significant variations. This provided them with a vital clue in detecting a narrative thread running through all seven stages of the Sigui. What they concluded, in summary, as reported by Rouch, was that the Sigui represented the enactment of the various stages of the epic Dogon myth of origin, which, in turn, paralleled the various stages of the human life cycle as the Dogon conceive it. Thus the first year referred to the origin of Death in primeval times when the first ancestor to die was crushed by the sandstone pillar, the second year referred to his funeral, while the third referred to his *dama*, a major ritual event that takes place approximately every five years among the Dogon in order to lift the mourning for those who have died in the interim and to send them definitively to the Land of the Dead. The fourth year of the Sigui referred to sexual procreation and the origins of language, the fifth to birth and the sixth to motherhood and nurturing. Finally, the seventh and final year referred to male circumcision. Taken as whole then, as outlined by Rouch, the Sigui appears to represent a collective triumph over death, not just by the physical process of birth but by the cultural forms of language, nurturing, and finally, circumcision, which is conceived as the ritual launching of a new generation.[17]

In presenting his interpretation of the Sigui, Rouch acknowledged that it was merely a working hypothesis about which not even he and Dieterlen were entirely agreed.[18] Certainly, there would appear to be many other possible strands of interpretation concerning the precise role of the societies associated with the extraordinary Dogon masks, for example, or about intergenerational relationships and political organization, or about the significance of the event in the context of gender relationships. Moreover, there are some more general theoretical questions that one might raise about the status of such explanations of ritual from a privileged perspective not available to any active participant.[19] But these are matters that should be left to others with more specialist knowledge of this particular cultural region. Here, the primary concern is not with the hermeneutics of the ritual event as such but rather with the filmmaking methods employed in this project.

The Praxis of the Sigui Filming Project

The Dogon material was first produced as a series of individual films, each corresponding to a different year of the Sigui. Rouch and Dieterlen are credited as the codirectors of all the films, while Gilbert Rouget is also credited in some sources with the codirection of the film corresponding to the first year, *L'Enclume de Yougou* (*The Anvil of Yougou*, 1967; see fig. 11.1 above). Rouch added a voice-over commentary only for the third film in the series, *La Caverne de Bongo* (*The Cave at Bongo*, 1969), giving up this practice when the Dogon complained in the feedback screenings that his voice prevented them from hearing what they themselves were saying. Some years later, in 1981, these individual films were amalgamated into what is often referred to as the "Sigui synthèse." This is a sort of shorthand for the very lengthy formal title, which is *Sigui 1967–1973: L'Invention de la parole et de la mort* (*Sigui 1967–1973: The Invention of Speech and of Death*). For this amalgamated version, the material presented in the series of individual films was reduced to just under half its total running time. With the addition of an introductory section outlining the history of the Dogon and their principal rites of passage, the result is a film with a running time of approximately 120 minutes.[20]

In both forms, these films are highly descriptive, representing in some ways a surprising reversion to the praxis of the films that Rouch made in the initial phase of his career. There are, to be sure, certain differences due to the technological advances made in the interim: the material is shot with synchronous sound, and Rouch makes abundant use of lengthy sequence-shots, particularly in the early films. But for all the technological advantages of the new equipment, the cinematography, taken as a whole, is not only rather unsophisticated but also strangely disengaged. For much of the time, the camera remains outside the action, a seemingly distant and uncertain observer. This is true even for the later films by which time, one might assume, Rouch would have got to know the subjects relatively well. Although the content of the images is undoubtedly highly dramatic and engaging, their execution is often unsteady and wavering. Rouch being resolute in his determination not to use a tripod, there are many shaky shots of both the dramatic cliff faces of the Bandiagara Escarpment and of the ritual action. Notwithstanding his strictures at other times regarding the zoom lens, there are quite a number of awkward examples of its use in these films.

In the "Sigui synthèse," the material is held together by an almost constant voice-over commentary. This is performed by Rouch himself and fulfils various different functions: it describes the progress of the film project itself, it provides some historical background, it explains what is going on at any given moment and it identifies the various locations through which the event is passing. It also paraphrases what people are saying in the few passages of conversation that occur in the film and provides some relatively straightforward interpretations of the symbolic significance of the ritual paraphernalia, the sinuous, snakelike movements of the columns of dancers, and so on. Perhaps the most striking use of the voice-over is the paraphrasing of the dancers' chanting and the elders' recital of the *sigi so*, the ritual language of the Sigui. To distinguish this ritual chanting from the more informational or interpretative passages of commentary, Rouch performs these passages in a more poetic, reiterative manner (fig. 11.2).

But notwithstanding these changes of tone and Rouch's undeniable virtuosity as a verbal performer, it has to be said that after a certain period the constant sound of his voice will seem rather wearing to some viewers. In that it acts as a barrier to direct engagement with the action of the film, it serves to reinforce the distancing effect produced by the disengaged cinematographic style. Given that he was by now working with fully synchronous sound, Rouch could have reduced his dependence on voice-over by using subtitles for both the chanting and the conversational passages if he had wanted. But as I noted in the previous chapter, he retained a lifelong antipathy to subtitles on the grounds that they "mutilate" the image and cannot capture the full meaning of what is being said.

Perhaps even more surprising than these relatively banal technical features is the absence of any clearly established characters in these films. After all, these films were made many years after Rouch's ethnofictional methods had radically transformed ethnographic film praxis by giving names, identities, and voices to a group of principal characters and by building the central narrative around them. During the early part of the Sigui project, Rouch was even simultaneously shooting *Petit à Petit*, which—for all its possible shortcomings, as discussed in the previous chapter—undeniably involves an intimacy and a direct personal engagement with the principal characters of the kind that had characterized Rouch's all Songhay films to a greater or lesser extent since *Bataille sur le grand fleuve*. But in the Sigui films, although a few of the most eminent men are named (notably Anaï Dolo, said to be 120 years old and witnessing his third Sigui, the first having been sensed while he was still in his mother's womb), there is no systematic attempt to establish any characters. Apart from a few rare moments, such as when some elders explain the significance of certain cave paintings, no subject ever addresses the camera.

Women are particularly noticeable by their absence in the Sigui films,

FIGURE 11.2. An elder chants the *sigi so*, the ritual language of the Sigui. © Fondation Jean Rouch.

other than as occasionally glimpsed spectators, though, as noted above, there are some important exceptions to this. For, throughout the cycle, the male dancers are joined by a number of *yasigine*, "the women of the Sigui," representing the ancestress Yasigui who participated in the first mythical enactment of the event. The *yasigine* are identified by the fact that they are holding an elaborately carved wooden staff surmounted by a half-gourd. This, as Dieterlen explains elsewhere, represents the ladle

FIGURE 11.3. *Left*, one of the *yasigine*, literally "women of the Sigui," holding the staff surmounted by a half gourd that is the emblem of their office. *Right*, a male dancer wearing women's jewelry. © Fondation Jean Rouch.

that Yasigui used to serve the male dancers with the millet beer prepared by the women at the first Sigui (fig. 11.3).[21]

There are also some interludes in the dancing when present-day Dogon women are shown supplying beer and also food to the dancers, or helping them dress in their ritual paraphernalia, which, interestingly enough, often consists of the women's own clothing and jewelry. But these interludes are covered in no more than a brief and distant manner by Rouch, and although he does link the remarkable transvestism of the male dancers in the latter phases of the Sigui to the themes of motherhood and nurturing, which are particularly pronounced at this stage of the cycle, he does not comment in the voice-over commentary on this striking displacement of women from a rite celebrating the collective rebirth of Dogon society.[22]

When challenged some years later about the absence of women in his African films, Rouch explained that it was quite impossible for a European man to film African women, since this would not be permitted by the local people. His own work among the Songhay contradicts this assertion to some extent, but this may well have been true in the case of the Dogon, whom he did not know so well. But even if there had not been any gender-related problems of access during the shooting of the Sigui films, it seems unlikely that women would have appeared in them to any great extent because the films are almost exclusively concerned with the ritual action itself, in which women play only a minor part. Although there are some sequences showing the preparation of the masks and other ritual paraphernalia by the men, and regular references to the ritual preparations of the male *olaburu* dignitaries who officiate during the ceremonies, there is only passing reference to the vast amount of labor that would have been required to prepare all the food and drink that is consumed during the event and which would primarily have been the responsibility of the women.[23]

Indeed, more generally, apart from some brief contextualization at the beginning of the "Sigui synthèse," there is no attempt to set the Sigui cycle within the everyday life of the Dogon, nor within any broader political or organizational context of Dogon society. The impingement of the wider world does break through at various points, but this is not because Rouch sought out these broader contexts but because their influence makes itself felt even when the Dogon are celebrating this most traditional of ceremonies. In fact, as is explained at the beginning of the "Sigui synthèse," many of the participants are migrants who have returned for the event from Abidjan and Accra, and there is even a brief shot in one of the later films of a number of them arriving with suitcases in their hands. For most of the time, however, these migrants are indistinguishable from their fellow Dogon since almost all the men are dressed in an identical traditional ritual costume. It is therefore almost surprising to discover, after a village chief dies and, as is customary, a mortuary mannequin in his likeness is set up on the roof of his house, that this mannequin is dressed in a modern soldier's uniform and helmet because, it transpires, the deceased had once served in the French colonial army (fig. 11.4).

But the most significant allusion to the presence of the wider world in these films does not take the form of such indices of modernity as dress and fashionable music as had been the case in the migration ethnofictions, *Jaguar* and *Moi, un Noir*. Instead, this wider world makes its presence felt most directly in the form of the threat to the continuation of the Sigui represented by the conversion of many Dogon to Islam. Thus toward the end of the film relating to the third year, we discover, in no more than a brief glimpse, that directly overlooking the plaza where the dancers have been enacting the memorial *dama* of the first culture hero, there is a new mosque with bright white walls and a gleaming star on top. Later, and more substantially, in the film relating to the sixth year, the

FIGURE 11.4. The mortuary mannequin of a recently deceased chief, testifying to his time as a soldier in the French colonial army. Both French and Malian flags are entwined around the flagpole. But the shawl of the mannequin is covered in traditional protective charms, while behind is the skin of a goat sacrificed in the deceased's honor. © Fondation Jean Rouch.

dancers make a dramatic about-face when they reach the point beyond which the Sigui cannot travel since it is no longer welcome in the Dogon villages further to the west since they have all converted to Islam.

At first sight, it seems rather extraordinary that twenty years later, and at a time when he was being fêted in Paris as one of the most innovative of contemporary French filmmakers, Rouch should be making films in a manner reminiscent of the praxis of the first phase of his career. In part, this might be explained by the fact that in many ways, Rouch found himself in the same situation with respect to the Dogon in the late 1960s as he had been with respect to the Songhay in the 1940s. For although he had some previous experience of the Dogon and considerable academic knowledge of their way of life, he did not have a personal network of the kind that he had developed over the years among the Songhay. Nor did he have any substantial knowledge of the Dogon language. As he frankly admitted, although they employed interpreters and even had a Dogon sound recordist, Ibrahim Guindo, during at least some phases of the shooting, it was frequently the case that neither he nor Dieterlen had any idea about what was going on as the ritual event was actually taking place. Often, it was only later in the edit suite or at one of the feedback screenings that they realized the significance of what they had recorded.

This lack of familiarity with Dogon society in general and the Sigui in particular, might well account for some of the uncertainty in Rouch's camerawork. But there are undoubtedly some more significant reasons for the particular outcomes of the Sigui films. Firstly, as Dieterlen's account of the project makes clear, the principal intention of the project was precisely *not* to make a character-led documentary but rather to produce a "document" in the classical Maussian-Griaulian manner. This document, she acknowledges, could later be edited and reconstructed for a general public, but the main purpose of the Sigui film project, at least as she conceived it, was to record the event as comprehensively and accurately as possible so that it could serve as the material for feedback screenings with the subjects.[24]

Secondly, but relatedly, many of the characteristics that I have described—the heavy emphasis on the exegesis of ritual performance, the absence of any systematic treatment of the organizational or political aspects of the event, the relative neglect of the everyday life of women and of work—echo the comments that have often been made by Anglo-Saxon scholars about the textual accounts of the Dogon produced over five decades by Griaule, Dieterlen, and their colleagues. Thus James Clifford, reiterating the views of Mary Douglas, observes that despite the comprehensiveness of the documentation, the account of the Dogon by the Griaulian team remains "curiously skewed" with little attention to "just how daily life is conducted, how circumstantial political decisions are actually made." The heavy emphasis on elaborately cross-referenced native theories of ontology and cosmology in Griaule's work, Clifford suggests, "never satisfies the nagging question: What are the Dogon really like?"[25] Much the same could be said of the Sigui films, suggesting that in this respect also we may detect the continuing influence of Griaule on his former student. After all, these films had originally been commissioned by Griaule, and Rouch made them in close collaboration with Griaule's long-term colleague and companion, Germaine Dieterlen. Indeed, the Sigui films could even be interpreted as an extraordinary *hommage* to Griaule, which in its sheer potlatch extravagance, masked the ambiguity that is sometimes evident in the sentiments that Rouch expressed about his late mentor.

Yet whatever the precise reasons for the form of these films, it is difficult to avoid the conclusion that relative to the vast amount of time and energy that Rouch expended in the filming of the Sigui, the final outcome is somewhat disappointing. It would seem, almost tragically, that the sheer volume of the material that he shot on the Sigui rather overwhelmed him. In a manner that is poignantly reminiscent both of the inability of Griaule and Dieterlen to get beyond the first volume of their masterwork on Dogon belief, *Le Renard pâle*, and of the many unfinished projects of his more distant intellectual ancestor, Marcel Mauss, it would appear that Rouch never managed to bring this, the most ambitious of his ethnographic film adventures, fully under his control.[26]

After the Sigui

Rouch completed the filming of the Sigui cycle in 1974, marking the end of a period of intense filmmaking activity. For, almost incredibly, the Sigui films were not the only films that Rouch made during the years in which the Sigui was taking place. In addition to shooting *Petit à Petit* back in Paris and reediting *Jaguar*, Rouch had continued to visit the Songhay throughout this phase of his career, shooting a large number of documentation films about spirit possession rites, as described in the last chapter. He even shot three other films among the Dogon. All three were on ritual subjects, and while one was a relatively short work of eighteen minutes, the others were major works of an hour or more in duration. Although these later Dogon films are more tightly structured than the Sigui films, they are similar in terms of general cinematographic praxis. That is, they are highly descriptive, featuring many long sequence-shots and a sonorous voice-over, with little development of character.

FIGURE 11.5. Dancers in *kanaga* masks (*left*) and in the longer *serige* masks, in the form of vertical snakes (*right*), during the *dama* for Ambara Dolo in 1974. (*Compare with Griaule's photographs in fig. 2.1 above, taken forty years earlier.*) © Fondation Jean Rouch.

Two of these late Dogon films concern funerals, namely, those of the ancient Anaï Dolo, who died in 1971, by then reputedly 123 years of age, and of the Hogon, who had first authorized the filming of the Sigui. The latter died suddenly in 1973 when Rouch just happened to be in Sanga.[27] Germaine Dieterlen is credited as codirector of both the film about Anaï's funeral and the third film made during this period, *Le Dama d'Ambara*. Shot in 1974, though not edited until 1980, this latter film concerns the *dama* for Ambara Dolo, who had appeared in the Sigui cycle films and who had acted as an informant, first with Griaule and later with Dieterlen and Rouch, since 1931. In contrast to the Sigui, the *dama* was a ceremony that Griaule had witnessed personally and that he had described in some detail in *Masques dogons*. Indeed, the continuity over time of the ceremony was so great that Rouch was able to base certain passages of the voice-over of *Le Dama d'Ambara* directly on Griaule's text, despite the fact that it had been written some forty years previously (fig. 11.5).[28]

Fittingly perhaps, given the reconnection with the work of Griaule, this spectacular, though somewhat disjointed, film on Ambara's *dama* brought Rouch's Dogon filmmaking to an end. Rouch was by now in his mid-fifties, and after such a vast expenditure of creative energy, it would have been quite understandable if he had been feeling somewhat anomic.

Indeed, many years later, he confessed that he did not know quite what to go on to at this point.[29] Certainly, the mid-1970s, marking the mid-point of his filmmaking career, represented something of a watershed for Rouch. Although he would continue to be extremely active into an advanced old age, shooting around forty-five films in the second half of his career, almost a third of his total oeuvre, and including a significant number of substantial feature films, the nature of his output was significantly different from that of the films from the first half of his career. The most noticeable difference is that ethnographic documentaries soon disappear from the repertoire. Rouch continued to work in the edit suite on his Dogon funerary films and on the "Sigui synthèse" for a number of years, but these had all been completed by 1981. Similarly, he continued for a while to make short documentaries about the Songhay but the last of these was shot no later than 1979. Instead, he dedicated an increasing amount of time to making fictional feature films.

In the first half of his career, Rouch had made a total of seven fictional features: two with his friends Damouré and Lam (*Jaguar* and *Petit à Petit*), two in Abidjan (*Moi, un Noir* and *La Pyramide humaine*), and his three New Wave films set in Paris. But in the second half of his career, he completed five more films with Damouré and Lam, though with the Bella shepherd, Tallou Mouzourane, replacing the Sorko fisherman, Illo Gaoudel, as the third of the troika of leading players. Rouch also made five other fictional feature films without his Nigerien friends, three of them in Paris, one in Italy, and one in Senegal. All of these films were made employing Rouch's usual improvisational methods and often in collaboration with young filmmakers. Two of the latter, *Folie ordinaire d'une fille de Cham* (1987) and *Bac ou mariage?* (1988), were based on preexisting theatrical works and therefore had a script. But, as in the shooting of *Gare du Nord* back in 1964, Rouch arranged to shoot these scripts in real time, therefore placing the requirement for improvisation onto the filmmakers with the all the attendant benefits, as he saw it, of risk and chance.[30]

However, Rouch also began to make films in what were, for him, entirely new genres. One of these consisted of a series of portraits of his friends or acquaintances. In terms of their general praxis, these films, which number about twelve, mostly involve what are, essentially, interviews between Rouch and the subject, or perhaps more accurately, conversations, sometimes conducted while walking, and shot as a series of sequence-shots. In some cases, a second camera crew is at work, filming Rouch in conversation with his subjects or even as he himself films. Although these films are ostensibly portraits of third parties, Rouch appears to be using them to take stock of his own life at this juncture.

The first three portrait films, shot between 1973 and 1977 are all sub-titled *Hommage à Marcel Mauss*, indicating an interest on Rouch's part to reconnect with the roots of his own anthropological inspiration. These films are about former pupils of Marcel Mauss—Tara Okamoto, a distinguished Japanese sculptor, Paul Levy, a similarly distinguished French theologian and sociologist, and most significantly of all, Germaine Dieterlen. A somewhat different form of self-assessment appears to be taking place in his 1978 portrait of his "friend" Margaret Mead at home in the Museum of Natural History in New York. A curiosity of this film is that the sound was recorded by John Marshall, the celebrated North American ethnographic filmmaker, who appears briefly in shot at the end of the film to perform a "mike tap." Two years later, Marshall again acted as Rouch's sound recordist in the shooting of a portrait of Captain Mori, a Japanese merchant marine captain who opened up the first commercial line between Japan and South Africa.

The shades of mortality hover around these portrait films, very explicitly in the case of the portrait of the Iranian historian Farouk Gaffary, shot in 1977 at what was then known as the Shah's Mosque in Isfahan. They are also present, somewhat less so but still hauntingly, in the conversation between Rouch and two fellow members of what he calls the European "ciné-mafia," Henri Storck and Joris Ivens. This latter film was shot in 1980, at Katwijk an Zee, a small seaside village near Amsterdam where Ivens had made his first and only fiction film, *Breakers*, some fifty years before. At one point, as the film was being shot on his birthday, May 31, Rouch suggests that they compare their ages: he is sixty-three, Storck is seventy-two, and Ivens is eighty-one.

The last three of Rouch's portrait films, shot between 1994 and 1999, are all dedicated to Germaine Dieterlen, showing her first at home, recollecting the time of her entry into the field of ethnology in 1920s, then in the field among the Dogon, and finally, in a film made a few weeks after her death at the age of ninety-five, showing Rouch himself as he evokes her memory by walking around her apartment in the company of Brice Ahounou, considering the objects that she had collected during her lifetime.

An entirely different genre, and also new for Rouch, is represented by a series of more poetic films, around ten in number, that he began to make in the late 1980s. Some of these films are poetic in form, others refer to poems, and some combine both. They deal with the most diverse subjects: the Arctic as perceived by Rouch while traveling through the ice floes on a Swedish icebreaker; a series of "ciné-poems" about Paris inspired by the early twentieth-century French symbolist poet Paul Fort;

in one film, the architect Gustave Eiffel's bridge across the River Douro at Porto is the subject while, in another, it is his famous Tower in Paris, illuminated for its centenary.

These more poetic films also include two portraits of museums, which like the portraits of individuals, mostly consist of a series of sequence-shots. One of these offers a portrait of the magnificent African art collection in the Fondation Maeght museum in Saint-Paul-de-Vence, not far from Nice, while the other is a portrait of Henri Langlois's Musée du Cinéma, then still located just across from the Musée de l'Homme, in other wing of the Palais de Chaillot. This was a place that was particularly dear to Rouch as he had visited it frequently in the dark days of the German Occupation at the same time as he was attending Griaule's lectures in the Musée de l'Homme. Two weeks after the completion of this film, the Musée du Cinéma was devastated by a fire and, in another *memento mori*, Rouch entitled the film *Faire-part*, a reference to the posters that are traditionally put up in French villages to announce the death of a member of the community.

At the same time as continuing to produce films at a remarkable rate, Rouch also travelled ceaselessly around the world, presenting his films in a broad variety of venues, often premiering them at prestigious film festivals, such as those in Berlin or Venice, but also screening them at more modest academic gatherings, such as the International Festival of Ethnographic Film of the Royal Anthropological Institute, first in London in 1985 and later at Manchester in 1990. Following the issuing of 8.5 hours of his principal works on video by the French Ministry of Foreign Affairs in 1981, retrospectives of his work were organized in forty-six different countries. Other lengthy retrospectives followed at Florence, Turin, and in Paris.[31]

By this stage, Rouch had become something of a *monstre sacré*, and he was showered with honorary degrees, lifetime achievement awards, and other such accolades by academic institutions, professional bodies, and film festivals all over the globe. From 1981 to 1985, he taught a series of summer sessions at Harvard University; from 1986 to 1991, he was president of the Cinemathèque française. He was also active in various UNESCO initiatives both in Paris and elsewhere. He played a leading part in setting up two of the most important documentary festivals in France, first the Cinéma du Réel at the Centre Georges Pompidou in 1977, and later, in 1981, the Bilan du Film Ethnographique festival at the Musée de l'Homme which, most fittingly, has recently been renamed in his honor as the Festival International Jean Rouch. And yet, ironically, although he may have been personally lionized, and his past work enthusiastically celebrated wherever he went, the films that he continued to make at this time did not, in general, receive the same degree of critical acclaim as the principal films from the first half of his career.

Two of the ethnofictions that he made with Damouré, Lam, and Tallou during the second half of his career did enjoy a certain degree of success. These were *Cocorico! Monsieur Poulet* (1975) and *Madame L'Eau* (1992). Although separated considerably in time, they both revolve around the theme of the ingenuity of Africans in adapting imported technology to their own needs. In the first case, the technology concerned is a Citroën 2CV van that Lam, as in real life at the time, used in his poultry wholesale business. With the help of Damouré and Tallou, he adapts the Citroën to local conditions, which includes floating it back and forth across the Niger River in three different ways because he does not have the necessary official permits to use the bridge. In the other film, *Madame L'Eau*, the technology at issue is a windmill-driven irrigation pump, which the intrepid adventurers go to Amsterdam to find and then bring back to apply to their drought-wracked fields. Both films are intended to be comedies, and although for my own personal taste, they suffer from the same ponderous humor and hammy acting as *Petit à Petit*, it seems that *Cocorico!* did very well at the box office in Africa.[32] Meanwhile, *Madame L'Eau* was well received by certain audiences in Europe, and in 1993 was awarded the International Peace Prize at the Berlin Film Festival.[33]

However, some of the other fiction films that Rouch made in this period of his career were quite unambiguous flops. Perhaps the most extreme example was *Dionysos*, released in 1984 and scripted by Rouch himself. The story is constructed around the arrival in Paris, in disguise, of the Greek god of nature and Bacchanalian celebration, Dionysos, to defend a thesis about the influence of Nietzsche on de Chirico before a doctoral committee in the courtyard of the Sorbonne. This he does successfully, leading to the sudden appearance of African spirit possession dancers. In the latter part of the film, he runs a workshop manufacturing Citröen 2CVs in the form of various animals of Greek mythology before finally escaping back to nature in the Bois Meudon when his disguise is discovered. Intended as some sort of fable about the continuing importance of giving free rein to the imaginary, even in industrial society, this film proved that Rouch's interest in Surrealist ideas and his association of these ideas with African ecstatic performance remained as strong as ever, some fifty years after his Damascene conversion experience on the rue Montparnasse. Rouch was very proud of this film, seeing it as intimately linked to his ethnographic work, but although the eminent philosopher Gilles Deleuze singled it out for particular praise, other commentators, even those normally sympathetic to Rouch's work, such as René Prédal, subjected it to a severe critical mauling.[34]

It is possible that at some point in the future the films that Rouch made in the latter part of his career will come to be appreciated in a manner analogous to Beethoven's Late Quartets, now highly regarded but once considered a disappointing decline from the work of the great composer in his prime. Indeed, even now, some of those who approach the Rouchian canon from the perspective of cinema and the arts rather than from that of anthropology, regard his later fictional features as being of particular interest on account of their originality in the handling of cinematic time and in their implicit assault on conventional understandings of narrative. However, these are matters that are beyond the remit of this book, which is to examine Rouch's work as an ethnographic filmmaker, and I shall therefore leave it to others more qualified than I to consider Rouch's later works in this light.[35]

However these later works eventually come to be regarded, Rouch's reputation as an ethnographic filmmaker will always be sustained by the remarkable series of films that he produced in an extraordinary burst of creativity in the fifteen or so years following the release of *Cimetières dans la falaise* in 1951: *Les hommes qui font la pluie*, *Bataille sur le grand fleuve*, *Les Maîtres fous*, *Jaguar*, *Moi, un Noir*, *Chronicle of a Summer*, and *The Lion Hunters* will surely all remain classics of ethnographic cinema. Even were all his other films to pass into oblivion, this small handful of *chefs-d'oeuvre* would alone secure a permanent and preeminent place for Jean Rouch in the history of the genre.

Cinema in Defiance of Mortality

In December 2006, almost three years after his death, the Dogon of the village of Tyogou held a funeral ceremony for Rouch, a rare honor previously extended to few outsiders, though among these numbered both Marcel Griaule and Germaine Dieterlen. This event, which took place over three days, was attended by Rouch's widow, Jocelyne, and was recorded by the filmmaker Bernd Mosblech for a documentary film. As is the Dogon custom, a mannequin stuffed with straw representing Rouch, dressed as he so often was, in a blue shirt and khaki trousers, was set up on the roof terrace of a house in the village while in the plaza below, a cow was sacrificed and dancers wearing *kanaga* masks performed. The mannequin was then carried on a bier to be buried in the cliff face of the Bandiagara Escarpment and Rouch's much-loved Aaton camera was smashed, symbolically bringing to an end his life's work (fig. 11.6).[36]

However, although one of the ritual purposes of a funeral ceremony, as the Dogon conceive it, is to dispatch the souls of the deceased on their journey to the Land of the Dead, Rouch's immaterial presence will con-

FIGURE 11.6. The funeral of Jean Rouch, as recorded in *Ich bin ein weisser Afrikaner* (2008), directed by Bernd Mosblech. *Top,* A mannequin representing Rouch's body, dressed in his familiar blue shirt and khaki trousers, is first displayed on a house terrace and then carried to the cemetery, wrapped in the traditional Dogon shroud, protected by magic charms (*compare with fig. 11.4 above, also with fig. 4.3 above*). *Bottom,* Pangalé, one of Rouch's closest Dogon associates, prepares to smash his Aaton camera, thereby representing the end of his life's work.

tinue to be felt on the Bandiagara Escarpment for a good while yet. For, just as Griaule had asked him to make a film record of the Sigui ceremonies of 1967–1973, so too did Rouch arrange for two of his own students to film the next Sigui, which is due to run from 2027 to 2033. In approaching the CNRS to set aside funds for this, Rouch suggested that the study of the Sigui should be conceived on the model of the natural sciences, whereby an experiment must be repeated four times for its results to be considered valid. He argued that Griaule should be considered the first person to have conducted the experiment to understand the Sigui, Germaine Dieterlen the second, and himself the third. Some years before he died, he provided for his successors, Nadine Wanono and Philippe Lourdou, to carry out the fourth and final experiment in the sequence.[37]

If the Dogon conceive of the Sigui as being an act of collective defiance of mortality, as suggested by Griaule in the epigraph to this chapter, then Rouch thought of ethnographic filmmaking as being an enterprise of the same kind. On this matter, he liked to quote Henri Langlois, first president of the Cinémathèque française, who once observed that "filmmakers never die, for every time their work is screened, they come to life again." However distinguished Jean Rouch's contribution may have been to other arenas of cinema, not only was he a uniquely creative ethnographic filmmaker, but he was also one to the last, remaining committed to ethnographic filmmaking throughout his life—and beyond.

THE CRAFT OF ETHNOGRAPHIC CINEMA

Introduction: Totemic Ancestors

In parts 1 and 2, I sought to identify the principles underlying the ethnographic filmmaking praxis of Jean Rouch by examining the ways in which they are made manifest in particular films. In this final part, I propose to approach the matter from the opposite direction, that is, to identify those principles directly, referring back, when concrete examples are necessary, to particular films discussed earlier in the book. This third part has four chapters, which, consecutively, will treat Rouch's praxis during the conceptualization and production phases of making a film, his approach to editing and other aspects of postproduction, and the key notion of "shared anthropology." These four chapters are then followed by a general summary and conclusion reflecting on legacy that Jean Rouch has left to ethnographic filmmakers working today.

But first, in this introduction, I shall consider the degree to which Rouch's praxis was itself influenced by the legacy of two particular filmmakers of the generation prior to his own. These "totemic ancestors," as Rouch used to call them, were the Soviet Constructivist filmmaker Dziga Vertov and the so-called "father of documentary," Robert Flaherty.[1] Although Flaherty was about fifteen years older, Vertov and he were more or less direct contemporaries in terms of their filmmaking careers since both of them were active from just before 1920 to around 1950. They never met one another, nor, it seems, did Rouch meet either of them. Nor did they have much contact with the anthropologists of their day: Flaherty may have had some contact, but Vertov almost certainly had none. "And yet," Rouch claims in his manifesto-essay "The Camera and Man," "it is to these two filmmakers that we owe all of what we are trying to do today."[2]

If this appreciation seems fulsome, it is but a pale shadow of the extravagant praise that, some years before, Rouch had heaped on Vertov and Flaherty in the lengthy entry on ethnographic film that he wrote for *Ethnologie générale*, an encyclopedia published by Éditions Gallimard.[3]

Rouch's enthusiasm for these two filmmakers is readily understandable. One of them, Flaherty, trained first as an engineer, like Rouch himself, and both of them were poets by inclination—even if, in Flaherty's case, this was not a sobriquet that he would have claimed. Thus, as a pair Vertov and Flaherty neatly complemented the two sides of Rouch's own background and personality. However, in terms of practical filmmaking, there were not only a great many differences between the two of them but also between their respective praxes and that of Rouch himself.

DZIGA VERTOV AND THE THEORY OF CINÉMA-VÉRITÉ

The differences between the praxes of Rouch and Vertov are particularly marked. Born Denis Kaufman in 1896 in a region of Poland that was then under the control of the Russian Tsarist state, he was about twenty when he changed his name to Dziga Vertov, a composite of Ukrainian and Russian meaning "spinning top." Not long afterward, he began to learn the craft of filmmaking through working as an editor of the newsreels that were distributed by agit-prop trains across the newly formed Soviet Union. After four years of this experience, in 1922, he started a sort of newsreel newspaper that provided commentary on issues of topical interest. He called this *Kino-Pravda*, a name that combined the Russian word for the adjective "ciné," *kino*, and *pravda*, truth, also the name of the official Bolshevik newspaper. Along with his brother Mikhail Kaufman, a cameraman, and his wife, the film editor Elizaveta Svilova, Vertov was also a leading figure of a group who dubbed themselves the *Kinoki*, literally "ciné-eyes." In 1923, this group published a manifesto in which they declared that the ciné-camera had introduced an entirely new way of viewing the world that would transform the visual arts and offer its own distinctive kind of truth. This truth was to be represented not by reproducing the world through literal images but rather by a particular process of montage, juxtaposing or superimposing shots in conjunction with various special visual effects, such as time-lapse photography, split screens, fast or slow motion, even running shots backward. Through these juxtapositions and manipulations, a sequence of images could provide commentary on one another and on the world at the same time. For the Kinoki, this was the distinctive truth that could be reached through the cinema and, recycling the name that Vertov had earlier given to his newsreel newspaper, they referred to it as *kino-pravda*.[4]

In 1929, Vertov produced the film for which he is now best known, *Man with a Movie Camera*, a life-in-a-day film, primarily about Moscow but also with some sequences from elsewhere. This was intended as a vehicle for the theoretical ideas of the Kinoki and involved Vertov's brother

Mikhail as the eponymous cameraman and his wife Svilova as the editor. Both she and Mikhail appear in the film, as does the hypothetical audience of the film, giving it a highly reflexive quality that served to distinguish it from most of the many other "city films" that were being produced by European directors around this time.[5] Shortly afterward, in 1931, Vertov produced one of the first documentaries featuring natural sounds rather than music on the soundtrack. This was *Enthusiasm*, which celebrates the achievements of the Stakhanovite miners of the Don River valley who had overfulfilled their five-year-plan production quotas. The soundtrack of this film was also subjected to an editorial montage so that the sounds both comment upon one another through juxtaposition, or on the image, mostly in a contrapuntal or evocative manner. But there are also some passages in the film in which the sounds have been synchronized with the images in a very literal realist manner, notably in one scene in which a politician, shot in relative close-up, gives a morale-boosting address to the miners.[6]

But despite his evident sympathy for the Soviet project, after these two films, Vertov's work fell out of favor in his own country because its generally modernist, nonrealist character did not sit well with the increasingly stringent norms of Stalinist Socialist Realism. When he died prematurely of cancer in 1954, Vertov was a largely forgotten figure in the Soviet Union. In France, by contrast, his reputation was actively sustained by certain leading intellectual figures writing about film, notably by the Marxist cinema historian Georges Sadoul but also by Edgar Morin, who wrote about Vertov in his book, *Les Stars*, published in 1957. However, despite this general enthusiasm for Vertov and the theory of *kino-pravda*, or *cinéma-vérité*, as it was translated very literally in France, his films remained very difficult to get hold of and, probably for this reason, the French authors of the period appear to have had only a limited understanding of what the theory of *cinéma-vérité* actually meant in practice. For the aspect of Vertov's approach that Sadoul, Morin, and others celebrated was not his formalist, montage-based methods as such, but his commitment to making films about the everyday and the modern, captured *sur le vif*, taken directly from life, rather than acted out in a studio, as was the practice of his Russian contemporaries Lev Kuleshov and Sergei Eisenstein. On these grounds, Sadoul situated *cinéma-vérité* in a realist tradition of cinema initiated by the Lumières—a line of descent that he would later repudiate—while Morin associated *cinéma-vérité*—with what seems in retrospect to be a similar lack of appropriateness—with the work of Jean Renoir, the Italian Neorealist Luchino Visconti, and Flaherty.[7]

Although Rouch later claimed to have come across the work of Vertov in the immediate postwar period, given the scarcity of Vertov's films in

France at that time, his exposure to them could not have been very great. For this reason, it seems unlikely that he would have had any more profound understanding of the theory of *cinéma-vérité* than the likes of Sadoul and Morin. In any case, even though he may have had some familiarity with Vertov's work beforehand, it was only through working on *Chronicle of a Summer* with Morin in 1960 that Rouch developed a real enthusiasm for Vertov's ideas. But while Morin seems to have been aware of certain differences between the approach that he and Rouch adopted and that of Vertov, Rouch, by contrast, lost no opportunity thereafter to stress what he saw as the similarities between Vertov's ideas and what he himself was trying to do.[8]

Completely at odds with the idea current among some of his present-day admirers that Rouch should be considered some kind of postmodernist *avant la lettre*, the aspect of Vertov's ideas that particularly appealed to Rouch was the quintessentially modernist proposition that the invention of the cinematographic apparatus had offered an entirely new way of understanding the world:

> Dziga Vertov . . . understood that the cinematographic way of looking was highly distinctive, employing a new organ of perception, the camera, which bore little relation to the human eye, and which he called the "ciné-eye." Later, with the appearance of sound, he identified a "radio-ear" in the same way, as an organ specific to recorded sound. . . . . Taken as a whole, he called this discipline *cinéma-vérité* (cinema-truth), which is an ambiguous expression since, fundamentally, cinema cuts up, speeds up, slows down, thereby distorting the truth. For me, however, "cinema-truth" has a specific meaning in the same way that "ciné-eye" does, designating not pure truth, but the truth particular to recorded images and sounds: "ciné-truth."[9]

Rouch also strongly identified with Vertov's experimentalism, quoting with approval in his *Ethnologie générale* panegyric, Vertov's defense of *Man with a Movie Camera* against those who criticized it at the time of its release for lacking sufficient popular appeal. Asserting his right not just to make popular films, Vertov had declared that it was also necessary from time to time to make "*films that produce films* . . . They are a necessary pledge of future victories."[10]

But although there may have been these elements of common ground between Rouch and Vertov at a general theoretical level, their respective ways of putting these ideas into practice could not have been more different. In the first place, as Morin noted, in Vertov's work there is a certain voyeuristic quality. At the heart of the Vertovian project "to catch life unawares," there is the ambition to be a "camera-thief," to film his subjects without them knowing and without their consent.[11] Some more recent commentators on Vertov's work have suggested that there is a more sinister side to his project, arguing that it was not so much voyeurism that Vertov practiced as surveillance and, as such, the eponymous man with the movie camera is a fittingly iconic symbol of the surveillance society that the Soviet Union of the late 1920s was increasingly becoming. Vertov's concern, it has been alleged, was not so much to catch life "unawares" as to catch it "red-handed."[12] Even if this is somewhat overstating the case, there is no denying the fundamental difference between Vertov's attitudes and Rouch's notion of "shared anthropology," central to which is the idea that any filmmaking project should take place within a collaborative relationship between filmmaker and subjects.

It is also difficult to see how Rouch, an inveterate storyteller if ever there was one, could really be sympathetic to the "death sentence" that Vertov declared on all forms of storytelling in films on the grounds that it was a bourgeois hangover from the theater.[13] But an even more fundamental difference concerns the precise nature of the distinctive truth that each thought the cinema could produce. For Vertov, this truth was primarily to be achieved in the edit suite: having used the camera to catch life unawares or red-handed, as the case may be, these little fragments of life were then to be subjected to intense manipulations in the edit suite through montage and special effects: it was in this way that "life facts" were to be transformed into "film facts."[14] In contrast, from a stylistic point of view, Rouch's films remained firmly within a realist register. Moreover, he was usually resistant to any wholesale manipulation of the original rushes in the edit suite. Montage of the kind in which juxtaposed individual shots are intended to provide some sort of commentary on one another, is extremely rare in his oeuvre, and when it does occur, as for example, in *Les Maîtres fous*, it can probably be attributed to the influence of the editor.[15] Similarly, I cannot think of a single example in any of Rouch's many films of a special visual effect, apart from the slow-motion sequences that he used in some of his collaborations with the ethnomusicologist Gilbert Rouget and the freeze frame that occurs in *The Lion Hunters* when his camera broke down. There is certainly nothing so radical as Vertov's cameraman appearing out of the top of a giant tripod or curled up inside a full glass of beer.

When challenged on the stylistic differences between his own films and those of Vertov, Rouch claimed that the reason that he was not able to adopt Vertov's montage-based strategies was that with the development of synchronous sound, it was no longer possible to juxtapose shots as freely as had been the case in the silent era when Vertov was first working.[16] What he had in mind was something known to all film editors, namely that if one were to create a montage of brief shots, each with its corresponding segment of synchronous sound, the aural effect would be a horrible cacophonous hiccupping. But it could be argued that in giving this particular reason for not using montage, Rouch was, in effect, merely reasserting his commitment to a naturalistic form of realism since this explanation does not allow for the possibility of removing the synchronous sound altogether and replacing it with music or some other form of continuous sound effect bridging the whole montage sequence.

However, I would argue that the most fundamental difference between the praxes of Vertov and Rouch is not merely technical or stylistic but epistemological. For Rouch, it was not the perception of the world that was transformed through the cinematographic apparatus but rather the world itself. For him, the distinctive truths to be reached through cinema were not constructed in the edit suite but rather were brought to light by the presence of the camera in the real world. This came about as the subjects in front of the lens were provoked by the performance of the filmmaker behind the lens to put on a performance of their own that, in ideal circumstances, could provide access to the world of their imaginaries, the world of their dreams. The exact nature of these revelations would depend on the context. In the extreme case, his filming of African possession rituals could provoke the adepts to go into trance and behave in the manner of the spirit possessing them. Meanwhile, in his European films and in his ethnofictions, the characters could be persuaded by the presence of the camera to express intensely private thoughts and sentiments that they would otherwise have kept to themselves. This ambition to transform the world through the use of the camera is clearly very different from Vertov's predilection for "catching the world unawares."

But if Rouch's conception of cinéma-vérité was different from that of Vertov, it was also very different from the meaning given to the term on the other side of the Atlantic by a group of North American documentarists who, at precisely the same time as Rouch and Morin, were also experimenting with a new portable, sound-synchronous documentary filmmaking technology. For at least some of those involved in this group, now most commonly referred to as the Direct Cinema group, and whose best-known directors included Ricky Leacock, D. A. Pennebaker, and the Maysles brothers, the term cinéma-vérité referred not to some truth particular to the cinema but rather to a literal representational truth accessed through cinematic means. Whereas Rouch hoped that the presence of the camera would "catalyze" subjects into putting on revelatory performances, the Direct Cinema group aspired to reduce their impact on their subjects to as close to zero as possible in order to get at a truth unadulterated by the act of filming.[17]

In the first of a series of interviews conducted by the documentary filmmaker James Blue with practitioners of the new methods, Leacock, who had studied physics as a student at Harvard University, drew an analogy between the strategy of the Direct Cinema documentarists and that of a laboratory physicist: although a physicist is aware that the instruments used to measure a phenomenon may have an influence on that phenomenon, he or she not only aims to reduce this to a minimum but also controls for this in order to be able to gauge the true measurement as accurately as possible.[18] By contrast, Rouch believed that the presence of the camera would inevitably affect the performance of the subjects, however discreetly it was operated. But far from devaluing the material that had been filmed, as the Leacock analogy suggested, Rouch thought that this provocation of extraordinary behavior increased its value. "What has always seemed very strange to me," he commented in his interview with James Blue, "is that, contrary to what one might think, when people are being recorded, the reactions that they have are always infinitely more sincere than those they have when they are not being recorded."[19]

Blue conducted these interviews in the wake of a meeting that took place in Lyons in 1963 involving a number of leading French documentarists, including Rouch, as well as certain members of the Direct Cinema group, amongst whom numbered Leacock. The general purpose of the meeting was to exchange ideas and see if the two groups could iron out their differences. The results were inconclusive, almost inevitably, since the two groups started out from what were long-standing and essentially irreconcilable philosophical postures—idealist on the French side, empiricist on the Anglo-Saxon side. But what was agreed was that in order to avoid further confusion, the term *cinéma-vérité* would be abandoned. From then on, the French documentarists would refer to what they did as *cinéma direct* while the North Americans, who had previously used various terms to describe their approach, including "Free Cinema" and "Uncontrolled Documentary" as well as "Cinéma Vérité" (often without the hyphen, sometimes without the accents) or even simply "Vérité" (with or without the accents), would refer thereafter to what they did as "Direct Cinema."[20]

The "direct" in both new names signaled the ambition, held by both groups, to reduce the amount of mediation involved in documentary filmmaking. This referred not only to a reduction in the amount of equipment employed in making documentary films, which both sides acknowledged inhibited relationships between filmmaker and subjects, but also in terms of the amount of directorial intervention involved on the part of the filmmaker. For although Rouch and his French colleagues did not aspire to a situation in which the presence of the camera would have no influence on the behavior of the subjects, they did not generally seek to direct their behavior either. On the contrary, they considered it crucial that it should be the subjects themselves who decided what their performance for the camera should be since this choice in itself would be revealing of those inner realities that they hoped to be able to bring out by the act of filming.

In effect then, the change from *cinéma-vérité* to *cinéma direct* merely shifted attention from the outcome or goal of the endeavor, that is, truth in some guise or other, to the minimally mediated process whereby this was to be achieved. A considerable amount of confusion continued to reign, as some commentators, including Rouch himself on occasion, tended to equate the essentially epistemological concept of *cinéma-vérité* with the technical strategy of *cinéma direct*. Moreover, although Rouch generally stood by the agreement and avoided the use of the term *cinéma-vérité* after 1963, the change of nomenclature did not diminish in any way his attachment to Vertov's ideas. Rather than use the forbidden term, he simply flagged his continuing affiliation to the Vertovian epistemology by the liberal use of the prefix *ciné-* in his subsequent commentaries on his filmmaking praxis. Thus, for example, almost twenty years after the Lyons meeting, we find Rouch declaring in an interview with Enrico Fulchignoni:

> With the camera to my eye, I am the "mechanical eye" as Dziga Vertov used to say, while my microphone is an electronic ear. With a ciné-eye and a ciné-ear, I am ciné-Rouch in a state of ciné-trance engaged in ciné-filming . . . That then is the joy of filming, "ciné-pleasure" . . .[21]

Rouch continued to make similar declarations for the remainder of his life. Moreover, the Vertovian prefix has also been widely adopted by third parties who have written about his work or who have reproduced his films after his death. But, as I shall argue in greater detail when considering Rouch's ideas about the "ciné-trance" in chapter 12, this evocation of a Vertovian pedigree serves as much to obscure as to illuminate the precise nature of Rouch's filmmaking praxis.

ROBERT FLAHERTY AND SHARED ANTHROPOLOGY

The parallels between the praxes of Robert Flaherty and Jean Rouch are much closer than those between Rouch and Vertov: if there are differences, these are more differences of degree rather than of kind. As such, they are differences that are only too easy to overlook amid Rouch's generous acknowledgments of his debt to the filmmaker whom he describes in his *Ethnologie générale* article as "without doubt the most modest and the most gifted of all filmmakers."[22]

Rouch frequently related that as small child, he was taken to see *Nanook of the North* shortly after it was released in 1922. It was the first film that he ever saw, and it left an indelible mark upon him. In an interview given when he was over eighty years of age, Rouch remarked that he still thought of himself in bed at night as being like the dogs in the famous last sequence of the film, curled up in the snow in a howling gale, intercut with their master Nanook asleep inside the nearby family igloo. Rouch was particularly captivated, both as a child and as an adult, by Nanook's "unforgettable smile" since this more than anything had brought home to him that despite his exotic appearance and remarkable way of life, Nanook was a fellow human being.[23]

In addition to the general humanistic quality of Flaherty's filmmaking, Rouch much admired the fact that Flaherty acted as his own cameraman. Being an engineer by training himself, Rouch was also much impressed by Flaherty's technical ingenuity. This not only permitted Flaherty to shoot under the extreme conditions of northern Canada, but even to develop and print his rushes without electricity on the spot. This he did by using the light of the sun controlled via a small hole cut in the wall of his cabin on the shores of the Hudson Bay. He also edited his own material on location and continued to do so right up until his last film, *Louisiana Story* (1948), though by this stage he not only had an editor working with him, Helen van Dongen, but also a cameraman. This second cameraman was none other than Ricky Leacock, later to become a leading figure of the Direct Cinema movement, as described above. Although Leacock did much of the hard labor, Flaherty continued to shoot some of the material himself, even though he was by now well into his sixties.[24]

What Rouch particularly appreciated about Flaherty's technical competence was his willingness to try out new things, which clearly prefigured his own love of experimentation. In the *Ethnologie générale* article, Rouch takes pleasure in reporting that while shooting *Moana* in 1923–1924, Flaherty was one of the first filmmakers to use Panchromatic film, which, with the aid of colored filters, allowed him to capture the deep azure blue of the skies of the South Seas.[25] Later, when making *Man of Aran* in 1933–1934 on an island off the west coast of Ireland, he experimented with new sound-recording equipment on location only to find that most of these field recordings were unusable. He therefore took his protagonists all the way to London and recorded their conversations and their cries in a professional sound studio—anticipating by some twenty years Rouch's own work with Damouré and Lam in a professional sound studio in Accra.

But what impressed Rouch more than anything else about Flaherty's way of working was the nature of his relationship with his subjects. It was Flaherty's custom to spend at least a year living with or near his subjects in order to get to know them as individuals and to understand their way of life. In the case of the Inuit, before he began to film them, Flaherty had spent as much as ten years working as a mining engineer in the region in which they lived. In this way, he was, Rouch observed, "an ethnographer without knowing it and without intending to be."[26] Far from looking down on his subjects in a patronizing or racist manner, as was typical of the attitudes of other filmmakers of the day toward ethnographic Others, Flaherty looked up to them. It was entirely consistent with this attitude that he should seek to engage the Inuit in the making of *Nanook*. Deploying his technical skills, he converted his camera into a projector and screened his rushes back to the Inuit so that they could discuss how to go about filming the following day. In doing so, as Rouch put it in "The Camera and Man," "he did not know that, with absurdly inadequate means, he had just invented both 'participant observation' . . . and 'feedback' with which we are still so clumsily experimenting."[27]

But notwithstanding these generous accolades to his "totemic ancestor" and the self-deprecating remarks about his own work, Rouch took the practice of shared anthropology much further than Flaherty ever did. First of all, Rouch gave his collaborators a much greater role in devising the content of his films than Flaherty gave to Nanook and his fellow Inuit. Flaherty asked the Inuit to adjust their house constructions, subsistence activities, their dress, and even their personal identities according to the requirements of his film. As is well known, he also asked the subjects of his films to revive practices that they had long abandoned: walrus hunting in *Nanook*, tattooing in *Moana*, and basking shark fishing in *Man of Aran*. By contrast, although Rouch might set up an initial situation in shooting his ethnofictions, he then allowed the protagonists to improvise largely along the lines that they themselves saw fit. Outside of the ethnofictions, he neither directed his subjects nor asked them to dress up or to dress down in any special way. In this regard, he had no sympathy for Robert Gardner's concern that the protagonists in *The Lion Hunters* were wearing old army boots. He was also very critical of Asen Balikci for arranging for tin cans and other evidences of modernity to be removed from the Inuit camp when he was making *The Netsilik Eskimo* films.[28]

Second, although Flaherty customarily spent prolonged periods with his subjects prior to shooting and arranged feedback screenings not only with the Inuit but also the Samoan protagonists of *Moana* and possibly the Aran Islanders as well, his motivation in doing so appears to have been primarily pragmatic, that is, he wanted to make sure that his subjects understood the nature of his enterprise and in the light of this understanding, offered suggestions about what should be filmed. Above all, as he put it to Nanook and his Inuit companions, he wanted to establish that when they were actually filming, the "aggie," as the Inuit called the filmmaking process, "would come first." Thus whatever their immediate inclinations when confronted with a walrus, he wanted them to understand that they should wait until he gave the signal before they attempted to kill it.[29]

In Rouch's case, although feedback screenings also had certain pragmatic purposes of this kind, at the same time they represented very much more than that. In fact, as we shall discuss at greater length in chapter 15, they formed the ethical cornerstone of his praxis, representing what he called—in a phrase nicely evoking his Maussian inheritance—an "audiovisual counter-gift," that is, but one in a prolonged series of exchanges with his subjects that he maintained over the course of his whole life.[30] In Flaherty's case, once he had cut a film, he never returned—to the best of my knowledge—to screen it in the communities where he had worked, and he certainly never completed more than one film in the same community.[31] Rouch's commitment to the "feedback" process was much more long-term: he did not show his protagonists the rushes merely in order to determine the next day's shooting but would come back months, or even years later with the completed film and present that to his subjects. Following this screening, he and his subjects would then typically devise a further filmmaking adventure. In this way, one of Rouch's films led on to another, and his subjects became active stakeholders in the realization of his projects. In some cases, this collaboration extended over more than fifty years.

In summary, if a line of descent can be traced from Vertov and Flaherty to Rouch, it is only with respect to certain aspects of their respective praxes, even in the case of Flaherty. In fact, when one makes a careful comparison of his work with theirs, it is difficult to endorse Rouch's claim that these "totemic ancestors" provided him with a model of how he himself should go about the practical processes of filmmaking. I would suggest, rather, that Rouch liked to acknowledge them as precursors, not because he aspired merely to copy what they did in a practical sense, but because he identified with them as kindred spirits, as filmmakers who shared his single-minded commitment to the medium of film as a unique and unprecedented way of promoting humanity's understanding of itself.

12 : Inspired Performance

He who never fails, never risks anything. What is the most interesting thing in life? Very probably to run risks. That for me is our profession.

JEAN ROUCH, 1967[1]

For me, as filmmaker and ethnographer, there is practically no frontier be-tween documentary film and fiction film. Cinema, art of the double, repre-sents a transition from the real world to the world of the imaginary, while ethnography, the study of other peoples' systems of thought, involves a per-manent criss-crossing from one conceptual universe to another, a form of acro-batic gymnastics, in which losing your footing is the least of the risks.

JEAN ROUCH, 1981[2]

Risk, Improvisation, and Grace

Many professional filmmakers would maintain that the key to a suc-cessful shoot is careful planning in order to ensure that the project un-folds in a systematic way, on time and within budget. In this way, they would claim, one minimizes the risk of unanticipated problems, which cannot but be a good thing. Jean Rouch, however, had very different ideas. Although he was not averse to careful preparation, he believed that an essential requirement for any successful filmmaking adventure was the presence of some element of risk and chance, to which the film-maker would be required to improvise an inspired response. This was an attitude that, in his youth, Rouch had much admired in the Surrealist poets, whose surrendering to the "objective chance" of the *rencontre* and whose reliance on automatism in the moment of artistic creation were but two different methods by which they sought to unleash the creative potential of their imaginaries. It was also an attitude that, in a different way, Rouch had appreciated in the musical performances of the African

FIGURE 12.1. Rouch shooting *Jaguar* in 1954, probably in Kumasi Market, with the Bell & Howell Filmo 70 that he bought in the Paris Flea Market in 1946. He went on using this spring-wound 16mm camera right up to the period 1959–1960 when he was shooting *La Pyramide humaine*, a film that was later blown up to 35mm and distributed to commercial cinemas. © Fondation Jean Rouch.

American jazzmen, as expressed particularly in their ability, at the height of a concert, to engage in the most elaborate solo improvisations, seemingly breaking away completely from the underlying musical rules as well as the performances of their fellow band members, but at the same time eventually achieving the most remarkable and satisfying harmony.

Rouch sought to apply these same creative methods in a highly pragmatic way to his own work as a filmmaker, as he explained in one of his major interviews with Enrico Fulchignoni:

> When shooting a ritual (a Songhay possession dance, for example, or a Dogon funeral), the filmmaker encounters a complex and readymade *mise-en-scène*, though he usually does not know who is directing it. Is it the priest sitting on his chair, or that nonchalant musician, or is it the lead dancer with a rifle? But if he wants to record an event that is about to get going and cannot be stopped since it seems to be driven by its own principle of perpetual motion, he will have no time to find anyone to give him the necessary guidance. He has to create his own *mise-en-scène* out of the reality before him, improvising his framing, his camera movements and the length of his shots, all subjective choices, the only key to which

is his personal inspiration. And, certainly, a masterpiece can be created if the inspiration of the observer is in unison with the collective inspiration of those whom he is observing. But this is so rare, it requires such a connivance, that I can only compare it to those exceptional moments of a jam session between the piano of Duke Ellington and the trumpet of Louis Armstrong, or the electrifying encounters between strangers as described on occasion for us by André Breton.[3]

This passage provides a convenient synthesis of some of the key principles of Rouch's shooting praxis. If a shot is be successful, the cameraperson must think quickly on his feet about where to position himself, what or whom to follow, how to frame his shots and so on. But for the best possible result, it is necessary for there to be an inspired performance on *both* sides of the lens, by the subjects as well as by the filmmaker. Moreover, these performances by subjects and filmmaker must be "in connivance," that is, in some sense in unison with one another. There must be skill, but also risk. For if the cameraperson is to improvise a truly inspired performance, one that is in unison with the performance of the subjects, there must be something at stake. He must be, as Rouch put it on another occasion, "a little bit afraid."[4]

There was also one further condition that was necessary, in Rouch's view, for any filmmaking venture to be successful. This was the presence of the "capricious little devil" that he referred to as *"la grace."*[5] As Rouch uses the term *la grace*, it has nothing to do with good manners or elegance, nor with the Christian concept of moral grace. Rather, his use of *la grace* is an allusion to the condition that Friedrich Nietzsche referred to as Dionysian, a completely amoral state in which creativity is spontaneous and intuitive rather than rational. Rouch believed that this *grace* could not be learned, taught, or made to happen: it simply arrived suddenly on its own account, or not at all. But unless it were present, one might as well give up any thoughts of shooting because there would be no possibility of it turning out well:

What is very strange is that even those whom I am filming, even those who are watching me film, know whether my filming has been successful. When my African friends see me filming a ritual or whatever, they will come to me at the end and say, "Ah, Jean, today it was very good," and other times, they will come and say, "It didn't work!" But you cannot provoke *la grace*, from time to time it just happens. I have often been in a situation where I have started to film for five or six minutes, or a complete roll of ten minutes, and then I have had to give up on account of the lack of a subject. There was not the necessary contact; it's difficult to explain.[6]

Yet although Rouch may have thought of his filmmaking as being ultimately dependent on the vagaries of this Dionysian grace, this does not mean that he went about his work without any sort of preparation. On the contrary, whether he was shooting an ethnographic documentary or an ethnofiction, he believed that it was necessary to engage in meticulous preparatory work. In his 1968 contribution to the *Ethnologie générale* encyclopedia, even perhaps somewhat at odds with the ideal-typical description cited above, he insists that prior to filming a ritual, an ethnographer should find out as precisely as possible what is going to happen and should even draw out a diagram of the ritual action. A film about a ritual, he observes, should never be "a film of discovery."[7] But careful preparation, in Rouch's view, could only take one so far. In order for a shoot to work out well, it was still necessary to improvise an inspired performance once the event got under way.

This principle of carefully preparing the ground but then trusting to chance and Dionysian grace for an inspired performance in the actual moment of execution was one that Rouch applied to all his filmmaking activities, not only when shooting but also later, back in the edit suite.

Scripts in the Oral Tradition

Although he may have believed in careful preparation as a general principle, Rouch rarely produced anything resembling a formal shooting script. The great majority of his documentaries concerned ritual events and these, as anthropologists have been aware since the writings of Arnold van Gennep in the earliest days of the discipline, usually have their own internal narrative with a beginning, a middle, and an end. Therefore, in order to arrive at a coherent film narrative, a filmmaker need only follow the event and then truncate it later in the edit suite with the possible addition of some "topping and tailing" footage that provides some sociological or interpretative context.[8] Many of Rouch's ethnographic documentaries were of this kind, with *Les Maîtres fous* providing one of the best examples. Of the relatively few that were not about ritual events, the best-known and most complex are about hunting, initially of hippopotami and later of lions. But these films too were constructed around particular events with their own internal narrative structure, climaxing with the killing of an animal, even if, by a curious coincidence, in all Rouch's hunting films, it happened that the alpha male managed to get away.[9]

Even when shooting a fiction film, Rouch had little time for a formal written script. He often claimed that whenever he found himself obliged by producers or research grant-givers to present some kind of outline of what he intended to do, he always ended up doing something quite different.[10] It was in this regard particularly that he saw virtually no difference between documentary and fiction filmmaking. Cinema pundits often make platitudinous comments about the permeability of the boundary between fiction and documentary. Most such statements refer to the fact that while supposedly making a "claim on the real," documentaries are often conceived and executed in accordance with a language developed within fictional cinema. But in Rouch's case, the relationship was the other way around: he conceived and executed his fiction films as if they were documentaries, without a script and with minimal direction, relying primarily on the protagonists to determine the way in which the action of the film would develop.

In the case of his documentaries, Rouch chose the subject matter for his films either on the basis of his prior anthropological interests or because they were suggested to him by his subjects following a "feedback" screening of a previous film. But for the ethnofictions, Rouch claimed that his film ideas usually came to him by an altogether more mysterious route, one that he conceived in a manner that again can be traced to his Surrealist background. No elaborate conceptualization was involved— rather, out of the blue, an idea would come to him that simply demanded to be made into a film. Thus, for example, the idea for *Moi, un Noir* came to him suddenly one lugubrious Sunday evening in January 1957 when he was sitting in a bar in Treichville, the poor migrants' quartier of Abidjan, capital of the Ivory Coast. The contrast between the ephemeral gaiety of the migrants' weekend activities and the hard grind of their daily lives weighed heavily upon him that particular evening. But he realized that neither by shouting his concern in the streets, and certainly not by writing a book popularizing the results of the surveys of migration that he was carrying out at that time, would he ever be able to communicate the profound pathos of the migrants' situation. Rather, it came to him "as a necessity" that he should make a film in which it would not be his own voice that expressed this extreme contrast between joy and pain, but rather the voice of one of those very migrants for whom Treichville "was both heaven and hell."[11]

Yet what came into Rouch's mind on such occasions was usually no more than a general story line. Rather than write out a detailed script, he would discuss his idea in general terms with his protagonists and identify a series of possible scenes. At this point, a great deal of research could go into developing the idea, though Rouch had a tendency to omit mention of this, preferring instead to emphasize the spontaneity with which one of his film ideas emerged. For example, in the case of *Jaguar*, Rouch would often claim airily that all that had been decided before the shoot began was that it would begin and end at Ayorou and that the protagonists would give away everything that they had earned on the Gold Coast in a single day. But in fact, as described in chapter 5, some three years before the shoot, accompanied by the protagonists, Rouch went on a research trip to the Gold Coast that lasted several months and during which they visited many of the locations that would later appear in the film.[12]

The principal protagonists of Rouch's fiction films were usually nonprofessional actors whom he knew very well and with whom he had worked many times before. Their own lives in reality were often either very similar to or in some sense related to the lives of the characters that Rouch asked them to play in his films. This was true not only of his ethnofictions, but also of his New Wave fictions and his later fictional works as well. Damouré Zika and Lam Ibrahim Dia are the recurrent 'stars' of his ethnofictions from the 1950s to the 1990s, while Nadine Ballot, Modeste Landry and a number of the other protagonists of *La Pyramide humaine*, shot in 1959–1960 reappear in *Chronicle of a Summer* and the New Wave films that he made back in Paris in the years immediately thereafter. In *Dionysos*, released in 1984, not only do some of Rouch's African friends appear, but also Germaine Dieterlen, Enrico Fulchignoni, and even Jean Sauvy, his old comrade from the Jeanpierjant expedition almost forty years before.

Once on location, having agreed in a general way with the protagonists about what would happen in a given scene, Rouch would then aim to film them without direction or interruption. In this way, Rouch could have his cake and eat it too: there was a general story line that all parties were agreed upon, but in shooting it, there was still an element of unpredictability because he never quite knew how his protagonists were going to perform their improvisations. He could therefore apply the same shooting strategy as he applied to the shooting of ritual events as described in the Fulchignoni interview, that is, even though he may have a general idea about what was going to happen, in the actual moment of shooting, he would still have to rely on his own spontaneity and inspiration in coordinating his own performance with that of his subjects.

Rouch's way of managing the shooting of his ethnofictions has been well described by Philo Bregstein, a Dutch filmmaker who made one of the first documentary film portraits of Rouch back in the 1970s.[13] Subsequently, he became a friend and a collaborator with Rouch on a number of fiction films, most notably on the late work *Madame L'Eau*, released in 1992, in which Damouré, Lam, and Tallou Mouzourane visit Amsterdam. Bregstein therefore had many opportunities to observe Rouch at firsthand, and his account of the Rouch's way of working confirms the general point that although he did rely on spontaneity and chance in the moment of actual performance, there was usually considerable careful preparation beforehand.

For while it was true that Rouch did not usually write out a formal script, Bregstein describes how he would work everything out in advance with his protagonists orally, thereby creating what Bregstein calls "a script according to the oral tradition."[14] On the morning of a shoot, whether it was taking place in Niamey, in Paris, or elsewhere, Rouch liked to meet with his protagonists at breakfast to discuss what they would do that day. Then, prior to shooting, they would go to particular locations without the camera and research the *mise-en-scène* in a very pragmatic way. This could take a matter of hours, with the protagonists very carefully walking through their parts, even taking into account the positions and trajectories of an imaginary camera. In *Rouch's Gang*, a film about the making of *Madame L'Eau* directed by Steef Meyknecht, Dirk Nijland, and Joost Verhey, there is a sequence showing the researching of the *mise-en-scène* of a scene to be shot amid the sand dunes along the Dutch coast. Interestingly, Damouré is absent and it is only Rouch, Lam, and Tallou who are involved. They explain to the filmmakers that this is the usual pattern: the three of them work out the logistics of a scene beforehand and then rely on Damouré to improvise once the filming actually begins.[15] But although there would generally be this careful preparation of the practical logistics of the *mise-en-scène*, there would usually be no rehearsal as such, so that when it came to the actual shooting, Rouch was still reliant on improvisation by the protagonists. According to Bregstein, both Damouré and Oumarou Ganda, the "star" of *Moi, un Noir*, had the impression that Rouch did nothing more than follow what they themselves chose to do, while Safi Faye, who played the Senegalese prostitute in *Petit à Petit*, reports that even when she asked Rouch to direct her, he refused to do so.[16]

In addition to rejecting the idea of a formal script, Rouch also had a "golden rule" that all the scenes of an ethnofiction should be shot in the chronological order of the story line, with only one take and one angle per shot.[17] In actual practice, as for example in the case of *La Pyramide humaine* described at length in chapter 6, under pressure from a producer wary about the budget or concerned about the coherence of the plot, Rouch would sometimes find himself obliged to shoot scenes out of their chronological order. But these were deviations from what he regarded as the ideal that he tried to avoid whenever he could. What he also tried to avoid, whether he was shooting a documentary or an ethnofiction, was the second take, that is, asking his protagonists to do something more than once. Every shot, he believed, should be an "unrepeatable adventure," since it was only in this way that in the moment of shooting would there be the elements of chance and risk that he considered essential to an inspired performance. Again, Rouch's actual practice did not always live up to the aspiration—one thinks particularly here of the seven takes of the first sequence shot of *Gare du Nord*, as described in chapter 9—but this does not detract from the importance to him of the "no second take" rule as an ideal.[18]

As the film progressed, Rouch and his protagonists always remained open to new ideas, with the result that the "script in the oral tradition" would often change radically. If a particular shot did not work out—if *la grace* was not present—a whole scene could be abandoned, reconceived, or simply left out of the final cut. As Bregstein puts it, the script "served as a springboard for diving into the film, at which point the script often fell overboard." Perhaps the most amusing example of this, frequently cited by Rouch himself, concerns *Cocorico! Monsieur Poulet*. In this case, the original "script in the oral tradition" was so constantly undermined by the breaking down of Lam's Citroën 2CV van that Rouch and his protagonists decided to make a virtue of necessity and turn these breakdowns into a recurrent plot point.[19]

This was the most usual pattern whereby Rouch went about shooting his fiction films. But notwithstanding his declarations about never working from a formal script, there were a number of occasions during his career, mostly in the latter part, when he did, in fact, do so. On two such occasions—when shooting *La Folie ordinaire d'une jeune fille de Cham* in 1986 and *Bac ou marriage?* the following year—the shooting was based on a preexisting theatrical script. But in these cases, with the aid of a second cameraman, Philippe Costantini, Rouch sought to shoot these scripts as much as possible in real time, never asking the actors to stop. In this sense, the actors' performances were also like those of the ritual dancers described in the Fulchignoni interview: in both cases, the subjects' performances conformed to a preexisting pattern, but both they and the cameramen were required to improvise the particular detail of their performances in the actual moment of shooting, making sure, at the same time, that they were in some sort of 'connivance' with one another.

However, there were at least two other occasions when Rouch was required to follow a script in a more conventional manner. Both these films were made in what were, for Rouch, unusual circumstances, in that they involved a large budget and a full professional crew. The two films in question were *Les Veuves de quinze ans*, shot in 1964 and released in 1966, and, twenty years later, *Dionysos*. In both cases, it appears that Rouch himself wrote the script, albeit in consultation with the actors. As a consequence of shooting with professional crews, with their great quantities of equipment, and their expectation of a daily shooting plan and precisely scheduled rest breaks, Rouch was obliged to abandon his usual improvisational procedures.[20] But although both films have their supporters, the general burden of critical opinion is that both were pretty much unmitigated disasters, confirming Rouch's own view that he could only make successful films if they involved a high degree of spontaneity.[21]

The Filmmaker Diver

For Rouch, the key to good practice while shooting a film, whether it was an ethnofiction or an ethnographic documentary, was to maximize his participation in the events being filmed. He was, as Edgar Morin said of him, a "filmmaker diver" who "plunged" into the world of his subjects.[22] This was an approach to shooting that was very different from that of his ethnographic filmmaking contemporaries in the Anglo-Saxon world. It was, for example, completely at odds with the quaintly futuristic vision extolled by Margaret Mead, whereby a 360-degree camera would be set up on a pole in the middle of a village to film life continuously, without the subjects being aware of it and without any intervention on the part of a filmmaker.[23] While even the most progressive of his North American ethnographic filmmaking contemporaries, such as John Marshall and Tim Asch, conceived of the camera as analogous to a scientific instrument, such as a telescope or a microscope, capable of observing human life in a detached objective manner, Rouch thought of it rather as a catalyst that when operated in an engaged, participatory manner could provoke the subjects into revelatory performances.[24]

This concern to participate directly in the lives of his subjects whilst shooting was more important to Rouch than technical quality per se. In general, he did not have a great deal of patience for technical virtuosity and in the latter stages of his career, his own camerawork would sometimes leave something to be desired. But he had a particular antipathy to what he would rather sneeringly refer to as "*la belle image*," by which he meant the perfectly crafted, conventionally beautiful image that professional camerapeople would seek to achieve at all costs, regardless of the effect on the spontaneity of what was going on in front of the lens. Although he was sometimes obliged to work with professional technicians when shooting his fiction films, Rouch had a particular aversion to the idea of working with them on an ethnographic documentary. In his manifesto-essay "The Camera and Man," he declares himself "violently opposed" to film crews and criticizes very severely the ethnographic filmmakers Asen Balikci and Ian Dunlop who had worked with them. Instead,

FIGURE 12.2. *Left*, Rouch, shooting on an Éclair NPR among the Dogon, is assisted by Tallou, who carries the camera battery. *Right*, the Dogon recordist Ibrahim Guindo records a wild track of a Dogon elder. © Fondation Jean Rouch.

he urges all anthropologists to follow his own example and shoot their own material, even if their technical skills are limited, because, in contrast to a brought-in professional cameraperson, only they have spent sufficient time in the field to know "when, where, and how to film."

As for sound recording, Rouch believed that it was essential that this function be fulfilled by someone fluent in the language of the subjects and therefore, usually, a local person. In "The Camera and Man," he argues that this is particularly necessary in an African village since more than one White person forms "a foreign body" that is in danger of being rejected.[25] For this reason, early in his own filmmaking career, he trained Damouré and Lam to record sound and Tallou to act as his camera assistant. Later, as sound recording became a more complex task, he trained a number of other recordists, including the Dogon, Ibrahim Guindo, and particularly the Zerma, Moussa Hamidou (fig. 12.2).

Throughout his career, Rouch worked in close collaboration with the leading audiovisual engineers of the day to develop more portable equipment that would enable him to increase his degree of participation in his subjects' lives. Among his collaborators were Stefan Kudelski, inventor of the portable Nagra reel-to-reel tape recorder which replaced the thirty kilogram Sgubbi that Rouch and Rosfelder had used in the early 1950s.

Another was André Coutant, inventor of the lightweight KMT Coutant-Mathot Éclair used by Michel Brault in the shooting of *Chronicle of a Summer*. This was the prototype from which Coutant later developed the Éclair NPR, the camera that was widely adopted from the mid-1960s onward by documentarists wanting to shoot in the handheld manner pioneered by Rouch and Brault. These users of the NPR included Rouch himself, who moved on to this camera after a relatively brief period in the early 1960s when he was shooting on a 16mm Beaulieu (fig. 12.3). Somewhat later, in the 1970s, Rouch was also closely associated with Jean-Pierre Beauviala, inventor of the Aaton camera that Rouch came to prefer in the latter part of his career. Not only was the Aaton lighter than the Éclair NPR, but much better balanced and easier to carry around, thereby further increasing the mobility of the cameraperson. Although Rouch undoubtedly appreciated the greater fidelity with which this more portable, sound-synchronous equipment reproduced the world, the increased participation in the life of his subjects that they enabled was equally important to him.

This concern for mobility and participation in the life of the subjects provided the rationale underlying most of Rouch's practical shooting strategies. From the beginning of his career, he used natural lighting whenever he could, and if this was not possible, he would try to make do with whatever artificial lighting was available on location. The same reasoning explained his antipathy to tripods. The story about how Rouch learned to shoot without a tripod on his first trip down the Niger in 1946 is one of the most repeated legends about his life, though as discussed in chapter 3, whether he actually broke it himself some way into the trip or lost it going over some rapids close to the start remains unclear. But whatever the precise circumstances of his *prise de conscience*, the fact remains that by the end of this trip, contrary to the prevailing wisdom, he had proved not only that it was perfectly possible to shoot a film without a tripod but that he could achieve a much greater degree of intimacy with his subjects since he was able to follow them around as they went about their business, rather than requiring them to come and perform in front of a static camera perched on a tripod.[26] This would remain one of the most cherished principles of his praxis for the rest of his days, even if, later in his career, due to the technical requirements of recording good synchronous sound, moving around with the subjects entailed a complicated ballet involving several people (see fig. 12.4, and compare with fig. 3.2, p. 40).

Rouch's antipathy to zoom lenses arose from a similar concern. He believed that zooms encouraged the illusion that it was possible to get closer to the subjects solely by adjusting the lens rather than by moving

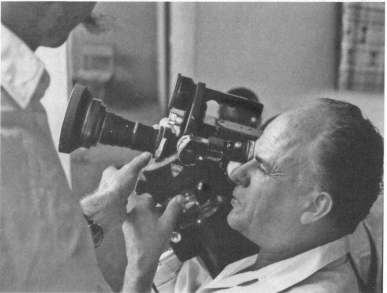

FIGURE 12.3. *Top*, Rouch shooting *Rose et Landry* on the Beaulieu R16 in the early 1960s (from *Cahiers du Cinéma* 24, no. 144 [1963]: 1). *Bottom*, shooting *Petit à Petit* in the late 1960s on the Éclair NPR, assisted by Philippe Luzuy. © Films du Jeudi.

physically into the heart of the action by means of what is known as a "tracking" or "traveling" shot. "The zoom can never replace the traveling shot," Rouch observed in an interview published in 1992. "Whether one is moving in or moving sideways, a traveling shot is a way of discovering

FIGURE 12.4. Walking with the Aaton. Rouch, *center*, walks backward while shooting Damouré, Tallou, and Lam on location in Holland for *Madame L'Eau* in July 1991. Moussa Hamidou, *left*, also from Rouch's "band," monitors the sound. Meanwhile, Rouch is guided by Eugène van den Bosch while the boom is operated by Bert van den Dungen. © MM Filmprodukties, photographer Bart Eijgenhuijsen.

the world."[27] Although he did occasionally use the zoom, it was usually only when circumstances beyond his control prevented him from getting any closer, as when he was filming the wounded lioness in *The Lion Hunters* and was afraid that she might attack, or when he wanted to give an overview of the serpentine movement of the massed ranks of Dogon dancers in the Sigui films. Rouch's preference was for fixed focus, wide-angle lenses which, with his characteristic playfulness, he would refer to as his "contact lenses" since in order to fill the frame when using a wide-angle, it is necessary to get physically very close to the subject. As so often with Rouch's jokes, behind this remark there was also a more serious point, namely, that the ethnographic filmmaker should always be striving for greater engagement with the subjects (fig. 12.5).[28]

From early on in his career, Rouch always shot in color even though back then it was considerably more expensive than monochrome stock. In part, this was simply because he considered it more realistic, but it was also because his subjects found it easier to "read" in feedback screenings. His first attempt at a feedback screening in the village of Wanzerbé had ended in failure because the film was in black and white, and the subjects had found this difficult to construe. In contrast, when he first showed his films to his subjects in color, they immediately understood what he was trying to do. "Color is life," he declared, "the world is in color. To suppress

FIGURE 12.5. The "contact lens." Rouch shooting *Madame L'Eau* in Niger, in April 1992, using his Aaton mounted with a wide-angle prime lens. © Steef Meyknecht.

color is to be the White man, taking refuge behind his writings."[29] Rouch particularly liked to use color stock in Africa because it poses less of a problem of contrast when shooting in tropical conditions, where for two or three hours either side of noon, the sunlight is not only typically very intense but also directly overhead, and as a consequence, the contrast ratio is very high. This results in burnt-out, featureless images in which the nuances of color, light, and shade are lost, and the modeling of bodies and objects is much reduced. In order to avoid these effects, shooting in tropical conditions should be confined to early in the morning or, as was more usual in Rouch's case, late in the afternoon. But, if anything, this time constraint was something that Rouch welcomed because, as Bregstein puts it, "this heightened the adventurous atmosphere of the shoot" since everyone knew that the filming had to be completed before the sun sank below the horizon.[30]

However, it is significant that in the Rouchian praxis, this participation in the life of the subjects did not usually involve any form of verbal dialogue during the actual process of shooting. He did engage in a great deal of dialogue with the subjects at other times, of course, both before filming, in the general course of his fieldwork or when discussing the "script in the oral tradition," and afterward, in the form of feedback screenings. But during the filming itself, Rouch was usually entirely silent, though there are some notable exceptions to this in his oeuvre. In *Chronicle of a Summer*, for example, Rouch himself appears in shot quite a number of times and engages in a conversational dialogue with the other subjects. Later in his career, in the "ciné-portraits" of his friends made in the 1970s and early 1980s, Rouch again appears in shot and even asks questions from behind the camera. But these are exceptions that prove the general rule. For the most part, and particularly in his ethnographic films, Rouch rarely speaks to his subjects and certainly never conducts anything even remotely resembling a formal interview. Indeed, formal interviews are seemingly so far from Rouch's thinking that he does not even mention them in "The Camera and Man."

The Dream Almost Beyond Reach

By the latter part of the 1960s, once the synchronous-sound technology had developed sufficiently, Rouch's ideal became, whenever possible, to shoot handheld sequence-shots, that is, prolonged shots that were so well executed that they could deliver an entire sequence that required no editing in the edit suite. This predilection for the prolonged sequence-shot arose from Rouch's fascination with the idea of shooting in real time. Not only did he believe that the sequence-shot showed the world as it really is, which he considered "very important", but it also posed a particular challenge to the filmmaker, forcing him to put on an inspired performance in response to the events going on around him.[31] It was an effect that Rouch tried to achieve not only in his documentaries, but also in his fiction films, most notably in *Gare du Nord*, a film of seventeen minutes that consists almost entirely of two sequence-shots.[32]

A particularly fine example of a handheld sequence-shot in one of his documentaries is to be found in *Architectes ayorou*, a film that Rouch made in 1970. This was executed with a fixed-focus, 10mm wide-angle "contact lens" and begins with the camera approaching a line of women as they pound vigorously at wooden mortars with long pestles, preparing millet flour for the midday meal of the house builders who are the principal subjects of the film. But as the camera gets closer, the women begin to sing a ballad about a handsome young man who left the village to work in Ghana, never to return. The mortars become a line of drums, the rhythm of the pestles producing a series of delicious percussive canons in counterpoint to the haunting, high-pitched singing of the women. Together, voices and percussion evoke a heartfelt longing for the lost man of the women's desires. Once the camera is adjacent to the women, it circles right round them, picking them and their impromptu musical instruments out one by one. At the end of the shot, the camera retreats to its initial position some 10–15 meters in front of the women, ending with a wide shot. This sequence-shot provides a good example of the ideal situation described by Rouch in the Fulchignoni interview since it shows how cameraperson and subjects can 'connive' to produce a small masterpiece. It also shows how the presence of a camera can have a revelatory catalytic effect since the pounding of the millet, undertaken in the first instance merely for the prosaic purpose of providing food, becomes instead a musical performance as the women respond to Rouch's act of filming them by breaking into song. Yet, for all its merits, this sequence-shot is only 2.5 minutes in duration.

For although Rouch may have been constantly striving to shoot sequence-shots from the mid-1960s onward, he found it difficult to shoot sequence-shots that were very prolonged. This was for the simple reason that a prolonged sequence-shot not only requires a high degree of skill on the part of the cameraperson but also sheer luck: the subjects may suddenly stop what they are doing, or move around in a way that it is impossible for the cameraperson to follow, however great his or her skill, or the cameraperson may stumble on a stone, bump into someone, or fall foul of any number of other contingencies. Rouch came to consider a sequence-shot of ten minutes, the maximum afforded by the standard 16mm magazine of 400 feet, to be "a dream almost beyond reach," and in 1992, he ruefully admitted that he had only managed to achieve it once in his career.[33]

This unique moment occurred in the shooting of *Les Tambours d'avant: Tourou et Bitti*, a film that Rouch shot in 1971, the year after *Architectes ayorou*. It was shot in Simiri, the same village in Zermaganda where, twenty years before, Rouch had shot *Yenendi, les hommes qui font la pluie*, a film about a spirit-possession ceremony in which the villagers appeal to Dongo, the Spirit of Thunder, to bring them rain.[34] The subject of *Les Tambours d'avant* is also a spirit-possession ceremony, though in this case the villagers seek the aid of the *gandyi bi*, the Black Spirits of the Bush, specialists in agricultural matters, to prevent pests from destroying their new millet crop.[35] The complete film is only eleven minutes long and apart from one brief shot at the beginning, consists almost entirely of the ten-minute sequence-shot. The experience of shooting this film was of crucial significance in the development of Rouch's notion of the "ciné-trance" and for this reason, we should consider it in some detail.

Arriving at Simiri on what was already the fourth day of the *gandyi bi* ceremony, Rouch and his Zerma sound recordist Moussa Hamidou discovered that the mediums had not been able to go into trance. This was despite the strenuous efforts of the musicians to attract the *gandyi bi* by playing their signature melodies on the single-stringed *godye* violin and various types of percussive instrument. The latter included the drums alluded to in the subtitle of the film, the *tourou* and the *bitti*, which the *gandyi bi* are thought particularly to favor (see fig. 12.6).[36] By 4:00 p.m.,

FIGURE 12.6. The *tourou* drum, used particularly for calling the *gandyi bi* spirits. © Fondation Jean Rouch.

as the light was beginning to fade, Moussa suggested to Rouch that they should at least take the opportunity to film the musicians' performance on the *tourou* and the *bitti* since these drums were played together with increasing rarity. This they duly did, as follows:

> After a preliminary shot outside the village and an opening title, the sequence-shot that makes up the main body of the film begins. It starts on the sun and then pans down, becoming a tracking shot that enters the village, passing a herd of tethered sacrificial goats on the left and, on the right, the disconsolate male medium Sambou Albeybu still waiting for inspiration. The tracking shot continues across the small earthen plaza and approaches the musicians who redouble their efforts as the camera glides over them, revealing the range of different instruments one by one. At this point, the music begins to peter out and the camera begins to withdraw, when suddenly there is a sudden cry of "Meat!" and Sambou goes into trance as he is possessed by Kure the Hyena, a leading *gandyi bi* spirit. The priests of the spirit-possession cult, the *zima*, approach Kure and engage him in a bantering dialogue, offering him "meat" in the form of sacrificial animals, in exchange for "grass," a good harvest. At this point, with the camera still turning, an old woman, Tusinye Wazi, hops across the plaza, shivering all over with the effects of possession by Hadyo the

Fulani Slave, also a *gandyi bi* spirit. The *zima* continue their negotiations with Kure, who is now threatening to leave unless he gets "blood." But as it is nearing the end of the magazine, the camera withdraws to the edge of the plaza. From here, it ends on a wide shot showing the young people looking on from the edge of the plaza, before finally panning up again to the sun, now setting and partially obscured by clouds.

A number of different elements of Rouch's filmmaking praxis come together in this short film. As with the sequence-shot in *Architectes ayorou*, Rouch was shooting with a 10mm wide-angle lens, which meant that even though his subjects were in the midst of a possession ceremony, he had to get very close to them to fill the frame. This was only possible because of his close relationship with them and their understanding of what he was doing. He himself was in a heightened state of excitement as he knew that he only had a maximum of ten minutes to shoot the event as the sun was already sinking in the sky. Most important of all, although he began to shoot with merely descriptive ethnographic objectives, the action developed into something much more interesting as a result of the presence of the camera.

For, Rouch claimed afterward, it was the fact that he was shooting a film that served to send the mediums into a trance state. In the middle of the shot, the drummers had given up and Rouch was about to turn off, but then, the *godye* violin player, seeing that Rouch was still shooting and assuming that this must be because he could see the spirits with this camera, began to play more energetically. This in turn encouraged the drummers to begin again, which then sent the principal medium into trance. In this way, the film represented for Rouch a good example of the positive benefits that can arise from the change in reality brought about the presence of the camera.[37]

Les Tambours d'avant also exemplifies Rouch's understanding of the interplay between subjectivity and objectivity that is involved in making a film in this particular way. Close to the beginning, over one of the preliminary shots outside the village, he explains on the commentary track that the film is "an attempt to practice ethnographic cinema in the first person." This is followed by a cut to black with the title "Un film de Jean Rouch" discreetly displayed in one corner. Only then does the sequence-shot proper begin, with Rouch commenting over it, "To enter into a film is to plunge into reality, and to be, at once, both present and invisible." Thus the film is presented as an unexpurgated slice of time involving a "plunge" into reality, echoing once again the analogy of the filmmaker-diver. But at the same time, it is presented as a view of this reality that is both intensively subjective ("ethnographic cinema in the first per-

FIGURE 12.7. The *zima* priest interrogates Sambou Albeybu, possessed by the spirit, Kure the Hyena. In the background, *left*, the *bitti* drummers. © Fondation Jean Rouch.

son") and authored ("Un film de Jean Rouch"). Through this interplay of the subjective and objective, the filmmaker can have the best of both worlds, being both an active participant whose presence provokes a reaction while still being "invisible" because he does not interrupt proceedings with questions and, being well known to the subjects, is treated as if he were an insider.

However, there is another way in which the film involves an interplay between the subjective and the objective that Rouch himself does not comment upon directly. That is, although the film is presented as an unexpurgated slice of time captured through an inspired performance, it is nevertheless structured by a series of highly conventional cinematographic narrative tropes. The sequence-shot begins with a pan down from the sun and then arrives at the edge of the village. As a tracking shot, it has a very pronounced subjective "point-of-view" feel as it enters the village. After this arrival trope, the film presents a "lack," namely, the absence of possession, but this is then progressively and, eventually, triumphantly resolved as the mediums go into trance (fig. 12.7). Finally, as if in summary, the camera withdraws to the edge of the plaza and the film ends with a wide shot of the setting sun as the children in the audience metaphorically look to the future.

It is not clear exactly how conscious Rouch himself was of this narrative structure at the time that he was shooting. But the fact that the sequence-shot begins and ends on the sun certainly suggests that this narrative shaping of the shot was intentional at some level of consciousness. So too does Rouch's commentary point, delivered as the camera withdraws toward the edge of the plaza, that he would have liked to have continued amid the dancers but wanted "to return to the beginning of my story." But whether or not it was consciously intended, there is clearly a considerable degree of narrativization going on. In effect then, although the full magazine sequence-shot of *Les Tambours d'avant* might have permitted Rouch to make a more profound "plunge into reality" than he was able to achieve either before or after, it did not represent a simple, descriptive "slice of time," but rather an authored work of cinema.

The Ciné-Trance

It was as a direct result of shooting *Les Tambours d'avant* that Rouch first began to develop his concept of the ciné-trance. He later described how, when he and the sound recordist Moussa Hamidou put down their equipment at the end of the take, they were trembling, aware that they had just been through a powerful experience. But Rouch did not attribute this merely to the physical exhaustion that it would be entirely reasonable to expect as a result of concentrating intensively over the course of executing a ten-minute sequence-shot. Rather, he thought that their trembling state was due to the fact that the engaging rhythm of the *tourou* and *bitti* drums had not only sent the two mediums into trance, but the two filmmakers as well. If the mediums were possessed by the spirits Kure and Hadyo, he and Moussa had been possessed by what he would later describe as a sort of "enthusiasm," which "cannot be defined but which is essential to poetic creativity." This was comparable, he suggested, to the German Romantic idea of *Stimmung*, a term which literally means "humor," "frame of mind," or "a tuning," as of a musical instrument, but which, Rouch claimed, defies translation in this more artistic sense.[38]

Rouch's ideas about the ciné-trance are explored at some length in an article that was first presented, in conjunction with a screening of the recently completed *Les Tambours d'avant*, at a celebrated CNRS conference about the African notion of the person in 1971. In this article, Rouch theorizes the ciné-trance through an extraordinary fusion of, on the one hand, Songhay-Zerma ideas about soul matter and, on the other, Vertovian ideas about *cinéma-vérité*.[39] Rouch explains that the Songhay-Zerma believe that every individual has a quality known as *bia*, variously glossed by the Songhay-Zerma themselves as "reflection," "shadow," or even "soul." Rouch, on the other hand, refers to it as "double," a term often used in the anthropological literature of West Africa to describe this phenomenon, which, in a variety of different forms, is a common feature of the religious belief systems of the region.[40] In death, this double, which is immortal, leaves the body, but even in life, it can take off on its own while its owner is dreaming and under certain other circumstances. In the course of possession, however, the medium's double is displaced or submerged by the double of the spirit. (Rouch admits to being uncertain as to whether the spirits actually have bodies—visible only to the *zima* priests—to which this double corresponds, or whether the spirits are nothing more than a double.) While possessed, mediums are no longer themselves but become like the spirits that have possessed them, dancing in ways that are suggestive of particular attributes or behaviors that are conventionally associated with those spirits. In effect then, they become the physical incarnation, literally, of the double of a spirit.

Rouch suggests that there is an analogy here between the condition, on the one hand, of mediums submerged by the double of the possessing spirit and, on the other, of filmmakers who become completely immersed in the reality that they are filming, thereby entering their own trance of cinematographic creativity. In the same way that the Songhay-Zerma mediums possessed by a spirit imagine themselves to be entering a world that is different from that of everyday experience, so too do "possessed" filmmakers enter a different reality when turning on the camera. Whereas the medium's "double" is taken over by the "double" of a spirit, the filmmaker is taken over by *Stimmung*, poetic creativity. It is this analogy that Rouch is alluding to when he refers to cinema as the "art of the double," as in the epigraph to this chapter. Here he appears to be suggesting that just as in the case of spirit possession, filmmaking similarly involves a transition from the world of the real to the world of the imaginary in which poetic creativity unleashed.

These arguments clearly reverberate strongly with the Surrealist ideas that Rouch encountered in his youth. However, in his discussion of the ciné-trance, they undergo a further transformation and are recast in a Vertovian vocabulary to make them applicable to the cinematographic experience. Rather than entering a trance of poetic creativity *tout court*, as one of his Surrealist poet-heroes might have claimed, the inspired filmmaker enters the ciné-trance. In this state, rather than revealing the truths embedded in the unconscious, as a Surrealist artist might have done through a poem or a painting, Rouch proposes that the filmmaker registers on his equipment the distinctive truths that only the cinematographic apparatus can reach, namely, those truths that Vertov sought to describe by the term *cinéma-vérité*.

Rouch claims that when he is in the ciné-trance, everything that he does is determined by this condition. In describing his actions, he attaches Vertovian prefixes to all the verbs. Thus when he films, he "ciné-looks"; when he records, he "ciné-listens"; and while editing, he "ciné-thinks" as he "ciné-cuts." Moreover, his film subjects too become involved in this world of *cinema-vérité* and become his accomplices in producing it. Rouch suggests that since they understand perfectly well what he is doing as a result of his many feedback screenings, his subjects react to his filmmaking as they would to those who are possessed by spirits, namely, by lending themselves to the performance on its own terms. As he "ciné-observes," they allow themselves to be "ciné-observed." In the most extreme case, as in the filming of *Les Tambours d'avant*, the subjects may go into their own kind of trance in response to the filmmakers' ciné-trance.[41]

Any experienced documentary filmmaker will probably recognize, at least to some degree, the state of mind that Rouch describes by the term ciné-trance. Many filmmakers will certainly be able to identify with Rouch when he says that while immersed in the ciné-trance, he feels able to free himself from the weight of anthropological and cinematographic theory and rediscover what he calls *la barbarie de l'invention*—a phrase that defies easy translation but which could be rendered as "raw creativity."[42] I am certainly aware from my own experience that a certain state of mind can arise when one has been filming an event over a prolonged period, particularly a long and repetitious ritual event, in a situation in which one knows the protagonists well and feels confident in one's relationship with them. Under these circumstances, banal considerations of technique can fall away and everything seems miraculously to "work," including not just one's own handling of the equipment but also the movements and reactions of the subjects within the frame. A sense of complicity is established between filmmaker and subjects, giving rise to a conviction that both parties are conspiring to produce a sequence of the highest quality.[43]

But although the ciné-trance may be a readily recognizable state of mind, whether Rouch's theoretical reflections on this condition stand up to close scrutiny is more debatable. There is, first of all, a significant mismatch between the Songhay,and Vertovian ideas that are central to the parallel that he seeks to draw. Even if one were to take both the Songhay and Vertovian theories at face value and consider them as true (in itself obviously a contestable proposition), the fact that one can identify certain analogies between them does not mean that they are referring to phenomena that are, in any genuinely meaningful sense, the same. Vertov's theories refer merely to one very particular form of perception, namely, the perception of the world afforded by the "ciné-eye." The distinctive truth about the world that the "ciné-eye" can offer, the *cinema-vérité*, is largely achieved in the edit suite as "life facts" are transformed into "film facts" through montage and special effects.[44] In contrast, when a Songhay medium becomes possessed, he feels that his body has been taken over by a spirit being. Surely only the most deranged Vertovian would believe the images on a cinema screen to be reality rather than a representation of it, whereas for the Songhay mediums, the spirits whom they incarnate in their dances are not mere representations but rather beings as real as their own bodies. In fact, as I suggested above, in drawing this analogy, Rouch is only able to make a bridge between Songhay and Vertovian ideas by introducing a third element, namely Surrealist or Romantic ideas about poetic creativity and then casting these in a Vertovian vocabulary. But here too there is a significant disjunction between the Songhay medium's belief that he has been invaded by some external being, and the Surrealist poet's belief that he is drawing on his own imaginary.

Rather than take Rouch's theory of the ciné-trance too literally, it would perhaps be more appropriate to explore it as a thought-provoking metaphor. Although there may be a fundamental ontological difference between the trance into which a spirit medium falls and the ciné-trance of the filmmaker, one thing that they do have in common is that while both are drawing in some sense on the unconscious mind, they remain structured by socially determined languages. Just as the possessed mediums in *Les Tambours d'avant* embody the doubles of Kure the Hyena or Hadyo the Fulani Slave by performing their dances in a highly conventional manner, so too Rouch, the filmmaker-diver, even though immersed deep within the ciné-trance, still shoots his sequence-shot according to the most conventional of cinematographic narrative tropes.

Moreover, whatever the shortcomings of Rouch's theoretical ideas about the ciné-trance, these do not detract from the value of the proposition, integral not just to his conception of the ciné-trance but also to his more general ideas about participatory shooting, that the production of knowledge about the world cinematographically should involve a process of mutual accommodation—or "connivance," as he puts it—between filmmaker and subjects. This element of exchange that lay at the heart of Rouch's shooting praxis represented not just a practical methodology but also an ethical posture and for this reason, we shall be returning to it again when we consider his ideas about "shared anthropology" in chapter 15.

13 : The Harsh Dialogue

[T]he reader [is invited] to consider the history of cinema in the light of the idea of freedom underwritten . . . by the great names of editing: Griffith, Eisenstein, Welles, Rouch, Godard.   DOMINIQUE VILLAIN, 1991[1]

To Edit or Not to Edit

In the view of Dominique Villain, author of *Le Montage au cinéma* and a distinguished film editor herself, Jean Rouch is one of the great figures in the history of editing, ranking in importance alongside D. W. Griffith, Sergei Eisenstein, Orson Welles, and Jean-Luc Godard. Yet, in comparison to his innumerable discussions and pronouncements about the practicalities of shooting, Rouch himself had relatively little to say about the process of editing. Moreover, from what little he did say, he seems to have had distinctly contradictory attitudes about this phase of the film-making process.

On the one hand, he would often assert the great importance of editing. In the catalog of African ethnographic films that he edited for UNESCO in 1967, for example, he observes that "it must not be forgotten that cutting a film remains the best way for the filmmaker to learn his craft."[2] In "The Camera and Man" in 1975, he again stresses the importance of editing, though on this occasion, he adds that the editing of a film should always be performed by someone who has had no involvement in the actual shooting. The advantage of bringing in such a "second ciné-eye" was that this person could look at the rushes and assess them on his or her own terms without being unduly influenced either by the original context of the shooting or by the filmmaker's intentions. Rouch acknowledged that the "dialogue" between this "objective editor" and the "subjective" filmmaker could be "harsh and difficult," but, he believed, the ultimate success of the film depended upon this exchange.[3]

On the other hand, despite these assertions about the great importance of working with an editor, Rouch seems to have worked hard to keep it to a minimum, be it by his practices on location or back in the edit suite. For, while on location, Rouch's ambition was to "to edit through the viewfinder." In this connection, he was fond of citing Vertov's observation that it is not only in the edit suite that editing takes place: it also takes place beforehand when a filmmaker chooses which subject among many possible subjects to shoot, and which way among many possible ways to shoot it.[4] In the earliest phases of his career, when he was still using a spring-wound camera that allowed shots of a maximum duration of twenty-five seconds, Rouch would use the interval required to rewind the mechanism to work out what his next shot would be. At the same time, he would change the angle or the framing in such a way as to enable one shot to follow directly on from the other in the edit suite if required.[5] This was surely good practice but, in effect, the more that it was successful, the more it made editing in the edit suite unnecessary.

The same was true of his predilection for the sequence-shot, which he used a great deal in the latter part of his career, once technological developments had made possible shots of several minutes' duration. As described in the previous chapter, Rouch's ideal sequence-shot would last the whole ten-minute duration of a standard 16mm magazine and would be shot so well that it could be inserted directly into the final version of the film, or even constitute the whole film itself, as in the case of *Les Tambours d'avant*. Again, the more prolonged a sequence-shot, the more it renders editing in the edit suite redundant. In short, whereas the conventional instruction in film schools is "shoot to edit," it seems that principle underlying Rouch's praxis would be more accurately summarized as "shoot so as not to edit."

Concerti à deux regards

Over the course of his career, Rouch worked with many of the most distinguished film editors in France. This was made possible through the unusual relationship that Rouch maintained with the producers of his films. With some notable exceptions, such as *Chronicle of a Summer* and *Les Veuves de quinze ans*, Rouch would usually begin shooting on a subject of his choosing, generally in West Africa and always on 16mm. The costs of this production phase of his films would usually be met by the CNRS as part and parcel of his position as a CNRS researcher. However, if he thought that the material had potential interest for an audience outside the academic world, he would show it to a producer. For much of his early career, this was Pierre Braunberger, the director of Argos Films. If Braunberger agreed about the potential popular interest of the material, then he would pay for a professional editor to work on it and, eventually, the edited film would be blown up to 35mm for cinema release.[6]

However, Rouch's first experience of working in this way was not with Braunberger, but with the newsreel agency Actualités françaises, which bought the rights to the material that he had shot during his descent of the Niger River with Pierre Ponty and Jean Sauvy in 1946–1947 and re-edited it for cinema distribution. But, as I described in chapter 3, when he saw the results, Rouch was deeply dismayed: not only had the editors at the agency given the film a dubious popular title, *Au pays des mages noirs*, but they had covered the images with excruciating canned music and a narration in the style of a sports commentary. Worst of all, in order to give the film an engaging climax, they had altered the chronology of the original material so that the sequence of a possession ceremony in which, prior to setting out, a group of hunters ask the spirit controlling the Niger River to release some hippopotami to them was presented instead as a ritual offering of thanks after the hunt. Yet although Rouch was unhappy with the way in which the chronology had been distorted, he also recognized that the newsreel editors, who were turning out two such films a week, really knew their business since by placing the ceremony at the end of the film, they had made it very much more dramatic. Putting his dismay to one side, he concluded that in future he too would always edit his films with reference to the ending.[7]

The working relationships that Rouch developed with the editors with whom he worked subsequently in his career were generally much more satisfactory, as Dominique Villain has described. Villain herself worked as an editor with Rouch on the short version of *Petit à Petit*, so although her descriptions of these relationships are tantalizingly brief, they are certainly based on firsthand experience. They provide a fascinating glimpse into these collaborations, or, as they were described by one of Rouch's later editors, Danièle Tessier, these *concerti à deux regards et quatre mains*, or "concertos for two ways of seeing and four hands."[8]

The editors with whom Rouch worked in the 1950s, though eventually destined to go on to great things, were still young and, like him, were at the beginning of their careers. As was generally the case in France at that time, according to Villain, most of these editors were women.[9] The status of editors was then so low in the hierarchy of the filmmaking industry that they were often not even named in the on-screen credits, particularly in the case of documentaries. This was certainly the fate of Renée Lichtig, who cut Rouch's early film, *Bataille sur le grand fleuve*, released in 1952. Lichtig was no more than twenty years of age at the time, but shortly afterward, she would go on to work with the legendary Hollywood director Eric von Stroheim on the synchronization of his 1920s silent classic, *The Wedding March*, and between 1958 and 1962, she cut the last three films of that towering figure of French cinema, Jean Renoir.

Prior to working with Lichtig, Rouch had thought that the services of an editor were as dispensable as the services of a cameraman. Although it had provided a useful learning opportunity, the experience of seeing his first film distorted by the editors of Actualités françaises had led him to believe that it was better to do one's own editing. But through working with Lichtig, Rouch came round to the view that it was not just useful, but absolutely necessary, to work with an editor. As described in chapter 3, while trying to edit the material that he shot on his descent of the Niger, Rouch had found it impossible to cut directly from one riverbank to the other since this involved crossing the imaginary line constituted by the movement of the canoe downriver.[10] But while cutting *Bataille sur le grand fleuve*, Lichtig proved to him that if there were no clearly defined line created by the movement of the canoe in which the camera was traveling, then it was perfectly possible to intercut scenes of hippopotamus hunting that had taken place on opposite banks of the river.

At first, Rouch was horrified by this suggestion, considering it the equivalent, if making a film about Paris, to intercutting shots of Notre Dame Cathedral with shots of Montparnassse. But he had to acknowledge that for someone who had had no direct personal experience of the location, the effect was not visible. At the same time, it was a device that allowed him to cut out many tedious shots of the hunters crossing back and forth across the river in their cumbersome canoes. As a result of this experience, he came to accept that not only were such editorial sleights of hand permissible, but that it was essential that the editing of a film be carried out by someone who had not been present at the shoot and who could therefore react in an entirely unprejudiced way to the material.[11]

Another editor with whom Rouch worked at the beginning of his career and who would later go on to achieve great eminence was Suzanne Baron. She and Rouch cut two films together. The first was *Les Fils de l'eau*, a compilation of extracts from various earlier films that Rouch had shot in the period 1948 to 1951. Later, Baron cut *Les Maîtres fous*, released in 1955, and one of the best known of all Rouch's films. Although also very young when she collaborated with Rouch, Baron had already worked as an (uncredited) editor for the celebrated feature director, Jacques Tati, on *Les Vacances de M. Hulot* (1953). Later, she would go on to become the editor of choice of Louis Malle and to work with many other well-known directors, including such luminaries as Frédéric Rossif, Joris Ivens, Volker Schlöndorff, and Werner Herzog.[12]

Of all the many legends that surround the life of Jean Rouch, one of the most frequently told, including in chapter 7 of this book, concerns the highly negative reaction of his closest friends and colleagues to the screening of a preliminary version *Les Maîtres fous* in the cinema of the Musée de l'Homme. His supervisor and mentor, Marcel Griaule, even told him that he should destroy the material.[13] The less frequently told coda to this story is that while Rouch was still wondering what to do after this distressing experience, Pierre Braunberger took him to show the film to the Hollywood film noir director Jules Dassin who was then living in France. (This was the height of the McCarthy era and Dassin had been hounded out of the United States on account of his leftist sympathies). Dassin not only strongly encouraged Rouch to defy his critics and preserve the film, but even suggested that it should be blown up to 35mm and prepared for general cinema release. Much encouraged by this response, Braunberger brought in Suzanne Baron to work on the film.[14]

Les Maîtres fous is perhaps the most tightly edited of Rouch's films and features a number of editorial devices that are highly unusual in his work, and which it is tempting therefore to attribute to the influence of Baron. These include particular individual cuts that have given rise to much comment in the literature on this film and to which I shall return when considering the more technical aspects of Rouch's editing praxis in the following chapter. What is not in doubt is Baron's role in improving the sound track of *Les Maîtres fous*. On location, the sound track had been recorded by Rouch's regular associates, Damouré Zika and Lam Ibrahim Dia, employing a tape recorder that, like his Bell & Howell camera, operated with a clockwork mechanism. Whereas the camera would run for only twenty-five seconds, the tape recorder ran for up to thirty minutes. Yet it was far from synchronous and although it was considered "portable," it actually weighed over thirty kilograms, so for most of the time, it remained in a single place with the microphone placed in a conveniently located tree.[15] This recording of live performance in the field was considered very advanced for the time, but the sound quality of the film remains poor by modern standards. Particularly poor was the quality of the sound recorded at the moments when Rouch was actually shooting since he had no sound-proofing for the camera, and the mechanism whirring away sounded like a "coffee-grinder." In order to overcome this problem, Baron cut out these passages of synchronous sound and replaced them with passages of nonsynchronous wild track recorded either just before or just after any particular shot.[16]

The quality of the sound editing in Rouch's films would take another big step forward under the influence of Marie-Josèphe Yoyotte who cut *Moi, un Noir* and *La Pyramide humaine*. At around the same time, she was also cutting *Les Quatre Cents Coups* (1959) for François Truffaut and Jean Cocteau's last film, *Le Testament d'Orphée* (1960). Later, Yoyotte would go on to work with a number of leading New Wave directors as well as on Rouch's own ill-starred feature, *Dionysos* (1984), though even her great skill was not sufficient to save this film from critical opprobrium. Indeed, of all the editors with whom Rouch worked, Yoyotte has probably been the most prolific, and she continues to be active as an editor of major feature films, with various highly distinguished awards to her name.[17]

Yoyotte encouraged Rouch to take an active interest in sound editing, and their first project together, *Moi, un Noir*, was certainly Rouch's most ambitious film up until that point in terms of the sound track. This film was shot by Rouch himself on his spring-wound Bell & Howell, so recording synchronous sound on location was impossible. Instead, as he had previously done with Damouré and Lam in the making of *Jaguar*, Rouch arranged for the actors playing the principal characters, Oumarou Ganda and Petit Touré, to improvise a commentary over the silent projection of a preliminary assembly of the film. The sound track was then built up through a complex mix of these improvised actors' commentaries, Rouch's own commentary voice, wild tracks of various kinds, plus a number of special sound effects and a broad variety of musical tracks.[18]

Rouch very much admired Yoyotte's inventiveness and as an example of this, he would tell the story of how they composed the sound track for the famous fight scene toward the end of *Moi, un Noir*. This takes place early one morning in the mud and the rain and involves the principal character, Robinson, and an Italian sailor whom Robinson discovers has spent the night with his girlfriend, Dorothy Lamour. Rouch had himself experienced how, when American B movies were screened in African cinemas, the spectators liked to accompany the fight sequences with cries and shouts that followed the rhythm of the punches being thrown by the actors. So when Yoyotte and he came to cut this scene, they covered the first part of the fight with music intended to encourage these responses.[19]

After he returned to work in Paris in the 1960s, Rouch continued to have the benefit of working with editors who were also working with the most celebrated feature film directors of the day. One of these was Jean Ravel, also one of the few male editors with whom Rouch worked in the course of his career. In addition to editing two of Rouch's less well-known ethnographic works, *Moro Naba* (1958–1960) and *Monsieur Albert, prophète* (1963), Ravel was primarily responsible for resolving the many editorial challenges posed by the innovative *cinéma-vérité* methods used in making *Chronicle of a Summer*. Rouch said of Ravel that he was an editor who could resolve transition problems that anyone else would find impossible. It was from him that Rouch learned that one can even perform a jump cut in the midst of someone talking, provided that it is timed to complement the cadence of what is being said. However, not all Ravel's solutions were entirely to Rouch's taste: although Rouch was party to it himself, he continued to have reservations about the strategy that Ravel developed in order to cut *Chronicle* to length, which consisted of reconstructing conversations by linking together questions and answers that originally had nothing directly to do with one another. Immediately after *Chronicle*, Ravel would go on to cut *La Jetée* (1962) for Chris Marker and *A Valparaíso* (1963) for Joris Ivens. Many years later, in 1987, he would return to work with Rouch on *Bateau-givre*, a film that was very different from *Chronicle* in that it had no commentary and the dialogues were of no significance.[20]

A number of the other editors with whom Rouch worked in the 1960s also worked with leading New Wave directors. Among these was the senior editor on *Gare du Nord*, Jacqueline Raynal, who cut several films for Éric Rohmer, while Claudine Bouché, who cut the largely disastrous *Les Veuves de quinze ans* for Rouch, also cut a number of François Truffaut's most successful films, including *Jules et Jim* (1961), *La Peau douce* (1964), and *La mariée était en noir* (1968). Both Raynal and Bouché then went on to distinguished careers after the New Wave era, though they did not return to work with Rouch himself.

Yet another editor with whom Rouch worked on a number of different occasions in the early 1960s was Annie Tresgot. She cut *La Punition* (1964) and *La Goumbé des jeunes noceurs* (1965), though she had evidently started working with Rouch some years beforehand since Claude Jutra describes her as working with him in the famously small cutting room of the Musée de l'Homme in 1961.[21] During this period, Rouch was extremely busy and often abroad, so after no more than a preliminary discussion, he would often leave the actual editing entirely up to her, giving her the impression that he had great trust in her judgment.[22] Later, Tresgot went on to become a distinguished documentary director-producer in her own right, whose works covered such diverse subjects as Algerian migrants in France, social change in the French countryside (notably *Les Enfants de Néant*, released in 1968, which she produced and which was directed by Michel Brault) and a series of portraits of Hollywood filmmakers including Billy Wilder and Elia Kazan.

Around this same time, Rouch also began working with Josée Matarasso, who cut *The Lion Hunters*, released in 1965. This was the first of three of Rouch's best-known films that would be cut by Matarasso, the others being *Jaguar* and the long version of *Petit à Petit*, both of which were cut in the period 1969–1971. Whereas Suzanne Baron, in cutting *Les*

FIGURE 13.1. Jean Rouch in an edit suite around 1962. © Annie Tresgot.

Maîtres fous, had emphasized the importance of the "punch" delivered by the first frame of a shot, Matarasso persuaded Rouch that it was last frame that was the most important because it endured, mingling with the images that followed. Rouch and Matarasso also appear to have developed a great mutual confidence, so that Rouch was happy to let her get on with the work alone. Villain reports that if Matarasso wanted to

FIGURE 13.2. Françoise Beloux with Rouch in 1991, in the very small edit suite, no longer extant, created out of the space at the head of a stairwell opposite the entrance to the cinema of the Musée de l'Homme. © Françoise Foucault.

be alone to cut some particularly difficult transition, all she had to do was make a small gesture and Rouch would leave the edit suite. On *The Lion Hunters*, Matarasso was assisted by Dov Hoenig, who went on to cut various major feature films in Israel and the United States. In the case of *Petit à Petit*, Matarasso was assisted by Dominique Villain in cutting the long, three-part first version but, due to Matarasso's many competing commitments, the cutting of the shorter ninety-two-minute version, which was the version that was later offered for general release, was actually mostly carried out by Villain.[23]

In the second half of his career, Rouch continued with this strategy of working with the same editor over a number of films in succession. Both of the DALAROUTA ethnofictions that he shot in the 1970s, *Cocorico! Monsieur Poulet* and *Babatou, les trois conseils*, were cut by Christine Lefort, while over the same period, Danièle Tessier cut a considerable number of his documentaries, including the major Dogon films, *Funérailles à Bongo* and *Le Dama d'Ambara*. But from the 1980s until the end of his life, Rouch worked almost exclusively on his major films with Françoise Beloux, an editor who had previously established her reputation in the 1970s through her work for Claude Lanzmann (fig. 13.2).

The "Napoleon" of the Edit Suite

As reported by Dominique Villain, the fundamental principle of Jean Rouch's approach to editing was free improvisation. In *Le Montage au cinema*, she cites a striking account by Josée Matarasso of the experience of working with Rouch:

> To cut with Jean Rouch . . . is to improvise on the editing table, to collaborate 100 % completely freely, quite outside the normal limits, following the often Surrealist lines of his thinking, "to enter into a film through emotion." You have to learn to feel for the shape of the sound, for the remark of one character that will set off the following shot.[24]

But this ethos of freedom did not mean that all was sweetness and light in the Rouchian *concerto à deux regards*. By contrast, Danièle Tessier's account confirms Rouch's own observation that it could sometimes be "harsh and difficult," precisely because editor and filmmaker were bound to have different points of view:

> The "birth" is sometimes turbulent, with the film being delivered in the midst of violent arguments; sometimes such a tension reigns that nobody dares enter the edit suite. Confrontation? That's inevitable, but there are also moments of collusion when ideas burst forth and everything links up clearly.[25]

True to his Surrealist tendencies, this ethos of improvisation in Rouch's edit suite was combined with a commitment to experimentation. It seems that he positively enjoyed struggling with editorial puzzles and he would go over them time and time again. Unconstrained by any conventional ideas of editorial practice, Rouch almost invariably found a solution to these problems. With tongue in cheek, Villain describes him as a "Napoleon" of the edit suite, because "he won all his battles."[26] As with his shooting, when he achieved these victories, he would attribute them to *la grace*, a term that, as we saw in the previous chapter, had a somewhat idiosyncratic meaning for Rouch, denoting a Dionysian state in which intuitive artistic creativity combines with random good fortune to produce a successful result.[27]

As described above, it was from observing the work of the editors of the Actualités françaises on his first film that Rouch learned that one should always cut a film with reference to the ending. Sometimes he would claim a more elevated model, suggesting that he was following Baudelaire, who composed his poems starting from the last line. However, by saying that he liked to cut his films in this way, Rouch did not actually mean that he cut them backward. The process was somewhat more complicated, as he explained to Villain:

> In cutting a film, you begin from the beginning, then you try to find out where you are going. Usually, I cut the first two-thirds, then the last third from the end. I have a theory that is perhaps a bit literary. I remember my French Composition lessons: you had to have an introduction followed by two parts and then a conclusion or third part, the so-called "synthesis." So you began with an introduction, got into the subject, the first part was usually a bit rough, you got on a bit better in the second part, arrived at a conclusion and wrote that up, then rewrote the second part, which in turn meant you had to change the first part, and then finally, you rewrote the introduction. Editing is like a narrative, like telling a story. Perhaps it's also like this in music, when the last note is prolonged and, as a result, becomes very important. . . . You begin from the tail. It's like Hitchcock's suspense, you give a sense in advance of the ending but without actually revealing it. The whole film heads toward it. Instinctively, that's what I do when editing.[28]

Villain emphasizes the rapidity with which Rouch worked in the edit suite. But, more generally, Rouch's relaxed attitude with regard to time was legendary. He would claim that he had learned in Africa not to wear a watch, considering it both a limitation and a *memento mori* that he could do without.[29] As a result, he was proverbially late for appointments. Unless under intense pressure from a producer, he showed a similar disregard for cutting his films according to any fixed schedule. Indeed, in order to give himself the luxury of being able to experiment with his films as long as he felt was necessary, he set up both his own edit suite and and his own sound-mixing facility at the Musée de l'Homme.

Not long after returning from a shoot, Rouch would generally look at the rushes, usually by himself. As there had been no shooting script, there could be no cutting script either. Instead, according to Philo Bregstein, while viewing the rushes, Rouch would write an extensive log, and these would become a sort of cutting script after the fact.[30] But once he had viewed the rushes, the images would be fixed in his mind and the precise date for editing took on less importance for him. In the case of some of his shorter films on very specific subjects, editing could be carried out shortly after the viewing. This happened, for example, with *Les Tambours d'avant* and the portraits of Mauss's former students. But sometimes years would elapse before he got round to editing more complex works. For example, *Mammy Water*, which was shot in 1954, was not definitively edited until 1966. *Le Dama d'Ambara*, shot in 1974, was not completed until 1980.[31]

Not only did Rouch shoot all his films, including the fictional works, as if they were documentaries, with no script, no second takes, and in chronological order, but he also edited them as if they were documentaries, working with the same sort of cutting ratios.[32] When shooting his ethnofictions, he usually ended up with what were, for a fiction film, many hours of rushes. In shooting *Petit à Petit* in 1967–1968, for example, he produced twenty-four hours of rushes.[33] This was similar to the twenty-five hours shot for *Chronicle of a Summer*, but that was a documentary. Given that *Petit à Petit* was a fiction film and that the rushes were entirely composed of what were, supposedly, first-and-only takes, twenty-four hours represented a vast amount of material. In cutting this material, Rouch was not choosing between various takes of the same shot, as one would normally do in the editing of a fiction film, but rather treating the material as if it were a set of documentary rushes, either cutting particular shots down in length or eliminating them completely. The cutting ratio of the 35mm version of *Petit à Petit* that eventually resulted from this process was 16:1, which is very high for a fiction film, though not at all unusual for a documentary shot on 16mm at that time.[34]

Editing by Successive Approximations

Rouch would often describe his editorial strategy as being based on the principle of "successive approximations," the design principle taught to him by Albert Caquot during his days as a student of engineering at the École des Ponts et Chausées. Transferred to the edit suite, what this meant was that Rouch progressed his edits by a process of trial and error, trying out various combinations, before finally selecting the one that he thought worked best. When this process of successive approximation entailed no more than the linking together of a few sequence-shots that had already been largely edited in the camera, then the editing that actually took place in the edit suite could be very brief. But if the subject of the film were more complex, then the editing could be very prolonged. Tessier compares the case of the fourteen-minute portrait film of the Japanese sculptor, *Taro Okamoto*, which took two hours to cut, with the editing of the eighty-minute *Funérailles à Bongo* that was not started until five years after the shoot and then took a further two years to complete.[35]

There were also a number of further reasons for the drawn-out nature of Rouch's editing schedules. One was simply that he was involved in many different things: if he was not engaged in some sort of project in Paris itself, he was off on an airplane to West Africa. Due to these many distractions, Rouch would often have to abandon a film in the middle of the edit and would only come back to it months or years later. Another reason for Rouch's prolonged editing schedules was that an integral part of the strategy of successive approximations involved screening cuts of the film to an audience and then recutting it in the light of the feedback. Rouch not only employed this feedback strategy with the subjects of his film as part of his practice of "shared anthropology," as described in earlier chapters, but also with what he called the "freemasonry" of editors around Paris, as well as with producers, colleagues or friends within his immediate circle.[36]

In this connection, one of Rouch's favorite stories concerned the time when he was working on a film with Suzanne Baron, early on in his career. Toward the end of the normal working day, the eminent director Jacques Tati would come into the edit suite and sit quietly in the corner, waiting his turn to work with Baron after-hours. Eventually, Rouch plucked up the courage to ask the great man what film he was working on, only to discover, to his astonishment, that it was *Les Vacances de M. Hulot*. This film, on which Baron had been one of three editors, had had its general release some four months earlier. But Tati explained that as a former mime artist, he knew that it took at least three months of public performance before a particular routine could be considered fully perfected and that the same applied, in his view, to films. Therefore, for several months after the release of his films, he would go in person to the cinemas where they were showing and then, on the basis of the audience's reactions, recut his films, often by minute amounts, taking out two frames here and three frames there.[37]

This attitude greatly impressed the young Rouch, and he would later apply it to his own practice of recutting his films in the light of the feedback that he received following screenings at film festivals or similar venues. In the 16mm era, this would have been an expensive strategy, since in order for a film to be shown at a festival, it would have been necessary to prepare, if not a fully married print, at least a double-band version with a mixed sound track and perhaps a fresh print of the image track as well.[38] Although this was a common enough strategy among feature filmmakers at the time, for most ethnographic filmmakers the cost of recutting and remixing after the presentation of a film at a festival would have been prohibitive. But although Rouch might have incurred certain laboratory costs for the reprinting of the image track, in other respects the costs involved in such a reworking would have been much reduced for him since he had both his own sound-mixing studio and his own editing suite at the Musée de l'Homme, and he usually carried out the sound mixing of the festival versions of his films himself.[39]

A number of Rouch's best-known films were recut after they had already been screened in public. As described in chapter 8, a festival version of *Chronicle of a Summer* was prepared for Cannes in 1961, but was then recut by Rouch when this screening suggested that a stronger ending was needed. But by far the most extreme example of recutting in the Rouchian canon is surely *Jaguar*. The first cut of this film was almost five hours long and was screened in private to Pierre Braunberger and Jules Dassin in 1955. At this screening, it was agreed that the material would work well with a voice-over improvised by the protagonists, though this was not recorded by Damouré and Lam until 1957.[40] This formed the basis of the sound track for the 2.5-hour version screened at the Cinémathèque in Paris shortly thereafter. But some years later, the film was recut again with additional voice-over material recorded by Damouré and Lam in 1960 and was then screened at the Venice Film Festival in 1967 with a running time of about a hundred minutes. A couple of years after that, around the same time that *Petit à Petit*, the sequel to *Jaguar*, was also being cut, *Jaguar* was recut yet again and released in the definitive eighty-eight-minute version.[41]

Rouch's editorial strategy of successive approximations and the many re-versions that he produced in the light of the feedback that he received certainly give the lie to what Philo Bregstein calls the "myth" that editing was of no importance to him.[42] However, the long drawn-out editing schedules that these practices entailed were only made possible by virtue of Rouch's very particular institutional circumstances. For most of the time, he was able to proceed at his own chosen pace, without either producers or academic authorities breathing down his neck, demanding some kind of output. But there was one circumstance that even Rouch, for all his ingenuity, could not avoid. For, in the end, the Napoleon of the edit suite also met his Waterloo: he simply ran out of time, as is the fate of Everyman. When he died, the editing of perhaps as many as a third of his works remained incomplete.

14 : The Fixing of the Truth

What is editing? It's a fixing of the truth.   JEAN ROUCH, 1992[1]

In the previous chapter, I suggested that there was something paradoxical about the fact that although Jean Rouch thought that it was essential to work with an editor, he always strove as much as possible to edit in the camera, the logical corollary of which was to make editing in the editing suite unnecessary. There is a similar paradox in his attitude toward the nuts and bolts of editing, which shall be our principal focus here. For, as we shall see, although Rouch may have been a Napoleon of the edit suite, dedicating himself with great energy to the resolution of technical problems, he only availed himself of a limited range of editorial weapons.

As I described in chapter 8, in the course of making *Chronicle of a Summer* in 1960–1961, Rouch became very perplexed about what he called the "devil of editing." As a result of the new portable sound-synchronous technology used in shooting *Chronicle*, the rushes had provided a much more faithful representation of the world than Rouch had been able to achieve in his earlier films. And yet, once back in the edit suite, he discovered, to his dismay, that under pressure from the producer, most of this painstakingly gathered material had to be jettisoned, while what remained was subjected to a radical reordering that showed scant respect for the reality of the original events. Rouch thought that the principles underlying this way of editing had been insufficiently thought through and compared the jettisoning of so much material to the amputation of a limb. The subsequent reordering of the material that remained he compared to Guillaume Apollinaire's practice of composing his poems from snatches of dialogue that he had heard in different bistros or, even more harshly, to the practice of cutting out isolated words from a newspaper and then pasting them together to send an anonymous letter.[2]

In the years immediately following the production of *Chronicle*, as we saw in chapter 9, Rouch tried various experiments to circumvent the dilemmas that the cutting of this film had posed for him. But these did not result in the development of anything like a new grammar of editing appropriate to the cutting of documentary films. On the contrary, they involved rather the minimizing of editorial interventions, relying instead on the inspiration of the cameraperson on location to decide what to include and what to exclude.

These attitudes remained with Rouch for the rest of his life, as exemplified by the rhetorical question-and-answer reproduced in the epigraph to this chapter. Posed some thirty years after his struggle with the "devil of editing" while cutting *Chronicle*, this remark suggests that for all that he subsequently sought to associate his work with Vertov's theory of *cinéma-vérité*, with its associated editorial strategy of montage and the abundant use of special effects, he continued to think of editing not as a means of delivering a distinctive truth about the world but rather as an act whereby, in the process of being transformed, the reality of the world is somehow betrayed.

Interestingly, however, the conclusion that Rouch drew from this, namely, that one should keep editorial interventions to a minimum, he applied only to the cutting of the image track. In relation to the sound track, he continued to be disposed to use the full panoply of tricks of the editor's trade. Furthermore, central to his editorial praxis was the superimposition of a poetic commentary that he always performed himself. So although Rouch may have set great store by preserving the objective integrity of the events represented in the images, the viewer's relationship to those images is always heavily mediated through the subjectivity of his oral performance. In effect, this involved what one might call a fixing of the truth in a somewhat different sense, that is, a fixing as in the final stage of a photographic process, in which a definitive form or coloration is imparted to an image.

The Straight Cut and Progressive Chronology

Not only in his documentaries, but even in his ethnofictions, Rouch showed a marked restraint in the use of visual transitions. He almost always used the straight cut: dissolves, fades, let alone anything so adventurous as a wipe, are virtually unknown in his films. On the other hand, no doubt assisted by his editors, he developed the straight cut into a fine art. Rather than rely, as is the most conventional practice, on moments of stability to make a cut, Rouch learned to use the movement within a shot to assist a transition. In a sense, this strategy was forced upon him by his shooting style. Particularly after he adopted the new technology and became committed to the sequence-shot, his shooting had a tendency to be unstable. It therefore became necessary to turn what might be considered, as one of his editors, Danièle Tessier put it, "an a priori defect in a style" into a virtue and cut according to the rhythm established by the movements of the camera.[3]

A very striking example of such cutting on movement is to be found in one of Rouch's earlier works, Les Maîtres fous, which was cut by Suzanne Baron. It occurs about four minutes into the film when a group of hauka cult members are seen approaching the camera in a taxi. As the taxi arrives at the level of the camera, there is a cut as it apparently passes the camera and continues down the road. The transition is entirely smooth, and it is only on closer inspection that one realizes that the incoming taxi is green, whereas the outgoing taxi is cream-colored. This remarkable metamorphosis is entirely obscured by the movement through one shot and into the next (fig. 14.1).

Although Rouch intended to invoke Vertov's concept of the kinoki in referring to his editors as a "second ciné-eye," his editorial style was completely different to that of his "totemic ancestor." Central to Vertov's editing practice was a particular form of montage, of the kind that Karel Reisz and Gavin Millar, in their classic manual on editing identified—even if rather debatably—as "Russian" or "intellectual" montage, that is, a sequence of shots in which each image makes some kind of comment on the adjacent images. They differentiate this from "British and American" montage, that is, a sequence of brief shots that, taken together as a series, merely provide information or context in a time-efficient manner.[4] But Rouch, with a number of significant exceptions, including those from Les Maîtres fous that I shall consider below, did not employ montage of any kind in his films. He also usually eschewed the special effects that Vertov absolutely relished, such as slow-, fast- or reverse motion, time-lapse cinematography, split screens, superimpositions, and so on. The only exception that I can think of here is the use of slow motion in the research films that Rouch made in conjunction with the ethnomusicologist Gilbert Rouget.[5]

Rouch was also very restrained in his manipulation of time in the edit suite. Cuts to different times or places outside the cumulative temporal diegesis of a film are a rarity. In editing his ethnofictions and also Chronicle of a Summer, he often departed from the real chronology of the rushes, but they were then reconstructed so as to represent a normally progressive, cumulative chronology within the diegetic world of the film. With the exception of a totally obscure flash-forward at the beginning of his late film, Madame L'Eau, I cannot think of any film in which Rouch uses a flashback or flash forward as a "hook" at the beginning of a film.

FIGURE 14.1. *Les Maîtres fous*,
A green taxi approaches (*top*) but
through cutting on movement
(*middle*) most viewers do not notice
that it is a cream-colored taxi that
emerges (*bottom*).

Usually, a Rouch film unfolds in time in a straightforward, cumulative manner from the first frame to the last.

However, as I have suggested, there are some important exceptions, of varying levels of sophistication. At the simplest level, Rouch does use illustrative cuts to another time and place on occasion, as in his late Dogon film, *Funérailles à Bongo*, when there is a cut from a nighttime shot of the elders chanting the *tegué*, the ancient sayings about the creation of the world, to a long shot of animal skulls that was clearly taken at some other time and place and over which the elders' chanting is continued. There are some more elaborate examples in *The Lion Hunters*, such as when Rouch cuts from the preparations for the hunt to show the hunters some months earlier collecting the plants from which they will make poison to paint on their arrowheads. Later on in the film, as they are preparing their traps, there is an even more startling cut to a metal workshop in Ghana, where an anonymous blacksmith is shown making the traps. But perhaps the best-known example in Rouch's work of such an editorial sortie to another time and place occurs just prior to the famous sequence at the end of *Moi, un Noir* in which Robinson talks about his Indochina experience as he walks along the banks of the lagoon at Abidjan with his friend Petit Jules. This scene begins with them sitting down, looking out over the water, which reminds Robinson of his childhood and leads him to reflect on the contrast between his happiness then and his present troubles. There is then a striking cut to an extended sequence of idyllic shots of children bathing in the river at Niamey, whom Robinson identifies in the voice-over as himself and his friends when he was young.

This last case could almost be considered an example of the rather different form of temporal excursus from the diegesis represented by the dream sequences earlier in *Moi, un Noir*, in which Robinson imagines, first, that he is a boxing champion, and later, that he is being welcomed into the bed of his girlfriend, Dorothy Lamour. But though they are meant to be dreams, in terms of their general visual style, these sequences are entirely realistic and within themselves conform to a conventional cumulative chronology. In this regard, they are no different stylistically from the rest of the film. The same is true of the dream sequence in which Raymond and Nadine get married in *La Pyramide humaine*. It could be argued that this makes them all the more effective since the viewer is not entirely sure until the dreams are over that they are, in fact, dreams. As such, Rouch could be said to be putting into practice the Surrealist project to break down the barrier between dreams and reality. But stylistically speaking, it remains the case that although Rouch may have been inspired by Salvador Dalí and shared the latter's Surrealist attitudes, his cinematic dream world is much less bizarre than the dream worlds that

Dalí himself conceived in his collaborations with Luis Buñuel, and later with Albert Hitchcock.

However, there is one film, *Les Maîtres fous*, in which there are numerous exceptions to these generalizations about Rouch's conservatism regarding the manipulation of time. This film has a very tight, tripartite structure, which, in itself, is unusual in his work. But it is the frequent use of montage that is its most distinctive feature. In the first of the three sections, there is a prolonged montage sequence of the kind that Reisz and Millar refer to as "British and American," in which the great variety of different jobs that Nigerien migrants carry out around Accra are summarized in a series of brief shots. The third section, in which the adepts of the *hauka* cult are shown back at their jobs the day after the ceremony, also features a montage sequence. In this case, however, there is a certain "Russian" flavor to the montage since the shots of them working away at their everyday jobs, smiling broadly, are intercut with shots of the same men the day before, in a state of trance, gorging themselves on dog meat with spittle running down their chins. The use of a visual flashback of this kind toward the end of a film to tie up the narrative and achieve a sense of closure is a much-used editorial device, but it is one that is highly unusual, if not actually unique, in Rouch's work.

However, it is in the central and most lengthy section of the film, dealing with the *hauka* cult ceremony itself, that there is the most striking example of "Russian" montage. For the most part, this section is cut in accordance with a conventional progressive chronology of the kind that is very common in Rouch's films. But suddenly, in the middle of this section, there is a cut from the cracking of an egg on the head of the statue of the *hauka* spirit Governor, situated alongside the dancing mediums in trance, to the "real" British governor reviewing colonial troops at the opening of parliament in Accra. This is perhaps the most-discussed cut in the whole of Rouch's oeuvre, though for reasons that I discussed at some length in chapter 7, its precise meaning is debatable. But whatever its significance, there is no doubt that some connection is implied in the juxtaposition of the two shots.[6]

Given Rouch's regular evocation of Vertov, it is tempting to conclude that these examples of "Russian" montage in *Les Maîtres fous* must represent some kind of debt to his "totemic ancestor." But it was not until some years after the cutting of *Les Maîtres fous* that Rouch started to show any particular enthusiasm for Vertovian ideas. Catherine Russell has suggested that these transitions should be considered rather as examples of Eisensteinian "dialectical" montage. This certainly ties in with Suzanne Baron's reported views about the importance of the "punch" delivered by the first frame of a shot, since this was also one of Eisenstein's editing principles. But whatever the precise nature of these examples of montage may be, the number of exceptions to Rouch's normal editorial praxis in *Les Maîtres fous* is so great that it seems very likely that they were due, at least in part, to the influence of Baron. Sadly, as she is also deceased and Rouch himself, to the best of my knowledge, did not talk or write about this particular aspect of their collaboration, this is a matter that is unlikely ever to be resolved.[7]

The *Trompe-l'oreille* and the "Opium of the Cinema"

Although Rouch barely mentions sound editing in his manifesto-essay "The Camera and Man," it was an aspect of post-production that interested him greatly. Such was the importance that he gave to sound editing that he believed that one should work with two independent edit-suites, one for picture, the other for sound. This indeed was the arrangement that he set up for himself in the Musée de l'Homme, with a film-editing suite fashioned out of a small corner at the head of the stairwell opposite the entrance to the museum cinema (as shown in fig. 13.2 above), while a sound-editing suite was set up in an equally small space, hidden behind the screen of the cinema (fig. 14.2).[8]

In the same way that Rouch set great store by improvisation and experimentation in shooting and picture editing, so he did in sound editing. He particularly enjoyed experimenting with special effects. As Dominique Villain observes, there is something rather paradoxical about the fact that although Rouch was generally averse to using special visual effects, he was very partial to what she calls the *trompe-l'oreille*, literally "ear-fooling," that is, a sound effect intended to persuade the listener into believing something about the soundscape of a scene that is not, in fact, the case.[9]

As one might well anticipate, Rouch did not like to use off-the-peg special sound effects bought from a library and would make a point of recording his own. Sometimes these additional effects would be entirely naturalistic—a tin can rolling on the ground, a child crying, the sound of distant traffic recorded out of the window of the edit suite itself— and they would be used merely to "sweeten," in other words, enrich or touch up the sound track. But in other cases, he intended these additional sounds to have some more metaphorical effect. A well-known example occurs in *Jaguar*: as Damouré travels into Accra in the back of an open-topped truck, he imagines himself being welcomed by crowds of people as if he were some kind of hero. On the sound track, one hears the roar of a crowd cheering and he waves his hand, as if he were a politician acknowledging his supporters, but the picture shows that in diegetic reality, there is barely a soul by the side of the road.

FIGURE 14.2. Rouch in the small sound-mixing suite behind the cinema screen of the Musée de l'Homme in 1990, with Patrick Genet, the sound recordist on a number of his later films. © Françoise Foucault.

Rouch was particularly fond of using the sound of birds and wind in a metaphorical way. Sometimes the "bird" sounds would be of his own manufacture: Villain reports that he once created a "bird" sound by making a recording of feet crunching on the gravel paths of the Jardin du Luxembourg and then playing it back at half-speed.[10] There are some interesting examples of the metaphorical use of both bird and wind sounds in *Madame L'Eau*. Relatively early in the film, as the "shameless Bella shepherd" Tallou flirts with Winneke, the lovely Dutch chauffeuse of their "jaguar" car, there is a lively chattering of tropical birds on the sound track. Tallou gives her a ring, declaring that they will always be brother and sister, but the tumultuous birds suggest that there is another agenda behind the gesture. Somewhat later, Philo Bregstein shows Damouré and Lam around a museum display about slavery in Africa. Even though they are plainly inside, as they look at the gruesome prints on the walls, there is an ominous wailing of wind in the background.

These metaphorical uses of sound effects can be contrasted with what might be termed a "structural" use. These are not common in Rouch's films, but there are a number of particularly striking examples. A relatively simple example occurs in *Chronicle of a Summer*. In the last shot of this film, after Rouch and Morin have said goodbye, and Morin is heading off down the Champs Elysées pursued by the "walking camera" of

Michel Brault, one hears the voices of Nadine and Marceline repeating their famous question from the scene right at the beginning of the film, "Are you happy, Monsieur? Are you happy?" These voices are mixed with the enchantingly melodious music produced by the music box of the young couple, the Cuénets, also featured early in the film, who had been the only respondents to reply positively to Nadine and Marceline's question. Whatever the doubts of the other subjects of the film, the effect, which is almost subliminal, is to make the viewer feel happy, not just on account of the euphonious character of the music, but also because, by taking us back to the beginning of the film, a satisfying sense of closure is achieved.[11]

A somewhat more complex example linking the beginning and end of a film is found in *Les Maîtres fous*. This film opens with a shot, taken from above, of a *hampi*, the large pottery vase that is central to the traditional Songhay *yenendi* rain-making ceremony. Based on a Kodakchrome slide taken in Ayorou by Rouch on his way to the Gold Coast in early 1954, this shot captures an important moment in the ceremony and shows a number of men with a finger placed on the edge of the vase.[12] This image of the epitome of tradition is accompanied on the sound track by calypso-like "highlife" music, which was the epitome of what was then modernity. Right at the end of the film, there is a similar juxtaposition, but this time, the other way around. Here, in the image, the adepts have returned to their everyday lives as laborers digging a trench for the Accra Waterworks company. But on the sound track, there is the plangent wailing of the *godye*, the single string violin by means of which the Songhay call the spirits. In both instances, the conjunction of sounds and images serves to underline a more general point that Rouch sought to make in his migration films, namely, that the Songhay migrants were part of both "modern" and "traditional" worlds and were, in fact, living in both at the same time (fig. 14.3).

This use of nonsynchronous music in *Les Maîtres fous* provides yet another example of how this film is unusual in the Rouchian canon. For, generally speaking, Rouch was highly circumspect about using nonsynchronous music in his ethnographic documentaries, be it intra- or extra-diegetically.[13] In "The Camera and Man," he refers to music as the "opium of cinema," declaring forcefully that it "can put one to sleep, lets bad cuts pass unnoticed or gives artificial rhythm to images that have no rhythm and never will have any." The story of his own *prise de conscience* about the inappropriateness of extradiegetic music was one that he particularly liked to tell. As described in chapter 3, it took place in the course of an open-air screening of *Bataille sur le grand fleuve* at Ayorou in 1954, during the same visit in which he took the photograph of the *hampi* used as the

FIGURE 14.3. The aural "book ending" of *Les Maîtres fous*. Over the first image, a scene from the traditional *yenendi* rain-making ceremony (*top*), one hears cosmopolitan "high-life" music; over the last image, showing the migrants' experience of modernity (*bottom*), one hears the traditional single string *godye* violin calling the spirits. Through these juxtapositions, the migrants are shown to be simultaneously living in both traditional and modern worlds.

first image of *Les Maîtres fous*. Even though it was a local hunting melody recorded on the portable Sgubbi, the audience objected to the superimposition of this music on the hippopotamus hunt that is the main focus of the film on the grounds that it would supposedly frighten away the hippopotami. Rouch concluded that thereafter he would have to be more careful in his use of such extradiegetic music. Yet he did not rule it out entirely and in "The Camera and Man," he approves its use if it "really supports an action."[14]

However, Rouch only applied these restrictions on the use of music to his documentaries. In his ethnofictions, there are many examples of nonsynchronous music, mostly in an extradiegetic form. In *Jaguar*, for example, the "Jaguar" hit song provides the leitmotif of the whole film, and is even repeated again briefly in *Petit à Petit*, which is essentially a reprise of *Jaguar*, in order to reaffirm the connection between the two films. But Rouch's most elaborate use of music is surely in *Moi, un Noir*. No doubt encouraged by Marie-Josèphe Yoyotte, who is an accomplished musician as well as the editor of this film, several different kinds of extradiegetic music are combined in the sound track, including a number of Caribbean and African songs as well as French ballads sung in an African accent. Working with an editor may often have involved a "harsh dialogue" in Rouch's view, but in this case, it resulted in a particularly melodious outcome.

Narration as Inspired Performance

Although Rouch did sometimes use music in his ethnographic documentaries, much more important in this genre of his filmmaking was narration, which he always performed himself. This narration could fulfill various different functions: it could provide essential contextualizing information, it could offer some interpretation—usually relatively low-key—of the significance of what was happening on the screen or it could paraphrase what was being said or chanted by the protagonists. On occasion, he would also use narration to perform what Tessier rather charmingly calls a "pirouette," by which she means a segue linking together two otherwise rather disparate sequences.[15]

As in all his filmmaking praxis, improvisation was a very important aspect of narration for Rouch, both in the intial conception of the words and then in performing them for the purposes of recording. In general, Rouch was a very able oral performer, even when speaking completely off the cuff. His style of speaking in public, whatever the context, was invariably elegant and poetic: his impromptu commentaries at the Bilan du film ethnographique festival will be remembered by all those who had the pleasure of listening to them. Although he often failed to answer the question and had a tendency to repeat the same familiar stories, the responses that he gave in his many interviews were always engagingly eloquent. All these qualities he brought to the formulation and performance of his narrations.

In the early films, Rouch's narrations have a reedy, declamatory quality and involve an almost exaggerated pronunciation of every syllable, a style that Rouch himself traced to his attendance at the Surrealist poetry readings of Paul Éluard and Jean-Louis Barrault in the 1930s.[16] Later, the narrations became more mellow, but they retained a certain lyrical quality, much admired, it seems, by French listeners, though regarded, it would probably be true to say, with some reservation by Anglo-Saxon audiences accustomed to more dispassionate narrational styles.

For Rouch, dispassionate narration was anathema. In the same way that he believed that effective shooting required intense participation in the world of the subjects, so too did effective narration require intense engagement with the film in its edited form. Just as filmmakers should seek to harmonize their shooting technique to the movements of the protagonists before their lenses, so too should narrators seek to harmonize their tone of voice and style of delivery to the subject matter of the film. In "The Camera and Man," he deplores the dry, supposedly "scientific" voice-overs produced by anthropologists "not wanting to confess their passion for the people they study." Equally unacceptable were voice-overs informed by "an ideological discourse through which the filmmaker exports notions of revolution that he has not been able to act upon in his own country." Both these forms of narration, Rouch believed, undermined the cinematic potential of a film:

> As long as an anthropologist filmmaker, out of scientism or ideological shame, hides himself behind a comfortable kind of incognito, he will ruin his films irreparably and they will join the documents in archives which only the specialists see.

It was precisely because he believed that a successful narration required an intense subjective engagement by the filmmaker that he usually insisted on narrating all his own films, even the English-language versions, despite his self-attributed "bad" English.[17]

As Jeanette DeBouzek has noted, in performing his voice-overs, Rouch assumed a variety of different forms of speech and tones of voice in accordance with which voice he was paraphrasing and/or the context of the particular passage of narration. The overall effect was what she refers to as "a cacophony of mixed voices."[18] These voices include, at one extreme, relatively even-toned ethnographic contextualization and at the other, reiterative paraphrasing of ritual chanting, in which Rouch himself adopts the inspired tone of voice of the protagonist(s). When recording the original French voice-over for *The Lion Hunters*, he learned from the editor, Annie Tresgot, that in order to differentiate these various voices, he should read the contextualizing commentary sitting down, but when he was paraphrasing the chants of the hunters, he should stand up, since this would have the effect of making his voice go up a couple of notes.[19]

But in many instances, the genres of speech overlap in Rouch's narrations as he often provides quasi-sociological commentary in reiterative poetic tones as if it were a ritual chant. An example of this occurs in the last section of *Les Tambours d'avant*, as Rouch seeks to underline the intergenerational continuity represented by the fact that the ceremony is being attentively watched by school-age children. Assuming a poetic timbre, Rouch intones, over the image of the *zima* priests negotiating with the spirit Kure the Hyena:

Sorciers, fils de sorciers, ancêtres de sorciers, d'un pouvoir plus fort que celui des marabouts [Sorcerers, sons of sorcerers, ancestors of sorcerers, of a power greater than that of the marabouts]

After Hadyo, Spirit of the Fulani Slave, has made her entrance, he returns to the theme as the camera withdraws to show the young people looking on from the edge of the plaza:

Pères de sorciers, grandpères de sorciers, les dieux maintenant attendent les sacrifices [Fathers of sorcerers, grandfathers of sorcerers, the gods now await the sacrifices]

The combination of the incantatory style of delivery and the reiteration, coupled with a poetic vocabulary that contrasts with the more sober sociological terminology that one might use when writing about the same event ("sorcerers" as opposed to "mediums" and "gods" rather than mere "spirits"), serves to give the film itself a ritualistic aura that mirrors and echoes the ritual character of the event that it presents.

In his interviews, Rouch liked to emphasize the spontaneity of these narrational performances. He told DeBouzek that they were totally improvised "according to chance, following my unconscious," and she suggests that, as such, they are analogous to the automatic writing of the Surrealist poets.[20] This was a point that Rouch particularly stressed in relation to the narration of *Les Maîtres fous*. He once described this as his first experience of entering the Vertovian ciné-trance, for, as he performed the narration, he felt as if he had been possessed by the process and had assumed a different persona. Certainly, as various authors have noted, the narration is of crucial importance in holding this film together. Others, however, have questioned whether this degree of integration between narration and action could really be achieved on the basis of an entirely improvised voice-over.[21]

A closer examination of how the narration of *Les Maîtres fous* came about reveals that although there was certainly an important element of improvisation involved in the final performance, as so often with Rouch's shooting and editing praxes, there was also a considerable degree of preparation beforehand. Even before he returned from the Gold Coast in 1955, Rouch worked together with one of the priests of the cult to produce an approximate translation of what the mediums were saying, which was often in a difficult-to-understand glossolalic combination of European and indigenous languages. Once back in France, he paraphrased these translations into French and combined these with more informational commentary points to produce a first version of the narration. It was this version that he rehearsed on at least two separate occasions when he screened rough cuts of the film, including the disastrous screening at the Musée de l'Homme and in the more private screening for the Hollywood film noir director Jules Dassin. It seems likely that he would also have rehearsed this version at other screenings of the rough cut to the "freemasonry" of Parisian editors or to his friends. Certainly, by the time he screened the rough cut to Dassin, it must have been reasonably well honed since Dassin suggested that it should be retained and used more or less as it was in the final film. But once Suzanne Baron became involved, as Rouch himself reports, he "began to work on the script with the editor," suggesting further, more carefully considered, refinements. It seems that Baron then took this script and used it as a basis for fine-cutting the image track, thereby accounting for the organic connection between narration and action.[22]

However, even with these adjustments, the narration script was not entirely finalized and in the definitive recording, there was still a need for some element of improvisation since Rouch had not decided how he should end it. The narration was recorded by André Cotin, a highly experienced sound engineer. Cotin encouraged Rouch to stand up and placed a microphone on a stand just below his mouth, carefully adjusting it so that Rouch's voice came out more base than normal. Cotin had heard Rouch perform the narration without using a text at a previous presentation of the film, and for this final recording, he encouraged him to perform it in the same way, making sure that he looked at the screen where a mute version of the film would be playing and speaking as if confiding a secret to the microphone.

Rouch was very nervous since, given the technology of the time, if he had made any mistake or one of the splices on the film had come apart, they would have had to begin all over again. He later recalled how as he began to speak, he felt that he had become possessed by someone other than himself. He could hear himself speaking in a strange voice that reminded him of the reedy voices of Paul Éluard and Jean-Louis Barrault as they performed at the Surrealist poetry reading that he had attended in 1937. It was this that he considered his first experience of the Vertovian "ciné-trance." But although he stammered a little, he managed to get through the whole film in a single take, even finding some words for the ending. These make up the well-known concluding passage in which he speculates whether the *hauka* mediums have found a way of absorbing the "mental disorders" of urban living that Europeans have yet to discover. Although, in retrospect, he considered this passage to be a little "awkward" and would later disclaim the general sentiments underlying it, he was still very pleased with the fact of it, since it had arrived "just like that," confirming once again his Surrealism-inspired faith in the value of spontaneity. However, it was a spontaneity for which a great deal of groundwork had been laid, and this would become the model for all his narrational performances in the future.[23]

The Master's Voice

When Jean Rouch first started making films, before the advent of portable synchronous-sound technology, there was no way of using the voices of the subjects themselves in an ethnographic documentary, except as postsynchronized voice-over. As described in chapters 5 and 6, this was the strategy that Rouch used very successfully in his ethnofictions *Jaguar* and *Moi, un Noir.* But once more portable synchronous systems became available in the 1960s, Rouch abandoned this post-synchronization strategy in making his ethnofictions and allowed the protagonists to speak in synch.

In the latter part of his career, Rouch also began to use synchronous speech in the series of personal portraits that he shot from the mid-1970s. But prior to that, with one very significant exception, even when synchronous speech was technically possible, he did not make use of it in his documentary films. This point is particularly pertinent to Rouch's Dogon films shot in the late 1960s and early 1970s, which represent his last major corpus of ethnographic work and which I discussed at some length in chapter 11. By this time, synchronous recording of voices on location was well established in documentary practice generally, partly as a result of Rouch's own pioneering efforts in this regard. But throughout this lengthy series of films among the Dogon, Rouch continued to use his own voice to paraphrase everything that his subjects were saying, whether it was ritual chanting or everyday speech. Through the many hours of these films, only on a few very rare occasions does a Dogon subject directly address the camera in synch.

The significant exception alluded to above was, of course, *Chronicle of a Summer,* which is covered from end to end with synchronized speech and is, moreover, widely regarded as establishing a new technical milestone in this regard. The exceptional character of *Chronicle* was something that arose in an interview that Rouch gave at the time of a screening of a selection of his films at the Margaret Mead Film Festival in New York in 1977. The interviewers press Rouch on why it is that the characters in *Chronicle* are shot in close-up, talking about complex ideas whereas in his African ethnographic films, the subjects are often shown in long shots engaged in action rather than speaking. The interviewers put it to him that whereas *Chronicle* emphasizes how its European subjects think, Rouch's ethnographic films on Africa emphasize how the subjects act. The implicit thrust of the interviewers' questions is that there is an unacknowledged racism in this differential use of synchronous speech. Given Rouch's pioneering role in providing a platform for African voices in his ethnofictions, not to mention the African voices in *Chronicle* itself, this would be a very harsh judgment. But although Rouch acknowledges that the interviewers are "asking good questions" and ones that he has not been asked before, the explanations that he offers are not very convincing.[24]

Although he was not able to mount a strong defense of his practice on this occasion, it would be most unjust to accuse Rouch of racism on this or any other matter. Nor is there any necessity to do so since there are a number of alternative reasons for the difference perceived by the interviewers. The first, and most obvious, reason has to do with language itself. For, true to the anthropological tradition of Griaule and Dieterlen in which he was trained, Rouch conducted most of his work in French. According to his closest associates, although he regularly visited the Songhay-Zerma for over fifty years, he never became entirely fluent in their language. As he himself admitted, he was "not very good at languages."[25] If his knowledge of Songhay was limited, we can surmise that his knowledge of Dogon was even more so. The reason why he was able to give a voice to the protagonists of his ethnofictions was simply that they all spoke in French. Damouré was Sorko, Lam was Fulani, and Tallou was Bella: they all spoke different first languages, but because they were all able to speak French, as could the principal sound recordist Moussa Hamidou, a Zerma, they could all work together on Rouch's ethnofictions.

However, when it came to Rouch's ethnographic documentaries, the great majority of which were about ritual performances of one kind or another, the subjects were clearly not speaking French. In the latter stages of his career, Rouch could have addressed this problem by the use of subtitles. By the time of the publication of "The Camera and Man" in 1975, the use of subtitles had become commonplace in North American ethnographic cinema, following the pioneering use of this device by John Marshall and Tim Asch when they were cutting Marshall's Kalahari material in the early 1960s.[26] But although Rouch is polite about Marshall's use of subtitles in the essay, he explains that he himself does not employ them because firstly, they "mutilate" the image and secondly, they cannot capture all the subtleties of meaning that are typically a feature of ritual speech, referring here to examples from *Un lion nommé "L'Américain"*, which he had recently been cutting. He acknowledges that paraphrasing might not be able to capture all these subtleties either, but argues that the answer is not to resort to subtitling. Instead, he suggests, these more recondite meanings should be elucidated through a "short pamphlet . . . which should henceforth accompany every ethnographic film."[27]

However, none of these reasons for eschewing subtitles really stand up to close scrutiny. Provided the camera operator leaves room for them at the bottom of the screen, subtitles need not obstruct the image and while they may not capture all the nuances of ritual speech, they are usually more than adequate to capture the essence of most other forms of speech. Even in the case of ritual speech, it would surely be better for the viewer to have some idea of their meaning, even if no more than partial, as opposed to none at all. Although the more arcane meanings of ritual speech could doubtless be thoroughly elucidated in a companion text, the reality is that notwithstanding the many pious statements as to their importance, accompanying texts are very rarely produced by ethnographic documentarists. Certainly none was produced by Rouch himself for *Un lion nommé "L'Américain"*.

In an interview with Colette Piault published in 1996, Rouch came up with yet another reason for not using subtitles, namely, that his often illiterate African subjects would not be able to read them. But as Piault rightly points out, this reason does not necessarily hold much water either. For if the subtitled film was about their own society, the Africans in the audience would not need to read the subtitles anyway: indeed, those audiences would need neither subtitles nor a paraphrasing voice-over to understand the film.[28] On the other hand, as Rouch argued elsewhere, in the multilingual states of modern Africa, by using a lingua franca, even if it was one of the former colonial languages, one would make a film about one ethnic group comprehensible by the members of any other ethnic group, even if they were illiterate.[29]

However, more important than the pros and cons of subtitling per se are the limitations imposed on Rouch's documentary repertoire by his preference for the narrational paraphrasing of his subjects' speech. For while his poetic declamatory style worked reasonably well when he was paraphrasing speech that was itself declamatory and poetic, as is the case with ritual chanting, for example, it was much less stylistically successful when it involved paraphrasing everyday speech, and more or less unworkable in situations in which there were several voices involved. Given that everyday interaction usually does involve several different voices, this effectively prevented Rouch from making any documentaries about everyday life unless they were in French—as was the case with *Chronicle of a Summer*, but very few of his other documentary films.

In his interview with Colette Piault, Rouch acknowledged that perhaps subtitling was not as bad as he had previously averred and he recognized that when he himself went to see a foreign feature film at the cinema, he preferred a subtitled version to one that had been dubbed. He even acknowledged that the subtitling of his French-language feature films, *Dionysos* and *Madame L'Eau*, into Italian and English, respectively, had actually added to the films because the subtitling had brought out certain meanings that would have escaped the viewer relying on speech alone.[30] But by this stage of his life, Rouch's career as an ethnographic filmmaker was effectively over, and this late conversion to the merits of subtitling, if such it really was, was therefore in vain.

Yet even if this conversion had come much earlier in Rouch's life, it seems doubtful to me that he would have ever have been able to make films about the everyday life of his African subjects anyway. Most prosaically, given his professed linguistic limitations, he perhaps would have had a certain difficultly in following the cut and thrust of their conversations. More importantly, everyday interaction simply did not lend itself well to Rouch's general filmmaking praxis. For this, as I have stressed throughout this part of the book, was all about performance, and on both sides of the lens. But the everyday, for all the dramaturgical metaphors used by some sociologists in describing it, is more about banal strutting and fretting than virtuoso performance. There was little then in the everyday to which Rouch might adjust his own performance.[31]

For Rouch, the very essence of filmmaking was an improvised but highly authored performance at all stages of the filmmaking process: in the field while shooting, in the edit suite while cutting, and in the sound studio while narrating. This authored performance even continued after the films had been released, since, for Rouch, it was very much part of the process of making a film to tour around the world with it afterward and to give improvised verbal performances about its significance at every screening, be it from the front of the cinema immediately afterward, or later in the many interviews that he conceded to his admirers. In short, from start to finish in the making of a film, there was an entirely firm claim to authorship at the heart of the Rouchian praxis. As we shall see in the next chapter, an awareness of this point is crucial to a proper understanding of his conception of "shared anthropology."

15 : Shared Anthropology

This is the start of what some of us are already calling "shared anthropology."
The observer is finally coming down from his ivory tower; his camera, tape re-
corder, and his projector have led him — by way of a strange initiation path —
to the very heart of knowledge and, for the first time, his work is not being
judged by a thesis committee but by the very people he came to observe.

JEAN ROUCH, 1975[1]

Every time I make a film, I kill Jean Rouch.   OUMAROU GANDA[2]

It is undoubtedly only too easy to idealize Jean Rouch's project of "shared anthropology," but equally, it is only too easy to be excessively cynical. Before either burdening this key concept of the Rouchian praxis with unrealistic expectations or rushing to some premature judgment, we should first to try and identify exactly what, in practical terms, Rouch meant by "shared anthropology." What kind of sharing was involved? And what kind of anthropology?

For Whom and Why?

Jean Rouch did not take up filmmaking in order to change the world but rather to celebrate what he discovered within it. As Jean-Luc Godard once said of him, he did not "track down truth because it is scandalous but because it is amusing, tragic, graceful, eccentric, what you will."[3] One searches in vain in his large warehouse of stories for anything akin to the story of his famously critical interlocutor, Sembène Ousmane, who would often relate that it was while sitting in a boat on the Congo River, he suddenly realized, as a sort of a epiphany, that cinema would be the most effective means to reach out to the great illiterate masses of Africa.[4] Rouch had no political project of this kind: indeed, throughout his life, although Joris Ivens was a personal friend, he remained suspicious, even disdainful, of figures such as Ivens and Chris Marker, who used their filmmaking as a form of political activism. If Rouch advocated any kind of political position, it was anarchism without militancy.[5] In Africa, in particular, he refused to become involved in any political movement, especially after the former colonies of West Africa had achieved political independence. He was on good personal terms with Kwame Nkrumah, the first prime minister of independent Ghana, and even started making a film with him after his political downfall, but finally backed away from the idea. In his interviews, he often lamented the state of postcolonial Africa on account of the corruption, the military dictatorships, and the decline in the standards of education, as he saw it. But he refrained from any such direct criticisms in his films, considering it "imperialistic" to project European values onto independent countries.[6]

However, due to a certain combination of circumstances—his particular personality, his disillusionment with the French establishment after the collapse before the German invasion in 1940, and his disgust at the attitudes of the French colonial personnel in Niger, the most militaristic and reactionary of French colonies in West Africa—he developed a way of making films that was historically progressive in the sense that far from observing his African subjects "like insects," as Ousmane would later suggest, he engaged them directly in the making of his films, thereby crossing the boundaries between European and African, filmmaker and subject, that no one had either thought to or had been able to do before.

But, in the last analysis, the purpose of all this boundary crossing was to make the films; it was not to achieve particular political objectives, such as combating racism or protesting economic dependence in the postcolonial world. If these were the messages that audiences could read in his films, then all well and good, since these were messages that he personally believed in, but this was not the primary reason for making the films in the first place. Moreover, to his enduring credit, Rouch never sought to legitimate his work in terms of its political significance, nor pass it off as some sort of altruistic venture to which he had dedicated his life for the greater good of his subjects. This is a point that he makes with admirable candor in "The Camera and Man":

> Everywhere. . . . the first question that is asked after the screening of an ethnographic film is: "For whom have you produced this film, and why?." . . . Strangely enough, my first response to this will always be the same: "For myself" . . . Of course, it will always be possible to justify [the use of a ciné-camera] for scientific reasons (the creation of audiovisual archives of cultures which are rapidly changing or in danger of disappear-

ing), or political ones (sharing in a revolt against an intolerable situation), or aesthetic ones (discovery of a fragile masterpiece in a landscape, a face, or a gesture that we simply cannot let fade away unrecorded). But actually, we make a certain film because there is suddenly that necessity to film, or in some quite similar circumstances, a certainty that filming must not occur.

As he further explains in this essay, although he might derive much pleasure from entering the "ciné-trance" while making his films, both in shooting and editing, he did not consider himself addicted to filmmaking, as if it were some kind of drug. It was just that "at certain times in certain places and around certain people, the camera (and especially the synch-sound camera) seems to be necessary." Here we might detect another echo of his youthful admiration for Surrealist poetry and painting and the importance its exponents gave to spontaneous expression of creative impulses. Yet even while freely admitting that he made his films in the first instance for his own "ciné-pleasure," Rouch claims that his "prime audience" was the subjects of his films since "film is the only method I have to show another just how I see him." But as it would "obviously be absurd to condemn ethnographic film to this closed circuit of audiovisual information," he does finally concede that he hopes that his films will be of interest, not just for anthropologists, but for "the greatest number of people possible, for all audiences."[7]

Yet while this might have been his mature understanding of his reasons for filmmaking, it seems that Rouch first took up the camera to achieve certain academic objectives. In "The Camera and Man," he reports that

> [i]n the late 1940s, young anthropologists followed to the letter the manual of Marcel Mauss ("you will film all of the techniques . . .") and brought the camera closer to man once again. Though some expeditions continued to have dreams of super-productions in 35mm . . . the 16mm camera was rapidly gaining ground.[8]

This is surely a reference to himself, since it is difficult to imagine who else might be included among this group of "young anthropologists," in the plural and, given the reference to Mauss, probably French, unless it is Roger Rosfelder, Rouch's fellow Griaule supervisee and filmmaking partner during the 1950–1951 expedition to the middle Niger River.

Certainly, as an anthropologist, Rouch had been trained in Maussian methods, though it seems unlikely that he ever met Mauss himself in person. By the time that Rouch began to study anthropology formally, in the immediate postwar years, Mauss was in a state of decline, having suffered a mental collapse following the German invasion in 1940. But Marcel Griaule, Rouch's supervisor, had himself been a student of Mauss and it was through him that Rouch was introduced to the Maussian approach. As described in chapter 1, in this approach, the first step in any research project is to produce a large body of particular items of data, or "documents," as they are referred to in the methodological manual to which Rouch refers in the passage cited above. Only once a substantial body of "documents" has been assembled should one begin the process of theorizing. While Mauss himself relied primarily on "documents" that he unearthed from bibliographic sources, he was a strong advocate of firsthand fieldwork and of the use of both photographic and cinematographic technology in the gathering of "documents."[9] The Maussian influence is not only very evident in Rouch's doctoral thesis, submitted in 1952, but also, indirectly, in the credits to the films that he and Rosfelder produced in their expedition of the previous years. Here the field recordings of musical performances that Rosfelder made using the newly available, portable Sgubbi tape recorder and which are used on the sound track of the film, are not referred to as "music," but rather as "original sound documents."[10]

This Mauss-inspired idea to use the camera as a data-gathering device to build up stocks of "documents" for later analysis and theoretical reflection also probably lies at the root of Rouch's lifelong interest in "salvage" ethnography. This might seem almost paradoxical for a filmmaker who positively celebrated cultural hybridization and innovation in his documentation of the "great adventure of African cities" during the period of his migration films. But although Rouch was certainly interested in the emerging world of late colonial Africa, his initial and perhaps primary interest lay in the traditional cultural worlds of the peoples living around the middle reaches of the Niger River. It was for this reason that when fully synchronous-sound technology became available in the mid-1960s he resolved to give up making films about urban migrants and return to the middle Niger to make films about cultural traditions that were either disappearing or in the process of being radically transformed.[11]

Although, as we have seen in earlier chapters, there was a vast methodological gulf between Margaret Mead's futuristic vision of a 360-degree camera that would collect ethnographic data without any form of intervention by a filmmaker and Rouch's own approach based on plunging into the reality of his subjects, they shared a common interest in building up stockpiles of ethnographic data for indeterminate future purposes. In his capacity as executive secretary and later chairman of the Comité International du Film Ethnographique et Sociologique or CIFES (a dependency of the UNESCO-funded International Union of Anthropological and Ethnological Sciences), Rouch was a strong advocate of using film in this way. This idea is clearly laid out in the "Resolution on Visual Anthropology" that he published in 1975 in collaboration with Paul Hockings, who was then cochairman with Rouch of CIFES. It appears among the appendices of *Principles of Visual Anthropology*, the volume edited by Hockings in which "The Camera and Man" appears and which is widely regarded as the foundational text for the academic subdiscipline of visual anthropology.

The opening lines of the resolution are as follows:

> Film, sound, and videotape records are today an indispensable scientific resource. They provide reliable data on human behavior which independent investigators may analyze in the light of new theories. They may contain information for which neither theory nor analytical schemes yet exist. They convey information independently of language. And they preserve unique features of our changing ways of life for posterity.[12]

The remainder of the resolution consists of a series of proposals for encouraging the systematic visual documentation of the rapidly changing cultures of the world. Although it envisages that the general purpose of this program of documentation should be "scientific study and education" and urges that "special attention" be given "to the needs of developing nations," it does not propose any more specific agenda, of either an academic or a political kind.

If Rouch's Maussian inheritance led him to believe that the production of visual "documents" was a legitimate end in and of itself, then his ideas about how these visual "documents" should be gathered and about fieldwork in general were greatly influenced by his supervisor Marcel Griaule and by Griaule's partner in life as in work, Germaine Dieterlen. As discussed in chapter 1, there are a number of aspects of Rouch's approach to filmmaking that can be traced to the influence of Griaule and Dieterlen's ideas about fieldwork. These include, crucially, the idea that in order to achieve a "deep knowledge" of a particular society, it is necessary to keep going back to the same community over a period of twenty or thirty years. Rouch's methods were also similar to those of Griaule and Dieterlen in the sense that he tended to work primarily in French and with a small group of select companions, namely, Damouré Zika, Lam Ibrahim, and the others. One may also discern a continuity, as James Clifford has done, between Griaule's proactive interview method, whereby he provoked his informants into revealing information that they would not otherwise have done, and Rouch's ideas about using the camera to provoke his subjects into revealing aspects of their imaginary that normally remained hidden.[13] Also like Griaule, Rouch tended to focus his attention on the public cultural rhetoric of the groups whom he studied with the result that the great majority of his films are about collective public performances of one kind or another, and there is very little emphasis on private domestic life and hence on the world of women.

But although these similarities are certainly striking, the differences between their respective methods are even more so. These mainly turn around what each considered the appropriate way to treat the subjects of their research. After he had been given access through his conversations with Ogotommêli in 1946 to the *parole claire*, the more arcane knowledge of the Dogon, Griaule became concerned to demonstrate that African mythology and cosmogony could be as complex as that of ancient Greece. But while he may have developed a great respect for African culture in the abstract, or at least the more religious aspects of it, his attitude toward his informants and their hold over this knowledge was quite the contrary, even after what Clifford suggests was his supposedly transformative encounter with Ogotommêli.[14]

Griaule's general approach to fieldwork is outlined summarily as part of the report on the Dakar-Djibouti expedition that appeared in the Surrealist journal *Minotaure* in 1933, but it is elaborated upon at greater length in the methodological handbook published posthumously by his daughter in 1957. From these accounts, it is clear that Griaule's approach was based on the basic assumption that his informants were seeking to obstruct his enquiries, either by professing ignorance when they knew about something perfectly well, or if necessary, by lying outright to protect some secret that they did not wish to reveal to outsiders. Therefore, in Griaule's view, the first task of the researcher was to break down this resistance. In the handbook, he suggests that an informant should be considered equivalent to the "guilty party" in a court of law, while the remainder of the society should be considered his "accomplices." In order to combat the informants' congenital mendacity, Griaule recommended that the researcher—compared variously in this text to a prosecution lawyer, judge, and even a bloodhound—should use whatever trick or stratagem was necessary to circumvent the informants' defenses, including putting on whatever "mask" was necessary in the interview situation (everything from "indulgent father" to "severe outsider," deploying apparent friendship or bribery as required) and using one informant's account to unsettle that of another.[15]

This shockingly unscrupulous approach, clearly the product of a colonial mentality whereby all indigenous knowledge is fair game, could not be further from Rouch's own attitudes. This is made abundantly clear in a telling passage in the introduction to Rouch's doctoral thesis, in which he advises the reader that he has omitted some of the secret knowledge to which he felt privileged to have been given access since he had prom- ised the Songhay that he would not divulge it to third parties. The lan- guage that he uses to justify this self-censorship is surely not coinciden- tal. "The ethnographer," he comments, "is not a policeman who extorts matters about which there is a desire neither to tell him nor show him."[16] The reference to a policeman in this passage, even if it was not intended as a direct allusion to Griaule's handbook, clearly represents a radical re- jection of the approach recommended by his supervisor.

Rouch thought of the relationship between researcher and subject not as one that should be based on maximizing the efficiency with which re- liable information might be extracted from the informant but rather as one that should be based on a principle of exchange. In this context, he suggested that his feedback screenings should be considered what he called—in a very Maussian phrase—an "audiovisual countergift," that is, a gift given in exchange for the trust that the subjects had shown in al- lowing him to film in the first place. By involving his subjects in this way, Rouch argued that the anthropological filmmaker would no longer be acting like an "entomologist," studying his subjects as Ousmane had al- leged, "like insects," in a disengaged, objectifying manner, but rather us- ing the screening of the film as a catalyst for the development of mutual understanding between observer and observed.[17] This mutuality was at the heart of Rouch's personal praxis. As he put it in an article published some four years before the extract from "The Camera and Man" repro- duced in the epigraph to this chapter:

> Knowledge is not a stolen secret later to be consumed in Western temples of learning, but rather is to be arrived at through an unending quest in which ethnographic subjects and the ethnographer engage with one an- other on a path that some of us are now calling "shared anthropology."[18]

In referring to knowledge as a "stolen secret later to be consumed in Western temples of learning," Rouch could surely have had no better ex- ample than the practice of Griaule, whose Dakar-Djibouti expedition brought back to Paris what Paul Rivet and Georges-Henri Rivière, then director and assistant director of the Musée d'ethnographie, respec- tively, unashamedly called a "booty" of museum objects numbering in excess of four thousand items. Nor was this mere metaphor, for, as Mi- chel Leiris reported in his travel journal with an almost boastful ironic candor, the expeditionaries were not above using all manner of subter- fuge and bribery, including the threat of calling the colonial police force, and even bare-faced theft, in order to acquire these items.[19]

Rouch's practice represented a radical break with this colonial intel- lectual inheritance. While Griaule thought of the ethnographic endeavor as a struggle to extract a nugget of truth from within a tangled skein of deceit in order to carry it off to Paris in triumph, Rouch's notion of exchange between subjects and researcher was based on the premise of collaboration in a joint creative project. While Griaule saw himself as "the bloodhound of the social fact," Rouch was the filmmaker who wanted to use his camera as Louis Armstrong had played his trumpet, always hoping to improvise unexpected harmonies with his subjects.[20]

Sharing Anthropology: From the Passive to the Performative

As Rouch conceived it, there were a number of different stations on the "path of shared anthropology." During the first stage, the feedback screenings, the sharing was relatively passive: Rouch screened the films, the subjects grew to understand why this strange European kept coming back with his camera, while Rouch grew to understand more about them. When he first began his ethnographic research, Rouch had tried giving his written works to the Songhay, but he had quickly discovered that they had no use for them, even when they were read out aloud by the village schoolmaster. On the other hand, when he started screening his films, not only did the Songhay understand his objectives more clearly, but they became participants in his cinematographic adventures.[21]

Initially, this participation on the part of the subjects consisted merely of commentary on the ethnographic content of the films. This proved particularly valuable many years later when he and Germaine Dieterlen came to make their series of films about the Dogon Sigui ceremony and had very little idea about what was going on in the actual moment of shooting. As we saw in chapter 11, by listening to the comments of the subjects during the feedback screenings, as well as to those of a ritual specialist, Amadigné Dolo, whom they took back to Paris to work with them in the edit suite, they learned a great deal about the symbolic significance of particular forms of dancing, the many items of ritual paraphernalia, the reasons for particular sequences of events and so on, none of which they would otherwise have understood.[22]

But the feedback screenings were only the prelude to what would become a much more active process of collaboration. For Rouch discovered, to his great delight, that at the end of a feedback screening, one or more members of the audience would typically come up to him and suggest an idea for a new film. These could be people who had been directly involved in the first film, or other members of the audience who had concluded that a film about their activities would be more interesting than the film that Rouch had just shown. Thus it was that after the screening of *Bataille sur le grand fleuve* at the very first feedback session, back in early1954, Damouré Zika and Illo Gaoudel, who had appeared in this film, suggested to Rouch afterward that they should make a "real" film, by which they meant a fictional film, about the migration of young men to the Gold Coast in which they would play starring roles. This would result in the filming of *Jaguar* later that year. In due course of time, when this film was completed, or at least existed in the form of a lengthy first assembly, Rouch moved the base of his migration studies to Abidjan and showed this cut of the film to the Nigerien migrants with whom he was working there. They claimed that their lives would be even more interesting to film than the lives of the migrants played by Damouré, Lam, and Illo in *Jaguar*. Rouch took them up on the suggestion and the film that resulted was *Moi, un Noir*.[23]

Nor was this the only string of films to be set off by the screening of *Bataille sur le grand fleuve* on that fateful evening in Ayorou. For on that same occasion, Rouch was also approached by another member of the audience, a certain Tahirou Koro, who belonged to the Gow subgroup of Songhay, who live in the region around Yatakala, about fifty miles west of Ayorou. He suggested that having filmed the hunting of hippopotami in this film, Rouch should now come to his region and film himself and his fellow Gow hunting lions with bow and arrow. It took Rouch some four years to take up this suggestion, and then a further seven years to complete the shooting. Every year that he returned to continue with the shoot, he would bring back a rough assembly of the material shot the previous year. On the basis of the feedback that he received on this material, he would plan together with the hunters what they should shoot that year. Eventually, in 1965, the original proposal made in 1954 resulted in *The Lion Hunters*. Three years later, Rouch returned with the completed film to Yatakala and screened that to Tahirou and his fellow hunters. Ashamed by the fact that the lion that they called "The American" had escaped them while they were shooting the first film and, moreover, was still at large, they resolved to go out and hunt for it there and then. Rouch followed them with his camera and the result was *Un lion nommé "L'Américain"*, finally released in 1972, almost two decades after the original screening in Ayorou that set off the whole series of films.[24]

The way that the screening of one film could lead to another was crucial to Rouch's conception of "shared anthropology" since the subjects who proposed an idea for a new film following a screening became not merely protagonists, but, as we might say today, active "stakeholders" in the new venture. Once he became interested in the work of Vertov, Rouch liked to present this chain effect as a vindication of Vertov's notion that more important than making a film as such was to make a film that would lead to the making of other films.[25]

FIGURE 15.1. A young man dressed in the "jaguar" style at the British Council screening of *Bataille sur le grand fleuve*, Accra, June 1954. © Fondation Jean Rouch.

Les Maîtres fous was yet another film that resulted from a screening of *Bataille sur le grand fleuve*, though not from the screening in Ayorou in early 1954. Later that same year, not long after he had begun working on migration to the Gold Coast, Rouch happened to discover that there were many Nigerien migrants in the Accra prison, probably for a variety of petty offences. In order to get to know them for the purposes of his survey, he asked the warden if he could show them *Bataille* "to improve their morale." It turned out that among the prisoners there were a number of *hauka* spirit mediums. They were greatly impressed by the nighttime possession sequence in *Bataille*, in which the Sorko hippopotamus hunters seek the *hauka* spirits' support. After the screening, the prisoners urged Rouch to show *Bataille* to their fellow *hauka* mediums on the outside.

Without necessarily being aware that he was doing so, Rouch acceded to this request by arranging an open-air screening of *Bataille* on the tennis court of the British Council in Accra in June 1954. This screening was attended by many members of the local Nigerien community, as well as by his wife Jane (fig. 15.1). But there appear to have also been some *hauka* mediums in the audience, for about two months later, when he happened to be in Togo, Rouch received a telegram from some *hauka* priests inviting him to come and film the annual gathering of the cult that was shortly due to take place near Nsawam, a small town in the foothills of the mountains, about twenty-five miles north of Accra. He accepted their invitation, and the result was *Les Maîtres fous*.[26]

Exceptionally, however, *Les Maîtres fous* was not a film that Rouch ever showed back to the protagonists. Rouch's standard explanation was that he was afraid that a feedback screening might have sent the subjects off into an uncontrollable trance.[27] However, this explanation is not entirely convincing. After all, Rouch had arranged many screenings of *Bataille sur le grand fleuve*, but there is no report that the powerful possession sequences in this film had ever resulted in any uncontrollable outbreaks of trance. Admittedly, the possession sequences in *Bataille* are briefer than those in *Les Maîtres fous*, which could conceivably have been a consideration. But I suspect that the most pressing reason that Rouch never showed this particular film back to the subjects was that, initially at least, it was banned by the British colonial authorities on the grounds that it involved disrespect to the Queen's representative, the governor. If Rouch had chosen to show it clandestinely to the protagonists, most of whom would presumably still have been living in Accra, he could have landed himself, and perhaps the adepts themselves, in all sorts of inconvenient trouble. Although the Gold Coast became independent some two years after the release of the film, by which time concerns about the dignity of the Queen might have been less important, in view of the accusations of racism that the film had provoked from African intellectuals in Paris, Rouch might still have considered it potentially very awkward to show the film in Accra.

If the mutual understanding that arises from feedback screenings can be considered to be a relatively passive form of shared anthropology while the proposal of new films that typically followed on thereafter constitutes a relatively active form, there is still another station on Rouch's "path of shared anthropology" that relates to the actual making of a new film. For, in Rouch's view, as we saw in chapter 12, in the ideal case, the shooting of a film should involve not just an inspired performance on the part of the filmmaker, but a performance that was "in unison" with an inspired performance on the part of the subjects. Here too then there is a sharing of anthropology since it is through this "connivance," as Rouch calls it, that the film is made.

This is a subject that Rouch addresses in the article that he wrote in 1971 in the wake of the experience of shooting *Les Tambours d'avant*, when it had seemed as if his filming might have sent the mediums into trance. In the ideal circumstance, he claims, when he is making a film and has entered the "ciné-trance," he is "ciné-observing" the subjects through the lens of the camera while they in turn play the role of the "ciné-observed," that is, they adjust their performance to the fact that he is filming, so if he has entered a trance, they are likely to do so too and vice versa.[28] The use of Vertovian prefixes in this context signals an important additional dimension to Rouch's understanding of this phase of the process of shared anthropology. For these seemingly innocuous prefixes are a reference to the core idea underlying Rouch's shooting praxis, that in these ideal circumstances, when film and subjects coordinate their performances in an inspired way, in a manner analogous to the transcendent moment of a jam session between Duke Ellington and Louis Armstrong, they are conspiring to enter the privileged domain of truth that Vertov called *cinéma-vérité*.

Moreover, in the concluding passage of this article, Rouch suggests that the coordination of performances to achieve the privileged truths of *cinéma-vérité* was something that could be extended by analogy to contexts in which the ethnographer did not even have a camera in hand:

> Once in the field, the simple observer undergoes a change. When he is at work, he is no longer the person who greeted the Elders at the entrance to the village. To recur to the Vertovian terminology again, he "ethno-looks," he "ethno-observes," he "ethno-thinks," while those before him undergo a similar change once they have come to trust this strange recurrent visitor: they "ethno-show," they "ethno-speak," they might even "ethno-think" . . . It is this "ethno-dialogue" that seems to me to be one of the most interesting tendencies of the ethnographic approach today.[29]

In this remarkable passage, Rouch appears to be announcing a "dialogical anthropology" at least a decade before such a thing became fashionable in the English-language anthropological literature. Even if one might be skeptical about the Vertovian pedigree of some of Rouch's ideas, as I have suggested at various points in this book one should be, no one could deny that in making statements of this nature, Rouch was far ahead of most other anthropologists of his generation in suggesting that anthropological knowledge should arise not from detached scientific observation but rather from engagement and mutual accommodation between subject and observer.

However, while all this is very laudable and undoubtedly historically progressive, a skeptic might still legitimately ask what benefits the subjects stand to gain from all this sharing of anthropology. While one should not underestimate the value nor the strength of documentary film subjects' interest in seeing their way of life valorized in some sense through the making of a film, there does not seem to be a great deal else for them to gain in the Rouchian conception of shared anthropology. For, as an "obstinate dissenter" might point out, Rouch's shared anthropology seems to have offered his subjects little more than some insight into why he kept visiting them, and then the opportunity to help him elucidate the ethnographic context of one of his films through a feedback screening. Eventually, when this elucidation was complete, they would have the opportunity to appear in another of his films, when the whole process could begin again. In short, "shared anthropology" sounds very grand, but what did it actually do for the subjects? In order to explore this question further, we should now look in more detail at the relationships between Rouch and his closest African companions.

A Band of "Adventurers and Amateurs"

There is a striking difference between the way in which Rouch envisaged his working relationships with his codirectors, at least as exemplified by Edgar Morin ("a violent game"), or with his editors ("a harsh and difficult dialogue"), and his description of his relationship with the subjects of his films. Whereas he spoke of his relationship with his cofilmmakers as fraught with tension and conflict, he would invariably refer to his relationships with his subjects as harmonious and collaborative.

From his earliest days in Africa, Rouch gathered around him a small group of local men who worked with him in a variety of ways over the years: they acted as his interpreters, they conducted surveys for his migration studies, they recorded the sound and took production stills for his documentaries, and they played leading parts as actors in his ethnofictions. They also drove his Land Rover, carried his equipment, and generally acted as his local fixers. In exchange, he benefited them in various ways, depending on precisely what he was doing and how they were involved: he paid them salaries to work as his research assistants while carrying out his migration research and he shared with them the profits of his filmmaking, usually on a fifty-fifty basis.[30] He often arranged for them to acquire certain skills, including those related to filmmaking, that would help to increase their earning power when they were not working for him. It also seems that, from time to time, he gave them substantial gifts of money.

He also afforded them opportunities to travel, which was something that they greatly appreciated. At first, this travel was to various other countries in West Africa, including Ghana, Burkina Faso, Mali, and Senegal. Later, Rouch enabled a number of his companions to travel with him to Europe: in 1967–1968, he took Damouré, Lam, and his sound recordist, Moussa Hamidou, to France, Switzerland, and Italy to shoot *Petit à Petit*, and then in 1991, he took them, and Tallou Mouzourane as well, to the Netherlands to shoot *Madame L'Eau*. In an interview recorded in 2003, Damouré and Moussa spoke of their great pride in being able to represent traditional Nigerien culture to Dutch people, as if they were ambassadors for their country.[31]

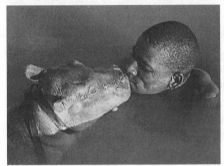

FIGURE 15.2. Damouré Zika. *Left*, clowning around with a baby hippo during the filming of *Bataille sur le grand fleuve*, 1951. *Right*, in a more contemplative mood during the filming of *Madame L'Eau*, 1992. © Steef Meyknecht.

Rouch felt entirely at ease in the company of this group of his closest African associates. Despite the cultural differences, he believed that they shared certain fundamentals in common, namely, a predisposition to look at life in a light-hearted manner, an inquisitiveness about the world, and a willingness to improvise a response to its challenges that depended more on personal ingenuity than on formal qualifications. "We are all amateurs, in the same sense as Flaherty—we love what we do," he comments at one point in *Rouch's Gang*, the film by Steef Meyknecht, Dirk Nijland, and Joost Verhey about the visit of Rouch and his companions to Amsterdam during the shooting of *Madame L'Eau*. Having introduced his "band" one by one, with examples of what they can achieve without any formal training—such as Lam's ability to roast a chicken by tying it to a car exhaust—he concludes that what they all have in common is that "we are all adventurers and amateurs."[32]

The first and surely the most gifted of Rouch's companions was the late Damouré Zika (fig. 15.2). When they met, Damouré was a member of the Sorko subgroup of the Songhay, who specialize in fishing the waters of the middle Niger, but it seems that originally he belonged to another group, the Kourteï.[33] He first met Rouch shortly after the latter arrived in Niger in late 1941. At the time, Damouré was still at school, though on the particular day that they met, he had skipped class and was fishing by the river when Rouch came to bathe. They struck up a conversation and soon developed a rapport. Whenever Rouch told the story of how they met, he would usually add that while he was the stronger swimmer, Damouré was better at swimming underwater, as if to suggest that they had complementary strengths.[34] In Philo Bregstein's film portrait of Rouch, Damouré claims, seemingly humorously though perhaps with good reason nevertheless, that he was disadvantaged in this swimming contest because he was suffering from malnutrition. But even though he may have lost the contest, it was evidently a meeting that Damouré cherished too, since sixty years later, he was still able to produce the swimming trunks that he wore on that occasion for the visiting filmmakers, Berit Madsen and Anne Mette Jørgensen![35]

Rouch would sometimes reflect on whether it was he who had chosen to meet his African friends, or whether it was they who had chosen to meet him.[36] Perhaps the Surrealist in him would have considered this encounter with Damouré a prime example of "objective chance" since both parties clearly found in the other something that they were looking for. But whoever motivated this first encounter, it was surely a *rencontre* as significant as any in Rouch's life for whenever he was in Niger, for the rest of his days, Damouré would invariably be by his side. Sixty-two years later, when Rouch met his death in an accident on a rural highway in Niger in 2004, traveling in the car with him, though fortunately not seriously hurt, was Damouré Zika.

Not long after their first encounter, Rouch employed Damouré as an assistant on his road-building project. Although only twenty-four, Rouch was in charge of some 10,000 Songhay-Zerma forced laborers working in the harshest conditions. Mechanization was minimal and stones were carried in baskets. Damouré had the job of "pointeur," which involved calling out a roll call of the workers every day. As described in chapter 1, when some of the laborers were killed by lightning, it was Damouré who introduced Rouch to his grandmother, a spirit possession priestess who ascertained, through organizing a possession ceremony, that it was Dongo, the powerful Spirit of Thunder, who was responsible. This awoke Rouch's interest in a practice that would become a lifelong fascination and shortly thereafter, assisted by Damouré, he began his first ethnographic enquiries into spirit possession among the Songhay-Zerma.[37]

If Damouré helped Rouch, Rouch also helped Damouré. As a child, Damouré had been taught by his father about traditional medicines, so Rouch arranged for him to train, first, as a paramedic in Niger, and later as a pharmacist in Paris. On the strength of these qualifications, Damouré managed the pharmacy at the University of Niamey for many years and when he retired, he set up his own clinic, with financial help from Rouch.[38] He also became something of a minor literary celebrity in France when the diaries of his travels with Rouch were published, through the good offices of Jane Rouch, in a French literary journal in 1956.[39] In addition to his presence in all of Rouch's ethnofictions, he also acted in at least two other feature films, one of which, *L'Exilé* (1980) was directed by another of Rouch's Nigerien associates, Oumarou Ganda.[40] Damouré reached old age as a wealthy man in local terms, with seven wives, thirty-five children, and a very large number of grandchildren. In an interview given to Berit Madsen and Anne Mette Jørgensen in 2003, he attributed this prosperity directly to the opportunities that Rouch had made possible for him when he was a young man.[41]

Damouré was also responsible for introducing Rouch to the other principal companion of his African adventures, Ibrahim Dia, most commonly referred to by his nick-name, "Lam," which was short for "Lamido," meaning "small chief." When Rouch and his wartime companions passed through Niamey during their descent of the Niger in 1946–1947, Damouré, who held a position in the French civil service at that time and who was therefore unable to travel with them into what was then the British colony of Nigeria, recommended that in his stead they should take Lam, then about fifteen. Lam was a Fulani, or Peul as this group is known in French, who are cattle pastoralists distributed widely throughout West Africa. As a young boy, he had lived in Nigeria for a period and had trained there as a marabout, a Muslim ritual specialist.[42]

Lam also benefited in various ways from his association with Rouch. He learned to drive while working with Rouch and whenever there is some driving to be done in the ethnofictions, it is Lam who does it, regardless of whether this involves driving an open-topped classic Bugatti touring car through the streets of Paris or Rouch's ancient Land Rover along the most isolated and pot-holed track in the Nigerien bush. At various periods of his life, when not working on one of Rouch's films, he used this skill as a way of earning a living, at the same time using the income that he derived from working with Rouch to buy himself the vehicles to do so. After working on *Petit à Petit*, he used the money to buy himself the 2CV van that features in *Cocorico! Monsieur Poulet* but which broke down so frequently that it was necessary to make this into a major plot point. Fortunately, *Cocorico! Monsieur Poulet* was sufficiently successful at the box office for him to upgrade later to a Land Rover of his own. Later, he became a wealthy farmer whose fields on the banks of the

FIGURE 15.3. Lam Ibrahim Dia at the time of shooting *Madame L'Eau*, 1992. © Steef Meyknecht.

Niger were irrigated with the aid of the appropriate technology windmill brought back from Holland as part of the narrative of Rouch's late film, *Madame L'Eau*.[43]

Although he had neither the flamboyant acting talent nor fluency in French of Damouré, Lam was often the originator of the principal idea behind an ethnofiction. In the films themselves, his role was to play the straight man. Without him as a foil, as Rouch discovered when they started shooting some scenes of *Petit à Petit* in Paris without Lam, Damouré simply could not do his improvisations. Later, Lam too was cast by Oumarou Ganda in one of his fictional features, playing the lead role in *Le Wazzou polygame* (1970). He died in 1997, and Rouch was much affected by his death.[44]

In *Jaguar*, the third of the three adventurers was played by Illo Gaoudel who, like Damouré, was a Sorko fisherman and like Lam, had also trained to be a marabout. He had previously appeared in a leading role in *Bataille sur le grand fleuve* and would also appear in *Petit à Petit*, though he did not go to Paris and only features in the scenes shot back in Niger. But in the later ethnofictions, from *Cocorico! Monsieur Poulet* onward, he is replaced as the third principal by Tallou Mouzourane, a member of the Bella ethnic group, who have very low prestige in the interethnic mosaic of the middle Niger since they were traditionally the slaves of the Tuareg. Rouch first met Tallou in late 1950, when Tallou was fifteen and suffer-

FIGURE 15.4. Tallou Mouzourane during the shooting of *Madame L'Eau*, 1991. © Steef Meyknecht.

ing from leprosy. As he was an orphan without a family, Rouch paid for the leprosy to be cured and took him under his wing. According to Claude Jutra, in the African view, having saved him from dying, Rouch then became responsible for his living.[45] In addition to supporting him personally, Rouch also helped Tallou to become affiliated with one of the leading families of Ayorou, thereby providing him with some degree of security during the droughts that regularly afflict the region.[46]

Even before he became one of the three principals, Tallou had helped Rouch out as a general "go-fer" during the period of his migration research and had even made minor contributions on screen. In *Jaguar*, we hear his improvised piano playing in the style of Dollar Brand over some shots of the interior of the Obuasi gold mine, while in *Petit à Petit*, we actually see him at the keyboard. Seemingly a volatile character in everyday life, in the scenes set back in Niger in this latter film he plays the role of Lam's unpredictable sidekick, alternately comical and irascible. His roles in the later ethnofictions represent a number of different variations on this persona, though with the comical becoming increasingly predominant. Sadly, Lam too has recently died.[47]

Another performer to receive support from Rouch after appearing in one of his films was Oumarou Ganda, the Nigerien migrant to Abidjan who was one of the two principals of *Moi, un Noir*. After the completion of that film, he continued to work with Rouch as a research assistant on his migration studies for a while and in the making of two of Rouch's subsequent films on the Ivory Coast, *Monsieur Albert* and *Rose et Landry*, both released in 1963. Later, in 1968, with strong encouragement from Rouch, Ganda returned to Niamey and trained as a feature filmmaker himself. He then went on to make a number of feature films, including *Cabascabo*, released in 1969, about the disillusioning experiences of a Nigerien Indochina veteran on his return home. This film enjoyed considerable success, winning a prize at the Moscow Film Festival and being selected to be shown at Cannes, the first film in Zerma to be so honored. Ganda went on to make at least two other feature films, but tragically, he was unable to fulfill his full potential before his premature death in 1981 at the age of forty-six.[48]

Yet others who went on to a filmmaking career after getting their first taste of filmmaking with Rouch included Moustapha Alassane and Safi Faye, both of whom appear in *Petit à Petit* though, as was the case with Oumarou Ganda, they were later trained in filmmaking methods that were very different from those advocated by Rouch. In Alassane's case, after studying in Canada, he became a pioneer within Africa of animated films on political and historical subjects, though he continued to make films in other genres, including the first Western to be produced in Africa, the medium-length *Le Retour d'un aventurier* (1966). This was a parody, as was his full-length feature film, *FVVA: Femme, Voiture, Villa, Argent* (1972), which made fun of the African nouveaux riches. Subsequently he became the director the Department of Cinema at the University of Niamey for 15 years. He also established the cinema at Tahoua, which was the first and may well be still the only cinema in Niger outside the capital, Niamey. Alassane remained a close associate of Rouch throughout his life. Indeed it was when Rouch was traveling to Tahoua to attend an event that Alassane had organized that he suffered his fatal accident. Alassane was also traveling in the car at the time of the crash, though fortunately, like Damouré, he was not seriously hurt.[49]

Safi Faye, meanwhile, is widely regarded as a pioneer of West African cinema and remains one of the best-known women directors of the region. In contrast to Rouch's other African associates, all of whom are Nigerien, Safi Faye is Senegalese and her involvement in *Petit à Petit* was the result of meeting Rouch at a film festival in Dakar in 1966. With his support, she then went on to study both anthropology and filmmaking in Paris. Although she has made a number of feature films and documentaries and currently works in television in Europe, her most widely cited film remains her early work *Kaddu Beykat* (*Peasant Letter*, 1975), a feature-length film in black and white about her natal village in Sen-

FIGURE 15.5. Moussa Hamidou demonstrates his recording skill in his backyard: "every time of day in the bush has its own sound." © Berit Madsen.

egal. Although she may have been trained in filmmaking methods very different to those practiced by Rouch, this film is reported to deal with a range of ethnographic topics within the framework of a fictional love story and, in this sense, it would appear to be not dissimilar in conception to a Rouchian ethnofiction.[50]

In addition to those who actually performed in front of the lens, there were many others who benefited directly or indirectly from working with Rouch in other ways. Surely the most important of these was Moussa Hamidou, the Zerma sound recordist who became a regular member of Rouch's "band' from 1959, when he was nineteen. Moussa had little or no schooling but learned to record sound by working with Rouch on the Ivory Coast. With Rouch's support, he later trained in Paris and was then appointed to a position at the Institut de la Recherche en Sciences Humaines (IRSH) in Niamey, where he established a large sound archive of music and oral traditions, not just from Niger, but also Burkina Faso and Mali.[51] With the income that he earned through this position and from his film work, both with Rouch and with Rouch's former protégés—he was the sound recordist on Oumarou Ganda's films *Cabascabo* and *Le Wazzou polygame* and on Moustapha Alassane's *Le Retour d'un aventurier*—he paid for an education for his children that has enabled them all to become professional people.[52]

In addition to sharing various material benefits with his companions and subjects, Rouch was also prepared to share the authorship of his films—though only to a certain degree. Even in his earliest documentaries, there is a notable tendency to acknowledge the contribution of the protagonists. In *Cimetières dans la falaise* and *Bataille sur le grand fleuve*, for example, the performers of musical "documents" are named in the on-screen credits, whereas perhaps most documentarists, even today, would probably just mix in traditional folk music on their sound tracks without any such acknowledgement. In *The Lion Hunters*, the eight principal hunters are not only named in the narration, but they are also all named in the on-screen credits, even Ali, "the apprentice" participating in his first hunt.

In shooting the ethnofictions, as I discussed extensively in chapter 12, Rouch gave his protagonists a remarkably free hand in improvising their dialogues. In recognition of their contribution to the films, both in terms of their role as actors, but also in the organization, Rouch formed a joint production entity with Damouré and Lam, the name of which was made up of the first syllables of their respective names—DALAROU. This collective name is reminiscent of the tripartite Jean Pierjant by-line with which Rouch and his two wartime colleagues, Pierre Ponty and Jean Sauvy, used to sign their reports when wiring them back to Agence France Presse during their descent of the Niger in 1946–1947. Later, when Tallou became more prominent in the ethnofictions, the tricephalous name was expanded so as to include the first syllable of his name as well. As a result, the entity acquired a quadricephalous moniker—DALAROUTA.

But for all that Rouch was prepared to acknowledge the contributions of his companions and protagonists, there remains a clear authorial *écriture* running through all Rouch's major films and there is certainly no mistake, as Marc Piault has put it, about who was the ultimate author.[53] Rouch may have conceded to his principal companions a major role in fashioning the films that they made together, a gesture that was unprecedented in ethnographic filmmaking. But in the last analysis it was he who initiated the films, it was he who shaped them in the edit suite (albeit in "harsh dialogue" with his editors), and it was he who distributed them afterward, usually traveling round the world with them to modulate their impact on the eventual audiences. As far as authorship was concerned, then, what this sharing of anthropology came down to was a process whereby Rouch engaged his subjects directly and profoundly in the conceptualization and shooting of his films, but in the end, the films that eventually emerged from the edit suite bore his unmistakable signature, overriding all others. For, whatever the tri- or quadricephalous

name in the credits might have been intended to imply, this acknowledgment of the companions' contribution was invariably *preceded* by another intertitle stating simply—"Un film de Jean Rouch."

"Killing" Jean Rouch

In summary, if his principal companions are any indication, Rouch's
"shared anthropology" was a project from which the subjects derived
considerable personal material benefits and to which they made a significant authorial contribution. Even if this authorial contribution was
always framed and shaped by Rouch's final authorship, it was a project in
which the subjects willingly participated and from which they apparently
derived considerable pleasure.[54] Even so, some of Rouch's critics have
suggested that his relationship with his principal companions, however
positive they personally might have considered it, was both paternalistic
and colonialist. The ethnofictions that he made with them, it has been
argued, are irredeemably marked by a colonialist vision since they generally show the subjects larking about in a childlike, innocuous manner,
celebrating a stereotypical and essentialist African *joie de vivre* without
any direct reference to the harsh political realities of the late colonial and
early postcolonial period.[55]

Certainly, not all Rouch's relationships with his film subjects were quite
so jocose as his relationships with his colleagues within DALAROUTA.
Rouch seems to have had an altogether more difficult relationship with
Oumarou Ganda. In an interview given in 1980, shortly before his death,
Oumarou said that he did not like *Moi, un Noir*, the film in which he had
starred, because it seemed to him to be false in certain parts. He particularly resented the suggestion in Rouch's commentary at the beginning
of the film that he had been driven from his home by his father who was
ashamed of him because he had been involved in the 1950s colonial war
in Vietnam, which the French had lost. This, he claimed, was completely
untrue. He also resented the fact that although they had developed the
film together, Rouch then took over the editing and finished it without
any further consultation with him. He acknowledged that later Rouch
helped him get training in Niamey, which allowed him to become a filmmaker too, but he claimed to have learned nothing from Rouch himself.
In fact, in his own work, he sought to distance himself completely from
his former patron. "Every time I make a film," he is reported as once having commented, "I kill Jean Rouch."[56]

Other African filmmakers and authors have also been particularly
critical of Jean Rouch's work, some virulently so. In preparing his contribution for the original special edition of *CinémAction* on Rouch's work

that was published in 1982, Pierre Haffner, a leading academic authority on African cinema, sought the opinions of a number of eminent African filmmakers about Rouch's work. Many declined on the grounds that they would have nothing positive to say. Among those who declined was Sembène Ousmane, who refused to make any further comment on Rouch's work after accusing him in 1965 of representing Africans "like insects" in his ethnographic films. Another leading African filmmaker told Haffner that for him, *Jaguar* was no more than a colonialist tale on a par with *Tintin in the Belgian Congo*. In a similar vein, another young African, as reported by Claude Jutra, told Rouch to his face that for him, *Moi, un Noir*, the film praised to the skies by Jean-Luc Godard and other French critics for being the first film to allow African voices to be heard, was yet another experience of "having his head held under water by a White man until he drowned."[57]

African screen studies scholars have been similarly negative. In one of the earliest academic studies covering African cinema, Teshome Gabriel lambasts *Les Maîtres fous* as "blatantly racist" and suggests that Rouch was "perhaps the unconscious tool and agent of French Imperialism in Africa" since "his films tend to reinforce existing prejudices that had been cemented by literature and the 'adventure stories' of the colonial era."[58] More recently, Nwachukwu Frank Ukadike asserts that "since its inception, Black African cinema has been struggling to reverse the demeaning portrayals presented by the dominant colonial and commercial cinemas which blatantly distorted African life and culture." Among the leading examples that he offers are not only feature films such as "the Tarzan jungle melodramas" and *The Gods Must Be Crazy* but also "the so-called ethnographic films of Jean Rouch."[59]

What both Gabriel and Ukadike hold particularly against Rouch, in common with even those African filmmakers who did consent to contribute to the special edition of *CinémAction*, is that he ignored the broader political context of the African world that he was representing. Not only that but, as they see it, his films were not informed by any agenda for addressing the many problems of developing Africa. As Gabriel put it, for him, Rouch presents an Africa that "is content with understanding nature and *coping with* the strains of everyday life, but in none of his works is there an Africa that wants to *change* its predicament."[60]

In part, these views have to be understood within the complex entanglements of the last period of the French colonial presence in Africa. Prior to 1960, when the colonies of West Africa achieved independence, there simply was no African cinema produced by Africans. Those francophone Africans who did manage to get training as filmmakers were often not permitted to make films in their own country. Such was the experience of the Senegalese filmmaker Paulin Vieyra, the first Black African to graduate from the French film school IDHEC, who was prevented from making a film in Senegal by the so-called Laval Decree that gave the power of veto on such matters to the governors of French colonies.[61] Moreover, this veto was applied not just to Africans, but also to those metropolitan French filmmakers who made films about Africa that were critical of the French authorities. It was for this reason that *Les Statues meurent aussi*, by Alain Resnais and Chris Marker, which criticized the export of African art, languished under a ban for some ten years from 1953 until after independence. Rouch's films were also subject to some degree of censorship at this time: for example, *Les Maîtres fous* was banned completely in the British colonies after it was released in 1955, while *Moi, un Noir*, released in 1960, was initially reduced by twenty minutes by the authorities of the newly independent Republic of Ivory Coast, though it was later restored to its full length. But otherwise, being mostly apolitical, certainly in intention, Rouch's films were not subject to rigorous censorship.

Under these circumstances of censorship and restriction on their own activities, it is readily understandable that African filmmakers should find it particularly galling to see Rouch fêted all over the world for his films about Africa, particularly when it was suggested that he was a "white Black," who had "given a voice to Africa" and who had "put the West to flight."[62] But in Rouch's defense, it must be said, firstly, that he should not be criticized for claims that he himself did not make: to the best of my knowledge, he never presumed to speak himself on behalf of Africa or Africans nor claim himself to be a "white Black"—on the contrary, he once declared that it would be "stupid" to make such a claim—though it is certainly true that many third parties, both African and European, have been somewhat over-anxious to award him this title.[63]

Rouch himself, with total justification, claimed only to provide a platform from which certain African voices could be heard that had not been heard before. Nor did he ever aspire to be a political filmmaker with an agenda for change. Instead, as I suggested at the head of this chapter, Rouch sought to find matters of interest, value, or beauty in the world as he found it. As the Beninois filmmaker and academic, Richard de Medeiros, comments in the *CinémAction* volume, there may be grounds for criticizing Rouch's films for lack of political contextualization, but there is no absolute reason why all films should be political in character. There should also be a place for films of an ethnographic sensibility that seek to discover value in the world as it is rather than as it should be.[64]

However, some of the criticism directed against Roush's films by African commentators appears to be based on the principle that the celebration of African life as it is represents some sort of endorsement of social or economic backwardness. While, for Rouch, the protagonists of his migration films are 'heroes of the modern world,' these critics see only victims of colonial or post-colonial oppression. Whereas for him, his possession ceremony films testify to the proud maintenance of traditional belief in the midst of modernity, for his critics they represent the glorification of primitivism. Those coming at his work from this angle have concluded that whatever Rouch's intentions might have been, the overall thrust of his films is to deny social progress in Africa, or worse, hold Africa and its inhabitants up to some kind of racist ridicule. Criticisms of this general kind are often directed against anthropologists, whether they are working in Latin America, Asia, or Africa, or even with marginal groups in the so-called "First World." But as in all these situations, it is surely the role of the anthropologist to identify and record the value in all forms of social life and, while not obstructing progressive change, to resist those changes that will merely result in the marginalization and degradation of those forms of life.

The potentially destructive consequences of social change were certainly a major preoccupation of Rouch, and one theme to which he often returned was the need to record the traditional forms of life in rural Africa before they disappeared. Indeed, this was central to his response to Sembène Ousmane when the latter accused him of filming Africans "like insects." Rouch defended himself and his fellow Africanists from this accusation by arguing that far from denigrating traditional African ways of life, they believed them to be as important as their own and that they had a solemn duty to record as much of this way of life before it was engulfed by social change.[65]

Rouch never developed this concern to preserve a record of traditional culture into a political project of some kind, along the lines, say, of the so-called "indigenous media" projects in present-day Australia, Brazil, Canada, and elsewhere, in which the valorization of traditional culture through filmmaking serves as a mode of resistance both to internal social disaggregation and to external pressures. But the record that Rouch left behind is still available to others for such purposes. Indeed, even in his own lifetime, he reported that his once much decried and supposedly "blatantly racist" account of the *hauka* cult, *Les Maîtres fous* was not only being screened in Niger for educational purposes but it had even stimulated a young Nigerien filmmaker, Inoussa Ousseini, to film a ritual event in the extreme east of Niger that appeared to be a variation on the same ritual theme.[66]

As de Medeiros concludes in his interview in *CinémAction*, there is a world of difference between referring to Rouch as an "African filmmaker" and referring to him as a "French filmmaker who has taken a great deal of interest in Africa." Whereas the first description will cause many people to take offence since it suggests that he was attempting to speak on behalf of Africa, the latter description is merely an accurate account of his situation and, as such, not controversial. Considered simply in this light, de Medeiros suggests, Rouch deserves to be respected as a pioneer whose vision was highly progressive for that time.[67]

Joking Relationships

As an inveterate crosser of social, cultural, and racial boundaries, it was almost inevitable that there should be some element of ambiguity in the relationships that Rouch developed on either side of those boundaries. One of Rouch's great personal skills was to be able to deal with this ambiguity. Joking relationships were central to his technique for doing so.

The ambiguity in Rouch's relationships with his principal companions is subtly portrayed in an early scene in *Rouch's Gang*. After a screening of *Jaguar* in a public cinema, the audience ask the "band' about their relationships with one another. Lam construes their relationship to Rouch as being based on more than just friendship, comparing it to a relationship of cousins, though one marked by "a joking relationship," which, he explains, means that they can both make fun of one another and ask one another for support. However, Tallou and Damouré immediately demur from this characterization. Tallou says that he considers Rouch more like a father, a point of view vigorously seconded by Damouré, who explains that, like sons, they feel that they can contact Rouch whenever they need help, be it materially or otherwise. But then Rouch himself intervenes, somewhat abruptly and apparently with some embarrassment, to say that he prefers to think of it as a relationship of cousins, since a relationship of paternity "is of no importance."

Clearly, Rouch was much happier with the implicit egalitarianism of a cousin relationship rather than with notion of a father-son relationship, with all its connotations of paternalism and colonialism. The irony, of course, is that in contradicting Tallou and Damouré quite so brusquely, Rouch leaves the spectator with the impression that it is their characterization that is the most accurate. Notwithstanding Rouch's denial of his "paternity" on this occasion, Damouré again refers to him in these terms close to the end of Berit Madsen and Anne Mette Jørgensen's more recent film about Rouch's "band." Brushing aside the opportunity offered by the filmmakers to speak skeptically about his relationship with Rouch, Damouré reiterates his appreciation of the fact that Rouch had given him

FIGURE 15.6. The band of "adventurers and amateurs." Lam, Rouch, Damouré, Tallou, and Moussa pose at a motorway service stop in the Beauce region, France, April 1993. © Christian Lelong.

a chance to make something of his life. It was in this sense that Rouch was like a father to him and with a father, Damouré insists, there can be no relationship of equality.[68]

The *bien pensant* might wince at this frank admission of hierarchy, but it clearly corresponds to certain realities of the West African situation. Moreover, this acknowledgment of hierarchy cannot be simply written off as some sort of false consciousness on the part of Damouré arising from his experience of colonialism as a young man. Hierarchical social formations have been a feature of West African life both before and since the period of European colonialism, and the attitudes associated with them sit uneasily with European ideals of egalitarianism. Besides, Damouré himself was a formidable character and a man of self-evidently great intelligence so to suggest that well into his seventies and almost fifty years after the formal ending of the French colony in Niger in 1960, he was somehow incapable of imagining himself the equal of Jean Rouch due to colonial false consciousness is frankly absurd.

But whatever the precise origins of the hierarchical component of the relationships between Rouch and his companions, it clearly was an intrinsic feature of those relationships, however much Rouch himself may have liked to imagine that that they were based entirely on a relationship of friendship between equals. The films that they made together may have been conceived and executed within a network of relationships that, for their era particularly, were remarkable for their egalitarian ethos. But within this network, Rouch's position was that of *primus inter pares*, the first among equals. If his trio of principal protagonists were the Three Musketeers, as they have been called, then he was d'Artagnan: they may have all worked together on the principle of "all for one and one for all" but, in the last analysis, everyone knew who was in charge.

Even if he was ultimately wrong about the cousin analogy, Lam was probably right on that night in the Amsterdam cinema to suggest that the relationship between Rouch and his companions was based on a joking relationship, as Rouch himself also frequently averred. For, as Jean-Paul Colleyn has pointed out, the *sanankuya*, as such relationships are known in West Africa, in common with joking relationships more generally, is a quasi-ritualized means of resolving social tensions, particularly those to do with ambiguities arising from differences in social status.[69] Even Rouch himself, in his response in the Amsterdam cinema—albeit in relation to Franco-German relations—describes a joking relationship as "a cathartic alliance" that "allows one to forget about old quarrels."

It is striking that Rouch maintained joking relationships in two very different directions in the course of his life, both of which were very important to him. On the one hand, there was his joking relationship with Marcel Griaule and on the other, there was his joking relationship with the Nigerien "band of adventurers." In the case of Griaule, the joking relationship allowed Rouch to be Griaule's faithful disciple while at the same time despising both his association with the Vichy government and his attitude toward his African subjects. In the case of his African companions, the joking relationship allowed Rouch to exercise an authority over them even while laughing and joking and speaking endlessly of their friendship with its implication of egalitarianism. Meanwhile, it allowed Rouch's companions to act as his loyal acolytes whatever they might personally have thought of the disparities in wealth and power that inevitably framed their relationship. In both situations, the *sanankuya* was remarkably effective. In relation to Griaule, it sustained Rouch through all the long years of the Sigui project while in relation to Damouré, Lam, and Tallou, it sustained them all over the course of a joint adventure in shared anthropology that lasted for more than fifty years.

16 : The Legacy of Jean Rouch

In the African religions that I know, if you do something important in your life-time, that's enough—you can be immortal. JEAN ROUCH, 1990[1]

By any measure, Jean Rouch is a major figure, possibly the greatest, among ethnographic filmmakers both past and present. Particularly in the earlier stages of his career, he was very much ahead of his time, anticipating by a long way certain intellectual positions that would later achieve the status of orthodoxies both in ethnographic filmmaking and anthropology more generally. Moreover, he left behind a large body of films about West Africa that will be a source not just of ethnographic evidence, but also of inspiration and debate for many years to come. David MacDougall has suggested that rather than think of ethnographic films as transparent representations of the world, we should now assess them as "sites of meaning-potential" that can be read at a variety of different levels and in a variety of different contexts.[2] If this is so, the "meaning-potential" of the films of Jean Rouch is vast, since the possibilities for reworking and reconsidering the significance of his films are boundless. For not only can each film be considered on its own, but each of his films can be used to comment on any number of others, while beyond the films lie his written works providing yet another dimension of intertextual insight and understanding. This linking of Rouch's filmmaking to his texts is what I sought to do in chapter 7 of this book in relation to *Les Maîtres fous*. But this is only one, even if an important one, of Rouch's works. Not only will this one film surely be reinterpreted many times again in the future, but there are many more that would merit this form of analysis.

This vast body of work will certainly assure Rouch a preeminent place in the history of ethnographic cinema. But what of his praxis, his particular way of making films—how valuable a legacy does that represent? This praxis has been the thread holding this book together and in this conclusion, my aim will be to summarize some of its most salient characteristics while at the same time offering an assessment of its value for future generations. However, if this is to be a genuinely useful exercise and not just an empty paean of praise of the kind that one sometimes finds in the English-language literature, our recognition of Jean Rouch's unparalleled achievements must be tempered by some degree of critical distance. We should begin then by recognizing that his most acclaimed ethnographic filmwork now lies in the relatively distant past, dating from the 1970s and before. Also, that he developed his praxis in a very different political climate, in the late colonial and early postcolonial period in Africa, and in relation to a cinematographic technology, 16mm film, that is now effectively obsolete, at least insofar as the great majority of ethnographic filmmakers are concerned. In these circumstances, it is not unreasonable to ask just how relevant the legacy of his praxis might be for the young anthropologist filmmakers of today just starting out on the "adventure of the real."

Anthropology in the First Person

The fundamental principle underlying Rouch's praxis, and one that can be traced, albeit in very different ways, both to his formation as an anthropologist by Marcel Griaule and his admiration for the work of Robert Flaherty, was the importance of a sustained participation on the part of the filmmaker in the world of the subjects. "Do you know what was the key to Jean Rouch's success?" his widow Jocelyne recently asked me, rhetorically. "It was his great openness to people."[3] Perhaps this openness was influenced by his experience of living among the Songhay, who, as reported by Paul Stoller, stress the role of participation in social life as a means of gaining wisdom.[4] But whatever its precise origins, the importance of participation was a principle that guided Rouch throughout his career.

Rouch was not afraid to admit the fact of this participation, nor its subjective nature. He often described what he did as "anthropology in the first person" and, inspired in part by his youthful encounter with Surrealism, he would frequently emphasize the importance of the individual filmmaker's subjective response to the situation in which he or she was filming. Moreover, he freely admitted that he made films, first and foremost, for himself: he was, he frequently commented, the first spectator of his films as he went about shooting them. The second set of spectators for his films, he claimed, were the subjects of his films, since he considered film the most effective means for showing his subjects just how he saw them. Only then, back in third place, did he consider that his films were for third parties.

FIGURE 16.1. Jean Rouch with Jocelyne in the Dogon men's *toguna*, meeting house, at Sanga, Bandiagara Escarpment, December 2003. © Philippe Costantini.

Though we should perhaps take this last assertion with a pinch of salt, it is undeniable that Rouch's praxis was very different from the ideas associated with the use of the camera for ethnographic purposes that were the common currency of his Anglo-Saxon contemporaries. For even the most progressive of the leading Anglo-Saxon ethnographic filmmakers of Rouch's era, such as John Marshall and Tim Asch, aspired in their theoretical pronouncements—albeit somewhat at odds with their actual practice—to use the camera as if it were some sort of objective recording device. Their preferred metaphors for the camera were drawn from the world of scientific instrumentation: for them, the camera was analogous to the telescope or the microscope, and their hope was that like these hero-instruments of the natural sciences, it would transform the discipline of anthropology by delivering data in an unprecedentedly objective manner.[5]

For Rouch, this idea of the camera was far too positivist—"that is Comte, exactly," as he once put it.[6] In his view, the use of the camera not only inevitably changed the world, but it did so in ways that were instructive. Rather than being merely a passive scientific recording device, capable of testifying only to what happened in front of it, he conceived of the camera as a catalytic instrument, one whose mere presence could provoke the subjects into producing a performance that revealed the beliefs, sentiments, attitudes and dreams that lay beneath the everyday surface of things and that, in the last analysis, were of primary importance in explaining the more visible forms of social behavior. In this regard, as we considered in greater detail in previous chapters, Rouch's praxis continued a long tradition in French anthropology, sharing with Mauss an interest in the intellectual underpinnings of the external manifestations of culture, and with Griaule, a commitment to provoking the subjects into revealing these, albeit with a camera rather than with interrogatory interviews, as was Griaule's characteristic method.[7]

It was this emphasis on participation in the Rouchian praxis that David and Judith MacDougall, and other early practitioners of Observational Cinema picked up on and developed in their own particular way to go beyond the idea of the camera as a scientific instrument.[8] In effect, as a direct result of this transfusion of Rouchian ideas, Observational Cinema was prevented from going any further down the route suggested by Marshall and Asch, and exemplified outside anthropology by the work of the Direct Cinema filmmakers whereby the new, more mobile, sound-synchronous technology would be used to achieve greater self-effacement in the hope of attaining some more objectively true representation of the world. In emphasizing that both the subjective engagement of the filmmaker and the equally subjective response of the subject were not merely inevitable but positively necessary and desirable, Rouch anticipated by a matter of almost twenty years the rejection in Anglo-Saxon anthropology of a natural sciences paradigm based on dispassionate objective observation and the associated rise of the so-called "literary turn" to which ideas of authorship, representation, and the relationship between anthropologists and their subjects were of central importance.

The Participatory Camera

It was the overriding importance to Rouch of participation in the lives of his subjects that provided the rationale for all his self-denying technical ordinances, such as the strictures on the use of the tripod or the zoom, the "violent" opposition to crews of professional technicians, the refusal to work with a script or repeat a take, and the suspicion of *la belle image*. For Rouch, all these restraints were necessary because too much equipment, too many people, an excessively "professionalist" concern with technique or visual aesthetics, or some over-elaborate preconceived idea about how the action should develop could all act as obstacles to the engagement between the filmmaker and the subjects. The benefits of such a participatory approach remains a lesson that still needs to be impressed upon young ethnographic filmmakers, many of whom, in my own experience, can be tempted to become overly concerned with technical or aesthetic matters as a way of demonstrating their professionalism, with the result that their films turn out to be remote and lifeless despite—or perhaps because of—their technical virtuosity.

But if the underlying rationale for all the features of the Rouchian praxis is primarily to ensure that there are no obstacles to the participation of the filmmaker in the world of the subjects, it is not always necessary to follow them to the letter. In making the Dogon films, Rouch declined to use a tripod even when engagement with the subjects could not have been an issue—for example, in the filming of geological features of the landscape or distant shots of massed ranks of dancers—producing unnecessarily poor, unstable shots as a result. There are also circumstances in which the zoom can be used discreetly, not just to avoid moving closer to the subject, which Rouch rightly decried, but to enhance the movement or the distribution of subjects within the frame. Similarly, while an excessive concern with aesthetic values may often be constricting, the rejection of *la belle image* should not become a pretext for a lack of attention to the basic cinematographic virtues of good framing, lighting, and movement, all of which can be accomplished by the skilful operator without inhibiting interaction with the subjects.

Indeed, if young filmmakers are looking for a model as to how to shoot, Rouch himself would not necessarily be the first person whom one would recommend. As a number of the leading French cinematographers of the 1970s acknowledged in a series of interviews given to René Prédal in 1981, Rouch's disregard for the constraining conventions then taught in film schools, his willingness to take risks with lighting and framing, to shoot handheld, and so on, had a liberating effect on the cinematographic practice of the day, directly inspiring the young cameramen who came under his influence, including figures as diverse as Nestor Almendros and Michel Brault.[9] But as these testimonies also suggest, Rouch was not an operator of the first rank himself, at least not in the later phases of his career.

The cinematography in Rouch's earliest work has a certain vital quality that contributes greatly to the overall sense of energy and dynamism that emerge from these films. Indeed, to my mind, the pinnacle of his achievement as a cinematographer is represented by *Moi, un Noir*, shot in 1957, which was the last film that he made in its entirety using the Bell & Howell that he picked up in the Paris Flea Market in 1946. As described in some detail in chapter 6, there are many ravishing shots in this film, and it is particularly interesting for the way in which he uses available light to good effect. The scene shot in the yard of the *goumbé* self-help organization toward the end of the film, particularly the sequence in which he dances with Nathalie while still operating the camera, is surely a candidate for being considered the most accomplished of his entire oeuvre.

But, ironically perhaps, although Rouch played a vital role in developing the new sound-synchronous technology, it is arguable that in terms of adjusting his personal cinematographic skills, he did not make the transition to the more sophisticated cameras of the 1960s as successfully as did some other ethnographic filmmakers—such as Robert Gardner or John Marshall—who also first learned their craft on the spring-wound cameras of the 1950s. Rouch himself often explained that when he was working with his Bell & Howell, he would consider how to execute his next shot while he was winding up the mechanism between takes. With the later battery-driven cameras, not only was such a degree of premeditation not forced upon him, but he was able to indulge his predilection for the long, unbroken sequence-shot. Shots of this kind require a great deal of both skill and luck to execute successfully, that is, steadily and without redundancy, and in Rouch's case, although sometimes they worked magnificently, as in the sequence-shots in *Architectes ayorou* and *Les Tambours d'avant* described in chapter 12, at other times, especially in his later films, they resulted in camerawork that was wavering and loose. Already by the early 1960s, the reviews in *Cahiers du Cinéma* were referring to his trembling hand, and as advancing age took its inevitable toll, this only became more apparent.[10] But given his positive celebration of amateurism, these were not matters with which Rouch concerned himself a great deal and the older he got, the less he cared about them.[11]

In view of his general disregard for formal standards of technical or aesthetic excellence, it seems rather strange at first sight that Rouch—in sharp contrast to his friend and contemporary Ricky Leacock—would remain resolutely hostile to video until the end of his days. But after an initial flush of enthusiasm, as represented by his optimistic remarks about the future of the medium in the conclusion to "The Camera and Man," he rejected video completely.[12] For many years, on account of his veto, films that had originated on video were not accepted for the Bilan Ethnographique film festival at the Musée de l'Homme. Eventually, in the 1990s, as video became the dominant medium of ethnographic filmmaking, Françoise Foucault, the principal organizer of the festival, finally managed to persuade him to accept films shot in this medium, but it required a great deal of tact on her part in order to bring about this situation.

Rouch's reasons for rejecting video were based in part on the visual quality of the image, which, particularly in the early days, was far inferior to that of film. The reverie that he liked to enter when watching films at the Bilan would undoubtedly have been much more difficult to achieve with the grainy image and the smeared colors that were typical of the first generation of video stock. He also had well-justified reservations about the longevity of the medium. But perhaps the main reason for his antipathy to video was because he felt that the very ease of use and the cheapness of the stock encouraged sloppy filmmaking. For Rouch, to run risks was the very essence of any form of filmmaking. Every shot should be an "unrepeatable adventure." But with video, it is only too easy to review what one has done and, if one does not like the first attempt to shoot a scene, have another go. This, Rouch felt, had profoundly negative consequences for the performances of both the filmmaker and the subjects. But while there was undoubtedly a great deal of truth to all these objections, Rouch's views about video, as Dirk Nijland has observed, served to distance him from younger generations of anthropologist filmmakers who, for good or for ill, have to learn to develop their skills in the context of the new medium rather than cling on to the vestiges of a technology that for most has become obsolete.[13]

Performance, Language, and the Everyday

If participation was the most fundamental principle underlying Rouch's praxis, the idea of performance was not far behind. For, in effect, Rouch's films were produced by a series of performances—in the field, in the edit suite, and in the dubbing studio, and, last but not least, in the cinema or seminar room. For, in these last two locations, as William Rothman has commented, Rouch took pleasure in presenting his films while performing a very particular sort of persona, one that Rothman describes as characterized by "joyfulness-tinged-with-melancholy."[14] Moreover, all these performances were usually in response to some kind of performance, or at least a reaction, on the part of third parties. In the field, shooting was a performance in response to the performance of the subjects; in the edit suite, it was a performance—albeit a "harsh dialogue"— in relation to the performance of the editor; in the sound studio, when recording his voice-overs, his performance was a response to the edited film itself as he allowed himself to "become possessed" by it, while in the cinema or seminar room, it was a response to the presence of the audience. In all these situations, success was achieved when the performances on both sides of the relationship were in some sense in unison with one another.

Although Rouch believed that it was important to prepare for all these performances—no ethnographic film should be an act of discovery, he once commented[15]—there was always a residue of uncertainty and chance separating the preparation from the performance itself. But for Rouch, as for his Surrealist poet-heroes, this was a positive matter because it was in this arena of risk between the potential and the actual that the performer was obliged to draw upon his creative inner resources, which by their very nature, were likely to produce performances that were more interesting, if not in some sense more true, than performances that represented merely the cranking out of ideas that were entirely rational, premeditated and controlled.

Rouch's ideal typical case of the filmmaker's performance while on location was the filming of a ritual event. As I described in chapter 12, Rouch believed that one should prepare very carefully for this, making the appropriate enquiries, even drawing out a sketch. But once the ritual had begun, then it was up to the filmmaker to come up with an inspired cinematographic performance commensurate with the ritual performance unfolding in front of him. When Rouch came to shoot his fictions, the same principles applied. Although there was generally no script to a Rouchian fiction, there was still meticulous preparation and detailed discussions with the actors about what each scene would contain. But once the shooting had begun and the actors were improvising their performances, then it was up to Rouch to respond to them, that is, to film them as if he were filming a ritual about whose general pattern he might have gathered some advanced knowledge but that he certainly could not stop. If there was an element of risk about this situation, then so much the better, since this could only improve the quality of both the filmmaker's performance and that of his protagonists.

This is certainly an exciting and inspiring way of conceiving of the process of shooting an ethnographic film, and it is one that will recommend itself immediately to all aspiring ethnographic filmmakers. But at the same time, one should recognize that it is a way of conceiving of the praxis of the ethnographic filmmaker that pertains only to a somewhat circumscribed arena of human experience. For it does not offer any clue as to how one should go about filming the petty routines of everyday life. In Rouch's ethnographic oeuvre, the vast majority of his films are about public ritual performances of one kind or another. If not, they are about hunting expeditions, which have a highly ritualized, performative element to them as well. When pressed about why he did not film everyday life, Rouch commented that one had to be a very great filmmaker to do so, and although he had managed to film some supporting scenes for his films about ritual events, he had never hit upon a satisfactory way of doing it in any more elaborate way.[16]

In fact, it seems that Rouch had difficulty even recognizing that a film about everyday life was a film at all. This is suggested by his reaction to *To Live with Herds*, the early film by David and Judith MacDougall that was awarded the grand prix at the Venice Film Festival in 1972 (also awarded to Rouch's own film, *The Lion Hunters*, in 1965). The MacDougalls' film is constructed around a series of scenes of everyday life among the Jie pastoralists of Uganda. Although Rouch was on the jury that awarded the prize to the MacDougalls, unanimously, his reported first response was, "This is not a film!" Indeed, more generally, he considered the MacDougalls' work, which, in contrast to his own, often concerns the routines of everyday life, to be "a wonderful positive approach . . . absolutely honest . . . something like *Le Paysan de Paris*, without Aragon, without the talent of a poet, because they are not poets."[17]

This overriding concern with public ritual events is entirely consistent with Rouch's formation as an anthropologist of the school of Griaule. But the reverse side of this particular coin is the relative neglect of the domestic domain in Rouch's films, which, in turn, resulted in the relative neglect of the world of women. As I discussed at greater length in chapter 11, when challenged about this, Rouch explained that in the African societies in which he worked, it would generally have been regarded as unacceptable for him to work more extensively with the women.[18] However, even while one might acknowledge that the realities of the societies where Rouch himself worked may have restricted his contact with women to a substantial degree, it remains the case that if young filmmakers were to follow Rouch's practice of filming only public, ritual events, in many societies this would result in the under-representation of domestic life and the world of women, even in situations in which there might not be any gender-related problems of access.

Another reason that Rouch would have had difficulty in making films about everyday life was his unwillingness to use the subjects' own language in his ethnographic films. At first sight, it seems highly paradoxical that although Rouch played a leading role in developing mobile synchronous-sound recording in documentary filmmaking generally, he was dismayed by the way in which the films based on this new technology showed "an incredible regard for the chatting of the people filmed, as if oral testimony were more sacred than the visual sort." Although he used interview techniques extensively in his survey work during the period of his migration studies in West Africa in the 1950s, he never used interviews in his ethnographic films, regarding any such dependence on speech as an "archaic habit" that television had inherited from radio and one that would disappear "quite soon."[19]

Moreover, it is not merely formal interviews but also informal conversations between subjects that are noticeable by their absence in his ethnographic films. The informal conversations that are central to the MacDougalls' films about the Turkana, and which include verbal exchanges not only between the subjects but also between the subjects and the filmmakers, Rouch once compared, somewhat disparagingly, to "translations of books."[20] Apart from one or two moments—including the remarkable episode in *Yenendi de Ganghel* (1968) when a medium possessed by Dongo, the Spirit of Thunder, acknowledges the camera—no subject ever directly addresses the camera in Rouch's ethnographic films.

Rouch was not alone among documentary filmmakers who first learned their craft in the era prior to synchronous sound in believing that the arrival of synchronous speech threatened to turn documentary filmmaking from an art form into a degenerate form of television journalism. Another ethnographic filmmaker of his generation who springs immediately to mind here is Robert Gardner. In addition to their aesthetic objections to speech-driven filmmaking, what Rouch and Gardner had in common, when working in culturally exotic locations, was a reluctance to use the indigenous language of their subjects. In Gardner's case, this may in part be because he has roved around the world making his films, never staying long enough in any one place to learn the language. By contrast, Rouch followed the injunction of his mentors Griaule and Dieterlen that it was necessary to keep returning to the same community for at least twenty years if one were to gain a "deep knowledge" of its system of thought. But, like them, Rouch always worked through interpreters and apparently did not consider it necessary to gain an equally "deep knowledge" of his subjects' language. As he himself readily confessed, he was "not very good at languages."[21] Although he frequently cites Songhay statements verbatim in his doctoral thesis and is reported to have had a day-to-day operational command of Songhay, his knowledge of the language was not, in fact, profound, while his command of Dogon was extremely limited. In the circumstances then, it is perhaps not surprising that he did not think it essential to give direct access to his subjects' speech in his documentaries.

The one great exception to all this is, of course, *Chronicle of a Summer*, which is covered from end to end with the subjects' speech and in a broad variety of forms—conversations of many different kinds, interviews both formal and informal, songs, even a soliloquy, namely, Marceline's famous muttered reflections on her concentration camp experience as she walks across the Place de la Concorde. But what also obviously marks out *Chronicle* among Rouch's documentaries, certainly in the first half of his career, is that it was in French. The same is also true of the ethnofictions and all of the films that he made on nonethnographic subjects throughout his career, one of the very few exceptions being the portrait of his friend, Margaret Mead, shot in 1978, which was in English. Until the 1970s at least, if the subjects of his documentaries are speaking African languages, Rouch paraphrases what they are saying in a French voice-over performed by himself, differentiating this from the tone of his narrator's commentary, by standing up for the former and sitting down for the latter, which, in effect, resulted in his voice having two different tones.[22] As we considered in chapter 14, this works well enough when the speech of the subjects consists of ritual chanting, particularly as Rouch adjusts the timbre of his voice and increases the poetic quality of the words to give the commentary a suitably ritualistic aura. But it is less successful when he has to switch between a ritual chanting voice, a commentary voice and then a voice paraphrasing everyday speech, as in the "Sigui synthèse," for example, and more or less unworkable when there is an exchange between his subjects involving several different voices.

Rouch might have resolved some of these linguistic problems if he had been prepared to use subtitles. But he retained a lifelong antipathy to using subtitles for reasons that were not entirely convincing. In reality, his objections to subtitles—principally that they "mutilated" the image and could not communicate all the nuances of meaning in the subjects' statements—rather than being coherent counter-arguments, seem to be more in the nature of a rationalization for not abandoning the eloquent and sonorous voice-overs that were so central to his praxis and which he clearly performed with such relish. Indeed, these voice-overs are so integral to Rouch's filmic *écriture*, that it is difficult to imagine his ethnographic documentaries without them.

This seems to have been Rouch's problem too and by the early 1970s, he appears to have arrived at some kind of impasse as to how to handle African languages in his documentaries. Although he continued to have no qualms about voicing over ritual chanting, as in *Les Tambours d'avant* (1972) and the Dogon ceremonial films (the last of which was completed in 1980), he seems to have become reluctant to voice over the more everyday conversations that he was increasingly able to capture with the more portable synchronous sound technology that he was by then using. Yet, at the same time, he could not bring himself to use subtitles which resulted in the effect that one finds in *Un lion nommé "L'Américain"* (1972), in which there are long passages of speech in an African language that is neither voiced over nor subtitled, and which are therefore incomprehensible to most viewers. Nor was this the only case, since in *Architectes ayorou* (1970) and in *Médecines et médecins* (1976), one encounters similar passages. Although it seems that very late in life, Rouch did eventually come round to recognizing that subtitles were not as bad as he had previously suggested, by then his career as an ethnographic filmmaker was effectively over, so he was never able to put this conversion, if such it really was, into practice.

Cinema and Truth

Although Rouch had a far more sophisticated understanding of the camera as a means of representation than his Anglo-Saxon documentary filmmaking contemporaries, he was not, by inclination, a theoretician. This is true as much of his ethnographic writing as of his writing and commentaries on cinema. His was a poetic rather than an analytical sensibility. He was above all a practitioner, always seeking the solution to any problem by a pragmatic experimental process of successive approximations, as recommended to him by Albert Caquot, his teacher when he was an engineering student at the École des Ponts et Chaussées, whom he continued to cite faithfully to this effect throughout his career.

Indeed, as Michael Eaton pointed out in the first major commentary on Rouch's work in English, Rouch's ideas about the evidential status of film had a tendency to be mutually contradictory.[23] In some contexts, he would emphasize the importance of subjective engagement on the part of the filmmaker in shooting his or her material, while on others, he would stress the importance of showing the world as it really is. Similarly, he would often extol the virtues of the camera as a catalyst that can provoke a performance on the part of the subjects, but at the same time, he played a leading role in developing a film technology that would minimize the impact on the subjects as they went about their lives.

But the context in which the contradictions at the heart of Rouch's ideas about the representational status of film were surely most evident was in relation to his struggles with what he once called "the devil of editing."[24] When making documentaries in the era prior to synchronous sound, Rouch not only constantly sought to edit while shooting, but at the same time, had no qualms about subsequently manipulating the rushes once back in the edit suite. As we saw in chapter 13, although he was initially reluctant to alter the literal account of the world recorded by his camera, his editors—first Renée Lichtig, then Suzanne Baron, and later Marie-Josèphe Yoyotte and Jean Ravel, each in their different way—convinced Rouch of the merits of editing in the edit suite. Thereafter, edit suite manipulations came to be central to his praxis up to and including *The Lion Hunters*, finally released in 1965, which was the last major film that Rouch shot using predominantly nonsynchronous technology.

But once Rouch was able to use the new technology, which was not only sound-synchronous but also permitted much longer takes, he seems to have become much less willing to engage in edit suite manipulations when making his ethnographic documentaries. As we saw in chapter 8, he considered the excisions that he was obliged to make in order to get *Chronicle of a Summer* down to the length required by the producer were tantamount to an amputation of a limb. Instead, as the technology developed, he preferred to do as much editing as possible through the viewfinder by shooting long, unbroken sequence-shots. This praxis is central to his later Dogon films, shot between 1966 and 1974, which typically consist of long aggregations of sequence-shots edited together with a minimal manipulation of chronology, or indeed any other editorial interventions in the image track. Sequence-shots were also a feature of the films that Rouch made among the Songhay during this period, and in 1971, he finally achieved his "dream almost beyond reach," namely, to shoot a complete film, *Les Tambours d'avant*, that consisted almost entirely of a single, unbroken sequence-shot of ten minutes, the maximum duration of a 16mm magazine of 400 feet.

But this strategy merely displaced rather than resolved the epistemological problem about the evidential status of the image posed by the "devil of editing." Instead of being dependent on decisions made *a posteriori* in the edit suite, the question of what to include and what to omit from any given scene would be resolved instead on location. Rather than being the product of a "harsh dialogue" between editor and filmmaker, the editorial structuring of the film became the result of a conjunction between "objective chance" and the inspired decisions of the filmmaker in the moment of filming a sequence-shot. But as I sought to show in chapter 12 when analyzing *Les Tambours d'avant*, the fact that a sequence-shot is unbroken and as such permits a "plunge into reality," as Rouch puts it in the narration of that film, does not mean that the representation of the world that it delivers is in any sense objective or unmediated. In *Les Tambours d'avant*, not only does the presence of the camera influence the event that is happening in front of it, seemingly causing the mediums to go into trance, but the manner in which Rouch chose to shoot that event, for all that it is unbroken, still conforms to the most conventional of narrative *topoi*. Even Rouch could not escape quite so easily from the "prison-house of language."

Moreover, as Rouch himself would on occasion acknowledge, the goal of shooting a sequence-shot as long as a standard 16mm 400-ft magazine would permit was, in reality, little more than a stylistic exercise.[25] For, clearly, the ten-minute duration of a 400-ft magazine is an entirely contingent matter. It became established at some point in the history of 16mm filmmaking technology for a mixture of commercial and technical reasons, and obviously bears no relation whatsoever to any considerations as to what might be an appropriate duration in terms of the content of a shot. Now that shots of an hour or more are perfectly feasible using professional video technology, the proposition that one should be constantly striving to keep a shot going as long as technically possible has become, in effect, absurd. It will become even more so with the imminent arrival of cameras mounted with hard drives that will permit shots of several hours in duration.

Rouch's limitations as a theorist are also apparent in his attempt to develop an epistemology for his filmmaking praxis by linking it to the ideas of Dziga Vertov. For several years after *Chronicle of a Summer* served to put the idea of *cinéma-vérité* into general circulation, it "cluttered up" discussions of documentary films at festivals and conferences, as one of the leading participants in such events has put it.[26] Indeed, it continues to cause confusion even to this day. Although Rouch generally obeyed the embargo on the use of the term that was agreed at the historic meeting between French and North American documentarists at Lyons in 1963, he simply used the alternative term proposed by Mario Ruspoli, *cinéma direct*, as if it were a synonym for *cinéma-vérité*. But this merely served to conflate the technique of working with the new mobile sound-synchronous technology, denoted by the term *cinéma direct*, with Vertov's theory about the nature of the knowledge of the world offered by the cinematographic apparatus, as denoted by the term *cinéma-vérité*.

Moreover, even though he may no longer have used the specific term *cinéma-vérité*, Rouch continued to link his work with Vertov by his use, at every available opportunity, of the prefix "ciné-" to describe what he was doing. In the same way that Vertov considered himself a *kinoki*, a "ciné-eye," so Rouch considered himself "ciné-Rouch in a state of ciné-trance engaged in . . . the joy of filming, ciné-pleasure."[27] But this enthusiasm obscured the fact that there was a major difference between his and Vertov's respective practices, at all stages of the production of a film. Where Vertov typically sought to capture the world unawares, Rouch always constructed his representations of the world through a prior process of exchange with the subjects. Where Vertov sought to break up the normal experience of reality through his use of montage and special effects, Rouch sought to preserve it both in his shooting technique and in the edit suite. Most importantly, while for Vertov the distinctive truths delivered by cinema were created by manipulations in the edit suite, for Rouch they were the truths revealed by subjects in response to the provocation of the camera.

The confusion caused by Rouch's attempt to give his ideas a Vertovian pedigree are particularly exemplified by his theory of the ciné-trance. Shorn of the Vertovian prefixes, this comes down to the proposition that if cinematographers become totally engaged in what they are doing and lend themselves entirely to the situation in which they are filming, they may enter a trancelike state in which they feel that both their physical movements and their technique are in harmony with the action in front of them. Meanwhile, on the other side of the lens, the subjects may be motivated by the presence of the camera to put on a special performance that reveals something of interest about their lives or their state of mind that they would not otherwise have exhibited.

Most contemporary ethnographic filmmakers would probably allow that both of these propositions are true, at least to some degree, and would agree that young filmmakers should be encouraged to develop the kind of engaged, participatory filmmaking strategies that make these effects possible. But whether these effects of participation in themselves give rise to some form of distinctively privileged truth, as Rouch believed, perhaps inspired at some remove by the Surrealist faith in automatism, is another matter altogether. Most contemporary filmmakers would probably find themselves more readily in agreement with the less ambitious conclusion reached by Edgar Morin regarding the making of *Chronicle*, namely, that however it is made, a film in and of itself cannot give rise to one single privileged truth, but rather to a variety of claims to truth that will often contradict one another. The relative value, significance or authenticity of these claims to truth will always be a matter for the filmmaker to judge by drawing on a variety of criteria and forms of evidence.

Fact and Fiction

Over the course of his career Rouch completed some seventeen fiction films, eight of them in the first half of his career that is the principal focus of this book. There were some common elements of praxis to all these first eight fiction films—no script, scenes improvised by the actors as they went along, shooting based on the principle of one-and-only takes—but they involved various, significantly different, relationships to ethnographic reality. As we discussed in chapters 5 and 6, the first two fiction films, *Jaguar* and *Moi, un Noir*, were both strongly anchored in particular ethnographic situations. In neither case did all of the characters in reality live precisely the sort of lives that they represented in the film. But they portrayed lives that were lived by many others from social and cultural backgrounds similar to their own and they acted them out in preexisting social situations. At the time that he made these films, Rouch was deeply engaged in a study of rural-urban migration in West Africa in which he had deployed an impressive range of conventional sociological research methods, including statistical surveys, formal interviews and focus groups. But he had turned to film, and fictional film in particular, as he felt that this was the most effective means at his disposal to represent the subjective experience of the migrants.

Rouch's third fiction film, *La Pyramide humaine*, shot in 1959–1960, marked a significant change in his praxis. First, it was not about the experience of rural-urban migrants but rather about relationships between European and African *lycéens*. But second and more significant, although it had some connection with the ethnographic reality of late colonial Abidjan, it portrayed a world of interaction between the two racial groups that did not in fact exist. Instead of reflecting a given ethnographic reality then, this film created another reality, a "surreality," as Rouch puts it in the commentary track early on in the film.

The same could be said for the two films that Rouch made toward the end of the first half of his career, *Petit à Petit* and *Cocorico! Monsieur Poulet*, released in 1971 and 1975 respectively. Both these films may have had an initial articulation with real life, but this was merely used as a point of departure from which to enter a "surreality." In the first case, the principal protagonist, Damouré, was indeed living in Paris at the time that the film was made as he was studying for pharmicist certification. But his "reverse anthropology" and his adventures with Lam and the others in the Alps, Mediterranean Italy, and the United States were an imaginative fabrication for the purposes of the film. Similarly, the story of *Cocorico! Monsieur Poulet* may have been based on Lam's real-life employment at the time as a itinerant poultry trader, but the floating of his Citroën 2CV van back and forth across the Niger River, the encounters with the "she-devil," and the three protagonists' spirit doubles were all, of course, complete fantasy.

The three fiction films that Rouch made between *La Pyramide humaine* and *Petit à Petit*—his three Parisian New Wave films of the first half of the 1960s, *La Punition*, *Gare du Nord*, and *Les Veuves de quinze ans*—were not motivated in any sense by ethnographic objectives. Rather, Rouch made these films as a means of carrying out a very specific experiment, which was to investigate whether fiction films could be made using the production methods of *cinéma-vérité*, that is, without scripts or studios, using dialogue improvised by the actors, the handheld "walking camera," and sound recorded on location.

But these films were also motivated, at least in the case of the first two, by another issue about which Rouch had become concerned during the postproduction of *Chronicle of a Summer* in 1960–1961. During the editing of this film, not only had Rouch been dismayed by the fact that in order to get it down to the required length, huge swathes of the rushes had to be consigned to oblivion, but he felt that these excisions were being made for reasons that had not been properly thought through.

However, when he came to cut *La Punition*, a film that he shot even before *Chronicle* had been completed and that was specifically intended to explore these issues, Rouch soon discovered that even though the shooting had been confined to two days, he still had to cut out a large amount of footage because the dialogues, which were improvised by the protagonists on the basis of no more than a framework story, contained many passages that were desperately dull. Therefore, when he came to make *Gare du Nord* a few years later, he worked intensively on a script with the protagonists beforehand and then, in the actual shooting, confined the main body of the film to two sequence shots that were both about ten minutes long. As a result, there was indeed much less elimination of material in the editing suite. But as both sequence shots went through several takes before they were considered acceptable, this film did not so much eliminate the problem of excision in the edit suite, nor lay down any well-considered new rules for doing so, as transfer the whole process of selection to the production phase.

In effect, then, in the work he produced in the early 1960s, one can see Rouch struggling with the same set of editorial problems in both his fiction films and his documentaries. But in the case of both genres, Rouch did not so much resolve the matter of how films should be cut down to length as displace the process of editorial choice from the edit suite to the location, leaving it to the cameraperson in the moment of shooting to make the decisions as to what should be included in the eventual film. Indeed, if one considers the evolution of Rouch's filmmaking praxis over the course of the 1960s, one can detect an increasing bifurcation in his work following the introduction of the new technology. On the one hand, there are his "straight" ethnographic films in which there is a heavy emphasis on preserving a literal record of the real in its totality, involving the pronounced use of sequence-shots and minimal interventions in the edit suite. On the other, there are his fiction films that become increasingly detached from any connection with a particular ethnographic reality and in the making of which, Rouch had no qualms about using the full panoply of editorial sleights of eye and ear to achieve the effects that he wanted. Indeed, it would seem that having struggled valiantly but in vain in the making of *Chronicle of a Summer* to unravel the Gordian knot of the status of truth in documentary filmmaking, Rouch decided that the most pragmatic strategy was simply to pass either side of it, alternately taking the low road of heavily descriptive films of ethnographic documentation, or the high road of fictional works of fantasy and imagination.

In terms of the legacy that they represent for young ethnographic filmmakers, I would suggest then that the value of Rouch's forays into fiction is mixed. The later works, from *La Pyramide humaine* onward, seem to me to be of lesser direct interest since their attachment to the empirical realities of a specific ethnographic milieu was sometimes rather tenuous. However, his first two works of fiction, namely, *Jaguar* and *Moi, un Noir,* both of which remain strongly embedded in particular ethnographic realities, continue to represent a potentially inspiring model of how the devices of fictional filmmaking may be used to represent the subjective experience of those ethnographic Others who are so often described in the ethnographic literature only in terms of external cultural traits and behaviors.

Equally importantly, these films continue to suggest an interesting alternative way for ethnographic filmmakers to work in situations in which more conventional participant-observational strategies might not be feasible, be it for practical or ethical reasons. Indeed, in recent years, a number of my own students have used techniques directly inspired by Rouch's work to make films in situations in which it would have been impossible for them to work in other ways. At the time of writing, the most recent and significant of these is *Transfiction*, shot by Johannes Sjöberg in 2007 as part of his doctoral field research amongst transvestites living in São Paulo, Brazil. In this film, the subjects improvise scenes from their everyday life experience, including situations such as being bullied at school, as a candidate for a job, or as the tenant of an apartment, on account of the prejudice against transvestites; it even includes scenes from the life of one protagonist who was a sex worker, this being one of the few avenues left open to transvestites as a means of earning a living (fig. 16.2). All these scenes would have raised serious ethical issues, let alone practical problems, had they been filmed in an observational manner. But, inspired by Rouch's example, Sjöberg was able to find a very effective way of surmounting these difficulties while representing the experience of his subjects in a vivid but ethnographically anchored manner.[28]

Sharing Anthropology

Throughout his life, Rouch was both viscerally opposed to racism and a profound admirer of African culture, which he sought to propagate and preserve through his films. In pursuing this project, Rouch collaborated with a particular group of Africans who became his constant companions over a period of decades. No one could reasonably deny that their collaboration represents a remarkable, unparalleled sharing of anthropology across boundaries of race and culture as well as time. But, as I argued in chapter 15, one should take care that in evaluating Rouch's notion of "shared anthropology," one does not to fall into an all-too-easy

FIGURE 16.2. Fábia and Bibi, principal protagonists of the Rouch-inspired ethnofiction, *Transfiction* (2008), directed by Johannes Sjöberg, a film about the life experiences of transvestites living in São Paulo, Brazil. © Éric Brochu.

presentism, either in exaggerating its progressiveness or in overemphasizing its deficiencies.

Even if Rouch's sharing of anthropology was unprecedented, one should also recognize that it had its limits. It was, in the first place, primarily a one-way project in the sense that, with the single exception of *Petit à Petit*, the ethnofiction in which Damouré and Lam visit Paris, the anthropology that Rouch shared with his African collaborators was the anthropology of their society rather than his. Rouch may have considered his African colleagues to be his friends, and they may have used this term of him as well on occasion, but they would also refer to him as a "father," implying a hierarchical relationship that Rouch was reluctant to acknowledge. Although Rouch's attitudes may have been extremely progressive for any European of his generation living in Africa, the reality was that it was generally he rather than his African colleagues who had the last word in the realization of their joint projects, and it was he who controlled the way in which they were then presented to the world.

It should also be acknowledged that while Rouch may have sought to share his admiration and understanding of African culture across the globe, and thereby could be said, with total justification, to have contributed greatly to the breaking down of prejudice on the part of Europeans and, by extension, to the development of intercultural understanding, this sharing of anthropology was not attached to any kind of political project on his part, neither of a conventional party political kind, nor of some form of indigenist politics, of the sort that one now finds associated with anthropology film projects in Brazil, Australia or Canada. As result, although the particular individuals with whom Rouch collaborated so profoundly appear to have benefited in many different ways from his sharing of anthropology, and although the films advance a historically progressive agenda, in the absence of any linkage with some more general political project, it is difficult to see how, in itself, this sharing of anthropology could have done a great deal to benefit the Songhay or Dogon *moyen* directly.

Indeed, the limitations of the practical effects of Rouch's sharing of anthropology were made sharply plain to Paul Stoller when he first started his doctoral research in Niger in the 1970s, following in the long shadow cast by Rouch's prior fieldwork. Although Stoller discovered that many of his informants remembered Rouch with affection, this was not universally the case, at least not with respect to his filmmaking activities. In the village of Wanzerbé, where some thirty years before Rouch had made one of his first films, Stoller was told that the people were fed up with being filmed and that they wanted no more of it unless they were paid a substantial sum. Even though Stoller made it clear that he had absolutely no intention of filming, he was completely unable to carry out any of his own research there.[29] Nor are these former subjects the only Africans to consider Rouch's film work in a negative light. As we saw in chapter 15, a number of African scholars and filmmakers have claimed that his project of sharing anthropology remained imbricated in an ethos that was, at best, anachronistic and at worst, colonialist.

On the other hand, even Rouch's most severe African critics would surely have to acknowledge his contribution to the creation of institutions aimed at fostering an appreciation of traditional African culture, not only within Europe but also in Africa itself. Not only did Rouch encourage a number of the Africans with whom he made films to become film-makers themselves—those such as Oumarou Ganda, Moustapha Alassane, Safi Faye, and Inoussa Ousseini—but he also played a leading role in the creation of a film school in Niamey where others could also receive training.[30] He also played a leading role in the creation of the Institut de la Recherche en Sciences Humaines (IRSH) in Niamey in 1964, whose objectives included the promotion of research into customary forms of knowledge and ways of living, and the development of an archive to preserve a record of these for future generations. Rouch maintained close ties with this institute for the remainder of his life and with his support, a number of his closest Nigerien associates were employed there, notably the sound recordist Moussa Hamidou.

Furthermore, while one should recognize that it is almost inevitable that Rouch's attitudes would have been influenced to some degree by the ideology of the colonial era in which he first went to Africa, and indeed by the continuing inequalities of North-South relationships after independence, one should also not underestimate the independence of mind that it would have required at the time to form the relationships that Rouch developed with Africans and their way of life. To get some sense of this, one need only compare Rouch's attitudes with those of his anthropological mentor, Marcel Griaule who although a great admirer of African culture in the abstract continued to think of Africans themselves as little more than liars intent on preventing his access to their cultural riches.

In short, viewed as a product of its time, Rouch's idea of shared anthropology was undoubtedly historically highly progressive, even if inevitably still marked to some degree by the particular context of the more general political and economic relationship between Europe and Africa in which it was developed. Yet, even today, who among contemporary anthropologists would feel sufficiently assured of the moral superiority or political significance of their own practice to throw the first stone? In its commitment to collaboration with the subjects of research, Rouch's idea of a participatory shared anthropology anticipated by several decades the "post-Malinowskian" fieldwork ethos as described by the Amazonist anthropologist Bruce Albert in which, in many parts of the world, there has been a significant shift from participant-observation to "observant participation," in which the participation is primary and the observation a privilege that the subjects of anthropological research may be willing to concede should they be sufficiently convinced of its value.[31] Considered in this light, Rouch's ideas about the sharing of anthropology based on an extended participatory immersion in the world of the subjects represent not so much an exact model for young ethnographic filmmakers to follow uncritically in every particular, but rather an example on which to build an appropriate ethical and political posture for their filmmaking praxis in a contemporary, postcolonial world.

The Adventure of the Real

On the evening of 18 February 2004, in the company of a group of his closest African friends and associates, including his wife Jocelyne, Damouré Zika, and Moustapha Alassane, Jean Rouch was travelling toward Tahoua, a town about three hundred miles northeast of the capital Niamey, where Alassane had organized a film screening. In the darkness on the country road, the vehicle in which he was travelling collided with a stationary truck, parked without lights. None of the others in the vehicle

FIGURE 16.3. Dancers in *kanaga* masks perform at the Dogon funeral of Jean Rouch in December 2006, bringing to a conclusion a story that began almost seventy years before when he first saw a photograph of *kanaga* masks in a Montparnasse bookshop window (*see fig. 2.1 above*). © Bernd Mosblech.

was seriously hurt, but the shock of the impact was too much for Rouch's already-fragile health and he died instantly. In all likelihood, he knew nothing of the event since he was asleep at the time.

Since he had died in Africa, Jocelyne concluded that it was his destiny to remain in Africa forever and, a week later, he was buried in Niamey in a simple tomb close to the wall of the Christian cemetery, a few meters from the Office of Public Works where he had been employed as an engineer when he first arrived in Niger in 1941. The funeral was attended by representatives of the Presidents of both France and Niger, and he was accorded military honors in recognition of his service in the Second World War. But the ceremony also incorporated certain traditional Songhay ritual elements, including the playing of the *godye* violin by the centenarian virtuoso Hamidou Yayé, whom Rouch had known since his earliest days in Niger. Some two years later, in December 2006, the Dogon also held a funeral ceremony for him, just as they had done for his mentors, Marcel Griaule and Germaine Dieterlen, burying a mannequin, dressed in his clothes and wrapped in a traditional shroud protected by magical charms, in a cemetery in the cliff face of the Bandiagara Escarpment close to Tyogou, the place where the Sigui traditionally begins.[32]

Jean Rouch did not die a rich man in a material sense but the value of the legacy that he left for the craft of ethnographic cinema was immense. For all practicing ethnographic filmmakers are indebted to him for showing by personal example that it is not necessary to depend on filmmaking professionals to make films, nor to be inhibited by an undue concern for technical standards or other such empty badges of professionalism. Some of the force of this example has undoubtedly been lost with recent technological developments. When Rouch started out, to go it alone, without technical expertise to hand, represented a much more daring gesture than it is today when the equipment that is available to ethnographic filmmakers is so much cheaper and easier to use. But the other skills involved in filmmaking—the more creative editorial skills to do with the conceptualization and realization of a film—remain as complex and difficult to acquire as they ever were. By showing that it was actually possible for an anthropologist to use a camera, not simply as some sort of scientific instrument for recording data but as a means of representation that could go beyond the mere description of cultural realities and could even embrace fiction, Rouch established an idea of the métier of ethnographic filmmaking as a creative, artistic activity of potentially broad horizons whose practitioners could engage in a lively exchange of ideas and practices with filmmakers from many other backgrounds and with very different agendas.

Every year, almost without fail, when we screen one of Jean Rouch's films at the University of Manchester as part of our introduction to the history of ethnographic film for undergraduates—usually *Chronicle of a Summer*, sometimes *Jaguar*, sometimes both—I receive the next day an enthusiastic e-mail from one of the students asking how he or she can become an ethnographic filmmaker. I suspect that this is something that would particularly have pleased Rouch, not merely because of the personal accolade that it implies, but because he believed, as did Vertov before him, that more important than just making films was the making of films that provoke the making of other films. And yet, an abiding enigma about Jean Rouch is that although there have been many who have been inspired by his example to become ethnographic filmmakers, he has had very few, if any, direct disciples. As Pierre Braunberger, the independent producer who produced many of Rouch's films, put it in the early 1980s, like the great feature film director Robert Bresson, Rouch had no immediate predecessors nor direct successors, but rather a profound influence.[33] There are many possible reasons for this, but one of the most important, surely, is that there is a broad variety about his work that was only given coherence by his own highly idiosyncratic genius.

When considered in detail, Rouch's filmmaking praxis may have been shot through with all kinds of ambiguities, both aesthetic and political. Particularly in his later years, his work was considered by some to be technically deficient. But none of these supposed flaws did anything to diminish its power to inspire. Even in the latter stages of his career, when the acclaim given to his new work was muted, Rouch still managed to enthuse succeeding generations of young filmmakers by touring the world with his earlier films or by holding court at the Bilan du film ethnographique festival at the Musée de l'Homme. Here, and wherever else he presented his films, he underlined his commitment to something that—to employ a turn of phrase that he himself liked to use—the world had never seen before, namely, an enthusiastic performance of the role of ethnographic filmmaker, engaged not in some sort of research sideline, an "accessory relaxation to fieldwork," as Malinowski once referred to photography, but rather in a lifelong vocation that had its own distinctive moral principles and its own very particular form of humanistic poetry.

Jean Rouch was a consummate teller of stories—a "fabulist" in Michael Eaton's word[34]—and he surrounded the vocation that he created for himself with its own Romantic mythology. In the last analysis, more than any particular body of filmmaking techniques that he might have developed, and more than any theories that he might have pronounced about the nature of cinematographic reality, more even than his concern to share anthropology with his subjects, it is his passion for the Adventure of the real and his willingness to experiment and to take risks in pursuing that Adventure that continues to strike a chord with young filmmakers coming across his work for the first time. This passion continues to burn through his films and continues to be, by turns, as inspirational and provocative as it was when he caused a scandal with the first screening of *Les Maîtres fous* in the cinema of the Musée de l'Homme more than half a century ago.

The Films of Jean Rouch

At the time of writing, all the original film materials of Jean Rouch, plus the associated 16mm magnetic audiotape, previously scattered around various institutions, have only recently been gathered together and deposited in the Archives françaises du film. These archives, which are located in the underground vaults of a former military fort on the outskirts of Versailles, are managed by the Centre National de la Cinématographie (CNC). Here, Rouch's films are currently being systematically accessioned under the supervision of Philippe Costantini, a director-cameraman who worked on a number of films that Rouch made toward the end of his career. Meanwhile, all the original reel-to-reel sound tapes, a large collection of textual materials relating to the films, not to mention Rouch's substantial collection of photographs, have been deposited in the Bibliothèque nationale de France (BnF). Eventually, further textual materials, including Rouch's travel diaries, currently in the process of being organized by Laurent Pellé of the Musée de l'Homme, and the extensive collection of his personal papers, which are being sorted through by Rouch's widow, Jocelyne, will also be deposited in the BnF. Only once all these materials have been properly accessioned in the BnF will it finally be possible to produce a comprehensive catalog of Rouch's film work. The listing of Rouch's films offered here should therefore be considered no more than an interim resource pending the eventual publication of a properly researched, definitive catalog.

A number of filmographies of Jean Rouch already exist, including those prepared by Houdaille (1981), Prédal (1996i), Pellé (1997), and Feld (2003). There is also the filmography on the Web site of the Comité du film ethnographique, also prepared by Laurent Pellé, and which can be accessed via http://www.comite-film-ethno.net/rouch/rouchfilm.htm. All these works are to a great extent dependent on prior listings prepared by Françoise Foucault in collaboration with Rouch himself. All are very useful, and I have drawn on them extensively. But taken as whole, they are uneven in their coverage and are sometimes mutually contradictory, due at least in part to the fact that in Rouch's own writings and statements, there is a good deal of contradictory information. To the data contained in these sources, I have added observations arising from my own viewings and all kinds of information gathered from the Web and elsewhere. In addition, there are quite a number of entries that have benefited from personal communications, notably from Françoise Foucault, Laurent Pellé, Philippe Costantini, and Brice Ahounou. Even so, despite all these additional inputs, I do not claim that this list represents anything like a definitive account of Rouch's films. Particularly in relation to the latter part of his career, I suspect that there are many errors of both omission and commission.

When the definitive catalog of Rouch's work does finally appear, it will certainly be a substantial work. For, in the course of a filmmaking career that stretched over 56 years (1946–2002), he may have shot as many as 140 films, possibly even a few more. However, this figure, which Rouch himself sometimes claimed and which is often repeated in secondary sources, should be treated with a certain degree of caution. While it is true that if every film on which Rouch began to work is included in the list of his films, then, as in this filmography, the total does indeed amount to around 140. But many of the films in this list would be works that were not completed, in the sense that although they may have been edited to some degree, they were never made up into definitive prints that could then be freely circulated. Some would consist of little more than titles given to a set of synchronized rushes. If one were to produce a list of Rouch's entirely completed films, it would feature "only" around 105 works.

Moreover, of these 105 completed films, no more than about half could be properly considered "ethnographic," even in the loosest sense of the term. Rouch also made about thirty-five other films, all relatively short, on social and economic development topics or on cultural subjects. These range from, at one extreme, three promotional films for a West African vehicle distributor to, at the other, a series of 'ciné-poems' about Paris and elsewhere. In the latter part of his career, he made around twelve short biographical films based on informal interviews with his friends and associates that, again, it would be difficult to qualify as "ethnographic." He also made some seventeen feature-length fiction films, but no more than half of these could be said to be based on ethnographic research. If all these films that it would be difficult to classify as "ethnographic" are discounted, along with those that either remained unfinished or that represent mere compilations of earlier films, the number of completed ethnographic films that Rouch made comes to no more than about fifty. But this still represents an average of almost one film a year over the course of a very long career and far outnumbers the oeuvre of any other ethnographic filmmaker, living or dead.

Periods and Categories in Rouch's Work

All the previous listings of Rouch's films have been based exclusively on chronological principles. While this is certainly the simplest way of classifying his films, it makes it difficult to appreciate the various different periods and categories of work that he produced. This difficulty is further exacerbated by the fact that many of Rouch's films were not finally edited and released until many years after they had been shot, and even then might be released in a number of different versions. A good example of this is *Jaguar*. This film was shot in 1954–1955 when Rouch was carrying out migration research on the Gold Coast. It was then edited into various versions between 1955 and 1967 but was not released in its definitive form until as late as 1969 or 1970, long after the Gold Coast had become the independent state of Ghana and long after Rouch had abandoned his spring-wound Bell & Howell camera in favor of more advanced synchronous-sound systems. However, in terms of the subject matter and the technology employed, as well as the general development of Rouch as a filmmaker, it is much more appropriate to consider *Jaguar* along with the other films that he shot in West Africa in the 1950s rather than in relation to those that he was producing around 1970. It was, for example, an important precursor to *Moi, un Noir*, shot in 1957, since in making this latter film, Rouch employed much the same improvisational techniques as those that he had first developed in making *Jaguar*.

In drawing up this list, I have grouped Rouch's films under a number of different headings, partly on the basis of the periods of his work identified in this book and partly on the basis of the type or category of work they represent. To some extent, periods and categories overlap and for this reason, some films appear more than once in the list. Here too, *Jaguar* can serve as an example since it appears both under the heading of films produced during the period of Rouch's migration studies between 1954 and 1960, and in the list of ethnofictions that he made in collaboration with Damouré Zika and Lam Ibrahim Dia at various points between 1954 and 2002. Similarly, *Petit à Petit* appears both in the list of Damouré and Lam ethnofictions, and in the list of films that I have identified as making up Rouch's 1960s "Parisian" period.

These groupings of Rouch's films are loosely sequenced on a chronological principle, though not exclusively. Thus, for example, although Rouch shot his first film among the Dogon in 1950, I place the category of Dogon films much later in the list, after the films that he shot in Paris in the 1960s, because the first Dogon film, *Cimetières dans la falaise*, was an isolated case and the main body of Rouch's Dogon films were not shot until the decade running from the mid-1960s until the mid-1970s. Similarly, I place the films that I classify as "Later Ethnographic Films in Niger, 1958–1981" *before* "Other West African Ethnographic Films, 1954–1971," even though the first film in the former category was made a few years after the first film in the latter category. This is because, again, the first film in the "Other West African films" category, *Mammy Water*, shot in 1954 but not released until 1966, was something of an isolated case. Otherwise, the two categories more or less overlap in the early years, but the films that Rouch made in Niger in this period were generally more important and certainly more numerous than the films that he made in other countries of West Africa.

I have also separated out all Rouch's fiction films and placed them in two categories at the end of the sequence. I appreciate that this is contrary to the spirit of Rouch's many pronouncements to the effect that, for him, there was no clear boundary between his documentary and his fiction films. But even while it may be true that documentary and fiction overlap in the Rouchian canon, I would argue that there is still a difference that it is worth signalling. At the same time, the placing of these fictional works separately at the end of the list serves to underline the fact that they took on an increased importance in the later stages of Rouch's career.

My hope is that this way of presenting Rouch's films will give the reader a better sense of the great diversity of his work. However, at the same time, I acknowledge that in breaking with the chronological principle, one loses a sense of the remarkable productivity of Rouch at certain periods of his career and the broad variety of different projects that he could sustain at any given time. In order to recapture these qualities, I also offer a more schematic presentation of his oeuvre in appendix 2, in which his films are plotted against an absolute timeline.

Format of Presentation

Unless otherwise stated, all the films in this list were originally shot in 16mm color stock by Jean Rouch himself and were produced by the Comité du film ethnographique of the Musée de l'Homme. As Rouch usually did his own sound editing, when there is a reference to "editing" in an entry in the list below, this should be taken as a reference to picture rather than sound editing, while the reference to "sound" in an entry should be taken as referring to sound recording in the field. When a third-party sound editor was involved, this will be indicated by the additonal title "sound editing."

The final version of Rouch's films took various different forms. He would usually start shooting a project on his own initiative with no more than the institititutional backing of the Comité and the funding that he received as a corollary of his position as a full-time researcher employed by the CNRS. Only later, at the editing stage, if the possibility of distribution outside academic circles were contemplated, would commercial production companies become involved. At this point, a professional editor might begin to work on the rushes. Once the editing was completed, these films could then be blown up to 35mm for cinema or festival release.

The films envisaged only for an academic audience would be mastered as 16mm prints. Or at least that was usually the intention. In fact, in many instances, accounting perhaps for a third of all his films, Rouch never fully completed the editing. In the case of some films, the sources simply state that the editing is incomplete, without giving any further details. In other cases, they state that the films in question exist only in a "double-band" version. This is when the image and the sound track have been edited but have not been "married," that is, processed in a laboratory so that the sound is transferred to an optical sound track running down the edge of the film. Instead, sound and image remain as two synchronized but separate 16mm "bands," one being a roll of positive celluloid film developed from the original camera negatives in a laboratory, while the other is a roll of magnetic tape onto which the original sound recordings made in the field on a reel-to-reel tape recorder have been transferred.

These two bands can simply be the "cutting copy," that is, the original rolls that were built up on the editing table so that, in effect, only one copy of the film exists. However, in this case, the quality of these rolls is generally very low because by the time that the editing has been completed, they will be spliced together by tape at all the joins where a cut has been made. The image track will usually be covered with dirt picked up in the edit suite and markings made by the editor, while on the sound track there will be abrupt transitions at all the cuts. In order to improve the quality of a double-band version, a common strategy is to make a fresh transfer of the sound material, mixing several different sound tracks in the process. This permits one not only to enrich the sound track generally, but also to smooth out all the cuts by cross fades between tracks. It would much improve the quality of the image track to make a new print also, but this is a very much more expensive process because it means sending the film back to the laboratory. In these circumstances, many filmmakers have opted for retransferring the sound, but leaving the image track as it is, held together by tape at the joins, while cleaning it up as much as possible.

In the instances in which one of Rouch's films is said to exist only in double-band, the sources do not indicate whether this means that consists simply of the 16mm rolls lifted off the editing table or a version that has been processed to some degree. But given that Rouch had sound-mixing facilities at his disposal in the Musée de l'Homme and, moreoveor, took a particular pleasure in carrying out his own sound mixes, it seems very likely that in most instances, the sound track in these double-band versions of his films would indeed have been mixed and transferred to fresh 16mm magnetic stock.

Where the information is available, I give the dates both of shooting and of release for a film, the latter being defined as the first public showing of the definitive version. However, Rouch was much given to preparing preliminary versions of his films for festivals or special screenings and then recutting on basis of the feedback. It is therefore often difficult to establish exactly when the definitive release took place. Where there is contradictory information on these matters in the sources, I give a range of dates. When I give only a date, without identifying whether this is the date of the shoot or the release date, this is because no further details are given in the sources and the date could be either or both. In these cases, it is often unclear what degree of editing, if any, the films have undergone. Since many of Rouch's films exist, or have existed, in a number of different versions, running times are particularly variable in the sources. Where there is some doubt on this matter, again I give a range of the running times indicated in the sources.

For most entries, I give an English translation of the title in adjacent brackets. When this is the title of the official English-language version of the film, I enclose it in inverted commas. Otherwise, it is my own translation. When no title is given in adjacent brackets, this should be taken to mean that the English title is, or in my view should be, the same as the French title.

Most entries are relatively brief, with cross-references to more detailed descriptions in the main body of text when they are available. However, when I consider a film to be of some importance but I have not dealt with it in the main body of the text in any detail, the entries tend to be more lengthy. Entries based on my own viewings are indicated with an asterisk adjacent to the title. Others are based on an amalgam of the various sources listed above. In cases in which I have relied particularly upon one or more of these sources, I cite them at the end of the entry.

Principle Acronyms and Terms

AMIP—Audiovisuel Multimedia International Productions

BBC—British Broadcasting Corporation

CFE—Comité du Film Ethnographique

CNC—Centre National de Cinématographie

CNRS Vidéothèque—Videotheque of the Centre National de la Recherche Scientifique, accessible via the web at http//videotheque.cnrs.fr.

CNRSH—Centre National de la Recherche en Sciences Humaines (Niamey)

La Fémis—École Nationale Supérieure des Métiers de l'Image et du Son

GREC—Groupe de Recherche et d'Essai de Cinématographique

IFAN—Institut Français d'Afrique Noire

INA—Institut National de l'Audiovisuel

INRSH—Institut Nigerien de la Recherche en Sciences Humaines (Niamey)

La Sept—a French television channel and production company now incorporated into ARTE

Les Films de la Pléiade—the production company of Pierre Braunberger that produced many of Rouch's early films. It later changed its name to Les Films du Jeudi.

NF1—a Dutch television production company

ORTF—Office de Radiodiffusion-Télévision Française, a French public broadcasting agency

RFO—Reseau France Outre-mer. A French television service to overseas départments.

SCOA—Société commerciale de l'Ouest africain, a French colonial trading conglomerate.

SODAPERAGA—An independent production and distribution company, founded by Pierre André Boutang, which works for the Centre National de la Cinématographie (CNC) in promoting the distribution of French films.

UNESCO—this refers to an entry in the UNESCO catalog on African ethnographic films published under the editorship of Jean Rouch in 1967.

The Distribution of Jean Rouch Films

Although the situation has recently improved, Jean Rouch's films remain difficult to get hold of. Those interested in screening 16mm or 35mm prints would be best advised to contact, in the first instance, the Comité du film ethnographique via e-mail at cfe@mnhn.fr or the Web site, http://www.comite-film-ethno.net. Prints of those of Rouch's films that were produced by Argos Films (26 rue Montrosier, 92200 Neuilly-sur-Seine, tel.: +33 1 47 22 91 26) or Les Films de la Pléiade, now known as Les Films du Jeudi (3, rue Hautefeuille, 75006 Paris, tel.: +33 1 40 46 97 98), may be available through the companies concerned.

However, an increasing number of Rouch's films are now available on DVD. Two excellent collections of some of the best-known films from the first half of Rouch's career were issued by Éditions Montparnasse in 2005 (a collection of ten films) and 2007 (a further three films), while a third collection, featuring his Dogon films, is due to be released in 2009 (see http://www.editions montparnasse.fr). Two of Rouch's best-known Parisian films are also available on DVD: *Chronique d'un été*, distributed by Argos Films and Arte Video (http://www.arte-tv.com), and *Gare du Nord*, which appears in the *Paris Vu Par* collection distributed by Atlantic Video (see http://www.atlanticdvd.com .au). A substantial number of Rouch's films, almost thirty in total, and mostly consisting of his more academic works, are distributed by CNRS-Audiovisuel, either in DVD or VHS (see http://www.cnrs.fr/cnrs-images/). His very first film, *Au pays des mages noirs* is also available on a DVD, released by Kinofilm, together with a new film by Dominique Dubosc, featuring Rouch commenting on the original film and reperforming parts of the voice-over narration.

Given the great interest in Rouch's work in the Anglo-Saxon world, it has long been a matter for regret that only a very small proportion of his works have been available in English-language versions. However, due to a recent initiative jointly undertaken by unReal and Watchmaker Films, there is every prospect that the situation will greatly improve in the near future. In the course of 2009, unReal and Watchmaker are due to release nine Rouch films on DVD with English-language subtitles, all based on new transfers from remastered originals. They will be available in two forms, one for the general public and the other in the form of research editions specifically designed for use in educational institutions. These films are to include *Les Maîtres fous* (1955), *Moi, un Noir* (1960), *La Pyramide humaine* (1961), *Chronique d'un été* (1961), *Jaguar* (1969–1970), *Petit à Petit* (1970), *La Goumbé des jeunes noceurs* (1965), and *Les Tambours d'avant* (1972). There are also plans to release further titles in the future. For more information, see http://www.unreal.as and http://www .watchmakerfilms.com.

In addition to these releases, the three films on the 2007 Éditions Montparnasse collection of DVDs are subtitled in English. (Unfortunately, this does not apply to the more substantial 2005 collection). These three films are *Cimetières dans la falaise* (1951), *Bataille sur le grand fleuve* (1952), *Cocorico! Monsieur Poulet* (1974–1975). In addition, the DVD versions of *Au pays des mages noirs* (1947), distributed by Kinofilm, *Gare du Nord* (1965), distributed by Atlantic Video, and *Le Dama d'Ambara* (1980), distributed by the CNRS, also include English subtitles. In the United States, a number of Rouch's films in English-language versions are distributed by Documentary Educational Resources (DER). These are *Les Maîtres fous*, *Jaguar*, *The Lion Hunters* (1965), and *Margaret Mead: Portrait by a Friend* (1978). DER also distribute a number of films about Jean Rouch (see http://www.der.org/films/filmmakers/jean-rouch.html).

In addition to the films listed above, which total seventeen, there are, to the best of my knowledge, only two other Rouch films that are available in English-language versions. These are *Capt'ain Omori* (1980), which I believe was originally recorded in English, and *Madame L'Eau* (1993), which exists in an English (and also Italian) subtitled version. The grand total of English-language versions of Rouch films therefore comes to nineteen films. This is a considerable improvement on the situation only a few years ago and there is every hope that the unReal/Watchmaker project will increase this number in the future. But even so, it remains the case that at the present time only a small fraction of Jean Rouch's total oeuvre is available in English-language versions.

*

Descent of the Niger, 1946–1947

These films were shot during the course of the expedition from the source to the mouth of the Niger River that Rouch carried out in conjunction with his two wartime colleagues, Pierre Ponty and Jean Sauvy between August 1946 and March 1947.

La Chevelure magique (Magical Hair). Codirector: Pierre Ponty. Incomplete, destroyed.

Rouch gave this title to a set of rushes that he and Pierre Ponty shot on an island near Ayorou on the middle Niger. It seems that this material was at least partly fictional. Unfortunately, it was never edited into a film: when the negatives were sent back to France to be developed, they were left out on an airstrip in excessive heat and were ruined. *Sources*: Suruge (2007), 14; Françoise Foucault, personal communication, September 2008.

*Au pays des mages noirs (In the Land of the Black Wizards). 13 min. Black and white. Codirectors: Pierre Ponty, Jean Sauvy. Edited and produced by Actuali-

tés françaises. Shot 1946–1947, released 1947. Reproduced both in the original version and in a new version with a voice-over improvised by Rouch in *Jean Rouch, premier film: 1947–1991*, directed by Dominique Dubosc, originally released in 1991, and rereleased on DVD with optional English subtitles in 2006 by Kinofilm.

The primary focus of this film is the hippopotamus hunting of the Sorko fishermen of the island of Ayorou. Before setting out on the hunt, the Sorko hold a possession ceremony in order to seek the permission of Harakoy Dikko, the spirit who controls the waters of the Niger and also to secure the support of the *hauka*, the spirits of power. This appears to be the same ceremony described in Rouch's doctoral thesis (Rouch 1989:257–258). On his return to France, Rouch and his colleagues were short of money and sold the rights to the newsreel company Actualités françaises. The newsreel editors thought that the possession ceremony would make a good climax so they simply put it at the end of the film, presenting it as if it were a ritual offering of thanks to the spirits (see chap. 3, pp. 42–43).

Feld (2003:347) mentions two other works that also appear to have been shot during this descent of the Niger, though it is not clear if they were ever distributed in any way. From the titles—*Chasse à l'hippopotame (Hippopotamus Hunting*, 50 min.) and *Chasse traditionelle à Bangawi (Traditional Hunting at Bangawi*, 12 min.)—it is evident that both works were about hunting. The first is clearly about the hunting of hippopotami, and the second may be also, since *bangawi* is the local name for a hippopotamus hunt. It seems very likely that these two works are merely different versions of the same set of rushes that was used to cut the hippopotamus-hunting sequence in *Au pays des mages noirs*.

Doctoral Research, 1948–1952

FIRST EXPEDITION, 1948–1949

Hombori. 60 min. Black and white. Shot in late 1948. Editing apparently incomplete.

This film was thought for a long time to have been lost, but a 16mm negative, without an accompanying sound track, but in a good state of conservation was discovered at the Musée de l'Homme in 2007. It is currently being restored at the Archives françaises du film. From a preliminary viewing of the negative, the film appears to be an account of Rouch's journey by horseback, accompanied by Damouré Zika, Lam Ibrahim Dia, and Douma Besso, to the Hombori mountains in eastern Mali. It includes a series of general views of village life as well as of everyday subsistence activities such as herding, iron working, weaving, and hunting. Rouch himself refers to this film rather dismissively as lacking any clear focus and therefore "almost impossible to edit and entirely unsuitable for projection to nonspecialist audiences." It is possible therefore that he never finished the film and that no sound track exists.

Sources: Philippe Costantini, personal communication, October 2008; Rouch (2008), 116.

La Circoncision (The Circumcision). 15 min. Secrétariat d'État à la Coopération. Shot in late 1948, released 1949.

This film follows the circumcision of forty boys in the Songhay village of Hombori in what is now Mali. It shows them being taken into the bush to be circumcised and then cared for until the evening, when they are brought out to sing the song of the circumcised. This film was apparently much appreciated by Marcel Griaule, Rouch's supervisor, and was awarded the Prix Misguich at the Short Film Festival, Paris, 1950. *Sources*: Rouch (2008), 81–87; Feld (2003c), 347.

Les Magiciens de Wanzerbé (The Magicians of Wanzerbé). 33 min. Black and white. CNRS/Secrétariat d'Etat à la Coopération. Shot in December 1948, released in 1949. Rereleased on DVD by the CNRS in 2008.

This film is set in the Songhay village of Wanzerbé, located about fifty miles west of the Niger River, close to the point where the borders between present-day Mali, Burkina Faso, and Niger meet. The principal subjects of this film are the *sohantye* ritual specialists whom Rouch refers to as "magicians" but whom in later texts are referred to as "sorcerers" (Stoller 1992:1) or "shamans" (de Heusch 1981). After preliminary scenes showing the Songhay trading with the Tuareg on market day and boys playing, the film follows one of the leading sorcerers of the village going about his work: collecting tree bark for magical charms, preparing medicines, and divining with cowrie shells. This is followed by a major scene showing a dance in the central plaza led by an elderly sorcerer that culminates with him vomiting up a small chain symbolizing his power. The film concludes with a sequence in which a group of sorcerers, accompanied by the village chief and all the village boys, go to the foot of a nearby mountain. Here, they sacrifice a white calf to the mountain spirit to ensure the fertility of the village. *Source*: Rouch (1989), 307–308, 317; see chapter 3, pp. 44–46.

Initiation à la danse des possédés (Initiation into the Dance of the Possessed). 21 min. CNRS/Secrétariat d'Etat à la Coopération. Shot in February 1949 and released later the same year. In August 1949, awarded a prize at the Premier Festival International du Film Maudit at Biarritz, presided over by Jean Cocteau. Rereleased on DVD by the CNRS in 2008.

This film was shot in Firgoun, a village on an island in the Niger River, upstream from Ayorou. The subject is a ceremony known as a *ganandi* (literally, "to make dance"), which has been put on by the local possession cult priest to initiate a young woman, Zaba, as a spirit medium. Zaba had been suffering spells of delirium through being randomly possessed by spirits. These had been so severe that she had lost the power of speech. The purpose of the *ganandi* is to teach Zaba how to perform the dances that will enable her to manage the spirits who are possessing her. Over the course of seven days, Zaba goes from being "empty" and secluded in a special hut to being capable of handling her possession by dancing in public in the manner associated with a variety of different spirits. On the final day, she emerges from the seclusion hut and dances with other initiated women, watched by visitors who have come from neighboring villages to witness her acceptance by the spirits. The next day, as the visitors leave, they give Zaba gifts to enable her to "open her mouth," that is, recover the ability to speak. *Source*: Rouch (1989), 261–264; see chapter 3, pp. 46–48.

SECOND EXPEDITION, 1950–1951

Cimetières dans la falaise (Cemeteries in the Cliff Face). 19 min. Assisted by Roger Rosfelder. Commentary points by Marcel Griaule and Germaine Dieterlen. IFAN/CNC/Musée de l'Homme. Shot in August 1950 and first released in 1951. Rereleased on DVD with optional English subtitles by Éditions Montparnasse in 2007.

The title of this film is given in the singular in most sources, but in the film itself, it appears in the plural. It was shot in August 1950 when Rouch and his colleague Roger Rosfelder visited Marcel Griaule and Germaine Dieterlen at their field station among the Dogon at Sanga in the Bandiagara Escarpment. While they were there, a Dogon man was drowned in a nearby river, and Griaule asked Rouch and Rosfelder to film his funeral rites. The film begins with two priests making a sacrifice to the water spirits in order to persuade them to release the body of the dead man. The corpse is discovered late one afternoon and next day is carried through the village in a serpentine fashion, to the sound of drums, bells, and wailing. Finally, it is hoisted up the cliff face to the cave that serves as the village cemetery. The film ends with some striking shots of water cascading over the cliff face. Griaule and Dieterlen assisted with the writing of the commentary, which features a number of typically Griaulian symbolic associations. See chapter 4, pp. 52–55.

Les Gens du mil (The Millet People). 45 min. Assisted by Roger Rosfelder. IFAN/Musée de l'Homme. Probably shot in September–October 1950, release date uncertain.

The sources provide very little information about the subject matter of this film other than that it is about the cultivation of millet. It was probably shot shortly after Rouch and Rosfelder arrived in Niamey during their 1950–1951 expedition. In an article describing this phase of the expedition, Rouch discusses the Songhay's dependence on a simple form of millet cultivation adapted to low precipitation and describes the measures that they take to protect the harvest against the *kurumey* sorcerers who are said to ride on the winds that blow in from the west. It seems likely that the film would have covered similar topics. *Source*: Rouch (2008), 139–145.

*Yenendi, les hommes qui font la pluie (Yenendi—the Rainmakers). 28 min. Assisted by Pierre Cros and Roger Rosfelder. IFAN/CNC/Musée de l'Homme. Shot in April 1951, released 1952. Rereleased on DVD by the CNRS in 2007.

This film was shot in Simiri, a village located about fifty miles north of Niamey, in the drought-ridden savannas of the Zermaganda region. The subject of the film is a possession ceremony known as a *yenendi* (meaning literally "to freshen the earth"), which customarily takes place annually on the fifteenth day of the seventh month of the dry season in order to ask the spirits controlling the weather to release the rains. This was the first of many films on *yenendi* that Rouch would make in Simiri between 1951 and 1979. See chapter 4, pp. 56–62.

*Bataille sur le grand fleuve (Battle on the Great River). 33 min. Assisted by Roger Rosfelder. Editor: Renée Lichtig. IFAN/CNC/Musée de l'Homme. Shot on various different occasions between February and May 1951. First released in 1952. Rereleased on DVD with optional English subtitles by Éditions Montparnasse in 2007.

This film represents a reprise of the topic of hippopotamus hunting, as previously shown in *Au pays des mages noirs*. However, in this film, which is in color, the hunting expedition is more comprehensively and expertly covered cinematographically. As it was edited under the direction of Rouch himself, he was able to ensure that the events were presented in the correct chronological order. This film marked a major step forward in Rouch's cinematographic development and was also the first film that he screened back successfully to the subjects, an event resulting in feedback screenings becoming a central feature of his methodology thereafter. See chapter 4, pp. 62–65.

Les Fils de l'eau (The Sons of Water). 69/75/88 min. Shot at various points between 1949 and 1951. Edited in 1953 (?) by Suzanne Baron. Produced by Les Films de la Pléiade. Blown up to 35mm for general cinema release in November 1958.

A compilation film featuring sequences from *Yenendi, les hommes qui font la pluie*; *La Circoncision*; *Cimetières dans la falaise*; *Bataille sur le grand fleuve*; and *Les Gens du mil*. Awarded a prize by the CnC. An English version may possibly exist (Michael Uwewedimo, pers. comm., 2002). *Source*: (Feld 2003c), 348.

Migration Studies, 1954–1970

*Les Maîtres fous (The Mad Masters). 28 min. Sound: Damouré Zika, Lam Ibrahim Dia. Editing: Suzanne Baron. Produced by Les Films de la Pléiade. Shot in August 1954, released 1955. Awarded the grand prix in the ethnographic category of the Venice Film Festival in 1955 (or 1957?). Available in an English-language version, with a voice-over by Rouch himself. Rereleased on DVD in the original French version by Éditions Montparnasse, 2005.

This film shows the annual gathering of the *hauka* spirit possession cult as practiced by Songhay-Zerma migrants to Accra, Ghana (then the Gold Coast). An introductory sequence presents the wide range of casual laboring jobs that the migrants carry out in the city. The film then follows the adepts of the cult as they travel by rural taxi to a clearing in the forest close to Nsawam, a town about twenty-five miles north of Accra. Here, they begin to dance, and soon become possessed by the *hauka*, spirits associated with the power of modern technology and colonial political power. While possessed, the adepts mimic the manners of the colonial authorities, and then sacrifice and consume a dog. But the next day, they are shown as smiling workers back in the city. The final commentary suggests that although their cult might seem bizarre, it serves as a way of reconciling the migrants to the difficulties of their lives in the city. This film caused great controversy at the time of its release and its significance continues to be a source of debate to this day. See chapter 7.

Jaguar. 88 min. Sound: Damouré Zika. Editing: Josée Matarasso, Liliane Korb, Jean-Pierre Lacam. Produced by Les Films de la Pléiade. Principal material shot in 1954–1955. First voice-over recorded in 1957 and a 150-minute version prepared for screening at the Cinémathèque in Paris. Second voice-over recorded in 1960 and additional sound mixed for a 100-minute version that was screened at the Venice Film Festival in 1967. The definitive version of 88 minutes was released in 1969 or 1970. Available in a version with English subtitles. Rereleased on DVD in the original French version by Éditions Montparnasse, 2005.

This film follows three young men, played by Damouré Zika, Lam Ibrahim, and Illo Gaoudel, as they set out from Ayorou on the middle Niger River to find work in what was then the British colony of the Gold Coast (now Ghana). Here they take a range of casual jobs and observe the strange customs of other ethnic groups of the region, both in the cities and in the countryside on the way. At the end of the film, they return to Ayorou, distribute all the goods that they have brought back with them in a single day, and return to their subsistence tasks. This film combined documentary footage with fictional scenes improvised by the protagonists as they went along. It was Rouch's first "ethnofiction" and served as the model for all his subsequent films in this genre. See chapter 5, pp. 72–81.

Moi, un Noir (Me, a Black Man). 73 min. Sound: André Lubin, Radio Abidjan. Editing: Marie-Josèphe Yoyotte, Catherine Dourgnon. Produced by Les Films de la Pléiade. Shot in 1957, awarded Prix Louis-Delluc 1959, though not released in its definitive form until 1960. Available in an English-language version. Rereleased on DVD in the original French version by Éditions Montparnasse in 2005.

This film presents the life of Nigerien migrants to Abidjan, capital of the Ivory Coast, as experienced by Oumarou Ganda, a young dockworker, and his immediate circle of friends. The material is structured as if it were taking place over a long weekend, contrasting the migrants' tough working conditions with the richness and variety of their leisure and cultural activities. This film employs the same ethnofictional methods as were used in the making of *Jaguar*, but whereas *Jaguar* presented migration as an amusing adventure, this film shows the lives of the migrants to be marked by poverty, exploitation, and conflict with the authorities. Their circumstances are only partially alleviated by the companionship afforded by the Nigerien migrant fraternity and a fantasy life that allows them to imagine that they are film stars or boxing champions. See chapter 6, pp. 83–91.

La Pyramide humaine (The Human Pyramid). 88 min. Camera: Louis Mialle, Roger Morillère, as well as Jean Rouch himself. Sound: Michel Fano, Guy Rophé. Editing: Marie-Josèphe Yoyotte, Geneviève Bastide. Produced by Les Films de la Pléiade. Shot in 1959–1960, released in 1961. Available in an English-language version. Rereleased on DVD in the original French version by Éditions Montparnasse in 2005.

This film is set in a mock-up of the elite Cocody *lycée* in Abidjan, Ivory Coast, where Europeans and Africans share the same classroom but have no social contact. Shot in the months leading up to Ivoirian independence, Rouch's aim in making this film was to explore whether it was possible for genuine friendship to develop between Africans and Europeans. Through his intervention, the two racial groups at the *lycée* do establish social contact, but this leads to arguments as well as friendships, though these arguments are as much to do with sentimental relationships as with interracial relationships as such. This was Rouch's first "psychodrama," that is, a film that, as he puts it in the commentary track, "instead of reflecting reality, creates its own reality." See chapter 6, pp. 91–100.

La Goumbé des jeunes noceurs (The Young Revellers' Goumbé). 26/30 min. Editing: Annie Tresgot. Les Films de la Pléiade. Shot and released in 1965.

This film shows migrants from Upper Volta (now Burkina Faso) at their workplaces and then follows them to a meeting at their *goumbé*, fraternity house, in Treichville, the migrants' *quartier* of Abidjan. The final part of the film features a dance competition in which, to begin with, the dancers follow the rhythm of the drums. But as they become inspired, it is the drummers who have to follow dance steps rather than vice versa. This was the first film in which Rouch was able to use a battery-driven camera that could generate sequence-shots up to three minutes long. *Sources*: Fulchignoni (1981), 19 and (2003), 167–168.

Royale goumbé. 10 min. 1967. Only available in a double-band version.

This film was made on the occasion of the marriage between a young woman from the Royale Goumbé, a self-help and cultural association in Treichville, the migrants' quartier of Abidjan (the same *goumbé* as featured in *Moi, un Noir*), and a young man from the Étoile filante (Shooting Star) *goumbé* of the more traditional African quartier of Adjamé. It shows the two groups getting together for a "jam session." Feld (2003c:383) lists an unfinished film with an identical title that I suspect may be the same film, though he dates it to 1957. *Sources*: Houdaille (1981), 61; Prédal (1996i), 219.

Later Ethnographic Films in Niger, 1958–1979

*La Chasse au lion à l'arc ("The Lion Hunters"). 77 min. Assistant direction: Damouré Zika, Lam Ibrahim, Tallou Mouzourane. Sound: Idrissa Maïga, Moussa Hamidou. Editing: Josée Matarasso, Dov Hoenig. Production: Les Films de la Pléiade. Shot on various expeditions between 1958 and 1965. Definitive copyright registered in 1965. Awarded the Golden Lion at the 26th Mostra Internazionale d'Arte Cinematografica in Venice in 1965. Available in an English-language version, with a voice-over performed by a Canadian voice artist. Rereleased on DVD in the original French version by Éditions Montparnasse 2005.

This film concerns the traditional hunting practices of the Songhay subgroup known as the Gow, who live in and around the village of Yatakala, about fifty miles to the west of Ayorou. Even further to the west, the savannas that stretch across the frontiers of Niger, Mali, and Burkina Faso, known as the "Land of Nowhere," are inhabited by Fulani and Bella cattle pastoralists whose herds are regularly attacked by lions. When the lions' depredations become too great, they call on the Gow, who are renowned for their hunting skills using bows and poisoned arrows. This film follows a group of Gow hunters through all the stages of the process, including the extended preparation of the poison, the consultation with diviners and spirits, the tracking of the lions and setting of traps, the shooting of the trapped animals and the chanting of praise songs to calm them in their death throes. Once the hunters return home, it shows the butchering and distribution of the meat. The seven shooting expeditions on which the film was based are presented as if they were only two, and the film as a whole is framed as if it were a hunting story sung at night by a musician playing the single-string *godye* violin. See chapter 10, pp. 201–208.

Hampi: Il pose le ciel sur la terre (Hampi: He Lays the Sky upon the Earth). 25 min. Shot in 1960, screened at film festivals in Cannes and Florence in 1962, definitive version not released until 1965.

Shot in the open-air museum of Niamey, capital of Niger, this film concerns the accessioning of a *hampi*, a large pottery water jar used for ritual purposes. As part of the process, a possession dance takes place and the adepts become possessed by Dongo, the Spirit of Thunder. A preliminary version of this film was awarded a prize at Florence in 1962. *Sources*: Jutra (1961a), 32–33; Moullet (1962).

Tambours et violons des chasseurs songhays (Drums and Violins of Songhay Hunters). 1965. Unfinished.

No further information available. *Source*: Prédal (1996i), 218.

Dongo horendi. 30 min. Assisted by Serge Moati and Charles Pidoux. 1966. Only available in a double-band version.

In Songhay, a *hori* is a festival, while *horendi* means "to put on a festival." Thus the literal meaning of the title of this film is "putting on a festival for Dongo." The film follows the initiation ceremony of Dyomansi, a new "horse," that is, medium, for Dongo, the Spirit of Thunder. A few days later, the initiate, who is an employee of a local educational television station, is asked what this ceremony has meant to him. *Sources*: Houdaille (1981), 61; Rouch (1989), 270.

Dongo yenendi, Gamkallé. 10 min.1966.

A film about a *yenendi*, a rain-making ceremony, offered to Dongo, the Spirit of Thunder, in the village of Gamkallé, on the outskirts of Niamey. Rouch considered this film as a first attempt to make a "ciné-portrait" of Dongo. *Source*: Houdaille (1981), 61.

Koli koli. 30 min. 1966. Only available in a double-band version.

This film shows young Gow hunters from around Yatakala racing their dogs, preparing guinea fowl traps, and performing traditional *fakarey* recitations at the end of the hunt. *Source*: Houdaille (1981), 61.

Daouda Sorko. 15 min. 1967.

The eponymous subject is a leading priest of the cult dedicated to Dongo, the Spirit of Thunder, in the village of Simiri, about fifty miles north of Niamey. In this film, he tells Damouré Zika, Rouch's associate, the creation myth about the *tourou*, the original family of spirits in the Songhay pantheon, of which Dongo is the most powerful and feared member. *Source*: Prédal (1996i), 219.

Faran maka fonda. 90 min. 1967. Only available in a double-band version.

Literally translated, the title of this film means "the path of Faran Maka," the latter being a Songhay divinity. The film is, in effect, a follow-up to *Daouda Sorko* and features the priest who was the subject of that earlier film describing the process of initiation into Sorko possession cults to Rouch's associate, Damouré Zika. They then go together to the sites along the middle Niger River where the events of the Sorko origin myth are thought to have taken place. *Source*: Houdaille (1981), 61.

Yenendi. 1967–1969.

In the years 1967 to 1969, as part of his broader project to produce a "ciné-portrait" of Dongo, the Spirit of Thunder, thought to be the deity principally responsible for bringing the rains, Rouch shot a number of films about *yenendi,* rain-making ceremonies. Some took place in rural villages, other in suburbs of Niamey. They include those shot in 1967 in the communities of Simiri (10 min.), Kongou (10 min.), Boukoki (25 min.), Kirkissey (10 min.), Goudel (10 min.), Gamkallé (45 min.), and Gourbi Beri (10 min.). Another film was shot in 1969 in Karey Gorou (10 min.). It seems that the editing of none of these films was completed. *Source:* Feld 2003c:383–384.

*Yenendi de Ganghel (Yenendi at Ganghel). 36 min. Shot in 1968, released in 1975 or after. Rereleased on DVD by the CNRS in 2008, though in this form, the film has neither a title nor screen credits.

The day after lightning burns down the house of a Fulani cattle herder close to Ganghel, a small Sorko fishing village some twenty miles from Niamey, a *yenendi* is organized to purify the village and call for rain. Rouch points out in the voice-over commentary that Ganghel was the place where a number of his laborers were killed by lightning in 1942 when he was a road engineer, an event which led to his first introduction to spirit possession. This present event is orchestrated by the head of the local village, Sanda, and by Pam Sambo, a leading *zima* priest and principal Rouch informant, who has come from Niamey for the purpose. With the aid of music provided by a group of drummers playing "talking drums" and by the more conventional possession cult orchestra of *gasu* calabash drums and the single-string *godye* violin, two mediums go into trance. One is male—Arkusa, a local peasant farmer and a respected medium, while the other is female—Kadi, a Niamey housewife. Arkusa is possessed by Dongo, the Spirit of Thunder, while Kadi is possessed by Dongo's "elder brother," Kyirey, the Spirit of Lightning. As a sign of the identity of the spirits possessing them, Arkusa is dressed in black and Kadi in a fiery red. The film then follows the process of possession through all its stages, largely through sequence-shots. At one point, Dongo approaches the camera and acknowledges Rouch and the rest of his filmmaking team, including a local sociologist and even the chauffeur. As the ceremony proceeds, a wealthy Niamey merchant becomes possessed by the spirit Zatao, a "slave" to Dongo, and he begins to dance around his spirit master. Nearby, Sanda is scattering medicinal powders on the surface of the water of a large *hampi* water jar. Everyone in the village must drink from this in order to be purified of the pollution caused by the lightning strike. Dongo himself purifies the ground where the lightning has struck but as the price of agreeing to bring rain, he requires the Fulani herder to sacrifice several head of cattle. This is a very high price, and the herder refuses. Other onlookers urge Dongo not to be so demanding. But Dongo will not modify his demand and departs in anger threatening that the millet crops will become no more than sterile straw. This dire prophecy would be fulfilled since the drought that began that year would last for another seven years. *Sources*: Ahounou (2000, 2007).

Les Pierres chantantes d'Ayorou (The Singing Boulders of Ayorou). 10 min. 1968. Editing not completed.

On the island of Ayorou, in the middle Niger, there is an outcrop of rocks covered in shallow depressions that are known as the "singing boulders." Children go there to beat out the latest drum rhythms, sometimes accompanying themselves on the guitar. *Sources*: Houdaille (1981), 62; Feld (2003c), 383.

Wanzerbé. 30 min. 1968. Only available in a double-band version.

In the village of Wanzerbé, located in the savannas about fifty miles west of Ayorou, and renowned for the power of its *sohantye* sorcerers, a possession ceremony is organized to ask the spirits to designate a successor to the leading sorcerer who has recently died. But no sooner have the spirits arrived than the niece of the priest who appears to have been nominated dies in childbirth. This is taken as a sign that the redoubtable Kassey, leader of the women sorcerers of Wanzerbé, is not in favor of the spirits' choice. *Source*: Houdaille (1981), 62.

*Un lion nommé "L'Américain" (A Lion called "The American"). 20 min. Assistant directors: Damouré Zika, Lam Ibrahim Dia, Tallou Mouzourane. Sound: Moussa Hamidou. Editing: Jean-Pierre Lacam. Production: Films de la Pléiade. Shot in 1968, released in 1970 or 1972. Rereleased on DVD by Éditions Montparnasse 2005.

This film was made after a screening of *La Chasse au lion à l'arc* to the protagonists. Stung by the shame of having let "The American" escape during their previous expeditions, as shown in the earlier film, the hunters go after him again, accompanied by Rouch's companions, Damouré, Lam, and Tallou. But they are no more successful this time and succeed only in trapping and killing one of the lionesses accompanying "The American." This film was shot on much better stock than the earlier film, and with synchronous sound. However, there is neither voice-over commentary nor subtitling, and as much of the dialogue is apparently in Songhay, many parts will be incomprehensible to most viewers. See chapter 10, pp. 208–210).

Yenendi de Yantalla (Yenendi at Yantalla). 40/60/68 min. 1969 or 1970.

In Yantalla, a district of Niamey, the priests organize a *yenendi*, a rainmaking ceremony, to call upon Dongo, the Spirit of Thunder, and his brothers, to bestow upon the community more rain and less thunder than in the preceding years. But the spirits are reluctant to appear (there are several failed attempts at possession) and reticent in their responses, which bodes ill for the year to come. *Sources*: Houdaille (1981), 62; Prédal (1996i), 220; Feld (2003c), 368.

Taway nya—La Mère (Taway nya—The Mother). 12 min. 1970. Only available in a double-band version.

An account of a mother with a two-year-old child living in the village of Liboré, on the outskirts of Niamey. *Sources*: Houdaille (1981), 62; Feld (2003c), 384.

Yenendi de Simiri (Yenendi at Simiri). 30 min. 1970 or 1971.

One of a number of films about *yenendi*, rain-making ceremonies, that Rouch shot in the village of Simiri, located about fifty miles north of Niamey. These films include *Yenendi, les hommes qui font la pluie* (1951), described above, and what is apparently another film with exactly the same title as *Yenendi de Simiri*, but shot in 1967, and somewhat shorter at ten minutes, on which the editing was incomplete (see *Yenendi 1967–1969*, above). In this later film, after three years of drought, the villagers ask the spirits to explain the reasons for their misfortune. But the spirits respond evasively, accusing the villagers of not being sufficiently respectful of traditional custom. *Sources*: Houdaille (1981), 62; Prédal (1996), 220; Feld (2003c), 368.

Rouch seems to have made at least two further films about *yenendi* in Simiri, both also apparently with the same title, *Sécheresse à Simiri* (1973, 30 min. and 1975, 10 min., see below). Later he also made a compilation film, which is given two slightly different titles in the sources, *La Grande Sécheresse à Simiri* and *Yenendi: Sécheresse à Simiri* (1974 or 1976, variously estimated at 120 and 238 min.). This draws on the various films that Rouch had made in the village since 1951. Houdaille (1981:64) mentions yet two more later films, also entitled *Yenendi de Simiri* (1977, 1979) but gives no further details other than that they are only available in double-band form.

*Architectes ayorou (Ayorou Architects). 30 min. 1970. Rereleased on DVD by the CNRS in 2008. In this form, the film includes neither a title, nor credits.

The people of the island of Ayorou, in the middle Niger, are developing an architecture that combines traditional materials and modern architectural styles, with rectangular buildings replacing the traditional beehive-shaped houses. The film begins with a number of shots of housebuilding and women preparing food, culminating in a scene in which there is a lively exchange about the distribution of this food, but as there is no commentary or subtitling, it is not clear what this is about to those who do not understand the local language. Midway through the film, a senior man emerges from a house and is interviewed in French. He explains some of the changes going on in house construction and also interviews a woman, but as this is also in the local language, and is not subtitled, the subject matter remains obscure. Later, the same senior man is shown in conversation with a group of other men, including a man from Ghana, whom Rouch speaks to in English. This group provides a few further details about the changes that have taken place. This film features a number of loose sequence-shots that wander over architectural features of the village, with much zooming in and out, and the sound is often of poor quality. However, it also includes a very well executed sequence-shot of a group of women singing as they pound millet in wooden mortars with long pestles. This shot was later included in the compilation film, *Rythme de Travail*, released in 1973or 1976 (see below). The contrast between this shot and the remainder of the film underlines the point that as a cameraman, Rouch was much more attuned to filming performance than he was to filming scenes of everyday life when nothing very much was happening. See chapter 12, pp. 269–270.

*Les Tambours d'avant: Tourou et Bitti (The Drums of Yesteryear: Tourou and Bitti). 10 min. Assistants: Lam Ibrahim Dia and Tallou Mouzourane. Sound: Moussa Hamidou. Sound editing: Philippe Luzuy. Shot 1971, released 1972. Rereleased on DVD by Éditions Montparnasse, 2005.

This film consists almost entirely of a single sequence-shot lasting almost the full duration of a standard 400 ft 16mm magazine. Arriving at the village of Simiri, fifty miles north of Niamey, where he had previously shot a number of films about *yenendi*, rain-making ceremonies (see the entry for *Yenendi de Simiri*, 1970–1971, above), Rouch and his Nigerien sound recordist Moussa Hamidou discover that a possession ceremony is underway to seek the help of the *gandyi bi*, the Black Spirits of the Bush, in combating an attack on the village crops by pests. The mediums have not been able to go into trance but they decide to film anyway and as the camera enters the village plaza, the musicians redouble their efforts and suddenly two mediums become possessed by spirits. The cult priests enter into negotiation with the spirits who demand "meat" and "blood", that is, animal sacrifices, in exchange for "grass," good crops. At this point, the magazine begins to run out and Rouch's camera retreats to the edge of the plaza, pulling back to show the general scene with children looking on and the setting sun. The experience of shooting this film, although very short, played a crucial part in the development of Rouch's concept of the "ciné-trance." See chapter 12, pp. 270–274.

*Tanda singui. 30 min. Sound: Moussa Hamidou. Editing: Danièle Tessier. 1972. Rereleased on DVD by the CNRS in 2008.

Literally translated, the title of this film means "putting up the shelter" and refers to the erection of a new shelter for the musicians who play at the ceremonies in the compound of Pam Sambo, the leading possession cult priest in Yantalla, a central district of Niamey. The camera enters the compound to find the cult members engaged in a possession ceremony, with the spirit known as Zatao, the "slave" of Dongo, the Spirit of Thunder, already there, behaving in his characteristically unclean ways. He is followed shortly afterward by the appearance of Serki, a chiefly spirit embodied in a woman medium, and then by a *hauka* spirit wearing a colonial helmet. But the adepts know that these spirits are not sufficiently important to inaugurate the new shelter and are waiting for Dongo. Finally he appears, possessing a man known to be one of his preferred mediums. Through this medium, Dongo offers advice to the cult members about the rainy season ahead, about what plants to use to cure a sick child, and other matters. He approves the shelter but warns the assembled company not to use the space for simulating possession and always to ensure that they respect the traditions of their ancestors. The film concludes with a shot of the musicians now installed in their shelter.

This is one of Rouch's less well-known films, but of those that he shot about possession ceremonies, one of his best. The first twenty minutes consist entirely of two sequence-shots, which achieve a remarkable intimacy in recording the process of possession, though at the expense of missing most of the erection of the shelter itself. The film also features a very low-key, reflexive commentary by Rouch, in which he describes the progess of his sequence-shots and at one point, compares his camera to the ritual axes with attached bells carried by the priests: both are considered by the local people to be signalling the presence of Dongo and to be repeating his praise words. When Rouch showed the edited version of the film back to the subjects, they pointed out that Mme Kountché, the wife of the general who would later become the military dictator of Niger, was in the audience. Rouch believed that she could even have been the sponsor of the event since she was known to want a shrine dedicated to Dongo close to her own home. He also surmised that if it had not been for the presence of his camera, she would probably have allowed herself to become possessed. Rouch intended to rerecord the commentary drawing attention to her presence, but it seems that he never got round to doing this. *Sources*: Houdaille (1981), 63; C. Piault (1996), 149, also (2007), 44; CNRS Videothèque, no. 529.

Horendi. 68 min. Sound: Hama Soumana. Editing: Danièle Tessier. Produced with the support of the CNRSH, Niamey. 1972. Rereleased on DVD by the CNRS in 2008.

The title of this film translates literally as "to put on a *hori*," a *hori* being the Songhay term for ceremony or festival. Here it is used to refer to a *ganandi*, literally "to make dance," the same ceremony as featured in the 1949 film, *Initiation à la danse des possédés* (see under "Doctoral Research, 1948–1952" above). But whereas the earlier film was shot in a rural location, this film was shot in a suburb of Niamey, at the house of the *zima* priest Pam Sambo. This second film concerns two women whom the *zima* had diagnosed some months before as being ill through possession by spirits. In the meantime, their families have gathered together the resources to pay for the musicians, dancers, and the priest himself to put on an initiation dance lasting seven days. This will establish a proper relationship between the women and the spirits possessing them by teaching them how to perform the dances conventionally associated with these spirits. This ritual process culminates with the two initiands being dressed in the clothing associated with the spirits possessing them: a striped black-and-white blouson in one case, a red one in the other. This is a film of documentation, simply recording various moments in the progress of the ceremony, without any form of explanation, neither in intertitle cards nor in voice-over. The film includes a number of slow-motion passages and in this regard appears to be a followup to *Porto-Novo*, the film that Rouch and the ethnomusicologist Gilbert Rouget had made the previous year in the capital of Dahomey (see under "Other West African Ethnographic Films" below).

Dongo hori. 20 min. 1973.

The title of this film means "ceremony for Dongo." In a new district of Niamey, on the way to the airport, an old *zima* priest, who is a medium for Dongo, organizes a ceremony to thank the all-powerful Spirit of Thunder both for the rain that he has brought in the past as well as for any that he might bring in the future. *Source*: Houdaille (1981), 63.

Rythme de travail (Rhythms of Work). 12 min. 1973 or 1976.

This is a compilation film bringing together three sequences from earlier films: a sequence-shot of young women pounding millet from *Architectes ayorou*; a peasant from Simiri singing as he weeds his fields during the rainy season, and a sequence from *Yenendi de Yantalla* of a skilled dancer dancing a secular dance after he has been unable to achieve possession. To these three sequences, Rouch intended to add the shot of pumping up a tire that opens the film *Un lion nommé "L'Américain"* but it would seem that he never managed to do so. *Source*: Houdaille (1981), 63.

Sécheresse à Simiri (Drought at Simiri). 30 min. 1973.

This film was based on the three visits that Rouch made to Simiri in 1973 to study the effects of the famine that was then afflicting the region and the way in which this was influencing ideas about Dongo, the Spirit of Thunder and the controller of the rains. The film shows that despite the *yenendi* rain-making ceremony offered to him in May, not only does Dongo not deign to allow sufficient rain, but in August, he sends his brother Kyirey to strike the spirit-house in the middle of the village with lightning. Notwithstanding a further ritual of purification, the harvests, filmed in October, are bad, and the priests attribute this misfortune to the abandonment of tradition. This is one of many films about *yenendi* that Rouch made in Simiri (see the entry for *Yenendi de Simiri*, 1970–1971, above). It also appears to be the first of two films about Simiri with the same title (see *Sécheresse à Simiri*, 10 min., 1975, below). *Sources*: Houdaille (1981), 62–64; Prédal (1996i), 220, 222.

*Boukoki. 8 min. Sound: Hama Soumana. Editing: Danièle Tessier. Made in collaboration with CNRSH (Niamey). 1973. Rereleased on DVD by the CNRS in 2008.

This film shows part of a *yenendi* rain-making ceremony taking place in Bukoki, a district of Niamey. The camera enters a crowd gathered around a *hampi*, the large ceramic water vessel that plays an important role in *yenendi* rituals though not visible at this point of the film due to the crush of people. A number of adepts have been possessed by spirits, including by the *hauka*, identifiable by the colonial helmets and the salivating mouths of their mediums. The crowd becomes rowdy and although some people are smiling, Rouch is obliged to hold the camera above his head to shoot. He follows some of the adepts into a nearby compound before returning outside where, finally, the *hampi* is revealed. The film consists almost entirely of a single sequence-shot, apart from a brief cut in the middle when camera is in the midst of the crowd and was probably jostled. Apart from a brief contextualizing comment at the beginning, the event is unexplained.

*Pam kuso kar. 12 min. Sound: Hama Soumana. Editor: Danièle Tessier. CNRS and CNRSH, Niamey. 1974. Rereleased on DVD by the CNRS in 2008.

The title of this film refers to the destruction of the *hampi*, the large ritual water jar of Pam Sambo, who died at the age of seventy in March 1974, having been the leading possession cult priest in Niamey since 1939. Sambo had also been one of Rouch's principal informants since 1957 and had appeared in a number of his earlier films, including *Hampi* (1960), various shorter films about rain-making *yenendi* in Niamey, *Tanda Singui* (1972), and *Horendi* (also 1972). The film opens with a shot of the road outside his compound, which Rouch inserted to make the point that possession cults do not only happen in rural locations but also in the city. In fact, this particular event took place only a short distance from the Roman Catholic mission. The camera enters the door of Pam's compound to reveal a considerable crowd sitting silently around the edge, with a group of women dancing slowly in the middle, a group of men sitting around the *hampi* in the center of the compound and at the end, in a shelter, four men playing calabash drums accompanied by a *godye* violinist. Also in the center of the compound, some other men are distributing the ritual garments that Pam used to give his adepts when they were possessed by the spirits. One or two women are crying out their grief, in short guttural yelps. Having surveyed the scene, the camera then retreats outside again. Apparently in its absence, the *hampi* is broken and the adepts become possessed in order to consult the spirits about the identity of Sambo's successor. This turns out to be an elderly woman, one Dyogonou.

Rouch tried to shoot this film as a single sequence-shot, but in fact there is a cut in the middle of the film and a couple of additional shots at the end, between which some time seems to have elapsed. When he later screened the completed film in Niamey, Pam's son was in the audience and was again moved to tears. A physicist by training, he asked Rouch whether this would disqualify him from ever achieving spirit possession. Rouch suggested that, on the contrary, the son's scientific qualification might one day allow him to discover, from the inside, a proper explanation for the phenomenon of possession, currently not at all well understood. *Sources*: Houdaille (1981), 63; Stoller (1992), xiii–xvi; Rouch (1989), 270, (1996b).

Toboy toboy tobaye. 13 min. 1974 or 1975. Only available in a double-band version.

The title of this film means "rabbit, little rabbit" and refers to the subject of the film, a dance that involves children dressing up as rabbits. This takes place at night during Ramadan, the Muslim period of fasting. *Source*: Houdaille (1981), 64.

Sécheresse à Simiri (Drought at Simiri). 10 min. 1975.

One of many films that Rouch made in Simiri, a village about fifty miles north of Niamey (see the entry for *Yenendi de Simiri*, 1970–1971, above). This appears to be the second of two films with the same title (see *Sécheresse à Simiri*, 30 min., 1973, above). Although the rainy season has been better than in the previous year, a large part of the harvest has been destroyed by the *dyeri-dyeri* army caterpillar. *Source*: Houdaille (1981), 64.

Sunna kuma, alt: Souna kouma. 30 min. 1975. Editing incomplete.

Both variants of the title of the film mean "remembering Sunna (or Souna)," a reference to the funerary ritual for Sunna, a *zima* priest of a district of Niamey who died in January 1975. This film shows the purification of those whom he had initiated and the nomination by the spirits of his son, Souley, as his successor. *Sources*: Houdaille (1981), 64; Rouch (1989), 270; Feld (2003c), 384.

Initiation. 45 min. 1975. Only available in a double-band version.

An initiation dance for a young woman possessed by Kyirey, the Spirit of Lightning. This would appear to be the same film as *Initiation des femmes* that Feld lists as being made in the same year and as "incomplete." *Sources*: Houdaille (1981), 64, Feld (2003c), 384.

Zomo et ses frères (Zomo and His Siblings). 20 min. 1975.

Probably the only film that Rouch shot in Super-8. After editing, the footage was enlarged to 16mm by the audiovisual engineer, Vincent Blanchet. This film offers a portrait of the family of Rouch's closest Nigerien associate, Damouré Zika, who at that time had ten children. Due to their great number, the children refer to their family as "The People's Republic" and to their father as "Mao." They lived in the district of Niamey named after Jomo Kenyatta, the late president of Kenya. They have a rock band called Gawey Youth and play instruments fashioned out of all kinds of materials. *Sources*: Feld (2003c), 377; Philippe Costantini, personal communication, October 2008.

La Grande Sécheresse à Simiri (The Great Drought at Simiri), alt. *Yenendi: Sécheresse à Simiri (Yenendi: Drought at Simiri).* 120/238 min. 1976.

A compilation film incorporating material from a number of earlier films about the droughts suffered by village of Simiri since 1951 when Rouch made his first film about a rain-making ceremony there, *Yenendi, les hommes qui font la pluie* (see the entries above for *Yenendi de Simiri*, 1970–1971; *Sécheresse à Simiri*, 30 min., 1973; *Sécheresse à Simiri* 10 min., 1975). Houdaille (1981:64) mentions yet two more later films, also entitled *Yenendi de Simiri* (1977, 1979) but gives no further details other than that they are only available in double-band form. It seems very unlikely that all these titles represent different films, but only by a thorough-going examination of the original materials will it be possible to establish a definitive list of the films that Rouch shot on the subject of *yenendi* at Simiri.

Faba tondi. 20 min. 1976.

The title of this film means "the protective stone" and refers to a "lightning stone" buried at the entrance to Simiri, a village about fifty miles north of Niamey, where Rouch shot many films about *yenendi*, rain-making ceremonies. The *zima* priest of the village, Daouda Sorko, relates how his great-grandfather had taken advantage of its protection when the village was invaded by Tuareg warriors from Aïr, located in the north of the present-day Republic of Niger. When his great-grandfather called upon Dongo, the Spirit of Thunder, he arranged for four of the Tuareg to be struck down with a lightning bolt. The stone supposedly left behind by the lightning bolt was then deposited in the village spirit-house. Every year, in recollection of this event, Douada sacrifices a red billy goat to the stone. *Source*: Houdaille (1981), 64.

Fête des gandyi bi à Simiri (Feast of the Gandyi Bi at Simiri). 30 min. 1977. Editing incomplete.

This film shows the last possession ceremony presided over by Siddo, a priest of the village of Simiri, fifty miles north of Niamey. The villagers appeal to the *gandyi bi*, Black Spirits of the Bush to protect their crops against predatory animals, but when they arrive, the spirits let it be known that Siddo will die within the year. *Sources*: Houdaille (1981), 64; Prédal (1996i), 223; Feld (2003), 384.

Le Griot Badyé (Badyé, the Griot). 15 min. Coproducer: Inoussa Osseini. 1977.

"Griot" is a term widely used in West Africa to describe an elder who is particularly knowledgeable about matters of ritual and belief. This film concerns a griot by the name of Badyé, who seeks inspiration from bird-song when composing his epic songs. *Sources*: Houdaille (1981), 64; Feld (2003c), 378.

Simiri siddo kuma, alt. *Siddo kuma.* 30 min. 1978 or 1979. Editing incomplete.

Literally translated, the title of this film means "Remembering Siddo of Simiri" and refers to the funerary ritual for the *zima* priest Siddo, of the village of Simiri, whose death was foretold in the earlier film, *Fête des gandyi bi à Simiri* (see above). The spirits themselves nominate his successor, Daouda Sorko, a priest who had also appeared in a number of Rouch's earlier films. *Sources*: Prédal (1996i), 223; Feld (2003c), 378, 384.

Other West African Ethnographic Films, 1954–1971

Mammy water. 18/19 min. Sound: Damouré Zika, Lam Ibrahim. Editing: Philippe Luzuy. CNRS/Les Films de la Pléiade. Although variously described as having been made in 1955 or 1956, this film was actually shot in 1954 though it was not sound mixed and definitively released until 1966. Rereleased on DVD by Éditions Montparnasse, 2005.

This film presents various scenes from the life of the Fanti fishermen of Cape Coast, southwest of Accra, a stretch of coastline dominated by the great colonial forts around Elmina. In addition to the fishermen's subsistence activities, the film also shows a wake for a local priestess and the ritual opening of the fishing season by the "King of Shama," at the mouth of the Pra River, southwest along the coast from Cape Coast.

Moro Naba. 27 min. Assisted by anthropologist Dominique Zahan. Editor: Jean Ravel. CNRS/IFAN. Shot November 1957. Released 1958–1960. Rereleased on DVD by the CNRS in 2008. Also available online through the CNRS Videothèque.

A film about the funeral ceremonies for the recently deceased Moro Naba, the traditional chief of the Mossi, a large and influential ethnic group of northern Burkina Faso (then still Upper Volta), and the election of his successor. In November 1957, Rouch was passing through the capital, Ouagadougou, on his way back from having filmed *Moi, un Noir* in Abidjan, when he learned that the Mossi had agreed that these events could be filmed for the first time. The funeral ceremonies last twelve days during which time the Moro Naba is represented in public by his eldest daughter. Wearing her father's clothes, she receives the Mossi dignitaries, village heads, and commoners, all of whom swear allegiance and make numerous sacrifices of chickens, even cattle. A mass is held in the cathedral: although the Moro Naba himself resisted conversion to either Christianity or Islam, many of his subjects are Roman Catholics. After the twelve days have lapsed, the mourning period is lifted, dancing begins, and a successor is elected. This turns out to be the deceased's eldest son and the film shows him receiving the dignitaries as they now swear allegiance to him. He then travels into the city to be presented officially to the government before, finally, being formally enthroned after a secret initiation ceremony. As Rouch's sound recorder was broken, he filmed these ceremonies mute and returned later to record the music and other effects, which were then postsynchronized. Despite this difficulty, the film was made to flow through the skill of the editor, Jean Ravel, who would later cut *Chronicle of a Summer.* The film was awarded a prize at the Festival dei Popoli in Florence in 1960, but it was banned by the government of the newly independent Republic of Upper Volta because the new chief tried to use it to promote Mossi political interests. *Sources*: UNESCO (1967), 186; Rouch (1996a); CNRS Videotheque, no. 583.

Sortie de novices de Sakpata (The Coming Out of the Sakpata Novices). 16 min. Codirected by Gilbert Rouget. Editing: Danièle Tessier. Shot in February 1959, released in 1963. Rereleased on DVD by the CNRS in 2008.

Sakpata is one of the principal divinities of the voudou cult practiced in the kingdom of Allada in the south of Benin (still known as Dahomey at the time that the film was shot). Initiation into the female cult associated with Sakpata involves a long period of seclusion during which the novices learn the particular songs and dances associated with this divinity. The first part of the film shows the novices as they come of out of their seclusion hut and dance alone in the village plaza, inviting onlookers to make a gift of money. The second part shows the dance that the novices perform three days later to mark the end of their seclusion, after which they leave their retreat and go to bathe in secret in a nearby pool. Then, dressed in new skirts, their faces covered by veils, they dance back to the village to the sound of drums, accompanied by their families and fellow villagers.

This was the first of a number of films that Rouch made in collaboration with ethnomusicologist Gilbert Rouget. Although Rouch was still using a spring-wound camera that would only permit a maximum take of twenty-five seconds, the sound recorder could play for much longer. The first part of the film is therefore cut on the basis of the sound track in order to preserve the integrity of the music and dancing, with pieces of black leader or cutaways inserted between shots to make up for the missing images corresponding to the time when the camera was being rewound. The wide shots in the DVD version of this film appear to be out of focus, though this could be an effect of the transfer from the original 16mm film. Other films on which Rouch and Rouget collaborated include *Batteries Dogon* (1966) and *Sigui no. 1: L'Enclume de Yougou* (1967) about the Dogon of Mali, and *Porto-Novo* (1970–1971), also shot in Benin. In contrast to this film, all these later films were all made with battery-driven cameras and synchronous sound. *Sources*: Rouget (1965), 127; CNRS Videotheque, no. 788.

Monsieur Albert, prophète (Monsieur Albert, the Prophet), alt.: *Albert Atcho*. 27 min. Assistant director: Oumarou Ganda. Editor: Jean Ravel (sometimes credited as codirector). Argos Films. Shot on 16mm in 1962. Blown up to 35mm and released in 1963.

A film about Albert Atcho, prophet of the Harrisist community in Bregbo, a community situated on the lagoon to the east of Abidjan, capital of the Ivory Coast. Originally from Liberia, Atcho set up the community in 1914 and was said to have converted 20,000 people to Christianity, though he himself remained a polygamist. Bregbo was primarily a therapeutic community for the mentally ill though economically it operated as a collective. Atcho himself continued to work as a fisherman and horticulturalist, even while acting as the community's prophet and healer. This film shows scenes of Sunday processions and ritual healing, led by Atcho, in which members of the community make public confessions of their sins and wash in holy water. *Sources*: Godet (1966); Prédal (1996i), 217.

Jackville. 20 min. Shot in 1964. Editing incomplete.

This film shows a ceremony of the Harrisist cult in Abidjan (see *Monsieur Albert, prophète* above). *Sources*: Prédal (1996i), 218; Feld (2003), 383.

Fêtes de novembre à Bregbo. 30 min. Codirector: Colette Piault. Shot in 1966. Only available in a double-band version.

This film covers a three-day festival at the Ivory Coast village of Bregbo, a center of the Harrisist cult as it developed around the healer and prophet Monsieur Albert (see *Monsieur Albert, prophète*, above). This shoot was facilitated by anthropologist and filmmaker, Colette Piault, and in recognition of her contribution, Rouch proposed to her that she be identified as codirector. However, the rushes covered the festival and nothing more, and although they were synchronized in the form of a double-band copy, they were never released in a more definitive form. This film was thought to be lost but was recently rediscovered in the Archives françaises du film. *Sources*: Colette Piault, personal communication, August 2007; Philippe Costantini, personal communication, October 2008.

Porto-Novo—La danse des reines; alt: *Porto-Novo, ballet de cour des femmes du roi* (*Porto Novo—the Dance of the Queens*, or *Porto-Novo, Court Ballet of the King's Wives*). 30 min. Codirected by Gilbert Rouget. Shot in 1969 and released in 1971. A new version of this film, directed by Rouget, was released by the CNRS in 1996 and then released again on DVD in 2008.

One of a number of films that Rouch made in collaboration with the ethnomusicologist Gilbert Rouget (see particularly *Sakpata*, 1963, above, and, below in the section "Dogon films," *Batteries dogon*, 1966). This film is about possession dancing at the royal court in Porto Novo in Dahomey (now Benin), on the occasion of the performance of new year rituals by the king. The film shows a sequence of six dances, mostly performed by the king's wives, though he himself, accompanied by his ministers, joins them at certain moments. The first four dances are each performed to a different drum and are associated with the four cardinal points. The fifth dance is performed to music that is almost exclusively vocal and composed by poets, while the sixth and final dance is performed to the sound provided by a line of calabash drums. The use of slow-motion filming permitted a precise analysis of the relationship between the dancing and the music, allowing the directors to establish that in these performances the musicians follow the dancers rather than vice versa. *Sources*: Houdaille (1981), 62; Stoller (1992), 192; CNRS Videotheque, no. 786.

West African Films on Other Subjects, 1957–1974

Baby Ghana. 27 min. Shot 1957. Only available in a double-band version.

This film shows the festivities following Ghanaian independence in March 1957. It has recently been restored by the Archives françaises du film. *Sources*: Houdaille (1981), 60; Philippe Costantini, personal communication, October 2008.

Niger, jeune république ("The Niger—Young Republic"). 56 min. Codirected with Claude Jutra. Assisted by Roger Morillère and Louis Boucher. Editors: Claude Jutra and Édouard Davidovici. Sound editors: Bernard Bordeleau and Marguerite Payette. Produced by Bernard Devlin for the National Film Board of Canada. Shot in 1960 and released in 1961.

In most sources, including the UNESCO catalog, Jean Rouch is credited only as an assistant to the Québecois filmmaker, Claude Jutra, who directed and scripted this survey of Niger immediately following independence for the National Film Board of Canada. The film carries a commentary spoken by Rouch and begins with scenes of the Independence Day celebrations at which the various different ethnic groups of the country pass in parade, each in their distinctive costume, as the new president, Hamani Diori, reviews the troops and makes a speech. The film then moves to rural areas to show the traditional mud architecture and ways of life of the Tuareg, Fulani, Zerma and Hausa. It also considers religious activities, including both Islam and traditional possession rituals. There is an interview with Damouré Zika and sequences in the Niamey hospital and the museum of the Institut Français d'Afrique Noire, as well as of the inauguration of the bridge over the Niger River. *Sources*: UNESCO (1967), 266; see also http://www.nfb.ca/collection/films/fiche/?id-17191.

Les Ballets du Niger (Ballet of Niger). 20 min. Black and white. 1961.

A film showing a performance by Nigerien dancers at the Théâtre des Nations in Paris. *Source*: Houdaille 1981:60.

Fête de l'indépendance du Niger (Niger Independence Celebrations). 21 min. Shot in 1961–1962.

No further details in the sources. This may be based on the same footage as *Niger, jeune république*, described above. *Source*: Prédal (1996i), 217.

Festival à Dakar (Festival in Dakar). Shot in 1962 or 1963. Only available in a double-band version.

At the first Panafrican Festival at Dakar in Senegal, Moustapha Alassane, whose early career as a filmmaker was supported by Rouch, is awarded the grand prix for an animation, *La Mort de Gandji (The Death of Gandji)*. In the evening, Duke Ellington plays *Black and Tan Fantasy* at the Sorano theater. *Sources*: Houdaille (1981), 60; Prédal (1996i), 217.

L'Afrique et la recherche scientifique (Africa and Scientific Research) 1962–1964. Production: UNESCO.

This film incorporates a number of shorter films on scientific research and its contribution to economic development. Three of these were shot on the Ivory Coast: *Abidjan, port de pêche (Abidjan, Fishing Port)*, 25 min., 1962; *Le Palmier à huile (The Oil Palm)*, 20 min., 1962; and *Le Cocotier (The Coconut Palm)*, 21 min., 1962/1963; while a fourth, *Le Mil (Millet)*, 27 min., 1963, was shot in Niger. Rouch found the making of these films "deadly boring," commenting that they were about "supposedly serious subjects that I never managed to understand" (Fieschi and Téchiné 1967:20). Prédal (1996i: 217) reports the existence of another film on what appears to be a related topic, *Urbanisme africain (African Town Planning)*, but describes it as "incomplete."

Rose et Landry (Rose and Landry). 28 min. Black and white. Codirected with Michel Brault. Camera: Georges Dufaux, with additional material shot by Jean Rouch. Sound: Marcel Carrière. Editing: Jean-Jacques Godbout. Production: National Film Board of Canada. Released in 1963. Awarded the Prix San Giorgio at the Venice Film Festival.

A film made for Canadian television, for which Rouch appears to have shot some material, without being the principal cameraman. Nor was he involved in the editing at any point. This film examines the significance of French culture in postcolonial Ivory Coast and its relationship to traditional African culture, as perceived by Modeste Landry, protagonist of *La Pyramide humaine*, *Chronique d'un été* and *La Punition*, who had recently returned after three years studying in France, and by his friend Rose Bamba. *Source*: Rohmer and Marcorelles (1963), 14–15.

Alpha noir (Black Alpha). 10 min. Editing incomplete. 1965.

A film about an adult literacy campaign in Mali. No further details in the sources. *Sources*: Prédal (1996i), 218; Feld (2003c), 383.

Rapports mères-enfants en Afrique (Mother-child relationships in Africa). 20 min. ORTF. Broadcast (?) in 1971.

No further information in the sources than the title, but presumably this was a program made for ORTF, the French government agency that held a monopoly on public broadcasting from 1964 to 1974. *Source*: Prédal (1996i), 221.

VW voyou (VW Rascal). 35 min. SCOA. 1973.

This film originated in a series of very much shorter films made for the French colonial trading conglomerate Société commerciale de l'Ouest africain (SCOA). These were humorous in nature and featured Damouré Zika and Lam Ibrahim Dia. They present the Volkswagen Beetle as a car that goes anywhere and can be used for anything. These films were originally intended to be shown individually as publicity films in cinema theaters. As this never happened, Rouch simply joined them all together into a single film. *Sources*: Houdaille (1981), 63; Feld (2003c), 373; Philippe Costantini, personal communication, October 2008.

Le Foot-girafe ou "l'Alternative" (*Giraffe Football or "The Alternative"*). 20 min. SCOA. 1973.
A publicity film for the French colonial trading conglomerate Société commerciale de l'Ouest africain (SCOA) promoting the Peugeot 403 and the Peugeot 504 Estate. The title is probably an allusion to the "game" invented by Rouch, as described by Claude Jutra, in which the driver of a car seeks to herd a giraffe through two trees that act as a "goal" (see Jutra 1960–61, 23). A possible example of the "game" in progress is the sequence close to the beginning of *La Chasse au lion à l'arc* in which a Peugeot is seen herding a giraffe at considerable speed across an open savanna (see fig. 10.1 above). *Source*: Houdaille (1981), 63; Feld (2003c), 373.

La 504 et les foudroyeurs (*The 504 and the Blasters*). 10 min. SCOA. 1974.
A publicity film for the French trading conglomerate SCOA, promoting the Peugeot 504 Estate and featuring Lam Ibrahim Dia and Tallou Mouzourane. The Peugeot is shown taking a new road in the Bandiagara Cliffs that the Dogon "blasters" open up with dynamite that they have made up themselves. *Source*: Houdaille (1981), 63.

*Médecines et médecins (*Medicines and Medics*). 15 min. Codirected by Inoussa Ousseini. Sound: Moussa Illo. Editing: Danièle Tessier. Coproduction with IRSH. 1976. Released on DVD by CNRS in 2008.
This film shows a clinic at work in rural Niger, but there is no commentary nor other form of explanation, so the precise location is not clear. A group of men are shown talking outside the clinic but mostly in an unsubtitled African language, presumably Songhay-Zerma. The camera then moves inside the clinic where Damouré Zika, who trained as a paramedic with Rouch's support, is seen in his white uniform, sitting at a desk. The central portion of the film consists of a remarkable series of sequence-shots of a surgical operation, carried out in a back room of the clinic, in very basic conditions. The window to the outside is open and at one point, Damouré enters and liberally sprays the room with what is presumably an insect repellent or perhaps an antiseptic. This operation appears to be an appendectomy, but the patient is fully conscious and apparently not in pain. There is a brief interview with the African surgeon in French, but this is difficult to hear since he is speaking through a surgical mask. After the operation, the patient is carried out on a stretcher and taken to what appears to be a windowless mudbrick ward behind the clinic. At the doorway of the ward, there is then an interview by Damouré, in the local language, of a woman *zima* priest who provides postoperative care. Damouré comments in French that both traditional healers such as her and modern

medicine are able to learn from one another at the clinic, though exactly what form this collaboration takes is not itself described. *Sources*: Prédal (1996i), 222; CNRS Videotheque, no. 702.

Damouré parle du SIDA (Damouré Talks about AIDS). 10 min.. Produced in collaboration with SODAPERAGA. Unfinished. Shot in 1992.

Damouré Zika, Rouch's close associate, who trained as a paramedic with Rouch's help, talks about AIDS with his two friends Lam and Tallou, under the admiring gaze of one of his wives, Lobo, also a nurse. Damouré says that AIDS is "a disease of love that can only be conquered through love" and that the right to love under the present circumstances only has one "passport"— the condom. He then gives a remarkable demonstration of how to use one. *Source*: Feld (2003c), 381.

Parisian Films: The New Wave and After, 1960–1971

*Chronique d'un été ('Chronicle of a Summer'). 90 min. Black and white. Co-directed with Edgar Morin. Camera: Roger Morillère, Raoul Coutard, Jean-Jacques Tarbès, Michel Brault. Sound: Guy Rophé, Michel Fano, Edmond Barthélémy. Editing: Jean Ravel, Néna Baratier, Françoise Colin. Produced by Argos Films. Shot 1960, released 1961. Awarded prizes at film festivals in Cannes, Venice, and Mannheim in 1961. Available in a subtitled English-language version. Rereleased on DVD in the original French version by Argos Films and ARTE, 2005.

For this, the first and most celebrated of a series of films that he made in Paris in the early 1960s, Rouch collaborated with the sociologist Edgar Morin to explore the attitudes of a group of young Parisians to work, love, the Algerian war, race, and life in general, over the course of the summer of 1960. Beginning with informal interviews in the street and discussions around dinner tables, the method of their enquiry gradually evolves as they get to know their subjects, going back with them to their homes and later going on holiday with them. But at the end of the summer, when they screen the rushes back to the subjects, the latter disagree about whether these images are really true to their lives. Rouch and Morin are left pondering what kind of truth can be represented through documentary cinema. See chapter 8.

La Punition (The Punishment). 58 min. Camera: Michel Brault, Roger Morillère, Georges Dufaux. Sound: Roger Morillère. Editing: Annie Tresgot. Production: Films de la Pléiade for the ORTF television channel. Shot in 1960. Broadcast on television and shown publicly at the UNESCO film club in 1963. General cinema release in 1964.

This is a fictional psychodrama, inspired by the Surrealist idea of the *rencontre*, the encounter between strangers. The principal character is a young student of philosophy, played by Nadine Ballot, previously a leading character of *La Pyramide humaine* (see under "Migration Studies" above) as well as of *Chronicle of a Summer*. Suspended from school for the day, Nadine wanders through Paris and has three encounters with men of a variety of ages and backgrounds. She proposes to each of them that they should abandon everything and run off together, but all of them refuse for one reason or another. Nadine returns to her parents' home in the evening, having discovered that the Surrealist notion of *l'amour fou*, crazy love, arising from an encounter with a stranger is an illusion. Shot over the course of a single weekend in October 1960, while Rouch was in the middle of editing *Chronicle of a Summer*, this film was made in reaction to his experience of having to cut down the rushes for *Chronicle* to a mere fraction of their original length. *Source*: Rohmer and Marcorelles (1963). See chapter 9, pp. 179–187.

Gare du Nord. 17 min. Camera: Étienne Becker. Sound: Bernard Ortion. Editing: Jacqueline Raynal. Production: Les Films du Losange. Shot in 1964, released in 1965. Released in 2006 on DVD with English subtitles by Madman Films, Australia.

The title of this film refers to the location in the somewhat tatty quartier around the famous railway station in the north of Paris. This is also a fictional "psychodrama" featuring Nadine Ballot and, like *La Punition*, also based on the Surrealist idea of the *rencontre*. Ballot plays Odile, who is desperate to escape from her life with her husband Jean-Pierre, played by the then up-and-coming film director and producer of this film, Barbet Schroeder. After an argument at home, Odile runs out into the street, where she meets a mysterious Stranger, played by the professional actor Gilles Quéant. He says that he is prepared to run off with her anywhere in the world, but if she declines his offer, he will kill himself. When offered the freedom that she thought that she craved, Odile cannot bring herself to grasp it, so true to his word, the Stranger jumps to his death from the railway bridge over which they are passing. This film consisted almost entirely of two sequence-shots and formed part of *Paris vu par* (released in an English-language version as *Six in Paris*), an omnibus film made up of a number of short sketches of Paris by leading New Wave directors, including Jean-Luc Godard, Éric Rohmer, and Claude Chabrol. This film has been recently declared to be the 'undeniable masterwork' of French cinema in the 1960s. *Sources*: Rouch (1965); Marie (2008). See chapter 9, pp. 187–192.

Les Veuves de quinze ans (*Widows at 15*) alt.: *Marie-France et Véronique* (*Marie-France and Véronique*). 24 min. Shot in 35mm black-and-white stock. Camera: Jacques Lang. Sound: Michel Fano. Editing: Claudine Bouché. Produced by Les Films de la Pléiade. Shot in 1964, released in 1966. Rereleased on DVD by Éditions Montparnasse 2005.

This film formed the French contribution to *Les Adolescentes* (alt.: *La Fleur de l'âge*), an international omnibus film also involving directors from Canada (Michel Brault), Japan (Hiroshi Teshigahara), and Italy (Gian-Vittorio Baldi). Although based on a fictional story, it aims to provide a portrait of Parisian teenagers in the summer of 1964, though they are all teenagers from the most elite stratum of Parisian society. These young people are shown to be lost in a swirl of materialism, rock-and-roll and drunken parties, matched only by the similarly dissolute attitudes of their parents. Although they might enjoy sexual freedom at an early age, only a minority are ever able to find true love. The film is structured around the friendship of two girls, the elegant Véronique and the more homely Marie-France. The former lends herself to this world of illusion, despite being aware of its faults, while the latter manages to resist it with the aid of regular consultations of the works of Baudelaire. Marie-France is finally rewarded when she becomes friendly with Marc, a nice boy who, although also sucked into the world of illusion, actually cares most of all about painting. In the final scene, Marie-France walks off in wide-shot with a worldly-wise avuncular figure, played by Gilles Quéant, who had previously appeared as the Stranger in *Gare du Nord*. He explains that although the chances of achieving happiness are but one in a thousand, one might just find it if one is sufficiently courageous. Shot in 35mm with a full professional crew, Rouch found making this film extremely tedious, comparing it to "forced labour, military service." *Sources*: Comolli (1964); Fieschi and Téchiné (1967); Veuve (1967). See chapter 9, pp. 192–195.

La Révolution poétique: Mai 68. 5 min. Shot in 1968. Unedited.

This title has been given to what appear to be no more than 200 feet of 16mm rushes covering the *événements* of May 1968 when left-wing students took to the streets and there were widespread workers' strikes, leading eventually to the political downfall of General de Gaulle. *Source*: Prédal 1996i: 219.

*Petit à Petit (Little by Little). Originally cut so as to be released in three parts: *Lettres persanes*, 78 min., *Afrique sur Seine*, 73 min., and *L'Imagination au pouvoir*, 79 min., but at the insistence of the producer, Pierre Braunberger, it was later reduced to 92 minutes and released at this length after being blown up to 35mm. Assistant director and assistant camera: Philippe Luzuy. Sound: Moussa Hamidou. Editing: Josée Matarasso (long version) and Dominique Villain (short version). Production: Les Films de la Pléiade in collaboration with CNRSH of Niger, and the Comité du Film Ethnographique. Shot in 1967–1968. Various versions released between 1969 and 1971. Rereleased in the 92-min. version in DVD by Éditions Montparnasse, 2005.

This is an ethnofictional reprise of *Jaguar*, though this time, Damouré Zika and Lam Ibrahim visit Paris rather than the cities of the Gold Coast. Back in Niger, "Petit à Petit," the trinket stall that they set up in Accra at the end of *Jaguar*, has now grown into a wealthy import-export business. In order to reflect their newfound status, Damouré, joined later by Lam, goes to Paris in search of some architects who will design a multistory building for them. Here, with Damouré mimicking the note taking and body measuring of early biological anthropologists, they study the customs of the natives. They also make visits to the Alps, to the Ligurian coast of Italy, and ostensibly, to the United States. Once the architects' drawings are done, they return to Niger with two girls whom they have picked up in Paris. One of these is Safi, a Senegalese prostitute, the other a French secretary and night-club dancer, Ariane. These two will swell Damouré's number of wives to eight, while Philippe, a tramp whom Lam befriends in Paris, will help out with herding Lam's cattle. But quarrels soon break out and the newcomers all leave. Damouré, Lam, and their old partner, Illo, conclude that money is not worth having if it produces such arguments, so they hand over Petit à Petit to some young managers and return to the simple lives they had at the beginning of *Jaguar*, before they ever took to the road in search of wealth and adventure. See chapter 10, pp. 210–217.

Dogon Films, 1950–1982

Cimetières dans la falaise (Cemeteries in the Cliff Face). 19 min. Shot 1950, released 1951.
　　See under "Doctoral Research, 1947–1952" above.

Batteries dogon: Éléments pour une étude de rythmes (Dogon Drums: Elements for a Study of Rhythms); alt: *Tambours de pierre (Stone Drums)*. 26 min. Codirectors: Germaine Dieterlen and Gilbert Rouget. Sound: Moussa Hamidou. Editing: Philippe Luzuy. Shot in 1964 and released in 1966. Rereleased on DVD by the CNRS in 2007.
　　This is a highly pedagogical work exploring a series of different rhythms played by the Dogon on percussive instruments made of wood, skin, and even stone. As well as being a film of ethnographic documentation, this film was also a technical experiment, intended to test out a newly developed lightweight system for achieving synchronous sound to the degree of accuracy of one one-hundredth of a second. Described by Rouch as an exercise in "cinémusicologie," it explores the subtle interaction between the right and the left hands in Dogon percussion. In the first part, the film shows various different rhythms being played by each hand separately, then being played together on a variety of media. The performers are mostly young goatherds being instructed by Amadigné Dolo, one of Germaine Dieterlen's principal informants. The final four minutes of the film consist of a remarkable sequence of both men and women dancing to these rhythms at a funeral. A short article describing the technical procedures developed in order to achieve sound-image synchronicity, as well as some of the ethnographic context, was published by Rouget in *L'Homme* in 1965. Without this text, it is difficult to make sense of the film. *Sources*: Rouget (1965); CNRS Videotheque, no. 587.

Sigui année zero (Sigui Year Zero). 15 min. Codirected with Germaine Dieterlen. Shot in 1966. Only available in a double-band version.

The Hogon, the paramount religious authority of the Dogon announces that the Sigui ritual cycle will begin the following year. This will be the first time that the cycle has been initiated since 1907. At the village of Yougou, where the cycle will begin, the elders consider the auguries of the event. They also discuss the messages that they will send to the young people living on the plains below the Bandiagara Escarpment or who have gone to Ghana and the Ivory Coast to work as migrant laborers. *Source*: Feld (2003c), 361–362.

Sigui no. 1: l'Enclume de Yougou (The Anvil of Yougou). 38 min. Codirected with Germaine Dieterlen and Gilbert Rouget. Shot in 1967. Release date unclear.

When they return to the Bandiagara Escarpment in January 1967, the film-makers find the village of Yougou full of people, as many of the migrant workers have now returned. Men and boys are shaved, while women and girls have given their jewelry to the blacksmiths to be reworked for the men to wear. Drums playing in the village square summon the dancers. They are all dressed in identical black trousers and white hoods (that supposedly make them look like fish, and thus symbolically associate them with fetuses in the womb). They also wear bandoliers of cowrie shells (a symbol of female genitalia). In the right hand, they each hold a fly swat, while in the left, they hold a three-pronged stool and a gourd for drinking millet beer. They enter the square in a serpentine dance line, led by drummers, but otherwise in strict order of age, with those who attended the 1907 enactment in front, and toddlers bringing up the rear. Elders declaim the *sigi so*, the secret language of the Sigui, while the younger dancers imitate the cry of the trickster spirit, the Pale Fox. After filling the square, the dancers continue their serpentine dance through the passageways of the village, before dancing on the flat roofs of the houses of deceased dignitaries of the Sigui, the *olubaru*. Here, they are greeted by a woman holding a staff surmounted by the symbolic drinking gourd of the *yasigine*, the twin sisters of the Pale Fox. The dancers then rest and drink millet beer prepared by the other women. The feast begins again the following afternoon, with a classic *rite de passage* in which the dancers pass in columns beneath branches of thorns. On the third day, they dance out of the village and along the steep paths of the cliff face, carrying the Sigui on to the next village, Yougu Na. *Source*: (Feld 2003c), 362–363.

Sigui no. 2: Les Danseurs de Tyogou (The Dancers of Tyogou). 26 min. Codirected by Germain Deiterlen. Shot in 1968. Release date unclear.

Men prepare their ritual dress before going to the village square of Tyogou to dance. The following day, they decorate the cave where the masks carved for this Sigui will later be kept. In the men's shelter, the *toguna*, from which all women are excluded, men prepare ritual paraphernalia and shave their heads. Then, in the afternoon, led by drummers and the elders, they dance in single file up the cliff path to the old village site. Here they dance on the square in a snake formation, singing the Sigui songs, chanting the *sigi so*, and crying out in imitation of the Pale Fox, the trickster spirit. After an interlude drinking millet beer while sitting on their stools, they begin dancing again, but this time in pairs, face to face. The next morning, the filmmakers visit the cave of the masks. Here they come upon a new and unpainted mask in the shape of a snake, decorated with a bird's head. They also see masks from 1908, 1848, and even 1788. The following day, the dancers perform again and then, on the third day, the Sigui leaves for the village of Koundou. *Sources*: Feld (2003c), 363–364; CNRS Videotheque, no. 518.

Sigui no. 3: La Caverne de Bongo (The Cave at Bongo). 38 min. Codirected by Germaine Dieterlen. Assisted by Amadigné Dolo, Lam Ibrahim Dia, Tallou Mouzourane. Sound recordist: Ibrahim Guindo. Edited by Philippe Luzuy. Shot in 1969. Release date unclear.

Apparently the only one of the original Sigui films to be fully completed as a free-standing film, with a voice-over recorded by Rouch and end credits. It begins in the cliff-side village of Banani, where the Sigui has arrived, but then moves on to village of Bongo, on the plateau above. Here the elders are shaving their heads, including old Anaï, said to be 120 years old and witnessing his third Sigui. Meanwhile, in a cave on the other side of the valley from the village, the *olubaru* dignitaries have been in seclusion for several weeks. Now they are making bull-roarers that will generate the "voices" of the ancestors. In the dancing plaza outside the cave, other elders prepare a circular clay mound, decorated with red and white squares. This represents the first human ancestor to die but who then returned in the form of a snake. The red and white squares represent the scales of his body. A pole protrudes from the center of the mound, crowned with a tuft of red feathers representing the rebirth of the ancestor. As the sun sets, the *olubaru* swing the bull-roarers to make them "speak." Once night has fallen, elders from the four villages around Bongo place the four great masks at the entrance of the cave. These include the new mask, which has now been painted red and white.

The next day, when the sun rises, the dancers are able to see the masks: the ones painted black, red, and white represent the dead snake while the those painted only red and white represent its restoration to life. Holding their ritual paraphernalia (the stools, fly swats and gourds) and dressed in their Sigui costumes, now supplemented by jewelry borrowed from their wives or sisters, the men dance in four lines in the plaza, representing the four different villages around Bongo. They dance in strict order of age, alternating dancing with drinking millet beer, all beneath the gaze of the masks and an elder chanting in *sigi so* from the mouth of the cave. At sunset, the drums gather around the clay mound, while fathers and brothers carry the youngest male children around the mound on their shoulders or in their arms, so that they can say that they too danced the Sigui. At nightfall, the dancers burn their old clothes, symbolically acknowledging that the generation into which they were born is now past. The final shot is from within the cave: the elders are shown in silhouette, the masks on the left, but through the mouth of the cave, one can discern a newly painted mosque, with what appears to be a gilded star glinting on top. *Sources*: Feld (2003c), 366–367; CNRS Videotheque, no. 525.

Sigui no. 4: Les Clameurs d'Amani (The Proclamations of Amani). 36 min. Co-directed by Germaine Dieterlen. Shot in 1970. Release date unclear.

The Pale Fox oracle at Bongo has declared that the Sigui should continue to Amani, a village about 20 miles away, down on the plains. But the Dogon require the filmmakers to ask the oracle whether they can go too. The answer is positive but the oracle warns of difficulties. They do indeed have difficulty getting there because the bridges are down, but when they arrive, everything is ready. Men and boys are shaved and ready while the elders are trying to establish the route followed by the Sigui in 1910: since then, houses have been built directly over the route. Here only the *olubaru* dignitaries are wearing cowrie bandoliers. Other men wear women's jewelry, women's loincloths crossed over their chests, and women's scarves to hold down their white hoods. The Sigui arrives, winding around the village in the usual serpentine manner. The mask prepared the year before is there and it is placed near the *toguna*, the men's shelter. Here, in a series of exchanges, two old men tell the Dogon creation myth in *sigi so*, the ritual language of the Sigui. The next day, the dancers visit the houses of deceased *olubaru* dignitaries and dance on their roof terraces. Then they return to the plaza to sing songs and hear the proclamations in *sigi so*. As shadows lengthen, an elder tells the creation myth in *sigi so*, punctuated by cries from the dancers imitating the Pale Fox. On the third day, they carry the Sigui to another village at the foot of the cliff nearby, where, under the gaze of a mask, they dance and engage in a lengthy exchange in *sigi so* with the elders of that village. *Sources*: Feld (2003c), 367–368; CNRS Videotheque, no. 569.

Sigui no. 5: La Dune d'Idyeli (The Sand-dune at Idyeli). 40/53 min. Codirected by Germaine Dieterlen. Shot 1971. Release date unclear.

Idyeli is located at the foot of a sand dune on the edge of the plain of Gondo, a further twenty miles or so to the southwest of Amani. (Idyeli is not to be confused with Ireli, which lies north of Amani and which is the village in which Rouch and Rosfelder filmed *Cimetières dans la falaise* in 1950). The night before the festival, the men climb up the sand dune and bury themselves in shallow burrows, where they remain without eating or drinking until the following day. Around 4:00 PM, as the sun begins to set, the men are called from their burrows by the *olubaru* dignitaries swinging bull-roarers. They emerge, wash themselves in the spring, and then, with the aid of their female kin, they dress in women's clothes, making themselves up and putting on bracelets and necklaces, before dancing in serpentine fashion into the village square where large vessels of millet beer await them. The next day, the Sigui will leave Idyeli and the plain behind, returning for the rest of the cycle to the plateau villages on top of the escarpment. *Sources*: Feld (2003c), 368–369; CNRS Videotheque, no. 543.

Sigui no. 6: Les Pagnes de Yamé (The Loincloths of Yamé). 50 min. Codirected with Germaine Dieterlen. Shot 1972. Release date unclear.

Yamé is a village on the plateau on top of the Bandiagara Escarpment and has three *toguna*, men's shelters. The *olubaru* dignitaries have withdrawn to one of these, while the rest of the men shave themselves and dress in women's clothing. Many are wearing skirts over their trousers, others wear jewelry: they have become "mothers" as this is the theme of this year's Sigui. But only the *olubaru* dignitaries are wearing cowrie-shell bandoliers on this occasion. As the dancers approach the entrance to the village, an old man tells the creation myth in *sigi so*, the ritual language. They are facing east, but the elder tells them to face west and then east again. In the past, they would have continued further to the west, but this would have taken them to the villages that have been Islamized and where the Sigui is no longer welcome. So the dancers return to one of the *toguna* in the village and drink beer, seated on their stools. The elders thank the dancers who then store their stools on the roof of the *toguna*. The next day, they meet briefly to drink more millet beer and perform a number of dances normally danced only by women, before dispersing in small groups to carry the Sigui to those few villages nearby that have not been Islamized. *Sources*: Feld (2003c), 372; CNRS Videotheque, no. 544.

Sigui no. 7: L'Auvent de la circoncision (The Circumcision Shelter). 18 min. Codirected with Germaine Dieterlen. Shot in 1974. Release date unclear.

This film shows a reenactment, by three *olubaru* dignitaries, of a simple ceremony of closure to the Sigui. This should have been filmed the previous year but this had been forbidden by the Malian government on account of an extreme drought. This seventh year ceremony takes place in the circumcision shelter close to the village of Songo, but as a result of the influence of Islam, the Sigui can no longer enter the village itself. The three *olubaru* dignitaries arrive at the shelter and sacrifice a goat. They sprinkle its blood on the altar of the ancestors and, in the morning, "refresh" the ancestral paintings on the wall of the cave by caressing them. As they do so, they explain to the filmmakers what these paintings signify. The paintings in the principal chamber show the spirit of water, Nommo, a silhouette of the Pale Fox, Sigui "satchels" (containers of words), and star constellations. Finally the *olubaru* leave, carrying some of the millet beer and singing Sigui songs. They will return without stopping to the village of Yougou, where the whole ritual cycle began in 1967. Here they will offer the beer to the elders, saying, "Here is the last of the Sigui beer. The Sigui is over." *Sources*: Feld (2003c), 375; CNRS Videotheque, no. 545.

Sigui, 1967–1973. L'Invention de la parole et de la mort (alt: *Sigui synthèse*). 120 min. Codirected with Germaine Dieterlen. Shot between 1966 and 1974. Released 1981 and 1996.

A synthesis of all the previous films about the Sigui, representing a reduction in overall running time by about half. In 1996, a different version of this synthesis, including some additional material showing Rouch and Germaine Dieterlen working with the Dogon, was produced by the Japanese television company NHK, which broadcast the material on its newly launched satellite service. *Source*: Prédal (1996c), 21–22. See chapter 11, pp. 220–234.

LATE DOGON FILMS

Funérailles à Bongo: Le Vieil Anaï, 1848–1971 (Funeral at Bongo: Old Anaï, 1848–1971). 70/80 min. Codirected by Germaine Dieterlen. Sound: Moussa Hamidou. Editing: Danièle Tessier. Shot in May 1972, editing not completed until 1979. Awarded a prize at the Venice Film Festival, 1979.

When Anaï Dolo died at 122, he had been present for three Sigui: one while in his mother's womb, one in 1909, and one in 1969, dying shortly thereafter in 1971. When Rouch arrived in 1972, Anaï had been dead for six months and funeral preparations were in hand. The film begins with a sequence of Anaï sitting outside his house in 1970, before showing the funeral blankets displayed around his house and the mannequin representing Anaï himself on the roof terrace. In this form, he will preside over his own funeral. Fluttering beside the mannequin, there are both Malian and French flags, the latter representing the time when Anaï had been involved in warfare against the French and had been injured despite his protective magical clothing. In the plaza, under the gaze of the great Sigui mask, this event is reenacted with much firing of old muskets. Anaï's family represent the Dogon while men from other villages represent the French. A nephew wears Anaï's magical cape. The Dogon are defeated but regroup in the village plaza before the statue of Anaï and chant courageously. Over the following days, the impurity of death will be ritually cleansed. Women are shaved, funeral blankets are washed, the Sigui mask is returned to the cave and the statue of Anaï is taken down. In evenings, in the darkness, elders repeat the *tegué*, the ancient sayings. They recount the creation of the world, of animals, of the Dogon, and incidents from the life of Anaï. The elders are shown initially in synch, but then there is a long cutaway over animal skulls and Rouch himself takes over the chant. The elders then consult the Pale Fox oracle to see if the time for dancing on the plaza has come. The answer is positive, so dancing begins again with further firing of muskets, though this time the battle is not against the French, but rather against death itself. A new statue has been put up, this time of Dyongou Sérou, the first ancestor to die. He is shown lying on a bier of antelope horns, recalling his original bier. The dancing reenacts his burial, including the sacrifice of a white cow offered in vain to God, who would not accept the sacrifice. Muskets are fired around the cow, women ululate and dance. Drums and cowbells sound in the background. One of Anaï's grandchildren fires at a target, thereby symbolically firing at the sun and at the Pale Fox, in order to ensure the rebirth of life. The participants then all gather for a final "chant of courage" on the village plaza to bid Anaï farewell. The next day, the very young great-grandson of Anaï is shown climbing up the cliff face. He will be Anaï's *nani*, his "correspondent," responsible for the rituals to accompany Anaï during his travels to the Land of the Dead, a journey that may take several months. Rouch repeats the *tegué* describing the postmortem journey as the boy completes his perilous ascent and disappears. *Sources*: Feld (2003c), 370–372; CNRS Videotheque, no. 581.

L'Enterrement du Hogon (The Burial of the Hogon). 18 min. Shot in 1973. Original release date not clear. Rereleased on DVD by the CNRS in 2008. In this form, the film has neither titles nor credits.

Rouch happened to be in Sanga when the paramount religious authority of the Dogon, the Hogon of the village of Lower Ogol, died suddenly in the night. The film documents events in the plaza of the village as all the men of the village conduct a sham fight against death, firing their muskets in the air while women ululate and wave gourds in the air. The crowd includes professional mourners as well as the genuinely bereaved. The priests, some with funeral blankets over their shoulders, carry the corpse, wrapped in a shroud, around the village plaza. Then, after sprinkling the body with grains of millet, they give it to the grave-diggers who carry it in a serpentine dancing procession toward the village graveyard, attended by a large crowd of people chanting and ululating. The film consists of a series of sequence-shots, without any form of explanation. Rouch had been forbidden by the Malian authorities to film dead bodies, but this one was covered in a shroud and, moreover, as he was the high priest, he was not considered by the Dogon to have died anyway. *Sources*: Houdaille (1981), 63; *Gardner* 2004; CNRS Videotheque, no. 501.

Funérailles de femme à Bongo (Woman's Funeral at Bongo). 20 min. Shot in 1973. Only available in a double-band version.

No further information in the sources. *Source*: Prédal (1996i), 221.

Le Dama d'Ambara (The Dama for Ambara). 60 min. Codirected with Germaine Dieterlen. Sound: Ibrahim Guindo. Editing: Danièle Tessier. Shot in 1974, but the editing was not completed until 1980. Rereleased on DVD by the CNRS in 2007.

Every five years, the Dogon hold a *dama*, a ceremony for those who have died in the interim. The purpose of the ceremony is to gather together the souls of the dead, which are believed to be still wandering in the vicinity of the village. The aim is to "enchant" the souls so that they are persuaded to leave permanently for the Land of the Dead and mourning for them can be brought to an end. This film concerns a particularly grand *dama*, lasting for three days, in memory of seven leading elders, including Ambara Dolo, who had died in 1971. Ambara had acted as interpreter and informant for Marcel Griaule and later for Germaine Dieterlen and Rouch himself since 1931. In certain passages, the voice-over commentary by Rouch follows very closely texts taken from the works of Marcel Griaule.

The film begins with a preliminary section in which, narrating over general views of the village and the surrounding environment, Rouch describes Dogon ideas about the origin of death and the purpose of the *dama*. In the company of another of his principal informants, Amadigné Dolo, Rouch then visits Ambara's son, Pangalé, at his house, where Pangalé is preparing masks for the event. Ambara himself is then shown in some archival footage. The ceremony begins with a parade of masks, representing a broad variety of figures, both human and animal. Leading the parade is the Pale Fox, master of disorder and inventor of the first *dama*, wearing a mask covered with eyes through which he searches in vain for his twin sister, Yasigui, from whom he was separated at the creation of the world. He is followed by the Fulani Horseman (represented by small boys), the Marabout (dressed in lurid green wigs and costumes and holding Koranic tablets), the Fulani Girl (represented by adult men, wearing breasts made out of a conical fruit), the Healer (the first man to die), the Turtledove (on tall stilts, representing the trees in which the Turtledove perches), Yasigui herself, the Hare, and particularly important, the *kanaga* masks surmounted by a cross with two arms (also representing the Pale Fox) and finally the very tall, serpentine *serigue* masks. Bringing up the rear, there is a mask representing modernity, the Policeman, who goes round administering "fines" to the onlookers, including seemingly to the film crew.

The masked dancers from all parts of the village join together to leap across a small gully, symbolizing the vagina of Yasigui, sister of the Pale Fox. They are preceded by elders carrying the stools on which the deceased sat to drink millet beer during the Sigui ceremonies of 1909 and 1969: these stools are then taken away and left to rot in a crevice in the nearby cliff face. This is the beginning of three days of dancing by the masked figures, at the end of which, some of the dancers go up onto the roof terraces of the houses of the deceased whose *dama* is being celebrated and dance there to enchant their souls. The masked dancers then lead the souls into the village plaza, where they dance out the creation myth for the last time. In the evening, the masks are returned to the House of Masks, while the souls leave the village for the Land of the Dead. *Sources*: C. Piault (1996), 151; Feld (2003c), 373–374; CNRS Videotheque, no. 590.

Le Renard pâle (The Pale Fox). Codirected by Germain Dieterlen. Unfinished. 1981.

Whereas in their earlier films, Rouch and Dieterlen had referred to Dogon myths in commenting upon the ritual events that they had filmed, in this film, their intention was to structure the film around one of the core Dogon myths concerning the trickster spirit, the Pale Fox, and the part that he played in the creation of the world. In 1981, Rouch reported that they had begun work on this project, but, like Griaule and Dieterlen's volume by the same name, it appears to have remained unfinished. *Sources*: Fulchignoni (1981), 26 and (2003), 179.

Songchamp-Dogon. 40 min. Assistant director: Philippe Costantini. 1982. Only available in a double-band version.

This film documents a conversation between Germaine Dieterlen and Enrico Fulchignoni about the Dogon, and the role of filmmaking in the relationships established with these people, first by Marcel Griaule, and later by Rouch and Dieterlen herself. *Sources*: Prédal (1996i), 224; Philippe Costantini, personal communication, October 2008.

Le Premier Matin du monde (The First Morning of the World). 1998.

The only information in the sources is that this film was shot in Mali. This fact, in combination with the title, suggests that it may deal with some aspect of Dogon cosmogony. *Source*: Feld (2003c), 383.

Personal Portrait Films, 1973–2002

*Taro Okamoto: Hommage à Marcel Mauss (Taro Okamoto: Homage to Marcel Mauss). 14 min. 1973 or 1974.

A portrait of the Japanese sculptor, Taro Okamoto, who was a student of Marcel Mauss at the École pratique des hautes études in Paris from 1930 to 1939. In this film, shot in his studio in Tokyo, the artist speaks about the influence of Mauss on his art, as well as on his way of thinking and living. *Sources*: Houdaille (1981), 64; Prédal (1996i), 221.

Paul Lévy: Hommage à Marcel Mauss (Paul Lévy: Homage to Marcel Mauss). 20 min. 1977.

As he comes out of the defence of a doctoral thesis at the Sorbonne, the sociologist and theologian Paul Lévy recalls his memories of Marcel Mauss. *Source*: Prédal (1996i), 223.

*Germaine Dieterlen: Hommage à Marcel Mauss (Germaine Dieterlen: Homage to Marcel Mauss). 20 min. 1977.

In the great circumcision shelter at Songo in the Bandiagara Escarpment, Germaine Dieterlen evokes the epic creation myths of the Dogon. Then at the site of the cave where the first inhabitants of Bongo took refuge, she leads a discussion about the architectural remains of previous human settlements. *Source*: Prédal (1996i), 223.

Ispahan: Lettre persane (Ispahan: A Persian Letter), alt.: *La Mosquée du chah à Ispahan (The Shah's Mosque at Ispahan)*. Additional camera: Hossein Taheridoust. 35 min. 1977.

Shot two years before the Iranian Islamic revolution brought about the fall of the Shah, and in the year in which Rouch was guest of honor at the Festival of Ethnographic Film in Isfahan, this film is based on a walking conversation between Rouch and the Iranian historian and cineaste Farouk Gaffary in the courtyard of what was then known as the Shah's Mosque. Rouch shot most of this conversation himself, though for certain parts, he passes the camera to an assistant, Hossein Taheridoust, who shows him talking to Gaffary. The two men discuss a wide range of topics such as the fact that in earlier periods of Islam it was possible to achieve communion with God through beauty. They also comment on the architecture of the mosque and the sentiment of calm that it inspires, even in those who are nonbelievers. They then sit down and discuss the ambiguous relationship that Islam has with cinematographic creativity and with sex, and also the fear of death on which both Christianity and Islam are based. *Sources*: Feld (2003c), 378; Françoise Foucault, personal communication, September 2008.

Ciné-portrait de Margaret Mead ("Margaret Mead: Portrait by a Friend"). 35 min. Sound: John Marshall, produced by Emilie de Brigard for DER and the American Museum of Natural History. 1978. Sound track in English.

Shot when Rouch was in New York for the film festival established in Mead's honor, this film shows her first in her office, then walking around the displays in the Pacific Hall, as she talks about her career as an anthropologist in response to questions by Rouch. Recording the sound is the leading North American ethnographic filmmaker, John Marshall. These scenes in the museum are mostly shot as a series of sequence-shots. Then Mead takes the filmmakers out into Central Park. On the way, they pass the grand equestrian statue of Teddy Roosevelt at the entrance to the museum. Marshall asks whether he should come down from his horse. "It's not a good horse," replies Mead evasively. In the Park, Rouch asks if she feels like a citizen of New York when she is there. Mead replies that she considers herself a citizen of the world, at home in a number of different places. After a pan off to Marshall in order to do a synchronising microphone tap, Rouch says goodbye and walks backward, leaving Mead as a small figure wearing a strange cape in the midst of Central Park.

Capt'ain Mori. 40 min. Sound: John Marshall. Sound track in English (?). 1980. Only available in a double-band version.

A portrait of the Japanese merchant marine captain who opened up the first commercial line between Japan and South Africa. This film was shot when Rouch was in Japan for a festival of films about the San "Bushmen," also attended by John Marshall, celebrated for his documentaries about these peoples of southern Africa. Mori describes his encounter with the South African writer, Laurens van der Post, who provided him with some protection from the racism institutionalized in the system of apartheid. This was the second of Rouch's portrait films for which John Marshall recorded the sound, the other being the Rouch's film about Margaret Mead, shot in 1978 and described above. *Sources*: Houdaille (1981), 64; Feld (2003c), 378.

Ciné-mafia. 33 min. Sound: Robert Busschots. Second unit camera and picture editing: Rogier Busschots. Second unit sound and picture editing: Dirk Nijland. Sound editing: Hans Panhuysen. Production: CFE and the Department of Anthropology, University of Leiden. 1980

This film was made on the occasion of Rouch being awarded the title of *doctor honoris causa* by the University of Leiden in May 1980 and consists of a conversation between himself, Henri Storck, and Joris Ivens in Katwijk an Zee, a small seaside village near Amsterdam where Ivens made his first and only fiction film, *Breakers*, in 1929. An intertitle at the beginning of the film, "Rencontre 1," indicates that this was supposed to be the first of several such meetings, though the subsequent meetings do not appear to have happened. Unusually for a film by Rouch, there are two independent units at work: Rouch himself, and another team recording Rouch recording the encounter. The sound recordist of this second unit was the leading Dutch visual anthropologist, Dirk Nijland, who appears in shot at one moment. The cameraman and editor of the second unit were the twin brothers Robert and Rogier Busschots. The conversation between the three members of the self-styled "ciné-mafia" starts outside the village church and then moves to a sort of seashore café, protected by glass screens from the wind. The conversation is initially intercut with extracts from their films, as they talk about how Storck and Ivens met, the world of avant-garde filmmaking in the 1930s, and the fact that all three of them made films about water. They compare their ages (Rouch was celebrating his sixty-third birthday that very day, Storck was seventy-two, and Ivens eighty-one) and discuss the inspiration that Robert Flaherty provided to all of them. They agree to meet again and to include Luc de Heusch, formerly Henri Storck's assistant. As in the Mead portrait, Rouch then leaves them walking backward, ending by panning off to the sea. This is possibly a cinematic reference to the shot that ends the walrus-hunting scene in *Nanook*, in which the mates of the captured walrus are shown watching from out at sea. *Source*: Nijland (2007c).

Portrait de Raymond Depardon. 10 min. Codirected by Philippe Costantini and Raymond Depardon with assistance from André Le Nôtre. Sound: Patrick Genet. Editing: Marie-Josèphe Yoyotte. Shot in 1983.

Based on a chance meeting late one afternoon in the Jardin des Tuileries in Paris, this film records an encounter between three cameramen-directors, Jean Rouch, Philippe Costantini, and the well-known photojournalist and occasional documentarist, Raymond Depardon. Each of the three filmmakers shows how he would film one of the female statues in the park. The film was cut by Marie-Josèphe Yoyotte who had first worked with Rouch on *Moi, un Noir* in the late 1950s. As a joke, Rouch added the name of André Le Nôtre, the seventeenth-century designer of the Jardin des Tuileries, to the film credits. *Source*: Philippe Costantini, personal communication, October 2008.

Hassan Fathi. 45 min. 1983. Editing incomplete.

This film is a portrait of the Egyptian architect Hassan Fathi who sought to develop an architectural style that drew on indigenous Egyptian models rather than models copied from the West. The second part of the film remains unedited. *Sources*: Prédal (1996i), 224; Feld (2003c), 384.

Germaine chez elle (*Germaine at home*) 35 min. Camera: Jérôme Blumberg. Sound: François Didiot. Editing: Françoise Beloux. Shot 1994. Only available in a double-band version.

Shot in her own apartment in Paris, this portrait of Germaine Dieterlen traces her career from its beginning in the Paris of the 1920s. It covers a wide range of topics, including her first encounters with jazz and with Marcel Griaule, her early work on the objects brought back by the Dakar-Djibouti expedition, her meeting with Marcel Mauss who encouraged her to engage in fieldwork, her discovery of Dogon country and the contribution of filmmaking to ethnographic research. *Source*: Philippe Costantini, personal communication, October 2008.

Germaine et ses copains (*Germaine and Her Pals*); alt: *Germaine dans la falaise* (*Germaine on the Bandiagara Escarpment*). 15 min. Editing: Françoise Beloux. Shot 1995–1996. Only available in a double-band version.

Shot at Sanga, the research base among the Dogon on the Bandiagara Escarpment which she had visited many times, this film shows Germaine Dieterlen meeting up again with her informants, Djamgouno and Pangalé, with whom she has worked for decades. It also evokes memories of her work with another informant, Amadigné Dolo, who as a very young boy had worked both with her and Marcel Griaule. *Source*: Philippe Costantini, personal communication, October 2008.

La Maison de Germaine (*Germaine's House*). 38 min. Camera: Jérôme Blumberg. Sound: François Didiot. Editing: Françoise Beloux. 1999.

In this film shot a few weeks after her death, Rouch offers an homage to Germaine Dieterlen in the company of an old friend of hers who frequently came to her house to play the piano. Rouch evokes her memory by drawing attention to various objects in the course of walking about her apartment with Brice Ahounou, who for a number of years, had been helping her to catalog her works. *Source*: Philippe Costantini, personal communication, October 2008.

Liberté, égalité: la thèse. Codirected by Bernard Surugue. Shot in 2001, released 2002.

A film made in homage to the late Théodore Monod following his death in 2000. *Source*: Surugue (2008), 292

Collaborative Films with Young Filmmakers, 1977–1997

Makwayela. 20 min. Codirected by Jacques d'Arthuys. 1977.

This is a teaching film that was made to demonstrate the technique of the sequence-shot to the students of the Institute of Cinema in Mozambique. It shows a group of workers from a bottling plant dancing and singing about their experiences as migrant laborers in the gold mines of South Africa. They denounce imperialism and apartheid in Barakolo, the miners' secret language. This would appear to be the same film as *Les chanteurs de la usine de bière de Maputo* (*Singers of the Maputo Brewery*), which was made during the first in a series of Super-8 workshops given by Rouch in Mozambique. These were organized by Jacques d'Arthuys in conjunction with the Mozambiqui Institute of Cinema and the French Ministry of Foreign Affairs. *Sources*: Houdaille (1981), 64; Diawara 1992:97–103; Philippe Costantini, personal communication, October 2008.

Enigma. 90 min. Codirection and script: Alberto Chiantaretto, Marco di Castri, Daniele Pianciola. Sound: Remo Ugolinelli, Stefano Savino. Editing: Françoise Beloux. Production: Kinowerke Cinema e Video, CNRS, INA, Commune de Torino, Regional Government of Piedmont and Fiat. 1986

A collaborative film made with a group of young Italian filmmakers and nonprofessional actors. The latter included Rouch's friends, the Swiss painter Gilbert Mazliah and the Dutch filmmaker Philo Bregstein. The story of the film begins when a wealthy patron of the arts invites a well-known forger, played by Mazliah, to paint a mural that the Italian Surrealist painter, Giorgio de Chirico had not managed to paint during his brief stay in Turin in 1911. Walking around the city in search of inspiration, the forger meets a group of children who want to go to Egypt in a submarine abandoned on the river Po. He then meets a philosopher, played by Bregstein, who recites Nietszchean texts from the summit of the famous Turin landmark building, the Mole Antoniella. He also meets an enigmatic young woman who turns out to be the wife of the patron of the arts. In the final scene, the forger manages to lure her away after presenting the forged de Chirico painting to her husband. Although this film began with a script written by Rouch's Italian collaborators, this was cast aside during the course of the production in favor of Rouch's improvisational methodology. *Sources*: Prédal (1996i), 225; Feld (2003c), 379–380; Bregstein (2007), 167.

Folie ordinaire d'une fille de Cham (*Ordinary Madness of a Daughter of Cham*). 79 min. Codirected by Philippe Costantini. Sound: Jean-Claude Brisson, Jean-Pierre Fénié. Editing: Françoise Beloux. Production: INA, RFO and CNRS. Shot in 1986, released 1987.

Based on a stage play by Julius-Amédé Laou, a young Caribbean writer, this film is structured around the presentation that a psychiatrist makes to his colleagues at a psychiatric hospital. This concerns the case of a woman who has been a patient in the hospital for more than fify years and who has come to believe that a newly arrived nurse from Martinique is her daughter. Having seen the original play at the theater, Rouch wanted to transfer this story to the famous psychiatric hospital of Sainte-Anne in Paris and shoot it there in real time, in the manner of *Gare du Nord* (see under "Parisian Films" above), but with the difference that there would be two cameras which would alternate so that it would never be necessary to stop the action. The playwright was enthusiastic, so Rouch asked Philippe Costantini, a young cameraman whose handheld shooting was very stable and who had worked with him on *Makwayela* (see above in this section) to shoot with a standard lens, while he himself provided more general cover with a wide-angle lens. In the event, they were not able to shoot in Sainte-Anne itself, but Rouch found another building of the same era and they used that instead. Their first attempt had to be abandoned when a lamp blew and the two principal actresses could not get back into character. They started again on the second day and although the intensity was not as great, this time they did manage to reach the end of the play. In the edit suite, however, they intercut the material from the two days. In doing so, Rouch discovered that whenever one cuts from a wide to a close shot, it is necessary to take out a few frames to recover synch. But although the film appears to have been a technical success, to Rouch's disappointment, the Institut National de l'Audiovisuel, who put up the money for the film, never arranged for it to be shown on television. *Sources*: Rouch (1996c); Prédal (1996i), 225; CNRS Videotheque, no. 706.

Bac ou mariage? (*Baccalauréat or Marriage?*). 70 min. Codirected by Fifi Tam-Sir Niane. Additional photography: Philippe Costantini. Sound: Jean-Claude Brisson. Editing: Françoise Beloux. Film script: Gérard Noyer and Fifi Tam-Sir Niane. Based on an original theatrical script by Djibril Tam-Sir Niane. Music: Irene Tassembedou. Production: La Fémis, INA, la Sept, les productions Philippe Dussart, the Senegalese Ministry of Culture and the French Ministry of Cooperation. 1988. Premièred at the Venice Film Festival, also shown at the Berlin Film Festival.

Rouch worked together with first-time director Tam-Sir Niane to create this film version of a popular Senegalese musical. Originally written as a theater play, Rouch shot it, handheld, on real locations in Senegal, as a series of sequence-shots of the actors performing various parts of the play without interruption. The film tells the story of Soukey, who, having just obtained her baccalauréat at her school in Dakar, learns that her parents have decided that in order to resolve the family's financial problems, she has been betrothed to an elderly man, already married, who is a very rich friend of her father's. Soukey's friends try to help her by arranging for the old duffer to be seduced by a very attractive young woman. Meanwhile, Soukey falls in love with Madou, who has recently graduated from the university. The situation is finally resolved when the father's friend is arrested for "financial irregularities." *Sources*: Prédal (1996i), 225; Dossou-Yovo (2003); Bregstein (2007), 172.

Boulevard d'Afrique (African Boulevard). Codirected by Fifi Tam-Sir Niane. 1989.

Prédal describes this film as being about the Ballets Africains, the troupe of Fifi Tam-Sir Niane, dancing in the streets of Paris (Prédal 1996i:225). However in some sources, this title, in the plural, *Boulevards d'Afrique*, is given as an alternative title for *Bac ou mariage?* See, for example, http://movies.nytimes .com/movie/120399/Boulevards-d-Afrique/overview.

Faire-part (The Announcement). 18 min. Camera: Jérôme Blumberg. Sound: François Didiot. Produced by GREC-CNRS and Fémis. Shot in July 1997 and screened at the Venice Festival later in the same year.

This film traces the history of cinema as conceived and presented by Henri Langlois in the Musée du Cinéma in the other wing of the Palais de Chaillot, across the small plaza from the Musée de l'Homme in Place du Trocadéro. Made in a single afternoon, in collaboration with a two-person film crew but with Rouch improvising a commentary, the film consists of five sequence-shots of ten minutes' duration. Two weeks later the Musée du Cinéma was devastated by fire, thus making this film the final testimony to Langlois' masterwork. This is reflected in the title of the film, which alludes to the obituary announcement, known as a *faire-part*, that is traditionally made in France when a member of the local community has died. *Source*: Feld (2003c), 382–383.

Later "Film-Poems" and "Promenades Inspirées," 1985–1998

Cousin-cousine, pirogue-gondole (Two Cousins—the Canoe and the Gondola). Editor: Françoise Beloux. 20 min. 1985. Only available in a double-band version.

This film appears to have been made while Rouch was attending the Venice Film Festival in 1984 to present his feature film *Dionysos*. It shows Damouré Zika and the ethnolinguist and filmmaker Mariama Hima, another of Rouch's Nigerien friends (later to become the ambassador of Niger in Paris), as they travel around Venice in a gondola. The original idea was to follow this up with a second shoot in Niger, in which they would be shown traveling on the river

Niger in a traditional pirogue, though this second part of the films was never made. *Sources*: Prédal (1996i), 224; Philippe Costantini, personal communication, September 2008.

Bateau-givre (Ice Ship). 35 min. 16mm enlarged to 35mm. Sound recording and sound editing: Patrick Genet. Picture editing: Jean Ravel. Music: Luc Ferrari. Production coordinator: Pascal-Emmanuel Gallet for the French Ministry of Foreign Affairs and the Swedish Film Institute. Shot in 1985–1986, released in 1987.

This film formed part of a trilogy of films, which were shot on board the Swedish ice-breaker *Frej*, and which were originally made for television under the collective title, *Brise-glace (Icebreaker)*. Rouch was one of three filmmakers (the others were Tittle Törnroth and Raúl Ruiz) who were invited to spend a couple of weeks on board the *Frej* and make a film on a subject of their choice. The proposal had a particular attraction for Rouch because his father had been a polar expeditionary. Although he shot it handheld in his customary manner and the film was cut by Jean Ravel, who many years earlier had worked on *Chronicle of Summer*, in other respects the film represents something of a break with Rouch's past practice in that there is no voice-over, nor any significant dialogue, but rather a mosaic of colors and shapes. It also features a complex stereophonic sound track recorded and later mixed by Patrick Genet. The film makes no attempt to explain the technical process of ice-breaking but simply shows the crew going about their work (they speak, but there is no subtitling) while the ship makes its way through the vast natural splendor of the ice. *Sources*: Prédal (1996g), (1996i) 225; Villain (1991) 87.

Couleur du temps: Berlin août 1945 (Color of Time: Berlin, August 1945). 10 min. Editing: Françoise Beloux. Production: Télé Image.1988.

In August 1945, when he entered Berlin as a lieutenant in the French Special Forces Armoured Division, Rouch wrote a memoir that was published shortly afterward in *Fontaine*, a Parisian arts magazine edited by Jean Cocteau. The title of the memoir, *Le Couleur du temps*, is a reference to the work of the poet Guillaume Apollinaire, who wrote a play in verse with this title that was published posthumously in 1918. Rouch's memoir was, in effect, his first film script, since he used it as the basis for the narration of this film, made some forty-three years later on the occasion of the inauguration of the French television channel, *La Sept*. *Sources*: Prédal (1996i), 225; Taylor (2003), 135; Feld (2003c), 380.

Promenade inspirée (The Inspired Walk). 30 min. Sound: François Didiot. 1989.

At the Fondation Maeght Museum in Saint-Paul-de-Vence, not far from Nice, in the South of France, Rouch lives out a dream in exploring a most beautiful collection of African art. *Source*: Prédal (1996i), 225.

Le Beau Navire (The Beautiful Vessel). 4 min. 1990.

This film was made in homage to the Eiffel Tower on the occasion of its hundredth anniversary. The title is an allusion to a poem of the same name by Baudelaire celebrating the beauty of a young woman, whose voluminous skirts remind the poet of a ship setting sail. Rouch invokes a similar analogy in relation to the Eiffel Tower as the poem is recited over a series of nighttime images of the tower, specially illuminated for the 1989 bicentenary celebrations of the French Revolution. *Source:* Thompson (2007), 185–186.

En une poignée des mains amies (Upon a Handshake between Friends). 35 min. Co-directed by Manoel de Oliveira. Camera: Jérôme Blumberg. Sound: François Didiot. Shot in 1996, screened at various festivals in 1997.

While enjoying a glass of vintage port on the banks of the river Douro in Porto, northern Portugal, Rouch agrees with his friend, the veteran filmmaker Manoel de Oliveira, that the bridge designed by Gustave Eiffel before he became famous for his tower in Paris, is the greatest work of modern architecture in the city. In less than five minutes, Manoel writes a poem and over the course of the next week, they realize their childhood dreams by travelling along the banks of the Douro on foot, by car, and in a helicopter. Amid the clouds, Rouch and de Oliveira declaim verses of a poem inspired by the wind, water, and friendship. *Source:* Feld (2003c), 382.

Faire-part (The Announcement). 18 min. Shot and released in1997.

See under "Collaborative Films with Young Filmmakers, 1977–1997" above.

Ciné-poèmes sur Paris (Ciné-poems on Paris). 18 min. Codirected by Sandro Franchina. 1998.

Originally commissioned by Jean-Michel Arnold, a senior figure in the audiovisual section of the CNRS, Rouch shot these "ciné-poems" in collaboration with Sandro Franchina, the Italian director and screenwriter best known for his documentary biographies of modern artists and sculptors. Like Arnold, Franchina was a former assistant of Henri Langlois. He had also been an assistant to Rouch in Paris in the early 1960s. Together, Rouch and Franchina made three films based on poems written in 1901 and 1902 by Franchina's maternal great-grandfather, the French Symbolist poet Paul Fort. *Sources:* Feld (2003c), 383; also the archives of the Torino Film Festival available at http://www2 .kwcinema.kataweb.it/torinofilmfestival/archivio.

Dalarou-Dalarouta Ethnofictions, 1954–2002

If one excludes what appear to have been a couple of false starts, Rouch collaborated with Damouré Zika and Lam Ibrahim Dia in the production of seven feature-length ethnofictions over a forty-eight-year period. By the time of the third in the series, *Cocorico! Monsieur Poulet*, released in 1975, the name DALAROU, an amalgam of the first syllable of all their names, begins to appear in the film credits. Later, as Tallou Mouzourane, a Bella shepherd and Rouch's "adopted son," took over from the Sorko fisherman, Illo Gaoudel, as the third of the "musketeers," the name was expanded to DALAROUTA. This composite name is reminiscent of the name "Jean Pierjant" that Rouch and his companions Pierre Ponty and Jean Sauvy adopted to file their journalistic reports while on their expedition down the Niger in 1946–1947. In both cases, the practice suggests Rouch's willingness to share the authorship of his works.

Jaguar. 88 min. Mostly shot 1954–1955. Final version released 1969 or 1970. See under "Migration Studies, 1954–1970" above.

Petit à Petit. 92 min. Shot 1967–1968. Released in various versions 1969–1971. See under "Parisian Films: The New Wave and After, 1960–1971" above.

Cocorico! Monsieur Poulet ("*Cock-a-Doodle-Doo, Mr. Chicken*"). 93 min. Les Films de l'Homme and DALAROU, with technical assistance from CNRSH (Niamey) and SCC (Paris). Sound: Moussa Hamidou and Hama Soumana. Editing: Christine Lefort. Music by Tallou Mouzourane. Production: Idrissa Maïga. First released in 1974 or 1975. Rereleased in DVD with optional English subtitles by Éditions Montparnasse, 2007.

The idea for this film was inspired by Lam's real-life job at the time as a poultry dealer. This consisted of travelling around the countryside in a decrepit 2CV Citröen van, buying up chickens and then re-selling them in the market at Niamey. The story begins when Lam and his assistant, played by Tallou Mouzourane, meet up with a "businessman," played by Damouré, who wants to join them. However, their enterprise is constantly undermined, partly because the van keeps breaking down, and partly because Damouré falls under the spell of a female "devil," played by a stewardess whom Rouch happened to meet. Another problem is that the van has no papers, so they cannot pass over the Niger River by the bridge, which is controlled by the police. They therefore have to float the van across, which they do in three different ways. Eventually, the "devil" releases Damouré from the spell, and they do manage to buy some chickens. As a poultry epidemic has broken out, the bridge has been closed to all other suppliers, and the three heroes, with their amphibious strategy, are the only ones who can get their chickens to the Niamey market. Given that chickens are now in very short supply, they are able to sell theirs for a very high price. *Source*: CNRS Videotheque, no. 589.

Babatou, les trois conseils (*Babatou and the Three Wise Counsels*). 92 min. Co-directed with Boubou Hama. Additional camera: Moustapha Alassane. Sound: Moussa Hamidou. Editing: Christine Lefort. Music: Dyeliba Badye and Daouda Kante. Association des cinéastes nigériens. Shot 1975–1976, released 1977.

This was the first feature film produced by the Association des cineastes ni-gériens and was very low-budget. The script was written by Boubou Hama, a leading Nigerien literary figure, educator, and politician, though this "script" was nothing more than a story line as most of the actors were illiterate. The film is set in the middle of the nineteenth century and relates the adventures of the shepherd Lam and his best friend, the hunter Damouré, who, accom-panied by two servants, including Tallou, go to seek their fortune by joining the slave-raiding expeditions of Babatou, a Gurunsi warlord and a real his-torical personage. However, Damouré is killed and after eight years, Lam re-turns to his village with very little of genuine value to show for his efforts, other than three pieces of advice offered by a wise elder in exchange for a slave girl: don't pass a village at night, don't cross a river in spate, never act in anger at night—wait until morning. Arriving home at night, Lam discovers a man sleeping next to his wife, but remembering the third counsel, decides to wait until morning before doing anything. In the morning, it is revealed that his presumed rival is his own son, whom he had not recognized because the son had become an adult in his absence. Although he encourages his son also to go to war, the film ends with Lam reflecting on all the misfortune brought by his involvement in warfare. The feats of Babatou are still remembered in Ni-gerien praise-songs to this day, but the film was intended as a denunciation of warfare and, as such, it was not appreciated by the dictator General Seyni Kountché, who came to power in Niger by means of a coup that took place while the film was still in production. *Sources*: Prédal (1996e); Feld (2003c), 375–376; Bregstein (2007), 166.

Les Deux Chasseurs (The Two Hunters). 1981. Unfinished.

In the manner of *Babatou* (see above) and involving the usual cast list of Damouré, Lam, and Tallou, this unfinished film was based on a historical sub-ject and revolved around a story about two men who claimed to be great hunt-ers but who in fact were tellers of tall tales. *Sources*: Houdaille (1981), 64; Brice Ahounou, personal communication, September 2008.

*Madame L'Eau. 103/120/125 min. Assisted by Philo Bregstein. Sound: Moussa Hamidou. Editing: Françoise Beloux. Production: NF1 (Netherlands)/ SODAPERAGA/BBC. Released 1992. Awarded the International Peace Prize at the Berlin Film Festival, 1993.

Originally based on an idea put to Rouch by his friend, the Dutch film-maker Philo Bregstein this film features Damouré, Lam, and Tallou. They play farmers ruined by drought who decide to go to Holland to discover whether Dutch windmill technology might provide a cheap and technologically appro-priate solution to their water irrigation problems. After touring around Hol-land in the company of Bregstein and the Dutch visual anthropologist Dirk Nijland in a "Jaguar" car (actually a large white Cadillac convertible), driven by the beautiful Winneke, they bring Frans, a Dutch windmill engineer, back to Niger. Here Frans assembles the simple prefabricated windmill that he has invented. This proves to be an immediate success, and the Nigerien farmers are able to irrigate their lands. Clearly intended as a parable about the relations between the North and South, and as an implicit criticism of the overly complex technological solutions to economic development that are so often lead to failure and dependency—"poisonous gifts," as Rouch once referred to them—the making of this film was documented in the film *Rouch's Gang* (1993), directed by Steef Meyknecht, Dirk Nijland, and Joost Verhey. This companion film was well received, but *Madame L'Eau* itself got very mixed notices: although it was awarded a prize at the Berlin Film Festival, the tone of reviews was rarely more than respectfully lukewarm. *Sources*: C. Piault (1996), 147; Bregstein (2007).

Moi fatigué debout, moi couché (*I'm Tired of Standing, I Lie Down*). 90 minutes. Assisted by Mahmoud Maiga, Brice Ahounou. Music: Hamidou Godyé. Editing: Françoise Beloux, François Didiot. Joint production with the Centre Culturel Franco-Nigerien in Niamey. Screened at various film festivals in 1997.

The principal "star" of this film is an acacia tree that has been struck by lightning, with the result that some of its branches are lying on the ground. According to local belief, if one dreams beneath such a tree, those dreams will come true. Clearly inspired by his youthful interest in Surrealism, this provides the cue for Rouch and his Nigerien friends to set off on various adventures to turn dreams into reality, assisted by Dongo, the Spirit of Thunder, and his mother, Harakoy Dikko, the spirit who governs the waters of the Niger River, as well as by Gaoberi, the talking spirit of the acacia tree itself. *Source*: Feld (2003c), 382.

Les Vaches merveilleuses (*The Wondrous Cows*). In production, 1997–1999.

This project arose from an idea proposed by Lam Ibrahim Dia, who died in 1997. It was based on Lam's encounter, while travelling through Sokoto State in northwest Nigeria in 1948 as a very young man, with a herd of hornless white cattle. Some preliminary scenes are shown being shot in *Mosso mosso*, a film about Rouch in the field made by the *Cahiers du Cinéma* critic, Jean-André Fieschi, and released in 1997. The project was reported by Feld (2003:383) as being still in production in 1999. However, it was never completed as a freestanding film and appears to have been incorporated instead into *Le rêve plus fort que la mort* (see below, also Surugue 2007:16).

Le rêve plus fort que la mort (*The Dream More Powerful than Death*). 88 min. Co-directed by Bernard Surugue. Camera: Gérard de Battista, Djingarey Maïga, Bernard Surugue. Sound: Moussa Hamidou. Editing: Françoise Beloux, François Didiot. Production: AMIP, IRD, CNRS Images, CNC, CFE, Clea Productions. Released 2002.

This was Rouch's last completed film and was made with the assistance of

Bernard Surugue and other cameramen, as he was no longer physically capable of handling the camera. It is based on a dream that the recently deceased Lam Ibrahim Dia had once had that he was stronger than death. This idea is explored in the film through three more specific dreams. In the first, Damouré Zika returns from Ghana in a convertible sports car, once again the "Jaguar" showing off his wealth, though now things have changed in his home country: the Niger River has become unpredictable and the Muslim ritual specialists, the marabouts, have forbidden animal sacrifices. In the second dream, a rehearsal of Aeschylus's play *The Persians,* led by the theater director Philippe Brunet, provokes the ethnologist and Hellenist scholar Dioulde Zaya to dream of the connections between ancient Greece and the Songhay empire, an association reinforced by the intercutting of scenes from the play with sequences of Songhay spirit possession. In the third dream, Tallou Mouzourane, who has spent a lifetime as the late Lam's cattlehand, finally takes over from him, leading a herd of hornless cattle with startlingly white hides. In the midst of the herd, Tallou begins to sing, calling upon the spirit of the deceased Lam, who thanks his "father" Jean Rouch for having come to meet him and his cattle. The spirits of the Niger River are then invoked by music on the single string *godye* violin performed by the Songhay ritual specialist, Hamidou Yayé, by then already over a hundred years old. *Sources*: Surugue (2007), 16–17; Bregstein (2007), 168; CNRS Videotheque, no. 1105.

Other Fiction Films, 1957–1990

Moi, un Noir (Me, a Black Man). 73 min. Shot 1957, released 1960.
    See under "Migration Studies, 1954–1970" above.

La Pyramide humaine (The Human Pyramid). 88 min. Shot 1959–1960, released 1961.
    See under "Migration Studies, 1954–1970" above.

La Punition (The Punishment). 58 min. Shot 1960, first released 1963.
    See under "Parisian Films: The New Wave and After, 1960–1971" above.

Gare du Nord. 17 min. Shot in 1964, released in 1965.
    See under "Parisian Films: The New Wave and After, 1960–1971" above.

Les Veuves de quinze ans (Widows at 15) alt.: *Marie-France et Véronique (Marie-France and Véronique)*. 24 min. Shot in 1964, released in 1966.
    See under "Parisian Films: The New Wave and After, 1960–1971" above.

Dionysos. 104 min. Additional camera: Philippe Costantini. Lighting: Antoine Georgeakis. Sound: Gérard Delassus. Script: Jean Rouch, Euzhan Palcy and others. Editing: Marie-Josèphe Yoyotte. Films du Jeudi/Antenne 2/CNRS. 1984.

This film demonstrated that Rouch's interest in the imaginary, first stirred by his encounter with Surrealism in the 1930s, was still running strongly some fifty years later. A preliminary scene in the Bois de Meudon, in which Rouch, on a bicycle, is surprised by three lightly clad Maenads, female followers of Dionysos, Greek god of nature, madness, and wine, establishes that the imaginary is still alive in modern society. In the first half of the film, Hugh Gray, in real life the American translator of the works of André Bazin, but here played by the French Amazonist anthropologist Jean Monod, defends his thesis at the Sorbonne before a committee featuring Germaine Dieterlen, Enrico Fulchignoni and Jean Sauvy, Rouch's old comrade from the 1946–1947 Jeanpierjant expedition. Gray's thesis involves the interpretation of the works of the painter de Chirico through the ideas of Nietzsche and an argument concerning the need for industrial societies to remain open to mythological forms of thinking. So successful is he in presenting these ideas that the committee finds itself within a de Chirico painting while African spirit possession cult dancers appear and become involved in the award of the diploma.

In the second part, Gray has become the head of an *atelier* where black and white workers (played by musicians rather than actual workers), working in harmony, construct Citroën 2CVs, but with a difference, turning one into a sacrificial bull in the workshop itself, and then creating a second carnavalesque 2CV in the form of a "perfumed panther" back in the Bois de Meudon. Linking the two halves of the film is a sequence set in the elevator in the Eiffel Tower in which Gray holds out a mirror to Rouch and asks him "Are you happy?" "Certainly," he replies, "this is ciné-pleasure." Rouch appears again in the last sequence of the film, after it transpires that the main character is not actually Hugh Gray, but an impostor, perhaps the god Dionysos himself. As this character disappears into the woods, exclaiming, "The god Pan is not dead," Rouch cycles off, declaring that he too "will continue to chase the imaginary through space and the passage of the seasons." Rouch was very proud of this film, and saw it as intimately connected with his ethnographic work. According to Jean Sauvy, he may even have seen it as the crowning achievement of his entire oeuvre, bringing together many different themes and many different people with whom he had worked over the years. But though the eminent philosopher Gilles Deleuze singled it out for particular praise, other normally sympathetic commentators subjected it to a severe critical mauling. *Sources*: Prédal (1996f); Walter (1996); Sauvy (2006), 193–213; Bregstein (2007), 166–167.

Enigma. 90 min. 1986.
See under "Collaborative Films with Young Filmmakers, 1977–1997" above.

Folie ordinaire d'une fille de Cham (Ordinary Madness of a Daughter of Cham). 79 min. Shot 1986, released 1987.
See under "Collaborative Films with Young Filmmakers, 1977–1997" above.

Bac ou mariage? (*Baccalaureat or Marriage?*).70 min. Released in 1988.

See under "Collaborative Films with Young Filmmakers, 1977–1997" above.

*Liberté, égalité, fraternité—et puis après? (*Freedom, Equality, Fraternity—And Then What?*). 95 min., alt.: *Cantate pour deux généraux* (*Cantatas for Two Generals*), 60 min. Produced by the Mission du Bicentenaire de la Révolution and SODAPERAGA. Shot 1989, released 1990.

This film was comissioned by the committee set up by the French government to celebrate the bicentenary of the French Revolution. Rouch's response was to ask two Black actors (one of whom was Brice Ahounou of the Comité du film ethnographique) to dress in eighteenth-century costume and speak to the professional actors playing historical personages in the official pageant about the possibilities for abolishing slavery after the Revolution. The second half of the film features a performance of a Haitian voudou ritual at night on the Champ de Mars with, in the background, the splendidly lit Hôtel des Invalides, where Napoleon's remains lie in pomp. This ritual event, which includes the cutting of the throat of a black cockerel, is presented as an attempt to reconcile the spirit of Toussaint-Louverture, the hero of the Haitian Revolution of 1791, with that of Napoleon, who as emperor, arrested the Haitian, brought him to France in 1802 and then threw him into prison, where he died a year later. A shorter version of the film with the alternative title, *Cantate pour deux généraux* was shown at the Berlin Film Festival in 1990. *Source*: Prédal (1996h).

Jean Rouch's Films by Year and Category, 1946–2002

Compilation films and some very minor works are not included. All years are approximate and many titles are abbreviated. Where release dates are very much later than production, this is indicated in brackets below the title. Some films appear twice because they can be classed under more than one genre.

	Descent of Niger, 1946–47	Doctoral Research, 1948–52	Migration Studies, 1954–70	Later Ethnographic Films (Niger), 1958–79	Other Ethnographic Films (W. Africa), 1954–71	Other Films (W. Africa), 1957–74
1946	*Au pays des mages noirs*					
1947						
1948		*Hombori.* *Circoncision.*				
1949		*Magiciens de Wanzerbé.* *Initiation à la danse . . .*				
1950		*Cimetières dans la falaise.*				
1951						
1952		*Les Gens du mil.* *Yenendi: les hommes qui font la pluie.* *Bataille sur le grand fleuve.*				
1953						
1954			*Les Maîtres fous.*		*Mammy Water (rel. 1966)*	
1955			*Jaguar (rel. 1970).*			
1956						
1957			*Moi, un Noir. (rel. 1960)*		*Moro Naba (rel.1959)*	*Baby Ghana*
1958						
1959				*La Chasse au lion à l'arc (shot 1958-1965, rel.1965.*	*Sakapata (rel. 1963)*	
1960			*La Pyramide humaine*	*Hampi (shot 1960, rel. 1965).*		

New Wave Period and After, 1960–71	Dogon Films, 1950–82	Personal Portrait Films, 1973–2002	Collaboration with Young Filmmakers, 1977–97	Late Film-poems 1985–98	Dalarouta Ethnofictions, 1954–2002	Other Fiction Films, 1957–90
	Cimetières dans la falaise					
					Jaguar (rel. 1970)	
						Moi, un Noir (rel. 1960)
Chronicle of a Summer. *La Punition*						*La Pyramide humaine*

Year	Descent of Niger, 1946–47	Doctoral Research, 1948–52	Migration Studies, 1954–70	Later Ethnographic Films (Niger), 1958–79	Other Ethnographic Films (W. Africa), 1954–71	Other Films (W. Africa), 1957–74
1961						Niger, jeune république.
1962					M. Albert prophète	Les Ballets du
1963						Niger.
1964				La Chasse au lion à l'arc (shot 1958-1965, rel.1965). Hampi (shot 1960, rel. 1965).		Festival à Dakar. Afrique et la recherche scientifique Rose et Landry.
1965			La Goumbé des jeunes noceurs			
1966				Dongo Horendi. Gamkallé. Koli koli.	Fêtes de novembre à Bregbo	
1967			Royale goumbé	Daouda Sorko. Faran Maka		
1968				Fonda. Wanzerbé. Yenendi de Ganghel (rel.1975). Un lion . . . Américain (rel.1970/2).		
1969					Porto Novo. (rel. 1971)	
1970				Yenendi de Yantalla. Taway Nya.		
1971				Architectes ayorou. Yenendi de Simiri. Tambours d'avant.		Rapports mères-enfants
1972				Tanda singui. Horendi.		
1973				Dongo hori. Sécheresse à Simiri. Bukoki.		VW voyou. Le Foot-giraffe.
1974				Pam kuso kar.		La 504.

New Wave Period and After, 1960–71	Dogon Films, 1950–82	Personal Portrait Films, 1973–2002	Collaboration with Young Filmmakers, 1977–97	Late Film-poems, 1985–98	Dalarouta Ethnofictions, 1954–2002	Other Fiction Films, 1957–90
La Punition						La Punition
Gare du Nord. Les Veuves de quinze ans.	Batteries dogon. (rel. 1966)					Gare du Nord. Les Veuves de quinze ans.
	Sigui: année zero					
Petit à Petit (final rel. 1971)	Sigui 1: Enclume de Yougou				Petit à Petit (final rel. 1971)	
	Sigui 2: Danseurs de Tyogou.					
	Sigui 3: Caverne de Bongo					
	Sigui 4: Clameurs d'Amani					
	Sigui 5: Dune d'Idyeli					
	Sigui 6: Pagnes de Yamé. Funérailles à Bongo (rel. 1979).					
	Enterrement du Hogon					
	Sigui 7: L'Auvent. Dama d'Ambara (rel. 1980).	Taro Okamoto			Cocorico! Monsieur Poulet. Babatou, les trois conseils	

	Descent of Niger, 1946–47	Doctoral Research, 1948–52	Migration Studies, 1954–70	Later Ethnographic Films (Niger), 1958–79	Other Ethnographic Films (W. Africa), 1954–71	Other Films (W. Africa), 1957–74
1975				*Souna kouna.* *Initiation.* *Zomo et ses frères.*		
1976				*La Grande Sécheresse. Faba tondi.*		*Médecines et médecins*
1977				*Fêtes de Gandyi Bi.* *Le Griot Badyé.*		
1978						
1979				*Simiri siddo kuma.*		
1980						
1981						
1982						
1983						
1984						
1985						
1986						
1987						
1988						
1989						
1990						
1991						
1992						*Damouré parle du SIDA*
1993						
1994						
1995						
1996						
1997						
1998						

New Wave Period and After, 1960–71	Dogon Films, 1950–82	Personal Portrait Films, 1973–2002	Collaboration with Young Filmmakers, 1977–97	Late Film-poems, 1985–98	Dalarouta Ethnofictions, 1954–2002	Other Fiction Films, 1957–90
						Babatou, les trois conseils
		Germaine Dieterlen. Paul Lévy. Ispahan.	*Makwayela*			
		Margaret Mead.				
		Capt'ain Mori. Ciné-mafia.				
		Raymond Depardon				
	Songchamp-Dogon					
		Hassan Fathi				
						Dionysos
				Cousin-cousine. Bateau-givre.		
		Enigma. Fille de Cham.				*Enigma. Fille de Cham.*
		Bac ou mariage?		*Couleur du temps.*		*Bac ou mariage?*
		Boulevard d'Afrique.		*Promenade inspirée.*		*Liberté, égalité, fratnernité*
				Le Beau Navire.		
					Madame L'Eau	
		Germaine chez elle				
		Germaine et ses copains				
			Faire-part	*Poignée des mains amies. Faire-part.*	*Moi fatigué, moi debout*	
				Ciné-poèmes.		

	Descent of Niger, 1946–47	Doctoral Research, 1948–52	Migration Studies, 1954–70	Later Ethnographic Films (Niger), 1958–79	Other Ethnographic Films (W. Africa), 1954–71	Other Films (W. Africa), 1957–74
1999						
2000						
2001						
2002						

New Wave Period and After, 1960–71	Dogon Films, 1950–82	Personal Portrait Films, 1973–2002	Collaboration with Young Filmmakers, 1977–97	Late Film-poems 1985–98	Dalarouta Ethnofictions, 1954–2002	Other Fiction Films, 1957–90
		Maison de Germaine				
		Liberté, égalité: la thèse			*Le rêve plus fort que la mort*	

Films about Jean Rouch and His Nigerien Associates

Jean Rouch and/or his Nigerien associates have been the subject of a large number of documentaries and filmed interviews, of which those listed below are no more than a selection. All films in the list are in color unless otherwise indicated. When directors' names are italicized, their films are referred to in this book.

Boussat, Marc-Arnaud (1997) Jean Rouch: paroles données. 15 min.

Boutang, Pierre-André (2004) Jean Rouch raconte à Pierre-André Boutang. 104 min. Prod.: IRD. Rereleased on DVD by Éditions Montparnasse in 2005.

Bregstein, Philo (1978) Jean Rouch and his Camera in the Heart of Africa. 75 min. Produced in collaboration with Dutch television, rereleased in 1986.

Brismée, Jean and André Delvaux (1962) Jean Rouch. Black and white. 50 min. Television series, 5 episodes. Prod.: Radio Télévision Belge Francophone (RTBF).

Cuello, Caroline (2004) Jean Rouch vu par . . . Prod: Nova Productions.

Donada, Julien and Guillaume Casset (1993) L'inventaire de Jean Rouch. 32 min.

Bergala, Alain (2005) Notes sur *Chronique d'un été*. 'Complément de programme' on the DVD version of *Chronique d'un été*. Prod: Argos Films and ARTE France.

Costantini, Philippe (2004) Jean Rouch et Germaine Dieterlen: L'avenir du souvenir. 52 min. Prod: AMIP, France5.

de Heusch, Luc (1983) Tracking the Pale Fox: studies on the Dogon 1931–1983. 48 min. Prod.: Le Centre de l'Audio-visuel à Bruxelles and RTBF in association with the CNRS and La Fondation belge pour les recherches anthropologiques (FOBRA).

Diawara, Manthia (1995) Rouch in Reverse. 52 min. Prod.: California Newsreel.

Dubosc, Dominique (1991) Jean Rouch, premier film: 1947–1991. Black and white and color. 26 min. Prod.: Kinofilm. Rereleased on DVD by Kinofilm (EDV 1488) 2006.

Fieschi, Jean-André (1997) Mosso Mosso, Rouch comme si. 73 min. Prod.: AMIP

Fulchignoni, Enrico (1982) Jean Rouch commente—entretiens avec Enrico Fulchignoni. Prod.: CNRS-CFE. Rereleased on DVD by Éditions Montparnasse in 2007.

Gardner, Robert (2004) Screening Room with Robert Gardner: Jean Rouch. 64 min. Prod.: Studio 7 Arts. Originally recorded in 1980.

Macintosh, Ann (2004) Conversation with Jean Rouch. 36 min. Prod. in collaboration with Documentary Educational Resources.

Madsen, Berit and Anne Mette *Jørgensen* (2005/2007) Friends, Fools, Family: Rouch's collaborators in Niger. First released in 2005 at 82 min.; rereleased in 2007 at 59 min. Prod.: Manche Film

Madsen, Berit and Anne Mette *Jørgensen* (2007) Damouré talks about Jaguar. 15 min. Prod.: Manche Film

Meyknecht, Steef, Dirk *Nijland* and Joost *Verhey* (1993) De Bende van Rouch (Rouch's Gang). 70 min. Prod.: MM Produkties.

Mosblech, Bernd (2008) Ich bin ein weisser Afrikaner: Abschied von Jean Rouch/ Je suis un Africain blanc: adieu à Jean Rouch. 55 min. Prod: Bernd Mosblech Filmproducktion/ SWR/ Arte.

Riolon, Luc and Bernard *Surugue* (2004) Le double d'hier a rencontré demain. Films de la Pléiade. Rereleased on DVD by Éditions Montparnasse in 2005.

Seligmann, Guy (1996) Les Dogon, chronique d'une passion (The Dogon—In Search of Sirius). 97 min. Prod.: ARTE/ SODAPERAGA. Rereleased on DVD by ARTE France in 2007.

Speckenbach, Jan (1995) A Few Minutes Jean Rouch. 39 min. Prod: Wagner and Taunus Television.

NOTES

Preface

1. Rouch (1965).

2. Jutra (1960), 32.

3. Since June 2006, it has been displaced in importance, most controversially, by the Musée Quai Branly, located on the opposite bank of the Seine, at the foot of the Eiffel Tower.

4. See htttp://www.ateliersvaran.com/presentation_origine.asp; Nijland (2007a), 33.

5. In this book, I use the term "Anglo-Saxon," as it is used in French texts, even those of an academic nature, to denote the British and all those who come from one of the major English-speaking former British colonies, that is, the United States, Canada, Ireland, southern Africa, and Australasia. In its most general usage, this classification does not take into account the personal cultural or ethnic affiliation of individuals, so someone who is, say, a Scottish Jew or an African American Black would also be Anglo-Saxon in this context. However, the meaning is also context-dependent, so in a more restricted context, such as a discussion of the population of the United States, a French author might well distinguish between "Anglo-Saxon" citizens, that is, those of British or northern European descent from those of Jewish or African American descent.

6. See appendix 1, pp. 366–367, for a more extended explanation of the term "double-band."

7. See Gauthier and Pellé (2000); also Nijland (2007a), 22, 24.

8. See http://www.comite-film-ethno.net/rouch/rouchbibli.htm for a comprehensive bibliography compiled by Laurent Pellé of the Comité du film ethnographique. See also the more select bibliography prepared by Steven Feld (2003d).

9. Thompson (1996), (2007).

10. Rouch's maternal uncles, Louis and Gustave Gain, were both distinguished explorers. Louis Gain, a biologist, was on the Charcot expedition, where his particular role was to study the penguins. It was through meeting Louis on this trip that Jules Rouch later got to know Jean's mother, Luce Gain. This was the basis for Jean's joke that he was "the child of the *Pourquoi Pas?*" (Taylor 2003:129; Merle des Isles 2005).

11. Fieschi and Téchiné (1967), 19

12. See Forbes (1996).

13. Gallet (1981).

14. Prédal (1982), 40; Bensmaïa (1996).

15. See, for example, Blue (1967); Freyer (1971); Roy-Leven (1996).

16. See Mundell (2004). This event underlined the fact that although Rouch's work is now much better known in Britain than it was at the height of his fame in France in the early 1960s, it remains primarily of interest to film scholars and visual anthropologists rather than to practicing film-makers.

17. M-H. Piault (1996), 48.

18. There are two different English-language translations of this essay. The one that I rely on in this book is by Paul Hockings and was published in the first edition of *Principles of Visual Anthropology* in 1975. However, the previous year, an entirely different translation of this article by Steven Feld and Marielle Delorme appeared in the first volume of *Studies in the Anthropology of Visual Communication* (Rouch 1974). In both cases, the translators chose to render the original French title, *La Caméra et les hommes* as "The Camera and Man," though in these more gender-aware days, it would perhaps be more appropriately translated as "The Camera and Humanity." It was not until 1979 that the article finally appeared in French, in a collection edited by Claudine de France (Rouch 1979). It appeared again in French, in a somewhat abbreviated form, in both the special editions of *CinémAction* edited by René Prédal. Both English-language versions have also subsequently been republished, Hockings's in the second edition of *Principles of Visual Anthropology* (Rouch 1995a) while the translation by Feld and Delorme appeared again in the recent collection of Rouch-related literature edited by Feld (Rouch 2003a).

19. For a list of the films available in English-language versions, see appendix 1, pp. 369–370.

20. Stoller has also written a number of other books about this region that provide a more general context for Rouch's films. These include Stoller (1989a), (1989b), (1995), (1997), and (2005).

21. See Hennebelle (1982); Haffner (1996). The criticism of Rouch's work by African filmmakers is discussed at some length in chapter 15.

Acknowledgments

1. These films have only recently been moved to the Centre national de Cinématographie (CnC) while the substantial collection of photographs and the paper archive associated with them have been moved to the Bibliothèque nationale de France (BnF).

2. Further details about the distribution of Jean Rouch's films are given in appendix 1, pp. 369–370.

Chapter One

1. Taylor (2003), 143.

2. Rouch (2003d), 103–104.

3. *Boutang* (2004); Sauvy (2006), 40–42.

4. Rouch (1997d), 207, (2003d), 104–106.

5. See Stoller (1992), 48–62.

6. Laurent Pellé, personal communication, March 2007. See also Masquelier (1993).

7. Rouch (1989), 19–28.

8. The number of laborers killed seems to have been subject to some inflation over time. In the 1970s, Rouch routinely referred to ten victims. By 1995, they had become "a dozen." Yet in his book, published in 1989 and based on his thesis drafted in the early 1950s, he states that there were only three. The exact date of the event in these various

sources also ranges from June to August 1942 (compare, for example, Rouch 1989, 242; Rouch 1995b, 222; Rouch 1995c, 418; and Rouch 2003d, 106).

9. The article "Aperçu sur l'animisme Sonrai" was published in *Notes Africaines* 20 (October 1943): 4–8. It was republished in 1997 (Rouch 1997b).

10. Rouch (2003d), 104–108; Sauvy (2006), 64–98.

11. Rouch (1989), 10, (2003d), 110.

12. Piault (2000), 114–116; *Seligmann* (1996).

13. Taylor (2003), 143.

14. This intellectualist tradition has been passed down over several generations of French anthropologists and in a variety of forms, not only through Griaule, but also through Claude Lévi-Strauss and Louis Dumont. In the most recent period, this tradition finds expression in such varied contexts as Pierre Bourdieu's concept of the *habitus* (Bourdieu 1977) and Philippe Descola's analysis of ideas about the relationship between nature and culture (Descola 2005).

15. James Clifford has suggested that this may be linked to the fact that in Mauss's era, academic anthropologists rarely did fieldwork themselves but instead relied on information gathered by missionaries, colonial officials, and the like (Clifford 1988a, 63).

16. Dieterlen (1988), 252.

17. Clifford (1988b), 123–125.

18. Dieterlen (1988). This book was first published in 1950 and was based on her own doctoral thesis.

19. Rouch (1989), 320–321.

20. The locus classicus for Malinowski's fieldwork method is the introduction to his *Argonauts of the Western Pacific,* first published in 1922. Although born and educated in Poland, Malinowski would still qualify as "Anglo-Saxon" in this context since he spent most of his academic career in the English-speaking world.

21. Douglas (1975), 139.

22. Rouch often refers to this visit as having taken place in August 1951 (see, e.g., Rouch 2003d, 112). However, it is clear from his photographic archive lodged at the Bibliothèque nationale that it actually took place in August 1950.

23. Rouch (2003d), 112. See also the first few pages of *Dieu d'eau* (1988, originally published in 1948), in which Griaule describes the scene as he and his three colleagues pursue their interrogatory investigations in the immediate vicinity of their field station at Sanga, first thing in the morning, on the day after their arrival.

24. See, for example Rouch (2003d), 111.

25. Rouch (1995b), 228; see also Taylor (2003), 140–141.

26. See Rouch (1956), 37.

27. Clifford (1988a), 77.

Chapter Two

1. Fieschi and Téchiné (1967), 19.

2. Mouëllic (2001).

3. See Jamin (1991), 84. The exact nature of the distinction between the terms *l'anthropologie* and *l'ethnologie* has changed over time in France. Until the 1930s, the term *l'anthropologie* was generally taken to designate the study of prehistory and what we would now call "biological" anthropology, while *l'ethnologie* designated the study of living and/or historically documented societies. But since the Second World War, as a term

for the discipline as a whole, *l'ethnologie* has been progressively displaced in France by *l'anthropologie sociale*, reflecting a change, championed notably by Claude Lévi-Strauss, that involved a movement away from cultural analysis in the Maussian manner toward a more sociological approach in the British tradition of social anthropology (though this was also French in origin in that it was initially largely inspired by a particular reading of the work of Durkheim). At the present time, the term "ethnology" would be considered rather anachronistic by most Anglo-Saxon anthropologists, who generally use instead the term "social anthropology" or, if they are from the United States, "cultural anthropology." In France, on the other hand, the term *l'ethnologie* continues to be widely used, without any negative connotations, to refer to work that goes beyond mere description—in making regional comparisons, for example—but that is not markedly theoretical. Meanwhile, the term "ethnography" continues to be widely used in both francophone and anglophone literature and is generally applied to texts that are primarily descriptive, though they may also involve some degree of theory, even if only by implication.

4. Rouch (1995b), 218.

5. Rouch (1989), 10; see also Price and Jamin (1988). Since its original appearance in 1934, *L'Afrique fantôme* has been republished several times, most recently in 2008 (see Leiris 2008).

6. Leiris (1930).

7. De Heusch (1995), 404.

8. Thompson (1995a), 9n.

9. Jamin (1991), 84–85; see also Price and Jamin (1988), 160–161; de Heusch (1995).

10. Griaule (1933b).

11. Rouch (1995c), 410.

12. Taylor (2003), 131–132; *Seligmann* 2006.

13. Rouch (1995c), 411–412.

14. Coeuroy and Schaeffner (1926); Jamin (1991), 87.

15. Clifford (1988b), 136. The legend is not entirely improbable since in his youth, Mauss had been a considerable athlete, from whence his interest in *techniques de corps*.

16. See Rouch (1995c), 415; and Mouëllic (2001), where Rouch specifically cites his first jazz experience as being the Armstrong concert in 1934. But in his 1990 interview with Lucien Taylor, he refers instead to the first concert that Duke Ellington and Louis Armstrong gave together in Paris "in 1941 or 1942" (Taylor 2003, 130). However, Marc Piault (pers. comm., September 2008) considers it very unlikely that African American jazzmen would have played in Paris during the Nazi occupation while Christopher Thompson (pers. comm., February 2009), on the basis of many conversations with Rouch, suggests that more important than these prewar or wartime jazz experiences for their influence on Rouch were his frequent postwar visits to clubs such as Le Lorientais (1946–1948), and from 1947, Le Bilboquet and Le Caveau de la Huchette.

17. Rouch (1995c), 415.

18. Mouëllic (2001).

19. See, for example, Char (2001).

20. In his memoirs, de Chirico is unflinching in his account of the shortcomings of the Surrealists. He describes Breton as "the classic type of pretentious ass and impotent *arriviste*" while he characterizes Éluard as "a colourless and commonplace young man with a crooked nose and a face somewhere between that of an onanist and a mystical cretin" (de Chirico 2001).

21. Fulchignoni (1981), 10 and (2003), 152; and Taylor (2003), 131.

22. Fulchignoni (1981), 7, and (2003), 148.

23. Rouch (1995a), 85–86. This text was in French when published in *Positif* in 1955. Here I have mostly reproduced Paul Hockings's translation of this text as it appears in "The Camera and Man" in the second edition of *Principles of Visual Anthropology*, except that in the last sentence I have substituted the term "mediums" for "masters" and "madmen" for "fools" since, given the date of the original *Positif* publication, this is undoubtedly a reference to the title of Rouch's then recently released film, *Les Maîtres fous*.

24. My thanks to Richard Werbner for this interpretation.

25. Taylor (2003), 132. As Elizabeth Cowie has pointed out, Freud was an ambivalent figure for many of those associated with Surrealism, for although he underlined the importance of the imaginary in the formation of individual consciousness, he also pathologized it (Cowie 2007, 208).

26. Taylor (2003), 139.

27. Richardson (2006), 91.

28. Lourdou (1995).

29. Rohmer and Marcorelles (1963), 6.

30. Remy (2000), 14–15.

31. Breton and Éluard were rather disappointed by the results of their enquiry. Many of their respondents appear to have failed to understand what they were driving at with their questions and gave rather banal answers (Breton and Éluard 1933).

32. Both these films are discussed at length in chapter 9.

33. Rouch (1995a), 89–90; Fulchignoni (1981), 8–9, 31–32, and (2003), 150, 186.

Chapter Three

1. Dieterlen (1995), 436.

2. Stoller (1992), 39–42; *Boutang* (2004); Surugue (2008).

3. This byline is sometimes reported to have been "Jean Pierrejean," including by Rouch himself (2003d, 110). However, the name that appears on one of the original reports in the Comité du film ethnographique archive at the Musée de l'Homme is "Jean Pierjant." This is also the name reported by Jean Sauvy in his memoir about Rouch (2006, 181). Some years after the expedition, Rouch published a brief account of the journey in *Le Niger en pirogue* (Rouch 1954).

4. Rouch (2003d), 109, Sauvy (2006), 135–136. Griaule's conversations with the Dogon sage would result in the classic text, *Dieu d'eau: Entretiens avec Ogotemmêli*, first published in 1948 (see Griaule 1985).

5. Stoller (1992), 34–38; Rouch (2008), 44–45.

6. Rouch (1995b), 219; Sauvy (2006), 102.

7. Mouëllic (2002); Rouch (2003b), 54; *Boutang* (2005); Surugue (2007), 13, 18n; Rouch (2008), 53.

8. See Taylor (2003), 136; Stoller (1992), 37.

9. Rouch (1995b), 220; *Dubosc* (1991).

10. Rouch (2008), 206–207.

11. See chapter 7 for an extended discussion of this film.

12. Rouch (1995b), 221. According to one of Rouch's many versions of this story, this first screening was also attended by Michel Leiris (which is entirely feasible since Leiris

then had both a post and an office at the Musée), and it was Leiris who suggested that Rouch screen the material at the jazz club. See, for example, *Dubosc* (1991); also Taylor (2003), 136.

13. Rouch (1995b), 221–222; *Dubosc* (1991).

14. Feld (2003c), 346, translates this title as "In the Land of the Black Magi." However, while the French term "les mages," may indeed designate the legendary Wise Men from the East featured in the New Testament, it has a less elevated connotation when applied to Africa, particularly in a colonial reference. In this context, I am advised that "les mages" would perhaps be more appropriately translated as "wizards," connoting a certain degree of respect, but also a residue of skepticism about their powers (Philippe Descola, pers. comm., July 2007).

15. See Fulchignoni (1981), 15 and (2003), 161; Colleyn (1992), 44; Stoller (1992), 39; Taylor (2003), 136; also *Dubosc* (1991).

16. See Rouch (2008).

17. This expedition is sometimes referred to in the sources as the Éxpedition Schoelcher, after Victor Schoelcher, the author and politician who played a leading role in bringing about the abolition of slavery in all French colonies in April 1848.

18. Rouch (2008), 81–87. See also Feld (2003c), 347.

19. Philippe Costantini, personal communication, October 2008.

20. See, for example, Stoller (1992), 1. Luc de Heusch (1981) refers to them as "shamans."

21. See the necklace in figure 1.2d, p. 5.

22. Rouch (1989), 308–309; Stoller (1992), 105–117. See also the description in Rouch (2008), 102–108.

23. This event is described at some length both in one of the *Franc-Tireur* articles (Rouch 2008), 89–98 and in Rouch's thesis (1989), 261–264.

24. See Rouch (1989), 149–150, 186n.

25. Rouch (1989), 150–151.

26. Literally translated, the name of this event was "The Festival of Condemned Film." This was a reference to a usage of the Symbolist poet Stéphane Mallarmé, who coined the term to refer to poets whose work broke new ground and were therefore 'condemned' by the critics who could not understand them (Cocteau 1965).

27. Rouch (1999); Surugue (2008), 286.

Chapter Four

1. Rouch (2008), 238.

2. See Rouch (2008), 122–124.

3. Rouch (1995a), 85.

4. The title of this film is often given in the singular, that is, *Cimetière dans la falaise*, even by Rouch himself. But as it appears in the film, it is in the plural. While Rouch recollects the visit to Griaule and Dieterlen as taking place in August 1951 (Rouch 2003d, 112), it is clear from the photographic archive that it actually took place in August 1950.

5. Hennebelle (1982), 167.

6. *Seligmann* (2006).

7. In discussing this film with Enrico Fulchignoni, Rouch refers only to Griaule's work on the script (*Fulchignoni* 1982), but Feld (2003c, 348) also credits Dieterlen. Given that

Griaule and Dieterlen generally worked very closely together, this seems more than likely.

8. See Dieterlen (1988), 252.

9. See *Fulchignoni* (1982).

10. See *Fulchignoni* (1982). Rouch explains that at first he was reluctant to shoot the mourners, given their apparent distress, but Griaule urged him to do so, explaining that most of them were professional mourners anyway. Interestingly, these shots of Dogon women have an intimacy that is absent from the Dogon films that Rouch made fifteen or more years later.

11. These films about the Sigui ritual cycle are discussed at length in chapter 11, pp. 220–234.

12. Rouch (2008), 139–145.

13. Rouch (2008), 146–193. It is possible, however, that some of this material was incorporated into *Jaguar,* the film that Rouch made during his subsequent expedition to the Gold Coast in 1954–1955.

14. I am grateful to Paul Stoller for the literal translation of the term *yenendi*, though he prefers to render this term as *yenaandi*. But given that this book is about Rouch's work, I have followed his preferred usage.

15. See chapter 1, p. 7. Also Rouch (1995c), 418.

16. See Piault (1997), 13; also Ahounou (2000), (2007). Christopher Thompson has drawn attention to the intriguing link between Rouch's interest in the figure of Dongo and the fact that his oceanographer father, Jules, was a meteorologist with a particular scientific interest in storms (Thompson 2007, 181).

17. See Villain (1991), 34, for a description of Rouch's *prise de conscience* about the need for an editor.

18. Rouch (2008), 207.

19. This sequence has a certain similarity to the sequence in *Nanook of the North* in which Nanook discovers the blowhole of a seal just in front of Flaherty's camera. As Rouch often talked about the influence of this film upon him, one wonders whether, consciously or not, it might have influenced him in setting up this sequence for *Bataille.*

20. Stoller (1992, 42) says that this crucial event took place in 1954, but Rouch himself (1995a, 93) maintains that it took place in 1953. It is not mentioned in Rouch's travel diary (Laurent Pellé, pers. comm., June 2008), nor in Jane Rouch's published memoir of the same journey (Jane Rouch 1956). However, Damouré Zika also wrote a travel diary for this part of the journey and although he does not report the screening either, he does state that the visit to Ayorou took place between 25 January and 8 February 1954 (Zika 2007, 36).

21. Fulchignoni (1981), 12–13, also (2003), 157–158.

22. Compare and contrast Rouch (1995a), 93, (1995b), 224; and *Fulchignoni* (1982).

23. Rouch (2008), 219–228.

24. *Speckenbach* (1995).

Chapter Five

1. This is a commentary point made toward the end of the film, *Jaguar*, released in various forms between 1957 and 1970.

2. These included the Scientific Council for Africa (CSA), set up in 1949, and the Com-

mission for Technical Cooperation in Africa (CCTA), set up in 1950. These agencies represented joint ventures by the governments of France, the United Kingdom, Belgium, Portugal, Rhodesia, and South Africa and in practice, they often operated in tandem (see Gruhn 1971, 459).

3. See Jane Rouch, *Le rire n'a pas de couleur* (1956), 9–55. Jane accompanied Jean Rouch on a number of his expeditions to Africa in the late 1950s and early 1960s. See also her equally amusing later account of some of these experiences, *Nous n'irons plus aux bals nègres*, published in 1984, particularly 28–82. Although mostly about Africa, this book also describes her experiences travelling in Latin America and Asia. Jane Rouch died in 1987.

4. Stoller comments that "a generation later," although migration to the Ivory Coast continued, Ghana was no longer a favored destination following the expulsion of Nigerien migrants in 1969 by that onetime student of anthropology, President K. A. Busia. However, this did not stop Nigerien migration: instead, Togo and Nigeria became the principal destinations (1992, 63, 69).

5. The methods as well as the results of Rouch's research into migration to the Gold Coast are reported in a lengthy article published in the *Journal de la Société des Africanistes* in 1956. An extensive summary in English is provided by Stoller (1992, 63–79).

6. See Rouch (1956), 179–181. Political events are much more prominently represented in the photographic record of Rouch's 1954–55 Gold Coast expedition.

7. I am grateful to Laurent Pellé of the Musée de l'Homme for the precise date and location of the principal photography of *Les Maîtres fous*. These data he extracted from Rouch's personal travel diary (pers. comm., July 2008).

8. Marc Piault (1997, 11) draws a parallel between Rouch's willingness to embrace modernity and the work of his contemporary Georges Balandier on the "colonial situation" in Central Africa. There are also many parallels with the work on African urban migration carried out in the 1950s by the Manchester School of social anthropology, headed by Max Gluckman (Banks 1996, 24–39; Werbner 1990). Rouch and the Manchester School had a number of research interests in common, and he visited Manchester on several occasions in the 1950s.

9. Fieschi and Téchiné (1967), 17.

10. There is some disagreement among regional specialists as to exactly what *kourmi* or *kurmi* means. Rouch suggests that it means "forest," while Thomas M. Painter reports that it is a Hausa word meaning, literally, "south." In the view of Murray Last, on the other hand, the term refers to a "forest beside a river" and as such, is a term applied to "the forest zone and the south generally" (Painter 1988, 97n).

11. In an interview given in 1967, Rouch states that he invented the character of Adamou as a device to encourage the sense that the voice-over commentary was like a story being told to a friend (Fieschi and Téchiné 1968, 17). However, this supposedly imaginary character appears to be closely modeled on Adamou Al Hadj Kofo, a Zerma migrant from Niger, who was a leading member of the francophone migrants' association in Accra and one of Rouch's principal informants for the sociological research on which the film is based (Rouch 1956, 36). Kofo is even given a screen credit alongside all the other principal protagonists in the opening titles and, according to Marc Piault (personal communication, September 2008), it is almost certainly his voice that one hears asking questions on the sound track.

12. See Damouré's account of these arrangements in *Madsen and Jørgensen* (2007). Also in Jørgensen (2007), 65–66.

13. Marshall and Adams (2003), 205.

14. Fieschi and Téchiné 1968, 17.

15. See Zika (2007), 28–35. As they head south from Ouagadougou, Damouré writes, at some point in late 1950, "we have to stop in places where it would be interesting to make films about Gold Coast migrants. . . . We arrive at a place where the trees are beautiful, tall. Very good, we must shoot films here." See also Rouch (2008),147–93.

16. Fieschi and Téchiné (1968), 17; Marshall and Adams (2003), 205–206. According to the *Cahiers du Cinéma* author, Alain Bergala, it was Roberto Rossellini who, on seeing a preliminary rough cut of the film in 1955, first suggested to Rouch that he should arrange for it to be narrated by the protagonists (Mundell 2004).

17. The origins and precise meaning of the term "ethnofiction" remain uncertain. See Sjöberg (2008a), particularly 19–28 for a recent discussion.

18. Rouch (1956), 117–118; Fieschi and Téchiné (1967), 18.

19. Painter (1988).

20. Rouch (1956), 194–195, (1997d), 207–208.

21. Jane Rouch (1956), 97; *Madsen and Jørgensen* (2007).

22. Rouch reports (2003b, 61) that Sean Graham, a former assistant of John Grierson who ran the colonial government film unit in Accra where Damouré and Lam recorded their voice-over and for whom Rouch had a high regard, also made a film called *Jaguar* based around the same popular song.

23. Rouch claims that as a teenage jazz enthusiast, he himself had adopted the zazouman style (see Mouëllic 2002; also chap. 2, p. 61).

24. Rouch (1956), 149; Jane Rouch (1956), 68–80.

25. Rouch (1956), 145.

26. Another version of the refrain, though not one that I have been able to detect in the film, is "Jaguar—been to, Jaguar—fridge full." In this case, the "been to" refers to the aspiration to have "been to" Britain to study, which is perhaps even more unlikely than the aspiration to own a sports car (Rouch 2003b, 61).

27. Ghana was the first sub-Saharan African state to achieve independence, in March 1957. But thereafter, under Nkrumah's government, the country became embroiled in a series of economic and political problems that eventually led to him being deposed in a military coup in February 1966.

28. Fieschi and Téchiné (1967), 18.

Chapter Six

1. Fulchignoni (1981), 17, and (2003), 165; Rouch (1999).

2. The detail about Oumarou being rejected by his father appears to have been a piece of poetic licence on Rouch's part and was later directly contradicted by Oumarou (Haffner 1996, 97–98).

3. Rouch (1957), (1960b), (1961), (1999).

4. Jutra (1960), 36–37. See also Jane Rouch (1984), 76–82.

5. See Colette Piault (1996b), 153.

6. The "Italian sailor" was actually played by Edmond Bernus, a French ethnologist from Rouch's circle of friends in Abidjan (Marc Piault, pers. comm., September 2008) while his voice was supplied later by Enrico Fulchignoni in the dubbing suite (Françoise Foucault, pers. comm., November 2008). This sequence was initially censored on the Ivory Coast, because it was deemed inappropriate for Whites and Blacks to be seen fighting in the newly independent republic. But, later, when the censored prints wore out and new

copies were ordered from Senegal, where the film had not been censored, the full version was shown on the Ivory Coast also (Rouch 1999).

7. The name "goumbé" derives from the name of a particular kind of drum that is played at the events organized by such associations.

8. Delahaye (1961), 7; Rouch (1999). See also Rouch (1958) for a transcript of this improvisational commentary by Oumarou.

9. Godard (1959), 22.

10. For further discussion of their collaboration, see chapter 13, pp. 282–283.

11. Godard (1959), 22.

12. Fulchignoni (1981), 18, also (2003), 166.

13. The term "psychodrama" was the name given to an approach to psychotherapy first developed by the North American psychiatrist of Austrian extraction, Jacob Levy Moreno, in the 1930s. This approach was subsequently adopted for purely theatrical purposes without any necessary associated therapeutic objectives. According to one authority, "Important in Moreno's theories were the concepts of role taking, spontaneity, creativity, tele (empathy), and catharsis. In the process of acting out conflicts and problems in interpersonal relations, the actors gained insight and were helped by the group process to remedy problem behavior patterns and improve coping skills" (Ozarin 2003). Although intended as an account of a psychotherapeutic process, this description parallels very closely Rouch's conception of the dramaturgical processes taking place in the making of *La Pyramide humaine*. See also Sjöberg (2008a), particularly pp. 166–172, for a more detailed comparison of Moreno and Rouch's ideas about psychodrama.

14. Fulchignoni (1981), 18, and (2003), 166.

15. Rouch (1960), 17; Hennebelle (1982b), 168.

16. Ten Brink (2007b), 138.

17. Ten Brink (2007b), 135.

18. Rouch (1999); ten Brink (2007b), 137.

19. Rouch (1960), 20; ten Brink (2007b), 136.

20. This cult featured in a number of Rouch's subsequent films, notably *Monsieur Albert prophète* (1963).

21. Ten Brink (2007b), 137.

22. In his memoir, Rouch admits that the reading of this poem by one of his Surrealist poet-heroes was his idea. The film also features a poem by Baudelaire and two by Rimbaud. These too were suggested by Rouch though he takes pleasure in the fact that after the filming, some of the students developed their own interest in poetry (Rouch 1960, 23).

23. Jones (2005).

24. Rouch (1960), 24–25.

25. Rouch (1960), 26.

26. Though perhaps the transformation in attitudes was not as great as Rouch imagined or hoped for. Alain later joined the Foreign Legion and went to fight against the independence movement in Algeria, where he was killed (Rouch 1999).

27. Anon. (1965b).

Chapter Seven

1. Piault (1997), 12.

2. Luc de Heusch, personal communication, October 2004. See also Rouch (1991); Stoller (1994), 84–85; Colleyn (1992), 48–49; Marshall and Adams (2003), 192. Rouch's com-

ment on Griaule's reaction seems to have been a canard symptomatic of the ambiguous relationship that he had with his mentor. Marc Piault (pers. comm., 2004) suggests that Griaule was probably shocked, not because of the way the film represented colonial authorities but because it undermined his long-term attempt to demonstrate that African culture is as aesthetically and intellectually refined as European culture. See chapter 15, pp. 314–317, for a more extended discussion of Rouch's "joking relationship" with Griaule.

3. Stoller (1992), 151.

4. Stoller (1992), 158.

5. Stoller (1992), 159; Fulchignoni (1981), 16, and (2003), 163.

6. Marshall and Adams (2003), 189. Although Rouch worked mostly with the Songhay-Zerma, *hauka* (variants: *haouka*, *hawka*) is actually a Hausa word meaning "madness." This is similar to the meaning of the Zerma term for the spirits of the cult, *zondom*. They are also referred to as *babule* in Hausa, meaning "spirits of fire," presumably a reference to the mediums' practice of scorching themselves with flaming torches (Olivier de Sardan 1993, 171n; Rouch 1989, 81; 1997b, 35).

7. Sardan (1993), 209n ; Marc Piault, personal communication, 2004.

8. In the original French version of the commentary, which is generally slightly more detailed than the English version, the last sentence referring to absorption of "our inimical society" is absent. As the English version was recorded some time later, one can only surmise that by then Rouch had become even more aware of the need to defend the film against accusations of racism.

9. Rouch (1995b), 222. This reproduces an article first published in 1988.

10. See Georgakas et al. (2003), 216–218. This reports an interview actually conducted in 1977.

11. See Rouch (1997d), 208 which reproduces an article originally published in 1990.

12. Rouch reports that the "real" Madame Salma, wife of an early twentieth-century French colonial official, was African (see Marshall and Adams 2003, 190).

13. Marc Piault reports (pers. comm., 2004) that in the French colonies, not only truck and train drivers, but also corporals could well have been Europeans, but that this is less likely to have been the case in the British colonies.

14. There are a number of editorial devices in *Les Maîtres fous* that are unusual in Rouch's work and it is therefore tempting to attribute these to the influence of the editor, Suzanne Baron. This is a matter that I shall explore at greater length in chapter 14, pp. 297–298.

15. See Stoller (1992), 152; Russell (1999), 224, 344n; also Taussig (1993), 242. It was this particular shot that appears to have prevented Rouch from getting cinema distribution in the UK. Following a screening of the film at the British Film Institute, the chairman of the Board of Film Censors told Rouch that although he had liked the film personally, there was no way he could approve its general release. When Rouch asked why not, he replied, "You just try cracking an egg on the head of the Queen of England and see what happens to you!" (Devanne 1998).

16. Stoller (1995), 132, 198–199. By accident, some years before Kountché took power, Rouch filmed Kountché's wife taking part in a spirit possession ceremony close to her home in Niamey, the Nigerien capital, on the occasion of a ceremony dedicating a shrine to Dongo that she herself had sponsored (see C. Piault 1996, 149; also 2007, 44).

17. Stoller (1992), 156.

18. Olivier de Sardan (1993) passim.

19. Lewis (1986a), (1986b), 102–103.

20. Boddy (1989), 125–131. Rouch himself seems to have been perfectly well aware of the similarities between the *hauka* and the various *zar*-like cults spread across West and North Africa since he alludes to various descriptions of these other cults in the final pages of his monograph, *La Religion et la magie songhay*. However, he refuses to draw any historical conclusions from these similarities, insisting rather on the entirely indigenous character of Songhay religion (1989, 321).

21. Lewis (1986b), 105.

22. Boddy (1989), 133.

23. This is the view of Marc Piault (pers. comm., 2004) who has worked for many years amongst the hausaphone Mawri of eastern Niger (cf. Piault 1970). He reports it as also having been the view of the late Nicole Échard, who worked precisely in the area of western Niger where the *hauka* cult first appeared.

24. See Rouch (1989), 91n. The white slave concubines were said to be "mostly from Romania," but perhaps this was merely another way of saying that they were Romanies, that is, gypsies? See also Marshall and Adams (2003), 193.

25. Olivier de Sardan (1993), 172.

26. Fugelstad (1983), 131; Rouch (1989), 80–82, 92n; Stoller (1992), 154–156.

27. Olivier de Sardan (1993), 173. Marc Piault (pers. comm., 2004) takes an intermediate position between Échard and Olivier de Sardan, suggesting that although there was no necessary association between politics and religion in the practice of the cult, the cult may have become a vehicle for political resistance on occasion.

28. Rouch (1989), 80, 83, 91n; Stoller (1992), 155–157.

29. Rouch (1997b), 27, 35.

30. Rouch (1989), 81–83, 91n; Marshall and Adams (2003), 190.

31. Stoller (1995), 1–12, describes an encounter with another such purely transgressive *hauka* by the name of Chefferi, the nonbeliever from the Red Sea.

32. Rouch (1989), 91n; Marshall and Adams (2003), 193–194.

33. Stoller (1995); Olivier de Sardan (1993), 198–199.

34. Marc Piault (pers. comm., 2004) reports that among hausaphone groups in eastern Niger, new *hauka* characters were also developed after independence, and the cult was certainly still visible around Niamey in 1992.

35. Rouch (1989), 24–28. Paul Stoller (pers. comm., 2005) comments that although the minority of Songhay living in urban centers may have been observant Muslims for a millenium, the impact in rural areas was minimal until "two to three generations ago."

36. Rouch (1989), 19–28 passim. However, with the rise of more radical fundamentalist forms of Islam in recent years, traditional possession cults throughout North and West Africa are under increasing pressure. See Masquelier (1993); Boddy (1995).

37. Muller (1971).

38. See Rouch (1989), 56–66, 91n. See also Stoller (1989b), 104–105; (1995), 30–35, 43.

39. See chapter 4, pp. 56–62.

40. See chapter 12, pp. 270–274.

41. Richard Werbner (pers. comm., 2004) suggests that the vision of the colonial governor on a horse could have served as a particularly powerful model of the *hauka* Governor "mounted" on his medium. In fact, in the celebrated cut to the parade ground in *Les Maîtres fous*, it is some cavalry soldiers who are mounted rather than the governor himself, but the general point is well taken.

42. Nor do we see the praise-singers whom Stoller reports as prominent in Songhay

possession ceremonies and who also play an important role in attracting the spirits (Stoller 1989b, 108, 112).

43. Rouch (1989), 158.

44. Olivier de Sardan (1993), 186–187.

45. Olivier de Sardan (1993), 200.

46. Stoller (1995), 37 ff.

47. See Georgakas et al. (2003), 218.

48. See in particular Stoller (1995), 35, 130–132 and passim.

49. Stoller (1989), 106. See also Boddy (1989, 134–135) who, with regard to the *zar* cult, explains that spirits actively desire to be embodied in a human being and may become disgruntled if not invited to do so, with negative consequences for the medium's personal well-being.

50. Marshall and Adams (2003), 190.

51. Rouch (1989), 302; Olivier de Sardan (1993), 203–204.

52. Rouch (1989), 259.

53. There is also further indirect evidence that witchcraft was present in the minds of the participants. At various points, two different *hauka* characters run flaming torches over their bodies. Stoller interprets this as a warning to any witches nearby, testifying to the power of the *hauka* (Stoller 1992, 157). Boddy (1989, 132) makes a similar point with regard to the *zar* cult in the Sudan.

54. Marc Piault, personal communication, 2004.

55. Masquelier (1993), 24.

56. Marshall and Adams (2003), 189.

57. Marc Piault, personal communication, 2004; see also Stoller (1992), 144.

58. Marshall and Adams (2003), 189.

Part Two

1. Jane Rouch (1984), 36–37. See also these pages for an insightful and amusing profile of her husband.

2. See Mundell (2004) for an account of the mutual influences of Rouch and Rossellini around this time, as reported by the *Cahiers du Cinéma* author, Alain Bergala in October 2004.

3. Nijland (2007a), 30–31, reports that among those who participated in this workshop were Jean-Luc Godard, Claude Chabrol, Eric Rohmer, Jean-Daniel Pollet, and François Truffaut.

4. Jutra (1960–61), 3:40. The people referred to here include the Senegalese filmmaker Paulin Viera; Serge Ricci, a film director who made a number of films in Africa; Annie Tresgot and Jean Ravel, both editors who worked on Rouch's films; and Pierre Braunberger, the producer of many of Rouch's best-known works.

5. See Rouch (1995a), 98 (first published in 1975), in which he looks forward to the day when those who are conventionally the subjects of ethnographic films will be able to make their own films using video technology.

6. Rouch attended a seminar in California in 1959, where he met many of the leading North American documentarists then working on the development of portable synchronous systems. There are many accounts of the development of this technology and its consequences for documentary filmmaking. Among others, see Rohmer and Marcorelles (1963), 16–22; Mamber (1974); Winston (1995), 144–47.

7. See Fulchignoni (1981), 19 and (2003), 168.

8. Rouget (1965).

9. Rouch (1995a), 94.

Chapter Eight

1. Morin (1962), 5.

2. Winston (2007), 298.

3. DiIorio (2007), 27.

4. Morin (2003), 265n.

5. Of Polish origin, Anatole Dauman (1925–1998) produced the early films of many directors who would later become leading figures of French cinema, including Chris Marker, Alain Resnais, Jean-Luc Godard, and Robert Bresson (see Gerber 1992).

6. Morin (2003), 229–231. It is interesting that Morin should choose the metaphor of the diver "plunging" into real-life situations to describe this way of working with a combination of participant observation and the new technology. There may be a reference here, even if unconscious, to Bronislaw Malinowski's comment in his famous methodological preface to *Argonauts of the Western Pacific* that it was from his "plunges into the life of the natives" that he discovered that "the behaviour, their manner of being . . . became more transparent and easily understandable than it had been before" (1932, 22).

7. See Morin (2003), 232. Marceline Loridan, one of the leading protagonists of the film gives a somewhat different account. According to her, it was Dauman who introduced Rouch and Morin to one another and suggested that they should work together (ten Brink 2007c, 146).

8. See Sadoul (1963), (1971); Rouch (1968), (1995a), 82–83; Fulchignoni (1981), 8, also (2003), 150; Ben Salama (1996), 127; DiIorio (2007), 30. See also the introduction to part 3 of this book, pp 244–254.

9. Rouch (1997e), 224.

10. Morin (2003), 231.

11. Just as the presence of the cameraman and his tripod had served to distinguish *Man with a Movie Camera* from Walther Ruttman's *Berlin: Symphony of a Great City* in the 1920s, so does the presence in front of the lens of Rouch and Morin in *Chronicle* serve to distinguish it from Chris Marker's "city film" about 1960s Paris, *Le Joli Mai*. For an interesting comparison of the representational strategies adopted respectively by Rouch and Marker, see Christie (2007).

12. Morin (2003), 232. See chapter 6, p. 92, especially note 13, for a discussion of "psychodrama." See also Sjöberg (2008a), 166–172, (2008b).

13. In an insightful recent article, Michael Uwemedimo has linked the use of this mode of enquiry reminiscent of a sociological questionnaire to a great enthusiasm among the mass media in France in the late 1950s for social surveys, polls, and *études psycho-sociales* that served to plot the emerging modernity of the country (Uwemedimo 2007).

14. Morin (2003), 232–234.

15. Georgakas et al. (2003), 215; Taylor (2003), 139.

16. See Georgakas et al. (2003), 210–211. In this interview, Rouch claims that all the subjects were members of a group called "Socialism or Barbarism" to which Morin himself also belonged. However, although some of the subjects were members of this group and there is also no doubt about Morin's left-wing sentiments at the time, Morin specifically distances himself from this group's views in his memoir (Morin 2003, 235).

17. Ben Salama (1996), 127. At this time, according to Marceline, Morin himself was "more to the left than the communists" and was particularly critical of the party's position on the independence struggle going on in Algeria (ten Brink 2007c, 146).

18. I rely extensively here on the excellent analysis of this scene by DiIorio (2007), 34–35.

19. Georgakas et al. (2003), 214.

20. Hennebelle (1982b), 169.

21. Maggi and Maggi (1996); Georgakas et al. (2003), 213; Rouch (2003e), 272.

22. A team of assistant editors was employed to do this but as there were 25 hours of rushes to deal with, it was a monumental task. "The girls who carried out that work," Brault commented later, "deserve to have their names engraved on the arch of posterity" (Maggi and Maggi 1996, 135).

23. Morin (2003), 256.

24. Morin (2003), 240. In a recent interview, Marceline reports that it was she who proposed the idea for this sequence to Rouch and Morin (ten Brink 2007c).

25. Morin (2003), 264, n.12.

26. See chapter 6, p. 85.

27. Much to Marceline's fury, one of the excluded scenes showed her and Jean-Pierre trying to patch up their relationship on a jetty by the seashore. This was retained in some early versions of the film but was later removed because, according to Morin, in order to overcome sound problems, it had to be subjected to so much cutting that it looked too staged (Morin 2003, 243; see also ten Brink 2007c, 145). The dialogue of this eliminated scene, which also appears in production stills associated with the film, is reproduced in Morin and Rouch (2003a), 320–321.

28. Morin (2003), 250–256.

29. Morin (2003), 264, n.16.

30. Rouch (1965).

31. Rohmer and Marcorelles (1963), 2–6.

32. "Vox pop," an abbreviation for *vox populi*, a Latin phrase meaning "voice of the people," is the standard documentary filmmaking term for the technique of asking the same short question in quick succession to a number of different people, usually randomly encountered in the street or some other public place. In the editing of this material, normally only a small selection of the responses will be retained. Although this is not the practice in *Chronicle*, after the first instance, the question is also usually left out because it is presumed that the audience will be able to remember it.

33. In addition to this major reworking of the chronology, there were many more petty examples of the manipulation of the rushes in ways that distorted their real chronology. Rouch himself later admitted that in the cutting of some of the conversations, certain comments are shown as if they were responses to remarks to which, in reality, they bore no direct relation. Dornfeld (1989) remarks that in cutting *À bout de souffle*, Jean-Luc Godard was much more open to the use of "jump cuts," and that even the North American practitioners of Direct Cinema were "rougher in their treatment of continuity codes."

34. Quoted in DiIorio (2007), 33.

35. Most of those who took part in the making of *Chronicle of Summer* apparently regarded it as being, on balance, a highly positive experience and a striking number thereafter became actively involved in filmmaking themselves. Perhaps the best-known case is that Marceline Loridan, who immediately after participating in *Chronicle* went on to make *Algérie année zero* (1962), a film about Algerian independence with her then boy-

friend Jean-Pierre Sergent. Later, she got to know Joris Ivens, indirectly through Rouch, married him and became an active collaborator on his film projects until he died in 1989. Among many other contributions, she encouraged Ivens to start using synch sound in the manner pioneered in *Chronicle*. More recently, she and Sergent collaborated on the screenplay for a fictional feature that she directed, *La Petite Prairie aux bouleaux* (2003), which is about a Birkenau survivor who returns to the camp after fifty years. Another of the principal protagonists, Marilou Parolini, became an active participant in the New Wave, writing the screenplays of several films with Jacques Rivette, and later with Bernardo Bertolucci, and working as a production stills photographer for Jean-Luc Godard on a number of his most important films. She also codirected the fictional short, *Aussi loin que mon enfance* (1971) with Jean Eustache. Prior to becoming a well-known political figure, Régis Debray went to Venezuela to work with Pierre Kassovitz on his documentary *Les Chemins de la fortune* (1964). As described in chapter 9 of this book, Modeste Landry and Nadine Ballot later collaborated with Rouch on a number of other projects, while Ballot also performed a brief cameo in François Truffaut's *Tirez sur le pianiste* (1960; Morin and Rouch 2003b; ten Brink 2007b, 2007c; DiIorio 2007, 42).

36. Michaud (1982); Serceau (1996); Goldman (1996); see also Lévesque (2004).

37. Morin (2003), 259–260.

38. DiIorio (2007), 42.

39. See chapter 1, p. 11.

40. See DiIorio (2007), 41; Ben Salama (1996), 126–127.

41. Rouch (1997e), 211.

42. See Piault (2000), 159n.

43. Ben Salama (1982), 136, and (1996), 127. The exact phrase that Morin uses is *"pot pourri."*

Chapter Nine

1. Aumont et al. (1986), 320.

2. Among other references in *Cahiers*, see Rouch (1960c); Jutra (1960, 1961a, 1961b); Delahaye (1961); Hoveyda (1961); Rohmer (1961); Weyergans (1961); Moullet (1962); Rohmer and Marcorelles (1963); Hoveyda and Rohmer (1963); Comolli (1964); Moullet (1964); anon. (1965a), 58; Ollier (1965); Godet (1966); Pierre (1967); Fieschi and Téchiné (1967); Fieschi (1968).

3. Moullet (1986), 35; see also Villain (1991), 134. According to Maxine Scheinfegel, there is even a direct allusion to *Moi, un Noir* in *À bout de souffle* (2008, 73).

4. Thompson (2007), 186. See also *Bergala* 2005 for the influence of Rivette and Godard on Rouch, and vice versa.

5. Truffaut (1985), 275. For the influence of *Moi, un Noir* on *Les Quatre Cent Coups*, see Delahaye (1961), 7; Rouch (1999); and chapter 6, pp. 88–89.

6. Scheinfeigel (2008), 69.

7. On the experimental attitudes of the Surrealists, see chapter 2, pp. 28–29. In relation to Vertov's experimentalism, see Rouch (1968), 445, 449.

8. Prédal (1996b), 18.

9. See chapter 2, pp. 29–31.

10. Prédal (1996b), 18. See also ten Brink (2007b).

11. Unless otherwise stated, the information about how Rouch went about filming *La*

Punition is taken from an interview that he gave to Éric Rohmer and Louis Marcorelles (1963).

12. I am indebted to Christopher Thompson for identifying this source.

13. Weyergans (1961).

14. Hoveyda and Rohmer (1963), 2–7. See Mundell (2004), for the mutual influences of Rossellini and Rouch, as reported by *Cahiers du Cinéma* author Alain Bergala.

15. Moullet (1964).

16. Serceau (1996), 171l; Thompson (2007), 182.

17. Moullet (1964), 50.

18. According to the *Cahiers du Cinéma* critic, Alain Bergala, this project was initially to have been produced by Roberto Rossellini. However, he did not like the proposals that were put to him by the New Wave directors and he dropped out. But the directors then found alternative sources of funding, and the project went ahead anyway (Mundell 2004).

19. Rouch (1965).

20. Rouch (1995c), 410n, 413.

21. I am indebted to Laurent Pellé of the Musée de l'Homme for alerting me to the fact that Caquot was possibly one of the designers of the bridge. I was able to confirm this by inspecting the plaque that hangs to this day on one of the central pillars of the bridge.

22. See ten Brink (2007b), 412. At around this time, Becker and Nadine were married, though I have not been able to establish whether this was before or after the shooting of *Gare du Nord*.

23. Maxime Scheinfeigel (2008, 170–179) has recently published a very interesting analysis of *Gare du Nord*, which I have drawn on at various points here.

24. Scheinfeigel (2008), 176.

25. Rohmer and Marcorelles (1963), 6.

26. Rouch (1965).

27. Ten Brink (2007b), 142.

28. Eaton (1979a), 19.

29. Marie (2008), viii, x.

30. The Canadian part was to be directed by Michel Brault.

31. According to Braunberger, this title was given to the film in order to get it past the censors whom, it was thought, would have taken a negative view if the film had remained with its original title, *Les Jeunes Filles*, "the young girls" (Serceau 1996, 171).

32. Veuve (1967), 90.

33. She confesses this in one of the longer scenes in the film in which she is shown doing a fashion shoot with a society photographer played by Maurice Pialat, who would later become a distinguished feature film director (Serceau 1996, 171).

34. Aumont et al. (1986), 320.

35. Fieschi and Téchiné (1967), 20.

36. Veuve (1967), 90.

37. Serceau (1996), 171.

Chapter Ten

1. Jutra (1961b), 116, 40.

2. Rouch (2003d), 111.

3. A "double-band print" is one in which the sound track, although transferred from the original reel-to-reel field tapes to 16mm magnetic tape, remains separate from the picture. A double-band print can only be viewed on an editing table or by means of a specially adapted projector. See appendix 1, pp. 366–367.

4. Fieschi and Téchiné (1967), 20.

5. The films concerned are *VW Voyou* (*VW Rascal*, 1973), *Le Foot-Giraffe* (*Giraffe Football*, 1973), and *La 504 et les foudroyeurs* (*The 504 and the Blasters*, 1974). See appendix 1, pp. 392–393 for further details.

6. See Rouget (1985, 1996).

7. See appendix 1, p. 7.

8. Rouget (1965).

9. Stoller (1992), 192.

10. Fulchignoni (1981), 19, and (2003), 168. Although Rouch did not make any further major films on urban migrants, he did return to Abidjan in 1967 to shoot a short unedited film about the marriage of a young woman from the Royale *goumbé* that had featured in *Moi, un Noir* (Houdaille1981, 61).

11. In an interview first published in 1991, Rouch claimed that he had shot "about fifty films" on spirit possession in Niger (Taylor 2003, 140). Although this appears to be something of an exaggeration, there is surely no doubt that Rouch shot an unprecedented number of films on this ethnographic subject.

12. See chapter 1, pp. 00–00.

13. This film has been the subject of an extended analysis by Brice Ahounou, a close associate of Rouch in Paris. Originally published in French, it has recently been translated into English (Ahonou 2000, 2007).

14. See chapter 4, p. 65.

15. See Stoller (1992, 124–125) who suggests that filming for *The Lion Hunters* began in May 1957, but in the credits of the film itself, it is stated that the first expedition took place in 1958.

16. Godard (1959), 22. See Jutra (1961a) for an account of the 1959 expedition.

17. C. Piault (1995), 151, and (2007), 45.

18. Quoted in Stoller (1992), 126.

19. Nijland (2007, 31) reports that Stefan Kudelski, the inventor of the Nagra tape recorder, supplied Rouch with an electric motor to be attached to the side of the camera to ensure that it would run at the same speed as the tape recorder. But this motor was very heavy and Rouch found it very difficult to achieve genuinely horizontal horizons when shooting. Nor does it appear to have been very effective in ensuring synchronicity because there are no extended shots in the film in which this is achieved.

20. C. Piault (1995), 152, and (2007), 46.

21. Marshall and Adams (2003), 200.

22. According to Stoller, the name given to the lion, Anasara, actually means "European" rather than "American" (1992, 122).

23. Rouch explains that the Gow are not considered a hereditary caste, as are blacksmiths among the Songhay, not least because it is widely believed that all the sons of a hunter who kills a lion will die in childhood. Anyone can choose to become a Gow hunter, provided that they have both the courage and technique to kill a lion (Marshall and Adams 2003, 197).

24. Marshall and Adams (2003), 201.

25. Naficy (2007), 99.

26. Marshall and Adams (2003), 203.

27. Rouch (1995a), 92–93.

28. See pp. 307–309.

29. See Houdaille (1981), 62.

30. In real life, Damouré lived in Paris for a prolonged period around this time while on a UNESCO internship to train as a pharmacist (Bregstein 2007, 166).

31. Viewed from the perspective of the present day, this scene strikes one initially as being something of a caricature of modern anthropology. However, it was precisely around the same period that *Petit à Petit* was being made, 1968–1969, that James Neel and his team were collecting blood samples from the Yanomami in Venezuelan Amazonia in a not dissimilar manner (Tierney 2000).

32. Somewhat disappointingly, the car she is driving is not actually a Jaguar, but an Austin Healey. For the association of the Jaguar sports car with a certain kind of cool comportment and a particular category of prostitute in the colonial Gold Coast, see chapter 5, pp. 79–81.

33. Fieschi (1968); Prédal (1996j), 233.

34. Fieschi and Téchiné (1967), 20.

35. This version appears to have been shown on French television in the early 1990s (Bregstein 2007, 174).

36. Fieschi (1968), 59.

37. Haffner (1996), 91; Thompson (2004–2005); Braunberger (1996), 171; Fulchignoni (1981), 27, also (2003), 181.

38. Although a first assembly of *Jaguar* of 2.5 hours was produced as far back as 1957, it was not until 1967 that a hundred-minute version was produced for the Venice Film Festival. This was subsequently reduced to the final running time of 88 minutes for general release in 1969 or 1970. Meanwhile, *Petit à Petit* was also edited in 1969–1970 and the 35mm version released in 1971. In the credits of this version, Josée Matarasso rather than Dominique Villain appears as the editor, but according to Philippe Costantini, currently working on a definitive archive of Rouch's films, this is an error (pers. comm., October 2008).

39. Fieschi and Téchiné (1967), 20.

40. Serceau (1996), 171.

Chapter Eleven

1. Griaule (1938), 819.

2. Rouch (2003d), 109–114. Here, as elsewhere, Rouch recalls this visit as having taken place in 1951. In fact, it is clear from both his personal diaries and from the photographic record that it took place in August 1950. See chapter 4, pp. 52–55, for a discussion of *Cimetières dans la falaise*.

3. Among the most important of these are Griaule (1938); Paulme (1940); Dieterlen (1941); de Ganay (1941); Griaule (1948/1985); Calame-Griaule (1965); Griaule and Dieterlen (1965); and Dieterlen (1982), though there are many other minor publications.

4. Among other contributions in the anglophone literature to this debate about the work of Griaule and his associates are Goody (1967); Douglas (1967/1975); Clifford (1988a); Van Beek (1991); De Heusch (1991); Calame-Griaule (1991); Van Beek (1992); Douglas (1995); and Wanono (2006). See also Piault (2000b). On the skeptical reaction of French anthropologists to Griaule's first reports on Dogon cosmology, see Rouch (2003d), 109–112.

5. Unless otherwise stated, the ethnographic detail about the Sigui in this chapter represents an amalgam of information gathered from Dieterlen's 1970 Lugar Memorial Lecture (Dieterlen 1971), Rouch's contribution to a festschrift in honor of Dieterlen originally published in 1978 (reproduced and translated into English as Rouch 2003d), Rouch's 1980 interview with Enrico Fulchignoni (Fulchignoni 1981, 19–26, translated in Fulchignoni 2003, 169–179), and from the Sigui films themselves.

6. "Joking relationships" (*relations à plaisanteries* in French) are a recurrent feature of the anthropological literature on Africa. As reported by Jean-Paul Colleyn, such relationships are referred to by the term *sanankuya* in West Africa and, as with joking relationships generally, represent a quasi-ritualized means of resolving social tensions, particularly those to do with differences in social status (Colleyn 2004, 540).

7. Prédal (1996c), 20; Rouch (2003d), 114.

8. Schaeffner (1933), 53.

9. Dieterlen (1971), 2. The computation of the sixty-year interval of the Sigui is one of the most controversial features of the entire Dogon ethnographic corpus. In their later works, both Griaule and Dieterlen claimed that the Dogon knew when to hold the festival by reference to the movement of a small "companion" star of the particularly bright large star, Sirius. However, although modern astronomers have indeed established that Sirius is orbited by a smaller, denser star, these orbits actually take closer to fifty than sixty years, and, more importantly, this smaller star is invisible to the human eye without the aid of powerful modern telescopes that the Dogon do not have. Even Rouch was initially skeptical about the validity of this claim, though he later consulted a paleoastronomer at the Massachusetts Institute of Technology who informed him that some two thousand years ago, both Sirius and its companion star would have been visible to the human eye (*Seligmann* 2006). If true, this might conceivably play some part in explaining the origins of the timing of the Sigui, but it would still not account for the disparity between the Sigui's sixty-year intervals and the star's current fifty-year orbits, nor would it explain how the Dogon discern those orbits under present conditions. A more immediately convincing explanation for the origin of the sixty-year interval, also suggested by Dieterlen, is that the number sixty is a basic figure in the system of numeration typical of the Mandé cultural-linguistic group to which the Dogon belong (Dieterlen 1971, 2). As for the actual computation of the interval, before he became immersed in Dogon cosmological theories, Griaule reported that the elders of Yougou, the village where the Sigui cycle always begins, computed the sixty-year interval simply by keeping a collection of cowrie shells to record the passage of thirty biennial beer-drinking festivals (Griaule 1938, 171; see also Leiris 2008, 155).

10. Griaule (1938, 215) reports that after the end of the festivities, some balls of the millet mash used in the preparation of the beer are preserved and from these, a liquid is derived to moisten the lips of any male babies born over the ensuing nine months.

11. Nadine Wanono, personal communication, April 2006.

12. Given that even in the Dogon's own oral tradition, it is recognized that they migrated to the Bandiagara Escarpment in relatively recent times, there is clearly some inconsistency here. Griaule refers to the people of Yougou as being "dupes" of a belief that a particular shelter in the cliff-face close to the village is associated with the death of the first ancestor (Griaule 1938, 167).

13. See Griaule (1938), 173–176; also Leiris (2008),165. Although Griaule's description of the progression of the Sigui generally concurs with that of Rouch and Dieterlen, he en-

visages it as only taking place over five years, and in the third year, he even suggests that it breaks out of the southwesterly progression and is carried in a northeasterly direction to the agglomeration of villages around Yanta.

14. Rouch (1995b), 228.

15. Prédal (1996c), 20–21.

16. Rouch (2003d), 122–124.

17. Rouch (2003d), 121; Fulchignoni (1981), 23, also (2003), 174.

18. Rouch and Dieterlen may have disagreed on the detail, but the general thrust of their interpretation is entirely consonant with Griaule's final conclusion in *Masques dogons,* an extract from which is quoted in the epigraph to this chapter, namely, that the fabrication of masks and the performance of masked dances are both means whereby the perpetuation of society is asserted in the face of consciousness of "the decomposition of death" (Griaule 1938, 819).

19. See Morphy (1994) for a discussion of an analogous case relating to the interpretation of Australian Aboriginal ritual on the basis of repeated viewings in the edit suite.

20. In 1996, a different version of this synthesis was produced by the Japanese television company NHK for screening on its recently launched satellite service. This version featured some additional footage of Rouch and Dieterlen working with the Dogon. See Prédal (1996c), 21–22.

21. Dieterlen (1987), 107–108.

22. The age of the *yasigine* varies considerably as the cycle progresses: in one of the early phases, the *yasigine* are female elders while in a later phase they are represented by a toddler carried on her father's shoulders.

23. See Georgakas et al. (2003), 217. It is notable that Dogon women appear in Griaule's films shot in the 1930s, seemingly without embarrassment, and even in Rouch's own film *Cimetières dans la falaise,* shot in 1950–1951, though this may be explained by the different circumstances of filming in earlier times. In the 1980s, Rouch and Dieterlen supported the training of a young Dogon specialist, Nadine Wanono, at the National Film and Television School, at Beaconsfield in the UK, so that she could make films about the everyday life of Dogon women (Nadine Wanono, pers. comm., April 2006, see also Wanono 1987).

24. Dieterlen (1995), 438–439.

25. Clifford (1988), 137–138. See also Douglas (1975).

26. For many years, copies both of the majority of the individual films and of the "Sigui synthèse" have been very difficult to come by. Happily, this situation is to be remedied by the release by Éditions Montparnasse, on DVD, of a number of Rouch's Dogon films, including the "Sigui synthèse." These are due to become available in the autumn of 2009 (Sophie Deswarte, pers. comm., July 2008).

27. The titles of these films are *Funérailles à Bongo: Le Vieil Anaï, 1848–1971 (Funeral at Bongo: Old Anaï),* which was shot in 1972 but not edited until 1979; and *L'Enterrement du Hogon (The Burial of the Hogon),* which was shot in 1973. In this same year Rouch also made an unfinished twenty-minute film about a Dogon woman's funeral at Bongo.

28. For a more detailed account of *Le Dama d'Ambara (The Dama for Ambara),* see appendix 1, pp. 403–404.

29. Taylor (2003), 141.

30. For more elaborate descriptions of the films that Rouch made in the second half of his career, see appendix 1. Specifically in relation to *Folie ordinaire d'une fille de Cham,* see Rouch (1996c).

31. See http://www.comite-film-ethno.net/rouch/rouchbio.htm

32. Georgakas et al. (2003), 224. See also Jørgensen (2007, 62–63) who has a very much more positive view of the film.

33. *Madame L'Eau* is perhaps the only one of Rouch's films to have been shown in its entirety on British national television. This came about through the initiative of André Singer, a producer with a doctorate in social anthropology. At that time, Singer was the series producer of the BBC 2 documentary feature series, *Fine Cut*.

34. Prédal (1996e, 1996h), 224; Walter (1996); Bregstein (2007), 166–167.

35. For appreciative assessments of Rouch's fiction films in this late period, see, for example, DiIorio (2005); Thompson (2007).

36. *Mosblech* 2008

37. Rouch (1995b), 230–231; Prédal (1996c), 22–23. Clearly, Rouch was expecting Wanono and Lourdou to be blessed with his own energetic longevity since they will both be around eighty years of age by the time the next Sigui is concluded.

Part Three

1. Rouch (1995b), 217, (2003), 267.

2. Rouch (1995a), 82.

3. Rouch (1968).

4. Rouch (1968), 440–444.

5. These other "city films" included *Rien que les heures* (1926), a portrait of Paris by the Brazilian filmmaker Alberto Cavalcanti, *Berlin—Symphony of a Great City* (1927) by Walter Ruttman, and *À propos de Nice* (1930), shot by Vertov's younger brother Boris Kaufman and directed by Jean Vigo, another filmmaker whom, on occasion, Rouch liked to claim as a precursor (Rouch 2003e:269).

6. It is notable that this example of synchronous sound recorded on location predates by some four years the British Documentary classic, *Housing Problems*, by Arthur Elton and Edgar Anstey, which is often cited as the first example of the use of on-location synchronous sound in anglophone documentary. See also Petric (1987), 58–59.

7. Sadoul (1963, 1971); DiIorio (2007), 30.

8. Morin (2003), 229–231.

9. Rouch (1997e), 224.

10. See Rouch (1968: 445, reiterated again (449), and also again in Rouch (1971), 14. The italics are in Rouch's original text.

11. Morin (2003), 230. See also Chamberlin (2006) who reports that Vertov laid great importance on filming people when they were otherwise distracted, considering "candid, concealed shooting" the best method of all.

12. See Chamberlin (2006), who cites Vertov himself drawing a parallel between the activities of the Soviet secret police and the work of the movie-camera.

13. Rouch (1968), 441–442. See also Petric (1987).

14. See Petric (1987), 3–4.

15. See chapter 14 below, pp. 297–298 for a discussion of the influence of the editor Suzanne Baron on the montage in *Les Maîtres fous*.

16. Colleyn (1992), 48.

17. Among the many texts on 'cinéma-vérité' in North America, see Mamber (1974); Hall (1991); Winston (1995), 148–163; Saunders (2007).

18. Blue (1965).

19. Blue (1967), 84.

20. Marcorelles (1963); Shivas (1996); Piault (2000), 159n.

21. Fulchignoni (1981), 8, see also (2003), 150.

22. Rouch (1968), 453.

23. See Rouch (1999).

24. See Leacock (2007).

25. However, Leacock (2007:27) reports that in experimenting with the Panchromatic film, Flaherty also discovered that it made his subjects look a golden gray rather than black and that in order to correct this, he later re-shot much of the film.

26. Rouch (1968), 453.

27. Rouch (1995a), 82.

28. Colleyn (1992), 46–47; Rouch (1995a), 88.

29. Ruby (2000), 67.

30. Rouch (1995a), 96.

31. Some fifty years after it was made, Flaherty's daughter, Monica, returned to Samoa with Ricky Leacock to show *Moana* to the subjects, much to their great enjoyment (Leacock 2007:28).

Chapter Twelve

1. Blue (1967), 86.

2. Rouch (1981), 31.

3. Fulchignoni (1981), 31, see also (2003), 185–186.

4. Rouch used this phrase when presenting *Jaguar* at the Origins of Visual Anthropology conference held in Göttingen in June 2001.

5. See Fulchignoni (1981), 32, also (2003), 186.

6. Fulchignoni (1981), 8–9, also (2003), 150. See also Rouch's observations about '*la grace*' in Ann Macintosh's biographical film (*Macintosh* 2004).

7. Rouch (1968), 463.

8. See Henley (2006b) for an extended discussion of this point.

9. Both the "Bearded One," the male leader of the hippopotamus herd in *Bataille sur le grand fleuve* (1951), and "the American," the male lion who was the principal quarry in both *The Lion Hunters* (1965) and *Un lion nommé "L'Américain"* (1972), managed to escape the hunters, despite being wounded.

10. Rouch (2003e), 266.

11. Rouch (2003e), 266–267.

12. See chapter 5, pp. 73–74.

13. *Bregstein* (1977).

14. Bregstein (2007), 170.

15. *Meyknecht, Nijland, Verhey* (1994).

16. Bregstein (2007), 168–169; ten Brink (2007d), 156–157.

17. Fulchignoni (1981), 32, also (2003), 186.

18. See Bregstein (2007, 172). It is not entirely clear whether the phrase the "unrepeatable adventure" was coined by Rouch himself or by Bregstein, but it seems entirely consonant with Rouch's attitudes. In French, the term "*répétition*" has the additional meaning of "rehearsal."

19. Fulchignoni (1981), 32, also (2003), 187; Bregstein (2007), 169–170. Bregstein's account of Rouch's development of a "script according to the oral tradition" is reminiscent

of Ricky Leacock's account of Flaherty working very hard at scriptwriting, which is contrary to the legend, spread by both his admirers and detractors, that he never worked to a script. Although it seems that Flaherty did actually write his scripts down on paper, he too was very much disposed to change his ideas as the production went along (Leacock 2007).

20. However, the account of the making of *Dionysos* published by Jean Sauvy suggests that even though there may have been a formal script, the production schedule remained fairly haphazard and subject to change (Sauvy 2006, 193–212).

21. Rouch described *Les Veuves de quinze ans* as being one of his least satisfactory filmmaking experiences though it was apparently a box office success (see chap. 6, pp. 193–195). With *Dionysos*, it was the other way round: Rouch was very proud of the result, but the film was critically panned.

22. Morin (2003), 230.

23. Mead (1995), 9–10.

24. Taylor (2003), 143.

25. See Rouch (1995a), 87–88.

26. See chapter 3, p. 39.

27. Colleyn (1992), 41. In this interview, Rouch admits that in the 1960s, when he first starting shooting with the Éclair NPR camera, which was very much heavier than the spring-wound cameras to which he had been accustomed, he did briefly try using a tripod when filming a ritual event among the Gourmantché of Burkina Faso. This was equipped with a Miller head that allowed much greater freedom in panning and tilting than older models. But despite this increased fluidity, Rouch soon abandoned the tripod because it locked him to a single spot and restricted all his shots to a single angle of view. As a result, he found himself zooming in and out "like the very devil."

28. Fulchignoni (1981), 11, 16, also (2003), 154, 162.

29. Fulchignoni (1981), 13, also (2003), 158, though the translation here is erroneous.

30. Bregstein (2007), 171.

31. Colleyn (1992), 42.

32. See chapter 9, pp. 187–192, for a discussion of this film.

33. Colleyn (1992), 41–42, 47.

34. See chapter 4, pp. 56–62.

35. In the film commentary, Rouch refers to "*sauterelles,*" grasshoppers, as causing the problem, though in describing the film elsewhere he says that it was "*chenilles processionnaires,*" army caterpillars (Rouch 1989, 185–186n). It is only too likely that the unfortunate villagers were suffering from both.

36. See Rouch (1989), 148–149, 186n, for a precise description of these drums and their mode of manufacture. There is an intriguing degree of homophony between the names of these drums and the names of two important classes of spirit whom the Songhay seek to contact through possession, namely, the primordial and very powerful *tôrou* (including Dongo and Harakoy Dikko) and the spirits of the bush, the *bi,* who are thought to be related to the original inhabitants of Songhay country, the *gabibi* or "black-skinned people." However, Rouch himself does not make any such connection, either in this film or in his writings, while the leading Songhay specialist, Paul Stoller (pers. comm., 2007), is also unsure whether it involves anything more than mere homophony.

37. Colleyn (1992), 41–42; Rouch (2003c), 101.

38. Rouch (1989), 186n. Rouch explains that this term was used by such diverse figures as the early nineteenth-century poet Friedrich Hölderlin, the philosopher Friedrich

Nietzsche, and the early twentieth-century painter Giorgio de Chirico, who was much influenced by Nietzsche and whose work had a powerful impact on Rouch when he was a very young man (see chapter 2, pp. 19–24).

39. Convenient republications of the original article are to be found in the second edition of Rouch's major work on Songhay religion (1989, 337–349) and in the more recent collection of ethnographic essays by Rouch (1997e). An abbreviated version is appended to his original interview in French with Enrico Fulchignoni (1981, 28–29). An English translation of this is offered in Steven Feld's edited volume, *Ciné-ethnography* (Rouch 2003c).

40. See Rouch (1989), especially 38–39; also Stoller (1995), passim.

41. See Rouch (1997e), 224–225, Rouch (2003c), 101. But see also his somewhat more sceptical comments in Colleyn (1992), 41–42.

42. Rouch (1997e), 226.

43. Comparing his own experience with that of Rouch, David MacDougall has written, "There is no doubt that film-making can induce a trance-like state in which the camera operator feels a profound communion with surrounding people and events and indeed feels possessed by a spirit emanating from them. In these curious ballets, one moves as though directed by other forces, and the use of the camera feels more than anything like playing a musical instrument" (1998b, 113). Even Robert Gardner, who on occasion has been somewhat sceptical about Rouch's notion of the ciné-trance has admitted to remarkably similar sentiments (compare Barbash 2001, 391 with Gardner and Östör 2001, 37).

44. See the discussion of Vertov's ideas on pp. 245–251.

Chapter Thirteen

1. This statement appears on the cover of Villain's book, *Le Montage au cinéma* (1991).

2. Rouch (2003b), 79.

3. Rouch (1995a), 91.

4. Rouch (1995a), 90–91.

5. Colleyn (1992), 42.

6. Anon. (1965a), 58.

7. Colleyn (1992), 44; Rouch (1995b), 221–222.

8. Tessier (1996).

9. Villain (1991), 58–64.

10. See chapter 3, pp. 39–41.

11. Villain (1991), 34.

12. Even earlier in her career, around 1948, Baron had worked as an assistant editor on a film directed by the Belgian documentarist Henri Storck about the Flemish painter Peter Paul Rubens. It was while working on this film that she first met the anthropologist and filmmaker Luc de Heusch, who was then Storck's assistant. Later she would cut three films for de Heusch, two about other distinguished painters (René Magritte and James Ensor) and a fiction film released in 1967, *Jeudi on chantera comme dimanche* (Luc de Heusch, pers. comm., 2004).

13. See chapter 7, pp. 103–104.

14. Mouëllic (2002).

15. Eaton (1979a), 6, reports that the tape recorder that Rouch was using was a "Scubitophone." I suspect that this would be the same Sgubbi machine that Rouch had used to shoot the films of his 1950–1951 expedition with Roger Rosfelder.

16. Devanne (1998).

17. At the time of writing, Yoyotte's latest film was *Deuxième souffle* (2007), directed by Alain Corneau, which represents a reworking of the 1966 film of the same name directed by Jean-Pierre Melville. Among many other recent films, she also cut *Himalaya* (1999), the quasi-ethnographic feature directed by Eric Valli. See http://movies.nytimes.com/person/117714/Marie-Josephe-Yoyotte/filmography.

18. See chapter 6, p. 90.

19. Villain (1991), 86–87.

20. Villain (1991), 88 ; Colleyn (1992), 44 ; Colette Piault (1996b), 156.

21. Jutra (1961b), 40. See p. 138 above.

22. Annie Tresgot, personal communication, November 2008.

23. Villain (1991), 87–88; Philippe Costantini, personal communication, October 2008.

24. Villain (1991), 88.

25. Tessier (1996), 168.

26. Villain (1991), 86.

27. Villain (1991), 33–34. See chapter 12, pp. 257–258.

28. Villain (1991), 16.

29. See *Bregstein* (1978); Taylor (2003), 146.

30. Bregstein (2007), 173.

31. Tessier (1996), 168; Prédal (1996i), 222.

32. A cutting ratio is the ratio of the total duration of the rushes to the duration of the definitive version of the edited film.

33. Villain (1991), 87n.

34. Alan Marcus, director of the Film Studies Programme at the University of Aberdeen, informs me that "shooting ratios in feature films . . . can vary widely, but the norm for a Hollywood studio picture might be from 8 to 1 to 12 to 1. An independent picture would be lower—perhaps 6 to 1" (pers. comm., 2008).

35. Tessier (1996), 168; Prédal (1996i), 221.

36. Tessier (1996), 168–169, Villain (1991), 35.

37. See Villain (1991), 94. Villain reports, no doubt on Rouch's authority, that this encounter took place while Rouch and Baron were cutting *Les Maîtres fous*. But as *Les Vacances de M. Hulot* was released in France in February 1953, and *Les Maîtres fous* was not edited until 1955, I suspect that it might have been the earlier film on which Rouch and Baron collaborated, *Les Fils de l'eau*.

38. See appendix 1, pp. 366–367, for an explanation of the terms "double band" and "married print."

39. Villain (1991), 42–44.

40. Exactly who was responsible for the suggestion that Jaguar should be voiced over by Damouré and Lam remains unclear. According to some sources, this idea originated with Roberto Rossellini after he saw a preliminary version of the film, possibly the same one shown to Braunberger and Dassin (see Mundell 2004).

41. See Fieschi and Téchiné (1968), 17; Colette Piault (1996), 153 and (2007), 46.

42. See Bregstein (2007), 173.

Chapter Fourteen

1. Colleyn (1992), 44. Rouch's exact words in French are "C'est quoi le montage? C'est un trucage de la vérité."

2. Rohmer and Marcorelles (1963), 2–6.

3. Tessier (1996), 168.

4. See Reisz and Millar (1999), 112–113. I am grateful to Lucien Taylor, who read a draft of this chapter, for pointing out the limitations of the Reisz and Miller distinctions based on nationalist labels. Not only are there significant differences between such classical Russian exponents of montage as Vertov and Eisenstein, but their cutting strategies are very different from those of current Russian directors, such as Alexander Sokurov, whose *Russian Ark* (2002) does not contain a single cut. However, if one takes into account the time at which Reisz and Millar were writing and in the absence of any widely accepted contemporary classification of styles of montage, I feel that their distinction, although inadequate, is sufficient for the limited purposes of this chapter.

5. These films include *Batteries Dogon* (1966) *Porto-Novo* (1971), and *Horendi* (1972). See appendix 1 for further details, pp. 397, 390, and 383–384.

6. See pp. 110–113.

7. See Russell (1999), 344; Villain (1991), 88. Luc de Heusch, a close friend and admirer of both Rouch and Baron, believes that her role in *Les Maîtres fous* has been widely underestimated. "Jean was a very good storyteller," he commented to me privately in October 2004, "but he was not really an editor."

8. According to legend, during the Second World War, this space was used by the Resistance network based at the museum for producing anti-Nazi propaganda leaflets.

9. Villain (1991), 42.

10. Villain (1991), 42.

11. One is reminded of Jean-François Lyotard's general comment about narrative that "all endings are happy endings" when they involve the final resolution of a dissonance (cf. Pinney 1992, 26).

12. Rouch (1995c), 427.

13. It is conventional in screen studies to identify two different kinds of nonsynchronous music within a film: intradiegetic (coming from elsewhere within the film, as with the Cuénets's music box in the last sequence of *Chronicle*) and extradiegetic (coming from completely outside the film, as with the "highlife" music in opening shot of *Les Maîtres fous*). See Hayward (2000), 84–85.

14. Rouch (1995a), 93–94. See pp. 64–65 for a more extended discussion of the reasons for the Sorko fishermen's objections. Interestingly, it does not seem to have occurred to either Rouch or the Sorko that the hippopotami would have been frightened off by his commentary voice!

15. Tessier (1996), 169.

16. Rouch (1995c), 427. See chapter 2, pp. 20–21.

17. Rouch (1995), 91–92, 96. Rouch came to insist on narrating the commentary of the English-language versions of his films, after his disappointment with the quality of the narration of *The Lion Hunters*, which was performed by a Canadian voice artist who injected what Rouch considered "false drama" into his performance (Marshall and Adams 2003, 202). However, if this narration is indeed a little awkward, far worse is the English-language narration of *Madame L'Eau*. This narration features many very Rouchian poetic flights of fancy that it would not be easy to translate into meaningful English under any circumstances, let alone for the purposes of a film narration. But what makes this narration particularly painful is the droll and distanced style of delivery adopted by the voice artist. This is very different from Rouch's own engaging manner, which had the effect of carrying the listener over any ellipses in the coherence of what he was saying.

18. DeBouzek (1989), 308. See also Colette Piault (1996), 150–151, and (2007), 44–46, who identifies "at least" four different types of commentary styles in Rouch's work.

19. C. Piault (1996b), 152, and (2007), 46.

20. De Bouzek (1989), 308.

21. Rouch (1995c), 427; Grimshaw (2001), 99; Russell (1999), 224.

22. Devanne (1998).

23. See Devanne (1998); Rouch (1995c), 427; Georgakas et al. (2003), 216. In recording the narration of *The Lion Hunters* a decade later, Rouch also prepared a text based on a rehearsal but then in performance allowed himself to become so possessed by the process that he put the text aside and assuming another persona and another accent, gave himself over completely to the commentary. See Colette Piault (1996b), 152, and (2007), 46.

24. Georgakas et al. (2003), 214–215.

25. Rouch (1995b), 228; see also Taylor (2003), 140–141.

26. MacDougall (1995c).

27. Rouch (1995a), 92–93.

28. C.Piault (1996), b154, and (2007), 48.

29. See Rouch (2003b), 80–81.

30. C.Piault (1996b), 154, and (2007), 48.

31. A very striking demonstration of both the strengths and weaknesses of Rouch's shooting praxis is to be found in the film *Architectes ayorou* (1970). This film features a magnificent improvised sequence-shot of a group of women pounding millet who break into song as Rouch's camera approaches. But the same film also features many wavering sequence-shots, with much awkward zooming in and out, as Rouch attempts to show the architectural features of the village where the film was shot.

Chapter Fifteen

1. Rouch (1995a), 96.

2. Karèche (2004).

3. Godard (1972), 129.

4. Murphy and Williams (2007), 51.

5. Taylor (2003), 139.

6. Georgakas et al. (2003), 214–215.

7. Rouch (1995a), 94–96.

8. Rouch (1995a), 85.

9. See chapter 1, pp. 9–12.

10. Films with credits of this kind include *Cimetières dans la falaise* (1951) and *Bataille sur le grand fleuve* (1952).

11. Fulchignoni (1981), 19, and (2003), 168.

12. Rouch and Hockings (1995).

13. Clifford (1988a), 77.

14. See Clifford (1988a), 8off.

15. See in particular Griaule (1933a), 10–12, and (1957), 59. See also the Dakar-Djibouti expedition travel journal of Michel Leiris (2008), 146, in which he expresses his fury because he believes that one particular elderly Dogon informant has purposefully misled him: "Amabibè Babadyi really is an old shyster . . . It would not take too much for me to strangle him."

16. Rouch (1989), 17–18.

17. Rouch (1995a), 96.

18. Rouch (1997e), 227.

19. Rivet and Rivière (1933), 3–5; see Leiris (2008), 103–105, 156–160.

20. Mouëllic (2001).

21. Rouch (1995b), 224.

22. *Gardner* 2004.

23. See Stoller (1992), 43; Fulchignoni (1981), 17, and (2003), 165.

24. See Stoller (1992), 43; Marshall and Adams (2003), 202–203; Houdaille (1981), 62.

25. See Rouch (1968), 445,449; and Rouch (1971), 14.

26. Rouch (1995b), 224.

27. See, for example, Marshall and Adams (2003), 192.

28. Rouch (1997e), 225.

29. Rouch (1997e), 227. But see also Fulchignoni (1981), 29, and (2003), 185, in which the same passage is reproduced but with the difference that the "ethno-observation" and the "ciné-observation" have been collated so that the researcher "ciné-ethno-observes."

30. Bregstein (2007). In the case of *Moi, un Noir*, Rouch claims to have given the actors 60 percent of the profits (Georgakas et al. 2003, 221).

31. See Jørgensen (2007), 68.

32. The producers of this excellent film chose to translate the title of the film *De Bende van Rouch* as *Rouch's Gang*, but for me, the term "gang" has certain unfortunate connotations—with violent street gangs, for example. I would refer instead to Rouch and his companions as a "band," as the Dutch title of the film suggests. Although this term has certain unfortunate musical connotations in English, generally it has more positive associations than "gang."

33. *Madsen and Jørgensen* (2005/2007). Damouré Zika died in April 2009, after a long illness, whilst this book was in production.

34. See Taylor (2003), 134, for a typical telling of this story by Rouch. There is some variation in the sources as to Damouré's date of birth, and therefore as to his exact age when he first met Rouch. According to Dussert (2007, 73), he was born at Niamey in 1924, which would have made him seventeen when he first met Rouch, which seems rather old for him to have still been at school. In contrast, in the film, *Rouch's Gang* (Meyknecht, Nijland and Verhey 1993), he is said to have been born in 1928. This would have made him thirteen when they first met, but this seems to be rather too young for Damouré to have started working as Rouch's assistant on the road-building project.

35. *Bregstein* 1978; Anne-Mette Jørgensen, personal communication, August 2008.

36. As, for example, in *de Heusch* 1983.

37. See chapter 1, p. 7, for a longer description of this event.

38. Bregstein (2007), 175. This clinic was named after Rouch's first wife, Jane. Here, Damouré provided free medical care to local people.

39. The literary journal in which Damouré's travel journal was published was the *Nouvelle nouvelle revue française* (sic), appearing in three separate installments in nos. 37–39 (Zika 2007, 7–9). Even before that, in 1949, Damouré had had a short story published in an anthology dedicated to naïve authors (Zika1949).

40. In addition to *L'Exilé*, Damouré also appeared in *L'Enfant lion*, directed by Patrick Grandperret and released in 1992.

41. *Madsen and Jørgensen* 2005/2007. See also Jørgensen (2007), 58, 70.

42. Stoller (1992), 38; *Meyknecht, Nijland, Verhey* 1992; Surugue (2007), 15–16; Rouch (2008), 44–45. There is some variation in these sources as to Lam's age: some would put him at nineteen when he met Rouch.

43. *Fulchignoni* 1982; Bregstein (2007), 175; Surugue (2007), 16.

44. See Fieschi and Téchiné (1967), 20; Jørgensen (2007), 63; Surugue (2007), 16.

45. Jutra (1960–1961), 1, 40. There is also some variation in the age attributed to Tallou in the sources. I suggest that he was 15 when he first met Rouch on the basis of a reference in a magazine article that Rouch wrote shortly afterwards (Rouch 2008:138).

46. Jørgensen (2007), 70–71. See also *Madsen and Jørgensen 2005/2007*.

47. Laurent Pellé, personal communication, June 2008.

48. Haffner (1996), 95–97.

49. Marc Piault, personal communication, September 2008. See also http://www.pariscinema.org/fr/2005/programmes05/alassane.html.

50. Haffner (1996), 90–91; ten Brink (2007d). See also http://www.bookrags.com/biography/safi-faye/.

51. Jørgensen (2007), 67–68.

52. *Madsen and Jørgensen 2005/2007*. Also Jørgensen (2007), 67–68, 70.

53. Piault (1997), 17–18.

54. Nor was it only Rouch's African subjects whose lives were transformed, apparently for the better, through taking part in his films. See chapter 8, p. 170.

55. Bregstein (2007), 174.

56. Haffner (1996), 97–99; Karèche (2004).

57. Haffner (1996), 89–90; Prédal (1996b), 15; Jutra (1961b), 44.

58. Gabriel (1982), 74–77.

59. Ukadike (1994), 2.

60. Gabriel (1982), 76.

61. Murphy and Williams (2007), 12.

62. This was famously the view of the philosopher Gilles Deleuze. See Ungar (2007), 111.

63. See Taylor (2003), 138.

64. Haffner (1996), 94.

65. Cervoni (1996), 106.

66. Rouch (1995b), 225–226.

67. Haffner (1996), 92.

68. *Madsen and Jørgensen 2005/2007*. See also Jørgensen (2007), 69–70. It is also interesting to note that though Rouch might deny his "paternity" in later life, in his writings in the early 1950s, he did sometimes refer to Damouré and the others as his "children" (e.g., Rouch 2008:137).

69. Colleyn (2004), 540.

Chapter Sixteen

1. Taylor (2003), 132.

2. MacDougall (1998a), 77.

3. Jocelyne Rouch, personal communication, March 2007. Jocelyne Lamothe and Rouch were married in 2002. His first wife, Jane, whom he married in 1952 and whose travels with Rouch were described in chapter 5, died in 1987.

4. Paul Stoller, personal communication, August 2007.

5. See, for example, Asch et al. (1973), 185.

6. Taylor (2003), 143.

7. See chapter 1, pp. 12–14, and chapter 15, pp. 315–317.

8. See MacDougall (1995).

9. Prédal (1996d).

10. See, for example, the review in *Cahiers* by Luc Moullet of Rouch's film, *Hampi: Il pose le ciel sur la terre,* shot in 1960, though only released in 1962. Moullet commends the quality of the film despite the "camera parksonienne" (Moullet 1962).

11. I retain a vivid memory of the occasion, at one of the last Bilan Ethnographique film festivals over which he presided, probably in 2001, when Rouch embraced a student from the Granada Centre, Richard Hughes, after a screening of Richard's film about a Chinese family restaurant in Kunming. "Remember," said Rouch, shaking his finger to emphasize the point, "always remain an amateur. *Always* remain an amateur."

12. Rouch (1995a), 98.

13. Nijland (2007a), 31. For a while, Rouch encouraged the training of students at Nanterre and elsewhere on Super-8 film. But Super-8 has its own particular technical problems and has also become obsolete as a medium of ethnographic filmmaking.

14. Rothman (1997), 104.

15. Rouch (1968), 463.

16. Hennebelle (1982), 167. See also Fulchignoni (1981), 13, and (2003), 158.

17. Taylor (2003), 145.

18. Georgakas et al. (2003), 217.

19. Rouch (1995), 94.

20. Taylor (2003), 145.

21. Rouch (1995b, 228; see also Taylor (2003), 140–141.

22. Colette Piault (1996), 152, see also (2007), 46.

23. Eaton (1979b).

24. Rohmer and Marcorelles (1963), 6.

25. Colleyn (1992), 42.

26. Fieschi (1979).

27. Fulchignoni (1981), 8, see also (2003), 150.

28. See Sjöberg (2008a, 2008b).

29. Stoller (1992), 8–10.

30. Surugue (2008), 289

31. Albert (1997).

32. See *Mosblech* (2008), also fig. 11.6 on p. 241.

33. Serceau (1996), 171.

34. Eaton (2004).

1999. Jean Rouch. *La Pyramide humaine* et *Moi, un noir.* http://perso.wanadoo.fr/cine.beaujolais/rouch.htm.

2003a.The camera and man. In *Ciné-Ethnography*, ed. Steven Feld, 29–46. Minneapolis and London: University of Minnesota Press. Originally published in this translation by Steven Feld and Marielle Delorme in 1974 in *Studies in Visual Communication* 1(1): 37–44.

2003b. The situation and tendencies of the cinema in Africa. In *Ciné-Ethnography*, ed. Steven Feld, 47–86. Minneapolis and London: University of Minnesota Press. Translated by Steven Feld and Marielle Delorme from the original 1967 article in the catalog, *Films Ethnographiques sur l'Afrique noire*, 374–408. Paris: UNESCO.

2003c. On the vicissitudes of the self: The possessed dancer, the magician, the sorcerer, the filmmaker, and the ethnographer. In *Ciné-Ethnography*, ed. Steven Feld, 87–101. Minneapolis and London: University of Minnesota Press. Previously published in this translation by Steven Feld and Shari Robertson in 1978 in *Studies in the Anthropology of Visual Communication* 5 (1):2–8. Originally published in 1971 in *La notion de personne en Afrique Noire*, 529–544. Paris: Centre National de Recherches Scientifiques.

2003d. The mad fox and the pale master. In *Ciné-Ethnography*, ed. Steven Feld, 102–126. Minneapolis and London: University of Minnesota Press. Translated by Steven Feld and Catherine Mazière from the original 1978 article published in French in *Systèmes de signes: Textes réunis en hommage à Germaine Dieterlen*, 3–24. Paris: Hermann.

2003e. The cinema of the future? In *Ciné-Ethnography*, ed. Steven Feld, 266–73. Minneapolis and London: University of Minnesota Press. Previously published in this translation by Steven Feld and Anny Ewing in *Studies in Visual Communication* 11(1): 30–35. Originally published in *Chronique d'un été*. Paris: Interspectacles, Domaine Cinéma.

2008. *Alors le Noir et le blanc seront amis: Carnets de mission, 1946–1951*, ed. Marie-Isabelle Merle des Isles with Bernard Surugue. Mille et une nuits, Arthème Fayard.

Joint publications with Edgar Morin

2003a. *Chronicle of a Summer: the Film.* In *Ciné-Ethnography*, ed. Steven Feld, 274–329. Minneapolis and London: University of Minnesota Press.

2003b. The point of view of the "characters." In *Ciné-Ethnography*, ed. Steven Feld, 330–342. Minneapolis and London: University of Minnesota Press.

Other Sources

Ahounou, Brice. 2000. Les dieux se fâchent à Ganghel. Divinités en colère et anthropologie visuelle. *Afrique Contemporaine* 196(4):17–26. Translated and republished as "Jean Rouch and the great Sahelian drought: Visual anthropology and the wrathful gods at Ganghel," in *Building Bridges: The Cinema of Jean Rouch*, ed. Joram ten Brink, 59–70. London and New York: Wallflower Press.

Albert, Bruce. 1997. "Ethnographic situation" and ethnic movements: Notes on post-Malinowskian fieldwork. *Critique of Anthropology* 17(1): 53–65.

Anon. 1965a. Sept questions aux cinéastes. *Cahiers du Cinéma* 161–162:14–61.

Anon. 1965b. Chacun ses dix. *Cahiers du Cinéma* 161–162: 126–127.

Asch, Timothy, John Marshall, and Peter Spier. 1973. Ethnographic film: Structure and function. *Annual Review of Anthropology* 2:179–187.

Aumont, Jacques, Jean-Louis Comolli, Jean Narboni, and Sylvie Pierre. 1986. Time overflowing. In *Cahiers du Cinéma, 1960–1968: New Wave, New Cinema, Reevaluating Hollywood*, ed. Jim Hillier, 317–323. Cambridge, Mass.: Harvard University Press. Based on an interview with Jacques Rivette originally published in *Cahiers du Cinéma* 204 (September 1968).

Banks, Marcus. 1996. *Ethnicity: Anthropological Constructions*. London and New York: Routledge.

Barbash, Ilisa. 2001. Out of words: The aesthesodic cine-eye of Robert Gardner. An exegesis and interview. *Visual Anthropology* 14:369–413.

Barnouw, Erik. 1983. *Documentary: A History of the Non-fiction Film*. Revised edition. Oxford University Press.

Bate, David 2007. Everyday madness: Surrealism, ethnography and the photographic image. In *Building Bridges: The Cinema of Jean Rouch*, ed. Joram ten Brink, 189–199. London and New York: Wallflower Press.

Ben Salama, Mohand. 1996. Entretien avec Edgar Morin. In *Jean Rouch ou le ciné-plaisir*, ed. René Prédal, 125–127. CinémAction, 81. Condé-sur-Noireau: Éditions Corlet-Télérama. First published in 1982 in *Jean Rouch: Un griot gaulois,* ed. René Prédal, 133–136. CinémAction, 17. Paris: L'Harmattan.

Blue, James. 1965. One man's truth: An interview with Richard Leacock. *Film Comment* 2 (3): 15–23.

———. 1967. Jean Rouch in conversation with James Blue. *Film Comment* 4 (2–3): 84–86.

Boddy, Janice. 1989. *Wombs and Alien Spirits: Women, Men and the Zâr Cult in Northern Sudan*. University of Wisconsin Press.

———. 1995. Managing tradition: "Superstition" and the making of national identity among Sudanese women refugees. In *The Pursuit of Certainty: Religious and Cultural Formulations*, ed. Wendy James, 17–44. London and New York: Routledge.

Bourdieu, Philippe. 1977. *Outline of a Theory of Practice*. Cambridge: Cambridge University Press.

Boutang, Pierre-André. 2004 (Film). *Jean Rouch raconte à Pierre-André Boutang*. 104 min. IRD. Rereleased on DVD by Éditions Montparnasse in 2005.

Bregstein, Philo. 1978 (Film). *Jean Rouch and His Camera in the Heart of Africa*. 75 min. Produced in collaboration with Dutch television, rereleased in 1986.

Bregstein, Philo. 2007. Jean Rouch, fiction film pioneer: A personal account. In *Building Bridges: The Cinema of Jean Rouch*, ed. Joram ten Brink, 165–177. London and New York: Wallflower Press.

Breton, André, and Paul Éluard. 1933. Enquête. *Minotaure* 3–4: 101–116.

Calame-Griaule, Geneviève. 1965. *Ethnologie et langage: La parole chez les Dogon*. Paris: Gallimard.

———. 1991. On the Dogon restudied. *Current Anthropology* 32(5):575–577.

Cervoni, Albert. 1996. Une confrontation historique en 1965 entre Jean Rouch et Sembène Ousmane. In *Jean Rouch ou le ciné-plaisir*, ed. René Prédal, 104–106. CinémAction, 81. Condé-sur-Noireau: Éditions Corlet-Télérama. Previously published in 1982 In *Jean Rouch: Un griot gaulois*, ed. René Prédal,133–136. CinémAction, 17. Paris: L'Harmattan.

Chamberlin, Carloss James. 2006. Dziga Vertov: The Idiot. *Senses of Cinema*. http://esvc001106.wic016u.server-web.com/contents/06/41/dziga-vertov-enthusiasm.html.

Chanan, Michael. 2007. Rouch, music, trance. In *Building Bridges: The Cinema of Jean Rouch*, ed. Joram ten Brink, 87–95. London and New York: Wallflower Press.

Char, René. 2000. The journey is done. In *Surrealist Painters and Poets: An Anthology*, ed. Mary Ann Caws, 21–23. Cambridge, Mass. and London: MIT Press.

Christie, Ian. 2007. Disbelieving documentary: Rouch viewed through the binoculars of Marker and Ruiz. In *Building Bridges: The Cinema of Jean Rouch*, ed. Joram ten Brink, 267–275. London and New York: Wallflower Press.

Clifford, James. 1988a. Power and dialogue in ethnography: Marcel Griaule's initiation. In James Clifford, *The Predicament of Culture: Twentieth-century Ethnography, Literature, and Art*, 55–91. Cambridge, Mass., and London: Harvard University Press.

———. 1988b. On ethnographic surrealism. In James Clifford, *The Predicament of Culture: Twentieth-century Ethnography, Literature, and Art*, 117–151. Cambridge, Mass., and London: Harvard University Press.

———. 1991. *Documents*: A decomposition. *Visual Anthropology Review* 7(1):62–83.

Cocteau, Jean. 1965. Préface au cinéma maudit. *Cahiers du Cinéma* 161–62:10–13.

Coeuroy, André, and André Schaeffner. 1926. *Le Jazz*. Paris: Éditions Claude Aveline.

Colleyn, Jean-Paul. 1992. Jean Rouch, 54 ans sans trépied. *CinémAction* 64: 40–50. Condé-sur-Noireau: Éditions Corlet-Télérama.

———. 2004. Jean Rouch, presque un homme-siècle. *L'Homme* 171–172:537–542.

———. 2005. Jean Rouch: An anthropologist ahead of his time. *American Anthropologist* 107(1): 112–115.

———, ed. 2009. *Jean Rouch. Cinéma et Anthropologie*. Paris: Cahiers du Cinéma /INA.

Comolli, Jean-Louis. 1964. Compte rendu de Venise 64. *Cahiers du Cinéma* 159:19.

Cowie, Elizabeth 2007. Ways of seeing: Documentary film and the surreal of reality. In *Building Bridges: The Cinema of Jean Rouch*, ed. Joram ten Brink, 201–218. London and New York: Wallflower Press.

DeBouzek, Jeanette. 1989. The "ethnographic surrealism" of Jean Rouch. *Visual Anthropology* 2:301–315

De Chirico, Giorgio. 2000. From *The Memoirs of Giorgio de Chirico*. In *Surrealist Painters and Poets: An Anthology*, ed. Mary Ann Caws, 25–32. Cambridge, Mass., and London: MIT Press.

De Ganay, Solange. 1941. *Les Devises des Dogon*. Paris: Travaux et Mémoires de l'Institut d'Ethnologie 41.

De Heusch, Luc. 1981. Possession and shamanism. In Luc de Heusch, *Why Marry Her? : Society and Symbolic Structures*. Cambridge: Cambridge University Press.

De Heusch, Luc. 1983 (Film). *Tracking the Pale Fox: Studies on the Dogon, 1931–1983*. 48 min. Le Centre de l'Audio-visuel à Bruxelles and RTBF in association with the CNRS and La Fondation belge pour les recherches anthropologiques (FOBRA).

———. 1991. On Griaule on trial. *Current Anthropology* 32(4):434–437.

———. 1995. Pierre Mabille, Michel Leiris anthropologues. In *L'Autre et le Sacré: Surréalisme, Cinéma, Ethnologie*, ed. Christopher W. Thompson, 397–405. Paris: L'Harmattan.

Delahaye, Michel. 1961. La règle du Rouch. *Cahiers du Cinéma* 120:1–11.

Descola, Philippe. 2005. *Par-delà nature et culture*. Éditions Gallimard.

Devanne, Laurent. 1998. Jean Rouch, cinéaste. http://www.arkepix.com/kinok/Jean%20ROUCH/rouch_interview.html.

Diawara, Manthia. 1992. *African Cinema: Politics and Culture*. Bloomington and Indianapolis: Indiana University Press.

Diawara, Manthia.1995 (Film). *Rouch in Reverse*. 52 min. California Newsreel.

Dieterlen, Germaine. 1941. *Les Âmes des Dogon*. Paris: Travaux et Mémoires de l'Institut d'Ethnologie 40.

———. 1971. Les fêtes soixantenaires chez les Dogon. *Africa* 41:1–11

———. 1982. *Le Titre d'honneur des Arou (Dogon-Mali)*. Paris: Musée de l'Homme/Société des Africanistes.

———. 1987. Postface. In Nadine Wanono, *Ciné-rituel de femmes dogon*, 105–108. Paris: Éditions du CNRS.

———. 1988. Essai sur la religion bambara. Second edition. Brussels: Éditions de la Université de Bruxelles. First published in 1950 in Paris by the Presses Universitaires de France.

———. 1995. Entretien avec Germaine Dieterlen à propos de Marcel Griaule et du cinéma ethnographique. In *L'Autre et le Sacré: Surréalisme, cinéma, ethnologie*, ed. Christopher W. Thompson, 433–441. Paris: L'Harmattan.

DiIorio, Sam. 2005. Notes on Jean Rouch and French cinema. *American Anthropologist* 107 (1): 120–122

———. 2007. Total cinema: *Chronique d'un été* and the end of Bazinian film theory. *Screen* 48(1): 25–43.

Dornfeld, Barry. 1989. *Chronicle of a Summer* and the editing of *cinéma-vérité*. *Visual Anthropology* 2:317–331.

Dossou-Yovo, Jean Baptiste. 2003. Jean Rouch: Derniers hommages. Clap Noir. http://www.clapnoir.org/actualites/rouch_derniers_hommages.htm.

Douglas, Mary. 1975. If the Dogon . . . In Mary Douglas, *Implicit Meanings: Essays in Anthropology*, 124–141. London and Boston: Routledge and Kegan Paul. First published in 1967 in *Cahiers d'Études Africaines* 28: 659–672.

———. 1995. Réflexions sur le renard pâle et deux anthropologies: À propos du surréalisme et de l'anthropologie française. In *L'Autre et le Sacré: Surréalisme, cinéma, ethnologie*, ed. Christopher W. Thompson, 199–218. Paris: L'Harmattan.

Dubosc, Dominique. 1991(Film). *Jean Rouch, premier film: 1947–1991*. Black and white and color. 26 min. Kinofilm. Rereleased on DVD by Kinofilm (EDV 1488) 2006.

Dussert, Éric. 2007. Damouré Zika, infirmier de santé, façonneur de langage. In Damouré Zika, *Journal de route*, 69–80. Paris: Mille et Une Nuits.

Eaton, Michael. 1979a. Chronicle. In *Anthropology, Reality, Cinema: The Films of Jean Rouch*, ed. Michael Eaton, 1–34. London: British Film Institute.

———. 1979b. The reproduction of cinematic reality. In *Anthropology, Reality, Cinema: The Films of Jean Rouch*, ed. Michael Eaton, 40–53. London: British Film Institute.

———. 2004. Jean Rouch 1917–2004. A valediction. http://www.rouge.com.au/3/rouch_valediction.html.

Feld, Steven. 1989. Themes in the cinema of Jean Rouch. *Visual Anthropology* 2:223–247.

———, ed. and trans. 2003a. *Ciné-Ethnography: Jean Rouch*. Minneapolis and London: University of Minnesota Press.

———. 2003b. Editor's introduction. In *Ciné-Ethnography: Jean Rouch*, ed. Steven Feld, 1–25. Minneapolis and London: University of Minnesota Press.

———. 2003c. Annotated filmography. In *Ciné-Ethnography: Jean Rouch*, ed. Steven Feld, 345–384. Minneapolis and London: University of Minnesota Press.

———. 2003d. Selective bibliography. In *Ciné-Ethnography: Jean Rouch*, ed. Steven Feld, 385–389. Minneapolis and London: University of Minnesota Press.

Fieschi, Jean-André. 1968. De "Jaguar" à "Petit à Petit" par Jean Rouch. *Cahiers du Cinéma* 200–201:55–60

———. 1979. Slippages of fiction: Some notes on the cinema of Jean Rouch. In *Anthro-*

pology, Reality, Cinema: The Films of Jean Rouch, ed. Michael Eaton, 67–77. London: British Film Institute.

Fieschi, Jean-André. 1997(Film). *Mosso Mosso, Rouch comme si*. 73 min. AMIP.

Fieschi, Jean-André, and André Téchiné. 1967. Jean Rouch—"Jaguar." *Cahiers du Cinéma* 195:17–20

Fischer, Michael M. J. 1997. Raising questions about Rouch. *American Anthropologist* 99 (1): 140–143.

Flaherty, Robert. 1996. Robert Flaherty talking. In *Imagining Reality: The Faber Book of Documentary*, ed. Kevin Macdonald and Mark Cousins, 36-43. London and Boston: Faber & Faber. Originally published in 1950 in *The Cinema*, ed. Roger Manvell, London: Penguin.

Forbes, Jill. 1996. Jean Rouch et la Grande-Bretagne. In *Jean Rouch ou le ciné-plaisir*, ed. René Prédal, 136–137. CinémAction, 81. Condé-sur-Noireau: Éditions Corlet-Télérama.

Freyer, Ellen. 1971. *Chronicle of a Summer* —Ten years after. In *The Documentary Tradition*, ed. L. Jacobs, 437–443. New York: Hopkinson & Blake.

Fugelstad, Finn. 1983. *A History of Niger, 1850–1960*. Cambridge: Cambridge University Press.

Fulchignoni, Enrico. 1981. Entretien de Jean Rouch. In *Jean Rouch: Une rétrospective*, ed. Pascal-Emmannuel Gallet, 7–29. Paris: Ministère des relations extérieures-Centre National de la Recherche Scientifique.

Fulchignoni, Enrico. 1982 (Film). *Jean Rouch commente—entretiens avec Enrico Fulchignoni*. CNRS-CFE. Rereleased on DVD by Éditions Montparnasse in 2007.

———. 2003. Ciné-anthropology. In *Ciné-Ethnography*, ed. Steven Feld, 147–187. Minneapolis and London: University of Minnesota Press.

Gabriel, Teshome H. 1982. *Third Cinema in the Third World: The Aesthetics of Liberation*. Ann Arbor, Michigan: UMI Research Press.

Gallet, Pascal-Emmanuel, ed. 1981. *Jean Rouch: Une rétrospective*. Ministère des relations extérieures-Centre National de la Recherche Scientifique. Paris.

Gardner, Robert. 2004 (Film). *Screening Room with Robert Gardner: Jean Rouch*. 64 min. Studio 7 Arts. Originally recorded in 1980.

Gardner, Robert, and Ákos Östör. 2001. *Making Forest of Bliss: Intention, Circumstance and Chance in Nonfiction Film; A Conversation between Robert Gardner + Ákos Östör*. Cambridge, Mass.: Harvard Film Archive and Harvard University Press.

Gauthier, Lionel, and Laurent Pellé. 2000. *Jean Rouch: Récits photographiques*. Paris: Éditions Muséum national d'Histoire naturelle and Musée de l'Homme.

Georgakas, Dan, Udayan Gupta, and Judy Janda. 2003. The politics of visual anthropology. In *Ciné-Ethnography*, ed. Steven Feld, 210–225. Minneapolis and London: University of Minnesota Press. Reprinted from *Cinéaste* 8:4, 1978.

Gerber, Jacques. 1992. *Anatole Dauman: Pictures of a Producer*. Translated by Paul Willemen. London: British Film Institute.

Godard, Jean-Luc. 1959. L'Afrique vous parle de la fin et des moyens. *Cahiers du Cinéma* 94:19–22

———. 1972. *Moi, un Noir*. In *Godard on Godard. Critical writings by Jean-Luc Godard*, ed. Jean Narboni and Tom Milne, 129. London: Secker & Warburg.

Godet, Philippe. 1966. *Monsieur Albert prophète*. *Cahiers du Cinéma* 174:78.

Goldman, Lucien. 1996. "Chronique d'un été," vu par Lucien Goldman. In *Jean Rouch ou* le ciné-plaisir, ed. René Prédal, 122–124. CinémAction, 81. Condé-sur-Noireau: Éditions Corlet-Télérama. First published in 1982 in *Jean Rouch: Un griot gaulois*, ed. René Prédal, 130–132. CinémAction, 17. Paris: L'Harmattan.

Gonçalves, Marco Antonio. 2008. *O Real Imaginado: Etnografia, cinema e surrealismo em Jean Rouch*. Rio de Janeiro: Editora Topbooks.

Goody, Jack. 1967. Review of Marcel Griaule, *Conversations with Ogotemmêli. American Anthropologist* 69:239–241.

Griaule, Marcel. 1933a. Introduction méthodologique. *Minotaure* 2: 7–12.

———. 1933b. Le chasseur du 20 octubre. *Minotaure* 2:31–44.

———. 1933c. Masques dogons. *Minotaure* 2: 45–51.

———. 1938. *Masques dogons*. Université de Paris, Institut d'Ethnologie (Musée de l'Homme). Travaux et Mémoires de l'Institut d'Ethnologie XXXIII.

———. 1957. *Méthode de l'ethnographie*. Paris. Presses Universitaires de France.

———. 1985. *Dieu d'Eau. Entretiens avec Ogotemmêli*. Paris: Fayard. First published in 1948.

Griaule, Marcel, and Germaine Dieterlen. 1965. *Le Renard pâle*. Vol.1, fasc. 1. Le mythe cosmogonique: La création du monde. Paris: Travaux et Mémoires de l'Institut d'Ethnologie.

Grimshaw, Anna. 2001. *The Ethnographer's Eye: Ways of Seeing in Anthropology*. Cambridge: Cambridge University Press.

Gruhn, Isebill V. 1971. The Commission for Technical Co-operation in Africa, 1950–1965. *Journal of Modern African Studies* 9 (3):459–469

Haffner, Pierre. 1996. Les avis de cinq cinéastes d'Afrique noire. In *Jean Rouch ou le ciné-plaisir*, ed. René Prédal, 89–103. CinémAction, 81. Condé-sur-Noireau: Éditions Corlet-Télérama. First published in 1982 in *Jean Rouch: Un griot gaulois*, ed. René Prédal, 62–76. CinémAction, 17. Paris: L'Harmattan.

Hall, Jeanne. 1991. Realism as a style in Cinema Verite: A critical analysis of *Primary. Cinema Journal* 30(4):24–50.

Hassan, Jibril. 2004. Oumarou Ganda: Une symbole du cinéma africain. Clap Noir. http://www.clapnoir.org/actualites/oumarou_ganda_un_symbole_du_cinema_africain.htm.

Hayward, Susan. 2000. *Cinema Studies: The Key Concepts*. Second edition. London and New York: Routledge.

Henley, Paul. 2006a. Spirit-possession, power and the absent presence of Islam: Reviewing *Les maîtres fous. Journal of the Royal Anthropological Institute* n.s. 12(4): 731–761.

———. 2006b. Narratives: The guilty secret of ethnographic documentary? In *Reflecting Visual Ethnography: Using the Camera in Anthropological Research*, ed. Metje Postma and Peter Ian Crawford, 376–401. Højbjerg and Leiden: Intervention Press and CNWS Publications.

———. 2007. Jean Rouch and the legacy of the "pale master": Filming the Sigui, 1931–2033. In *Building Bridges: The Cinema of Jean Rouch*, ed. Joram ten Brink, 39–57. London and New York: Wallflower Press.

Hennebelle, Guy. 1982. Conclusion (un peu) polémique: Cinéma ethnographique et cinéma d'intervention social: Des frères ennemis? In *Jean Rouch: Un griot gaulois*, ed. René Prédal, 164–175. CinémAction, 17. Paris: L'Harmattan.

———. 1996. Jean Rouch et l'éthique du cinéma ethnographique. In *Jean Rouch ou le ciné-plaisir*, ed. René Prédal, 76–79. CinémAction, 81. Condé-sur-Noireau: Éditions

Corlet-Télérama. Originally published in 1982 in *Jean Rouch: Un griot gaulois*, ed. René Prédal, 47–49. CinémAction, 17. Paris: L'Harmattan.

Houdaille, Marie-Hélène. 1981. Filmographie. In *Jean Rouch: Une rétrospective*, ed. Pascal-Emmanuel Gallet, 34–64. Ministère des relations extérieures-Centre National de la Recherche Scientifique. Paris.

Hoveyda, Fereydoun. 1961. Cinéma vérité ou réalisme fantastique. *Cahiers du Cinéma* 125: 33–41.

Hoveyda, Fereydoun, and Éric Rohmer. 1963. Nouvel entretien avec Roberto Rossellini. *Cahiers du Cinéma* 145:2–13.

Jamin, Jean. 1991. Anxious science: Ethnography as a devil's dictionary. *Visual Anthropology Review* 7 (1): 84–91.

Jones, Graham. 2005. A diplomacy of dreams: Jean Rouch and decolonization. *American Anthropologist* 107(1): 118–20.

Jørgensen, Anne Mette. 2007. Filmmaking as ethnographic dialogues: Rouch's family of "scoundrels" in Niger. *Visual Anthropology* 20 (1): 57–73.

Jutra, Claude. 1960–61. En courant derrière Rouch I, *Cahiers du Cinéma* 113:32–43; II, *Cahiers du Cinéma* 114:23–33; III, *Cahiers du Cinéma* 116:39–44.

Karèche, Boudjemâa. 2004. Hommage à Jean Rouch. Le cinéaste et anthropologue de l'Afrique n'est plus. http://www.algerie-dz.com/article10.html.

Leacock, Richard. 2007. Robert Flaherty's contribution to film making. In *Memories of the Origins of Visual Anthropology*, ed. Beate Engelbrecht, 25–29. Frankfurt: Peter Lang.

Leiris, Michel. 1930. Le "caput mortuum" ou la femme de l'alchimiste. *Documents 2* (8):461–466.

———. 1933. Danses funéraires Dogon (Extrait d'un carnet de route). *Minotaure* 1: 73–76.

———. 2008. *L'Afrique fantôme*. Mesnil-sur-l'Estrée: Gallimard. Originally published in 1934, republished in 1951 and 1981.

Lévesque, Robert. 2004. Un échec essentiel. *24 Images* 119:49.

Lewis, Ioan. 1986a. Possession cults in context. In I. M. Lewis, *Religion in Context: Cults and Charisma*, 24–50. Cambridge: Cambridge University Press.

———. 1986b. The power of the past: African "survivals" in Islam. In I. M. Lewis, *Religion in Context: Cults and Charisma*, 94–107. Cambridge: Cambridge University Press.

Loizos, Peter. 1993. *Innovation in Ethnographic Film: From Innocence to Self- Consciousness, 1955–1985*. Manchester: Manchester University Press.

Lourdou, Philippe. 1995. "Mettre en circulation des objets inquiétants": Ethnographie et surrealisme. In *L'Autre et le sacré: Surréalisme, cinéma, ethnologie,* ed. Christopher W. Thompson, 307–314. Paris: L'Harmattan.

MacDougall, David. 1995. Beyond observational cinema. In *Principles of Visual Anthropology*, ed. Paul Hockings, 115–132. Second edition. Berlin and New York: Mouton de Gruyter.

———. 1998a. Visual anthropology and the ways of knowing. In David MacDougall, *Transcultural Cinema*, 61–92. Princeton, New Jersey: Princeton University Press.

———. 1998b. The subjective voice in ethnographic film. In David MacDougall, *Transcultural Cinema*, 93–122. Princeton, New Jersey: Princeton University Press.

Macintosh, Ann. 2004 (Film). *Conversation with Jean Rouch*. 36 min. Produced in collaboration with Documentary Educational Resources.

Madsen, Berit and Anne Mette *Jørgensen*. (Film). 2005/2007. *Friends, Fools, Family: Rouch's Collaborators in Niger*. First released in 2005 at 82 min.; rereleased in 2007 at 59 min. Manche Film

Madsen, Berit and Anne Mette *Jørgensen*. (Film). 2007. *Damouré Talks About Jaguar*. 15 min. Manche Film

Maggi, France, and Gilbert Maggi. 1996. Entretien avec Michel Brault. In *Jean Rouch ou le ciné-plaisir*, ed. René Prédal, 133–135. CinémAction, 81. Condé-sur-Noireau: Éditions Corlet-Télérama. First published in 1982 in *Jean Rouch: Un griot gaulois*, ed. René Prédal, 119–121. CinémAction, 17. Paris: L'Harmattan.

Malinowski, Bronislaw. 1932. *Argonauts of the Western Pacific: An Account of Native Enterprise and Adventure in the Archipelagoes of Melanesian New Guinea*. Second impression. London: Routledge. First published in 1922.

Mamber, Stephen. 1974. *Cinema Verite in America: Studies in Uncontrolled Documentary*. Cambridge, Mass., and London: MIT Press.

Mandelbaum, Jacques. 2004. Jean Rouch, sorcier blanc de l'Afrique et du cinéma. *Le Monde*, 21 February, Section Culture: Disparition, 24.

Marcorelles, Louis. 1963. La foire aux vérités. *Cahiers du Cinéma* 143:26–34.

Marcus, Alan. 1995. *Relocating Eden: The Image and Politics of Inuit Exile in the Canadian Arctic*. Hanover: University Press of New England.

———. 2006. *Nanook of the North* as primal drama. *Visual Anthropology* 19:201–222.

Margulies, Ivone. 2007. The real in-balance in Jean Rouch's *La Pyramide humaine*. In *Building Bridges: The Cinema of Jean Rouch*, ed. Joram ten Brink, 125–133. London and New York: Wallflower Press.

Marie, Michel. 2008. Preface. In Maxime Scheinfeigel, *Jean Rouch*, vi–x. Paris: CNRS Éditions.

Marshall, John. 1993. Filming and learning. In *The Cinema of John Marshall*, ed. J. Ruby, 1–133. Philadelphia: Harwood Academic.

Marshall, John, and John W. Adams. 2003. Jean Rouch talks about his films. *American Anthropologist* 80: 1005–1022. Republished in *Ciné-Ethnography*, ed. Steven Feld, 188–209. Minneapolis and London: University of Minnesota Press.

Masquelier, Adeline. 1993. Narratives of power, images of wealth: The ritual economy of the *bori* in the market. In *Modernity and Its Malcontents: Ritual and Power in Postcolonial Africa*, ed. Jean Comaroff and John Comaroff, 3–33. Chicago and London: University of Chicago Press.

Mead, Margaret. 1995. Visual anthropology in a discipline of words. In *Principles of Visual Anthropology*, ed. Paul Hockings, 3–10. Second edition. Berlin and New York: Mouton de Gruyter.

Merle des Isles, Marie-Isabelle. 2005. *Destins d'explorateurs de l'Antartique à l'Asie centrale, 1908–1950*. Paris: Éditions de la Martinière.

Meyknecht, Steef, Dirk *Nijland* and Joost *Verhey*. 1993 (Film). De Bende van Rouch (Rouch's Gang). 70 min. MM Produkties.

Michaud, Samuel. 1982. Rouch et le cinéma-vérité: Un detour par le "direct." In *Jean Rouch: Un griot gaulois*, ed. René Prédal, 111–118. CinémAction, 17. Paris: L'Harmattan.

Morin, Edgar. 1962. Preface. In Luc de Heusch, *Cinéma et sciences sociales: Panorama du film ethnographie et sociologique*. UNESCO: Rapports et documents en sciences sociales, no. 16. Republished in English in 1988, in *Visual Anthropology* 1:99–156.

———. 2003. Chronicle of a film. In *Ciné-Ethnography*, ed. Steven Feld, 229–265. Minneapolis and London: University of Minnesota Press. First published in English in *Stud-*

ies in Visual Communication 11, no. 1 (1988): 4–29. Originally published in French in 1962 in *Chronique d'un été*. Paris: Interspectacles, Domaine Cinéma.

Morin, Edgar, and Jean Rouch. 2003a. *Chronicle of a Summer*: The Film. In *Ciné-Ethnography*, ed. Steven Feld, 274–329. Minneapolis and London: University of Minnesota Press. Previously published in this translation by Steven Feld and Anny Ewing in *Studies in Visual Communication* 11(1). Originally published in French in 1962 in *Chronique d'un été*. Paris: Interspectacles, Domaine Cinéma.

———. 2003b. The point of view of the "characters." In *Ciné-Ethnography*, ed. Steven Feld, 330–342. Minneapolis and London: University of Minnesota Press.

Morphy, Howard. 1994. The interpretation of ritual: Reflections from film on anthropological practice. *Man* 29:117–146.

Mosblech, Bernd. 2008 (Film). *Ich bin ein weisser Afrikaner: Abschied von Jean Rouch/ Je suis un Africain blanc: adieu à Jean Rouch*. 55 min. Bernd Mosblech Filmproducktion/ SWR/ Arte.

Mouëllic, Gilles. 2001. Jean Rouch: Comme Armstrong jouait de la trompette. *Jazz Magazine*, no. 514.

Moullet, Luc. 1962. Petit journal: Petites choses cannoises. *Cahiers du Cinéma* 133:34.

———. 1964. Le mensonge suspect. *Cahiers du Cinéma* 155:48–50.

———. 1986. Jean-Luc Godard. In *Cahiers du Cinéma, 1960–1968: New Wave, New Cinema, Reevaluating Hollywood*, ed. Jim Hillier, 35–48. Cambridge, Mass.: Harvard University Press. Originally published in *Cahiers du Cinéma* 106 (April 1960).

Muller, Jean-Claude. 1971. Review of *Les Maîtres fous*. *American Anthropologist* 73: 1471–1473.

Mundell, Ian. 2004. "Rouch isn't here, he has left." A report on *Building Bridges: The Cinema of Jean Rouch*, French Institute, London, October 5–14, 2004. http://www.senses ofcinema.com/contents/festivals/05/34/jean_rouch_conference.html.

Murphy David, and Patrick Williams. 2007. *Postcolonial African Cinema: Ten Directors*. Manchester and New York: Manchester University Press.

Naficy, Hamid. 2007. Ethnography and African culture: Jean Rouch on *La Chasse au lion à l'arc* and *Les Maîtres fous*. In *Building Bridges: The Cinema of Jean Rouch*, ed. Joram ten Brink, 97–108. London and New York: Wallflower Press.

Nijland, Dirk. 2007a. Jean Rouch: A builder of bridges. In *Building Bridges: The Cinema of Jean Rouch*, ed. Joram ten Brink, 21–35. London and New York: Wallflower Press.

———. 2007b. Cinémafia—Jean Rouch with Joris Ivens and Henri Storck. In *Building Bridges: The Cinema of Jean Rouch*, ed. Joram ten Brink, 221–233. London and New York: Wallflower Press.

Olivier de Sardan, Jean-Pierre. 1993. La surinterprétation politique: Les cultes de possession *hawka* du Niger. In *Religion et modernité politique en Afrique noire*, ed. J. F. Bayart, 163–213. Paris: Karthala.

Ollier, Claude. 1965. Cinéma-surrealité. *Cahiers du Cinéma* 172:50–51.

Ozarin, Lucy. 2003. J. L. Moreno, M.D.: Founder of psychodrama. *Psychiatric News* 38 (10): 60. http://pn.psychiatryonline.org/cgi/content/full/38/10/60.

Painter, Thomas M. 1988. From warriors to migrants: Critical perspectives on early migrations among the Zarma of Niger. *Africa* 58(1): 87–100.

Paulme, Denise. 1940. *Organisation sociale des Dogon (Soudan français)*. Paris: Éditions Domat-Montchrestien.

Pellé, Laurent. 1997. Bibliographie et filmographie de Jean Rouch. In Jean Rouch, *Les Hommes et les dieux du fleuve: Essai ethnographique sur les populations songhay du moyen*

Niger, 1941–1983, 271–278. Paris: Éditions Artcom. htttp://www.comite-film-ethno
.net/rouch/rouch.htm.

Petric, Vlada. 1987. *Constructivism in Film:* The Man with the Movie Camera, *a Cinematic
Analysis*. Cambridge: Cambridge University Press.

Piault, Colette. 1996a. "Parole interdite," parole sous contrôle . . . In *Jean Rouch ou le
ciné-plaisir*, ed. René Prédal, 140–147. CinémAction, 81. Condé-sur-Noireau: Éditions
Corlet-Télérama. Translated and republished in 2007 in *Visual Anthropology Review*
23(1):38–42.

———. 1996b. Parole dominée, parole dominante . . . In *Jean Rouch ou le ciné-plaisir*,
ed. René Prédal, 148–160. CinémAction, 81. Condé-sur-Noireau: Éditions Corlet-
Télérama. Translated and republished in 2007 in *Visual Anthropology Review* 23(1):
43–53.

Piault, Marc-Henri. 1970. *Histoire mawri: Introduction à l'étude des processus constitutifs
d'un état*. Paris: CNRS.

———. 1996. Une pensée fertile. In *Jean Rouch ou le ciné-plaisir*, ed. René Prédal, 46–55.
CinémAction, 81. Condé-sur-Noireau: Éditions Corlet-Télérama.

———. 1997. Preface. Regards croisés, regards partagés. In Jean Rouch, *Les Hommes
et les dieux du fleuve: Essai ethnographique sur les populations songhay du moyen Niger,
1941–1983*, 7–20. Paris: Éditions Artcom.

———. 2000a. *Anthropologie et cinéma: Passage à l'image, passage par l'image*. Paris: Éditions Nathan.

———. 2000b. La *yasigui* et le renard pâle. Mythes, controverses, images . . . *Cahiers
d'études africaines* 159. Éditions EHESS. http://etudesafricaines.revues.org/
document24.html.

Pierre, Sylvie. 1967. Le regard brûlant du conteur. *Cahiers du Cinéma* 192:65–66.

Pinney, Christopher. 1992. The lexical spaces of eye-spy. In *Film as Ethnography*, ed. Peter
Crawford and David Turton, 26–49. Manchester: University of Manchester Press.

Prédal, René, ed. 1982. *Jean Rouch: Un griot gaulois*. CinémAction, 17. Paris: L'Harmattan.

———. 1996a. Ed. *Jean Rouch ou le ciné-plaisir*. CinémAction, 81. Condé-sur-Noireau:
Éditions Corlet-Télérama.

———. 1996b. Rouch d'hier à demain. In *Jean Rouch ou le ciné-plaisir*, ed. René Prédal,
12–18. CinémAction, 81. Condé-sur-Noireau: Éditions Corlet-Télérama.

———. 1996c. Le ciné-plaisir. In *Jean Rouch ou le ciné-plaisir*, ed. René Prédal, 19–39.
CinémAction, 81. Condé-sur-Noireau: Éditions Corlet-Télérama.

———. 1996d. Jean Rouch et l'évolution des techniques de prises de vues, 161–164.
CinémAction, 81. Condé-sur-Noireau: Éditions Corlet-Télérama. Originally published
in 1982 in *Jean Rouch: Un griot gaulois*, ed. René Prédal, 142–147. CinémAction, 17.
Paris: L'Harmattan.

———. 1996e. 1976: "Babatu, les trois conseils". Entretien avec Jean Rouch. In *Jean
Rouch ou le ciné-plaisir*, ed. René Prédal, 189–195. CinémAction, 81. Condé-sur-
Noireau: Éditions Corlet-Télérama.

———. 1996f. "Dionysos," utopie et pluri-ethnisme. In *Jean Rouch ou le ciné-plaisir*,
ed. René Prédal, 198–201. CinémAction, 81. Condé-sur-Noireau: Éditions Corlet-
Télérama.

———. 1996g. 1987: "Brise-glace," prélude au regard documentaire. In *Jean Rouch ou le
ciné-plaisir*, ed. René Prédal, 204–205. CinémAction, 81. Condé-sur-Noireau: Éditions
Corlet-Télérama.

———. 1996h. 1990: "Liberté, égalité fraternité . . . et puis après." In *Jean Rouch ou le ciné-plaisir*, ed. René Prédal, 211. CinémAction, 81. Condé-sur-Noireau: Éditions Corlet-Télérama.

———. 1996i. Filmographie. In *Jean Rouch ou le ciné-plaisir*, ed. René Prédal, 214–226. CinémAction, 81. Condé-sur-Noireau: Éditions Corlet-Télérama.

———. 1996j. Bibliographie. In *Jean Rouch ou le ciné-plaisir*, ed. René Prédal, 227–236. CinémAction, 81. Condé-sur-Noireau: Éditions Corlet-Télérama.

Price, Sally, and Jean Jamin. 1988. A conversation with Michel Leiris. *Current Anthropology* 29 (1):157–174

Reisz, Karel, and Gavin Millar. 1999. *The Technique of Film Editing*. Second edition. Oxford: Focal Press. Originally published in 1968.

Remy, Michel. 2000. The entrance of the medium. In David Gascoyne, *A Short Survey of Surrealism*, 13–22. London: Enitharmon Press.

Richardson, Michael. 2006. *Surrealism and Cinema*. Oxford: Berg.

Riolon, Luc and Bernard *Surugue.* 2004 (Film). *Le Double d'hier a rencontré demain*. Films de la Pléiade. Rereleased on DVD by Éditions Montparnasse in 2005.

Rivet, Paul, and Georges-Henri Rivière. 1933. La mission ethnographique et linguistique Dakar-Djibouti. *Minotaure* 2:3–5.

Rohmer, Éric. 1961. Le goût de la beauté. *Cahiers du Cinéma* 121:18–25.

Rohmer, Éric, and Louis Marcorelles. 1963. Entretien avec Jean Rouch. *Cahiers du Cinéma* 144:1–22.

Rothman, William. 1997. *Documentary Film Classics*. Cambridge: Cambridge University Press.

Rouch, Jane. 1956. *Le Rire n'a pas de couleur*. Seventh edition. Paris: Gallimard.

———. 1984. *Nous n'irons plus aux bals nègres: Le tiers monde en miettes*. Paris: Scarabée and Compagnie.

Rouget, Gilbert. 1965. Un film expérimental: *Batteries Dogon*, éléments pour une étude des rythmes. *L'Homme* 5 (2): 126–132.

———. 1985. *Music and Trance: A Theory of Relations between Music and Possession*. Trans. Brunhilde Biebuyck. Chicago and London: University of Chicago Press. First published in French in 1980 by Éditions Gallimard.

———. 1996. *Un Roi africain et sa musique du cour: chants et danses du palais à Porto-Novo sous le règne du Gbèfa (1948–1976)*. Paris: CNRS Éditions.

Roy-Leven, G. 1996. Jean Rouch interviewed by G. Roy-Leven. In *Imagining Reality: The Faber Book of the Documentary*, ed. Kevin MacDonald and Mark Cousins, 264–268. London and Boston: Faber and Faber.

Ruby, Jay. 1989. A filmography of Jean Rouch, 1946–1980. *Visual Anthropology* 2 (3–4): 333–367

———. 2000. *Picturing Culture: Explorations of Film and Anthropology*. Chicago and London: University of Chicago Press.

Russell, Catherine. 1999. *Experimental Ethnography: The Work of Film in the Age of Video*. Durham and London: Duke University Press.

Sadoul, Georges. 1963. Actualité de Dziga Vertov. *Cahiers du Cinéma* 144:23–34.

———. 1971. *Dziga Vertov*. Paris: Éditions Champ Libre.

Saunders, Dave. 2007. *Direct Cinema: Observational Documentary and the Politics of the Sixties*. London and New York: Wallflower Press.

Sauvy, Jean. 2006. *Jean Rouch tel que je l'ai connu: 67 ans d'amitié, 1937–2004*. Paris: L'Harmattan.

Schaeffner, André. 1933. Peintures rupestres de Songo. *Minotaure* 2: 52–55.

Scheinfeigel, Maxime. 2008. *Jean Rouch*. Paris: CNRS Éditions.

Scheinman, Diane. 1998. The "dialogic imagination" of Jean Rouch. Covert conversations in *Les Maîtres fous*. In *Documenting the Documentary: Close Readings of Documentary Film and Video*, ed. Barry Keith Grant and Jeannette Sloniowski, 188–203. Detroit: Wayne State University Press.

Seligmann, Guy. 1996 (Film). *Les Dogon, chronique d'une passion*. 97 min. ARTE/ SODA-PERAGA. Rereleased on DVD by ARTE France in 2007.

Serceau, Daniel. 1996. Entretien avec Pierre Braunberger. In *Jean Rouch ou le ciné-plaisir*, ed. René Prédal, 170–171. CinémAction, 81. Condé-sur-Noireau: Éditions Corlet-Télérama. Originally published in 1982 in *Jean Rouch: Un griot gaulois*, ed. René Prédal, 158–160. CinémAction, 17. Paris: L'Harmattan.

Shivas, Mark. 1996. Richard Leacock. In *Imagining Reality: The Faber Book of Documentary*, ed. Kevin Macdonald and Mark Cousins, 254–258. London and Boston: Faber & Faber.

Sjöberg, Johannes. 2008a. Ethnofiction: Genre hybridity in theory and practice-based research. Ph.D. dissertation. University of Manchester.

———.2008b. Ethnofiction: Drama as a creative research practice in ethnographic film. *Journal of Media Practice* 9 (3): 229–242.

Speckenbach, Jan. 1995 (Film). *A Few Minutes Jean Rouch*. 39 min. Wagner and Taunus Television.

Stoller, Paul. 1989a. *Fusion of the Worlds: An Ethnography of Possession among the Songhay of Niger*. Chicago: University of Chicago Press.

———. 1989b. *The Taste of Ethnographic Things*. Philadelphia: University of Pennsylvania Press.

———. 1992. *The Cinematic Griot: The Ethnography of Jean Rouch*. Chicago and London: University of Chicago Press.

———. 1994. Artaud, Rouch and the cinema of cruelty. In *Visualizing Theory: Selected essays from V.A.R., 1990–1994*, ed. Lucien Taylor, 84–98. New York and London: Routledge.

———. 1995. *Embodying Colonial Memories: Spirit Possession, Power, and the Hauka in West Africa*. New York and London: Routledge.

———. 1997. *Sensuous Scholarship*. Philadelphia: University of Pennsylvania Press.

———. 2005. *Stranger in the Village of the Sick: A Memoir of Cancer, Sorcery, and Healing*. Boston: Beacon Press.

———. 2009. *The Power of the Between: An Anthropological Odyssey*. Chicago: Chicago University Press.

Surugue, Bernard. 2007. Jean Rouch and the sacred cattle. In *Building Bridges: The Cinema of Jean Rouch*, ed. Joram ten Brink, 9–19. London and New York: Wallflower Press.

———. 2008. Les jalons de la vie de Jean Rouch. In Jean Rouch, *Alors le noir et le blanc seront amis: Carnets de mission, 1946–1951*, 283–293. Mille et une nuits, Arthème Fayard.

Taussig, Michael. 1993. *Mimesis: A Particular History of the Senses*. New York: Routledge.

Taylor, Lucien. 2003. A life on the edge of film and anthropology. In *Ciné–Ethnography*, ed. Steven Feld, 129–146. Minneapolis and London: University of Minnesota Press. First published in 1991 in *Visual Anthropology Review* 7(1):92–102.

Ten Brink, Joram, ed. 2007a. *Building Bridges: The Cinema of Jean Rouch*. London and New York: Wallflower Press.

———. 2007b. *La Pyramide humaine*: Nadine Ballot. In *Building Bridges: The Cinema of Jean Rouch*, ed. Joram ten Brink, 135–142. London and New York: Wallflower Press.

———. 2007c. *Chronique d'un été*: Marceline Loridan Ivens. In *Building Bridges: The Cinema of Jean Rouch*, ed. Joram ten Brink, 145–152. London and New York: Wallflower Press.

———. 2007d. *Petit à Petit*: Safi Faye. In *Building Bridges: The Cinema of Jean Rouch*, ed. Joram ten Brink, 155–163. London and New York: Wallflower Press.

———. 2007e. From "caméra-stylo" to "caméra-crayon" et puis après . . . In *Building Bridges: The Cinema of Jean Rouch*, ed. Joram ten Brink, 235–248. London and New York: Wallflower Press.

Tessier, Danièle. 1982. Le Montage: Concerto à deux régards et quatre mains. In *Jean Rouch ou le ciné-plaisir*, ed. René Prédal, 168–169. CinémAction, 81. Condé-sur-Noireau: Éditions Corlet-Télérama.

Thompson, Christopher W., ed. 1995a. *L'Autre et le Sacré: Surréalisme, cinéma, ethnologie*. Paris: L'Harmattan.

———. 1995b. Du sacré comme puissance au sacré comme jeu. In *L'Autre et le Sacré: Surréalisme, cinéma, ethnologie*, ed. Christopher W. Thompson, 7–19. Paris: L'Harmattan.

———. 1995c. De Buñuel à Rouch: Les surréalistes devant le documentaire et le film ethnographique. In *L'Autre et le Sacré: Surréalisme, cinéma, ethnologie*, ed. Christopher W. Thompson, 263–281. Paris: L'Harmattan.

———. 1996. Aventure, ethnologie et hasard. In *Jean Rouch ou le ciné-plaisir*, ed. René Prédal, 69–73. CinémAction, 81. Condé-sur-Noireau: Éditions Corlet-Télérama.

———. 2004–2005. Time in the cinema of Jean Rouch. htttp://www.der.org/jean-rouch/content/index.php?id=compose_time.

———. 2007. Chance and adventure in the cinema and ethnography of Jean Rouch. In *Building Bridges: The Cinema of Jean Rouch*, ed. Joram ten Brink, 181–187. London and New York: Wallflower Press.

Tierney, Patrick. 2000. *Darkness in El Dorado: How Scientists and Journalists Devastated the Amazon*. New York and London: W. W. Norton.

Truffaut, François. 1985. *The Films in My Life*. Trans. Leonard Mayhew. New York: Touchstone. Originally published in French in 1975.

Ukadike, Nwachukwu Frank. 1994. *Black African Cinema*. Berkeley, Los Angeles, and London: University of California Press.

Ungar, Steven. 2007. Whose voice? Whose film?: Jean Rouch, Oumarou Ganda and *Moi, un noir*. In *Building Bridges: The Cinema of Jean Rouch*, ed. Joram ten Brink, 111–123. London and New York: Wallflower Press.

Uwewedimo, Michael. 2007. Inventing the interview: The interrogatory poetics of Jean Rouch. In *Building Bridges: The Cinema of Jean Rouch*, ed. Joram ten Brink, 251–264. London and New York: Wallflower Press.

Van Beek, Walter E. A. 1991. Dogon restudied: A field evaluation of the work of Marcel Griaule. *Current Anthropology* 32(2): 139–167.

———. 1992. On myth as science fiction. *Current Anthropology* 33(2): 214–216

Veuve, Jacqueline. 1967. Jean Rouch in conversation. *Film Comment* 4 (2–3): 90–91.

Villain, Dominique. 1991. *Le Montage au cinéma*. Paris: Éditions *Cahiers du Cinéma*.

Walter, Robert. 1996. Jean Rouch parle de "Dionysos": "Une expérience inséparable de mes films ethnographiques." In *Jean Rouch ou le ciné-plaisir*, ed. René Prédal, 202–204. CinémAction, 81. Condé-sur-Noireau: Éditions Corlet-Télérama.

Wanono, Nadine. 1987. *Ciné-rituel de femmes dogon*. Paris: Éditions du CNRS.

———. 2006. From spatial analysis to virtual wonder. In *Reflecting Visual Ethnography: Using the Camera in Anthropological Research*, ed. Metje Postma and Peter Ian Crawford, 252–269. Højbjerg and Leiden: Intervention Press and CNWS Publications.

Werbner, Richard 1990. South-Central Africa: The Manchester School and after. In Richard Fardon, ed., *Localizing Strategies: Regional Traditions of Ethnographic Writing*, 152–181. Edinburgh and Washington: Scottish Academic Press and Smithsonian Institution Press.

Weyergans, François. 1961. La photo du mois. *Cahiers du Cinéma* 123:53.

Winston, Brian. 1995. *Claiming the Real: The Documentary Film Revisited*. London: British Film Institute.

———. 2007. Rouch's "second legacy": *Chronique d'un été* as reality TV's totemic ancestor. In *Building Bridges: The Cinema of Jean Rouch*, ed. Joram ten Brink, 297–311. London and New York: Wallflower Press.

Yakir, Dan. 1978. Ciné-trance: The vision of Jean Rouch. *Film Quarterly* 21(3): 1–10. http://der.org/jean-rouch/content/index.php?id=crack_cine.

Zika, Damouré. 1949. Les aventures de Mekoy (Celui qui a une bouche). In *Anthologie de la poésie naturelle*, ed. Camille Bryen and Bernard Gheerbrant, 164–165. Paris: K Éditeur.

———. 2007. *Journal de route*. Paris: Éditions Mille et Une Nuits. Previously published in 1956 in three separate installments in the journal *Nouvelle Nouvelle Revue française*, nos. 37–39.

INDEX

The letter f following a page number denotes a figure. All italicized entries beginning with a capital refer to films, publications, or sometimes proper names. Unless otherwise indicated, they refer to films by Jean Rouch. Numbers in bold following the titles of Rouch's films refer to entries in the listing of films in appendix 1. These provide summary details of the films. All italicized entries without capitalization refer to words in French or other foreign languages.

collaborations with young filmmakers. *See* film works by Jean Rouch: collaborations with young filmmakers

Colleyn, Jean-Paul, xvii, 337, 452n6

colonialism, European, in West Africa, 2, 78–79, 82; representation in *hauka* cult, 101–34 passim

Comité du Film Ethnographique (CFE), x, 69, 363, 366

Comité International du Film Ethnographique et Sociologique (CIFES), 313

commercial films by Jean Rouch, 197

Commission for Technical Cooperation in Africa (CCTA), 440n2

Congo (Belgian colony), 156, 166

Convention People's Party (CPP), Ghana, 70

Costantini, Philippe, 262, 363, 451n38; as additional cinematographer, 410, 411, 417; as archivist, 363; as assistant director on Rouch's films, 405; as codirector, 407, 410; as photographer, 340f

Côte d'Ivoire. *See* Ivory Coast

Cotin, André, 305

Couleur du temps, Le, 24, **412**

Cousin-cousine, pirogue-gondole, **411–12**

Coutant, André, 157, 265

Coutard, Raoul, 157, 158f, 168

Cowie, Elizabeth, 437n25

Croccichia, Major Horace ("Wicked Major" *hauka* spirit), 117

Cros, Pierre, 57

Dahomey. *See* Benin

Dakar (capital, Senegal), 214, 328, 391, 411; Rouch's time at, 7–8

Dakar-Djibouti expedition, 1, 221, 408; colonial fieldwork methods of, 315–16, 460n15; connections with Surrealism, 17, 18, 19, 21

DALAROU, DALAROUTA (production companies), 286, 330, 414

Dalí, Salvador, xiv, 16, 17, 20, 28; dream sequences, 296–97; visit to Port Lligat, 67

Dama d"Ambara, Le (codirector, Germaine Dieterlen), 286, **403–4**; funerary rite for Griaule and Dieterlen's informant, 235; Griaule's texts used in voice-over, 235; long lapse between shooting and editing, 288

Damouré parle du SIDA, **393**

Damouré Zika, 43, 56, 67, 179, 204, 209, 299, 392, 411, 415; acting roles with directors other than Rouch, 325, 461n40; age when he first met Rouch, 461n34; *Bataille sur le grand fleuve*, role in dramatization of, 62, 64f; death of, 461n33; family, film about, 386; fiction films with Rouch, number of, 236; improvisational talent of, 216–17, 261, 326; introduces Rouch to his priestess grandmother, 7, 324; introduces Rouch to Lam, 38; injured in Rouch's fatal car accident, 324, 358; *Jaguar*, leading role in, 72–81, 298; *Jaguar*, performs voice-over with Lam, 74, 137, 291; meeting with Rouch as example of "objective chance," 324; paramedic, pharmacist, 324–25, 353, 391, 393–94, 451n30; *Petit à Petit*, leading role in, 25, 210–17; "pointeur" for Rouch, 324; portraits, 77f, 80f, 323f, 336f; relationship with Rouch over sixty-two years, 322–25, 335–36, 336f; Sorko ethnic group, member of, originally Kourteï, 307, 323–24; sound recordist, acts as, 101, 282, 388; suggests making "a real film," 65–66, 318; travel diary and other writings, 73–74, 325, 439n20; wealth in old age, 325. *See also* Lam Ibrahim Dia

Danseurs de Tyogou, Les. See *Sigui no. 2: Les Danseurs de Tyogou*

Daouda Kante, 414

Daouda Sorko (film, Jean Rouch), **3**

Daouda Sorko (priest of Dongo cult, Simiri), 378, 387

d'Arthuys, Jacques, 409

Dassin, Jules, advises on *Les Maîtres fous*, 282, 291, 305

Dauman, Anatole: biography, 446n5; *Chronicle of a Summer*, producer of, 147–48, 156, 167, 171, 173, 446n7

Davidovici, Édouard, 391

De Battista, Gérard, 416

De Chirico, Giorgio: referred to in Rouch's films, 239, 409; as Surrealist painter, 20, 23f, 24, 28, 29, 436n20

De Ganay, Solange, 37

De Gaulle, General Charles, 82

De Heusch, Luc, 18, 407; defends *Les Maîtres fous*, 104; on Suzanne Baron, 459n7

De Medeiros, Richard, 333, 334–35
De Oliveira, Manoel, 413
De Sade, Marquis Donatien Alphonse
    François, 184
De Vos, George, xvi
DeBouzek, Jeanette, 303, 304
Debray, Régis, 154, 159f, 165, 448n35
Delahaye, Michel, 176–77
Delassus, Gérard, 417
Deleuze, Gilles, 239, 462n62
Depardon, Raymond, xii, 407
DER (Documentary Educational Re-
    sources), 369, 406
Descola, Philippe, 435n14
Deux Chasseurs, Les, **415**
development in Africa, social and eco-
    nomic, films about. *See* film works by
    Jean Rouch: development in Africa, so-
    cial and economic, films about
Devlin, Bernard, 391
Di Castri, Marco, 409
Di Gioia, Herb, xxivf
Didiot, François, 408, 411, 412, 413, 416
Dieterlen, Germaine, xxi, xxiii, 1–2, 7, 16,
    37, 41, 218–19, 241, 307; *Batteries dogon*,
    codirector, 198; *Cimetières dans la fal-
    aise*, role in scripting commentary, 438–
    39n7; death, 9, 237; *Dionysos*, role in,
    260, 417; Dogon funeral for, 240; *Essai
    sur la religion bambara*, published the-
    sis, 12; fieldwork, views about, 10f, 11,
    13–14, 196, 314; film portraits by Rouch,
    237, 405, 408–9; Marcel Mauss, meeting
    with, 408; portrait of, 10f; Rouch's high
    regard for, 9; Sigui ceremony, interpre-
    tation of, 221–22; Sigui films, codirector
    of, 143–44, 145, 219, 224, 234, 317; Sigui
    films, conception of as documents, 233
Dieu d'eau (book, Marcel Griaule), 435n23,
    437n4
DiIorio, Sam, 171–73
Dionysos, 239, 262–63, 283, 309, **417–18**,
    456nn20–21
Dionysos, Greek god of Bacchanalian cele-
    bration, 239, 418
Diori, Hamani (President of Niger), 391
Direct Cinema group, xvi, 139, 165, 341,
    447n33; differences with Rouch regard-
    ing meaning of *cinéma-vérité*, 149, 174,
    249–51

disturbing objects (*objets inquiétants*). *See*
    Surrealism
documents (ethnographic data): Sigui
    films as "documents," 233; "sound docu-
    ments," term used by Rouch to refer
    to music, 65, 313; term originated by
    Mauss, 11, 172, 313
Documents (Surrealist journal), 17, 18, 19, 27
Dogon (ethnic group of Bandiagara Es-
    carpment, Eastern Mali), 13, 14, 144,
    218–36 passim; circumcision, 226; con-
    troversy over Griaule's account of, 219–
    20; Dakar-Djibouti expedition, encoun-
    ter with, 18, 22f; drumming, 397; films
    by Rouch about, 52, 54–55, 198, 219,
    224–36, 397–405; Griaule's treatment
    of, 315; historical migrations, 220–21,
    452n6; Islam, effects on, 220–23, 231–33;
    joking relationship with plains-dwelling
    groups, 9, 221; *kanaga* masks, 20, 22f,
    29, 235f, 240, 359f; Ogotemmêli, inter-
    views with Griaule, 37; origin of Death,
    226; origin of language, 226; Pale Fox or-
    acle, 225, 400; population numbers, 220;
    serige masks, 235f; Sirius and its com-
    panion star, controversy about, 452n9;
    toguna men's house, 340f, 398–99
—funerary rites, 54–55, 55f, 439n10; Anaï,
    funeral of, 402–3; *dama* ceremony, 226,
    231, 235, 235f, 403–4; firing of muskets,
    ululation, 402–3; Griaule and Dieter-
    len, funerals for, 240, 359; Monzé the
    Hunter, funeral of, 19–20, 22f; mortu-
    ary mannequins, 231, 232f, 241f, 402;
    nani "correspondent" on journey to
    Land of the Dead, 403; Rouch, funeral
    for, 240, 241f, 359; serpentine danc-
    ing, 373, 403; *tegué* creation sayings,
    296, 402
—Hogon, paramount chief: funeral filmed
    by Rouch, 235, 403, 453n27; Rouch and
    Dieterlen seek permission to film from,
    224, 398
—Sigui ceremony, 144, 219–34; arrange-
    ments to film in 2027, 241–42; birth
    symbolism, 400–401; bull-roarers as
    "voice" of the ancestors, 399, 400;
    and circumcision, 226, 401; as collec-
    tive male *rite de passage*, 221, 398, 400,
    452n10; conclusion of, 401; cowrie

film works by Jean Rouch (*continued*)
other West African groups, 69, 197–98,
388–90; on the Songhay, 38–49, 56–65,
70–72, 101–34, 196–210, 236, 370–75,
376–87
—fictional works (other than ethnofictions), 91–100, 176–95, 236, 366, 394–
97, 409–11, 412, 417–19; ethnographic
reality, relationship to, 352–55; mixed
value of for ethnographic filmmakers,
354–55; New Wave, films forming part
of, 176–95, 353, 394–96
—migration, films about, 67–91, 101–34,
199, 374–77
—Paris, films set in, 145–95, 210–17, 394–
97, 405, 407–9, 410, 411, 413, 417–18, 419
—portrait films, 236–37, 405–9
filmmaking, Rouch's praxis: "anthropology in the first person," 339; authorship, claim to, 272–74, 309, 330–31; *barbarie de l'invention*, raw creativity, 276;
camera as catalyst, 263, 270, 272, 340–
41, 349; definition of praxis, xvii–xviii;
grace, Dionysian, 257–58, 287; performance, importance of, 344–45; risk and
chance, importance of, 38, 236, 255–58,
260, 263, 344–45; *Stimmung*, as poetic
creativity, 274–75, 456n38; theorist,
Rouch's limitations as, 349–52; value of
Rouch's legacy, 338–61
—camera technology: Aaton, 240, 241f,
265, 267f, 268f; Arriflex 16mm, 157,
159f; Beaulieu R16, 203, 265, 266f; Bell
& Howell Filmo 70, 35, 38, 50, 55, 60f,
70f, 93, 101, 139, 140, 203, 256f, 342;
Éclair Cameflex CM3 (35mm), 157, 158f;
Éclair NPR, 217, 264f, 265, 266f, 456n27;
KMT Coutant-Mathot Éclair, 157–58,
159f, 265; Miller tripod head, rejection
of, 456n27; Super-8, 386, 409, 463n13;
video, rejection of, 138–39, 343–44
—camerawork, shooting technique, 255–
77; abandonment of the tripod, 39, 40f,
265, 342; *belle image*, disdain for, 263,
341–42; "crossing the line," early problems with, 39–41; difficulty in adapting
to sound-synchronous systems, 343;
dollies, improvised, 160–62; editing
through the viewfinder, 140; film crews,
"violently opposed" to, 263–64, 341;

lighting, 90, 265; limitations of in later
career, 342–43, 460n31, 463n10; *Moi,
un Noir*, apogee of, 88, 342; participatory camera, 263–69; sequence-shots
(*plans-séquence*), 141, 189–90, 192, 197,
198–99, 200, 238, 269–74, 279, 343, 350–
51, 383, 385; slow-motion cinematography, 198, 294; tracking (traveling) shots,
53f, 88–89, 140, 161–62, 266; walking
with a camera, 157–58, 159f, 179, 267f;
wide-angle as "contact lens," 267, 268f,
272; zoom lens, use of, 140, 265–67, 342,
460n31
—ciné-trance, xii, 201; and *cinéma-vérité*,
274–77, 320–21, 351–52; experience of
while narrating voice-over, 305; limitations of concept of, 276–77; Surrealist
resonances of, 275–77
—directing: absence of women, domestic
sphere in Rouch's ethnographic work,
14, 52, 228–31, 314–15; collaboration
with other directors, variable quality
of, 146, 224; color film, preference for,
267–68; dialogues, Rouch's antipathy
to in documentaries, 142, 268–69, 346–
47; "golden rule" (chronological order
and one take), 261–62; improvisational
methods, 73, 81, 95, 260–61, 345; origin
of film ideas, 259; participatory "filmmaker diver," 148, 150, 263–69, 341–42,
446n6; preponderance of films about
ritual, 14, 52, 314–15; psychodrama, 92,
151–52, 442n13; realist aesthetic, 149;
recurrent use of same actors, 260; research prior to shooting, 73–74, 92,
142–43, 258, 259–60; "scripts in the oral
tradition," 73, 179, 258–63; scripts shot
in real time, 187–92, 236, 262, 410–11;
scripts written with actors, 192, 195,
258–59, 262–63, 456n20; use of language, French versus indigenous, 306–
9, 347–48; "vox pop" interviews, 151f,
167–68, 300, 447n32
—editing, general, 278–309; anguish
caused by, 179, 191; compared to amputation of a limb, 166, 350; compared
to collecting phrases in a bistro, writing with letters cut from newspapers,
292; consequences of sound synchronicity for narrative, 141–42; cutting ratios,

165, 289, 458nn32–34; "devil of editing," 167, 191, 292–93, 349–50; dream sequences, 28, 86–87, 96, 96f, 296–97; duration, variable, of edits, 288–89; feedback screenings to peers and recutting, 290–91; "harsh dialogue" between director and editor, 278–79, 287; logging, 288; montage, forms of, 294, 297–98; "Napoleon" of the edit suite, 287; narrative structure, 42–43, 258, 273–74, 280, 287–88; principle of "successive approximations," 166, 289–91; "punch" of the first frame versus lingering effect of the last frame, 284–85, 297; rapidity of, 288; second "ciné-eye," need for, 61, 278, 281; Surrealist tendencies, 287; temporal progression, 294–97; unfinished films, 291

—editing, picture: editing in the viewfinder, 55, 140, 273–74, 279; jump cuts in mid-sentence, 284; visual transitions, cutting on movement, 293–94, 295f

—editing, sound: aural "bookends," 169, 299–300; festival sound mixes by Rouch himself, 290; *Les Maîtres fous*, elimination of camera noise, 282; *Moi, un Noir*, complex mix of, 90; music, 42, 64–65, 90, 179, 300–302; sound effects, 283, 298–300; wild tracks, 74, 90

—narration: ciné-trance while narrating voice over, 305; voice-over by protagonists, 74, 86, 93–94, 94f, 137, 291; voice-over by Rouch, 142, 183–84, 227–28, 293, 302–6, 308–9, 348

—shared anthropology, xxii, 310–37, 355–58; break with colonial practice, 316–17, 358; "connivance" in performance as form of, 257, 277, 320–21; credits as example of, 204, 330; ethical practice, as form of, 254, 277; feedback screenings as "audiovisual countergift," 63–65, 224, 253–54, 267, 316, 317–20, 439n20; limits to, 356–58; Rouch's relationship with Damouré, Lam, and other protagonists, 322–31, 335–37, 355, 462n68

—sound recording, 46, 48; development of sound-image synchronicity, 139–40, 158, 198; Edison wax cylinders offered by Griaule, 38; lavalier microphones, 159f, 160, 179; local sound recordists, use of, 233, 264, 282; Nagra reel-to-reel

recorder, 51, 158, 177, 179, 263, 450n19; radio microphone, 160, 161f; Sgubbi reel-to-reel recorder, 50–52, 53f, 65, 101, 139, 158, 263, 282, 301

—subtitling: late conversion to, 348; Rouch's aversion to, 142, 210, 228, 307–9

Films de la Pléiade, Les (Les Films du Jeudi), 69, 369, 374–77 passim, 380, 388, 394, 396, 417

Films de l'Homme, 414

Films du Losange, Les, 395

Films in My Life, The (autobiography, François Truffaut), 177

Fils de L'eau, Les, 137, **374**, 458n37

Firgoun (Western Niger), 2, 41, 46, 371, 372

Fischer-Møller, Knud, xxivf

Flaherty, Monica, 455n31

Flaherty, Robert: admiration by Rouch, 252–53; differences between Flaherty and Rouch, 253–54; influence on Rouch, 150, 209, 244–45, 251–54, 323, 407, 439n19; scriptwriting, approach to, 456n19; as "totemic ancestor," 244, 253–54

Flea Market (Paris), 35, 38, 50, 101, 139

Folie ordinaire d'une fille de Cham (codirector, Philippe Costantini), 236, 262, **410**

Fondation Maeght museum (Saint-Paul-de-Vence, South of France), 238, 412

Fontaine (arts magazine, edited by Jean Cocteau), 412

Foot-giraffe, Le, 197, **393**

"For a New *Cinéma-Vérité*" (article, Edgar Morin), 149

Forman Lecture (given by Jean Rouch, 1989), xxiii

Fort, Paul, 237, 413

Foucault, Françoise, xxiv, 286f, 299f, 343, 363–64

Fournier, Alain, 183

France Observateur (magazine), 149

Franchina, Sandro, 413

Franc-Tireur (magazine), 43

French Soudan. *See* Mali, Republic of

Freud, Sigmund, 27, 171

Friends, Fools, Family (film, Berit Madsen and Anne Mette Jørgensen), 335–36

Fulani (West African pastoralists, also known as Fulan, Peul), 2, 122, 204, 206, 325

Lomé (capital of Togo), 68, 74

Loridan, Marceline, 300, 446n7, 447n17, 447n27, 447n35; concentration camp experiences, 155, 160–61, 162f, 165, 174, 448n35

Lorientais, Le (jazz club), 41, 436n16

Louisiana Story (film, Robert Flaherty), 252

Lourdes et ses miracles (Georges Rouquier), 154

Lourdou, Philippe, 28, 218n, 241, 454n37

Lubin, André, 90

Lumière brothers, Auguste and Louis, 246

Luzuy, Philippe, 266f; as editor, 388, 397; *Petit à Petit*, various roles in, 213–14, 396; as sound editor, 382

Lyons (France), meeting of French and North American practitioners of *cinéma-vérité*, 250–51

Lyotard, Jean-François, 459n11

MacDougall, David, xxivf, 196, 338, 341; on the ciné-trance, 457n43; Rouch's comments on work of, 345, 346–47

MacDougall, Judith, 196, 341, 345, 346–47

Madame L'Eau, 260–61, 267f, 322, **415–16**; awarded prize at Berlin Film Festival, 239; flash forward in, 294; screening on British television, 454n33; sound effects, 299; subtitled versions, 309, 370; voice over narration, 459n17

Madsen, Berit, 79, 324, 325, 329f, 335

magic, magicians. *See* Songhay: sorcery, sorcerers (*sohantye*)

Magiciens de Wanzerbé, Les, 3, 44–46, **372**

Magritte, René, xiv, 16, 28, 457n12

Maïga, Djingarey, 416

Maïga, Idrissa, 204, 414

Maïga, Mahmoud, 416

Maison de Germaine, La, 237, **408**

Maîtres fous, Les, xvi, xvii, xx, 7, 41, 70–72, 74, 101–34, 198, 240, 295f, **374–75**

—assessments of: banned on the Gold Coast and in the UK, 104, 443n15; cult as counter-hegemonic parody, 103–4, 108, 114–15, 126–27, 128, 132–33; cult as therapy, 106–7, 107f, 129–30, 305; feedback screening to protagonists, absence of, 319–20; a "foundational film," 102;

international prizes, 105, 137; *Marat/Sade*, Peter Brook, inspired by, 105; Musée de l'Homme première, 103–4, 282, 360; *Les Nègres*, Jean Genet, inspired by, 105; racism, accusations of, 104–5, 320; used for educational purposes in Niger, 105, 334

—content: animal sacrifice, 108–9, 131, 133; demonstrated that spirit possession occurred in urban as well as rural contexts, 200; dog, consumption of, 113, 114f, 130–32; eggs, cracking on the head of Governor, 110–13, 111f, 112f, 130, 297; globalization and "the great adventure of African cities," 102; *hauka* spirits in film, nature of, 109–10; invitation to make film by telegram, 319; montage, unusual presence of, 248, 294, 297–98; music, aural "bookend," 300, 301f; narrative structure of, 258; psychological derangement shown in, 108–9, 109f, 133, 305; sexual impotence, curing of, 108–9, 129–30; sound effects, 300; "thick inscription," as example of, 134; title, ambiguity of, 105; voice-over narration, 106, 304–6, 443n8; witchcraft, references to, 129; *zima* priest, role of, 108–9, 109f, 129–30, 133. *See also* spirit possession: *hauka* spirits

Makkah (Mecca), 116, 127

Makwayela (codirector, Jacques d'Arthuys), **409**

Mali, Republic of (formerly known as French Soudan), 2, 36, 37, 43, 50, 196, 201; Dogon films, location of, 52, 136, 198, 218

Malia. *See* Red Sea

Malinowski, Bronislaw, 13, 360, 435n20, 446n6

Mallarmé, Stéphane, 438n26

Mammy Water, 69, **388**; long lapse between shooting and editing, 288

Man of Aran (film, Robert Flaherty), 252

Man Ray, 18, 29, 30f

Man with a Movie Camera (film, Dziga Vertov), 149, 245–46, 247, 446n11; *Chronicle of a Summer*, similarities and differences to, 150, 152, 177, 248

Manchester School of Anthropology, 440n8

Scheinfeigel, Maxime, xvii, 177, 448n3, 449n23

Schlöndorff, Volker, 281

Schoelcher, Victor, 438n17

Schroeder, Barbet, 189, 190f

Scientific Council for Africa (CSA), 439n2

SCOA (Société Commerciale de l'Ouest Africain), 197, 392–93

scripts. *See* filmmaking, Rouch's praxis: directing

Seabrook, William B., 18

Séchan, Edmond, 39

Sécheresse à Simiri (two films with the same title), **384**, **386**. See also *Grande Sécheresse à Simiri, La (Yenendi: Sécheresse à Simiri)*

Sembène Ousmane. *See* Ousmane, Sembène

Senegal, 7–8, 136, 236, 333, 410–11

Senghor, Blaise, 104

sequence-shot. *See* filmmaking, Rouch's praxis: camerawork

Sergent, Jean-Pierre, 154–55, 159f, 448n35

sexuality. *See* film works by Jean Rouch: sexuality, presence of in

Sgubbi sound recorder. *See* filmmaking, Rouch's praxis: sound recording

shared anthropology. *See* filmmaking, Rouch's praxis: shared anthropology

shooting. *See* filmmaking, Rouch's praxis: camerawork

Si (Sonni Ali), founder of Songhay empire, 45

sigi so ritual language. *See under* Dogon: Sigui ceremony

Sigui 1967–1973: camerawork, disengaged, 227; characters, absence of, 228; feedback screening of, 224; final outcome disappointing, 234; as homage to Griaule, 224, 234; informants, Rouch and Dieterlen work with on, 224–25; *L'Invention de la parole et de la mort* (Sigui synthèse, codirector, Germaine Dieterlen), 227–34, **402**; Islam, references to, 231–33; Pale Fox gives permission for, 225; social and political context, absence of, 231–34; stages, interpretation of meaning of with aid of repeated film viewings, 225–26; voice-over, 227–28, 348; women, absence of,

228–31, 453n23. *See also* Dogon: Sigui ceremony

Sigui année zero (codirector, Germaine Dieterlen), **398**

Sigui no.1: L'Enclume de Yougou (codirectors, Germaine Dieterlen and Gilbert Rouget), 223f, 227, **398**

Sigui no. 2: Les Danseurs de Tyogou (codirector, Germaine Dieterlen), **398–99**

Sigui no.3: La Caverne de Bongo (codirector, Germaine Dieterlen), 227, **399–400**

Sigui no.4: Les Clameurs d'Amani (codirector, Germaine Dieterlen), **400**

Sigui no.5: La Dune d'Idyeli (codirector, Germaine Dieterlen), **400–401**

Sigui no.6: Les Pagnes de Yamé (codirector, Germaine Dieterlen), **401**

Sigui no.7: L'Auvent de la circoncision (codirector, Germaine Dieterlen), **401**

Sigui synthèse. See *Sigui 1967–1973*

Simiri (Zermaganda region, Western Niger), 5, 6f, 200; resistant to Islam, 57; *Tambours d'avant*, location of, 270–74; *yenendi* films, location of, 56–58, 59f, 381, 384, 386–87

Simiri siddo kuma, **387**

Simondé, Roger (French boxer), 21

Singer, André, 454n33

Sjöberg, Johannes, 355, 356f

Socialism or Barbarism (political group), 446n16

SODAPERAGA, 394, 415, 419

sohantye. See Songhay: sorcery, sorcerers

Somba (ethnic group, northern Benin), 74, 75–76

Songchamp-Dogon, **405**

Songhay

—films by Rouch about, 38–49, 56–65, 70–72, 101–34, 196–210, 236, 370–75, 376–87

—general ethnography: millet cultivation adapted to low precipitation, 56; precolonial empire, 2–3; religion (*see* Islam; spirit possession); seasonal migration, 6; woman, high status, portrait, 5f; Si (Sonni Ali), founder, Songhay empire, 45

—Gow subgroup, 65, 69, 201–10, 450n23; portrait of hunter, 5f; preparation of traps and *fakarey* recitations, 377; Tahirou Koro, hunt leader, 65, 201, 204–6, 209–10, 318